A SHORT TEXTBOOK OF SURGERY

UNIVERSITY MEDICAL TEXTS

General Editor

SELWYN TAYLOR

D.M., M.Ch. (Oxon.), F.R.C.S.
Dean of the Royal Postgraduate Medical School
Surgeon, Hammersmith Hospital

A Short Textbook of Medicine
(Third Edition)

J. C. HOUSTON
M.D., F.R.C.P.
Physician and Dean of the Guy's Hospital Medical School, London

C. L. JOINER
M.D., F.R.C.P.
Physician, Guy's Hospital, London

J. R. TROUNCE
M.D., F.R.C.P.
Professor of Clinical Pharmacology and Sub-Dean of Guy's Hospital Medical School

A Short Textbook of Medical Microbiology
(Second Edition)

D. C. TURK
D.M., F.R.C.P., M.C.Path.
Consultant Clinical Bacteriologist, Radcliffe Infirmary, Oxford;
Honorary Consultant, Oxford Public Health Laboratory

and

I. A. PORTER
M.D., M.C.Path.
Consultant Bacteriologist to the Ayrshire Area Laboratory Service

A Short Textbook of Chemical Pathology
(Second Edition)

D. N. BARON
M.D.
Professor of Chemical Pathology, Royal Free Hospital School of Medicine, London

A Short Textbook of Gynaecology and Obstetrics

G. D. PINKER
M.B., F.R.C.S. (Ed.), F.R.C.O.G.
Consultant Gynaecological Surgeon and Obstetrician, St. Mary's Hospital

D. W. T. ROBERTS
M.Chir., F.R.C.S., F.R.C.O.G.
Consultant Obstetrician and Gynaecologist, St. George's Hospital, London

A Short Textbook of Orthopaedics and Traumatology

J. N. ASTON
M.B., F.R.C.S.
Orthopaedic Surgeon, St. Bartholomew's Hospital, London

A Short Textbook of Psychiatry

W. L. LINFORD REES
B.Sc., M.D., F.R.C.P., D.P.M.
Professor of Psychiatry, St. Bartholomew's Hospital Medical College, London

A SHORT TEXTBOOK
OF
SURGERY

SELWYN TAYLOR
D.M., M.Ch., F.R.C.S.
Dean, Royal Postgraduate Medical School
Surgeon, Hammersmith Hospital

LEONARD COTTON
M.Ch., F.R.C.S.
Surgeon, King's College Hospital

THE ENGLISH UNIVERSITIES PRESS LTD
ST. PAUL'S HOUSE   WARWICK LANE
LONDON EC4

ISBN 0 340 05117 5 paperback
ISBN 0 340 05116 7 boards

First printed 1967
Second edition 1968. Reprinted 1970

Printed and bound in Great Britain
for The English Universities Press Ltd
by Richard Clay (The Chaucer Press), Ltd,
Bungay, Suffolk

EDITOR'S FOREWORD

'Books must follow sciences, and not sciences books'

FRANCIS BACON (1561–1626)

The double burden of editing the 'University Medical Texts' and also being an author of one of the books in the series weighs heavily on the writer. However, for the latter task of producing a Short Textbook of Surgery I have received splendid assistance.

A Short Textbook of Surgery is one of the new series of books which is being published with the intention of offering up to date, low-priced textbooks suitable for qualifying and postgraduate students. The scientific foundations of surgery are so important and the theory and practice of the subject changes so quickly at the present time, that any textbook is out of date within a very few years. What the surgical student requires therefore is a convenient and expendable manual of current practice, rather than a large and comprehensive work which he might be tempted to retain and use for the rest of his life.

A textbook such as the present one should be looked upon as an introduction to the subject and rather as a key to open the door. For wider reading the student, of whatever age, should be encouraged to consult original sources and to make full use of a medical library. To this end a few references to major works and monographs have been added under the title of 'Further Reading' at the end of many of the chapters.

The practitioner anxious to keep abreast of the times will find this a refreshing textbook to consult. Not only is due emphasis given to modern developments in surgery, but the references at the end of each chapter will enable him to seek further information which he may not readily be able to find elsewhere.

SELWYN TAYLOR.

AUTHORS' PREFACE

There is a very real need for a short and inexpensive textbook of surgery, and this is what we have tried to produce. There are a number of large, good but also very expensive textbooks; however, the shorter books at present available are mostly only suitable for revision and for use by those who already have a good working knowledge of the subject. Surgery in all its aspects is changing rapidly at the present time, so that any textbook is out of date in a few years. Since this volume is inexpensive, it can be looked upon as expendable.

At the end of many chapters will be found a brief guide to further reading. This should help the student to broaden his outlook by consulting some of the major works of reference and original sources of material in the library. In orthopaedics and genito-urinary surgery, references to further reading will be found at the end of the introductory chapters. Many practitioners may welcome a book of this size, for in it will be found the basic principles of surgery clearly outlined, the indications for operation and the techniques presently available. For them the references at the ends of chapters will make it easy to find answers to problems which cannot of necessity be provided in so compact a text as this.

The student of today may reasonably ask why he need learn anything about surgery, since he will not be called upon to perform an operation unless he elects to go through a long period of specialised training. The answer is that someone must always make the first decision as to whether the patient needs medical or surgical care. Moreover, many conditions which were treated medically yesterday are sent to the surgeon today, and vice versa. Next, every medically qualified person should know the general principles of asepsis and bacteriology and the present-day problems of cross-infection, stemming, as they largely do, from widespread use of antibiotics. In recent years subjects like shock, electrolyte balance and maintenance of blood volume have undergone a silent revolution, and their basic principles should be a part of the armamentarium of anyone caring for the sick. Surgical pathology has largely moved from the post-mortem room to the operating theatre, and anatomy likewise has left the dissecting room for the operating table.

The great divide which used to lie between medicine and surgery is fast disappearing. This is because so many of the specialties; pulmonary, cardiac and endocrine, to mention only three, have bridged the gap not only by the joint endeavour of physician and surgeon but also by the advances in clinical and basic research which each has contributed. This two-pronged attack on disease means that the student can no longer divide his knowledge into separate and tidy compartments of medicine and surgery, and anyone using this book would be well advised to read the companion volume *A Short Textbook of Medicine* in conjunction with it.

Any new textbook must of necessity have many imperfections, no matter how careful the planning, how thorough the revision. We accept the responsibility for these and welcome the constructive criticisms which have helped us to improve the book in this second edition. We have leaned heavily on colleagues in certain specialised sections of the text, and are especially indebted to the following: R. Q. Crellin, orthopaedic surgeon of King's College Hospital, and J. J. Maccabe, neurosurgeon at the same hospital and the Guys–Maudsley neurosurgical unit. D. A. Packham genito-urinary surgeon at King's College Hospital has kindly read through chapters 25–27. M. W. L. Gear, lately registrar at King's College Hospital, provided much material for the chapters on accident surgery and bone disease.

SECOND EDITION

It is good that a new edition should be called for within a year of publication and we welcome the opportunity it gives of correcting mistakes and bringing the text up-to-date. We are particularly grateful to all those who have written with suggestions and emendations. Especial thanks for help with this edition go to Lawrence Garrod, Peter Flute, Hedley Berry, Derek Packham, James Maccabe, Robin Crellin, John Cobbett and Brian Sykes.

LEONARD COTTON
*King's College Hospital
Medical School,
London S.E.5.*

SELWYN TAYLOR
*Royal Postgraduate Medical School,
Hammersmith Hospital,
London, W.12.*

October, 1968.

CONTENTS

CHAPTER ONE

INTRODUCTION

Surgery is as old as man, and its evolution has been moulded in every age by current technical and scientific advances, not forgetting the demands made upon it by social customs and religion. It is both an art and a science, while its practice largely depends on the human relations between doctor and patient.

It is extremely difficult to define where surgery begins or ends, and its separation from medicine is largely based on the very different paths which the two disciplines took in ancient times. Originally surgery, as it was then known, was something of a menial task, and those who performed it were usually itinerant craftsmen who could let blood or cut for the stone. They entered the patient's house through the servants' quarters, while the physician used the front door, and to this day a surgeon is addressed as Mister in the British Isles, a constant reminder of these lowly beginnings; the retention of this title nowadays is probably only a form of inverted snobbery, as in other countries a surgeon is addressed as Doctor. The Barbers, who were the people usually called upon to let blood, united with the surgeons and received a Royal Charter from Henry VIII through the good offices of Thomas Vicary, but this union was not to last long, and it is only in comparatively recent times that surgeons have taken their place in the practice of medicine, using that word in its widest sense.

The word surgeon is derived from two Greek words, 'cheir', a hand, and 'ergon', work. Surgery has been defined as that part of the art of medicine which deals with the treatment of disease and injury mainly by operative methods, but although this may define the end product, the modern surgeon has to build his knowledge on a sound foundation of the basic sciences, especially physiology, pathology and anatomy, as well as on a broad understanding of general medicine.

It is no longer possible for a surgeon merely to be a craftsman. He must know about the physiology and biochemistry of the body fluids if he is to maintain his patient in good fluid balance before, during and after operation; he must be familiar with the intricacies of protein metabolism if he is to maintain his patient in good nitrogen balance; and in addition he has to know something of the mechanism of blood clotting and the problems of blood grouping. A sound knowledge of bacteriology and the way cross-infection occurs has become even more important with the introduction of new and potent antibiotic agents. These drugs have been used so widely that many new resistant strains of organisms have been bred, with the result that particularly virulent bacteria can now spread from one patient to another in the wards, via the operating theatre, and sometimes through the agency of the surgeon or nursing staff as they go about their duties from patient to patient.

A hundred years ago infection was easily the most dangerous complication of surgical operations, but with the advent of Lister's method of antisepsis, and later asepsis, this problem was temporarily solved. Today, however, infection is once again one of the major problems of surgical management, and it does not appear that a solution is likely to be found by the introduction of more and more potent antibiotic drugs. Indeed, at the present time it appears to be made even more difficult thereby.

The surgeon must also be familiar with the wide variety of materials used in his craft. Many substances today can be implanted in the tissues and remain there without being extruded as a result of cellular reaction; such materials are woven into tubes to replace blood vessels, shaped into prostheses for the replacement of bones, joints or heart valves, and play an ever-increasing part in all branches of surgery. The surgeon must still be a true craftsman in so far as he is dependent on tools and instruments in his work, and these may be exceedingly complex and require skilful maintenance. In some countries institutes have been created purely for the development of surgical tools and appliances, and it is possible that in this mechanical age technological aids will become of greater and greater importance.

The medical student who finds that he has no particular inclination towards surgery as a career will early in his studies ask himself the question: how much do I need to know about surgical techniques if I am not going to practise surgery in later life? He may wonder if attendance in an operating theatre is really necessary, or if he need assist in the dressing of wounds in the wards and accident department. The answer is that anyone who is going to qualify as a doctor should have a certain basic knowledge of surgery. This should include some idea of the scope of problems involved and of the possibility and range of treatment that is presently available. He should know, from close observation, something of the ordeal which the patient must undergo in the pre-operative, operative and postoperative period, for without such information he will find it impossible to give sound advice or assist later when his own patients require operation. The best way of obtaining such information is to be responsible for the care of surgical patients in the wards: obtaining a really good case history when the patient first arrives, with adequate information about social background, family diseases and occupational hazards. This careful interrogation should lead up to a useful doctor–patient relationship. He should make a thorough physical examination of his patient and then assist the surgeon at operation, and subsequently familiarise himself with the progress of that patient to health and eventually back to work. A close study of a few patients in this manner will give the student a better insight into the scope of surgery than a more superficial study of a much larger number of patients.

Finally, a good working knowledge of psychology is essential for anyone who is involved in the handling of surgical patients. The treatment offered by a surgical operation is unique among all kinds of therapy; it is approached by the patient in a different frame of mind than is treatment by drugs, whether taken by mouth, injection or any other route. The mental approach to an operation is not only different but it is often reflected in the different atmosphere which prevails in the medical and surgical wards of a hospital.

CHAPTER TWO

SHOCK, LOSS OF BLOOD AND ITS REPLACEMENT, STATES OF ABNORMAL BLEEDING

SHOCK

It is difficult to define shock, because the term has been applied to so many clinical states including fainting, the effects of blood-, plasma-, electrolyte- and water-loss, severe infection, trauma, anaphylaxis, adrenal failure and toxaemia. All of these may produce a similar clinical condition because all are associated with deficient tissue perfusion resulting in tissue anoxia. The clinical features of shock are:

Hypotension, rapid pulse (except in fainting), pallor, cold sweating extremities, subnormal temperature, rapid respiration, thirst, scanty concentrated urine, restlessness and alertness (except in fainting).

There has been much confusion in the past about the causes of shock, because for long it was thought there must be some toxic factor responsible. Substances such as histamine and adenosine were thought to be liberated early in shock and, among other clinical changes caused hypotension. Only since blood transfusion has been widely used has it been appreciated that in so-called 'traumatic shock' patients can usually be fully restored by increasing their blood volume by blood transfusion alone. The vast majority of shocked patients suffer from a depleted circulating blood volume (hypovolaemia) either due to a loss of whole blood or to plasma, water and electrolytes. A toxic factor may be added in severe infections, such as general peritonitis or septicaemia, or from the toxins that are liberated in long-standing strangulation of bowel.

The word shock should always be qualified, viz. *hypovolaemic* shock in cases where body fluids are depleted and *neurogenic* shock where pain is the prominent feature and the condition readily relieved by analgesics and opiates.

Anaphylactic shock is the state of profound hypotension resulting from the injection of some foreign protein into a person who has acquired sensitivity to it. Examples are reaction to horse-serum proteins in anti-tetanus serum or even such trivial injuries as insect stings. The reaction may be so severe as to cause immediate death. The condition is thought due to release of large amounts of histamine or histamine-like substances which cause extreme vasodilatation. If time allows, the condition can usually be corrected by injections of antihistamines, steroids and vasoconstrictors, the most powerful of the latter being adrenaline.

The rôle of the *adrenal glands in shock* is incompletely understood. A shock-like state is seen when both adrenals are destroyed by medullary haemorrhage (Waterhouse Friderichsen syndrome), an occurrence happening usually in children who have suffered from overwhelming infection. In some cases of shock due to oligaemia or toxaemia the blood pressure remains low, despite replacement of the blood volume and correction of acid–base disturbances. In these occasionally the intravenous infusion of hydrocortisone given empirically is dramatically successful in saving the patient. Perhaps the best example of adrenal dysfunction in shock is in those patients who have been given steroids for some reason in the past who, when given an anaesthetic or during an operation, become severely shocked. In these patients adrenal function has been depressed by the administration of steroid hormones, and may remain depressed for as long as two years after the medication has ceased. The stress of anaesthesia or operation calls for the increased secretion of cortical hormones which cannot be met, and shock or even death ensues. Patients undergoing operation should be questioned about whether they have ever had treatment with adrenal cortical steroids, and if they have should be prepared before operation by the injection of 100 mg. of cortisone twice daily for two days. Patients who are on steroid maintenance therapy, either because their adrenals have been removed surgically or because they are suffering from Addison's disease, must have their regular dosage of cortisone considerably increased before operation or when they have infection.

The use of noradrenaline in severe shock does not seem so favoured as a few years ago. Hypotension can be corrected by the intravenous infusion of 2, 4 or 8 microgrammes per litre of noradrenaline, but the effect is transitory, and progressively more and more of this drug must be given. Its specific use is for hypotension following removal of an adrenal tumour, especially the phaeochromocytoma, when the blood pressure does not respond to the injection of hydrocortisone.

Toxaemic, septic or endotoxic shock are terms used to explain shock associated with bacterial infections, septicaemia and strangulation. In these states the powerful toxins of bacteria are responsible, and their effects are often fatal. Antibiotics given intravenously are often effective in combating bacterial growth, but if the action of the toxins is prolonged and the infection not rapidly brought under control the condition may be irreversible and fatal. An example is the toxaemia associated with release of a strangulated hernia. A patient may appear well with strangulated intestine, especially if only part of the bowel is affected (Richter's hernia), until the strangulation is relieved and bacterial toxins released and absorbed into the general circulation. A state of irreversible shock may ensue, and death follows. Often the organisms responsible are clostridia, and attempts have been made to combat the toxaemia by the intramuscular injection of antitoxins (anti-gas gangrene serum contains antitoxins to *Clostridium welchii, septique* and *oedematiens*). Toxaemic shock remains one of the most serious problems, for the results of its treatment are so often poor.

Hypovolaemic shock is dangerous because it is associated with deficient oxygenation (hypoxia) of vital tissues, such as the brain, heart and kidneys. The sluggish circulation allows the accumulation of metabolites (metabolic acidosis), and so not only must the hypovolaemia be corrected by blood transfusion but electrolyte and acid base disturbances must be corrected as well. Usually sodium bicarbonate is infused intravenously to correct the acidosis. How much is gauged by analysis of blood gases. So-called irreversible shock is less and less diagnosed these days with the wider appreciation of the need for accurate fluid replacement of the correct composition and as more is being learnt of the metabolic changes that may complicate shock-like states.

Disseminated intravascular coagulation may account for irreversible shock. Constriction of arterioles and dilatation of capillaries allows increasing stasis, sludging and thrombosis in dilated capillaries and venules.

HAEMORRHAGE

Haemorrhage occurs most commonly after wounding, less often from a mucosal surface such as the gastro-intestinal tract or into a body cavity such as the peritoneum in ruptured ectopic pregnancy or aneurysm. Occasionally haemorrhage is a result of some defect in the blood-coagulation mechanism or in the structure of the vessel wall.

Classification of Haemorrhage

Haemorrhage may be arterial, venous or capillary. It may be *revealed* as in external haemorrhage or *concealed* as in haemorrhage into a body cavity or for example into the pregnant uterus.

1. *Arterial Haemorrhage*

This is pulsatile, bright red in colour and issues from the proximal end of a vessel. *Primary* arterial haemorrhage occurs at the time of injury; *reactionary* haemorrhage occurs within 24 hours after injury, and is produced by the rise in pressure which follows the hypotension caused by primary haemorrhage or anaesthesia; *secondary* haemorrhage occurs much later, usually seven to ten days after injury or operation, and is usually due to infection causing bleeding from vascular granulation tissue.

Examples of reactionary haemorrhage are wound haematoma after thyroidectomy, which, in the first 24 hours after operation, may seriously endanger life by compression of the trachea. In extradural haemorrhage the middle meningeal artery is torn by a fracture of the sphenoid or parietal bones. Bleeding is arrested because of the hypotension produced by concussion; as the conscious level improves the blood pressure rises, and so bleeding starts again and signs of intracranial compression appear.

Examples of secondary haemorrhage are post-prostatectomy haematuria, which commonly occurs post operatively about the fifth to tenth day following infection of the prostatic bed. Haemorrhage after haemorrhoidectomy may occur following infection at the site of ligature of a haemorrhoid pedicle.

2. Venous Haemorrhage

This occurs in a steady stream, is dark in colour and issues from both ends of a vessel. It is easily controlled by external pressure or by reducing the venous pressure by elevation of the part above the level of the heart. An example is haemorrhage from a ruptured varicose vein.

3. Capillary Haemorrhage

This causes oozing from a wound surface. Oozing from the gum after dental extraction is usually capillary in type.

Effects of Haemorrhage

The effects of haemorrhage depend partly on the volume of blood lost, but most of all on the speed at which it is lost.

1. Acute Severe Haemorrhage

Severe haemorrhage may be defined as the loss of a volume of blood sufficient to cause a fall in blood pressure and frequently necessitating blood transfusion; the fall in blood pressure may be transitory, producing fainting or giddiness, or it may be prolonged as part of the syndrome of shock produced by hypovolaemia (see p. 6).

The body's immediate reaction to severe haemorrhage is a selective vasoconstriction mediated by nervous reflexes designed to spare the brain and heart from anoxia at the expense of the gut, skin and kidneys, and thus to reduce the size of the vascular bed. Later, over a period of 48 hours, there is an attempt to restore the blood volume by haemodilution. Thirst increases the intake of oral fluids. There is a shift of fluid from the interstitial compartment into the plasma to increase the circulating blood volume. The release of hormones such as antidiuretic hormone and aldosterone restrict the excretion of water and sodium in urine.

There are a number of changes at the site of bleeding which help to arrest it locally. These include contraction of the bleeding vessel, retraction of its intima and media inside the adventitia and curling up of the internal elastic lamina. All these changes help to plug the open end of the bleeding vessel and are more marked in a lacerated vessel than in one cleanly incised. They are assisted by a fall in blood pressure, increased coagulability of the blood after haemorrhage and platelet agglutination that helps plug the vessel and hastens clotting by the release of thromboplastin. Arrest of haemorrhage is hindered by movement, by deficiency of blood-clotting factors and platelets. Prolonged bleeding is likely in conditions such as haemophilia, jaundice and thrombocytopoenia.

2. Chronic Haemorrhage

Chronic haemorrhage usually follows repeated small bleeds and produces symptoms insidiously. These symptoms may include tiredness, faintness, blackouts and dizziness. Other symptoms include swelling of the ankles, angina, claudication and, sometimes, a low fever, especially if the haemorrhage is concealed. Examination of the blood shows hypochromic anaemia. At first the red cells are normal in size (normocytes), later they are small (microcytes) and deficient in haemoglobin (hypochromic). There may be an increase in reticulocytes, especially following sharp episodes of bleeding.

It is most important in the investigation of this common problem to differentiate iron deficiency due to chronic blood loss from other anaemias. Almost always in men and commonly in women a cause for the blood loss can be found. Investigation should include a careful enquiry into abnormal bleeding and a deficiency of iron in the diet. The common causes of iron-deficiency anaemia due to blood loss are haemorrhoids, menorrhagia, peptic ulcer and, most important of all, alimentary carcinoma. Physical examination must include rectal and vaginal examination, proctoscopy and sigmoidoscopy. The faeces must be tested for occult blood, the urine for microscopic haematuria. The blood-urea level may be raised and be associated with depression of bone-marrow function. Radiological examination of the alimentary tract by barium enema or meal is often necessary to complete the investigations. Finally, laparotomy may be necessary if no cause can be found for the bleeding.

Estimation of Blood Loss

In most cases estimation of the volume of blood lost must be purely clinical. In external haemorrhage the patient's own estimate or that of a witness is usually exaggerated; in closed injuries it is more usual for the clinician to underestimate the volume of blood lost, e.g. in fractures. The degree of pallor, the level of blood pressure and the volume of blood required to restore the patient's well-being and blood pressure to a reasonable level are all useful indices. It is important that the blood pressure should not be allowed to remain for long under 90 mm. Hg, for below this level the kidneys may not excrete urine. The haemoglobin and haematocrit level are of no value in acute blood loss, but are of help when haemodilution has occurred or for example after plasma loss due to burns.

Direct measurement of the circulating blood volume can be made by injecting red cells labelled with radio-active chromium or human serum albumin labelled with radio-active iodine, but the technique is not as yet widely used. At operation, blood loss can be fairly accurately assessed by weighing swabs and by measuring the volume of blood aspirated by the sucker. Measurement of the central venous pressure via a catheter in the superior vena cava is very useful in assessing the effects of transfusion after severe blood loss. Failure of the pressure to rise after transfusion is evidence of incomplete restoration of the normal circulating blood volume. Blood is infused until the central pressure begins to rise.

Treatment of Haemorrhage

The treatment of haemorrhage includes local measures designed to arrest the flow of blood and, when necessary, replacement of blood by transfusion.

1. *Local Treatment*

If bleeding is external or revealed it may be controlled by pressure at the site of the injury, application of a pad of dressings and wool overlain by a crêpe bandage, or by pressure at an arterial pressure point nearest and proximal to the site of bleeding. A cavity such as a bleeding tooth socket or an oozing wound may be packed and pressed upon. Bleeding from veins is best treated by laying the patient flat and elevating the part to lower its venous pressure, after which a compression bandage can be applied. Spurting arteries may be clipped by arterial forceps and ligatured. Coagulation by diathermy is useful for small vessels at operation. Hot packs assist arrest of oozing by shortening the coagulation time of blood. Cold packs applied to the neck may induce reflex vasoconstriction in the pharynx after such operations as tonsillectomy and adenoidectomy and help to slow down bleeding. Another method of arresting haemorrhage is to insert a suture of the mattress type which under-runs the bleeding point and, when tied, firmly obliterates it.

Vasoconstrictor substances, such as adrenaline, are useful to stop oozing from wounds such as bleeding tooth sockets; adrenaline mixed with saline in very dilute solution (1:250,000) and widely infiltrated subcutaneously produces a dry operating field. Adrenaline must never be injected into the fingers, for there it may cause vasospasm and even digital gangrene. Ergometrine (0·2 mg) is given for the arrest of postpartum haemorrhage by causing vasoconstriction in the uterus; vasopressin may be injected intravenously with great caution to control haemorrhage due to portal hypertension by its action in constricting mesenteric arterioles and thus reducing portal flow to the liver and lowering the portal venous pressure (see p. 342).

Assistance to clotting can be provided by spraying wounds with human or bovine thrombin. Gelatin foam and alginates (surgical) hasten clotting by providing an enormous surface area on which it may occur; they are rapidly absorbed and do not form foreign bodies. Vitamin K (10 mg.) is given by intramuscular injection to patients with jaundice to avoid any tendency to bleeding from prothrombin deficiency. Fresh blood transfusions, fresh frozen plasma and antihaemophilic globulin concentrates are of great value in bleeding due to blood dycrasias. Excessive bleeding during prostatectomy and in states where the blood fibrinogen level is reduced, e.g. during delivery, may indicate the need for administration of epsilon amino-caproic acid intravenously.

2. *General Measures*

Splintage of fractures is important, for movement may cause pain and further hypotension. If the blood pressure is low, elevation of the feet helps to maintain the cerebral circulation. Severe pain is best relieved by morphia, which in cases of urgency may have to be given intravenously. Where the peripheral circulation is sluggish the effects of morphia injected subcutaneously are very slow. In such cases it should not be repeated, and preferably should be given intravenously. It should, however, be avoided altogether in cases of cranial, abdominal or thoracic injury, where it may mask physical signs.

3. *Blood Transfusion*

Blood transfusion is required where blood loss is so great that life is in peril, or where the blood volume must be rapidly restored because of the need for an urgent operation. If time permits, blood of the same ABO and Rh groups as that of the patient should be used. Accurate cross-matching takes 2–4 hours; an emergency cross-match may be performed in 20 minutes, but in cases of great urgency it is permissible, though potentially wasteful of valuable blood, to give group O, Rh negative blood without matching. The use of a 'plasma expander' such as dextraven may allow time for emergency cross-matching. It is important not to transfuse Rh-negative patients with Rh-positive blood, because antibodies may be formed which, in women, may cause haemolytic disease of the newborn, and in any case may cause reactions due to incompatibility after future transfusions. Rh-positive blood is only permitted if Rh-negative blood is unavailable or in the elderly, where repeated transfusions are unlikely.

Blood for transfusion should be kept in a refrigerator at a temperature of 4–6° C., when it can be used for 21 days; it must not be frozen. It must be discarded if there is any evidence of haemolysis, as shown by staining with haemoglobin of the supernatant plasma. Blood is now given through plastic disposable giving sets, which are less likely to produce febrile reactions or thrombophlebitis than the red rubber sets that were formerly used. The largest possible needle is inserted percutaneously, through which a plastic cannula is passed. Veins of the arm are preferred, especially those near the wrist; veins in the leg should be avoided for transfusion, because deep vein thrombosis is a risk and the patient's movements are restricted. If a transfusion must be given rapidly a Higginson's syringe may be attached to the inlet tube of the blood bottle, with great care in pumping to avoid air embolism. Better still, a Martin's pump may be used, in which the flow of blood is speeded by the pressure of an eccentric cam rotating and pressing on the tubing of the giving set. Massive bleeding at operation may be counteracted by direct infusion into the aorta.

Transfusions may slow down because the needle slips out of the vein or the vein goes into spasm or clots. The needle site should be inspected for haematoma, a warm pad over the vein may relieve spasm or the vein may be syringed through with sodium citrate. The height of the bottle may be raised to increase the head of pressure where the circulation is slow and when the infused blood is cold and viscous.

Complications of Blood Transfusions

Reactions due to incompatibility are infrequent so long as grouping and cross-matching is scrupulously carried out. Reactions include tachycardia, rigors and transient jaundice; much more rare is pain in the loin followed by oliguria and anuria. In any case of reaction the transfusion should be stopped at once, and the blood should later be checked for a cause of incompatibility. If oliguria or anuria occur this should be treated as described on p. 366. It is important to obtain a history of previous transfusions in a patient who is to be given blood, for antibodies may be present that may cause haemolytic reactions. Accurate cross-matching is essential in such patients.

Jaundice is usually transient and requires no treatment, except that the patient's blood and the transfused blood should be checked for causes of incompatibility, including haemolysis due to the use of old, heated, over-cooled or, very rarely, infected blood. Rarely, virus hepatitis may be transmitted by transfusion, it has a long incubation period up to 120 days.

Transfusion of too large a volume of blood is very dangerous, for cardiac failure may ensue. A careful watch must be kept during large transfusions on the degree of distension of the veins in the neck and for the appearance of moist sounds at the bases of the lungs. Where transfusions must be given to a patient with a diminished cardiac reserve it is wise to give packed cells. Packing is achieved by aspirating the supernatant plasma above the red cells of two bottles of blood, thus allowing the red cells of two bottles to be given in the volume of one. Packed-cell transfusions are viscid and slow to flow, the addition of heparin (10 mg./ 550 ml. of blood) is useful in preventing clotting at the site of the insertion of the needle. Packed cells must be given within 24 hours of their preparation.

Thrombophlebitis is less common with the plastic disposable giving sets now in common use, but it is still likely during prolonged transfusion. Infection may be associated with phlebitis and may cause pain and swelling at the site of insertion of the needle, with extension around the vein in the form of cellulitis and lymphangitis. Infections are extremely painful, and can usually be avoided by percutaneous insertion of the needle and by meticulous aseptic technique, but chemical phlebitis may still occur. Septicaemia is rare because of the self-sterilising properties of blood, but may follow infection of donor blood during sampling for cross-matching or during its collection. Donors should be excluded if they have been in contact with hepatitis or have had syphilis or malaria.

Usually blood need not be heated prior to transfusion, as haemolysis may result from overheating. Only in rapid massive transfusions need there be concern about the temperature of stored blood (4° C.), for large volumes of cold blood may cause ventricular fibrillation. Warming of blood must be very carefully controlled at 37° C. Citrate intoxication follows rapid transfusion, especially if there is impairment of liver [function. It is in the liver that citrate is normally metabolised, and in each 550-ml. bottle of blood 140 ml. is citrate solution. Evidence of citrate intoxication is failure of the transfusion to elevate the blood pressure and occasionally cardiac irregularities. Prophylaxis is achieved by giving 10 ml. of 10% calcium gluconate for every 2 pints of blood when blood must be given fast to shocked patients, to those with liver disease and to children.

Allergic reactions, urticaria and other skin rashes are uncommon and respond to antihistamines. Siderosis in which haemosiderin is deposited in the liver, spleen, kidney and reticulo-endothelial system follow repeated transfusions in chronic anaemia.

STATES OF ABNORMAL BLEEDING

Blood Coagulation

Normal clotting of blood is the result of a very complex chain reaction, the first feature of which is contact between blood and a foreign surface, such as damaged or irregular endothelium. This sets up a series of substrate to enzyme transformations, the enzyme being shown with a suffix as in the scheme below.

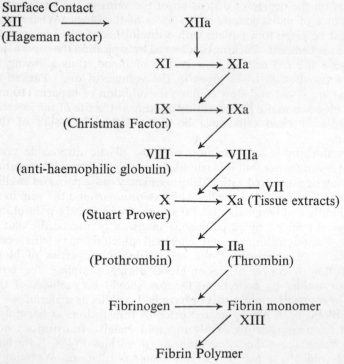

Platelet phospholipid and ionised calcium catalyse many steps in the sequence.

Abnormal Bleeding States

Abnormal bleeding may be due to defects in the blood, in the platelets or in the vessel wall.

1. *Defects in the Blood*

Haemophilia is an inherited disease of man transmitted by women who are carriers; women can only be affected if a haemophiliac marries a carrier. The tendency to abnormal bleeding is the result of a deficiency of antihaemophilic globulin (Factor VIII) that results in inadequate formation of fibrin after injury. The clotting time is often prolonged (normally 5–10 minutes) but it may be normal, the partial thromboplastin time is a more sensitive test, the bleeding time is normal (1–4 mins.). The prominent features of the disease are abnormal bleeding after injury and bleeding that is very difficult to arrest. Bleeding after tooth extraction, circumcision and tonsillectomy may be fatal. Haemarthrosis going on to arthritis and joint contracture is common, as is haematoma and extensive bruising after trivial or unnoticed injury.

Bleeding due to haemophilia can now be treated by the intravenous infusion of antihaemophilic globulin concentrate, either human or animal, human cryoprecipitate, or by the use of fresh frozen human plasma stored at −25° C. Essential operations can be performed so long as adequate pre-operative replacement therapy is available and replacement of the necessary factor must be continued until the wound has healed. Reference Centres hold stocks of these substances. All haemophiliacs should carry a green identification card issued by these centres once the diagnosis has been made. Christmas disease is an identical condition, except that it is due to deficiency of Christmas Factor (Factor IX). Treatment is the administration of fresh frozen plasma.

A deficiency of factors V, VII, X and prothrombin may be congenital, but more often it is due to disease of the liver and steatorrhoea. The prothrombin time is rapidly restored to normal by intramuscular injection of vitamin K (10 mg. twice daily for several days), treatment which must be given before operation on the jaundiced patient if dangerous haemorrhage is to be avoided.

A deficiency of fibrinogen in the blood is rarely congenital, but it may appear during complicated labour and prolonged operations. It is detected by a prolonged thrombin clotting time, and must be treated by blood transfusion and administration of human fibrinogen. It is more common after intra-uterine death of the foetus and following delivery accompanied by severe postpartum haemorrhage. Evidence of hypofibrinogenaemia may be failure of blood to clot after passage of the placenta.

2. *Platelet Deficiency*

There are many causes of thrombocytopenia, some of which are known, including blood diseases—leukaemia, aplastic anaemia, infections and drug idiosyncrasy. The cause of many, the idiopathic group, is unknown. In thrombocytopenia there may be mucosal haemorrhages together with bruising and purpura; purpuric spots are minute haemorrhagic spots in the skin which do not blanch on pressure and may coalesce to form large bruises.

In these states the bleeding time is prolonged, the clotting time is normal, Hess's test is positive,* the platelet count is diminished. Treatment obviously depends upon the cause. Platelet transfusions and cortisone are useful modern therapeutic aids. In a few cases where thrombocytopenia persists and in which there are numerous megakaryocytes in the bone marrow, splenectomy may be followed by a dramatic rise in the number of circulating platelets.

3. Defects in the Vessel Wall

Purpura and mucosal haemorrhage may be due to vessel-wall abnormalities such as the allergic purpura of the Henoch–Schönlein type, in which the alimentary tract, joints and kidney are involved. It may be secondary to many serious diseases including scurvy, infections, drugs, toxins, hepatic, renal and cardiac failure. In addition, there are rare congenital abnormalities, such as the diffuse angiomata of hereditary haemorrhagic telangiectasia; an abnormality of the elastic tissue of vessels in pseudoxanthoma elasticum and, in Von Willebrand's disease, defects in both vessels and plasma clotting factors.

In these conditions the bleeding time may be prolonged, Hess's test may be positive, the clotting time and the platelet count is normal. Occasionally there are no abnormal findings apart from the bleeding.

Investigation of Abnormal Bleeding

Patients quite often claim that they bleed easily, and obviously it is important for the surgeon to ensure before an operation that no defect exists in the patient's blood that may cause troublesome or even fatal postoperative haemorrhage.

Investigation of such a case includes a full clinical history, physical examination for signs of blood dyscrasia and a careful enquiry into the family history. The haemoglobin should be estimated and a blood-film examination made. If this indicates a deficiency of platelets a platelet count should be performed. The bleeding time should be measured and Hess's tourniquet test undertaken. Partial thromboplastin and prothrombin times should be measured, and if they show any abnormality, then more complicated investigations, such as the assay of individual clotting factors, should be performed, in which deficiencies of many of the factors involved in clotting can be measured.

---

* In this a cuff used for measuring blood pressure is inflated around the upper arm to midway between the systolic and diastolic pressure for 5 minutes. Normally very few or no petechiae appear unless there is a vessel defect or platelet deficiency.

FURTHER READING

Scientific Foundations of Surgery (1967) edited by Wells, C. and Kyle, J. Heinemann Medical Books, London.

Morrison, P. L. (1961) *Blood Transfusion in Clinical Medicine.* Blackwell, Oxford.

Biggs, R. O., Macfarlane, R. G. (1962) *Human Blood Coagulation.* Blackwell, Oxford.

Hardaway, R. M. et al. (1967), Intensive study and treatment of Shock in Man. J. Amer. med. Ass., *199*, 115.

Hardisty, R. M. and Ingram, G. I. C. (1965) *Bleeding Disorders, Investigation and Management.* Blackwell, Oxford.

CHAPTER THREE

FLUID BALANCE AND NUTRITION

Among the many reasons for the safety of modern surgery, one of the most important is greater knowledge of the fluid and other nutritional needs of man. Such knowledge is essential not only for the preparation of patients for operation but also for recognition and accurate replacement of deficiencies and maintenance of basic requirements, both before and after operation. Further advances will come when techniques are found for measurements of ions and nutrients within the cells. At present much is known of the changes that occur in extracellular fluids, but little is known of the concomitant variations within the cells. Cellular factors must play an important rôle in the control of wound healing, a complex process only superficially explored at present. However, it is obvious clinically that healing is greatly influenced by the nutritional state of the patient, so it is of paramount importance that the patient should be in the optimum state of nutrition before surgery and that this state should be preserved as far as possible after it.

FLUID BALANCE

In the patient undergoing surgical operation the nutritional requirements which must be considered are:

1. Water.
2. Salts.
3. Carbohydrate.
4. Protein.
5. Vitamins and iron.

Of these, correct administration of water and salt is paramount, because deficiency or excess of either may have short-term disastrous effects, whereas deficiencies of carbohydrate, proteins, vitamins and iron have long-term consequences, which, though important, do not require urgent and rapid correction. For this reason water and salt metabolism will be considered first.

Normal Body Water

In the normal healthy adult about 60% of body weight is water. Body water is distributed through two main compartments. The extracellular (plasma and intercellular) fluid lies outside the cells and makes up about a quarter of the total. The rest of the total body water lies inside the cells. In children the extracellular compartment is relatively greater than in the adult, making up about 50% of the total body water. The partition of water in the human body can be very roughly expressed as below:

70-kg. man—total body water
(the weight usually taken 50 litres
for the 'average man')

Intracellular 35 litres
Extracellular 15 litres
Interstitial 11 litres
Plasma 4 litres

Composition of Body Water

Each of the fluid compartments and all the secretions of the body except urine and sweat have the same osmotic pressure, though their compositions may differ, i.e. they are normally isotonic. Their osmotic equivalent is 0·9% saline.

The principal ions in extracellular fluid are sodium, chloride and bicarbonate. The protein content of interstitial fluid is minimal (less than 0·1 mg. %) as compared with plasma (6–7 g. %). Chemical analysis of the plasma or serum gives a fairly accurate estimate of the concentration of ions in the whole of the extracellular compartment. The principal ions in intracellular fluid are potassium and inorganic phosphate, but these intracellular substances cannot easily be measured directly.

Measurements of the concentration of various salts are expressed in milli-equivalents per litre. The equivalent weight of an element is that which will combine with or replace one gram of hydrogen. An equivalent can also be defined as the atomic weight divided by the valency expressed in grammes. Equivalents are more useful than measurements in grammes, because ions interchange in proportion to their equivalent weights and not in proportion to their masses. Estimates of salts in body fluids are expressed in milli-equivalents because the amounts measured are small. A milli-equivalent is a thousandth of an equivalent. Electrolytes are estimated by flame photometry, in which serum is vaporised in a flame of burning coal gas. The intensity of light produced by sodium and potassium can be measured and compared with a standard solution. Chloride is estimated electrometrically after precipitation with silver nitrate.

The buffer systems in blood play an important rôle in preventing changes in the normal acid–base balance and thus preserve the normal hydrogen-ion concentration (pH 7·4) in blood. Buffers are combinations of a weak acid and a base, the acid acting to donate hydrogen ions and the base accepting them. The three most important buffer systems in plasma are bicarbonate, protein and phosphate. Of these the bicarbonate system is most easily measured. Broadly speaking, the concentration of bicarbonate reflects changes in metabolism that may affect acid–base balance, e.g. in uraemia and diabetic ketosis. The *standard bicarbonate* is the concentration of bicarbonate in fully oxygenated blood, when the pCO_2 (see below) is 40 mm. Hg and the temperature 38° C.

Respiratory disorders that may affect acid–base balance, for example, hyper- or hypo-ventilation, can conveniently be investigated by estimating the partial pressure of carbon dioxide in arterial blood, that is the part of the total gas pressure that is contributed by carbon dioxide (pCO_2). The pCO_2 of arterial blood (except in certain lung diseases) is the same as the pCO_2 of alveolar air, which determines the blood concentration of dissolved CO_2 and H_2CO_3 and therefore affects the hydrogen-ion concentration.

It must be stressed that changes in the serum concentration of ions are late and reflect gross changes of salt and water balance. Repeated estimations are often of more value in showing trends than isolated measurements. The concentration of blood urea should also be measured, and the standard bicarbonate and pCO_2 when necessary. The concentration of serum proteins and the haematocrit are of value in revealing haemoconcentration. The urine osmolality and specific gravity are useful in detecting a renal defect. The normal range of concentrations are:

Sodium	140–145 m.eq./l.
Potassium	4·0–4·5 m.eq./l.
Chloride	105 m.eq./l.
Urea	20–40 mg. %
Standard bicarbonate	24–27 m.eq./l.
pCO_2	34–46 mm. Hg
Protein	6–7 g. %
Urine osmolality	200–1,200 milliOsmols/l.
Urine specific gravity	1·006–1·036
Urinary urea, N_2	10–15 g./24 hrs.

Normal Fluid Balance

DAILY INTAKE		DAILY OUTPUT	
Fluid in drinks	1,500 ml.	Urine	1,400 ml.
Fluid in food	1,000 ml.	Insensible fluid loss	1,000 ml.
		Faeces	100 ml.
	2,500 ml.		2,500 ml.

Insensible loss is inevitable, in that it continues under all circumstances but varies with the temperature and humidity of the atmosphere. It includes sensible and insensible perspiration and losses in respired air, practically all water loss, for the loss of salt in perspiration is negligible unless the volume is excessive. Urine output is adjusted so that total output balances intake, so the volume of urine in the normal individual is a rough index of adequate fluid intake. The volume of water in faeces is the residue of the vast volume (8,000 ml./24 hours) of fluid secreted into the gastrointestinal tract, almost all of which is re-absorbed under normal circumstances, leaving only that excreted in faeces (100 ml.).

Disturbances of Fluid Balance

The commonest disorders of fluid balance met with in clinical practice are the result of *diminution of fluid intake* due to deprivation, or inability to take fluid, *losses from the gastro-intestinal tract*, such as from vomiting, diarrhoea, gastric aspiration or entero-cutaneous fistula, and loss of *circulating-blood volume* from haemorrhage, trauma and shock.

In surgical practice pure water depletion is rarely met, almost always there is an associated loss of salts, for example, in vomiting and diarrhoea or in loss of blood during operation or postoperatively.

In *severe vomiting* from, for example, pyloric obstruction, hydrogen, chloride and potassium ions are lost. The hydrogen-ion concentration in blood falls and the standard bicarbonate rises to high levels. There is raised bicarbonate excretion in the urine provided adequate fluid is available.

The combination of low serum potassium and a raised standard bi-carbonate, hypokalaemic alkalosis, can only be rectified with potassium supplements additional to saline. Associated with these upsets in acid–base balance, the level of blood urea may climb to a surprisingly high level up to, say, 100 or 150 mg. % as a result of dehydration; a rapid fall in the level of urea may occur when appropriate ions and water are replaced. A rise in blood pH may also be associated with a decreased concentration of ionised calcium to the point of causing tetany.

Where losses occur from the upper small intestine as well as from the stomach, as for example in duodenal fistula, high intestinal obstruction and biliary fistula, more bicarbonate may be lost than hydrogen ions. The standard bicarbonate level in the blood may then fall with a rise in hydrogen-ion concentration. Correction must aim at replacing bicarbon-ate as well as water, sodium, potassium and chloride secretion.

Hypokalaemia (potassium deficiency) may result from prolonged vomiting from fistulae or ileostomy, or from small intestinal loss from diarrhoea. Since potassium is mainly an intracellular ion, plasma potas-sium concentration gives little indication of the total body potassium balance. Serum potassium falls late and only when there is gross potassium depletion.

Loss of intracellular potassium results in a shift of both hydrogen and sodium ions into the cells. This loss of hydrogen ions from the plasma pro-duces a rise in the standard bicarbonate which accounts for the alkalosis which frequently accompanies potassium depletion. Potassium loss, as for example in severe vomiting, is usually accompanied by an excessive loss of chloride over sodium. The presence of hypochloraemia results in defective conservation of both potassium and hydrogen ions by the kidney. The urine may therefore remain persistently acid. Chloride and potassium must be given to correct this state.

Losses of water and salts lead to a reduction in the volume of extra-cellular fluid (normally 15 litres), producing collapse with peripheral circulatory failure, low blood pressure and oliguria. The blood-urea con-centration may rise, but falls rapidly to normal as the deficits are replaced (pre-renal uraemia, see p. 365). Thirst is surprisingly absent, though the signs of water and salt loss are obvious, inelastic skin, dry tongue, etc.

Concentrations of serum electrolytes may be spuriously high if water is lost in excess of salts because of haemoconcentration. High concentrations of serum proteins or a raised haematocrit may be very useful in showing haemoconcentration and the course of haemodilution that follows if water is replaced in excess of salts.

The converse states of *water and salt excess*, really drowning of the patient, are usually iatrogenic, being the result of careless or ignorant treatment. Water excess may follow the use of hypotonic or electrolyte-free fluids, or by excessive water absorption from, for example, rectal infusions of water (rarely used nowadays). Signs of overhydration include oedema, ascites, 'moist sounds' at the bases of the lungs, engorged neck veins and cardiac failure. Children may have convulsions due to cerebral oedema. Excessive blood transfusion may have the same effects. Sodium excess may be induced by excessive infusion of normal or hypertonic saline and by the administration of corticosteroids. Oedema results from excessive sodium in the extracellular compartment, into which water passes to maintain tonicity.

Hyperkalaemia (potassium excess) is likely in anuria from failure to excrete potassium, or in massive transfusions because, as stored blood ages, potassium tends to shift from the red cells to the plasma.

Variations in lung ventilation may cause profound changes in acid–base balance. For example, underventilation of the alveoli may occur in poliomyelitis affecting the respiratory muscles, barbiturate poisoning, chest and head injuries and postoperatively. Patients are especially affected if they have lung disease, such as chronic bronchitis, and emphysema. Underventilation results in a rise in the carbon dioxide level in the alveoli, and hence a rise in the partial pressure of carbon dioxide in arterial blood (pCO_2) accompanied by a fall in blood pH.

Overventilation usually occurs in anxious patients or in artificial respiration, and results in a fall in the arterial pCO_2 and a fall in hydrogen-ion concentration (hence a rise in pH) in the blood. Tetany may occur.

Respiratory changes affecting acid–base balance are becoming of greater importance today due to the common use of respirators and prolonged artificial respiration after operations and in cases of deep coma. A small rise in pCO_2 may produce a rapid bounding pulse, hypertension, hot hands and small pupils. Confusion, drowsiness and a coarse tremor may follow. A large rise may cause coma and extensor plantar responses.

Fluid Balance after Surgery

In the first 24 to 36 hours of the postoperative phase salt and water are retained. Water retention and fluid restriction result in the urine being of small volume, concentrated and of high osmolality. In this early phase potassium and nitrogen excretion is increased. These changes are the result of the stimulus of trauma acting on the adrenal cortex, which secretes an excess of mineralocorticoids and the pituitary which secretes anti-diuretic hormone. These changes are 'normal' responses to trauma,

KING'S COLLEGE HOSPITAL
DAILY FLUID BALANCE (MLS)

Name .... Age ....Ward.............. Hosp. No.................

INTAKE (ML)

DATE														
	D	N	D	N	D	N	D	N	D	N	D	N	D	N
Oral														
Parenteral:														
Saline														
Glucose														
Saline Glucose														
Saline Glucose														
Plasma														
Blood														
TOTAL														

OUTPUT (ML)

	D	N	D	N	D	N	D	N	D	N	D	N	D	N
Insensible Loss (1000 in 24 hrs.)														
Urine														
Suction														
Vomit														
Fistula														
Fæces P.R.														
TOTAL (24 hours)														
BALANCE														

ANALYSES

	D	N	D	N	D	N	D	N	D	N	D	N	D	N
Sodium (125-150 mEq/L)														
Potass. (3.5-5.5 mEq/L)														
Chloride (95-108 mEq/L)														
Bicarb. (21-30 mEq/L)														
Blood Urea (20-40 mg %)														
Haemoglobin														
Haematocrit														
Plasma Proteins														
Weight														

S.F. 700/62

FIG. 1. Specimen fluid-balance chart

they cannot be prevented and are thus 'obligatory'. They are not harmful and require no treatment. Following the period of salt and water retention there is a phase of diuresis with secretion of urine of low osmolality and high salt content. In the early postoperative phase, so long as there are no abnormal losses of salt and water, fluid balance can be maintained by 2 litres of 4·3% dextrose in one-fifth normal saline in 24 hours given intravenously, or by 60–90 ml. of water given orally every hour.

Most surgical patients who are dehydrated either before or after surgery usually suffer from a deficiency of both salt and water. In the assessment of the patient's condition, the history, the duration of the illness, the nature and volume of all abnormal losses, and the volume of oral intake give a rough guide to the magnitude of deficiencies of fluid and salts. It is impossible to assess losses into dilated bowel or into the peritoneal cavity unless they are removed at operation, when they should always be carefully measured.

In the postoperative period accurate fluid-balance charts (see Fig. 1) are essential. Examination may reveal a dry tongue, inelastic skin, hypotension and peripheral circulatory failure. Repeated serum electrolyte and urea estimations are of great value, but it must be remembered that because of haemoconcentration the values may be higher than expected from known fluid losses. Any patient on intravenous therapy for more than 3 days should have serum electrolytes measured. Haemoglobin, haematocrit and plasma proteins give some index of haemoconcentration. Repeated measurement of urine specific gravity or osmolality is of use in following the results of therapy, and occasionally may suggest a severe renal defect, especially if a water load of 1 litre fails to produce a more dilute urine. Estimation of urinary urea gives some evidence of renal function, especially in differentiating the oliguria of haemoconcentration from that due to renal impairment.

Maintenance of fluid balance is achieved by replacement of abnormal losses, the volume of which must be added to the normal daily requirement of fluid. Most initial losses are from the gastro-intestinal tract, and should be replaced by isotonic saline. Where there is loss of protein, as in burns and peritonitis, plasma or blood must be given and, invariably, blood loss must be replaced by blood. Potassium must be replaced in vomiting, diarrhoea and ileus, but great care must be exercised in its administration until it is certain that renal function is adequate. Its administration must be controlled by repeated serum estimation and, if necessary, electrocardiography. 1 g. of potassium chloride (13 m.eq.K) in 500 ml. of saline should be given over 4 to 6 hours, up to 6 g may be needed in 1 day. If possible, potassium should be given orally in the form of enteric coated capsules (slow release K).

Gross disturbances of acid–base balance are infrequent in surgical practice. If the cause is reversible the body can usually correct such states by compensatory mechanisms, such as the buffer capacity of blood, renal excretion and respiration. In renal failure, diabetes and after cardiac arrest it is sometimes necessary to give alkaline fluids intravenously, sodium bicarbonate or one-sixth molar sodium lactate. Where loss of base has occurred, as in profuse diarrhoea or intestinal fistula, administration of isotonic saline supplies adequate sodium, the excess of chloride being excreted in the urine. Loss of chloride and hydrogen ions in vomiting can be replaced by isotonic saline, occasionally potassium supplements must be given, and calcium may be needed if tetany occurs.

NUTRITION

The nutritional state of patients must always be considered so that deficiencies may be corrected when possible before operation and prevented after it.

Before Operation

Starvation is the commonest nutritional problem met in surgery, either the result of obstruction of the upper alimentary tract (e.g. oesophageal obstruction, pyloric stenosis) or from losses resulting from profuse diarrhoea or intestinal fistula. In such cases the urgent need for an operation may allow only correction of water and salt losses. If time allows, replacement of carbohydrate, protein, iron and vitamins over a period of a week or more may dramatically improve the state of the patient and greatly enhance the chances of a successful operation.

If one considers the malnourished patient who can only take a fluid diet orally, an easily assimilable and restorative daily diet is one of 2,400 calories made up of 1 litre of milk, protein digest (complan) to contain 50 g. of protein, fat emulsion, to contain 80 g. of fat and 60 g. of added glucose. Such a diet contains 90 g. of protein, 160 g. of fat and 200 g. of carbohydrate. Vitamins (especially B_1, B_2 and C) and iron may be added. Extra fluids will be necessary to make up the usual maintenance volume of 2,500 ml. Fat has a very high calorific value (9 calories/g., in contrast to carbohydrate, 4 calories/g.) and can now be given in specially prepared emulsions orally or, with care, intravenously.

The safety of intravenous solutions used for parenteral nutrition has now been established. A source of calories and nitrogen is needed. Glucose in concentrated solution produces an osmotic diuresis and local thrombophlebitis. Fructose only enters the urine in small amounts and is more easily metabolised in starvation. A 20% solution of fructose will provide 800 cals per litre. Fat emulsion prepared from soya bean (Intralipid) has proved relatively free of serious side effects and is readily absorbed. A 20% solution of Intralipid will provide 1800 cals per litre. Pure solutions of essential amino acids (Trophysan) are now available for simultaneous administration with a source of calories.

After Operation

It is important not to forget the metabolic requirements of the patient being fed intravenously. For short periods of time, 2 or 3 days, this is not important, as deficiencies can be made up rapidly later. In oliguria and anuria calories must be supplied to depress tissue catabolism, and thus prevent the accumulation of nitrogenous substances such as urea in the blood (see p. 368).

B

At least 1,500 calories must be supplied daily to minimise tissue break-down, even more in katabolic states such as anuria. On the usual maintenance volume of 2,500 ml. of 4·3% dextrose in $N/5$-NaCl solution per day only 500 calories are given, but the deficit can rapidly be corrected once oral feeding can be started.

The phase of negative nitrogen balance that follows surgery is usually rapidly corrected once normal feeding can be resumed. Occasionally, in prolonged illness, especially after severe protein loss in diarrhoea and intestinal fistula, protein supplements must be given. Needs for protein are usually satisfied by the régime described on p. 23. Administration of amino acids and calories intravenously may be tried when food cannot be taken by mouth. Parenteral administration of vitamins is essential in states of malnutrition, coma and severe protein loss, and additional vitamin B complex is called for when broad-spectrum antibiotics are being taken.

FURTHER READING

The Scientific Basis of Surgery (1965) edited by Irvine, W. T. J. & A. Churchill, London.

Wilkinson, A. W. (1960) *Body Fluids in Surgery*. E. & S. Livingstone, London.

Moore, F. D. (1959) *Metabolic Care of the Surgical Patient*. Saunders, Philadelphia.

Taylor, W. H. (1965) *Fluid Therapy and Disorders of Electrolyte Balance*. Blackwell, Oxford.

Le Quesne, L. P. (1957) *Fluid Balance in Surgical Practice*. Lloyd Luke. London.

CHAPTER FOUR

BURNS, WOUNDS AND THE SCOPE OF PLASTIC SURGERY

BURNS

Burns and scalds kill some 700 persons each year in England and Wales. Young children under three years and old persons over sixty-five years make up a large proportion of those who die. In the majority the accidents causing these deaths could be prevented. Such measures as the enforcement of safety guards to all fires, the use of flame-proof materials for children's clothes especially pyjamas (now in force), discouraging the wearing of nightdresses by little girls and close supervision of children in rooms containing fires, all these could help to reduce the appalling mortality of burns. Widespread propaganda is essential to make people aware of the problem. Once this is achieved, perhaps it will become obvious that the consequence of Guy Fawkes' celebrations can only be avoided by banning the sale of fireworks. The case of burns is perhaps the most obvious one of prophylaxis being more rational and effective than the treatment of sequelae. Apart from the fatalities that burns cause, the total cost must include the misery of prolonged and painful invalidism, repeated dressings and anaesthetics and the plastic repair of severe scarring and loss of function.

Types of Burns

Burns are usually due to flame, some result from electric current or lightning, strong chemicals may burn. Scalds follow injury from boiling water or steam. Burns are usually classified in terms of their depth and the capacity of the body for their spontaneous healing. In *superficial burns* there is reddening and blistering of the skin, changes which allow healing without scarring in up to 2 weeks. In *partial thickness burns* the destruction of the Malpighian layer is incompete, and regeneration of skin can occur from islands of germinal epithelium. Sweat and sebaceous glands penetrate beyond the basal layers of the epidermis, and from their epithelium regeneration can also occur. The speed of repair may be very much delayed by the occurrence of infection. Deep burns or *full thickness burns* involve death of tissue at least beyond the Malpighian layer of the epidermis. No regeneration is possible in the burnt area; healing from adjacent less damaged skin is slow and complicated by scarring and contracture.

The Effects of Burns

Severe burns imperil life from the effects they have on the body as a whole; locally they cause pain, discomfort, scarring and deformity.

Local Effects

Obviously the changes produced by heat will depend on the intensity of the stimulus and the area to which it is applied. The minimal effects are erythema and blistering, the maximal are necrosis or charring to a variable depth, even down to bone. In between these extremes there may be cyanosis, yellowness or brown-staining of the skin, which may look dead and lack its normal sheen. Deep burns are insensitive to touch and pinprick: small thrombosed veins may be visible through the semi-transparent eschar. Superficial burns and very deep burns are easily recognised, but in many partial thickness burns it is difficult to assess depth until inflammation resolves or necrotic skin separates, a process that may take several weeks.

At the site of the burn there are the changes of inflammation, alone or combined with those associated with tissue necrosis. In the inflamed skin intense vasodilatation occurs, with capillary damage that allows the exudation of plasma. There follow the usual changes of inflammation, diapedesis of cells into the damaged tissues, formation of granulation tissue and, later, fibrosis. If the lesion is at all deep or extensive, vessels and red cells may be destroyed to cause anaemia and, with the loss of plasma, hypovolaemia.

The raw surfaces with their covering of exudate, that are left after burning, form an excellent culture medium for pathogenic organisms. Unless stringent measures are taken to exclude organisms from burns, infection is inevitable and very serious, because it delays healing and greatly increases the discomfort of the patient. Antibiotics are only temporarily effective, because strains of organisms resistant to their action rapidly colonise the granulating surfaces.

From about the second to the fourth week the necrotic parts of the burnt skin begin to separate, to leave areas of pink granulation tissue exuding serum or pus. This phase, in patients with extensive burns, may be associated with flares of infection, toxaemia and severe illness, often accompanied by malnutrition due to loss of protein. In partial thickness burns the granulation tissue may be stippled by islands of regenerating skin. In such cases, so long as infection can be held in check, healing will occur spontaneously with little scarring. Areas of full thickness burn form large ulcers, in which healing can only occur from the periphery unless skin grafting is carried out.

Electric burns may be due to heat alone, or they may be the result of electricity itself. In the latter case there are commonly burns at the site of contact and where the electrical charge leaves the body. Electric burns can be assumed to be full thickness in depth, and should be treated as such.

Burns of the head and neck or those due to the inhalation of steam may cause injury to the mucous membrane lining the upper respiratory tract. Obstruction to respiration from oedema of the glottis may follow and be so severe that tracheostomy is required for its relief.

General Effects

The most important general effect of a burn is the exudate of plasma, that is water, electrolytes and protein that leaks from the dilated and damaged capillaries at the site of injury. The volume of exudate is proportional to the area burnt; if this is large, then, because the loss is from the extracellular compartment, there is hypotension and hypovolaemia with haemoconcentration, the latter being shown by an increase in the haematocrit and an increase in all the serum electrolyte values. The greatest loss of exudate occurs in the first 8 hours after burning, it ceases after about 48 hours.

In deep and in extensive burns there is in addition loss of red-cell mass, abnormal haemoglobin metabolism and to some extent an increased fragility of red cells, factors which contribute to anaemia when the volume of plasma water has been corrected. Later in the phase of recovery, anaemia may be caused by sepsis, malnutrition and blood loss from grafting operations.

Nausea and vomiting are common after burns, and may necessitate parenteral feeding. In the early phase nausea and vomiting are due to ischaemia of the gut, part of the general hypovolaemia. Later acute dilatation of the intestine may occur due to paralytic ileus. The heavy protein loss in the plasma exudate, the failure of normal ingestion of food, the negative nitrogen balance that follows injury and the katabolic effects of fever and sepsis, all these influences add up to severe protein deprivation and malnutrition. Much of the hypercatabolism is due to obligatory heat loss from evaporation of water from the surface of the burnt area. Malnutrition may be fatal if it is uncorrected. Delay in healing and failure of skin grafts to 'take' are manifestations of poor nutrition resulting from burns.

Treatment of Burns

The treatment of burns is to be considered under the headings of first aid, recognition and treatment of hypotension and hypovolaemia, local treatment and, lastly, plastic repair. It is important not to forget tetanus prophylaxis.

First-aid Treatment

It is most important to assess the severity of the burn to decide whether or not hospital treatment will be necessary. Minor superficial burns require only the application of a sterile dressing and observation at suitable intervals until healing has occurred. More severe burns should be covered by sterile towels and the patient referred to hospital for treatment. No attempts should be made to dress the injuries with antiseptics or antibiotics. Once the patient has reached hospital an assessment should be made of the need for resuscitation by intravenous therapy, and the need for admission to hospital. The burns should be examined with full aseptic ritual. Many moderately severe burns can conveniently be treated in the out-patient department so long as resuscitation is not required and the extent of the burn is not so great as to interfere with the patient's movements. Out-patient treatment involves less chances of cross-infection, and may well suit the patient's convenience.

Resuscitation

The need for resuscitation is assessed by the extent and depth of the burn and the degree of hypotension and peripheral circulatory failure. If the burn covers more than 15–20% of the body surface, intravenous therapy will be needed. Wallace's 'rule of 9' gives an easily remembered guide to the areas of certain parts of the body surface. Eighteen per cent is allowed for each surface of the trunk, 9% for each upper limb, 18% for each lower limb and 9% for the face. There are many charts and diagrams available from which the necessary volume of intravenously administered fluid and its composition can be calculated. Very roughly it can be said that 2 ml. of fluid is needed for each 1% of body surface area burnt per kilo. body weight. Half of this volume should be given as normal saline and half as plasma. Of the total volume one third is given in the first eight hours; one third in the next sixteen hours and the remaining third in the next 24 hours. The rest of the normal requirement is given by mouth or, if there is vomiting, it is given intravenously and supplemented by volumes of normal saline equal to any additional losses.

If more than 20% of the body surface is burnt or if there are extensive deep burns a quarter of the added fluid should be compatible blood and three-quarters plasma. Occasionally, if severe hypotension persists, then hydrocortisone may be given intravenously, though its administration is empirical and its value has not been fully assessed.

Progress of resuscitation is assessed by improvement in the general well-being of the patient, the pulse and the state of the peripheral circulation. An adequate secretion of urine each hour is a very good sign of satisfactory progress. A rising haematocrit level indicates the need for further transfusion, as do raised electrolyte values.

The best relief of pain is given by morphia, which can be used in appropriate doses at all ages. Occasionally it should be given intravenously if urgent relief of pain is needed.

Local Treatment of Burns

Once resuscitation of the patient is completed, then local treatment should be started. The principles are first to allow natural healing without delay by avoidance of infection and malnutrition as far as possible, and secondly, the early recognition of full thickness burns that will require skin grafting.

Initially extensive burns should be cleansed under the analgesia produced by intravenous morphia. General anaesthesia is not usually required and may be hazardous in the difficult phase of shock. All clothing is removed, together with any material adherent to the burn, blisters are snipped and the whole area washed with 1% cetrimide. A decision must then be made as to whether treatment by exposure or by occlusive, pressure-dressing technique should be instituted. These methods appear mutually contradictory, for pressure dressings are applied to suppress exudation, whereas, in the exposure method, exudation is permitted and crust formation encouraged by placing the patient in a warm, dry room. Each method has its place, exposure is particularly suited for the face and perineum, which are impossible to bandage; the fingers should not be exposed, because severe burns, especially circumferential burns, lead to crust formation, which may produce severe contractures of the digits. The limbs or trunk heal well with either exposure or pressure dressings.

A pressure dressing comprises first a layer of non-adherent gauze, such as tulle gras covered by gauze, wool and finally a crêpe bandage. It acts to some extent by preventing exudation by external pressure and also by absorbing any fluid that does leak. Once the dressing becomes soaked, organisms can pass through it from the exterior, so changes of dressings must be performed whenever it is considered they have become ineffective in excluding bacteria. Such dressings should be carried out with full aseptic techniques, preferably in air-conditioned dressing rooms, for the possibility of cross-infection from such burns dressings is very great. Pressure dressings should also be changed if there is fever or if the dressings become malodorous. Fingers are dressed individually to avoid contact between damaged surfaces.

Burns to be exposed are, after initial cleansing, wrapped in sterile towels and later bared in a cubicle which has been heated above the environmental temperature if that is cool. Such burns exude diminishing amounts of fluid for up to 48 hours, and the drier the atmosphere, the shorter the period of exudation. A coagulum forms over the burn, which rapidly becomes painless and surprisingly comfortable. It can be expected to remain clean, if not completely sterile, for 10–14 days, when the crust begins to separate. Superficial burns heal in that period, but adherence of the crust suggests a greater depth of burning that may later require grafting. After 10–14 days the coagulum should be removed under general anaesthesia and any deeply burnt areas grafted with skin if they are free from gross infection.

Antibiotics may be given systemically or locally. It should be remembered that their effect is short-lived because colonization with antibiotic resistant organisms occurs so readily. The dangerous organisms are streptococci, staphylococci and B. Pyocyanea. Long courses of cloxacillin will deal with streptococci and prevent staphylococcal septicaemia.

Pyocyanea infection can be controlled locally by exposure and the application of sulphamylon, gentamycin and 0·5% silver nitrate solution. Systemically invasion by B. Pyocyanea may be prevented by the administration of Colomycin or Pyopen when operation is contemplated.

If burns are without doubt full thickness in depth they should be excised and grafted at the earliest opportunity. Electric burns are usually full thickness and should be grafted. Usually the depth of a burn is in doubt, and so it is often necessary to wait 2–3 weeks for separation of sloughs before the need for grafting becomes obvious.

Plastic Repair of Burns

So soon as it becomes apparent that full thickness burns have been sustained, grafting of skin should be undertaken. Grafting is unlikely to be successful unless the patient's nutrition has been adequately maintained. In those suffering from extensive burns, as soon as oral feeding can be started, protein supplements, such as complan, should be given with vitamins and iron. Anaemia needs correction by blood transfusion. The area to be grafted should be free of gross contamination with staphylococci B. Pyocyanea and streptococci, and the granulations should present a relatively dry, flat, pink surface. At this phase antibiotics are of little use in preparing the surfaces for grafting. Mechanical removal of sloughs is best achieved by frequent application of wet dressings soaked in antiseptics such as eusol, sodium hypochlorite (Milton) or repeated immersion of the burnt area in saline baths.

Grafting is usually performed by the application of split skin or Thiersch grafts. These are grafts cut from normal skin of the patient at a plane which passes through the Malpighian layer but not deep to it. Sheets may be cut to cover the whole area needing grafting or, in large burns, more economically by the 'postage stamp' method, in which the grafts are cut in 2-cm. squares and applied 1 cm. apart. It is useful to cut more skin than necessary, anticipating that some grafts will not adhere because of infection. Surplus skin can be preserved by refrigeration at 4° C. for 3–4 weeks, and can be applied to the burnt surface without further anaesthesia. The grafts may be enclosed by pressure dressings or, preferably, they are exposed; the method to be used depends on the situation of the burn. For example, on the face exposed grafts heal well.

Further plastic surgery may be necessary to deal with impaired function following scarring or to improve cosmetic appearance. Joint contractures are likely in burns that cross flexures; keloid formation is common in children and where there has been considerable infection. Reconstruction of injured structures, such as eyelids or contracted orifices, may demand more complicated plastic surgery, for example a full thickness burn of an eyelid will need early grafting, say in the first week, for fear of corneal exposure leading to ulceration, perforation and blindness.

WOUNDS

Problems arising from the infliction of wounds, intentional or accidental, are among the commonest in surgery. It is therefore important to have detailed knowledge of types of wounds, their treatment, their healing and the complications that may arise from them. Considering how much of surgery is to do with wounds, it is remarkable how little is known of the complex mechanism of wound healing and its derangements. Though it is possible to describe in detail the gross and microscopical appearance of wounds, little is known of what makes them heal.

Types of Wounds

Wounds may be incised, lacerated or contused. Severe contusion, for example by crushing or friction, may seriously devitalise skin almost to the point of necrosis, yet healing may still occur, so long as contamination with foreign bodies and organisms which may lead to infection does not occur. Even without infection, necrosis or gangrene may appear at an interval if the contused skin slowly dies, perhaps because of poor blood supply. Wounds may be of the 'de-gloving' or 'scalping' type when flaps of skin are raised by injury which may appear healthy when they are replaced but slowly necrose because of insufficient blood supply coming through the base of the flap. Wounds causing loss of substance often cannot be completely closed, and necessitate immediate plastic repair, so long as there is no gross contamination and the interval from wounding is not too great.

Injuries to skin of a minor degree may have serious consequences if its blood supply is reduced by arterial occlusion or if the drainage of blood is impaired by venous disease, especially if there is oedema. Such minor injuries may not even break the skin surface, yet these so-called sub-cutaneous injuries may later be followed by gangrene or ulceration. Skin which is insensitive because of peripheral neuritis or other nervous diseases, such as syringomyelia or tabes dorsalis, may react badly to trauma. Ulceration of a deeply perforating type or even gangrene may occur.

Healing of Wounds

From the clinical point of view wound healing is generally described as primary or first-intention healing and secondary or second-intention healing (or healing by granulation). Cleanly incised wounds without loss of substance heal most rapidly, so long as contamination by foreign bodies or organisms does not cause delay. The gap between the wound edges fills with blood clot and serum, in which fibrin forms a matrix on which fibroblasts and angioblasts grow from the wound edges. The smaller the gap, the more rapidly the clot becomes organised; firm union can be expected in 3–4 days, but not firm enough to permit any undue strain. By 7–10 days the granulation tissue formed between the skin edges has become far less vascular, and fibroblasts have contracted to collagen, which forms the basis of the scar. Uneventful healing of this type is called primary or healing by first intention.

If the wound becomes infected or if there is loss of substance and failure to approximate the skin edges, then the wound heals by second intention or by granulation. Granulation tissue is pink and vascular, becoming paler and contracting as healing progresses. Such wounds can only heal from the base and from the edges. This type of healing is anticipated and indeed wanted when abscesses are drained, and cavities must heal from the base. Granulation tissue is defined as inflammatory tissue composed of fibroblasts and angioblasts infiltrated by inflammatory cells, in the early phase polymorphonuclear leucocytes predominate, in the later phase mononuclear cells are in excess. Healing by granulation is inevitably followed by scarring, which may later seriously interfere with function.

Wound Suture

For optimum healing wounds should be shaved of hairs for 1–2 inches around them and cleaned with antiseptic detergents, such as 1 % cetrimide. Eyebrows should not be shaved, and extensive shaving of the scalp should be avoided. The edges of the wound should then be approximated meticulously so that the space between them is reduced to the minimum. Up to 8 hours from the time of injury primary suture can be carried out with maximum hope of success, but after this time the wound is more likely to become infected, and optimum healing cannot be expected in all cases. Immediate or primary suture can still be performed up to 24 hours after injury, but after this time healing by granulation should be permitted. Occasionally, after an interval of 3–4 days, when active inflammation has subsided and granulations are clean, delayed primary suture may be considered at which the wound is completely excised and closed. Administration of antibiotics in such cases aids the success of the operation. If granulating wounds are relatively clean at 10–14 days, then secondary suture may be performed after wound excision. It should not be forgotten that all patients who have suffered penetrating wounds should be immunised against tetanus (see p. 58).

The technique of wound suture should be meticulous and atraumatic. After shaving and cleansing of the wound complete haemostasis is secured. Sutures should approximate the full thickness of the wound and be inserted at centimetre intervals and tied only just tightly enough fully to approximate the wound edges. Vertical mattress sutures are particularly suitable for accurate approximation of skin. Wounds swell after injury, and sutures tied tightly cut in and cause necrosis. Drains should only be inserted if there is great fear of haematoma in very vascular situations. They may also be used where there is a possibility of infection. Prophylactic antibiotics are rarely indicated; only if fever, throbbing pain or swelling occurs should they be given.

Local analgesia with a 1% solution of lignocaine infiltrated into the wound edges is usually adequate for primary suture, except in children or the very apprehensive, in whom preliminary pre-medication with a barbiturate is very helpful. Fine silk sutures suffice for most situations; in the face fine monofilament nylon on atraumatic needles inserted shallowly through the skin gives a better cosmetic result. Sutures are usually safely removed on the eighth to tenth day. In the head and neck they may be removed about the fourth or fifth day. The earlier sutures are removed, the less scarring is left; on the face sutures can be removed early because of the good blood supply to the facial tissues and their rapid healing with good cosmetic results. The surgeon often inserts absorbable catgut sutures subcutaneously so that skin sutures may deliberately be removed early. If this is done, as in incisions for removal of the thyroid, skin sutures can safely be removed on the second or third day after operation. Deep sutures are used where the subcutaneous tissue is thick to prevent 'tenting' of wounds, allowing the accumulation of deep haematomata, prone to infection. Deep tension sutures through all layers of the abdominal wall are unnecessary, except for the repair of wound dehiscence.

Contused or lacerated wounds must be carefully cleaned with cetrimide. All foreign bodies should be removed and all loose tags of fascia or muscle excised. Wound edges should be inspected carefully and any devitalised skin removed. Full excision of the wound edges is rarely necessary in civilian practice, but was found essential in wartime.

Flaps of skin may be sutured back in position after being carefully cleaned, so long as the base of the flap is at least twice the width of its length. For narrower flaps the subcutaneous fat should be removed and the skin replaced as a full thickness graft with its attached pedicle. A blue flap is more likely to heal than a white one. If skin is completely avulsed it should be cleaned and after its subcutaneous fat has been removed the skin should be replaced as a full thickness graft.

If there is a loss of subcutaneous tissue the edges may be undercut to allow approximation without tension. Occasionally, lengthening of the wound into an S-shaped or stellate form may allow a defect to be closed. Larger gaps may necessitate plastic repair by formation of advancement or rotation flaps (see p. 37).

Complications of Wound Healing

Haemorrhage may be the earliest complication of wounding, see Chapter Two. Sepsis is common, especially in contused wounds and in wounds that are contaminated by clothing, earth and other foreign bodies. Wounds that cannot be sutured because of an interval of more than 24 hours between the injury and its receiving medical attention inevitably become infected. Sepsis may occur any time after injury and cause throbbing and tension, which is only relieved after release of pus or removal of one or two sutures at the maximum site of tension. Subcutaneous haematomata are very likely to become infected, hence the need for meticulous haemostasis before a wound is closed. Dressings after suturing should be as infrequent as possible, and where convenient, for example on the face or perineum, wounds are best left exposed and protected only by some plastic seal such as 'nobecutane' or, more old-fashioned, tincture of benzoin in ether (Whitehead's varnish). Exposed wounds less often become infected than closed ones, because dressings tend to become soaked in exudate and allow the growth of organisms.

Failure of healing usually follows infection. It may also indicate a poor arterial blood supply or poor venous drainage. Although it is known that vitamin C plays a part in wound healing, this is very rarely a factor in man, because deficiency to the extent of frank scurvy must be present before healing is affected. Wounds may fail to adhere because of premature removal of sutures. Every wound should be carefully inspected before sutures are removed, and if there is any doubt as to the integrity of the wound, then only alternate sutures should be removed, leaving the rest for another day.

Wound dehiscence after abdominal surgery or 'burst abdomen' is rare, but potentially serious. In such cases there is failure of healing, and about the sixth to tenth day the wound gives way to allow protrusion of the intestines and other viscera. Usually there is some warning of impending rupture, for peritoneal fluid leaks through the wound for a few days before the skin breaks because subcutaneous rupture may have been present for some time. All layers of the abdominal wall are usually affected. Infection may be a factor, but dehiscence can occur under sterile conditions. Old people, the malnourished, those with great abdominal distension and those with cancer have all been said to be prone to burst abdomen, but in fact the cause is not known. Use of unabsorbable sutures in the abdominal wall repair, such as nylon or wire, certainly reduces the incidence of burst abdomen, and it is possible that some people react badly to catgut and fail to heal normally with it. When such burst wounds are repaired with wire or nylon the wounds usually heal more rapidly than in primary healing. The first-aid treatment of a burst wound is simply to cover the area with sterile towels and take the patient to the operating theatre for toilet of the wound and suture under general or local anaesthesia.

Cosmetically unsightly scars may follow wound healing complicated by infection, especially in healing by granulation. Such scars may be accepted by the patient if they are not on exposed surfaces and if they do not interfere with function. Keloid formation (see p. 124) is particularly common in children and coloured persons and in wounds complicated by slow healing and infection also in pregnancy. Often it is best to wait for a year before advising plastic surgery for unsightly scars until the vascularity of the scar is at its least and contraction has ceased. Obviously if there is a severe functional defect operation is called for earlier. Keloid will often disappear if injections of triamcinolone are given directly into it on a number of occasions.

The capacity for regeneration of a specialised tissue depends upon the ability of its cells to undergo mitosis. In tissues in which mitosis continues into adult life, such as the skin, the lining of the gastro-intestinal and respiratory tracts and other epithelial surfaces, active regeneration occurs by growth inwards from the edges of the wound. If the full thickness of the epithelium has not been lost, then regeneration can occur from the depths of the wound as well as from its edges. For example, skin may regenerate from sebaceous and hair follicles in the base of a wound.

Blood and reticulo-endothelial tissues rapidly regenerate following depression of their activity by cytotoxic drugs and X-rays. A good example of regeneration is the power of colonisation that preserved marrow cells have when they are injected into the circulation. Such cells have the capacity to spread throughout the skeleton and restore the marrow completely.

Endocrine glands and such glands as the liver are composed of stable cells which, though they normally cease to multiply in the adult, retain a potential for mitosis, which may be initiated by a variety of stimuli. In the central nervous system there is no power of cell multiplication, and no regeneration can occur after birth. Injury causes gliosis, which of itself may cause disabilities such as epilepsy. Peripheral nerve cells cannot multiply, but their axons may regenerate and function again as long as they can enter appropriate Schwann sheaths peripherally. Injury to muscle, cartilage and tendon can only be restored by scar tissue.

Plastic Repair

This subject will be dealt with more fully in the next section, but in brief the measures available for correction of scarring are excision of the scar, with careful resuture of the wound and skin grafting of defects either by split thickness grafts or by full thickness grafts, free or pedicled. Wide excision of fibrous tissue deep to the skin may pose problems of repair and filling of dead space.

THE SCOPE OF PLASTIC SURGERY

Plastic surgery is concerned with repair and reconstruction. Although much of this work is carried out by specialist surgeons in special units, especially those operations that have to be staged over many months or even years, many problems of plastic surgery are dealt with by surgeons of all specialties, because all surgeons are concerned not only with the appearance of their patients but also with the functional results of their operations. Frequently the plastic surgeon acts in close liaison with other surgeons, for example, in the repair of skin defects after compound fractures and the reconstruction of the pharynx after excision of a growth of it. The borders of the speciality of plastic surgery are ill defined, but because plastic techniques enter so many fields, it is important that the principles of repair and reconstruction should be widely known.

Much of the surgery of congenital abnormalities is performed by the plastic surgeon. Reconstruction of the cleft palate and lip is performed by him in close co-operation with the dental surgeon and the speech therapist. Other congenital deformities, such as 'bat ears', are unsightly and yet easily corrected by reconstruction; webbed fingers interfere with function and are disfiguring; haemangiomata may need excision and complicated reconstructive operations.

In the surgery of trauma, treatment of the more complicated injuries to the face and jaws is carried out by plastic and dental surgeons. Other facets of plastic surgery are the repair of extensive loss of skin and other tissues from injury or surgical excision and the treatment of burns at all stages. Plastic repair usually takes place when healing has been achieved and the full effects of scarring have become obvious. It is vital that the surgeon excising a growth should not be deterred from the widest possible excision by inability to carry out reconstruction necessary to preserve function and appearance. Plastic repair in the face and neck after excisional surgery is often carried out immediately after a growth has been excised.

So-called cosmetic surgery is an important part of plastic surgery. Excision of unsightly scars, remodelling the nose, especially after injury, reshaping the breast affected by scarring or massive hypertrophy are all examples of this work.

In this chapter many examples of repair and reconstruction have already been mentioned. It is now convenient to summarise the principles upon which this type of surgery are based. These principles do not differ from surgery of any type, but in the surgery of repair their neglect is more serious than elsewhere.

1. Haemostasis must be complete, for haematoma under grafts or skin flaps may be disastrous. There must be precise approximation of wound surfaces for successful healing.

2. Complicated reconstructive surgery should be performed in the absence of infection. Infected wounds may have to be grafted temporarily to allow healing and clearance of infection so that more extensive plastic surgery can be carried out later.

3. Skin closure must be exact and without tension. All tissues must be handled with great gentleness. Clumsy technique may make all the difference between success or failure, for example in reconstruction by a pedicled flap of skin.

4. Both surgical incisions and the wounds left after excision of scars should, as far as possible, lie in skin creases or what are known as Lange's lines. Lange's lines are lines of elastic tension in skin which pull linear wounds into an elliptical shape. Wounds closed in these lines heal well with minimal scarring; for example, in the neck the lines run transversely, and so the transverse incisions made for thyroidectomy produce scars that are usually cosmetically very satisfactory.

5. Fibrosis deep to the skin must be widely excised if contractures and deformities are to remain corrected.

Grafting Procedures

Skin grafts are either partial thickness or full thickness in depth and in addition are either free or pedicled; pedicle grafts are fashioned with a blood supply preserved through their bases and used as flaps or tubes.

Partial thickness grafts are most widely used, for they will take on infected surfaces, and the most commonly performed grafting operation is that done for infected burns. So long as infection is not caused by virulent organisms and so long as the granulating surface is flat and exuding relatively little, a high percentage of successful 'takes' can be expected. Such grafts have the disadvantage of leaving a cosmetic defect, especially if they are applied in patches. The patchwork appearance often persists, with some keloid formation making the scarring between the grafts more obvious. Partial thickness grafts contract over a period of 3–6 months, and may then cause interference with function. They are accepted by almost any surface except bare cortical bone and tendon. Because partial thickness grafts are cut in a plane that runs through the Malpighian layer regeneration of skin can occur in the donor area; hence further grafts can be taken from the same site after some weeks. Partial thickness grafts preserve well if stored in sterile tubes at 4° C. for up to 3–4 weeks.

When extensive areas of burnt skin have to be grafted it may be very difficult to find large enough donor areas. For this purpose 'skin banks' have been formed of homologous skin grafts. However, the use of skin homografts is limited by the immune response. They are accepted for about 6 weeks, but unless the skin is taken from an identical twin, a rare event, they are rejected at about that time. Attempts to prolong the period of acceptance of homografts have not so far met with any success.

Full thickness grafts take much less readily than partial thickness grafts and free grafts less readily than pedicled grafts. Infection, haematoma or a poorly prepared site for grafting may all cause failure, with sloughing of the graft. Full thickness free grafts (Wolfe grafts) are occasionally used for slice injuries of the tips of the fingers and for defects in the hand after excision of Dupuytren's contracture or after excision of tumours on the face. Useful donor sites are the post-auricular skin and the skin of the abdominal wall. A pattern is cut of the size of the defect to be covered, and an area of skin of this size is excised from the donor area. The graft is sutured in place meticulously and pressure applied by dressings to prevent haematoma accumulating.

Full thickness flaps of skin are used either flat or converted to tubes. Such flaps are essential to cover cortical bone, for example in compound fractures with loss of skin substance, where tendons are bared and where large areas of full thickness skin have been removed by injury or by the surgeon. The flap must have an adequate blood supply coming through its base and must not be too long in relation to its breadth. Normally the base should be twice as broad as its length to provide sufficient blood supply. Wide undercutting is necessary to fashion the flap, and this of itself may allow a skin defect to be closed without tension (advancement flap). Occasionally a flap is cut and rotated laterally to cover an important area (rotation flap). For example, the defect over say the frontal area of the cranium left after excision of a large rodent ulcer may be covered by skin moved from a parietal flap based on the superficial temporal artery. This leaves a defect within the hair line in the parieta area which can be covered by a partial thickness graft.

Tubed pedicle grafts are less often used, but are essential for the transfer of skin from a greater distance than can be allowed by a pedicled flap. The skin of a flap is first raised but left attached at the ends. Its cut surfaces are sutured to form a tube, and the defect underneath it grafted with partial thickness skin grafts. The tube is left for at least 3 weeks, after which one end is detached and joined to its receptor site. Again after several weeks, when it is judged that the tube is adequately vascularised, the other end is separated and moulded to the size and shape required. Such staged operations are suitable for, say the transfer of skin from the arm or supraclavicular area to the face.

FURTHER READING

Muir, I. F. K., and Barclay, T. L. (1962) *Burns and Their Treatment.* Lloyd-Luke, London.

Douglas, D. M. (1963) *Wound Healing and Management.* E. & S. Livingstone, Edinburgh.

McGregor, I. A. (1965) *Fundamental Techniques of Plastic Surgery.* E. & S. Livingstone, Edinburgh & London.

Wound Healing (1966) Edited by Illingworth, C. J. & A. Churchill, London.

CHAPTER FIVE

INFLAMMATION AND CROSS-INFECTION

Inflammation is the reaction of living tissues to an injury which does not destroy them. When tissue is destroyed inflammation occurs at the junction with healthy tissue, forming a line of demarcation from the dead part. The term inflammation is usually restricted to the early vascular and cellular responses which are part of the defence mechanism of the body, while the later reconstructive changes are referred to as repair.

The causes of inflammation are conveniently grouped as follows:

1. *Infection* by bacteria, viruses and parasites.
2. *Physical agents* which include trauma, heat, cold, electricity and ionizing radiations.
3. *Chemical agents* such as acids and alkalis.

ACUTE INFLAMMATION

Pathology

There is an initial dilatation of blood vessels, especially the capillaries and arterioles, due largely to the release of histamine, 5-hydroxytryptamine and other vasodilators as a result of the injury. Serum, white blood cells and antibodies pass through the capillary walls into the tissues. There is a slowing of the blood flowing through the vessels, while the overall volume is increased because of the vasodilatation.

The exudate may contain much fibrin, especially in staphylococcal infection, and this helps to wall off the inflammation. It also contains white cells, especially polymorphonuclear leucocytes, which are amoeboid, and phagocytose bacteria. At the same time the number of these cells in the general circulation rises from a normal count, which lies between 5,000 and 10,000 per cu. mm. up to as much as 40,000.

In an overwhelming and possibly fatal infection the white cell count may fall, i.e. leucopenia or the polymorphs may disappear, i.e. agranulocytosis, due to depression of the function of the bone marrow by bacterial toxins.

Symptoms and Signs

There are four cardinal symptoms and signs:

1. Redness (rubor) of the skin due to dilated blood vessels.
2. Heat (calor) due to increased blood flow.
3. Swelling (tumor) due to the presence of exudate in the tissue.
4. Pain (dolor) due to pressure on the sensory nerve endings.

Results of Inflammation

The course of inflammation varies according to the type of infection or injury and the efficiency of the body's responses:

1. *Resolution* is a complete return to normality—fibrin digested, cells phagocytosed, exudate absorbed and blood flow back to normal. Because the tissue damage is minimal, no scarring results.

2. *Suppuration* commonly follows bacterial infection. Pus consists of liquefied tissue cells, leucocytes, bacteria (dead and alive), cholesterol and fat globules.

3. *Fibrosis* results when tissue has been destroyed by suppuration or prolonged infection leading to incomplete resolution. It is a feature of the infection caused by slow-growing organisms, such as tubercle bacilli or actinomycosis. Destruction of tissue by burns or other types of trauma can only be replaced by fibrosis. The destroyed tissue separates and is discharged, the defect is invaded by fibroblasts that eventually contract to fibrocytes that make up scar tissue.

4. *Ulceration* may follow inflammation of or near to an epithelial surface. An ulcer is a persistent breach of an epithelial surface.

5. *Gangrene* is a form of necrosis, usually with some colour change in the tissues, most often due to cutting off of the blood supply to a part, which may then separate as a slough.

Treatment

(a) *General.* Severe inflammation demands bed rest and a generous intake of fluids by mouth, fluids because appetite is depressed and because fever and sweating deplete the volume of body water. If the patient is very ill and vomiting the fluid must be given intravenously. Antibiotics are frequently required, and given preferably after the organism has been identified and its sensitivity determined in the bacteriological laboratory. Usually it is not possible to wait the necessary 2–3 days for this to be done, so immediate treatment is begun with a wide-spectrum antibiotic such as ampicillin. When the sensitivity tests are available a change of antibiotic may be necessary. Often the type of organism can be forecast, aiding the choice of antibiotic, for example staphylococcus aureus in hand infections, coliforms in urinary infection.

(b) *Local.* The affected part is rested. Local heat is comforting and may speed resolution, it can be applied in fomentations or radiant heat for superficial lesions and short-wave diathermy for deeper ones. Elevation of a limb reduces congestion and oedema and may lessen pain. As soon as suppuration occurs, the pus is evacuated through an incision.

CHRONIC INFLAMMATION

This is the result of a long-continued mild stimulus which provokes a marked proliferation of the tissues. Chronicity may be the end-result of acute inflammation when some structures develop considerable local resistance, as in osteomyelitis and empyema, or it may be the result of low-grade inflammation from the outset. There are three main groups of conditions causing chronic inflammation:

(a) Specific granulomatous infections, of which tuberculosis, syphilis and actinomycosis are the most important.

(b) Infection by pyogenic organisms of virulence diminished or attenuated by antibiotics, especially if given in inadequate doses.

(c) Foreign bodies such as non-absorbable sutures, compounds containing silica which was used in glove powder, silica and asbestos dust inhaled in mining and calculi may all cause chronic granulomata.

Histologically there is great proliferation of fibroblasts and fibrocytes in which small vessels show obliterative endarteritis. Lymphocytes, macrophages and plasma cells predominate, while polymorphs are very scanty. In long-standing infection and suppuration amyloid disease may develop, with infiltration of certain organs, especially the liver, spleen, kidneys and intestines, with an extracellular waxy amorphous substance. This amyloid material is a glycoprotein which stains orange with Congo-red.

ULCERATION

A persistent breach in any epithelial surface is called an ulcer. The main causes can be grouped as follows, often more than one cause operates at the same time:

1. *Physical.* Pressure, e.g. bedsore or plaster sore, intense heat, cold, friction, chemicals, irradiation.

2. *Infection.* Acute infections, e.g. Staphylococcal, may lead to local gangrene and ulcer formation. Chronic infection, e.g. syphilitic gumma, tuberculosis, fungal infection.

3. *Vascular Insufficiency.* Gangrene of skin follows arterial thrombosis secondary to atherosclerosis. Varicose veins and the sequelae of thrombosis of the deep veins of the legs are particularly prone to produce leg ulcers because of the waterlogging of tissues which accompanies venous stagnation leading to impaired nutrition of the skin.

4. *Sensory Loss.* Deficient sensation, e.g. as occurs in peripheral neuritis and syringomyelia, allows the individual to sustain injury without pain, and ulceration follows. Trophic ulcers on the sole of the foot arise from anaesthesia of the overlying skin.

5. *Malignant Disease.* The skin or mucous membrane may be the site of a neoplasm, e.g. rodent ulcer or epithelioma, which breaks down and ulcerates, or tumours may secondarily involve the epithelium and progress to ulceration.

6. *Haematological Disorders.* In blood dyscrasias, such as spherocytosis, sickle-cell anaemia, hypersplenism and reticuloses, ulceration of the leg may occur.

It is convenient to consider ulceration as passing through three stages. The first is *extension*, in which there is active destruction of the epithelium, e.g. bursting of an abscess. Discharge is copious, the floor of the ulcer is shaggy and there is a zone of acutely inflamed tissue surrounding it. In the second or *chronic* stage sloughs separate from the base of the ulcer, which becomes adherent to nearby structures, there is little discharge and the surrounding skin becomes fibrotic and often pigmented. The third stage is that of *repair*, the base of the ulcer becomes covered by velvety vascular granulations, the edge shelves and becomes less well defined as the epithelium grows in.

Treatment

The treatment of any ulcer, acute or chronic, depends on finding the cause and dealing with it. Local treatment includes dressings, coping with infection, discharge and sloughs, and measures to aid or speed healing such as rest in bed, splintage and supportive bandaging. On the whole, antibiotics are of little value in clearing up the infection on the surface of the ulcer, except in specific infections such as tuberculosis. If one type of organism is cleared from an ulcerated surface another type will usually replace it, usually one resistant to the antibiotic used. In addition, skin hypersensitivity to locally applied sulphonamides and antibiotics is common. Mild chemical antiseptics are more useful, such as proflavine hemisulphate or 5-aminoacridine in a dilute solution. If there is a profuse discharge an antibiotic aerosol spray containing neomycin, bacitracin and polymyxin (polybactrin) is very useful in drying it up. The aim should be to make the surface of the ulcer clean and dry. Sloughs are usefully removed by gauze dressings soaked in half-strength hypochlorite solution (Milton). Adhesion of dressings is prevented by the application of special gauze impregnated with silicone (non-adherent dressings). Elevation of the limb and application of pressure dressings removes oedema. Some ulcers will heal if the cause is removed, rest provided and infection curbed. In some the defect is so great as to require plastic procedures, such as skin grafting, to speed healing.

The investigation and treatment of the commonest site of ulceration, the leg, is dealt with in more detail in Chapter Nine.

GANGRENE

Death of a portion of tissue large enough to be seen by the naked eye is called *gangrene*. Smaller groups of dead cells are referred to as *necrosis*. The piece of dead tissue is called a *slough* which, after separation, leaves an ulcer; so many of the causes of gangrene are the causes of ulceration. Gangrene is the term more often used to describe death of tissue from arterial occlusion. Gas gangrene is due to anaerobic infection (see Chapter Six); severe physical trauma, burns, frostbite, prolonged immersion in cold water and trauma may be followed by gangrene. Diabetic gangrene may be due to arterial disease, neuritis or infection, or by a combination of these factors. Chemicals such as phenol, strong acids or alkalis may destroy skin, causing gangrene. Drugs such as ergot or adrenaline may cause gangrene by producing arteriospasm.

The terms 'wet' and 'dry' gangrene are more of historic than practical interest. The appearance of a limb affected by gangrene depends upon the amount of fluid present in it at the time of onset of the disease or injury, the speed of change and the incidence of infection. Where both veins and arteries become blocked by thrombosis it is possible for the limb to swell and show gangrenous changes in an oedematous limb. Venous gangrene is a condition in which the veins of the leg alone become obstructed by thrombosis, producing gross swelling and death of tissue.

In dry gangrene typically a digit becomes shrunken and blackened and, so long as infection does not occur, the dead part may fall off to leave a slowly healing ulcer. The line of demarcation which delineates the gangrene is due to granulation tissue forming where the dead and living tissues join.

In wet gangrene more extensive necrosis has occurred, allowing spreading cellulitis and infection with severe toxaemia.

INFECTION

Infection is the invasion of the body by micro-organisms in such numbers and of such virulence that they produce inflammation, the intensity depending on the type of organism and its aggressiveness, the local resistance of the tissues and the general defence mechanisms of the body. A razor cut of the face heals rapidly and well because there are few organisms present and the blood supply is excellent, but a wound from nail-scissors on the toe of an old person with atherosclerosis and diabetes may lead to massive infection, gangrene and loss of the toe or even the limb.

Entry of Infection

Micro-organisms enter the body as a complication of wounds (including those made by the surgeon), in droplets or dust through the nose and lungs and in contaminated food or water entering the alimentary tract. Many parts of the body are normally inhabited by micro-organisms but these only become pathogenic if they pass to another site, e.g. *Esch. coli* proliferating in the urinary tract having travelled from the colon or rectum. Many people carry organisms pathogenic to others with no ill-effect to themselves, e.g. *Staphylococcus aureus* in the nose of a doctor or nurse, typhoid and diphtheria in carriers.

Spread of Infection

The virulence of micro-organisms depends on their capacity for spreading and multiplying in the tissues. Their toxicity depends on the strength of the toxins they produce:

Exotoxins are released from bacteria. An example is the specific exotoxin of tetanus bacilli, which lowers the threshold of excitability of the anterior horn cells of the spinal cord. Endotoxins are released from the bodies of dead bacteria and are usually non-specific in their actions.

Some enzymes are produced by bacteria which may help to localise or alternatively to diffuse the inflammatory process.

Coagulase is produced by some pathogenic staphylococci which convert fibrinogen to fibrin, and hence the pus that is formed by such organisms is thick, and a well walled-off abscess is a feature of the inflammation. The capacity of some organisms to produce coagulase is used by the bacteriologist as a test of pathogenicity, coagulase-positive staphylococci are pathogenic, coagulase-negative staphylococci are usually non-pathogenic.

Fibrinolysin which dissolves fibrin is produced by streptococci. Hence a lesion caused by streptococci is rapidly spreading, the pus that is formed is characteristically thin.

Haemolysins are produced by many bacteria, for example anaerobes—red cells are destroyed and pigment liberated.

Leucocidin destroys white cells which are an important defence against infection.

COMPLICATIONS OF INFECTION

Bacteria spread not only locally through tissues and along fascial planes but may also gain entry into the lymph or blood streams. Organisms multiplying in the lymphatics cause lymphangitis showing as red, tender streaks along the course of lymphatics to the regional lymph nodes which become large and tender—lymphadenitis.

The presence of organisms in the blood stream is called bacteraemia. It may not be serious for blood has a very great potential for self-sterilisation. Transient bacteraemia is probably common and unsuspected in most cases. The transient bacteraemia that follows dental extraction may be serious if the patient has a damaged heart valve, because subacute endocarditis may arise. If it is known that a person with a heart abnormality must have teeth extracted it is customary to give penicillin cover at the time of the extraction.

Septicaemia is the multiplication of bacteria in the blood, and is always a serious and often fatal complication. Severe toxaemia, a high fever and tachycardia should always raise suspicion of septicaemia and indicate the urgent need for blood culture to identify the organism and its sensitivity to antibiotics.

In pyaemia fragments of septic thrombus enter the blood. These particles may be arrested in smaller blood vessels, especially in the kidneys, lungs and brain, where they may form metastatic abscesses.

RESISTANCE TO INFECTION

The body is well protected against the entry of micro-organisms. The skin is an excellent barrier, and most organs have their own special defences, e.g. the ciliated mucous membrane of the respiratory tract and upper air passages. The function of the processes of inflammation is to resist and deal with infection, immune responses help further to resist bacterial invasion.

Immunity is the ability of the body to resist organisms or foreign substances, such as toxins, foreign cells or the products of cell breakdown. *Natural immunity* depends on the mobilisation of leucocytes and the intrinsic capacity of the body to deal with foreign materials by producing antibodies. We know far more about *acquired immunity*, for measures to promote immune reactions have played an enormous part in the protection of the health of peoples.

Examples of *acquired immunity* include:

1. An attack of the disease building up a reserve of natural antibodies preventing further attacks, e.g. measles rarely recurs.

2. Dead organisms in suspension (vaccine) may be injected to induce an active immunity which may be permanent, e.g. poliomyelitis or temporary, e.g. typhoid.

3. A vaccine of living organisms which have been attenuated or weakened by chemicals or special methods of culture may be injected to produce active immunity, e.g. B.C.G. vaccine (a strain of attenuated tubercle bacilli). The attenuated poliomyelitis virus may be given by mouth in the prophylaxis of poliomyelitis.

4. In vaccination the virus of vaccinia (cowpox) is scratched into the skin and provides a stimulus to increased immunity against a similar virus disease, variola (smallpox). Pure exotoxins are used in the prophylaxis of tetanus and diphtheria. The toxins are rendered harmless by precipitation with formalin, alcohol or aluminium hydroxide; the substances, toxoids, that result are active immunologically.

Passive Immunity can be conferred by the injection of specific antibodies in serum obtained usually from an animal, sometimes from a human being, immunised either from having suffered from the disease being treated or as a result of the response to injections of vaccines or toxins. The immunity conferred lasts only a short time, but may be extremely valuable, e.g. antitetanus serum (A.T.S.) and convalescent measles serum. The disadvantage of this type of treatment is its short-lived effect and, if an animal serum is used, the possibility of causing anaphylactic shock. Before any such sera are given, a close enquiry must be made into the history of allergy, and it is usual to perform a skin test by injecting a minute test dose intraepidermally to see what reaction it produces. If either human serum or purified human gamma globulin is given, there is no such risk and this precaution is unnecessary.

THE SURGERY OF INFECTION

The use of antibiotics has removed most of the fears of infection. Septicaemia and pyaemia are rarities nowadays, and when they occur are usually treatable with success. The surgeon still, however, has an important rôle to play in deciding when antibiotics should be used, which antibiotic is likely to be effective, when it should be abandoned and when to drain for pus. It is important to realise that not all infections require antibiotics. Antibiotic therapy can sterilise an abscess, but pus must be evacuated, for it cannot be absorbed, and unless drained will usually come to a surface and discharge spontaneously. Antibiotics have a grave disadvantage in that where they are only partially successful against organisms, infection may be dampened down but not completely rendered inactive. A low-grade inflammation may persist, encouraging the formation of an excessive amount of vascular granulation and fibrous tissue. Discharge may be prolonged and induration and scarring exaggerated.

The important indication for antibiotic therapy is cellulitis, that is inflammation spreading in areolar tissue, usually subcutaneous tissue, which may resolve or go on to suppuration, sloughing or necrosis. Cellulitis is commonly associated with lymphangitis, lymphadenitis and, in the days before chemotherapy, commonly went on to fatal septicaemia. It is the effect of chemotherapy in dramatically limiting spreading infection that has been so striking in preventing the most serious effects of infection.

Acute Abscess

An acute abscess is a circumscribed collection of pus surrounded by a zone of inflammation called the pyogenic membrane. Abscesses often tend to enlarge by following lines of least resistance, usually in fascial planes, and so may come to ramify widely. In some tissues, e.g. the breast, the abscess cavity becomes loculated, and if only one part is drained the rest may continue to suppurate. Abscesses which are not drained may discharge spontaneously, e.g. an appendix abscess may discharge into the rectum. If drainage is efficiently carried out the cavity collapses and the granulation tissue in the wall of the abscess is replaced by fibrous tissue. Delayed healing may be due to inefficient drainage or because the walls of the abscess cavity are too rigid to contract. For example, an abscess in bone or in the pleural space (empyema) is held open by the rigidity of its walls. The presence of a foreign body, such as a non-absorbent suture, a faecolith or a calculus, may produce a persistent discharge from the site of the abscess cavity. Persistence of infection always suggests the possibility of some underlying disease, such as a neoplasm or chronic granuloma.

An abscess causes pain, typically throbbing. Overlying it there is brawny swelling, tenderness on palpation and pitting due to oedema. When pus forms, the sign of fluctuation can be elicited, but only if it is superficial; beneath dense inelastic structures like fascia an abscess may be under great tension. Fever results and sometimes rigors. The white-cell count may rise to 15,000 to 40,000 cells per cu. mm. Most of the white cells in the blood are polymorphonuclears. The severity of local and general symptoms depends on the type of organism and the response it evokes in the tissues. Some abscesses reach a large size almost silently, while others cause intense local reaction even at an early stage.

Treatment

Pus in an abscess should be drained as soon as it forms. If the abscess is pointing an incision is made over the site of maximum fluctuation or tension. In some cases, e.g. for an empyema of the chest, drainage must be carried out at the most dependent point. All loculi within the abscess cavity should be broken down gently to leave a single cavity. On the whole, it is better rather to over-incise than to under-incise, and the rule should be that in an abscess of any size it should be possible to put a finger into the cavity and explore it thoroughly, breaking down any septa. Pus should be sucked out, expressed or mopped out. Where the diagnosis is in doubt, then it is wise to take a small part of the wall for histological examination. Drainage of pus is usually followed by dramatic improvement in symptoms, fall in temperature and fall in leucocyte count. Recurrence of symptoms and signs of infection indicate loculation of the abscess and the need for further drainage. It is wrong to pack abscess cavities firmly with gauze, because the packing may delay healing. All that is necessary is to insert a gauze wick to keep the edges of the opening into the abscess apart so that healing can occur from the base of the abscess up to the surface.

Chronic Abscess

Chronic abscesses contain pus, but often there is little evidence of inflammation around them. Some acute abscesses become chronic for the reasons that have already been mentioned, but some are due to organisms such as tuberculosis which excite only a low-grade inflammatory reaction, and the abscesses they form are called *cold abscesses*. In such chronic abscesses there is no urgency for drainage—more important is the diagnosis of the causative organisms and the cause for chronicity. Chemotherapy for the specific condition may allow the abscess to become static or even calcify. Sometimes if the abscess approaches the surface of the skin it is necessary to aspirate or express it. Where a chronic abscess is due to a granuloma, neoplastic disease or a foreign body, then the abscess must be opened, explored and biopsy of the wall taken to find the cause.

A *sinus* is a narrow track blind at one end lined by granulation tissue. It usually leads from an abscess cavity, which may be quiescent, to the skin or any of the body surfaces. The reasons for the persistence of a sinus are the same as those previously mentioned for chronicity of an abscess. A *fistula* is a narrow track which joins two epithelial surfaces, e.g. fistula-in-ano joins the anal canal to the peri-anal skin.

The causes of sinus and fistula are alike, one difference is that a fistula will not heal once its lining becomes epithelialised. In addition, the constant passage of secretions, such as faeces, urine and cerebro-spinal fluid, may prevent spontaneous closure.

In days gone by chronic suppuration was not uncommonly followed by the development of amyloid disease. In this condition a waxy material is deposited in the walls of blood vessels and in the connective tissue stroma of the liver, kidney, spleen and indeed any organ. In the blood there is a diminution in the level of serum albumen and a rise in the globulin. If the dye congo-red is injected intravenously it is taken up by the amyloid and disappears rapidly from the blood stream—a test which can be used diagnostically. The condition is always fatal eventually.

ANTIBIOTICS

Antibiotics are chemotherapeutic agents which kill or inhibit the growth of bacteria. These substances which can be extracted from moulds or bacilli are often made synthetically. Sulphonamides are chemical compounds that have a bacteriostatic action, that is they prevent the division of organisms. From the point of view of treatment of infection, antibiotics can be grouped into three main categories:

1. Those active against gram-positive organisms, e.g. staphylococci and streptococci; penicillins (including penicillin G, penicillin V, methicillin and cloxacillin), erythromycin, novobiocin, fusidic acid, vancomycin and bacitracin.
2. The wide-spectrum antibiotics active against gram-positive and gram-negative organisms; tetracycline, streptomycin, chloramphenicol, ampicillin, kanamycin, neomycin, gentamycin and cephaloridine.
3. Chiefly active against gram-negative organisms; polymyxins and carbemicillin.

The choice of an antibiotic depends on many factors, ideally it is made in consultation with a bacteriologist after he has had time to culture and identify the organism and its characteristics. Laboratory tests may take several days, during which treatment must be maintained, so that it is important that the surgeon should know the characteristics of the common infecting organisms, the relative seriousness of the clinical conditions they cause and their probable response to different chemotherapeutic agents.

Bacteria vary in their sensitivity to antibiotics and their capacity to produce resistant strains. *Staph. aureus* has over the years become resistant to many antibiotics; *Strep. pyogenes* is rarely resistant except to tetracycline, never to penicillin. Equally, some antibiotics have a tendency to encourage the emergence of resistant strains of bacteria, streptomycin is notorious for the rapidity with which resistant organisms appear when it is used. Tetracycline and chloramphenicol induce resistance more slowly. Resistance to penicillin has developed because a small proportion of naturally occurring staphylococci produce penicillinase, an enzyme which destroys the antibiotic. They occur in hospitals where penicillin is widely used. Fortunately new penicillins are being synthesized which are impervious to penicillinase, such as cloxacillin.

When it becomes necessary to use an antibiotic, pus should be sent to the laboratory so that the sensitivity of the infecting organism can be determined, a process that takes a minimum of 18 hours. Meanwhile it is usually desirable to start treatment right away. The surgeon tries to forecast the causative organism and the likelihood of its sensitivity to antibiotics. For severe staphylococcal infection in hospital, a penicillinase-tolerant penicillin is indicated, such as cloxacillin or methicillin, since most hospital staphylococci are nowadays resistant to benzyl penicillin and tetracycline. In domestic practice and in less severe infections and in the Casualty Department, penicillin G is still effective in most cases. For gram-negative bacilli the antibiotic of choice is streptomycin, tetracycline and even sulphonamides still have their place. For organisms resistant to the commonly used antibiotics kanamycin or polymyxin is of use, but these substances do have the serious drawback of having side effects, such as renal damage. The following table shows the sensitivity of the commoner organisms to most of the available antibiotics:

Antibiotic	Staph. aureus	Strep. pyo- genes	Strep. faecalis	Clos- tridium	E. coli	Ps. pyo- cyanea	Proteus
Penicillin	SR	S	s	S	R	R	sR
Cloxacillin, methicillin	S	S	R		R	R	R
Ampicillin	SR	S	s		SR	R	SR
Streptomycin	SR	s	sR	R	SR	sR	SR
Kanamycin	S	s	s	R	SR	sR	SR
Neomycin	S	R	s	R	SR	sR	SR
Vancomycin	S	S	S	S	R	R	R
Polymyxin, colistin	R	R	R	R	S	S	R
Bacitracin	S	S	s	S	R	R	R
Erythromycin	SR	S	S	S	R	R	R
Novobiocin	SR	s	SR	s	R	R	sR
Tetracycline	SR	SR	sR	S	SR	R	sR
Chloram- phenicol	SR	S	S	s	SR	R	SR
Sulphonamides	SR	SR	R	sR	SR	sR	SR

S = Sensitive. s = moderately sensitive.
R = Resistant.
SR = Normally sensitive but resistant strains are common (resistance may rarely be seen in any organism to almost any antibiotic).

Prophylaxis

Under special circumstances prophylactic chemotherapy may be justified, but it is clearly likely to lead to the development of resistant strains of bacteria or colonisation by other organisms. It must be remembered that many infections are due to mechanical causes. For example, postoperative lung infections mostly follow collapse of segments of the lung. Wound infection is most often due to haematoma or tissue trauma. If prophylactic chemotherapy is given to prevent infection in, say, a collapsed lung, or haematoma in a wound, it is likely that resistant organisms will be encouraged to grow or other organisms will colonise the damaged tissues. Prophylactic chemotherapy is essential for colonic resection, insertion of protheses and thigh amputation for isehaemia. It is useful when there is some established infection that cannot be cleared up pre-operatively, e.g. a severe bronchitis. It should always be given in patients with damaged heart valves, who may develop endocarditis following surgery. There is no indication that prophylactic chemotherapy of itself in any way diminishes the incidence of wound infection or promotes the healing of the wounds.

Untoward Reactions

The first antibiotic to be used on a wide scale was penicillin, and it is emarkable how few complications it produced. Penicillin still remains the safest of all, and this is also true for the newer penicillinase-tolerant penicillins. Some patients become hypersensitive and develop troublesome skin rashes. Sensitivity is common in nurses giving injections of penicillin. Rarely severe allergy may result, and very rarely sudden death may occur if penicillin is injected into a sensitive person.

Sulphonamides occasionally produce a measles-like skin eruption, but their greatest hazard is blockage of the renal tubules by crystals, with resulting haematuria and anuria. Chloramphenicol very rarely produces aplastic anaemia, and should never be given in repeated courses to children, in whom it is especially liable to produce blood dyscrasias, often fatal. All broad-spectrum antibodies taken by mouth reduce the bacterial flora of the gut, and this can produce nausea, vomiting, diarrhoea and vitamin-B deficiency. Diarrhoea is common, and occasionally a fulminating entero-colitis due to resistant *Staph. aureus* overwhelms the patient.

The polymyxins may cause kidney damage, and are to be avoided in the patient who has renal disease. Streptomycin and gentamycin can damage the vestibular branch of the eighth nerve; neomycin, kanamycin, vancomycin, the auditory. Normal doses may be toxic if renal function is impaired allowing accumulation of the drug.

CROSS-INFECTION

Sepsis due to cross-infection has become a major problem in surgica wards. Infection arising in clean surgical wounds may lead to a prolonged stay in hospital, danger to other patients, prolonged invalidism, failure of the surgical procedure and even death. 'Clean operations' are those in which infections should not happen, for example, hernia operations and operations on bones and joints. Infection in the wound is not inevitable, but may be unavoidable where the alimentary tract is opened, where a drain must be inserted, or obviously after any operation for an inflammatory condition.

Where control of sepsis in hospital is efficient the incidence of infection in clean wounds should be no more than 2–5%. In recent years outbreaks of infection have occurred in many hospitals, in which 25% or more of wounds have become infected. It is often difficult to define wound sepsis. slight redness around an incision may be transitory, tiny beads of pus may discharge around stitch holes. Patients often leave hospital early, and it is not until they attend the Out-Patient Department that a discharging wound is found. Sepsis may only be revealed after several weeks, when an abscess discharges from a wound, usually with a suture around which the infection has arisen.

The increase in hospital sepsis has come with increasing reliance on antibiotics and slackening of standards of sterility in the wards and operating theatres. In addition, since the war there has been an ever-increasing load of surgical operations performed in hospitals which were built for much less busy conditions. When antibiotics were first introduced their effects were almost magical, but as resistant organisms have proliferated, especially in hospitals, it has become increasingly realised that antibiotics are now only effective against established infection, and must not be used as a prophylaxis against wound infection.

Before the Second World War the great fear, especially in maternity hospitals, was the haemolytic streptococcus. Fortunately this organism is never resistant to penicillin, and so it is no longer a serious problem. The new scourge is *Staphylococcus aureus*, because penicillin-resistant strains and penicillinase-producing staphylococci are increasing in incidence every year. Staphylococci are normally carried in the noses and throats of a considerable number of people, and cause them no harm. In hospital the flora changes so that noses and throats become colonised by virulent staphylococci, which may be unnoticed by the carrier, though they may be a common cause of furuncles in the nose, boils on the skin and whitlows. The change in flora in the nose is encouraged by the presence of minute amounts of penicillin and other antibiotics in the air in hospitals, liberated in the preparation of solutions of these substances, which suppresses sensitive strains and allows proliferation of resistant organisms.

Not all pathogenic staphylococci cause serious infections. Strains can be differentiated by phage-typing. Bacteriophages are viruses which lyse bacteria. Different types of bacteriophage can be grown which specifically lyse certain types of staphylococci. By phage-typing it is possible to trace the source of an outbreak of infection. A common strain of staphylococci causing serious infection has been Phage Type 80.

A striking example of the way in which nasal carriage of staphylococci spreads in hospital is the incidence in nurses in training. Only 20% of nurses entering a preliminary training school from civilian life carry staphylococci in their noses; after 3 months in hospital 80% have become carriers, and a high percentage of the organisms grown from their noses are both penicillin- and tetracycline-resistant. It is obviously impractical to try to eliminate this carriage of staphylococci. More important are stringent measures to improve sterilising procedures and the care of wounds in the wards and operating theatres. Constant awareness of the possibility of wound infection enables sepsis rates to be kept to the minimum. No one knows why, when there are so many staphylococcal carriers, so few of them cause wound contamination, or why outbreaks occur sometimes explosively in epidemics. Careful recording of wound infection enables the warning signs of such outbreaks to be detected and active measures to be taken for their curtailment.

Although most is said and written about cross-infection due to staphylococci, it must not be forgotten that other organisms can be as serious. In urological wards *Proteus* and *Ps. pyocyanea* can spread from patient to patient, usually in those with indwelling catheters. In paediatric practice outbreaks of diarrhoea due to Salmonella infection and certain types of pathogenic *Esch. coli* may occur. In maternity wards streptococcal infection can still be serious.

Sources and Control of Infection

Control of infection in hospitals is a vast problem, with many facets. It is important that everyone coming into contact with the patient should be fully conversant with the routes by which infection spreads and the rules of discipline that must be obeyed if sepsis is to be minimised. The problem will be considered under the following headings:

1. The patient.
2. The patient's attendants.
3. Central Sterile Supply Department (C.S.S.D.), instruments and fluids.
4. The operating theatre.
5. The wards.
6. Control of infection.

1. *The Patient*

Patients may bring infection into hospital. Their noses and throats may harbour pathogenic staphylococci or be colonised by them in hospital. Such carriage of organisms is especially likely in those who have previously been admitted to hospital for another illness. Cutaneous infection, discharging wounds and pulmonary infection should be looked upon with suspicion. A particularly dangerous patient is the old man admitted with staphylococcal pneumonia coughing up virulent organisms that may spread to the occupants of a whole ward, both patients and nurses. Those affected should be isolated and the organisms identified bacteriologically. In some hospitals where sepsis has been a serious chronic problem, dramatic results in reducing it have been achieved by giving all patients a cream to insert into their noses containing neomycin and bacitracin.

Extensive skin preparation of patients before operation is not considered necessary nowadays. Most surgeons accept a moderately wide shaving of the operation area (not from the nipples to the knees, the extent formerly advocated for preparation of the abdomen). A bath or preferably a shower and a scrub all over with soap containing hexachlorophane effectively reduces skin carriage of pathogenic organisms. Operations through areas of skin showing infected boils or furuncles should be avoided.

2. The Patient's Attendants

No nurse, doctor or other person who has any active cutaneous infection should attend a patient. Particularly dangerous is the healing boil, apparently innocuous and only slightly discharging. Such lesions should be cultured and the person only allowed to perform hospital duties if certified free of infection. In the wards and operating theatres soap containing hexachlorophane is effective in reducing cutaneous flora. This reduction is short-lived, and during a long operation organisms may come to the surface in sweat and sebaceous secretion from the depths of the skin. Because gloves are commonly punctured during operation, organisms may be liberated into the wound even after an efficient 'scrub up' of the hands. Some epidemics of wound infection have been traced to certain individuals who persistently carry staphylococci not only on their hands but in their noses and on the perineal skin. Frequent use of hexachlorophane soap in bathing is usually effective in clearing these organisms.

The commonest mode of cross-infection is by contact, so handling of wounds should be minimised, and dressings should be performed by a no-touch technique. Before and between operations and wound dressings the hands, forearms and nails should be scrubbed for 2 minutes, with massage into the skin of a generous amount of hexachlorophane cream. Hands should be dried with disposable paper towels and not on a sodden ward towel used by 40–50 people. Masks covering the nose and mouth are worn for dressings and operations. Masks contain an impermeable layer of tissue that prevents passage of organisms. The function of a mask is to direct the breath containing organisms posteriorly behind the doctor's or nurse's ears. Clouds of organisms are liberated in speech, so talking should be reduced to the minimum. Masks should be changed between operations.

3. C.S.S.D., Instruments and Fluids

Control of infection in hospital has been made easier by the establishment of the Central Sterile Supply Department. In this department dressings, instruments and syringes are packed and sterilised before delivery to the wards. Special packs are prepared for ward procedures, such as intravenous cutting down sets, tracheostomy, catheterisation, gastric intubation, etc. The use of disposable plastic and paper has simplified many procedures. Standardisation of methods is essential. Sterilisation is achieved in hot-air ovens and by autoclaving. Many plastic materials, such as catheters and nasal gastric tubes, now come from manufacturers enclosed in polyethylene packs sterilised by gamma-radiation.

In most operating theatres instruments and dressings are sterilised by autoclaving. A few years ago a survey of hospital sterilisation procedures revealed that most hospitals' autoclaves were inefficient and obsolete. Modern automatic electric autoclaves sterilise by steam under pressure which is then removed by vacuum extraction in a cycle of 7 minutes.

Fluids, such as sterile water, saline and antiseptics (cetrimide, chlorhexidine), used in operating theatres and wards must truly be sterile. Preferably they should be prepared in the C.S.S.D. They should be frequently changed, for some organisms can grow in even strong antiseptics.

4. The Operating Theatre

All persons entering an operating theatre should wear gowns and masks, and wear clean boots, shoes or overshoes. The patient should have his hair covered with a hat made of gauze, blankets from the ward should be exchanged for theatre blankets before entering the anaesthetic room. Clean anaesthetic equipment is used for each patient.

Much attention has been given in recent years to the type of ventilation required in operating theatres. Preferably the air should be filtered and humidified, and it should be possible either to heat it or cool it to provide satisfactory working conditions. The pressure of the air in the operating theatre should be slightly greater than that in the corridors outside to avoid any suction effect, infected air being sucked from the wards into the operating theatre. A similar type of positive-pressure ventilation is ideal for rooms in which patients with infection are isolated or where dressings are to be carried out. The work of the operating theatre should be arranged so that during at least one day a week the theatre is empty, so that its walls and floors can be washed with antiseptic solution.

The skill of the surgeon is most important in reducing the chance of infection, no undue tissue trauma, avoidance of haematoma and minimal operating time are all important. Wounds can be exposed to the air after surgery with safety if they are protected by a thin film of plastic applied in an aerosol spray (Nobecutane). Under gauze and strapping wounds tend to become soggy, and once a dressing is sodden, it loses its protective value. Of course, if there is a discharge or drain an occlusive dressing must be applied.

5. The Wards

Dressings should be done as infrequently as possible, and only at a time of day when dust is at its minimum, e.g. at least an hour after bed making and ward cleaning. A clean trolley washed down with antiseptic is used for each patient, preferably the dressing is performed in a special room set aside for dressings off the main ward. Ideally this room should be artificially ventilated and the air pressure slightly higher than outside to prevent any suction effect. Dressings and instruments come from the C.S.S.D.

prepacked and sterilised. Paper towels are used and thrown away. All contaminated instruments are put into paper bags and returned to the C.S.S.D.

Ward cleaning is done in such a way as to minimise dust dissemination. Floors are oiled and polished, vacuum cleaners remove dust, but must be of a type that does not allow it to be blown about. Blankets are made of cotton that can be boiled. Woollen blankets harbour organisms and cannot be boiled. Mattresses are covered with plastic sheeting that can be washed with antiseptic.

Systems of bladder and chest drainage are used that are closed and do not permit organisms to gain entry. Disposable bladder drainage sets are made in plastic as one unit so that once a catheter is passed into the bladder the system is completely closed. It is important when the thorax is drained with suction that organisms are prevented from being disseminated into the ward air through the outlet of the suction machine.

6. *Control of Infection*

So far the measures that have been described are those which should be routinely followed to minimise hospital infection. Next comes the supervision of the hospital to ensure that the routine is being followed and to detect the occurrence of infection before an epidemic arises. Lastly, some of the measures to be instituted in established infection will be mentioned.

Every hospital should have a Control of Infection Committee chaired usually by a bacteriologist, with representatives of the medical and nursing staff and staff from the C.S.S.D. This committee recommends new methods and assesses their effectiveness. All cases of infection are reported to it.

Every ward keeps a sepsis book, each patient's condition is recorded and every week the record is sent to the Hospital's Control of Infections Officer, usually a bacteriologist, who can then see at a glance where infection is occurring and how frequent or how serious it is.

Wards should have side rooms where patients suspected of developing infection can be isolated. Unexplained fever and redness or tenderness of wounds are all suspicious signs. 'Infectious precautions' taken by nurses include wearing gowns, masks and gloves for dressings of their patients. Clothing, cutlery and bed linen are all kept separate from those in the main wards. All persons entering the room must don a gown and a mask kept in the room for the purpose. The surgeon remains in charge, but consults with the bacteriologist over problems such as choice of antibiotics. Abscesses may need to be drained.

After the patient has been discharged the whole room is thoroughly washed out with an antiseptic or is fumigated. All bedding is removed for sterilisation, all furniture is washed with antiseptic.

There is a place for some patients with serious infection who are a danger to their fellows, even in a side room, to be removed to an infectious wing or even to a fever hospital, which usually has empty beds nowadays

C

and has facilities for isolation. Such cases include infected burns, chronic discharging sinuses (empyema, fistula) where highly virulent organisms are being discharged.

Isolation rooms should preferably have artificial ventilation, but it should be arranged that the air evacuated from the room cannot enter the hospital again.

FURTHER READING

General Pathology (1962) edited by Lord Florey. Lloyd-Luke, London.
Williams, R. E. O., and Shooter, R. A. (1960) Hospital Infection, Causes and Prevention. Lloyd-Luke, London.
Humphrey, J. H., and White, R. G. (1964) Immunology for Students of Medicine. Blackwell, Oxford.

CHAPTER SIX

SPECIFIC INFECTIONS

ANAEROBIC INFECTIONS

Anaerobic infections are rare, but so dangerous when they occur that it is vital that they should always be kept in mind so that prophylactic measures can be undertaken which are extremely effective. Treatment of an established infection often fails, with loss of life or limb. The two most important infections are tetanus and gas gangrene. Anaerobic streptococcal infection is uncommon, but may spread from the gut and vagina to wounds after operation.

Tetanus

Tetanus is caused by the *Clostridium tetani*, a gram-positive bacillus which forms spores, drumstick in appearance, that are extremely resistant to physical agents such as desiccation and heat. The organism occurs in soil, especially when it is heavily manured. In hospital, infection has occasionally been traced to catgut, wool for padding plaster casts and plaster of Paris. Any wound, however superficial, may be contaminated but it is especially in deep wounds and wounds contaminated by soil that tetanus organisms are most likely to grow. Very rarely a second operation, for example exploration of an old fracture, may light up a latent tetanus infection.

The bacillus produces a powerful exotoxin that travels along nerve sheaths to the central nervous system, where it lowers the threshold of excitability of the motor neurone cells of the cranial and spinal nuclei. Increased excitability of the motor cells leads to painful and exhausting muscle spasms caused by the most trivial stimuli. The effect of the toxin persists for a variable length of time, but if the muscle spasms can be relieved and if the patient's general condition can be maintained until the effect of the toxin has waned survival can be expected.

Symptoms

The incubation period usually lies between 5 and 15 days, but tetanus may be delayed for up to several weeks, especially in someone who has previously been immunised. Tetanus is always a serious infection, but usually the later the onset, the more localised are the spasms to the site of the infection and the better the chance of survival. Infection may be prevented or modified by prophylactic immunisation.

At first there is pain in the region of the wound, with spasm and twitching of nearby muscle groups. Tachycardia, fever and increased reflex excitability may develop. There may be evidence of pyogenic infection in or around the wound. As the neurotoxin spreads more widely, there is stiffness of an increasing number of muscles. The masseter muscles go into spasm early (trismus). Later, spasm of the facial muscles (risus sardonicus), posterior trunk muscles (opisthotonus) and respiratory muscles occur, with, at the end, generalised convulsions initiated by the slightest disturbance by touch, light or sound. In these spasms bones may be fractured or muscles ruptured. Death results from pain, exhaustion, toxaemia, respiratory infection and respiratory failure. Because the disease is rare, the possibility of its occurrence may not be considered, especially in those cases of delayed and slow onset. Unfortunately in its early phase the disease is easily mistaken for hysteria.

Treatment

Tetanus can be prevented with certainty by active immunisation with tetanus toxoid. This is a pure antigen prepared from culture filtrates, and is given by intramuscular injection in 1-ml. doses in three injections. The first and second are separated by 6 weeks, and the second and third by 6 months. Booster doses are given every 5 years for full protection and at the time of injury. It seems likely that immunisation conveys some protection for life, even without successive booster doses, so long as an injection of toxoid is given at the time of injury. In Britain all parents are now offered immunisation of their babies from the age of 2 months with the triple antigens of diphtheria, pertussis and tetanus. If there is evidence that immunisation has been completed in children, then all that is necessary at the time of injury is to give 1 ml. of toxoid.

Patients who have not been actively immunised must be given passive immunity by the injection of antitetanus serum (1,500 units given intramuscularly). At the same time the first injection of a course of toxoid can be started. If, instead of this, 'adsorbed toxoid' is used antitetanus serum does not interfere with the development of active immunity. All such patients are advised to return for their second and third toxoid injections. 'Adsorbed toxoid' is tetanus toxoid precipitated with aluminium hydroxide. Formol toxoid, which is precipitated with formalin, is not so potent.

Although antitetanus serum is extremely effective in preventing tetanus, it has serious drawbacks. It is prepared from the serum of horses and commonly causes symptoms of allergy, which may be delayed for 2 or 3 weeks. Serum sickness can be very unpleasant, with rashes, effusions into joints, fever and malaise. Serious anaphylaxis may occur at the time of injection, with fainting or even sudden death. For this reason a test dose of 0·1 ml. of serum must always be injected intradermally and the site of injection inspected after 20 minutes to see if any local reaction, erythema or oedema, or any generalised symptoms occur. Adrenaline must always be immediately available to combat any serious hypotensive effects. Enquiry should be made for a history of previous injections of serum and any allergic history of asthma, hay fever, urticaria, eczema or migraine before antitetanus serum is given. If reactions to a test dose do occur careful assessment should be made of the danger of a full injection weighed against the danger of contracting tetanus. Another drawback of antitetanus serum is that if a previous injection of antiserum has been given subsequent injections may be ineffectual.

For all these reasons a campaign for active immunisation against tetanus must be energetically pursued. In some quarters it has been held that antitetanus serum administration is more dangerous than the chances of acquiring tetanus and that the use of antiserum should be replaced by tetanus toxoid and penicillin. It must be appreciated that 6 weeks elapses before active immunity can be produced by two injections of toxoid, and in this time fatal infections can result. Tetanus still causes about 30 deaths per year in England and Wales, and before abandoning prophylaxis by antiserum good evidence will have to be produced that chemotherapy is effective and safer than antitoxin. To reduce the number of antiserum injections patients with minor injuries, scratches and clean lacerations may be given toxoid and one injection of a long-acting penicillin. When tetanus is a serious possibility antitoxin should be given.

Established Infection

Penicillin should be given in large doses, for the bacillus is often sensitive to it. The wound should be inspected and, unless it is completely healed, it should be opened, drained and if necessary excised. The value of antitetanic serum at this stage of the disease has never been proven, but it is customary to give large doses (20–50,000 units) half intravenously and half intramuscularly, though not intrathecally as was formerly practised.

The patient must be nursed in a darkened quiet room and disturbance kept to a minimum. Heavy sedation with barbiturates or paraldehyde is started, though not to the degree of respiratory depression. If the muscle spasms are severe and respiration embarrassed, then tracheostomy, mechanical respiration and paralysis of muscles by relaxant drugs (flaxedil, curare) may be needed for as long as the neurotoxin acts. The tracheobronchial tree is sucked out frequently to prevent the accumulation of secretion; food is given through a naso-gastric tube. This regimen has significantly reduced the mortality of the infection from about 80% to 15%.

Gas Gangrene

Gas gangrene is a clostridial infection due to gram-positive spore-bearing organisms, of which three types predominate, *Cl. welchii*, *septicum* and *oedematiens*. It should be remembered that other organisms form gas in wounds or in visceral infection, for example some types of *Esch. coli* and some streptococci. The gas-forming clostridia are particularly prone to grow in deep wounds contaminated by soil, especially if damaged muscle is present. The incidence of these infections is very much higher in wartime, and in the 1939–45 war became a serious problem when fighting moved from the desert, where infection was rare, to France, where contamination of wounds with heavily manured soil was common. Infection may also appear around colostomies, empyema drainage tubes and in infected wounds after peritonitis. The diagnosis of gas gangrene should always be a clinical one, since the finding of the organism in a smear or culture does not necessarily mean clinical infection. When it does occur the infection is often associated with other organisms, including staphylococci, streptococci, *Esch. coli*, *B. pyocyanea* and *B. proteus*.

Signs and Symptoms

The incubation period is short, 1–3 days after injury. The patient feels ill with fever and tachycardia. The wound is unusually painful, discharges serous fluid and emits a characteristic musty odour once smelt never forgotten. The skin is first pale and then purplish, with blebs of fluid on its surface. Crepitus under the skin can be felt and gas bubbles seen in the discharge and, in radiographs, in tissue planes. Death may occur from overwhelming toxaemia, septicaemia and extensive gangrene.

Treatment

Prophylaxis. Débridement is the term applied to the excision of wounds. The surgeon uses it as a prophylactic against the development of infection, including gas gangrene. All dead tissue, skin, fascia, muscle, loose bone and any foreign bodies are removed; contused structures are excised until freely bleeding tissue is met. In wartime such wounds were left open, covered by loose packing and sutured by delayed primary suture after a period of 4 days. In civilian injuries primary closure is usually safe, so long as careful observation and chemotherapy are maintained. Once gas gangrene is diagnosed or even suspected, large doses of penicillin should be given (1 mega unit 4 times a day), and polyvalent gas-gangrene antiserum containing antibodies to the three common clostridia (9,000 units intramuscularly). It must be admitted that the effectiveness of antiserum has never been proven. Swabs of the wound should be taken and cultured anaerobically.

Established Infection. When infection is established the wound must be opened and drastic excision of all infected tissue performed. All muscle that fails to contract or bleed when cut must be excised. There are characteristic colour changes in the muscles, which may be brick red, dark green or black. In the past amputation was often necessary to save life, but more recently the use of hyperbaric oxygen has proved very useful. In this method of treatment patients are placed in a special pressure chamber filled with oxygen under a pressure of 2 atmospheres.

Infection in postoperative wounds, around colostomies and drainage tubes usually responds to chemotherapy and drainage of the infection.

TUBERCULOSIS

In Britain the incidence of tuberculosis has fallen steeply during the last fifteen years, mainly due to the efficacy of chemotherapy, which, besides producing cure in many cases, has also minimised the spread of the disease. Other reasons for the decreased incidence of the disease include the detection of early cases by mass radiography and raising the immunity of those especially at risk, for example, nurses, by injection of attenuated tuberculous bacilli (B.C.G. vaccine) in those who are negative to tuberculin tests. Pasteurisation of milk and tuberculin testing of cows should eliminate infection of lymph nodes, bone and joints in this country. The disease is still common among immigrants, especially Indians and West Indians, and in many countries tuberculosis still presents a major problem. A strong family history of tuberculosis probably indicates a genetic predisposition to the disease. Improvement of social conditions has and will increasingly aid, the elimination of tuberculosis.

Pathology

The causative organism is *Mycobacterium tuberculosis*, a thin, rod-shaped organism which stains red with hot carbol-fuchsin (Ziehl Neelsen technique). Because the stain resists decolorisation by strong acids, mycobacteria are known as acid-fast bacilli. There are two types, the human and the bovine, distinguishable by their cultural characteristics. The human type is usually spread via infected sputum, the bovine type by infected milk. The organisms gain entry to the body through the respiratory and alimentary tract, tonsils and skin. Local lesions may develop, with further spread by lymphatics or less often by the blood stream.

The course of tuberculosis is very variable, depending much upon the dose and virulence of the bacilli and the degree of resistance of the host. It also depends upon whether the infection is a first infection (primary complex), for then there is a marked local tendency to healing and great enlargement of regional lymph nodes. In second infections hypersensitivity is a feature, evidenced by an exudative lesion with much oedema and an acute inflammatory cell reaction. As chronicity develops, infections are characterised by varying amounts of fibrosis, tissue damage, cavitation and caseation. Caseous (i.e. like cheese) tissue is the necrotic liquefied material that is a typical though not invariable feature of the tuberculous process. In it tubercle bacilli may lie dormant for many years, but can at any time become active and cause recrudescence of the disease. It should be remembered that once a tuberculous infection has been contracted, it may recur at any time in a person's lifetime. Collections of caseous material simulate abscesses, but because of their avascularity and the absence of signs of inflammation they are usually called 'cold abscesses'. Tuberculosis is a destructive disease accompanied by fibrous tissue replacement that seriously interferes with function, for example, stenosis may occur in a bronchus as a result of tuberculous infection.

The *tubercle follicle* is the fundamental lesion of tuberculosis. Usually many are seen showing as small rounded white spots on the surface or in the depths of the affected organ. Microscopy shows a central area of caseation surrounded by a zone of reticulo-endothelial (epithelioid) cells and a variable number of Langhans-type giant cells. These are syncytial cells, often very large and containing many nuclei lying at the periphery. Outside the epithelioid cells are lymphocytes, and outside them fibroblasts. Such lesions may heal by fibrosis or caseate and coalesce to form larger foci of disease with local destruction of tissue.

Tuberculosis spreads by local extension and by involvement of regional lymph nodes. Organisms may enter the blood stream by invasion of veins or occasionally via the thoracic duct. Tuberculous bacteraemia may be transitory and be responsible for infection of such organs as the kidneys, bones or joints. In miliary spread many systems may be involved by an infection which, before the days of chemotherapy, was overwhelming and rapidly fatal. Occasionally tuberculosis spreads along epithelial surfaces or through the subepithelial lymphatic plexuses of such tubular structures as the bronchus and ureter or through the potential body cavities, pleura, peritoneum or meninges.

Diagnosis

Although symptoms, signs and radiology give strong indications of the diagnosis of tuberculosis, it is essential to make a certain diagnosis either by culture of the tubercle bacillus or, failing this, by finding histological evidence of a typical tuberculous pathological process. The treatment of tuberculosis may extend over years, and once begun, it is usually not possible to obtain bacteriological confirmation of the presence of the disease.

Acid-fast bacilli can often be seen in pus, sputum, urine, cerebrospinal, synovial and ascitic fluid. Some specimens may reveal positive results only after special concentration methods and microscopy of the deposit. Whether acid-fast bacilli are seen or not, all specimens are cultured on Dorset's egg or Lowenstein–Jensen media on which the bacteria may appear in from 2 to 8 weeks. The sensitivity of the bacilli to antibiotics can be tested on these cultures. More and more resistance to tuberculostatic drugs is being met nowadays, especially in persons who have previously been treated for tuberculosis, and so it is of vital importance to detect resistant organisms as early as possible. Inoculation of a guinea-pig with infected material is the most sensitive test for tuberculosis, and should be carried out where there is special difficulty in diagnosis. Six weeks after inoculation the guinea-pig is killed and searched for evidence of tubercle follicles or caseous foci.

Microscopical examination of diseased tissue may reveal acid-fast bacilli, caseation and typical giant cells. The finding of tubercle follicles is suggestive, but not diagnostic, of tuberculosis, for there are many other diseases which are characterised by the presence of non-caseating tubercle follicles, for example, sarcoidosis, leprosy, regional ileitis and foreign-body granuloma.

Tuberculin tests produce evidence that the patient has had previous contact with tuberculosis but are rarely of diagnostic value in proving active disease. A positive reaction in children under the age of 2 years is strongly suggestive of a recent infection. A negative test in an adult suggests that tuberculosis can be excluded, but this is not wholly reliable. The test is performed by the intradermal injection of 0·1 ml. of Old Tuberculin in increasing concentrations from 1 : 10,000 to 1 : 10. In children the Heaf method is used, in which a special instrument with a number of needle points is used to prick a minute quantity of tuberculin into the epidermis. In either method the test is read at 48 hours when, in a positive reactor, the skin is reddened and oedematous around the site of injection.

The erythrocyte sedimentation rate is raised when the disease is active and is a useful guide to progress, satisfactory healing being associated with a fall in sedimentation rate. Occasionally a lymphocytosis is associated with tuberculosis, but this is unlikely to be of diagnostic value.

Treatment

Chemotherapy has revolutionised the treatment of tuberculosis, both in dramatically reducing the mortality and also by lessening its spread from cross-infection. Before chemotherapy, reliance was placed on the sanatorium régime, which was designed to increase the resistance of the patient and to isolate him from his fellows. An important feature of the sanatorium régime was rest, both of the whole of the body and, if possible, of the local focus by such methods as plaster immobilisation or collapse therapy for lesions in the lung. It is still essential to examine members of the patient's family to find carriers or those apparently symptom free who may have the disease.

Tuberculous bacilli become resistant to the use of chemotherapeutic drugs used singly, but if two or three are given simultaneously they appear to act synergistically, and the chance of developing drug resistance is reduced. Streptomycin in 1-g. daily doses is given intramuscularly, para-aminosalicylic acid 5–15 g. and isonicotinic acid hydrazine 200–400 mg. daily given by mouth. Daily injections of streptomycin are given for 6–8 weeks and thereafter 2–3 weekly for 4 months. The oral drugs must be continued for up to 2 years. Careful watch must be kept for the most serious side effect of streptomycin, that is damage to the vestibular and auditory nerves. Early evidence of such damage is produced by complaints of dizziness and tinnitus. If the drug is continued permanent vestibular damage is likely to result. In some patients sensitivity to streptomycin is obvious very early in the course of treatment, and a decision must then be made as to whether the danger of the infection is greater than the disability produced by side effects. If tuberculous bacilli become resistant to streptomycin other drugs are available, including rifampicin, viomycin, cycloserine and ethionamide. These new drugs are not so effective as streptomycin, and are potentially more dangerous in their side effects, so that they should only be used if it is absolutely necessary.

The sanatorium régime depends upon a period of bed rest followed by graduated exercise, the amount depending upon the activity and progress of the disease. A high-calorie diet with added vitamins, extra milk, fresh air and sunshine are all needed to improve general resistance to the disease. Many patients with pulmonary, skeletal and urogenital tuberculosis still benefit from the st.ict discipline of the sanatorium.

Progress of the disease is followed by the sense of well-being of the patient, absence of fever and a lowering of the pulse rate. The erythrocyte sedimentation rate should fall steadily to normal. Bacilli should disappear from the sputum or urine. Radiological evidence of healing is shown by calcification and disappearance of lesions. In the lungs signs of fibrosis and contracture may appear. Fibrosis produced by the healing of tuberculous lesions can cause harmful sequelae, for example, stenosis of a bronchus may prevent a lung cavity from closing, contraction of the bladder may cause intolerable frequency of micturition. Any sign of reactivation of the disease is a signal for a stricter sanatorium régime.

Surgery may be needed to excise foci, such as infected lymph nodes and costal cartilages. Healing may be hastened especially by arthrodesis of the spine or hip joint; caseous abscesses may be evacuated as a matter of urgency, in paraplegia from tuberculous disease of the spine. Amputation is still occasionally needed for disease that cannot be controlled, for example in the ankle or knee joint of an adult.

ACTINOMYCOSIS

Actinomyces are normal inhabitants of the mouth. Human actinomycosis is caused by *Actinomyces israeli*, a gram-positive filamentous, branching organism. It is anaerobic, but can grow under micro-aerophilic conditions, and is commonly part of a mixed infection with coliform and fusiform organisms. In pus discharging from an actinomycotic lesion 'sulphur granules' may be seen, microscopy of which shows radiating groups of club-shaped organisms, the central being gram positive and the peripheral gram negative.

The lesions of actinomycosis occur most commonly in the face, neck and jaws. The lung may be affected, and very rarely the caecum. The organism gains entrance to the body through an abrasion or tooth socket, and a history of a recent dental extraction is common. Caecal disease may present, with symptoms and signs suggesting appendicitis or as a sinus in the abdominal wall some weeks after appendectomy. In the lung an abscess may form which may rupture to produce an empyema or a sinus through the chest wall. Abscess in the liver follows an infection in the alimentary tract; such abscesses are rare, and have a characteristic honeycombed appearance. It is a feature of actinomycosis that its abscesses may track far and wide and give rise to distant sinuses and fistulae.

In the face and neck the characteristic feature of actinomycosis is induration of the skin and subcutaneous tissues, which break down and discharge pus, often containing sulphur granules. Lymph nodes are rarely infected. The jaw may become swollen not by true bony infection but by involvement of periosteum and soft tissues. Recurrent abscess formation in the face and neck or in the right iliac fossa should always be investigated for actinomycosis. Repeated microscopy of pus for the typical colonies of the organism followed by their culture must be performed.

Treatment

Before the use of penicillin, actinomycosis was often a fatal infection. Iodides in very large doses were then the mainstay of treatment. Penicillin must be given in large doses (500 000 units four times daily) for 3 months at least, followed by weekly injections of a long-acting penicillin for 3 more months. Shorter courses are likely to be followed by recrudescence of the disease. Rarely, if the organism is resistant to penicillin, tetracycline may be effective. Drainage of abscesses is necessary. If recurrence occurs penicillin is usually still effective.

LEPROSY (HANSEN'S DISEASE)

Leprosy is caused by the *Mycobacterium leprae*, and is an infection widespread in Asia and Africa. There are two types—the *lepromatous*, contagious and rapidly progressive and the *tuberculoid*, non-infective and slow in development. The disease affects the skin, which becomes ulcerated and scarred, with hideous deformities. Peripheral nerves become thickened, and patches of cutaneous anaesthesia develop with paralysis. Diagnosis is made from the clinical signs and recognition of the organisms in scrapings from the cut dermis, nasal swabs and smears, and biopsies of skin lesions.

Treatment takes years, and is continued until scrapings or biopsy are repeatedly negative. Dapsone (diaminodiphenyl sulphone) in doses increasing from 50 to 600 mg. is given twice weekly or Solapsone (sulphetrone) as 50% solution by mouth in doses increasing from 0·1 to 2·5 ml. twice weekly. Physiotherapy both active and passive, wax baths for hands and much reconstructive surgery is necessary. Tendon transplants for paralyses such as wrist and finger flexors and arthrodeses to restore stability make the treatment a long-term one. Iron therapy is usually necessary.

VENEREAL DISEASES

Syphilis

Syphilis is caused by the spirochaete *Treponema pallidum*, and is usually contracted during sexual intercourse. A syphilitic mother may transmit the infection to her unborn child. The disease is usually classified into three stages.

1. Primary Stage

The primary lesion is the *hard chancre*, a raised inflamed area or ulcer which is characteristically indurated and painless, with greatly enlarged regional lymph nodes, which are also painless. The ulcer arises within a few days or weeks of exposure to infection. It occurs in the male on the prepuce or glans penis and in the female on the labia or cervix. Extra-genital sites include the anus, lip, breast and abdominal wall. The ulcer heals even without treatment, to leave a fine papery scar.

The diagnosis is made by microscopical examination for spirochaetes of fluid exuding from the ulcer under dark-ground illumination and by the treponema immobilisation test, in which antibodies in the patient's serum are detected by their power to immobilise live spirochaetes cultured in rabbit testis. Serological tests for syphilis become positive about 2–4 weeks after the appearance of the chancre. The Wassermann reaction is said to be positive when a non-specific antigen reacts with syphilitic serum in the presence of complement which is used up, thereby preventing the haemoly-sis of sheep's red cells by haemolytic serum used as an indicator. The Kahn reaction is technically simpler and is a precipitation test. False positives are not uncommon, especially in low titres; repeated tests are therefore important in the diagnosis.

2. Secondary Stage

Secondary lesions usually appear 2–3 months or even later after the primary infection. There are many manifestations, including enlarged lymph nodes, especially in the posterior triangle of the neck. Erythema-tous or papular skin rashes, which are typically coppery in colour, may affect the scalp and extend to the hands, feet and flexor surfaces of the limbs. Mucous patches with raised white and ulcerating surfaces are seen in the mouth and on the fauces ('snail track' ulcers). Condylomata, large flat moist papules which are highly infective, may be seen round the anus and vulva. Cellulitis, periostitis and epididymitis also occur, but are un-common.

3. Tertiary Stage

The tertiary phase may not arise for many years after the appearance of the primary infection. The characteristic lesion is the gumma, a chronic granuloma characterised by fibrosis, endarteritis obliterans and an in-filtration of chronic inflammatory cells, among which plasma and mono-nuclear cells are prominent. The lesion may necrose and if it lies near an epithelial surface an ulcer is formed which has typical vertical punched-out edges with a dirty slough covering the ulcer base.

More diffuse granulomatous changes may affect bones, the meninges and brain, major vessels and viscera. Bones may become diffusely thickened by osteoperiostitis. Involvement of the meninges, brain and spinal cord may cause general paralysis of the insane and tabes dorsalis. Involvement of the dorsal columns of the spinal cord renders joints insensitive and disorganised (Charcot's joints). Scarring of the aorta may go on to aneurysm formation and aortic valve incompetence. Narrowing of the ostia of the coronary arteries causes angina. The manifestations of tertiary syphilis are so diverse that it is difficult to describe them all. Any tissue of the body can be involved.

Treatment

Penicillin is the mainstay of treatment for syphilis. For early cases, procaine penicillin 600,000 units intramuscularly is given daily for 10 days (20 days if the Wassermann reaction is positive). A single intramuscular injection of 2·5 million units benzathine penicillin is an alternative. In late cases, especially when the cardiovascular system and brain are affected, penicillin may produce severe reactions (Herxheimer reactions), with fever, malaise and aggravation of the manifestations of the disease. To avoid these reactions bismuth 0·2 g. weekly is given for 4 weeks, followed by penicillin 600,000 units in daily doses for 10 days extended to 15–20 days if there is cardiovascular or cerebrovascular disease. After treatment the Wassermann and Kahn tests must be followed for 2 years and the cerebrospinal fluid examined before a final cure can be claimed.

Congenital Syphilis

Syphilis may be conveyed to the foetus through the placental circulation of a syphilitic mother after the fifth month of pregnancy. Miscarriage and still-birth of syphilitic babies is common. Congenital syphilis is entirely preventable so long as a Wassermann test is done in all women early in pregnancy and all those reacting positively are treated.

Congenital syphilis is rarely seen in this country. It has many manifestations in children, including bullous skin eruptions, mucous patches or ulcers in the mouth and palate, and infection and scarring (rhagades) at the corners of the mouth and around the nose. Nasal discharge may be followed by destruction of nasal bones, giving rise to a saddle-shaped nose. There may be tenderness in bones and joints due to periostitis, which may go on to the typical sabre deformity of the tibia. Another cause of a painful joint is epiphysitis, causing pseudo-paralysis in the newborn. The skull may be thickened by periostitis with prominent bossing of the parietal or frontal regions. Hydrarthrosis of joints may occur in older children (Clutton's joints). The permanent incisor teeth may be notched (Hutchinson's teeth) and the molars conically shaped (Moon's molars). Deafness is common, and interstitial keratitis may cause blindness around the age of puberty. The nervous system may be affected with varying degrees of mental defect; a juvenile form of tabes dorsalis may arise if the spinal cord is affected.

Treatment is as for the acquired disease. Prevention is more important than cure.

Soft Chancre (Chancroid)

Soft chancre is a venereal disease of tropical countries, and is caused by the bacillus *Haemophilus ducreyi*. A painful ulcer appears on the genitals a few days after infection. Ulceration is rapid and deep, with a copious foul discharge. The regional lymph nodes are greatly enlarged and matted together (bubo). The diagnosis is made by microscopical examination of the discharge for the causative organism and, in chronic cases, by the use of a specific skin test (Reenstierna's test), in which a vaccine of the organism is injected intradermally. The condition responds to sulphonamides, streptomycin and tetracycline. Healing leaves disfiguring scars.

Gonorrhoea

Gonorrhoea is a purulent infection of the urethra caused by the *Neisseria gonorrhoeae*. Less often the rectum and vagina may be infected, and very rarely nowadays the conjunctiva of the newborn infant. Urethritis presents with dysuria, followed by a copious discharge of yellowish pus 2–8 days after exposure to venereal infection. The most common complication of urethritis is epididymo-orchitis. Damage to the urethral mucosa may lead, months or years later, to fibrosis and urethral stricture. Infection may also pass proximally in the male to cause prostatitis and vesiculitis, which may present acutely or, more often, chronically.

In women salpingitis, pelvic cellulitis and Bartholinitis are common complications, and sterility may be a sequel. There is a marked tendency to chronicity, with persistent discharge from the urethra. Symptoms of gonorrhoea tend to be less severe in women, who may be highly infective and yet unaware of their condition. In children conjunctivitis and vulvovaginitis may rarely be caused by gonococcal infection. Uncommon late complications of gonorrhoea are synovitis and arthritis.

Diagnosis

Gonococci are difficult to culture unless the urethral discharge is plated out immediately on warm chocolate agar plates and incubated in an atmosphere of 10% carbon dioxide. In smears of pus, taken from the urethra before micturition, the presence of gram-negative diplococci *within* polymorph leucocytes usually suffices for the diagnosis to be made. Passage of urine into two glasses confirms that infection comes from the anterior urethra if the first glass contains sediment and threads. In women cervical smears should be examined.

Later in the disease examination of secretion obtained from the urethra after massage of the prostate is a useful guide in men to cure or to the presence of chronic infection. The gonococcal complement fixation test is only of value in the diagnosis of late complications, such as arthritis.

Treatment

Those affected should abstain from sexual intercourse until all signs have resolved, usually for about 6–8 weeks. Penicillin has been most effective in the control of gonorrhoea, though in recent years penicillin-resistant strains have become more and more common. The use of penicillin has the drawback of masking syphilis acquired at the time of gonorrhoea though latent because of its longer incubation period. A combined injection of 600,000 units of procaine penicillin and 500,000 units of soluble penicillin given intramuscularly cures the majority of gonococcal infections. Blood is taken for Wassermann and Kahn reactions at the time of initial treatment and 3 months later. If penicillin does not cure, tetracycline is given by mouth. If penicillin has been used a final Wassermann test must be performed 6 months after treatment.

After treatment it is important to be sure that the infection has really been cured. Urethral secretions are examined in men before they micturate after urine has been held for 3 hours. In men and women smears and cultures from the urethra should be examined at weekly intervals for 3 weeks, and then monthly for 3 months.

Non-specific Urethritis

Not all urethritis is gonococcal, the clinical presentation may be similar, but no bacterial cause may be found. In non-gonococcal or non-specific urethritis the incubation period is usually longer and the course milder, without serious local complications, apart from epididymitis and an uncommon association of urethritis, iridocyclitis and arthritis (Reiter's syndrome). The disease mostly occurs in men, in whom the diagnosis is made by exclusion of gonorrhoea. The results of treatment are variable; tetracycline is tried first, and sulphonamides, chloramphenicol and streptomycin are effective in some patients. In addition, cortisone is often used in the treatment of Reiter's syndrome. In both men and women trichomonal infection must first be excluded.

Yaws

Yaws is due to a spirochaetal disease that closely resembles syphilis, occurring in tropical countries. The causative organism is the *Treponema pertenue*, which has the same morphological characteristics as *Treponema pallidum* and gives rise to positive Wassermann and Kahn reactions 3–4 weeks after the primary infection. It is acquired by direct non-venereal contact or by sexual intercourse. In the primary stage an ulcer appears on the arm or leg, which heals to leave a papery scar. Secondary skin rashes occur 1–3 months after the primary infection. The tertiary lesions are much like those of syphilis; skin and bone lesions are especially common, whereas visceral and nervous lesions are rare. Penicillin offers effective treatment of the disease, a single injection of 1,000,000 units of procaine benzyl penicillin results in a high proportion of cures.

Lymphogranuloma Inguinale

Lymphogranuloma inguinale, also known as lymphogranuloma venereum, is another venereal disease that occurs in tropical countries but is occasionally seen in temperate climates, principally in coloured immigrants. It is caused by a virus which gives rise to an ulcer on the genitals 1–2 days after intercourse. Three or four weeks later there is swelling of the inguinal nodes, which become matted, break down and discharge. In women severe swelling of the vulva (esthiomene) may occur. Rectal strictures arise in women from inflammation passing from the cervix and vagina around the rectum in the pararectal lymphatics.

The diagnosis is made by Frei's test, the intradermal injection of an antigen derived from pure cultures of the causative virus. A positive reaction is denoted by wheal formation and redness at the site of the injection. The virus may be cultured by injection of it into the yolk sac of a fertile egg; a complement fixation test is also available. Tetracycline and chloramphenicol are used in the treatment of the condition. High rectal strictures can be very difficult to treat; repeated dilatation usually suffices, but in some cases surgical repair or even colostomy may be necessary.

HYDATID DISEASE

Hydatid disease is caused by the tapeworm *Taenia echinococcus*. The adult worm lives firmly attached to the mucosa of the small intestine of the host, usually the dog, although the wolf, jackal, fox and kangaroo can all act as definitive hosts. Eggs passed in dog faeces may be ingested by intermediate hosts, including cattle, sheep and man, in whom the larval phase proliferates. Embryos are liberated in the duodenum, from where they enter small veins of the portal system and are mostly filtered from the blood in the liver. Some reach the lungs and some enter the arterial circulation to lodge in any organ. Many embryos die, but some produce hydatid cysts containing numerous scolices, which represent the heads of future worms. The cycle is completed by a dog eating tissues from an intermediate host. Man is usually infected by eating food or drinking water contaminated by dog faeces that contain eggs. The disease is therefore found where man, dogs and sheep live in close proximity, for example, in Australia and Iceland. It is uncommon in Great Britain, though a number of cases occur in the southern part of Wales.

Hydatid cysts may occur in any organ, but common sites are the liver and lung. The cyst wall is formed by three layers—an inner germinal layer, from which project daughter cysts and brood capsules, forming scolices. Outside the germinal layer is a soft, laminated membrane in which no nuclei or cells can be seen. Outside that there is the ectocyst, a dense fibrous capsule formed by the host. Cysts cause symptoms from their size and the pressure they exert by growth. Occasionally a cyst may rupture, causing anaphylactic shock and spread of the disease. Fibrosis and calcification, and, in many cases death of the parasite occur, but one can never be entirely certain of this fact. Suppuration is unusual.

The diagnosis is made by recognition of hooklets and scolices in the cyst fluid and by the Casoni test, in which hydatid fluid is injected intradermally and produces an inflammatory wheal if hydatid disease is present. A complement fixation and precipitation test are also available.

Cysts may grow so large as to require removal, especially those in the lung, liver and brain. It is important to kill the parasite before the cyst is enucleated, as rupture of the cyst with liberation of larvae may spread the disease. It is usual to isolate the cyst with packs soaked in formalin, to aspirate fluid from the cyst so that it can be filled with 2% formalin. The cyst is then enucleated from within its ectocyst. There is no specific chemotherapy.

AMOEBIASIS

Amoebiasis is due to the protozoal parasite *Entamoeba histolytica*. It is common in the tropics, but not unknown in temperate regions. The usual route of infection is ingestion of food or water contaminated by human excreta containing amoebae in their cystic form. The cysts hatch in the large intestine into active amoebae, which invade the submucosa of the colon. Small ulcers may be seen at sigmoidoscopy showing undermined edges, which go deeply as far as the muscle coat; typically the mucosa intervening between the ulcers appears normal. The symptoms are those common to any dysenteric infection—passage of loose stools, blood and mucus—and the condition must always be differentiated from bacillary dysentery, which may occur concurrently.

The diagnosis can only be made by recognising the *Entamoeba histolytica* in the stool. A number of specimens of freshly passed stool are examined in a smear placed on a warmed microscope stage. The characteristic features of *Entamoeba histolytica* are that it is actively motile, and phagocytoses red and white cells. It is similar in morphology to a non-pathogenic amoeba commonly found in faeces, *Entamoeba coli*. Typical sigmoidoscopic appearances are helpful, and biopsies and smears taken through the sigmoidoscope may show the causative organism.

Amoebic ulcers may bleed, perforate and cause peritonitis or a pericolic abscess. Intestinal obstruction may follow inflammation and adhesion of loops of bowel. Granulomata or amoebomata may reach massive size, due to fibrosis in the colon, producing signs simulating a malignant growth. Amoebic hepatitis is a common complication, and may go on to abscess formation. The abscess may be very large, and characteristically contains pus resembling anchovy sauce. Such abscesses may rupture from the liver into the pleura or lung; from the lung they may be coughed up.

Emetine is the specific drug for amoebiasis. It is given as emetine hydrochloride 60 mg. daily by intramuscular injection until acute symptoms have been controlled, usually in 4–5 days. The drug is very toxic, and the patient must be kept in bed while it is given. When the acute phase has subsided emetine and bismuth iodide is given by mouth in 60-mg. doses daily for 12 days. Amoebic hepatitis is best treated with chloroquine, 400–800 mg. daily by mouth, but injections of emetine are also effective.

SCHISTOSOMIASIS

Schistosomiasis (Bilharziasis) is caused by *Schistosoma haematobium* in Africa, *S. mansoni* in Africa, South America and the West Indies, and *S. japonicum* in Japan. The cercariae penetrate the skin of men wading in water infested by snails, and after entering the venous system infect the bladder and, less commonly, the rectum. The disease is seen throughout the African continent, and is most common in Egypt. Haematuria is the first sign, followed by fibrosis of the bladder wall, frequency and pain. Carcinoma of the bladder is a common complication. Prophylaxis is difficult, because the snails are not easily killed. It is usually impracticable to prevent people wading or bathing in infected lakes or rivers. Recent irrigation projects and building of dams has caused a spread of the snail, so the problem of prevention is causing even greater concern. Treatment is unsatisfactory, antimonials are partially effective.

FILARIASIS

Filariasis is due to infection by a nematode, *Wuchereria bancrofti* or *Malayi*, which enters the blood stream of man by the bite of an infected mosquito. The main symptoms result from blockage of the lymphatics by the adult worms, which may grow up to 7 cm. in length. Elephantiasis of the legs and scrotum results. The embryos of the parasite are typically only seen in blood films taken at night. Treatment is a month's course of diethyl carbamazine (banocide) to kill the parasites. Massive lymphoedema may require surgical treatment, for example, the scrotum may be massively enlarged and need amputation.

FURTHER READING

Turk, D. C., and Porter, I. A. (1965) *A Short Textbook of Medical Microbiology*. English Universities Press, London.

Anders, C., Lowbury, E. J. L., and Taylor, S. (1964) 'The Surgery of Infection' in *Recent Advances in Surgery*, Ch. 2. Churchill, London.

Prescribers' Journal. An independent journal issued free to all medical practitioners in the United Kingdom. Published by H.M. Stationery Office.

CHAPTER SEVEN

MALIGNANT DISEASE

NATURE OF TUMOURS

The word tumour comes from the Latin *tumor*, which means a swelling, but the word is used surgically in the restricted sense of a new growth or neoplasm. A tumour is the result of an excessive and abnormal growth of tissue that is unrelated to the needs of the body and which continues after the initiating stimulus has ceased to act. It is important to distinguish between the growth of tumours and that of certain other forms of tissue. *Regeneration* is growth made in response to tissue damage, and ceases when healing is complete. *Hyperplasia* is growth which may be excessive but is made in response to a body need and ceases when the initiating stimulus is removed. *Hamartoma* is a name given to a group of congenital malformations which consist of an abnormal mixture of tissues, one component of which may grow to excess. Such a lesion may grow while body tissues are growing, but does not show the progressive growth which is typical of a tumour.

Benign and Malignant

By long usage, tumours are subdivided into benign and malignant, although the distinction between these two is not always clear cut. They are also classified according to their tissue of origin.

Benign	*Malignant*
Closely resemble tissue of origin	Often atypical, with incomplete differentiation
Grow by expansion, remaining localised	Grow both by expansion and infiltration of nearby structures
Well-defined capsule	Capsule rarely formed
Few mitotic figures	Usually many mitotic figures, some of which are abnormal
Typically slow growing	Variable growth, often more rapid than benign tumour
Growth localised, no distant spread	Growth locally invasive, and spreads to distant organs by lymph and blood (metastasis)
Usually harmless, does not directly endanger life	If left, endangers life by its progressive spread

Classification Of Tumours

Tumours arising from epithelial cells may be:

Benign	Malignant
Benign tumours of skin are very common and named according to the predominant tissue	Carcinoma is a malignant epithelial growth, and is classified according to tissue of origin
Papilloma from surface epithelium	Epithelioma from surface epithelium
Adenoma from glandular epithelium	Adenocarcinoma from glandular epithelium

Tumours arising from connective tissue may be:

Benign	Malignant
According to tissue of origin:	Sarcoma is a malignant growth of connective tissue. If well differentiated it is named after tissue of origin—liposarcoma, chondrosarcoma, osteosarcoma, fibrosarcoma
Lipoma—fat	
Fibroma—fibrous tissue	
Chondroma—cartilage	
Osteoma—bone	
Haemangioma—blood vessel	If undifferentiated it has a descriptive
Leiomyoma—smooth muscle	title, e.g. spindle-cell sarcoma

Spread Of Malignant Tumours

Malignant tumours spread by *direct infiltration* and by distant metastasis. Direct infiltration of adjacent tissues is a characteristic of malignancy, although how the tumour does it is not fully known; proliferation of cells, loss of cohesion, motility and the production of substances which assist spreading, like hyaluronidase, are all involved.

The mechanics of direct spread is also important. Soft tissues, body cavities, natural tissue planes and channels allow unimpeded growth, whereas fascial planes, capsules and bones often prevent or deflect direct spread of the tumour.

Growth in continuity or *permeation* can occur, along with lymphatics and blood vessels, and is common with carcinomas, e.g. a hypernephroma invades the renal vein.

Metastasis is caused by malignant cells which are dislodged from the primary tumour and travel, typically via lymphatics or blood vessels, to new sites, where they produce *secondaries* often in a distinctive pattern.

Metastasis by lymphatics is the commonest form of spread of carcinoma, but is uncommon with sarcoma. Tumour cells lodge in a regional lymph node, and thus continue to grow. They may pass into the thoracic duct and escape into the blood stream.

Metastasis by blood vessels is typically due to invasion of a vein by the tumour, and occurs with carcinoma and sarcoma. Tumour cells in the systemic circulation will lodge in the lungs, those in the portal system in the liver and those reaching the left side of the heart may then be distributed anywhere in the body. Many tumour cells and emboli degenerate and disappear.

Metastasis in body cavities is due to direct spread, in the peritoneal cavity it is called *transcoelomic* spread, for example, when carcinoma of the stomach produces metastases in the ovaries (Krukenberg's tumours). Implantation in a scar may follow a surgical attack on the primary tumour. It occurs typically after mastectomy for breast cancer, and may appear after a great number of years.

Some idea of the extent of the problem of malignant disease is shown by the figures below, which are taken from the Registrar General's return for England and Wales, an area with a population of between 45 and 50 million. The figures show the number of deaths recorded in one year, 1961.

Total Population England and Wales,
46 million, 1961

	Men	Women
Lung	20,289	3,652
Stomach	7,784	6,004
Breast	81	9,286
Rectum	2,919	2,428
Oesophagus	1,356	1,055
Thyroid	97	278

Cause of Malignancy

The cause of malignant disease is not known, but it must not be forgotten that cancer is not one disease, but a great multiplicity of them, and there are many contributory causes.

Age. Carcinoma is rare in the young, but occurs more commonly after the age of 40, and two-thirds of those dying from cancer in the British Isles are over 60. However, no age is immune.

Sex. Certain tumours show a predisposition to occur in certain sexes. Thus, carcinoma of the lung and stomach are more common in men, and carcinoma of the breast, gall bladder and thyroid are more common in women.

Races. Some people appear particularly susceptible to certain tumours, while others appear relatively immune. Clearly many factors may be at work, but there does seem to be a certain pattern in the distribution of malignant disease among the different races of the world. For example, carcinoma of the cervix of the uterus is rare among Jewish women, however, circumcision is universal among Jewish men, and it may be that this removes some carcinogenic factor. Carcinoma of the liver is common among the Bantu in South Africa, but not among the white population, and may well be related to malnutrition. Lung carcinoma is particularly common among cigarette smokers in North America and Europe.

An interesting sidelight on the incidence of malignant change has been investigated in recent years as a result of the discovery that individuals with certain blood groups are more likely to develop malignant change in certain organs, especially the stomach. Thus, it has become possible to relate some of the patterns of malignant disease seen in the world by studying the distribution of blood groups.

Yet another interesting approach to the problem of causation of malignancy is that recently provided by Burkitt. He discovered that a lymphoma occurring in children with a distinctive pattern of metastasis only arose under certain climatic conditions in Africa, so that the disease was limited geographically and not racially or dietetically.

Chemicals. Repeated exposure to certain chemicals carries a risk of malignant change, and the first disease for which compensation was granted in Great Britain was carcinoma of the scrotum in chimney sweeps. In this case the hydrocarbons of the soot were the carcinogenic factor. Tar, a great many other coal products and arsenic are also capable of inducing a malignant change in the skin. A group of chemicals related to the aniline dyes when excreted in the urine cause malignant change in the urinary tract, and it is now known that 2-amino-1-naphthol is the substance responsible for producing bladder tumours in those working with these dyes.

Hormones. Continued dosage of the experimental animal with oestrogens can lead to a malignant change of the breast, and thus it is possible that this is one of the factors at work in producing malignant change in women (see Chapter Fifteen). Almost 50% of human breast cancers appear to depend on oestrogens for continued growth; this hormone dependence is the basis for the operations of oophorectomy, adrenalectomy and hypophysectomy in the control of metastatic carcinoma.

Ionising Radiation. Radium, X-rays and emanations of radio-active isotopes are among the most potent causes of malignant change in man. Radium, discovered by Marie Curie, was the first radio-active substance to be identified, and occurs naturally in the earth in deposits of pitchblende. Many radio-active substances or isotopes are now manufactured in atomic piles. The word isotope was coined by Professor Soddy in 1912. It is well known that the scars of X-ray burns can later undergo a cancerous change, and it is now thought that doses of radiation from many other sources, such as cosmic radiation and the fall-out, following the explosion of nuclear bombs, may very rarely affect the bone marrow and produce leukaemia.

The early workers with X-rays developed skin cancer, and the girls who painted luminous figures on watch dials with thorium-containing paint were liable to osteosarcoma of their bones. Thyroid carcinoma may develop in children who have received irradiation for so-called enlarged thymus.

Chronic Infection. Long-standing sepsis is occasionally complicated by a malignant change. It is seen, though very rarely, in chronic ulcers of the leg, either associated with varicose veins or chronic osteomyelitis.

Carcinoma of the tongue is more commonly seen in those with syphilis.

Chronic Irritation. The continued abrasion of the tongue by a septic or rough stump of a tooth, or irritation to the buccal mucosa by an ill-fitting denture, can lead to the development of carcinoma.

Hereditary Factors. Some tumours show a clear predilection for certain genetic types. *Polyposis coli* is a familial disease in which multiple polyps occur in the colon and rectum in childhood and frequently undergo malignant change in early adult life. *Neurofibromatosis* or von Reckling-hausen's disease is the development of multiple tumours, mainly on the peripheral nerves, it is a familial disease and the tumours occasionally become sarcomatous.

DIAGNOSIS OF MALIGNANCY

Cancer Education

In a few countries, mainly those which enjoy a high standard of living, an attempt has been made to disseminate information about the symptoms and signs which malignant disease may produce. The idea is to encourage people to examine themselves, and when they discover suspicious symptoms or signs, that they should then consult their doctor. Instruction has been given to women as to how they may examine their breasts each month in the hope that breast cancer will be discovered at an early stage, and that by this means more effective treatment will ensue.

It is an excellent thing if people can be encouraged to go to their doctor early when suspicious signs arise, and also if they can be taught to realise that, diagnosed early, malignant disease can often be treated with success. The only criticism of this form of propaganda is that a few individuals may be encouraged to become hypochondriacs, but these exist in every community, and this is a small price to pay if a majority of people have their carcinomas treated earlier and more effectively.

Cancer Detection Clinics

A number of valuable diagnostic aids are now available for screening large sections of the population for malignant disease.

(*a*) Smears of vaginal secretion when examined by the Papanicolaou technique can show when carcinoma of the cervix is present, and women are being encouraged to present themselves regularly for examination at special clinics for this cytological examination.

(*b*) *Sputum.* This can be examined for malignant cells, and with the enormous increase in the incidence of bronchial carcinoma in men in Britain and North America, this has become a valuable diagnostic service.

Mass Radiography

By this means large sections of the population have regular chest X-ray examination, and although this was primarily intended for the detection of tuberculosis, it is equally successful in showing carcinoma of the lung, which is frequently silent in its early stages.

The Individual Patient

The diagnosis of malignant disease in the individual patient depends so much on the site of the tumour that only a few clinical findings are common to all patients with malignancy. However, if the possibility of cancer is always kept in mind it is less likely to be missed. Careful history-taking is a prerequisite for all good surgery and medicine, and is particularly important here. Many patients with malignant disease develop anorexia and loss of appetite which may precede other symptoms. Thus, loss of weight, not otherwise explained, is particularly significant in the older patient. Similarly, the patient should be closely questioned about general health, as the early signs of cancer may be entirely non-specific. In the later stages of malignant disease the trained observer is unlikely to miss the diagnosis, even in the absence of localising signs, because the loss of weight and energy, often associated with anaemia, is accompanied usually by a distinctive sallow complexion, especially when the tumour involves some part of the alimentary tract.

The clinical examination must be thorough and meticulous, with especial attention paid to likely sites for malignant disease, such as the breasts. Rectal and vaginal examination, both digitally and by inspection endoscopically, must always be included. Radiographs of chest, the alimentary tract following the introduction of barium, and the renal and biliary tracts can be performed on patients without admission to hospital. More specialised tests may require admission, and some of these are mentioned below, but it must never be forgotten that clinical findings must always over-ride laboratory and ancillary tests, when these are apparently in conflict.

Endoscopy

Instruments are available which can be inserted into every orifice in the body and allow the surgeon to remove a sample of tissue (biopsy) from any area which appears suspicious of a malignant change. The bronchoscope, oesophagoscope and cystoscope are typical examples of endoscopes through which biopsies can be taken. The tissue is sent to the pathologist, and histological examination can reveal if a malignant change has taken place.

Isotopes

Malignant tumours usually show more cellular activity than normal body tissues, and this activity is associated with a more rapid turn-over of, among many substances, phosphorus, which is incorporated in nuclear protein material. Thus, radio-active phosphorus may be concentrated in greater amounts in malignant tumours than the surrounding tissue, and this can be used as a diagnostic aid in locating brain tumours.

Frozen Section

Even at operation, the surgeon may be unable to decide if a mass of tissue is malignant or benign. A small piece may then be sent to the pathologist, frozen and cut in a cryotome and after staining, an immediate diagnosis can often be made. The preparation and examination of a frozen section may only take 15 minutes, and the operation can then be completed according to what is reported.

General Management

The general management of a patient suspected of malignant disease is best illustrated by taking an actual example. A man goes to his doctor complaining of indigestion, and is then suspected of having carcinoma of the stomach. He is referred to a specialist in the hospital, who examines him carefully, giving special attention to palpation of the abdomen and obtaining a blood count, which may show anaemia, and arranging a barium-meal examination, which may reveal an ulcer or filling defect in the stomach. If the diagnosis is still in doubt, gastroscopy is performed so that the interior of the stomach may be inspected, and a test meal is carried out to see if free hydrochloric acid is secreted. In some clinics it may be possible to submit samples of resting juice aspirated from the stomach for microscopical examination to see if malignant cells are present, a technique described as exfoliative cytology. Finally, if a firm clinical impression still remains that malignant disease is present, even after all the tests have been found to be negative, a laparotomy is performed in order that the stomach can be examined by direct palpation and if necessary opened for a closer inspection of the mucosa.

A technique of value when it is desirable to do less than a laparotomy is *peritoneoscopy*, which allows limited inspection of the abdomen by an instrument rather like a cystoscope, which is passed through a small incision in the abdominal wall.

Treatment

There are at the present time four principal ways in which malignant disease can be treated: surgical excision, radiation therapy of various kinds, the use of hormones and finally chemotherapy, especially the cytotoxic drugs. The general principles underlying the use of these will be outlined here, but further details will be found in other parts of the book.

Surgery

Since time immemorial man has tried to remove malignant tumours, and those that were accessible, such as rodent ulcers and epitheliomas of the skin, were probably treated in this way many thousands of years ago. However, it was not until Virchow described the pathological changes which take place in malignant disease that a rational approach to cancer surgery was made.

In most parts of the body the principle of treating malignant disease is to excise not only the malignant tumour but a wide margin of healthy surrounding tissue, and if the tumour has spread to regional lymph nodes, to excise them in continuity with the primary lesion. Usually the excision will have to be of the whole organ involved, but this may not be practicable in all cases. For example, in early carcinoma of the breast it is usual to perform the operation of radical mastectomy, or some modification of it, introduced by Halsted, i.e. excision, in one block, of the whole breast and overlying skin, underlying pectoral muscles and the lymphatic and areolar tissue in the axilla. Since, however, the disease may have spread to the lymph nodes lying along the internal mammary vessels, or the supra-clavicular space, the disease may well have escaped beyond the excised area by the time of operation. Many surgeons do not include the pectoral muscles unless they are obviously involved.

Malignant change may not be localised to one area of the organ, for example, in carcinoma of the tongue and of the thyroid gland the disease is often multicentric, therefore total glossectomy or total thyroidectomy may be necessary. When malignant disease has spread widely in the body and there are distant metastases it is rarely useful to excise the primary tumour. Occasionally, however, metastasis is single, or there may be only two or three secondary deposits, and then a radical surgical approach is justified. Hypernephroma, which is a malignant tumour of the kidney, may sometimes be treated this way.

Radiation Therapy

The discovery of X-rays by Roentgen in 1895 opened up a new era in the treatment of malignant disease, since it was soon realised that these rays could burn or destroy the skin, and that the cells of ovary and testis were particularly susceptible. Cells which are actively dividing appear to be much more sensitive to X-rays than the other cells of the body, and although all the tissues are damaged when irradiated, it is usually the cancer cells which show most destruction, since it is they which are grow-ing and dividing most rapidly. In addition, the X-rays can be directed fairly accurately at the area which is to be treated, thus sparing the other tissues.

All forms of ionising radiation produce similar effects in living tissues, and these radiations may be obtained from radium, X-ray machines and radio-active isotopes. The unit of measurement of radiation is the *rad*, which is defined as the absorption of 100 ergs when 1 g. of tissue is irradiated.

Different varieties of malignant tumour have different sensitivities to ionising radiation. Highly radio-sensitive lesions often melt away when irradiated, and in this group are lymphosarcoma, seminoma and medulloblastoma. Moderately sensitive lesions are squamous-celled carcinoma of the skin and some carcinomas of bronchus. Resistant lesions include those which grow slowly and are relatively avascular, but also include some fast-growing lesions. Malignant melanoma and many sarcomas are included in this rapidly growing resistant group.

X-ray Therapy

There are three kinds of ionising radiation: *alpha-particles*, which have very little penetrating power and can be stopped by a sheet of paper. *Beta-particles*, which are electrons and according to their energy have varying degrees of penetration; for the most part they can be stopped by quite thin layers of metal. *Gamma-rays*, which are electromagnetic waves, and therefore in the same spectrum as the ultra-violet and infra-red rays, but since they are of much shorter wavelength, they have greater penetrating power. X-rays are in this latter range, and those of high voltage are more penetrating than those of low voltage.

Low-voltage Therapy

X-rays of low voltage, that is under 100 kilovolts (kV) have little penetration, but are useful for the treatment of skin cancers, i.e. rodent ulcer and epithelioma. The machine is placed very close to the tumour and a small dose given.

Medium-voltage Therapy

Most radiotherapy machines in use in the world probably still fall into this group, that is between 100 and 200 kV. They are used for treating volumes of malignant tissue (that is tumours) of the order of those found in the breast, axilla, neck, especially larynx and pharynx.

The limiting factor in this form of treatment is the dose which the skin receives, because this will be damaged before the deeper tissues. To avoid this a number of different 'ports' of entry are used, and thus any one area of skin receives less radiation than the underlying tumour, which receives the sum of all the treatments.

Super-voltage Therapy

X-rays of extremely high voltage, and therefore very short wavelength and great penetration, are now being used more and more, but the machines needed to produce them are extremely expensive. The Van de Graaff generator can produce rays of the order of 2 meV, that is two million electron volts, the linear accelerator 5–10 meV and the cyclotron and synchotron up to 20 meV. Neutron beams generated by the latter can be used to bombard material, which in turn becomes radio-active and irradiates the tissues.

Cobalt and Radium Therapy

Radium was the first substance used for the irradiation of malignant disease. It gives off alpha- and beta-particles and also very penetrating gamma-rays. It is usually placed in ½- or 1-mg. amounts in platinum needles, which can be inserted into the tissues and so irradiate a volume of the tumour. Such a *volume implant* is the usual form of treatment for cancer of the tongue.

If a larger quantity of radium, radio-active cobalt or radio-active caesium is placed in a suitable screened container, or *bomb*, a beam of rays can be directed from it on to a malignant lesion in much the same way as an X-ray machine is used. Radio-active cobalt ^{60}Co, is a much cheaper source of rays than radium, but the half-life of ^{60}Co is only about five years, whereas radium has a half-life of over 1,500 years. *Half-life* is the physicist's way of describing how long radio-active material takes to decay, and is the time during which half the energy of the isotope will have been emitted as radiation.

Radio-active Isotopes

A radio-active element is one with the same atomic number as its stable counterpart. Its chemical properties are unchanged, but its nucleus is unstable and gives off radiations, until it is no longer radio-active. The time it takes to do this may be days, as with sodium (^{24}Na), years, as with cobalt (^{60}Co), or a thousand years or more, as with radium.

Certain elements are concentrated in particular tissues in the body. When such elements can be made radio-active they can be used for local irradiation of tissues, the most important of these is iodine. Others, including phosphorus, are mentioned elsewhere in this book. Cobalt, ^{60}Co is now largely replacing radium as a source of radiation in beam therapy and caesium, ^{137}Ca, is used in a similar manner. Radio-active gold (^{198}Au) is employed in the form of gold grains and seeds, which can be implanted into a tumour and, since they do not react chemically with the body, they can be left in place indefinitely. ^{198}Au is also used in a colloidal suspension injected into the pleural or peritoneal cavities in the treatment of malignant effusions.

Endocrine Therapy

A number of malignant tumours in the body are said to be 'endocrine dependent' (see p. 185), and therefore if the supply of hormone can be cut off it may be possible to arrest growth or even cause regression of a tumour. This is especially so in the case of breast cancer, which is sometimes 'dependent' on oestrogens (p. 191). Well-differentiated metastases from thyroid carcinoma may function and be under the control of the anterior pituitary via its secretion of thyroid-stimulating hormone (TSH). When a patient with such metastases is given thyroxine by mouth the pituitary secretion of TSH is inhibited and the metastases may regress.

Chemotherapy

A number of chemical substances have been elaborated in recent years which have a toxic effect upon dividing cells, and can therefore be used to destroy malignant tumours. The limiting factor must always be the toxicity of the drug on the normal tissues of the body, and the most vulnerable tissues are almost always those which manufacture the white and red blood cells.

These substances can be used in many ways. They may be injected or instilled locally as, for example, into the pleural cavity. They may be used regionally by intra-arterial infusion, whereby a block of tissue, as for example, floor of mouth and tongue, may be treated, for example, by infusing the external carotid artery. When a malignant lesion occurs in the head and neck region, and is unsuitable for excision or further irradiation, infusion therapy may offer good palliation. Even greater amounts of cytotoxic drugs may be given if the part affected can be excluded from the general circulation, for example, by a tourniquet around the root of a limb. The limb is perfused via cannulae inserted into the main artery and vein, which are connected to a pump oxygenator, by which oxygenated blood is circulated through the excluded limb. Perfusion can only be performed for periods of an hour or so, where infusion can be maintained for days. In perfusion a larger amount of cytotoxic drug can be given, whereas by infusion less can be given but for a much longer time.

In addition to giving cytotoxic drugs for local therapy by infusion and perfusion, it is also possible to administer them intravenously and so maintain a steady systemic concentration. In addition, some of these compounds can be given by mouth. The merits of these different methods have yet to be evaluated fully.

FURTHER READING

Kunkler, P. B., and Rains, A. J. H. (1959) *Treatment of Cancer in Clinical Practice*. Livingstone, Edinburgh.

Lee Clark, R. (1961) *Cancer Chemotherapy*. Thomas, Springfield, U.S.A.

Davies, A. (1964) 'The Use of Cytotoxic Agents in Surgery', in *Recent Advances in Surgery*, Ch. 4, ed. Selwyn Taylor, Churchill, London.

Ackerman, L. V., and Butcher, H. R. (1964) *Surgical Pathology*. 3rd ed. Mosley, St. Louis.

Wright, G. P. and Symmers, W. St.C. (1966) *Systemic Pathology*. Longmans, London.

CHAPTER EIGHT

DISEASES OF ARTERIES

ATHEROSCLEROSIS

Atherosclerosis is the commonest disease of arteries and is the commonest cause of death. In 1960 the Registrar General for England and Wales recorded 198,000 deaths from diseases of the circulatory system, of which 143,000 were due to arteriosclerotic and degenerative disease of the heart and 14,000 were due to diseases of arteries. In recent years the range of treatment for atherosclerosis has been greatly widened. As yet, the commonest site of the disease, the coronary arteries, can rarely be treated surgically, but in such sites as the peripheral arteries of the lower limb, the aorta, the carotid and renal arteries the effects of occlusion of these vessels are more and more being dealt with by the surgeon.

Aetiology

The causes of atherosclerosis are unknown. Much interest is now being focussed upon diet. The disease is rare in the Bantu African in his native habitat, but becomes common when he is brought into a civilised community. It is rare in rice-eating Japanese. The rôle of fats has excited much interest recently, especially the relation of atheroma to eating saturated fatty acids such as are found in animal fats and oils. Diet rich in unsaturated fatty acids, as in vegetable oils, may prove of value in preventing or arresting atherosclerosis. No evidence has as yet been produced of such an effect. It is known that atheroma is commoner and manifests itself at an earlier age in the presence of hypercholesterolaemia, which is seen typically in myxoedema and diabetes. In rabbits a diet rich in cholesterol produces a disease of arteries similar to atherosclerosis.

The disease is often localised to the bifurcation of vessels and near the origins of main arteries. Hypertension is a common concomitant. These factors have suggested that stress or trauma may have an effect in localising the disease, though not in causing it. Heredity may play a part in the racial distribution of the disease, though this is difficult to separate from environmental factors such as diet. The disease is certainly far less common in women before the menopause. Symptoms rarely appear before the age of fifty years except in diabetics, but examination of vessels such as the aorta shows fatty streaks in the intima from birth onwards and fibrotic changes which become most obvious from the fourth decade.

Pathology

The largest and the medium-sized arteries become thickened and tortuous, with firm plaques in their walls which may become calcified.

Segments become totally occluded by thrombus, with many tortuous collaterals around the blocked segment. Less often localised stenoses may occur.

Microscopy shows deposition of lipoid substances in plaques in the subintimal plane. It is possible that these deposits have originally been mural thrombi which have degenerated and have become covered by new intimal endothelium. The lumen of the vessel becomes irregular and presents favourable conditions for thrombosis. Sub-intimal plaques may ulcerate into the lumen and open a route for dissection. Haemorrhage in the sub-intima may cause total occlusion. Plaques may calcify and may be detected by X-rays as longitudinally disposed flecks of radio-opacity.

In the media there is fibrosis of smooth muscle and degeneration of elastic tissue, especially in the internal elastic lamina. If thrombosis has occurred, then the inner part of the media merges imperceptibly into the organised thrombus.

In the adventitia there is fibrosis and increased vascularity of such a degree as to suggest an aseptic inflammation. The vessels are intimately attached to surrounding structures, such as veins and vascular sheaths, and can only with difficulty be separated from them.

Localisation

The disease is always generalised, but often its impact is most severe on certain localised sites. In the lower limb, the aortic bifurcation (*aorto-iliac disease*) and the superficial femoral artery (*femoro-popliteal disease*) are most often affected especially where the superficial femoral artery passes through the adductor hiatus. The upper limb is rarely affected unless there has been trauma, for example, from a crutch or cervical rib.

The bifurcation of the common carotid artery is a common site for stenosis or plaque formation. Stenosis of the renal artery near its origin from the aorta is one cause of hypertension. Narrowing of the origin of the superior mesenteric artery can cause abdominal pain.

ATHEROSCLEROSIS OF ARTERIES OF THE LOWER LIMB

Next to coronary and cerebral disease, atherosclerosis most commonly affects the peripheral arteries of the lower limb. It is in the lower limb that the surgeon most often has to treat the effects of ischaemia.

1. *Symptoms and Signs*

Symptoms of ischaemia are often produced by localised thrombosis secondary to atherosclerosis and much more rarely by stenosis. Pain may be of two types—intermittent claudication and rest pain. The most serious effect of ischaemia is gangrene.

Intermittent claudication is muscular pain produced by exercise, relieved by rest and reproduced by further exercise. It is typically felt in the calf, and is usually due to occlusion of the superficial femoral artery below the level of the profunda femoris and above the popliteal. Claudication results from poor blood supply to the calf muscles. Muscles need a five fold increase in blood flow in exercise, and if this cannot be supplied, then accumulation of metabolites in the muscles results in pain, which causes the patient to stop.

In patients who have calf claudication no pulses can be felt below the level of the femoral artery. The onset is usually insiduous. At first the patient can walk 400–500 yards or more before pain occurs, but usually the claudication distance shortens to 100 yards over a period of months or years. Claudication occurring in less than 100 yards is a severe handicap, and below 30 yards the patient is virtually immobilised. Often there is spontaneous improvement in claudication distance in the first year, and this is worth anticipating in cases of recent onset.

If claudication occurs in the buttock or thigh there is stenosis or occlusion of the iliac arteries, usually near the bifurcation of the aorta and often involving both iliacs. In such cases one or both femoral pulses may be weak or absent, and often a systolic murmur can be heard in the groin below a stenosed vessel. Impotence may be a symptom in younger subjects.

Rest pain is a more serious symptom, because it warns of impending gangrene. It is usually due to occlusion of the superficial femoral artery, often extending to the popliteal artery or with additional segments of thrombosis or stenosis in the vessels below the knee. Less often only the distal arteries below the level of the popliteal artery are affected. The pain may be intractable. It is continuous, often worse at night and often partially relieved by hanging the leg down. The toes may be red and tender, with hyperaesthesia, paraesthesia and numbness. The pain is due to ischaemia of nerves and skin.

Gangrene or necrosis of tissue, usually associated with blackening or other colour changes, may be preceded by *pregangrene*. Pregangrenous changes include severe rest pain, discoloration of the skin and swelling of the foot. The occurrence of infection may hasten the onset of gangrene. There is often a long history of claudication before the onset of gangrene.

2. *Investigations*

Patients with ischaemia of the legs frequently have diabetes (known or unknown), and so the urine must always be tested for sugar. Anaemia is common, and may aggravate the symptoms. Arteriography is used for those in whom surgery is contemplated, to confirm the diagnosis of a localised occlusion and to assess the condition of the vessels above and below the block. The technique is performed percutaneously under local analgesia unless the patient is apprehensive. If the vessels below the inguinal ligament are to be visualised a needle is inserted into the femoral artery (percutaneous femoral arteriography). If the aorta or iliac arteries are to be examined the aorta is punctured by a long needle inserted alongside the lumbar vertebrae (translumbar aortography), the patient lying in the prone position. If there is a full and bounding femoral pulse on one side retrograde catheterisation of the aorta with a fine polyethylene catheter passed through a cannula inserted into the femoral artery may be preferred (retrograde aortography). Radio-opaque medium is injected rapidly, and radiographs of the parts to be examined are swiftly taken. In patients to be submitted to surgery a general assessment of the cardiovascular system, including an electrocardiogram, must be made. Special tests, such as oscillometry (measure of the amplitude of pulsation), plethysmography (measurement of blood flow) and skin temperature measurement before and after induction of reflex dilation, are rarely required except for research purposes. Plain radiographs of the limbs are of little value— they may show calcification, but this does not necessarily indicate occlusion of vessels.

3. *Treatment*

The conservative treatment of peripheral ischaemia includes the treatment of diabetes and correction of anaemia. Vasodilator drugs are of no value, though alcohol is comforting. Smoking is thought to be vasoconstricting, therefore it should be stopped. Reflex heating by cooling the extremity by exposure to room temperature and heating the rest of the body is of some value in acute ischaemia. Analgesics, such as codeine, physeptone and pipedone, are helpful, but opiates should be avoided for fear of addiction. Patients often improve with rest in bed with the leg kept horizontal.

The feet must be kept clean. Extremes of heat and cold must be avoided. Fungus infection should be eradicated and the heels protected from pressure. Antibiotics may be needed to control infection and, if possible, gangrene should be kept dry by exposure to room temperature and local antibiotic sprays. Great care should be exercised in cutting nails, if possible a chiropodist should attend to the feet.

The vast majority of claudicants need only reassurance. Half are likely to improve, progress to gangrene is rare (2%), only 15% are so crippled that operation is needed. The cause of their symptoms should be explained, and they should be instructed to slow down their activities. They should avoid walking, and when they must walk they should walk slowly. The administration of phenindione as a prophylaxis against further thrombosis has been tried, but there is no evidence that it is effective.

The indications for surgery are *crippling claudication* and *threatened loss of limb*.

D

Three operative procedures are available for peripheral ischaemia:

1. Direct arterial surgery.
2. Lumbar sympathectomy.
3. Amputation.

The decision as to which procedure should be adopted is made by a process of exclusion. The aged, the decrepit, the bedridden and all those unlikely to walk again can only be treated symptomatically or by amputation if gangrene develops. Those who have had recent coronary thrombosis or who have severe angina pectoris must be treated medically or by amputation. The remainder who are considered fit for surgery should be submitted to angiography to prove the localised nature of the block and to assess the condition of the vessels above and below it. The condition of the arteries distal to the block is critical to the success of grafting procedures below the inguinal ligament. There must be at least one patent artery to the ankle to guarantee success.

If the patient is fit and if angiography shows a suitable picture direct arterial surgery can be performed. Two procedures are favoured.

1. *Thrombo-endarterectomy* is used mostly for occlusions above the inguinal ligament in the aorta and iliac arteries. In this operation the abdomen is widely opened, and after mobilisation of the affected vessels the thrombus and surrounding atheroma is carefully enucleated by meticulous dissection. A smooth plane of cleavage is found in the media and, though the vessel is left thin, it is adequate to withstand arterial pressure. An aneurysm never occurs, long term results are excellent in 90% of cases.

2. *Arterial grafting* is used mainly in the vessels below the inguinal ligament. In this operation a graft is inserted by-passing the block and anastomosed above to the common femoral artery and below to the lower popliteal artery. The best graft is the patient's own long saphenous vein (autogenous vein graft). Cadaveric arterial homografts have proved less satisfactory because they thrombose or after 3–5 years they may show aneurysm formation. Plastic prostheses which cause little reaction to the surrounding tissues can be used for aorto-iliac disease but have fallen out of favour when used below the inquinal ligament because of a high incidence of thrombosis within a year of insertion. With autogenous vein grafts used for femoro-popliteal disease limbs can be preserved for at least 2 years in 70% of cases if the patients are well selected. It is important to appreciate that these operations do not arrest the disease but only relieve symptoms. The results must be considered in relation to the fact that only the most severe cases are operated on.

Lumbar sympathectomy is employed where arterial reconstruction is impossible and for moderately severe ischaemia with rest pain and early colour changes of the Raynaud type. Swelling of the limb and established gangrene are contra-indications, except in young subjects with localised arterial disease in vessels distal to the popliteal artery. In the operation of lumbar sympathectomy the second and third lumbar sympathetic ganglia are removed together with their rami through a lumbar incision and an extraperitoneal approach to the lateral aspect of the lumbar vertebrae.

Unfortunately amputation is still the most common operation performed for gangrene. Local amputation of toes, amputation through the metatarsals or above the ankle joint (Syme's) are occasionally successful in diabetics and in atherosclerotics who have distally sited disease. Below-knee amputation is worthwhile if the patient is young and is likely to walk again, but, because of a precarious blood supply, the skin flaps are slow to heal and must be left open, to heal by granulation. A Gritti-Stokes type of amputation provides a long stump with preservation of proprioceptive sensation. The femur is divided at the level of the adductor tubercle and the patella denuded of articular cartilage is sutured to the end of the femur. A mid-thigh amputation is performed if the femoral pulse is weak or absent.

ATHEROSCLEROTIC ANEURYSM OF THE AORTA

Aneurysm of the aorta is becoming more common as the average age of the population increases. Whereas 30 years ago syphilis was the usual cause of thoracic aortic aneurysm, today this is rare, but atheromatous aneurysm of the abdominal aorta is common.

Pathology

An aneurysm is a pathological dilatation of a vessel which forms a sac partly filled with blood or clot. The dilatation is due to loss of muscle and elastic fibres in the media and their replacement by fibrous tissue. Fibrous tissue tends to give way under sustained and pulsatile pressure, and so rupture is inevitable. It is known that 60–70% of aneurysms rupture within 2 years of their recognition. The aneurysm is usually asymmetrical, the anterior wall giving way most. It may be fusiform or saccular. The major part of the cavity is filled by clot laid down in concentric layers, with fibrosis and calcification at the periphery. The aneurysm is usually welded by fibrous tissue to surrounding structures, for example, the inferior vena cava.

Clinical Features

Aneurysms are occasionally found during abdominal examination when they are causing no symptoms. A mass is felt with prominent expansile pulsation in the position of the aorta. Usually a lateral edge can be felt, and it is possible to outline the upper limit of the aneurysm unless it extends above the renal arteries. Auscultation reveals a systolic murmur in most cases. The pulses below the aneurysm are usually full and bounding. In cases of doubt, when it is possible that the aorta is being more easily felt than usual, for example in a thin or hypertensive person, a plain radiograph of the abdomen is of value, because aneurysms are so often calcified in their outer layers.

The symptoms of aneurysms are due either to pressure on surrounding structures or to rupture. Pain may be due to pressure on vertebrae or nerves or may warn of impending rupture. Rupture may cause sudden death, but more often there is pain for some days or weeks and possibly signs of peritoneal irritation if there has been leakage of blood into the peritoneal cavity or extra-peritoneal tissues. Renal colic, anuria and haematuria may follow involvement of the renal vessels.

Treatment

If an aneurysm of the abdominal aorta is increasing in size, or if it is causing any symptoms, it should be resected. Whether symptomless aneurysms should be treated is a matter of controversy. The results of treatment of ruptured aneurysms are so bad that some believe all symptomless aneurysms should be excised. However, the operation is extensive, and the subjects are often old with widespread arterial disease and usually other disabilities.

At operation the abdomen is widely opened and a full exploration carried out to exclude other causes of abdominal pain. The aorta above the aneurysm is freed as far as the renal vessels, and the iliac arteries are mobilised below. The aorta is transected and the sac of the aneurysm opened and evacuated of clot. The iliac arteries are divided below to leave the shell of the aneurysm *in situ*. Continuity is restored by insertion of a plastic prosthesis made of Teflon or Dacron between the aorta and the iliac arteries.

ANEURYSMS IN OTHER SITES

Atherosclerotic aneurysms are less common in vessels other than the aorta. The iliac, common femoral, popliteal, subclavian, axillary, brachial and carotid arteries may all be the site of aneurysm formation. Occasionally there are multiple aneurysms suggesting a general deterioration in the condition of the arteries. If possible, peripheral aneurysms should be excised and replaced by grafts. Syphilitic aneurysms should be resected after a course of penicillin. Proximal ligation (Hunterian) still has a place in the treatment of popliteal aneurysm.

DISSECTING ANEURYSM OF THE AORTA

Dissection of the aorta occurs in the atheromatous and in the hypertensive. Usually a horizontal split in the intima immediately distal to the sinuses of the aortic valve allows blood to enter the media. A twin-barrelled aorta is formed which terminates usually fatally by rupture either externally into the thorax, pericardium or abdomen. Spontaneous internal rupture back into the aorta at a more distal level allows decompression of the dissection and spontaneous cure, with occasional prolongation of life for several years. Dissection may progress along the branches of the aorta, causing ischaemia of the brain or limbs. If the renal vessels are dissected anuria and uraemia may result.

Dissection produces severe retrosternal or epigastric pain of sudden onset radiating to the back and associated with shock. Coronary thrombosis, arterial embolism, perforated peptic ulcer and pancreatitis may be closely simulated. Signs typically vary from hour to hour, limbs may become ischaemic and pulses disappear. Murmurs may appear in the aortic area. Chest radiography may show a widening of the aortic shadow.

Treatment is difficult. Many die suddenly, many are never fit for surgery. If the general condition is satisfactory and there is no evidence of renal failure retrograde femoral aortography should be performed to confirm the diagnosis by showing a filling defect in the aorta or a double channel. Operation usually requires the use of cardio-pulmonary by-pass because the ascending aorta has to be occluded. The aorta is divided and the aneurysm replaced by a plastic graft. The aortic valve often has to be repaired.

ARTERIAL STENOSIS

Renal Artery

Stenosis of the renal artery has been recognised as an infrequent cause of hypertension. The cause of stenosis is usually atheroma, but congenital, fibrous and muscular strictures are sometimes found. Hypertension following renal artery stenosis is akin to hypertension produced experimentally by placing an occluding clip on one renal artery (the 'Goldblatt kidney'). It appears that the ischaemic kidney liberates a hormone renin which produces hypertension and damages the opposite kidney.

Facts which suggest renal artery stenosis are hypertension under the age of 45 and asymmetry of the size of the kidney outlines in abdominal radiographs and in the intravenous pyelogram. Pyelography may show a denser contrast in the renal pelvis of an ischaemic kidney than in the normal. Collection and examination of urine separately from both ureters (divided renal flow estimation) shows that urine from an ischaemic kidney contains less sodium and chloride and is of smaller volume than that from the opposite side. A systolic murmur may be heard over the stenosed renal artery. Methods are now being used for screening hypertensives by the injection of hippuran containing radio-active iodine and following its passage through the kidneys separately and synchronously by twin scintillation counters. Confirmation of stenosis can only be obtained by aortography. This is performed by the retrograde femoral route and requires a series of quick exposures so that the rapid course of radio-opaque contrast medium can be followed through the kidneys.

If stenosis is confirmed and thought to be the cause of hypertension, then the artery is explored and the stenosis treated either by thrombo-endarterectomy or with a by-pass graft, for example by the use of the splenic artery anastomosed end-to-side to the renal artery distal to the stenosis. Occasionally it is only possible to remove the kidney, but this is to be avoided if possible, as it may potentially be a better functioning organ than its fellow because the stenosis protects its vessels against the effects of a high blood pressure. The results of surgery for renal artery stenosis are variable and more refined methods are needed to indicate those amenable to correction. It is difficult to know if stenosis of a renal artery is the cause or the result of hypertension.

Carotid Artery

Localised plaques of atherosclerosis are commonly found near the bifurcation of the common carotid artery and at the origin of the vertebral artery from the subclavian. These plaques may give rise to intermittent hemiplegia, hemianaesthesia and blindness. Vertebral artery stenosis, may cause vertigo and falling down. Stenosis occurs first, but, as thrombus is deposited on the atheromatous plaque, the vessel may eventually be totally occluded—the effect of which is often permanent hemiplegia.

The intermittent nature of the neurological symptoms and signs suggests the diagnosis, which may be confirmed by hearing a systolic murmur over the carotid bifurcation on auscultation. Angiography is performed by passage of a catheter from the femoral artery to the aortic arch so that all four arteries to the brain can be visualised, carotids and vertebrals. It is common to find stenosis or occlusion of one or both carotids. If a carotid bifurcation is found to be grossly stenosed it is explored and 're-bored' by thrombo-endarterectomy. As the carotid artery supplying the brain must be occluded in this operation for up to 20 minutes, the stenosed area may be excluded by placing a temporary circulatory by-pass around it or through it using a plastic tube. Operations for carotid artery stenosis are often performed under local analgesia to assess the effects of carotid occlusion.

Subclavian Steal Syndrome

Patients may present with episodes of vertigo, falling down and unsteadiness. A loud murmur is heard over the root of the neck and the radial pulse on the affected side may be weak or absent. Arch angiography reveals stenosis or occlusion of the subclavian or innominate artery proximal to the origin of the vertebral artery. Symptoms are caused by reversal of blood flow down the vertebral artery on the affected side thus starving the base of the brain of blood. Correction is achieved by endarterectomy of the occluded vessel.

Superior Mesenteric Artery

Mesenteric artery stenosis is a rare cause of abdominal pain, which is worse after food and causes nutritional deficiency and steatorrhoea. Stenosis of the superior mesenteric artery occurs close to its origin from the aorta. If the diagnosis can be made, thrombo-endarterectomy or by-pass graft can be performed.

THROMBO-ANGIITIS OBLITERANS (BUERGER'S DISEASE)

Thrombo-angiitis is a clinical syndrome of occlusive arterial disease in young men aged 20–40 years which may be preceded by migratory phlebitis. Heavy smoking may possibly be a factor, and also fungus infection of the feet. The site of the disease is usually in distal arteries below the mid-calf level. Claudication and gangrene are common, all four limbs may be affected, but visceral vessels are rarely affected. Many surgeons believe that this is not a true disease entity, but merely atherosclerosis presenting at an early age and in a distal situation.

Opportunities to see the microscopical appearances of the active stages of the disease are rare. However, they are described as showing an acute inflammatory condition of the whole neurovascular bundle. Organised thrombus is seen in the arteries with preservation of the elastic laminae and media. Arteriography shows the disease to be distally sited in tibial or plantar arteries, with a characteristic fine network of collaterals.

In the treatment of this disease smoking must be stopped. Rest pain may be relieved by lumbar sympathectomy. Gangrene of toes may be treated by sympathectomy and local amputation or below-knee amputation. Direct surgery on the affected arteries is usually impossible because of the distal localisation of the disease and the small size of the affected vessels. Occasionally there is improvement with cortisone, which should be tried if rest pain is severe and amputation likely. Recently it has been shown that smoking interferes with the oxygen-carrying power of haemoglobin in these subjects. This fact is a potent reason for forbidding smoking in arterial disease.

MEDIAL CALCIFICATION (MONCKEBERG'S SCLEROSIS)

Vessels are often seen in radiographs because the media is calcified either wholly or in part. It does not necessarily indicate occlusion or narrowing of the vessels, but atherosclerosis may be associated with it. Medial calcification is occasionally a feature of overdosage with vitamin D and of hyperparathyroidism. Of itself it has no clinical significance.

GANGRENE IN DIABETICS

It is now recognised that what was formerly called 'diabetic gangrene' is in fact gangrene due to three factors.

Ischaemia

Atherosclerosis is common in diabetics who develop symptoms from it approximately 10 years earlier than non-diabetics.

Neuropathy

Peripheral neuritis, to which diabetics are particularly prone, leads to insensitive skin. Trauma may be followed by gangrene, neuropathic joints (Charcot's type) and perforating ulcers.

Infection

Diabetics are prone to infection which, if severe, may of itself lead to gangrene.

It is important in any case of gangrene in the diabetic to assess the relative importance of each of these three factors. If neuropathy and infection predominate, and especially if pedal pulses are present, then local amputation is often successful. Removal of toes, sometimes all the toes, and removal of infected metatarsals may be all that is necessary. Below-knee amputation often results in satisfactory healing.

TRAUMA TO ARTERIES

Injuries to arteries are usually associated with open wounds. Arteries may be cut across partially or completely, they may go into spasm, or they may become thrombosed after contusion. A traumatic aneurysm may form if there is partial division of an artery and if blood leaks into the surrounding tissues, making for itself a capsule of surrounding structures and laminated clot. A puncture wound may traverse both artery and vein and produce an arteriovenous fistula.

Injuries to arteries give rise to the signs of acute ischaemia. There is severe pain made worse by movement, whether active or passive. There may be paraesthesia and numbness or eventually complete anaesthesia and paralysis. The periphery becomes cold. Initially there is pallor of the skin and, if ischaemia persists, marbling of the skin and finally gangrene, with a line of demarcation separating it from normal skin. Pulses are absent below the level of the injury. Murmurs may be heard at the site of the injury if a traumatic aneurysm or arterio-venous aneurysm is developing. These signs and symptoms refer to complete ischaemia. They are modified or absent if the collateral circulation recovers rapidly and if distal thrombosis is prevented or does not occur. They indicate the need for urgent treatment because severe ischaemia for more than a few hours may lead to irreversible damage to nerves and muscles.

1. *Wounds*

Severe haemorrhage from a major artery should be controlled by pressure proximal to the wound and rarely by a tourniquet, which, if it must be applied, must be released every 30 minutes. Emergency blood transfusion and exploration of the wound must be carried out in the operating theatre so that repair may be undertaken.

If the haemorrhage ceases spontaneously the distal pulses and peripheral nerves must be examined, and if there is any suggestion of arterial damage the wound must be explored. It is valuable in all cases of possible arterial injury to auscultate the site of the injury, because the presence of a murmur may indicate a developing aneurysm.

2. *Spasm*

Spasm may follow contusion from a fracture or foreign body, pressure of a haematoma (especially if it is held under tension by fascia) and injection of thiopentone intra-arterially. The danger of prolonged spasm is of the thrombosis that follows it.

If reduction of a fracture is not followed by improvement in the volume of the peripheral pulses, the artery should be exposed, blood clot released and any foreign body removed. If there is still no improvement the artery should be painted with a 2·5% solution of papaverine sulphate and finally it should be forcibly distended by the injection of saline. It is essential to restore blood flow or muscle contracture (Volkmann's), and gangrene of the digits may follow.

If thiopentone (Pentothal) has been injected intra-arterially by accident the patient complains of pain in the fingers. The needle should be left in the vessel, and 25 mg. of tolazoline (Priscol) should be injected. The operation should be abandoned and heparinisation maintained by continuous I–V injection for at least 10 days until the fear of arterial thrombosis has passed. The use of 2·5% thiopentone and avoidance of injection at the elbow are important prophylactic measures.

3. *Contusion and Thrombosis*

Thrombosis may follow contusion of an artery or prolonged spasm, especially if the vessel is atheromatous. The artery must be explored and the thrombus removed from the damaged segment. A vein graft may be necessary if the vessel is extensively contused.

4. *Traumatic Aneurysm*

Days or even months after a perforating injury of a limb a pulsatile swelling may appear which, if it is left, may compress surrounding structures, including veins and nerves. It may eventually rupture externally or become infected. Usually there is a history of profuse haemorrhage at the time of injury. A systolic murmur may be heard over the course of the vessel, even before the aneurysm has developed. Peripheral gangrene occasionally occurs if the aneurysm enlarges to a considerable size.

The presence of a traumatic aneurysm demands operation. The artery proximal to the aneurysm must be exposed so that it can be occluded at will. The aneurysm is opened and the mass of clot contained within it removed. The artery must be freed and either repaired or a segment of it is excised and replaced by an autogenous vein graft.

5. *Traumatic Arteriovenous Aneurysm*

Evidence of a communication between an artery and a vein may be apparent immediately after an injury or not for months or years. A pulsatile swelling appears which may cause pain and may compress veins and nerves. Peripheral gangrene may arise. The physical signs of arteriovenous aneurysm are distension of superficial veins which may pulsate and which contain blood with a high oxygen saturation. A continuous machinery murmur may be heard over the aneurysm, abolished by pressure on the artery feeding it. There may be a collapsing pulse, a wide pulse pressure and an increase in the size of the heart if the communication is large and near the heart. Pressure on the artery proximal to the fistula may slow the heart rate and produce a rise in the systolic blood pressure (Branham's sign).

The diagnosis is confirmed by angiography. At operation an attempt is made to separate the vein and artery and to repair them by suture or graft. Adhesions may make this impossible, in which case the artery and vein must be ligated both proximal and distal to the aneurysm, quadruple ligature. It may be possible to save the artery only by sacrifice of the vein in some cases.

RAYNAUD'S SYNDROME

It is common to see patients, mostly women, who show pallor of the fingers due to hypersensitivity to cold. After the pallor passes off a burning, painful redness follows. If the patient's fingers are warmed while they are still pale they become very painful and blue. It is thought that there is a 'local fault' in the smaller vessels of the hands and feet, usually in the digital arteries, which makes them hypersensitive to cold. Recent work has suggested that such vessels are hypersensitive to circulating pressor amines such as adrenaline, noradrenaline and serotonin. It may be that the peripheral blood in such cases is more viscous than normal. Pallor is due to spasm of small arteries and arterioles. Redness is due to the reactive hyperaemia that follows the release of spasm. Persistent cyanosis of digits (acrocyanosis) is a similar disorder that merges imperceptibly into Raynaud's syndrome.

It is difficult to give a satisfactory classification of the causes of this syndrome, because, although many factors are known which may produce colour changes in the cold hand, these factors apply only to a very small proportion of the patients who are affected. Obviously a great deal of further research and investigation will be required to sort out this complicated problem. The vast majority are best described as idiopathic, but a number of factors can be listed as below:

Arterial Disease. Raynaud's syndrome may be a feature of any arterial disease especially atherosclerosis of small vessels in elderly men.

Thoracic Inlet Syndrome. This includes cervical rib and costoclavicular pressure.

Disease of the Central Nervous System. There may be vascular symptoms associated with such diseases as syringomyelia, syphilis and poliomyelitis.

'Collagen' Diseases. In this group may be included scleroderma, dermatomyositis cryo- and macroglobulinaemia and disseminated lupus erythematosus.

Drugs. Ergotism may be manifested by intense ischaemic changes in the hands and feet, going on to gangrene.

Trauma. Injury to vessels from frostbite or prolonged immersion in water may be followed by hypersensitivity to cold.

Occupation. It is well known that workers with vibrating tools may develop Raynaud's syndrome, and must then cease this type of work.

'Hereditary Cold Fingers'. A large proportion of those complaining of Raynaud's syndrome are girls and women ranging in age from puberty to about 25–30 years who complain of intense pallor and pain in the hands on exposure to cold. There is often a strong hereditary background and often a psychogenic factor. This condition never progresses to true organic disease. In older subjects hypothyroidism may be associated.

Raynaud's Disease. There remain a few women who show the colour changes of Raynaud's syndrome which cannot be explained and in whom all the factors listed above have been excluded. They are usually of an age around the menopause. The symptoms vary greatly in severity, and a few go on to digital gangrene from thrombotic and fibrotic occlusion of digital and palmar arteries. The majority never progress to gangrene.

Investigation

In the investigation of Raynaud's syndrome the known aetiologica factors can usually be excluded by clinical examination. Investigations include X-rays of the thoracic inlet and hands and occasionally the Wassermann reaction, tests of thyroid function, blood examination for L.E. cells, sedimentation-rate estimation and examination of the serum proteins. Angiography is rarely indicated.

Treatment

In a small percentage of cases a specific cause can be found and treated. If an abnormality of the thoracic inlet can be diagnosed the supraclavicular fossa is explored to excise a cervical rib or bands of fascia. If no cause can be found and if compression of the neurovascular bundle between the clavicle and the first rib is suspected, then the anterior inner end of the first rib is removed, allowing the vessels to fall back from the clavicle.

In the vast majority of patients simple measures such as avoidance of cold and wet, wearing gloves, extra socks and boots instead of shoes suffice. Vasodilator drugs have proved of no value. Sympathectomy is disappointing for the hand, for improvement is often only short-lived, though it is very effective for the foot. After removal of the second and third thoracic sympathetic ganglia there is temporary improvement, but relapse can be anticipated within 2 years. However, for many patients, symptoms are so severe that they are prepared to accept even temporary relief from an operation. Sympathectomy for the upper limb is rarely complete because of accessory ganglia which are inaccessible and because of collateral nerve sprouting which occurs if denervation is incomplete. Lumbar sympathectomy produces complete and permanent denervation of vessels below the knee, and hence is usually permanently effective.

Because of evidence that Raynaud's syndrome is due to hypersensitivity to circulating pressor substances, and because of the occurrence of minor endocrine defects in older women, treatment has been advocated in which triiodothyronine, reserpine and androgens are used separately and together. As yet the full value of these drugs is unknown, many patients fail to respond and come to sympathectomy, notwithstanding its short-lived effects in the hand.

ARTERIAL EMBOLISM

The commonest sites from which a thrombus may embolise to peripheral arteries are the left atrial appendage, especially if atrial fibrillation is present, and the left ventricle from an area of infarcted muscle due to a recent coronary thrombosis. Other less common sites are a plaque of atheroma, from an aneurysm and very rarely from a thrombus in a deep vein if a patent foramen ovale exists, paradoxical embolus. In subacute endocarditis infected emboli may lodge in the peripheral arteries and cause gangrene or a mycotic aneurysm.

Emboli tend to lodge at the sites of bifurcation of arteries. Their effects depend on the size of the vessels occluded, the extent of thrombosis that spreads distal to the occlusion and the anatomy and efficiency of the collateral circulation. In some sites, for example, the brain, an embolus may be small and yet disastrous because it lodges in some vital area, for example, the posterior cerebral artery, when partial blindness may follow.

It is often difficult to distinguish between acute arterial thrombosis and embolism. In early cases with severe ischaemia it is preferable to treat acute thrombosis as embolism.

1. Lower Limb

The embolus may lodge at the aortic bifurcation, the origin of the profunda femoris or the bifurcation of the popliteal artery. The signs and symptoms are those of severe acute ischaemia, the extent depending upon the level of the block. Popliteal occlusion leads to ischaemia of the foot, femoral up to the mid-calf and iliac or aortic to one or both knees. It is usually easy to localise the obstruction by finding absence of pulses distal to it.

If the occlusion persists for more than 6–10 hours, irreversible changes up to gangrene may occur. Anaesthesia is a sign of severe persistent ischaemia. Not uncommonly, the period of severe ischaemia may be short and followed by full recovery. In such cases it must be presumed that the embolus has passed into some less-important artery or that the anatomy of the collateral circulation is such as to allow efficient restoration of blood flow and prevention of distal thrombosis.

2. Upper Limb

Embolism in the upper limb is less common than in the lower. An embolus may lodge in the third part of the subclavian artery or at a lower level. If a major vessel is obstructed gangrene may follow, but spontaneous recovery is more usual because of the excellent collateral circulation in the arm.

Treatment

Any method of treatment for arterial embolism produces relatively poor results, mainly because of the possibility of recurrent embolus in the same or other sites and also because of the poor general state of these patients, many of whom may be in cardiac failure or have other serious disorders.

It is vital to treat embolism within 6–10 hours of the onset of symptoms, or propagation of thrombus distal to the embolus will preclude recovery.

1. *Heparin.* Intravenous heparin should be given at once as a first-aid measure to prevent distal thrombosis; 10,000–15,000 units (100–150 mg.) can be given as a loading dose.

2. *Embolectomy.* If there is no improvement in an hour, or if anaesthesia has developed, embolectomy must be performed. The heparin effect must first be reversed by intravenous injection of protamine sulphate (1 mg./ 100 units of heparin given). The best results are obtained within 6–10 hours of embolism, rarely is there any hope of recovery after 24 hours.

The artery is exposed above the level of the embolus and is occluded temporarily proximal to it. The artery is opened and the embolus gently withdrawn. A Fogarty catheter is passed down the artery in the leg as far as the ankle. The tiny balloon on the end of the catheter is inflated and the catheter is withdrawn bringing with it the distal thrombus. The catheter is passed repeatedly until a good back-flow of blood is obtained. The operation can be performed under local analgesia. For a saddle embolus at the aortic bifurcation Fogarty catheters can be passed retrogradely from the femoral arteries to dislodge the embolus.

3. *Conservative Régime.* Because the results of embolectomy are often poor and because of the bad general condition of these patients, many believe that arterial emboli should be treated conservatively and not by operation. A good case can be made out, especially in the grossly unfit, for

such measures as sympathetic block followed by heparinisation and phenindione therapy. The infusion of low-molecular-weight dextran ('Rheomacrodex') has been reported to be of value.

RARE ARTERIAL DISEASES

Recourse to textbooks of general medicine should be made for information about such rare diseases as polyarteritis nodosa, temporal arteritis and 'pulseless disease', syphilitic arteritis and mycotic aneurysm.

FURTHER READING

Kinmonth. J. B., Rob, C. G., and Simeone, F. A. (1962) *Vascular Surgery*. E. Arnold, London.
Indications and Techniques in Vascular Surgery. (1963) edited by Martin, P. E. & S. Livingstone, Edinburgh & London.
Hershey, F. B. and Calman, C. H. (1963) *Atlas of Vascular Surgery*. Mosby, St. Louis.
Allen, E. V., Barker, N. W., and Hines, E. A. (1962) *Peripheral Vascular Diseases*. 3rd ed. W. B. Saunders, Philadelphia & London.

CHAPTER NINE

DISEASES OF VEINS

VARICOSE VEINS OF THE LOWER LIMB

Varicose veins are veins which are irregularly dilated, tortuous and lengthened. The commonest site for varicosity is in the lower limb, less common sites are in the submucosa of the anal canal—haemorrhoids, in the submucosa of the oesophagus—oesophageal varices, in the pampiniform plexus—varicocele and, rarely, around an arterio-venous fistula.

Approximately 20% of the population has varicose veins; in the vast majority the cause is unknown and must be called idiopathic. All that can be said of their development is that there is some 'weakness' in the wall of superficial veins and that heredity and hormonal influences play a subsidiary but important part. Deficiency of the venous valves both in number and competence is probably secondary to venous dilatation and not a cause of it.

In the varicosity associated with occlusion of deep veins due to thrombosis, venous obstruction may play a part. A raised venous pressure causes oesophageal varices and very rarely varicocele secondary to a renal tumour. A high venous pressure may also be responsible for the varicosity associated with traumatic and congenital arterio-venous fistulae.

Clinical Features

Varicose veins of the leg are either primary (idiopathic) or secondary to venous thrombosis. The long saphenous vein is more often affected than the short saphenous, and the left leg more often than the right. Women are more commonly affected than men (ratio 5:1). In two-thirds of patients there is a strong familial history. Pregnancy causes varicose veins to become more obvious, and the symptoms which they cause are made worse by menstruation. Patients who have varicose veins complain of aching (especially premenstrually), the cosmetic defect they cause, haemorrhage and phlebitis. Other effects of varicose veins are secondary to failure of the calf muscle pump to clear the limb efficiently of blood, viz. oedema, eczema and ulceration.

Varicose veins are usually visible, especially the tortuous tributaries of the main saphenous trunks. The main veins are often better felt than seen, especially in fat patients. When the patient stands the saphenous vein can be identified, if it is considerably dilated, as a compressible swelling in the groin or above the knee. Helpful confirmation of the presence of a dilated vein is given by eliciting a cough impulse or a thrill and by tapping the vein at the knee and feeling an impulse in the groin.

The Trendelenburg test proves the possibility of retrograde flow of blood down the long saphenous vein, and hence incompetence of the valve at the saphenofemoral junction.

Trendelenburg Test

The patient lies supine, the leg to be tested is elevated and the saphenous vein occluded in the groin by pressure with the thumb. The patient

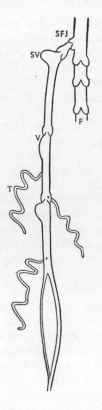

FIG. 2. The varicose long saphenous vein. F, femoral; SFJ, vein saphenofemoral junction; SV, saphena varix; V, varix; T, tributary

stands and the thumb is removed. The test is positive if the vein is seen to fill with blood downwards towards the foot. It is negative if the veins fill slowly from below. A combined result is recorded if there is rapid filling of veins below the knee before, and retrograde flow in the thigh after, release of the thumb, indicating an incompetent sapheno-femoral valve and incompetent communicating veins.

Pathology of Varicose Veins

Examination of the varicose long saphenous vein (Fig. 2) shows that it is cylindrically dilated through most of its course. Immediately below the venous valves there are prominent dilatations which project and form visible swellings if they lie near the skin. The largest of these forms the saphena varix and occurs within a few centimetres of the end of the long saphenous vein. Cylindrical dilatation of a vein produces incompetence of its valves. The number of valves varies from two to twenty and has no relation to the occurrence of varicosity. The tributaries entering the varicose, long saphenous vein are markedly tortuous in appearance. The initial histological change in the long saphenous vein is a marked hypertrophy of the medial muscle and an atrophy of the elastic tissue; after long-standing dilatation the hypertrophic muscle is replaced by fibrous tissue.

These changes in idiopathic varicose veins stop abruptly at the junction of the superficial and deep veins, whether at the junction of the saphenous main trunk with the femoral vein or at the junction of communicating veins with the deep veins; the deep veins are unaffected. In varicose veins secondary to deep vein thrombosis the deep veins are rigid and valveless over a variable extent of their course. Although the deep veins may originally have been completely occluded by clot, recanalisation restores the calibre of the vessel over a period of two years, but with destruction of its valves. The valves guarding communicating veins are destroyed allowing reversal of blood flow to occur from deep to superficial veins.

The Effects of Varicose Veins

Varicose veins decrease the efficiency of the calf-muscle pump which has the function of promoting the venous return to the heart. Normally, when the calf muscles contract blood is impelled towards the heart both in the deep and superficial veins. If there is incompetence of valves guarding the openings of communicating veins (including the sapheno-femoral junction and the termination of the short saphenous vein) into the deep veins, then, when the calf muscles contract, some blood will flow retrogradely down the superficial veins. Hence the efficiency of the mechanism of clearance of blood from the limb is reduced. Retrograde blood-flow in varicose veins occurs continuously during exercise and transiently during change of posture from lying to standing (as in the Trendelenburg test). It is abolished by firm elastic bandaging, which, if it covers the calf muscles and extends to the root of the toes, restores the efficiency of the calf-muscle pump by obliterating the superficial veins. Varicosity secondary to damage to the deep venous valves following thrombosis places an increased burden on the calf pump. Even if dilated superficial veins are removed swelling may persist because of deep venous incompetence. Only firm bandaging is effective in speeding the venous return.

The impaired venous return is reflected by changes in the venous pressure. The venous pressure in the superficial veins of a patient standing at rest, whether with or without varicose veins, is the hydrostatic pressure (the weight of a column of blood from the heart to the ankle, approximately 90 mm. Hg). Exercise reduces this pressure to 30–40 mm. in the normal limb, but if varicose veins are present the pressure may not fall or may fall only to a relatively small extent.

The effects of retrograde blood flow and failure of the venous pressure to fall during exercise are peripheral venous stasis and oedema. The first sign of inadequacy of the calf-muscle pump to cope with venous incompetence is swelling of the ankle. This may be delayed for years, or may never occur. When it does occur it is a sign of decompensation, just as in cardiac disease swelling of the ankle is evidence of failure of the right side of the heart.

Treatment

Varicose veins can be treated either by injection of sclerosants, by operation or by pressure bandaging. Operation includes removal by stripping of dilated main venous trunks and division of incompetent communicating veins where they enter deep veins.

1. *Injection of Sclerosant Substances*

Sclerosant injections are indicated for tortuous venous tributaries in the absence of main saphenous trunk dilation. Hence minor varicose veins causing only cosmetic defect or residual tributaries left after stripping operations are particularly suitable.

The most commonly used sclerosant is 5% ethanolamine oleate, which acts by irritating and damaging the intima of the vein and by shortening the clotting time. The patient first stands to allow the vein to fill; a light rubber band is applied around the leg above the vein to be injected. The patient then lies flat, a needle attached to a syringe containing no more than 2 ml. of sclerosant is inserted into the vein and the band is released. The sclerosant is slowly injected, the needle withdrawn and the vein massaged up and down to spread the sclerosant. The patient must not move the leg for 5 minutes.

The advantages of this method are comfort for the patient, achievement of wide thrombosis and the rarity of spill-over into the deep veins.

Recently the indication for sclerosant therapy have been widened. Fegan has pointed out that if the injection can be given at the site of incompetent perforating veins a more efficient thrombosis can be achieved, especially if the leg is tightly bandaged for 6 weeks to keep the damaged endothelial surfaces in apposition until firm fibrosis occurs. This type of treatment is called compression sclerotherapy.

2. *Removal of Saphenous Trunks by Stripping*

Stripping operations are performed for dilatation of the main saphenous trunks to reduce retrograde blood flow. If the main saphenous veins can be felt either in the groin, thigh or behind the knee it can be assumed that they are sufficiently dilated to be permitting retrograde blood flow, and if there are symptoms they should be removed. Aching pain, swelling of the ankles, eczema, ulceration and recurrent phlebitis are all indications for stripping if the saphenous veins are enlarged.

In the operation of stripping the end of the long or short saphenous vein is exposed and the veins are divided flush with the femoral or popliteal veins. All nearby venous tributaries must be divided, or recurrence may occur. The long or short saphenous vein is next exposed at the ankle and a flexible vein stripper passed up the vein within its lumen. A firm crêpe bandage is applied and the vein pulled out by traction on the stripper in the groin or behind the knee. The patient must get out of bed next day and exercise the leg freely, for immobilisation in bed is likely to be followed by deep venous thrombosis and pulmonary embolism. Following the operation crêpe bandages must be worn for 3–4 weeks or longer until all swelling has subsided. Patients must be warned that approximately 8 weeks must be allowed for the reaction in the legs to settle down completely before the full benefit of the operation can be appreciated. After this time the legs are inspected and any residual varices treated by injection of sclerosant.

If there has been a history of deep venous thrombosis one should be much more guarded about offering benefit from an operation on the veins. Operation on the superficial veins may be beneficial so long as there is no great swelling or induration and when the superficial veins are very large. In such cases it is often much safer simply to divide the saphenous veins flush with the deep veins rather than carry out the larger operation of stripping. With these operations may be added division of other incompetent communicating veins. Patients must be warned, however, that the legs can never be fully restored to normal because of the damage to the deep venous valves which has resulted from the previous thrombosis and that they must always wear elastic support.

3. *Division of Incompetent Communicating Veins*

Varicose veins may recur after stripping operations even when the entire main trunk has been removed if communicating veins have become incompetent. The commonest sites of communicating vein incompetence are:

'*Mid-Hunter perforator*'—immediately above the adductor tubercle joining the long saphenous vein to the femoral in Hunter's canal.

'*Ankle perforating veins*'—lying behind the posterior borders of the subcutaneous surfaces of the tibia and fibula below the level of the bellies of the calf muscles.

The communicating branch between the long and short saphenous vein behind the tibial condyles.

Indirect communicating veins that mostly lie over the calf muscles and connect superficial veins with intramuscular veins.

Communicating veins can be localised by the presence of many fine tortuous tributaries which tend to be greatest in number around the sites of communication or by feeling defects in the fascia over them. If two venous tourniquets are applied to a limb and the subject made to exercise, the superficial veins between the rubber bands should remain full when an incompetent communicator lies between them. They should be marked with skin ink and later explored and divided flush with the deep veins. A history of previous deep thrombosis does not rule out such an operation so long as the leg is not grossly indurated or oedematous.

4. *Elastic Support*

Elastic stockings are recommended during pregnancy, for the old, those unfit for operation and after deep vein thrombosis.

ULCERATION OF THE LOWER LEG

It has been estimated that there are about a quarter of a million persons suffering from ulcers of the leg in Great Britain; the majority are women, because venous disease and deep venous thrombosis are so much more common in women. There are many causes of ulcers of the leg and many patients with ulcers, so it is important to have simple methods of elucidating the differential diagnosis. Below are set out in general terms the causes of ulcers, together with an approximate estimate of the frequency of occurrence of each.

Venous	75%
(¾ Primary; ¼ Secondary to deep vein thrombosis)	
Arterial	5%
Traumatic	10%
Miscellaneous	10%

The last group though small includes a large number of disorders, such as blood dyscrasias—acholuric jaundice, hypersplenism, leukaemia, sickle-cell anaemia, chronic inflammatory disease—syphilis, tuberculosis and pyogenic osteomyelitis, congenital arterio-venous shunts, epithelioma, hypertension, diabetes, ulcerated skin diseases and diseases affecting joints and muscles—poliomyelitis, rheumatoid arthritis and hemiplegia.

Differential Diagnosis

1. *Venous Ulcer*

A typical venous ulcer lies immediately above the malleoli, more often on the medial surface of the shin and is associated with either varicose veins, oedema, pigmentation or induration. In about one-quarter of this group there is a clear history of deep venous thrombosis, but others may have had less severe degrees of thrombosis unnoticed or forgotten.

2. *Arterial Ulcers*

Arterial ulcers are usually a manifestation of arteriosclerotic gangrene. They arise in the elderly and cause severe pain. Sites are the shin, dorsum of foot and over the tendo Achillis. The pulses at the ankle are absent and there is evidence of severe peripheral ischaemia. Occasionally a limb may show the vasospastic changes of Raynaud's syndrome, which may contribute to persistence of an ulcer.

3. *Traumatic Ulcers*

There is a history of injury. The ulcer lies on the shin and is often slow to heal because of associated venous disease and oedema.

It should be possible to diagnose the cause of 90% of ulcers of the leg from:

(i) the site of the ulcer;

(ii) the signs of venous disease or a history of deep venous thrombosis;

(iii) the presence of severe peripheral ischaemia;

(iv) a history of injury.

In the remaining 10% further investigations should be carried out, such as urine test for sugar, full blood count, red-cell fragility test, abdominal examination for splenomegaly, measurement of blood pressure and radiography of the leg for bone changes. Phlebography is of help when the history suggests a deep venous thrombosis, and then it is useful to confirm that the deep veins have been damaged and to what degree.

An epithelioma may arise de novo, in a long-standing ulcer, at the orifice of a sinus of chronic osteomyelitis, in the scar of a burn or X-ray therapy. The ulcer has hypertrophic edges, erodes bone and is very painful. Biopsy should be performed if there is any suspicion of malignancy. Diffuse congenital arterio-venous fistulae are rare, but easily recognised by the occurrence of varicose veins or ulcer in the young (that is under 20 years). The affected leg is longer than normal and warm. Superficial extensive plane naevi are common on the skin. Pulses are full in volume, venous oxygen saturation is high, murmurs may be heard over the arteries of the affected leg. Chest radiography and electrocardiogram may confirm enlargement of the heart.

Treatment

The treatment of venous and traumatic ulcers (85% of the total) is pressure bandaging. The treatment of the remaining 15% is that specific to the disease causing the ulcer. In general, it can be said that it is simple to heal an ulcer of the leg; the difficulty is to keep the ulcer healed.

1. *Pressure Bandaging*

The action of the pressure bandage is to assist the calf-muscle pump by obliterating superficial and communicating veins and by maintaining even pressure over the calf muscles despite their changes in shape during the contractions of exercise. The elastic sleeve must therefore cover the calf completely to assist the pump and must extend from the root of the toes to prevent peripheral oedema. Once the sleeve is applied, exercise should be encouraged, literally to squeeze oedema out of the limb. The girth of an oedematous limb may be reduced by 3 cm. or more in a week by proper application of a pressure bandage.

Numerous types of elastic support are available, and they can be graded in order of effectiveness. *Porous adhesive bandages* are most efficient, but there is a danger of producing cutaneous sensitivity reactions to the adhesive. These reactions can be reduced if a sleeve of gauze tubing is applied to the leg first. The bandage must extend from the root of the toes to the tibial tubercle and include the heel. It must be firmly applied, and each turn should overlap its predecessor by half the width of the bandage. Reduction in the size of the leg is rapid at first, and necessitates frequent changing of the bandage, either once or twice weekly. If it is left longer the skin becomes abraded and discharge from the ulcer saturates the coverings. These factors cause irritation and may increase ulceration. With correctly applied bandages an ulcer can be expected to heal in 8–12 weeks.

Heavy Webbing Elastic Bandage applied over a gauze sleeve is suitable for the patient who cannot tolerate adhesive bandages or whose ulcer is discharging profusely because it is inflamed. Infection can be treated with aerosol sprays of mixtures of neomycin, bacitracin and polymyxin. As it dries the ulcer can be painted with simple applications, such as 1% aqueous solution of gentian violet applied to the ulcer three to four times a day until it has crusted over. The bandage is only applied by day, and can be tightened as the swelling is reduced.

Elastic Stockings must be accurately fitted after the swelling has been reduced to the minimum by elastic bandaging. Elastic stockings are particularly suited to the patient with a healed ulcer, the pregnant woman, the patient who has previously suffered deep venous thrombosis, the old and those unfit for operation.

Crêpe Bandages are the least efficient in the control of swelling, but they are not bulky and they are easy to apply. They are most useful for the patient who has recently had an operation on the superficial veins. They will control swelling of tender legs temporarily.

2. *Operation*

Those patients who have gross dilatation of superficial veins should have them removed by stripping after the ulcer has been healed. Stripping of either or both long and short saphenous veins is usually all that is necessary, despite the possible existence of incompetent perforating veins. Reduction of retrograde blood flow, and hence assistance to the calf-muscle pump, may prevent recurrence of ulceration for many years. Presumably there is some critical level of efficiency of the pump beyond which the leg cannot compensate. Routine division of all incompetent communicating veins is difficult and requires long operations and may cause painful postoperative disability. If an ulcer recurs after vein stripping incompetent communicating veins should be identified and divided.

Lumbar sympathectomy should be performed only if there are signs of ischaemia. Deep vein ligation has not proved to be a satisfactory method of dealing with the post-thrombotic state.

VENOUS THROMBOSIS

Detailed knowledge of venous thrombosis is important, for it is so common, it cannot be anticipated, and its effects may be disastrous to life and limb. In the majority of patients the cause is unknown, in fact little can be added to the original postulates of Virchow (1856) that venous thrombosis is due to three factors, intimal damage, stasis and an abnormality of the clotting mechanism.

Injury to the intima may follow direct contusion or pressure from a pillow or sling. Slowing of the circulation is a well-known feature of the early postoperative period, during pregnancy and in varicose veins; in all these conditions venous thrombosis is common. No factor in the clotting mechanism has ever been found responsible for thrombosis, though it has been assiduously sought after. Thrombosis is certainly common in blood dyscrasias such as leukaemia, polycythaemia and anaemia. There is an increase in the number and stickiness of platelets in blood after splenectomy when thrombosis is common. The association of thrombosis with malignancy (Trousseau's sign) has never been explained. No abnormal clotting factors have been discovered to account for thrombophlebitis migrans, in which attacks of superficial and deep thrombosis occur over the years in many different sites.

Local anatomical features may determine the location of thrombus in certain veins, for example, in the large sinus-like veins in the soleus muscles and in tortuous varicose tributaries of the long saphenous vein.

Pathology

A thrombus begins as an aggregate of platelets which become adherent to the vein wall. Fibrin accumulates over the platelets, with blood cells in its meshes. The proportions of fibrin, platelets and red and white cells determine the appearance of a thrombus—that is whether it is red or white. Usually there is a zone of white thrombus firmly attached to the vessel wall, on which is deposited soft red thrombus which may protrude as a long filament floating in the blood stream, part of which may break off and embolise. Clot differs from thrombus, in that clot has no regular structure, fibrin and cells being randomly arranged. In thrombus there are zones of differing structure which are laid down as it grows.

After the third or fourth day from its initiation a thrombus shows signs of organisation following the invasion of fibroblasts and angioblasts from the vessel wall, to which it becomes fused inseparably. At the same time clefts appear in the granulation tissue which coalesce and eventually recanalise the occluded segment. Even massive thrombi in large veins may show such extensive recanalisation that phlebography after a period of two years or more usually shows a vessel of normal calibre, though with irregularity of its wall.

Although the vein is efficiently recanalised, thrombosis and recanalisation destroys its valve cusps so that retrograde blood flow during exercise may occur. Many thrombi fibrose and become calcified. Such calcification is almost invariable in thrombi in pelvic veins, where they are commonly seen in abdominal radiographs and frequently cause difficulty when they must be distinguished from ureteric calculi.

SUPERFICIAL VENOUS THROMBOSIS

Superficial venous thrombosis or phlebitis is common. It is commonest in varicose veins, and may follow injury, infection of veins or injection of them with irritating substances, such as sclerosants, thio-pentone and strong glucose solution.

The affected veins become tender and inflamed, often with surrounding cellulitis or periphlebitis. Suppuration is rare. Resolution usually occurs after 2–3 weeks. Embolism is not to be expected because of the fixity of the thrombus to the vein wall. Occasionally, in the leg, thrombus may spread from the superficial to the deep veins, from where embolism may occur. For this reason parenteral therapy through the veins of the leg should be avoided. Occasionally there is a steady spread of thrombus along superficial veins, especially the long saphenous vein to the femoral vein in the groin.

Migratory thrombophlebitis is uncommon. Attacks of phlebitis may occur in either superficial or deep veins at random anywhere in the limbs at times separated by months or over periods of years. Rarely migratory thrombophlebitis is a precursor or concomitant of thrombo-angiitis, and rarely it is associated with recurrent pulmonary embolism. In Mondor's disease there is phlebitis of superficial veins near the breast or in the ante-cubital fossa. Hard tender cords appear which resolve spontaneously after a few weeks. Trauma and infection are occasionally factors, but the basic cause of the disease is unknown.

Treatment

In cases of minor severity it is only necessary to await spontaneous resolution and to treat symptoms by elastic support and analgesics. If an infective element is suspected antibiotics should be given. If phlebitis is spreading, anticoagulants may be necessary after admission of the patient to hospital. In cases of migratory thrombophlebitis the patient may need long term anticoagulants for a period of years. Pain is often severe in phlebitis, and a short course of phenylbutazone, 200 mg. twice daily for 1 week, is often valuable in relieving pain. The drug is said to have 'anti-inflammatory effects', but should be used with care, especially in patients with a history of previous peptic ulcer, as occasionally there is idiosyncrasy and severe gastro-intestinal bleeding and purpura.

DEEP-VEIN THROMBOSIS OF THE LOWER LIMB

Deep-vein thrombosis is common in the calf muscles after operation, childbirth and in cases of anaemia and infection. Pelvic operations and a complicated postoperative course are other possible factors. The incidence of calf-vein thrombosis is approximately 3–5% of all operations.

The commonest site of deep-vein thrombosis is usually in the soleus muscle just above its junction with the tendo Achillis in the midline. If a finger is firmly pressed on the tendo Achillis at its insertion into the calcaneum and run up towards the muscle bellies of the calf the patient flinches as the site of thrombosis is passed. Often both legs are symmetrically affected. There may be slight fever before the occurrence of pain. Other common sites of thrombosis are the femoral, iliac and pelvic veins, in these the thrombus may not produce any clinical signs.

Oedema of the ankle usually does not appear unless thrombus extends into the popliteal vein and obstructs the venous return. If massive spread occurs to the femoral or iliac veins gross oedema collects in the thigh and the lower leg, with distended collateral veins, especially in the groin. If there is spread to the inferior vena cava both legs are swollen and perhaps also the buttocks, abdominal wall and genitals. Collateral veins are often visibly distended over the abdomen and thorax. In such extensive thromboses the patient may be shocked and is often ill with a high fever, especially if there is infection in or near by the veins. Rarely there is a steely blue discoloration of the leg associated with recurrent progressive and massive venous occlusion (phlegmasia caerulea dolens). Such patients are often severely shocked, with a limb which progresses to venous gangrene. Venous gangrene is rare, and occurs usually in the very old, the very ill and those with advanced carcinoma. It is usually a terminal and fatal illness.

Treatment

Deep-vein thrombosis should be treated by anticoagulants (see p. 112), so long as there is no fear that they may produce haemorrhage. Up to about 6 days after an operation haemorrhage from a wound or a suture line is a serious hazard, and so in this period anticoagulants should only be given if embolism has occurred. Fortunately it is unusual for deep-vein thrombosis to occur in less than 6 days after an operation.

It is difficult to give a precise régime for the treatment of deep-vein thrombosis, as so much depends on the extent of venous occlusion and personal opinions as to the merits of heparin and phenindione. A tentative scheme is as follows:

For thrombi limited to the calf muscles, intravenous heparin for 24 hours, followed by phenindione therapy for 6 weeks. As soon as the prothrombin time is adequately prolonged the patient, if fit, should be up and about.

For major ilio-femoral thrombosis, thrombectomy should be seriously considered, that is operation to clear the femoral and iliac vein of thrombus to prevent embolism and the sequelae of damage to the deep venous valves. For those unfit for thrombectomy or after thrombectomy heparin should be given intravenously for about 10 days, followed by phenindione for several weeks. Adequate prolonged heparinisation is usually dramatically successful in slowing the spread of thrombus, the leg decreases in size and well-being is improved.

If there is *oedema* a gauze sleeve should be applied from the toes to the groin and overlain by a fairly tight elastic bandage (Bisgaard bandage). If there is fever, blood culture should be performed and antibiotics given for fear of septicaemia and pyaemia. Patients with extensive thrombosis are often very anaemic, and for them urgent blood transfusion must be considered.

Major vein ligation femoral, or inferior caval, should only be performed for repeated pulmonary emboli from recurrent deep-vein thrombosis. The vena cava can be partially interrupted by a series of mattress sutures or a plastic clip specially made to allow partial occlusion of the vena cava. The operation should be followed by anticoagulant therapy. Further thrombosis and embolism may still occur so the role of thrombectomy and inferior caval occlusion is not yet clear.

Phlegmasia caerulea dolens is difficult to treat. Shock should be treated, heparin injected immediately, the limb elevated and bandaged. Thrombectomy may be indicated.

Active exercises should be encouraged to limit the extent of thrombosis by speeding the venous return. Many patients so affected have terminal conditions so the mortality is high.

ANTICOAGULANT THERAPY

Anticoagulants cannot dissolve formed thrombi, but, by limiting their extent, severe damage to the deep veins can be avoided and the chances of pulmonary embolism reduced. Two anticoagulants are in common use—heparin and phenindione.

Heparin

Heparin or mucoitin polysulphuric acid is the normal anticoagulant in blood. It is formed in the mast cells and prepared for use in the human from mammalian lung. Its action is to neutralise thromboplastin in shed blood, an immediate action that lasts from 4 to 6 hours, and which can at any time be reversed by the injection of protamine sulphate, 1 mg. of which inactivates 1 mg. (100 units) of heparin. To be effective heparin must be given by intravenous injection, preferably through an indwelling needle of the Gordh or Mitchell type. It is given by continuous intravenous infusion, and the does must be controlled by repeated *clotting times* so that the coagulation time is maintained at a level twice the normal (normal 4–8 minutes). The initial loading dose is high, 10,000 units or more, for there is often some initial resistance to the drug; later, because the clotting time is more easily prolonged by heparin, the dose must be reduced.

Phenindione

Phenindione inhibits the formation of prothrombin by the liver. It is slow and cumulative in action; its full effect is delayed for from 24 to 36 hours The action of phenindione can be reversed, but only more slowly than that of heparin by the use of fresh blood transfusion and intramuscular injection of vitamin K_1, 500–1,000 mg. Daily prothrombin time estimations are performed to follow the effect of treatment; a dose of phenindione is then given which maintains the prothrombin time at twice the normal level. On the first day 150 mg. is given, on the second 100 and on the third and subsequent days the dose is adjusted according to the thrombin time. Long-term therapy over months or years is fairly safe, and the prothrombin time need only be measured at weekly intervals. The patient must be warned that haemorrhage may occur—bleeding gums, haematuria and bruises—and this event may necessitate stopping the drug.

Aperients such as liquid paraffin interfere with the absorption of the drug. Alcoholic excess must be avoided. Broad spectrum antibiotics potentiate phenindione. Idiosyncrasy may cause rashes and even renal damage up to the point of anuria. Phenindione is a dangerous drug that must be prescribed with care.

Attempts to dissolve thrombi with an enzyme, streptokinase have produced equivocal results. Streptokinase activates plasminogen normally found in blood to plasmin that will dissolve recently formed fibrin. The results of treatment with streptokinase are so far inconclusive.

PULMONARY THROMBO-EMBOLISM

Pulmonary embolism remains one of the most serious of postoperative complications. No test has been found to warn of its happening, and such measures as early ambulation after surgery have not proved effective in diminishing the mortality of embolism. Embolism occurs in 3–5% of operations, fatal embolism in 0·1%. Recurrent embolism is fatal in 20% of cases.

The majority of emboli originate from the deep veins of the lower limb, mostly from the calf muscles, some come from the iliac and femoral veins and others from pelvic veins. Occasionally, even at post mortem, no source can be found, and it must then be presumed that infarction of the lung has occurred from pulmonary-vein thrombosis, which is clinically indistinguishable from pulmonary embolism. Pulmonary embolism is not restricted to surgical patients, it is a common cause of death in all manner of disorders, especially cardiac failure. Post-mortem examination of patients dying in medical wards shows 10% to have had pulmonary embolism, but not necessarily fatal emboli. Repeated incidents of embolism with or without deep-vein thrombosis is a feature of cardiac disease such as mitral stenosis and is less often seen in thrombophlebitis migrans.

Clinical Features

Sudden death follows massive embolism, which may be unheralded or possibly preceded by a sudden urgent desire to defaecate. Death in the lavatory or on the bedpan is not an uncommon incident. More often pulmonary embolism causes sudden pleuritic pain with dyspnoea, the pain possibly radiating to the shoulder if the diaphragm is irritated. If the infarct is large there is shock with a fall in blood pressure. In the early phase there may be no signs in the chest clinically or in radiographs. Later haemoptysis and pleuritic rub and signs of pulmonary collapse may appear. Occasionally, in the early postoperative period after an abdominal operation a patient may suddenly collapse and become very ill with thoracic or abdominal pain. It may then be very difficult to distinguish coronary thrombosis, pulmonary embolism and leakage from an intra-abdominal suture line. The electrocardiogram in such an event may be of great value in determining the differential diagnosis between coronary thrombosis and pulmonary embolus. Pneumonia in the postoperative period should be thought suspicious of embolus, especially that occurring about the 10th to 12th day. It is especially likely to be the cause if the sputum is not purulent.

Treatment

The anticoagulant régime described on p. 111 is instituted. Before the sixth postoperative day the danger of haemorrhage from anticoagulant therapy may be real, and in such a case one must weigh up the chances of further embolism against the danger of haemorrhage. Morphia (10–15 mg.) may be injected to relieve pain.

Many patients suffering from a large pulmonary embolus survive long enough for the diagnosis to be confirmed and consideration of pulmonary embolectomy. Cardiac catheterisation and angiography confirm the diagnosis. In such patients pulmonary embolectomy with cardio-pulmonary by-pass may be dramatically successful. Usually the inferior vena cava is interrupted to prevent further embolism.

Many attempts at prophylaxis of embolism have been made, but there is little evidence that the incidence of fatal pulmonary embolism has been affected by them. Raising the heels on sponge rubber on the operating table to relieve pressure on the calves may be valuable. Deep-vein ligation before operation was practised extensively in America, but has not been widely used elsewhere. The use of prophylactic phenindione in old people who need operations following trauma, such as pinning of a fractured femur, has recently been shown to be effective in reducing the incidence of pulmonary embolism.

FURTHER READING

Dodd, H., and Cockett, F. B. (1956) *Pathology and Surgery of Veins of the Lower Limb*. Livingstone, Edinburgh.

Fegan, G. (1967) *Varicose Veins*. Heinemann Medical Books, London.

CHAPTER TEN

THE LYMPHATIC SYSTEM

ACUTE LYMPHANGITIS AND LYMPHADENITIS

Acute lymphadenitis is always secondary to some focus of infection such as a cut or abrasion. Sometimes, however, the source of infection may be difficult to find. The organisms pass along the lymphatic channels and grow there and in the lymph nodes. The regional lymph nodes are affected, and the infection is usually limited to them; they become painful and tender and later enlarged. Because of the spread of inflammation beyond their capsule, the nodes frequently become matted together and to surrounding tissues. The skin over the nodes may become reddened. Occasionally the inflammatory process proceeds to cellulitis and even suppuration.

Red lines in the skin arising from the region of the infected source and passing towards the regional nodes mark the position of the inflamed lymphatic channels. Nowadays acute lymphangitis is rather uncommon; it is usually due to haemolytic streptococci, and penicillin is of the greatest value in treatment.

Treatment consists in dealing with the source of infection. If a patient is ill he should be put to bed. The limb should be rested. An appropriate antibiotic should be given. If suppuration occurs, the abscess should be drained.

CHRONIC ENLARGEMENT OF LYMPH NODES

This is a common and important problem for diagnosis. There are a multiplicity of causes, both infective and non-infective. If doubt exists, then a biopsy and histological examination of a node should make the diagnosis clear. Enlargement of nodes may be classified as follows:

1. Chronic Inflammation

Non-Specific

Chronic lymphadenitis results from septic absorption from chronic ulcers, tonsils, bad teeth or other septic areas. The behaviour of the enlarged nodes depend on the virulence of the infection. Usually they are tender but not adherent to one another. They may, on occasion, go on to suppuration. Occasionally there is remarkably little tenderness, and this fact gives rise to difficulty in diagnosis. Treatment consists in dealing with the infected source. If the nodes remain enlarged, then the diagnosis may be in considerable doubt, and biopsy of one of the nodes should be performed.

Specific

(a) *Tuberculous Adenitis* may occur at any age, but quite often in young people under the age of twenty. The tubercle bacilli gain access to the lymphatic system via some breach of the surface epithelium of such organs as the tonsils, gastro-intestinal tract or pulmonary tree. The nodes most commonly affected are the cervical, bronchial and mesenteric. The infection is at first limited by the capsule of the lymph nodes. Later periadenitis causes the nodes to become matted to one another and later to deeper structures and to the skin. Frequently the necrotic tissue in the node liquefies and forms a cold abscess. It is called 'cold' because there is none of the hyperaemia usually seen with infection, and therefore it does not feel warmer than the surrounding tissues. If the abscess discharges on to the skin chronic sinuses result. Calcification of the nodes occurs commonly when the disease is no longer active.

Although the above description is typical of tuberculous adenitis, it may present in other and less typical ways, often there is secondary infection due to pyogenic bacteria, and then the nodes become tender, painful and may contain some yellow pus. Occasionally the nodes remain rubbery and discrete.

Cervical Lymphadenitis is the commonest tuberculous condition requiring surgical treatment, and is less serious than tuberculosis elsewhere in the body. Almost invariably it is due to milk-borne bacilli, and the portal of entry is by the tonsils or adenoids. Nowadays this condition is much less common in Great Britain than formerly since the introduction of pasteurisation of milk and tuberculin testing of herds of cows. In many countries it is still frequently encountered.

The jugulo-digastric group of nodes draining the tonsils are the most commonly affected. More rarely those in the posterior triangle, the submandibular and the lower deep cervical or supraclavicular groups may also be involved.

Symptoms and Signs

Typically the nodes are at first small, discrete, mobile, painless and not tender on palpation. Later they tend to become larger and matted together due to periadenitis. Sooner or later they become caseous and liquefy, but the pus remains within the capsule of the mass. Later still the nodes may coalesce and form a larger cold abscess, with a false fibrous capsule around it. These abscesses may burst through a small opening in the deep fascia of the neck and spread into the subcutaneous tissue—thus forming a 'collar-stud' abscess. Later still, if untreated, the skin becomes involved and chronic multiple sinuses result.

Prophylaxis. Prevention is better than cure, and the elimination of tuberculosis from cattle and the pasteurization of milk has virtually eliminated this condition in England, Sweden and the United States.

Treatment. As with tuberculosis elsewhere, general treatment is of the utmost importance. Bed rest is rarely called for, but depends upon the general condition of the patient. Fresh air, sunlight, good food and tubercle-free milk are the essentials. Calciferol 50,000–100,000 units daily for 7 days is of benefit. Systemic treatment with streptomycin, PAS and INH should be given whenever the disease is not regressing.

If treatment is started at an early stage the above measures may well be sufficient. However, if an abscess has formed a small incision should be made and the contents of the cavity expressed. If a localised group of nodes does not respond to the above treatment, then excision should be performed to prevent further abscess formation and unsightly sinuses. The jugulo-digastric group of lymph nodes are the commonest requiring excision. They are removed *en masse*, avoiding spillage of caseous material. Great care is taken to avoid damage to important structures such as the accessory nerve and the cervical branch of the facial nerve. The jugular vein is often adherent to the nodes. Diseased tonsils may require removal, and if so they should, if possible, be removed before the operation on the cervical lymph nodes.

(b) *Syphilitic Lymphadenitis*. In the primary stage of syphilis enlargement of the nodes draining the chancre may occur and the lymph nodes may become very large. Suppuration does not follow unless there is a secondary pyogenic infection. In the secondary stage there is enlargement of many of the nodes in the body, including very often those in the posterior triangle of the neck. The nodes are small, firm and painless.

2. Malignant Nodes

(a) *Metastasis*

In lymph nodes this is common. The primary tumour is usually carcinomatous, being either squamous or columnar celled. Metastasis to nodes from sarcomata is much less common.

Although the lymph nodes are at first firm, later they become stony hard, painless and are not tender on palpation.

(b) *A Primary Malignant Growth*

Arising in lymph nodes this is rare, but lymphosarcoma, a very malignant tumour, may arise from lymph nodes, particularly in the cervical group or from the lymphoid tissue in the tonsillar region or mediastinum. It is a firm, painless, rapidly growing tumour and spreads to adjoining lymph nodes and infiltrates nearby structures. Histology shows masses of cells resembling lymphocytes.

Excision of a local growth at an early stage is occasionally feasible. The great majority are treated by irradiation. The first response may be dramatic, but recurrences are more resistant to subsequent courses of radiotherapy.

3. The Reticuloses

Various diseases are now known to arise as a result of proliferation of lymphoid or lymphoreticular tissue. In most instances the lymph nodes are the first to be affected. Sooner or later other lymphoid tissue is involved, such as the spleen, liver, Peyer's patches in the small intestine and the bone marrow. Examination of the blood and bone marrow and biopsy of a lymph node are required to establish the diagnosis.

The reticuloses comprise a complex group of diseases, but the more important ones of surgical interest can be classified as follows:

Haemopoietic	Leukaemias
Unknown	Hodgkin's disease (Lymphadenoma)
	Sarcoidosis
Neoplastic	Lymphosarcoma
	Reticulosarcoma
	Multiple myeloma
	Ewing's tumour
	Giant Follicular Lymphoma (Brill Symmer's disease).
Metabolic	Gaucher's disease
	Schuller-Christian's diseases

Hodgkin's Disease (Lymphadenoma)

Although the cause of this disease is unknown, it has many aspects which resemble those of malignancy. It often occurs in young adults, but may occur at any age.

Clinical Features. The first sign is usually painless enlargement of groups of lymph nodes, most commonly in the neck, but sometimes in the groin and axilla. At first the nodes are discrete and rubbery, but later may become matted together. Sometimes other lymphoid tissue is affected first. Enlargement of abdominal nodes and infiltration of the bowel with Hodgkin tissue may result in abdominal pain or bouts of diarrhoea. Involvement of mediastinal nodes and lung tissue may make the patient present with dyspnoea and cough. Such patients may have fever of the Pel-Ebstein type, which lasts for a week or two, with intervening afebrile intervals. As the disease progresses, there is increasing weakness, malaise, loss of weight and anaemia. In the majority of patients the spleen and the liver eventually become enlarged. Almost any organ can become infiltrated with Hodgkin Tissue, and this may result in bizarre symptoms, such as pain in the bones, pressure on nerves, resulting in palsies and, in the case of skin, severe pruritus. The patient may experience pain localised to foci of disease whenever he drinks alcohol. The diagnosis of Hodgkin disease can only be established with certainty by removing a lymph node and examining it under the microscope. The histological features are loss of the normal architecture of the lymph node, reticulum-cell hyperplasia, eosinophil cells and giant cells of the Reed–Sternberg type.

Treatment. Radiotherapy is the treatment of choice, especially when the disease is limited to one or two groups of nodes. The nodes become smaller and symptoms, if present, are relieved. Remissions may last for a few months to a year or two, but the disease inevitably recurs, except in a very small group which may be free of it for up to 20 or 30 years. Subsequent radiotherapy has progressively less effect. At this stage, or if the disease is more widespread at the beginning, intravenous nitrogen mustard may be given, in a dosage 0·1 mg./kg. body weight daily for three successive days; it is most convenient to give it in a saline infusion. Steroids such as cortisone sometimes produce a temporary improvement in general well-being, so does transfusion with fresh blood. Some patients may survive 10 years or so, but the majority are dead in 4–5. Rapidly progressive forms of the disease will kill the patient in 6 months. Cyclophosphamide may produce long remission.

4. Other Causes

(a) *Glandular Fever* (Infectious Mononucleosis)

This is a virus infection and is very variable in its presentation. The incubation period is from 5 to 14 days. There is an enlargement of lymph nodes, which are rubbery and slightly tender on palpation. There is an irregular fever, often accompanied by a sore throat, splenic enlargement and rash. Examination of the blood reveals an absolute and relative lymphocytosis, characteristic mononuclear cells and a heterophil antibody (Paul–Bunnell reaction).

(b) *Lymphogranuloma Inguinale*

This is a tropical venereal disease, but is not rare in temperate climates where there is a mixed population of white and Negro races. In England it is mainly encountered in those coming from tropical climates. The lesion is caused by a virus.

Usually the primary lesion in the genital region is missed and the patient presents in the secondary stage. These lesions appear 2–6 weeks after exposure to infection. Constitutional symptoms are usually minimal. Lymph nodes in the groin enlarge, particularly those lying medially. The nodes increase in size, become matted together and may break down to form chronic sinuses. In the female other complications may occur. The rectum may become involved in the inflammatory process, with resultant stricture and fistula formation between the rectum and vagina.

LYMPHOEDEMA

Chronic lymphatic obstruction results in oedema, which is at first soft and pitting but which later becomes hard and non-pitting. The subcutaneous tissue becomes thickened and is very prone to repeated attacks of inflammation, cellulitis and erysipelas. The toes are usually spared. Lymphangiography is useful in difficult cases to distinguish lymphoedema from venous oedema. An intravital dye is injected into the digital webs. An incision on the dorsum of the foot usually reveals a lymphatic stained blue. The vessel is cannulated with a very fine needle and injected with an

E

ultra fluid iodized oil that is radiopaque. Lymphoedema may be distinguished from oedema due to venous disease by the absence of history of thrombosis, varicose veins or stasis changes in the skin, induration and pigmentation.

Primary Lymphoedema

This is due to a congenital imperfect development of lymphatics in which the lymphatics may be diminished in size and number, or may be absent or varicose. The oedema may be present at birth, but much more often appears later, usually in women at 15–30 years or even later. Only one leg is usually affected. Milroy's disease is a familial condition of lymphoedema of the legs. Cellulitis and erysipelas are common complications.

Secondary Lymphoedema

This may be due to:

(1) *Trauma*, especially surgery and irradiation. Following a block dissection of the lymph nodes in the groin or after radical mastectomy, lymphoedema of leg or arm may result.

(2) *Infection*—recurrent attacks of cellulitis or erysipelas may result in lymphatic obstruction with lymphoedema later.

(3) *Malignant Cells* permeating the lymphatic system may result in lymphoedema (e.g. in the arm following involvement of the axillary lymph channels and nodes).

(4) *Parasites*, filaria bancrofti may lodge in lymphatics chiefly in the groin, resulting sometimes in gross oedema and thickening of the subcutaneous tissues in the scrotum and legs.

Treatment in the early stages consists in elevation of the limb and pressure bandaging. Infection must be controlled, particularly by the use of antibiotics. More advanced cases can be benefited only by plastic operations. These involve removal of the skin and subcutaneous tissue of the leg. The grossly thickened subcutaneous tissue is then removed from the skin and the skin replaced over the denuded area. The operation on the leg is carried out in stages, one area at a time. Lymphoedema of the arm after mastectomy often has a venous component due to scarring around the axillary vein which can be relieved by freeing of the vein of scar tissue.

CONGENITAL DILATION OF LYMPHATIC VESSELS

(a) Capillary Lymphangioma

This consists of brownish or wart-like excrescences in the skin. On examination with a lens, small vesicles can be seen.

(b) Cavernous Lymphangioma

This consists of masses of lymphatic cysts and is termed cystic hygroma when it occurs in the neck and axilla as a soft lax multilocular cyst that transiluminates brilliantly. It is a developmental abnormality of lymphatics and is treated by excision.

(c) *Lymphangiectasis*

This rarely gives rise to enlargement of the tongue or lips. It may affect the subcutaneous lymphatics of the lower limb, e.g. in Milroy's disease.

FURTHER READING

Yoffey, J. M., and Courtice, F. C. (1956) *Lymphatics, Lymph and Lymphoid Tissue*. 2nd ed. Edward Arnold, London.

Kinmonth, J. B., Rob., C. G., and Simeone F. A. (1962) *Vascular Surgery*. Edward Arnold, London.

CHAPTER ELEVEN

AFFECTIONS OF THE SKIN AND ITS APPENDAGES

ACUTE INFLAMMATION

Carbuncle

A carbuncle can be defined as cellulitis in fatty and areolar tissue due to an organism which is so potent as to produce necrosis of tissue. It is almost always due to the *Staphylococcus aureus*. The essential feature of a carbuncle which distinguishes it from cellulitis is a central slough of necrotic tissue which is slow to separate and discharge. A carbuncle is almost always in subcutaneous tissue, rarely it occurs in the kidney, where it produces fever and is difficult to diagnose. Diabetics commonly develop carbuncles, which may be a presenting feature of their disease. Common sites are the subcutaneous tissue of the back of the neck and the back of the hand.

A localised red, brawny, painful swollen area of skin develops which may extend over several square centimetres. A number of grey points appear in the inflamed area, which later discharge pus. The openings coalesce and the slough is slowly discharged. A large cavity is left which eventually heals by granulation.

The majority of carbuncles respond to chemotherapy alone. Penicillin is tried first and is given by intramuscular injection of 300,000 u. of procaine penicillin daily; if an immediate response is not obtained ampicillin in an oral dose of 1g daily for 5–7 days should be given and a swab of pus examined for identification of the causal organism and its sensitivity to antibiotics. Incision is not required, but it may be necessary to excise the slough when it is very slow to separate. The urine must be tested for the presence of sugar in all patients with carbuncle and in all cases of recurrent skin sepsis.

Boils

A boil is an infection or abscess in a hair follicle or in an apocrine gland such as is found in the axilla or perineum.

Boils are treated by simple expression of pus or incision if the abscess is large. Chemotherapy is only used if cellulitis extends beyond the boil, or if it is sited in a dangerous area such as on the face or in the nose, where spread to the intracranial venous sinuses rarely produces thrombophlebitis. Recurrent boils are difficult to treat; autogenous vaccines are disappointing in their effects. Surgery may occasionally be required to excise recurrently infected apocrine glands in the axilla or perineum.

Cellulitis

Cellulitis is spreading inflammation of fatty or areolar tissues. The commonest organisms responsible are streptococci or staphylococci, but many other organisms may cause cellulitis, for example, the anaerobic organisms responsible for gas gangrene. Cellulitis is dangerous, because it may spread locally to important structures, for example, tendon sheaths, bones and joints, or more distantly to cause lymphangitis and septicaemia. The presence of cellulitis demands urgent chemotherapy and immobilisation of the affected part to prevent local and general complications.

Erysipelas

Erysipelas is an inflammation of the epidermis due to streptococci which spreads rapidly. In the past it was very contagious, but is now rarely seen except in aged, ill-nourished patients or as a complication of lymphoedema. The face and scrotum were common sites. There is fever and malaise, the affected part of the skin becomes vividly red, with small vesicles at the periphery. The margins of the inflammation are well defined and advance rapidly. Treatment with intramuscular penicillin is most effective, with ichthyol paste locally to sooth the irritation.

CHRONIC INFLAMMATION

Pyogenic Granuloma

Pyogenic granuloma usually arises at the site of an unhealed wound or infected benign tumour such as a papilloma. A spongy red mass of granulation tissue arises which may be very vascular and may simulate a tumour. It is treated by daily cauterisation with silver nitrate or by curettage under local analgesia and application of a cautery to its base.

Lupus Vulgaris

Chronic tuberculous infection of the skin is rarely seen nowadays. Its surgical importance lies in the occasional appearance of squamous carcinoma at the site of healed lupus, especially in scars produced by radiotherapy, which was many years ago employed in the treatment of this disease.

WARTS AND CORNS

Warts

Warts are localised areas of hyperplasia of the prickle-cell layer of the skin due to a filterable virus. The dermal papillae are enlarged secondary to downgrowth of the epidermis (acanthosis). Many types are described: plane, common, plantar, filiform and condylomata acuminata. They are often multiple on the hands and face. Crops of warts may appear and disappear spontaneously. Plantar warts (verrucae) show as a translucent central zone deep to a thickening of the epidermis, usually over a metatarsal head. Their unusual appearance may be due to pressure, they may be spread through contact.

Warts may be removed by curettage under local analgesia or, if multiple, under general anaesthesia. Plantar warts respond to repeated soaks with 10% formalin solution, treatment with salicylic acid plaster (50%) or excision. Vulval or penile warts can be painted with 25% podophyllin resin in liquid paraffin, which is washed off after 24 hours.

Corns

Corns and callouses are formed of hard keratin. They form in response to pressure from badly fitting shoes or as a result of postural deformities of the foot, for example, pes cavus, prominent calcaneum.

Callouses are treated by correction of the deformity if this is possible or relief of pressure by the provision of better or special shoes. Application of 10% salicylic acid in acetone helps to soften the keratin and enables it to be pared away painlessly.

Keloid

Keloids are localised overgrowths of vascular collagen fibres. They are particularly common in the skin of surgical incisions and at the site of infected burns, especially in children and in pregnancy. There is a constitutional factor for many Negroes, and some white people always develop keloid at the site of an incision or wound, and such keloids tend to recur after excision. Radiation burns may become extensively keloidal. Scars become heaped up, vascular and pink, rarely prominent tumours form. Later, keloids may shrink to pale papery scars.

Attempts to prevent keloid formation have included the use of soft X-rays after operation or the use of cortisone, but the results of such treatment are unpredictable. Recently injection of triamcinolone directly into the scar tissue has been found very effective though rather painful. Local surface application of triamcinolone under occlusion by an adhesive tape causes flattening of the keloid.

CYSTS OF THE SKIN AND SUBCUTANEOUS TISSUE

Sebaceous Cysts

Sebaceous cysts are very common. They are thought either to be retention cysts of sebaceous glands or hamartomata of sebaceous glands. Hamartoma can be defined as a malformation of tissue which normally occurs at the site of a tumour or cyst and is to be distinguished from teratoma, in which the tissues may be foreign to those normally found at the site of the tumour.

The scalp, scrotum and vulva are particularly affected. Sebaceous cysts are subcutaneous, except at the punctum or duct which leads on to the skin. The cyst is lined by squamous epithelium and is filled by sebum, which may occasionally discharge through the punctum. Malignant change is almost unknown. Secondary infection is common, especially on the face and neck. Occasionally a prominent horn (sebaceous horn) forms of inspissated sebum and keratin.

Treatment is by enucleation under local analgesia. Extensive shaving of hair on the scalp is unnecessary. If infection is present, incision and evacuation of pus should be carried out. Some cysts are destroyed by infection, but some recur.

'Benign Calcifying Epithelioma'

This term is a misnomer, it represents a calcified variant of a sebaceous cyst. A hard subcutaneous tumour forms, typically in children. Treatment is by enucleation.

Dermoid Cysts

Dermoid cysts are identical in appearance to sebaceous cysts, except that they are wholly subcutaneous, having no punctum. They are filled by sebum and lined by squamous epithelium. Two types are recognised—*congenital* at the sites of embryonic fusion, such as the *external angular dermoid* of children lateral to the outer canthus of the eye (see p. 180), and *implantation or sequestration dermoids*, in which a fragment of skin has been driven into the dermis by injury or operation. Treatment of both is by enucleation, which must be complete, or recurrence may occur. *Tubulo-dermoids* form along embryonic tracks such as the thyroglossal tract—a thyroglossal cyst or branchial cyst is a tubulo-dermoid.

Benign Tumours of Skin

1. *Papilloma*

Papillomata are warty tumours of the epidermis. Microscopy shows marked keratinisation with a variable downgrowth of skin papillae. Such tumours should be excised under local analgesia, all should be examined histologically, because clinical diagnosis is often incorrect, and malignant tumours such as melanomata and squamous-cell carcinoma may present as papillomata. Confusion is especially likely in pigmented and infected, ulcerated papillomata.

Keratoses are similar histologically to papillomata, but they are less horny, and may often be flat and pigmented. They may bleed and become infected. Some arise from exposure to intense sunlight—*solar keratoses*; some appear in old age—*senile keratoses*; and some appear in response to *chronic irritation* from irradiation, working with tar products and administration of arsenic by mouth for long periods.

Keratoses need not be excised unless they are a result of chronic irritation by light, irradiation or by chemicals. If malignancy is suspected they should be excised.

2. *Histiocytoma* (Sclerosing Haemangioma)

Histiocytoma is a firm, well-defined, non-ulcerating tumour arising from the dermis but fixed to the epidermis. It usually projects slightly above the surrounding skin. The leg is a common site, Microscopy shows subepidermal fibrosis, with fat cells and many vessels. Haemosiderin may be present and may easily be mistaken for melanin, and the tumour for a malignant melanoma. Treatment is by excision under local analgesia.

3. *Keratoacanthoma* (Molluscum Sebaceum)

This is a tumour of the skin which closely simulates in appearance and microscopically a squamous-cell carcinoma. A single firm hemispherical nodule appears which rapidly grows in a few weeks to a size of about 2 cm., with ulceration and crusting. Over a period of about 6 weeks the centre falls out to leave an ulcer with prominent rolled edges. Spontaneous healing usually occurs in 2–3 months. The face, nose, fingers and hands are common sites. The tumour more often occurs in men over the age of 50 years.

The diagnosis is purely clinical, because the microscopical appearances are so like those of carcinoma. Under local analgesia the tumour should be curetted to leave a flat base, which can then be cauterised.

4. *Melanoma* (see p. 129)

Malignant Tumours of Skin

1. *Basal-cell Carcinoma* (Rodent ulcer)

Basal-cell carcinoma is common. It arises usually on the face above the level of the lips, but at other sites, such as breast, anus and umbilicus, it is not unknown. It is unusual under the age of 40 years. Men and women are equally affected. Long exposure to intense sunlight is a factor, and hence it is common in the tropics and in Australia. It may persist unchanged for many years, but it tends to grow slowly, to become fixed and eventually to erode structures such as bone and cartilage. In a neglected case the eye may be destroyed and the dura mater exposed.

A firm disc-like nodule appears in the epidermis which ulcerates, crusts over and bleeds. Its edge has a typically 'pearly' lustre. Cystic change is common; another variant is formation of a prominent horn of keratin. Pigmentation is uncommon. It is only locally malignant, and does not metastasise to lymph nodes. Occasionally multiple superficial rodent ulcers occur.

Histology shows a tumour of the basal layer of the epidermis. The tumour comprises prominent club-shaped processes of cells surrounded by typically palisaded basal cells which have large and deeply staining nuclei. There is often extensive spread beneath an apparently normal-looking epidermis. Clear areas in the tumour processes indicate cystic change and are to be distinguished from the 'pearls' of squamous carcinoma.

In the treatment of rodent ulcer, radiotherapy and excision are found to be equally effective. Excision should be performed if the diagnosis is in doubt, when the tumour recurs after radiotherapy and for involvement of bone and cartilage. If radiotherapy is used a dose of 900 rads over a period of 2–3 weeks is usually adequate. If excision is used it must be fairly wide because of subepidermal spread of the tumour and because multicentric change is common.

2. Squamous Carcinoma

Squamous carcinoma usually arises spontaneously, but may follow prolonged exposure to sunlight, tar, mineral oils, arsenic and soot. It may also arise in the scars of healed lupus vulgaris and following radiotherapy or in sinuses due to osteomyelitis or in chronic ulcers of the leg. Common sites are the hands and face; men are more commonly affected than women at an age usually over 40 years.

The tumour begins as a nodule, warty mass or ulcer, the latter having typical rolled everted edges. It spreads locally and may be fixed and invading deep structures. Distant metastases occur in regional lymph nodes and are usually late in appearance. Microscopy shows a tumour of the 'prickle-cell' layer of the epidermis. Processes composed of malignant cells infiltrate the dermis and often, in the well-differentiated tumours, there are typical 'squamous pearls', zones of concentrically arranged keratinous cells like the cross-section of an onion.

Squamous carcinoma is usually treated by wide local excision, with repair of the defect by plastic surgery. Where wide excision is impracticable or if the patient is unfit, radiotherapy may be preferred. The regional lymph nodes are examined monthly, and if they are found to be enlarged, removal of them by a block dissection is performed.

Occasionally, superficial intra-epidermal squamous carcinomata are seen on such sites as the face and genitals (Bowen's disease). These are of low malignancy and can be treated equally well by irradiation, excision, or even in extensive cases by currettage.

3. Secondary Tumours in Skin

Secondary nodules either in the subcutaneous tissue or in the epidermis are most commonly due to carcinoma of the breast, less often a growth in the bronchus or alimentary tract may be the cause. Only those secondary to breast carcinoma are amenable to therapy by endocrine treatment (see p. 188). Usually such deposits occur in the terminal phase of malignancy.

HAEMANGIOMA (NAEVUS)

A naevus is by definition a birth mark, it is a term applied to haemangioma and melanoma, both of which may be considered to be hamartomata or malformations

Haemangioma

Haemangiomata are divided into capillary and cavernous types.

Capillary haemangiomata

These may be apparent at birth or shortly after. They vary in size from a pin head to those which cover wide areas of the body surface. If extensive they often conform to the shape of a dermatome or body segment. Capillary haemangiomata are bright red in colour and may be raised and spongy, or they may be flat. Pressure causes blanching. Ulceration and infection may occur and lead to disappearance of the malformation by scarring. The natural history of angiomata is that 80% can be expected to disappear before the age of 6 years, the centre becomes pale first and finally the tumour disappears, leaving either no scar or minimal skin changes. Various types are seen, including 'strawberry marks' and telangiectases; Campbell de Morgan spots occur in older patients and persist, as does the 'port-wine stain', which is present from birth. Microscopy of these tumours shows angioblastic tissue with vascular clefts and embryonic vessels.

Treatment depends on situation and age. If spontaneous resolution can be awaited this is the best course, for this leaves little or no scar. Two thirds can be expected to disappear by the age of 5–6 years. Ulceration and infection may hasten resolution. Those that do not resolve should be excised. If, for cosmetic reasons, the tumour must be treated early the application of carbon dioxide snow may hasten resolution. Telangiectases can be coagulated in the centre by a guarded diathermy point. Port-wine stains are the most difficult to treat. Excision and grafting, even with tattooing of the grafted area, often produces a poor cosmetic result, which may even be worse in appearance than the original lesion.

Cavernous haemangioma

This involves both skin and subcutaneous tissue. It is dark blue and contains many large cavernous spaces full of blood. Skin or mucosae may be affected. Most of these tumours practically disappear by the age of 6, but when they do not resolve they should, if possible, be excised. Other methods which have been tried with varying success are injection with hypertonic saline or boiling water. Radiation must only be used in children for tumours which endanger life, for example, angioma of the pharynx, obstructing respiration, or if there are extreme cosmetic defects.

BENIGN MELANOMA (NAEVUS)

The common mole (intradermal melanoma) is brown, with a smooth, hairy or warty surface. Most people have 10–20 moles on their bodies. Microscopically the lesion is entirely dermal. Beneath a normal or thinned epidermis masses of polygonal 'naevus cells' (melanocytes) stream down as far as the subcutaneous tissue. Signs of 'activity' in the basal-cell layer of the epidermis, hyperchromatic or abnormally sized nuclei, increased mitoses and lymphocytic infiltration denote *junctional change*, which, after puberty, may be considered premalignant.

Moles on the palm of the hand, under the nail, sole of the foot and genitals are usually of the junctional type. All moles below the knee should be looked upon with suspicion. Only a small number become malignant, but it is typically in this group that malignancy arises.

Melanomata in the young may clinically and microscopically arouse suspicion of malignancy, but, before puberty, malignant change is extremely rare. A *blue naevus* is dark blue, rarely becomes malignant and histologically shows a clear zone separating the epidermis from the tumour.

MALIGNANT MELANOMA

Malignant melanoma usually arises at the site of a benign melanoma. Indications of possible malignant change are increase in size of the tumour, deepening pigmentation, ulceration and bleeding. Occasionally, tumour masses may appear with depigmentation (amelanotic melanoma). 'Incontinent' pigment may stream out of the periphery of a tumour, staining the surrounding skin. Microscopically malignant change is indicated by wide infiltration, increased cellular pleomorphism, anaplasia and mitoses. The growth spreads locally to invade nearby structures, and sometimes to produce skin nodules. Lymph nodes are invaded by tumour emboli. Blood-borne metastases may occur to any tissue, often many years after apparent successful treatment. Widespread malignant melanoma may be associated with excretion of pigment in the urine.

Benign melanomata should be removed if they are subject to recurrent trauma and for cosmetic reasons, especially if they lie on the hand, sole, genitals or below the knee. Increase in size, deepening of pigmentation, spread of pigment around the tumour, bleeding and ulceration are all indications for removal.

Only surgical excision of moles is permissible. Biopsy, diathermy and curettage are forbidden, because such tampering may initiate malignancy and may produce widespread metastases. If excision is carried out for cosmetic reasons or for fear of the results of repeated trauma a clear margin of at least 2 mm. must be allowed. If there is fear of malignancy a wider margin of 2 cm. is allowed, and if malignancy is confirmed at a later date, even wider excision may be performed. If malignant melanoma can be diagnosed clinically then it should be widely excised, that is by excision down to and including the deep fascia with a 5-cm. clearance of skin around the tumour. Such a clearance inevitably calls for plastic repair by skin graft.

Following operation, the regional lymph nodes are examined monthly and only removed if they become enlarged. If they are involved at the time of diagnosis of malignant melanoma both tumour and nodes must be removed, but the chances of arresting the disease at that stage are remote. It is not believed of value nowadays to remove the skin and deep fascia between the primary growth and regional lymph nodes as was formerly practised. Radiotherapy has not been of much value in the past because the tumour is highly radio resistant to conventional radiotherapy. The more recent methods of giving intensive radiotherapy, such as with the cobalt unit, do show that in some sites malignant melanomata are moderately sensitive to irradiation. Intralymphatic therapy by injecting radioactive iodised oil shortly after excision of the primary growth seems promising. The isotope is concentrated in the regional lymph nodes.

Malignant melanoma is highly malignant. However, if it is widely excised at an early phase reasonably successful results can be achieved. Figures for survival for 5 years as high as 72% have been claimed for such early cases. Cytotoxic drug therapy is now used, especially with drugs of the phenylalanine mustard group that may be selectively metabolised by pigmented tumours. These drugs are given intravenously by repeated injections, intra-arterially by infusion over a period of days or best of all by local intra-arterial perfusion. In the latter the main artery and vein of a limb are cannulated and perfused by a pump oxygenator. A tight tourniquet excludes the limb from the general circulation so that a very high dose of cytotoxic drug can be given to the tumour for a short period. In most patients any improvement is short-lived.

NAILS

Ingrowing Toe-nail

The nail develops from a germinal matrix which lies deep to the demilune and deep to the nail fold. It extends to the lateral nail folds and a little beyond them. The sterile matrix of the nail bed takes no part in nail growth.

Ingrowing toe-nail mostly affects the great toe. Other toes may be similarly deformed, but ingrowth only causes symptoms in the great toe. The nail is usually more curved than normal in the transverse plane, its lateral edge lies deeply embedded in the nail groove on one or both sides, and often a sharp spike of nail projects from one corner. The lateral nail folds are often unusually prominent and appear to ride up around the nail as pressure is placed on the toe. Causes of ingrowth are ill-fitting shoes, cutting the nails too short and trauma to the nail bed.

Occasionally it occurs in infants. Usually young adults are affected. The ingrowing nail first causes pain as its sharp distal spike presses on the sensitive nail groove. Later a paronychia may arise, often with prominent granulations along the side of the nail.

Prophylaxis entails meticulous cutting of the nails, leaving no sharp spicules at the corners and leaving the nail to project from the nail grooves. If the nail is causing pain from a sharp spike left at its corner this may be cut away obliquely and the nail lifted out of its groove by elevation with a sharp pair of pointed scissors. The patient should be seen regularly to see that the nail grows out of the nail grooves. When infection is established removal of the nail under a local ring block (see p. 134) relieves pain immediately. The new nail should be observed as it grows at monthly intervals and watched to see that it does not grow in again. If there is a history of recurrent ingrowing nail, then the nail bed should be excised.

Excision of the nail bed should be performed under a local ring block of the great toe. Only the germinal matrix need be excised, but this must be widely performed, or nail rudiments may grow again through the scars of the excision. The nail folds are widely undercut and left to cover the raw area. Absence of a nail leaves little cosmetic deformity.

Onychogryphosis

Thickened deformed nails occur in the elderly, often after a crush injury of the toe which has damaged the nail bed. Such nails are ugly and may be painful. They may be removed once, but if the deformity recurs, then the nail bed should be excised.

Subungual Conditions

1. *Haematoma*

An injury causes blood to collect under the nail, causing great pain due to tension. Infection may follow with osteomyelitis if there is an underlying fracture. A radiograph should be performed to exclude bony injury. To relieve pain, under a ring block, the free edge of the nail is lifted, the epidermis incised and blood released.

2. *Exostosis*

Subungual exostosis usually arises in young adults, sometimes following trauma. An excrescence of cancellous bone projects from the dorsal surface of the distal phalanx lifting up one or other side of the nail. An exostosis is characteristically covered by thickened horny epithelium.

The importance of this condition is that it is commonly mistaken for a wart or, if infected, paronychia. It should be diagnosed clinically, and the diagnosis should be confirmed radiographically. Treatment involves excision of the exostosis under general anaesthesia—the nail is removed, the horny epithelium over it cut away and the excrescence removed completely by bone forceps.

3. *Glomus Tumour*

Glomus tumour gives rise to exquisite pain, usually under the nail, but sometimes in other parts of the finger. Glomus tumours have been described in other sites. The agonising pain and localised tenderness suggests the diagnosis. Under local analgesia the nail should be removed and, if a tumour is present, this is seen as a tiny encapsulated nodule pinkish in colour and easily enucleated. Such tumours are malformations of arteriovenous anastomoses (glomus organs) normally found in the finger. Histology shows sheets of argentophil cells, nerve fibres and vessels.

4. *Melanoma* (see p. 126).

Subungual melanoma is particularly liable to become malignant.

Paronychia (see p. 135)

SWEAT-GLAND TUMOURS

Tumours of sweat glands are rare. Occasionally isolated benign subcutaneous tumours prove after removal to be *Hidradenomata*, tumours of apocrine glands in the axilla or vulva, or *Syringomata*, minute nodules which may be diffusely scattered over the body.

'*Turban tumours*' produce gross deformity of the scalp, which is covered by prominent bosses and nodules. Such tumours may show a basal cell or cylindromatous pattern derived from sweat glands. The tumour is rare and often too extensive for excision.

FURTHER READING

Moyer, C. A., Rhoads, J. E., Allen, J. G., and Harkins, H. N. (1965) *Surgery, Principles and Practice*, Ch. 24, 3rd. ed., Pitman, London.

CHAPTER TWELVE

THE HAND

The largest part of surgery of the hand deals with sepsis. An illustration of how commonly the hand requires attention was shown in a survey in the Casualty Department of King's College Hospital, where out of 735 patients attending in a week for dressings, 240 were seen in the septic-hand clinic. Other conditions which will be described in this chapter are injuries and diseases of tendons and nerves, cysts and tumours of the hand and finally contractures.

SEPSIS OF THE HAND

Although the seriousness of hand infections has diminished since the introduction of antibiotics, in that septicaemia and massive local infection are rare, incapacity for work may still be prolonged and contracted, useless fingers may still occur if the principles of treatment are not fully understood. Most hand infections of any severity should be treated in the hand clinic of an Accident Service or Casualty Department.

General Principles

Infection of the hand most often follows injury; the causative organism is almost always the staphylococcus; rarely the streptococcus may be a cause of spreading inflammation.

Prior to Operation

Rest is important in relieving pain and aiding the localisation of infection. A sling may suffice, but in severe infection bandaging the hand and

FIG. 3. The hand in the position of function on a plaster of Paris front slab

forearm to a plaster of Paris slab in the position of function (Fig. 3) is very effective. At night the hand should be elevated to reduce swelling. If the patient is pyrexial he or she should rest in bed.

The value of local heat is difficult to assess; its value is probably only to give symptomatic relief by acting as a counter-irritant. The use of heat has declined since the introduction of chemotherapy. The kaolin poultice is messy and ineffectual, short-wave diathermy is comforting.

Chemotherapy must be given where there is cellulitis and lymphangitis. If pus is diagnosed incision should be performed as soon as possible; antibiotics rarely sterilise pus and need only be given if cellulitis is associated. When chemotherapy is required penicillin is usually given first, procaine penicillin 500,000 units per day intramuscularly for 5 days. If there is no response to penicillin after 48 hours, then tetracycline or cloxacillin should be given, 0·25 g. four times a day for 5–7 days. Organisms resistant to antibiotics have not proved to be a serious problem in the case of the septic hand, despite the fact that surveys show every year an ever-increasing percentage of penicillin-resistant organisms in Casualty Departments.

Analgesics should not be forgotten, aspirin 300–600 mg. and codeine 30–60 mg. are usually adequate for relief of pain, and barbiturates, e.g. butobarbitone, 100–200 mg., should be given to ensure sleep.

Operation

All operations on the hand require anaesthesia either local or general. A block of the digital nerves is very satisfactory for distal infections of the

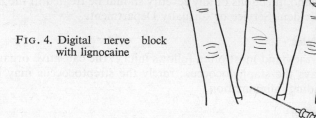

FIG. 4. Digital nerve block with lignocaine

fingers. In this procedure, after cleaning the finger with cetrimide and surgical spirit, 2 ml. of 1 % lignocaine is injected into the soft tissues on either side of the base of the finger (Fig. 4). *Adrenaline should never be injected, as it may cause arterial spasm and gangrene.* Incisions can be made after a period of 5 minutes has elapsed from the time of the injection of lignocaine. General anaesthesia with gas and oxygen, supplemented with either trichlorethylene or halothane, is employed for other hand infections.

Incisions are performed when pus is diagnosed. In the hand the occurrence of tension indicates pus; elsewhere one may wait for fluctuation, but in the hand irreparable damage may follow incision delayed after pus has formed. Incisions should be made over the maximum site of tension; the finger-tip should be avoided if possible, unless pus is pointing at that site. Note should be made of the position of the digital arteries and nerves, which lie just dorsal to the mid-lateral line. On the whole it is better to over-incise than to under-incise. Any septa in the abscess cavity should be broken down with mosquito forceps and any sloughs excised. In the hand incisions should follow the transverse creases of the palm. Drains are unnecessary if incisions are adequate and sloughs are excised. If they are felt to be necessary nothing more than a wick of tulle gras need be inserted merely to separate the wound edges for no more than 48 hours.

Severe and potentially dangerous sepsis in the hand is best explored under general anaesthesia; a tourniquet should be used, and good operating conditions must be available so that a careful dissection can be performed by an experienced surgeon to eradicate the focus of infection without damage to vital structures. Major procedures should preferably be carried out after the patient has been admitted to hospital, even if this is only possible for a day or two.

After Operation

Dressings should be as infrequent as possible. The patient should be seen the day after operation, but the dressings need not be disturbed for 48 hours, at which time the wound should be inspected. At 48 hours it is vital for careful assessment of progress to be made. If there is any doubt of satisfactory resolution of inflammation, then the hand should be radiographed to exclude osteitis or pyogenic arthritis, and a swab should be taken of the wound to determine the causative organism and its sensitivity to antibiotics. Finally, the opinion of someone experienced in the problems of the septic hand should be obtained. At this phase it may be necessary to change the antibiotic from penicillin to a broad spectrum antibiotic such as tetracycline, cloxacillin or methicillin.

Rest in a sling or plaster is maintained until there is no pain or it is seen that the infection is resolving. The best sign of resolution is wrinkling of the skin around the infection, which is often more obvious on the dorsum of the hand, where the tissues are normally lax and where swelling is more obvious than on the front of the hand. Active movements should then be encouraged, preferably under the supervision of a physiotherapist.

TYPES OF INFECTION

At least 75% of infections of the hand are due to paronychia, pulp-space infection, osteitis and web-space infection. These infections form the group which will be described first because they are so common. The second group is less common, but very important because it can produce such disastrous results in the hand. This group comprises septic arthritis, tenosynovitis and palmar-space infections. Lastly, there is a miscellaneous group of conditions—erysipeloid, virus infection, apical abscess and carbuncle.

1. Paronychia (Fig. 5)

In acute paronychia the nail fold is reddened, tense, tender and throbbing. In this phase the infection may be aborted by penicillin, but if pus forms, as shown by a yellow bleb deep to the nail fold, then, after a digital nerve block, the nail fold should be incised laterally and elevated to release pus. If the abscess extends under the nail the proximal half of it should be removed. Should the infection lie lateral to the nail fold, pus may be evacuated by removing the cuticle over it and if there is extension of infection under the nail the lateral edge of it can be cut away as far as necessary. A non-adherent dressing is applied, and rapid resolution of the inflammation can be expected.

Chronic paronychia is fairly common. It affects particularly those who

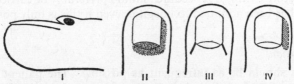

FIG. 5. Paronychia: (i) pus in nail fold; (ii) lateral extension; (iii) incision of nail fold; (iv) unroofing of lateral extension

work with their hands in water, for example, barmaids and cleaners. The nail fold is swollen, intermittently painful and occasionally discharging small amounts of pus. Most chronic paronychia are due to monilial infection, some to non-specific pyogenic organisms. Chronic paronychia is difficult to treat. Gloves must be worn and local applications, such as Castellani's paint (carbol fuchsin), should be brushed well into the nail fold daily for several months. Fungous infection of the nail may be associated with chronic paronychia; the nails lack lustre, are brownish, brittle and crumbly. Often several nails are infected, the toe-nails should also be examined. Such cases are best treated by the dermatologist, who uses fungicides, such as nystatin locally and griseofulvin orally. In cases resistant to treatment removal of the nail and gentle curettage of the nail bed may be unavoidable, at which time the nail bed should be painted with a fungicide. When the diagnosis is in doubt culture of the fungus and examination of the nail for hyphae may help.

2. Pulp-space Infection (Fig. 6)

Infection of the terminal pulp-space compartment of the finger is the commonest type of hand infection and the most important, because inadequate treatment or delay in treatment can so rapidly result in serious consequences.

Infection of the pulp causes cellulitis of the fatty and areolar tissue, which may be so intense as to cause necrosis and thus a carbuncle. The infection is close to the distal phalanx, which is commonly eroded by osteitis, especially in its distal two-thirds. The proximal third of the phalanx is supplied by the cruciate anastomosis of the digital arteries around the joint, the distal two-thirds by terminal branches of the digital arteries. Because the skin of the pulp is attached to the bone by numerous fibrous septa (Fig. 6), tension is an early feature which may compress or thrombose the terminal branches of arteries supplying the distal part of the phalanx. The terminal interphalangeal joint is near to the pulp

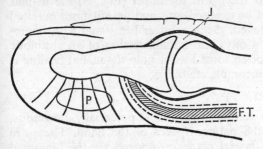

FIG. 6. Pulp space—P, J, joint, F.T., flexor tendon

and may be involved by infection; the synovial sheath of the flexor tendon sheath is liable to be infected near where the tendon is inserted into the base of the distal phalanx.

As soon as a diagnosis of pus can be made it should be released by an incision made over the site of maximal tension or where an abscess is obviously pointing usually over the volar surface of the pulp. A disc of skin is removed to leave a hole for drainage and removal of sloughs (medallion incision). Subcuticular abscesses should be saucerised by removing the dead skin overlying them, and sloughs should be excised. Digital nerve block with lignocaine provides excellent operating conditions and allows ample time for a careful exploration of the digital pulp. Chemotherapy is only necessary if there is spreading cellulitis, and incision may have to be postponed for 24 hours till spreading infection has been arrested.

3. Osteitis

If the patient presents with a pulp which has been converted into a bag of pus, or if at 48 hours after incision resolution is obviously not progress-

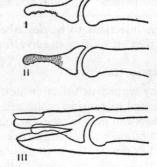

FIG. 7. (i), (ii) X-ray signs of erosion of distal phalanx due to infection. (iii) 'Fish-mouth' incision of pulp complicated by osteitis

ing satisfactorily, radiographs of the finger should be undertaken to exclude or to confirm the complication of osteitis. These radiographs may show erosion of the under surface of the terminal phalanx or decalcification of part or whole of the distal two-thirds of the terminal phalanx (Fig. 7). If osteitis is diagnosed, then the distal pulp should be split by a lateral incision which extends round the tip of the finger (Fig. 7); the palmar surface of the phalanx should be exposed, pus and granulations curetted out and any sequestrum removed. Such a finger heals well with immobilisation in plaster for 3 or 4 days and administration of an antibiotic such as cloxacillin. There is often some loss of pulp tissue, but healing is usually rapid and otherwise uncomplicated.

4. Web-space Infection (Fig. 8)

Infection in the interdigital webs is common and potentially dangerous, because it may spread into the palmar spaces of the hand. These are potential spaces bounded by fascial planes prolonged via the lumbrical

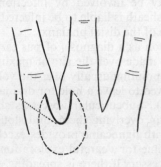

FIG. 8. Web space infection;
(i) incision

canals which run along the radial aspects of the bases of the fingers. The web becomes swollen and painful and is often surrounded by spreading cellulitis, for which chemotherapy must be given. Once tension is obvious, incision must be carried out under general anaesthesia. It suffices to split the digital web either longitudinally or horizontally (Fig. 8) and to insert a pair of sinus forceps to evacuate the pus. Complications are rare, extension into the palmar spaces is possible but very rarely met.

The infections to be described next are far less common, but it is vital that they are diagnosed early, for they may have such serious effects.

1. Septic Arthritis

Any wound or infection adjacent to an interphalangeal joint must be suspected of causing septic arthritis. There is periarticular swelling with stiffness and pain in the joint, but these signs are often masked by adjacent suppuration and cellulitis. A suspicion of joint infection should call for a second opinion, for so rapidly do joint surfaces become damaged or destroyed by pyogenic infection that it is vital to observe the finger frequently and to treat it actively. In recent years it has become obvious that this type of infection is one of the most serious that can occur in the hand, mainly because the diagnosis is so often difficult to make and treatment is thereby often delayed.

If arthritis is suspected the finger should be radiographed. The earliest radiographic sign is widening of the joint space by effusion, a feature which can only be appreciated by careful comparison with other joints. The finger should be splinted in plaster of Paris and a potent antibiotic such as methicillin given. Radiographs should be performed daily, and if foci of infection appear in the phalanges adjacent to the joint (Fig. 9) they should be explored under general anaesthesia, a tourniquet should be

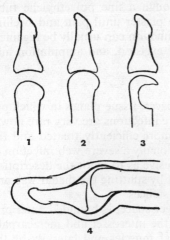

FIG. 9. Septic Arthritis. (1) Effusion with increased joint space; (2) Cartilage erosion with narrowed joint space; (3) Bony erosion by infection; (4) Pathological dislocation

applied and after incision necrotic foci should be curetted out of the phalanges. If the infection does not resolve rapidly the joint should be opened and pus evacuated. If the causative organism is sensitive to antibiotics normal function may be secured, but if damage to the articular cartilages has occurred fibrous ankylosis can be expected. Ankylosis must only be allowed to occur in flexion if a useful finger is to be obtained. If the infection is treated late, then pathological dislocation or a persistent sinus may follow, producing a useless finger that can only be dealt with by amputation.

2. Suppurative Tenosynovitis

Infection of tendon sheaths is very rare. The diagnosis is easily made. The finger is held semiflexed and completely rigid by muscle spasm. The slightest attempt at movement causes severe pain and is actively resisted. Tenderness is exquisite and localised along the midline of the finger; it is maximal at the proximal ends of the digital sheaths which lie over the metacarpal heads. Very rarely the ulnar bursa may be involved from the sheath of the fifth finger. Usually infection follows a perforating injury of the sheath or extension of a severe pulp-space infection.

Inflammation in the synovial sheath produces tension and obliterates the blood supply to the tendons, which comes rather tenuously by the vincula that cross between the parietal and visceral layers of the synovial sheaths. Untreated, this tension causes sloughing of tendons, and hence a useless finger.

Treatment is urgent, the patient should be admitted to hospital, systemic chemotherapy given and operation performed using a tourniquet in the operating theatre. If the infection has arisen in the terminal pulp, then this should be explored, pus evacuated and the synovial sheath exposed. If the sheath is bulging it should be opened and washed out with penicillin solution, 1,000 units/ml., introduced through a fine polyethylene tube. The finger should then be immobilised in plaster until pain and swelling have subsided. With early treatment full function can usually be regained. In late cases sloughing tendons may need excision, and amputation may become inevitable.

3. Palmar-space Infection

The palmar spaces are only potential spaces, tissue planes in which pus may accumulate and spread. In fact, space infections are very rare nowadays, presumably because hand sepsis is more efficiently treated and the use of antibiotics curtails cellulitis. Occasionally a severe web infection of the first interdigital space may be so extensive as to merit the description of a thenar-space infection. Drainage of it by splitting the thenar web and insertion of sinus forceps to evacuate pus suffices.

The mid-palmar space, which is the larger space, is bounded anteriorly by the palmar aponeurosis, posteriorly by the interossei and metacarpals, medially by the fascia over the hypothenar muscles and laterally by the septum that passes from the third metacarpal to the palmar aponeurosis separating it from the thenar space. Its extensions via the lumbrical canals offer a pathway of infection from the web spaces of the second, third and fourth fingers to the hand. Treatment involves incision and drainage through the web spaces or, very rarely, by a direct approach through the palmar aponeurosis made by an incision in a transverse crease of the hand. Such extensive operations should only be performed after application of a tourniquet and using the facilities of a general operating theatre.

Lastly, there is a miscellaneous group of infections of the hand which, though important, rarely give rise to complications. On the whole, they are easily recognised.

1. Erysipeloid

This is a specific infection due to the erysipelothrix rhusipathiae. It is an infection of the epidermis of the finger affecting particularly butchers and fishmongers. The finger becomes swollen and painful with a lilac hue. The margin is serpiginous and well circumscribed, but pus never forms. The infection is self-limiting over a period of about 6 weeks, and its spread can be arrested by the administration of penicillin or streptomycin.

2. Herpes

Virus infections of the finger are fairly common. Herpes simplex for some reason is an infection common among nurses. The finger presents infected vesicles, cellulitis and sometimes superficial suppuration. Antibiotics have little effect, and after a period of a few weeks the infection subsides spontaneously. Very rarely herpes zoster may occur and be difficult to diagnose. Pain and vesiculation occurs on the finger, and only after a few days does it become obvious that the infection follows a nerve-root distribution. There is no specific treatment; after a few days spontaneous resolution occurs.

3. Apical Abscess

Subcuticular abscess is common, especially in nurses. A subcuticular bleb appears, usually under the centre of the edge of the nail. All that is needed for its treatment is 'unroofing' of the abscess by excising the cuticle with a sharp-pointed pair of scissors, a painless procedure, because the cuticle is dead. It is important to inspect the base of the abscess when the pulp is squeezed, because an apical abscess may in fact be part of a collar-stud abscess communicating by a minute track with a pulp-space infection. If a sinus is present going down to the pulp it must be traced and the pulp drained after a digital nerve block has been performed.

4. Carbuncle

Carbuncles usually occur on the dorsum of the finger in relation to hair follicles. Chemotherapy suffices for a cure, incision is rarely required to release pus, healing is often slow because of the time taken for a slough to separate. The urine should be tested to exclude diabetes.

INJURIES TO TENDONS

Injuries to tendons are fairly common in the hand, both to extensor and flexor tendons and to tendons at the wrist. Repair of such injuries in many cases demands very specialised and highly skilled techniques if full function is to be restored.

Extensor Tendons

Extensor tendons may be divided by injury anywhere along their course. Special instances are division at the insertion into the base of the distal phalanx, division of the middle slip of the tendon over the proximal phalanx and division of the common extensor tendons on the dorsum of the hand. In all cases the affected part of the finger cannot be actively extended, though passive movement is free.

Quite trivial injury may avulse the tendon from its distal insertion producing a semi-flexed distal phalanx the 'mallet finger'. Spontaneous ruptures of the mallet type and of other tendons are common in rheumatoid arthritis. If the middle slip of the extensor tendon is divided over the proximal phalanx a typical deformity of flexion of the proximal interphalangeal joint arises with hyperextension of the distal joint—the so-called boutonnière or button-hole injury. The hyperextension of the distal joint is due to the uncompensated action of the lateral slips of the extensor tendon which pass round the side of the proximal joint and often escape injury. Division of common extensor tendons over the dorsum of the hand causes loss of extension at the metacarpophalangeal joint; the interphalangeal joints can still be extended by interossei and lumbricals which are inserted into the extensor expansion which is intact. Rupture of the extensor pollicis longus tendon is usually a spontaneous and late complication of Colles' fracture or rheumatoid arthritis causing inability to extend the distal joint of the thumb. Usually extensor tendon suture is carried out at the time of primary wound suture, but only by a surgeon skilled in this type of work.

Mallet fingers can be immobilised on a special plastic splint in a position of hyperextension of the distal interphalangeal joint and flexion of the proximal joint, so long as the finger can be immobilised within 24 hours of tendon rupture and so long as the immobilisation can be maintained for 6 weeks. The disability of a mallet finger is often slight and is accepted by the patient. A few, in whom full function is vital, for example, a concert pianist, need tendon repair at open operation. Those who come too late for plaster immobilisation and complain of loss of function may be treated by arthrodesis of the distal interphalangeal joint. Ruptures of the extensor pollicis longus tendon are treated by tendon transplantation from an adjacent muscle, such as extensor carpi radialis, or by a free tendon graft from palmaris longus or a dorsal extensor tendon of the foot.

Flexor Tendons

Flexor tendons may be divided within the digital fibrous flexor sheath, in the palm or at the wrist. Whereas suture of extensor tendons is simple and relatively free of complications, flexor tendon repair is much more difficult, especially in the fibrous flexor sheath, where adhesions may cause stiffness or complete rigidity of the finger. In all cases it is best to close skin wounds and to repair tendons at a secondary operation. Damage within the fibrous flexor sheath usually necessitates the employment of a tendon graft. Repair in the palm can be performed by direct suture so long as too great a degree of retraction of the divided ends of the tendon has not occurred, otherwise a tendon graft may have to be inserted. At the wrist direct suture is usually possible after fairly extensive mobilisation of tendons and muscles.

TENOSYNOVITIS

Pyogenic tenosynovitis has been described on p. 139.
Traumatic tenosynovitis commonly affects the dorsal extensor tendon

sheaths, causing pain and swelling around the tendons and, at some phase, fine crepitus, which can be elicited when the tendons are put into action. Typists and others performing repetitive hand movements in their work are particularly prone to this form of inflammation. Rest from work, strapping, immobilisation in plaster for 2 or 3 weeks—any of these methods can be expected to be followed by resolution of the inflammation.

Stenosing tenosynovitis or de Quervain's disease is a more chronic form of inflammation of the tendon sheaths of abductor pollicis longus and extensor pollicis brevis at the wrist. Pain, local tenderness, swelling and often crepitus occurs around both these tendons, and may persist for weeks or months. Injection of 25 mg. hydrocortisone into the painful area is often effective in relieving pain; otherwise the sheaths should be laid open, an operation which is simple and dramatically effective.

Trigger finger is due to a localised thickening in a tendon sheath that constricts a tendon or blocks its movements in certain ranges. The finger appears to stick in mid-flexion, but can be forced passively past this point. The thickened area of tendon sheath usually lies in the proximal end of the fibrous flexor sheath. All that is necessary is to expose the constriction and to divide it at open operation.

A compound palmar ganglion is an effusion into the ulnar bursa, due to chronic inflammation, which surrounds the flexor tendons and extends from the wrist above and almost to the heads of the metacarpals below. The transverse carpal ligament lies across the bursa, and so distension of the bursa produces fluctuant swellings above the wrist and in the palm which, because they are in communication, show the sign of cross-fluctuation. Cross-fluctuation is elicited by compressing one swelling and feeling an impulse transmitted to another. Compound palmar ganglia are mostly due to tuberculous infection, but a few are due to a non-specific type of inflammation often associated with rheumatoid arthritis. Clinically the two types may be indistinguishable. The synovial sheaths are thickened by granulation tissue and fibrinous deposit and often contain numerous 'melon-seed bodies' composed of fibrin. Tuberculous infection may go on to caseation, cold abscess and sinus formation unless active measures are taken. In addition, tendons may be destroyed by the tuberculous process. If tuberculosis is diagnosed from the history and by bacteriological and histological examination chemotherapy is given, followed by excision of the diseased tissues and a period of chemotherapy postoperatively. In the non-specific cases operation is less often necessary.

NERVE INJURIES

The ulnar and median nerves are often injured by wounds at the level of the wrist with partial or complete division.

Median Nerve

Division of the median nerve at the level of the wrist results in paralysis of the small muscles of the thumb—opponens, flexor and abductor pollicis brevis, paralysis of the lateral two lumbricals and anaesthesia of the radial three and a half fingers. The sensory loss is a more serious handicap than the motor, for the long flexor of the thumb and the adductor pollicis can between them compensate for loss of opposition, the most important movement of the thumb. The pathognomonic test of loss of median-nerve function is inability to abduct the thumb, that is to carry the thumb in a plane at right angles to the flat of the hand. The position of deformity of the hand after median-nerve division is one of partial flexion of the first and second fingers with some hyperextension at metacarpophalangeal joints. This deformity results from paralysis of the first two lumbrical muscles. The thenar nerve supplying the thenar muscles may rarely be damaged by injury or by incautious incisions in the thenar eminence for sepsis of the hand. It should be remembered that the thenar nerve arises from the median nerve approximately 1 inch below the lower margin of the transverse carpal ligament.

Wounds involving the median nerve should be treated by primary suture of the skin and secondary suture of the nerve delayed for 2–3 weeks after injury when the nerve sheath is thickened by fibrosis and when regenerative activity in the nerve is at its maximum. During the period of nerve regeneration the hand should be supported by some form of 'elastic' splint that keeps the thumb in the position of opposition and allows active and passive movements of the fingers.

Carpal-tunnel Syndrome

In this syndrome pain occurs in the distribution of the median nerve, sometimes with wasting of the small muscles of the thumb which is due to compression of the nerve by the transverse carpal ligament. Division of the ligament dramatically and permanently relieves the pain. A period of immobilisation in a splint with the wrist in the mid-position may also be effective. Carpal-tunnel syndrome may follow a fracture of the wrist, be associated with arthritis of the wrist, or more often it may arise for no obvious reason. It may occur in early pregnancy when it is thought that tissue water retention may cause pressure on the median nerve. Diagnosis may be difficult, especially where the pain radiates up the arm. Cervical spondylosis must be differentiated. In the tourniquet test, application of a sphygmomanometer cuff inflated to occlude the brachial artery will often reproduce the pain of carpal-tunnel syndrome. Measurement of nerve conduction time may show delay of the nerve action potential at the carpal ligament.

Ulnar Nerve

Division of the ulnar nerve at the wrist produces paralysis of the hypothenar muscles, the interossei, the adductor pollicis and the medial two lumbricals. In addition, there is anaesthesia of the fifth finger and the ulnar half of the fourth finger. The extensive motor paralysis is much more serious than the sensory loss which, because of overlapping in cutaneous nerve supply, may be confined to a small area on the ulnar border of the hand. The position of deformity is characteristic, the fourth and fifth fingers are held hyperextended at the metacarpophalangeal joints and flexed at the interphalangeal joints. The second and third fingers are not deformed because of the median-nerve supply to the first and second lumbricals.

The position of deformity of the fourth and fifth fingers arises because of the direction of action of the interossei. The tendons of these muscles pass anteriorly to the axis of rotation of the metacarpophalangeal joints which they flex, and posteriorly to the proximal interphalangeal joints which they hyperextend because they join the extensor expansions over the proximal phalanges. When these muscles act they flex the metacarpophalangeal joints and extend the interphalangeal joints. Paralysis of their action causes hyperextension of the metacarpophalangeal joints and flexion of the interphalangeal joints. There is in addition marked wasting of the interossei as shown by hollows appearing between the metacarpals making the extensor tendons more obvious.

Treatment is as for any peripheral nerve repair, secondary suture 2-3 weeks after primary wound healing and effective physiotherapy to prevent joint stiffness by passive movements during the period of regeneration. Splints should be worn of the knuckle-duster or 'lively' Exeter type that prevent deformity and stretching of muscles and yet allow full movements.

WASTING OF THE SMALL MUSCLES OF THE HAND

The small muscles of the hand are supplied by the eighth cervical and first thoracic segments. It is important in the diagnosis of the cause of wasting of these muscles to assess first whether it is due to a segmental or peripheral nerve lesion, secondly, whether the median or ulnar nerve is at fault and lastly, if the lesion is in a peripheral nerve, at what level it has occurred. The pattern of sensory loss helps to establish the type of nerve lesion, and so a knowledge of the dermatomes of the upper limb is essential for the differentiation of segmental and peripheral nerve lesions (Fig. 86). When the eighth cervical and first thoracic nerve segments are involved the area of sensory loss lies along the inner side of the upper and lower arms and extends into the ulnar border of the hand, whereas lesions of the seventh cervical segment produce sensory loss and pain down the dorsum of the arm to the back of the middle finger. When the fifth and sixth nerves are involved pain and loss of sensation may occur over the shoulder region.

The segmental lesions which may cause wasting of the small muscles of the hand include such entities as compression of nerve roots or the spinal cord from prolapsed intervertebral discs, cervical spondylosis and spinal tumours. Diseases of the central nervous system include poliomyelitis, amyotrophic lateral sclerosis, disseminated sclerosis and syringomyelia. Compression of trunks or cords of the brachial plexus may occur from a cervical rib, aneurysms in the supraclavicular region, apical lung tumours or compression between the clavicle and the first rib.

The characteristics of wasting of the small muscles of the hand due to median- and ulnar-nerve lesions have already been described. The median and ulnar nerves are usually damaged by injury, and the history or the presence of a scar will indicate the level at which damage has occurred. Occasionally ulnar-nerve lesions are due to cubitus valgus or increased carrying angle at the elbow causing a delayed traction injury of the ulnar nerve where it lies in the groove behind the medial condyle of the humerus. Such lesions occur in adult life following fractures in childhood of the supracondylar type; occasionally ulnar neuritis may occur spontaneously without any history of trauma, in which case the nerve is often thickened and tender behind the elbow. The function of flexor carpi ulnaris is preserved in ulnar neuritis because its nerve supply is given off from the ulnar nerve above the elbow, an important sign in localising the level of damage to the nerve. It is treated by transplanting the nerve to the front of the elbow.

CYSTS AND TUMOURS

Cystic swellings in the hand, especially in the fingers, are common and most often due to dermoid cysts and ganglia. There are no tumours specific to the hand, but synovioma may be found in this situation and will be described in this section.

Ganglion

A ganglion is a myxomatous degeneration of fibrous tissue found most commonly in relation to tendon sheaths and joint capsules. A cavity appears in fibrous tissue which is often multilocular and is filled by a jelly-like mucinous material. Common sites of ganglia in the hand are over the tendons of the wrist, especially on the dorsum, and near to flexor tendons in the palm or finger. Some communicate with joints, some become tense and very painful. The swelling produced by a ganglion is rounded and mobile until adjacent tendons are put into action; characteristically ganglia transilluminate brilliantly. Some can be ruptured by external pressure, but recurrence is common after this manoeuvre. Most need excision, an operation that must be performed using a tourniquet to provide an avascular field and a full aseptic technique.

Dermoid Cysts

Most dermoid cysts in the hand are implantation dermoids, that is cysts formed by the growth of minute fragments of skin which have been driven in by injury. Rounded subcutaneous swellings are formed which are often yellowish in colour if they lie near the surface; transillumination is impossible because the content is sebum. Histological examination of a dermoid shows a squamous-celled lining, whereas a ganglion has no specific structure, being composed of fibrous tissue alone. Dermoid cysts are treated by excision.

Synovioma

Synovioma can occur in or near any tendon or joint; benign synoviomata are uncommon, but when they occur the hand and wrist is a favourite site. Smooth, rounded, hard subcutaneous swellings are formed which are very like ganglia except that they are opaque to transillumination. The tumour is solid and composed of collagen, spindle cells, foamy macrophages and giant cells of the foreign-body type. Clefts which are typical of synovial tissue may be found in the tumour. Treatment involves complete excision. A highly malignant form of sarcoma, malignant synovioma, is rare. Amputation is necessary for its treatment.

CONTRACTURES OF THE HAND

Contractures of the hand are common and mostly affect the fingers. Their causes include nerve palsy, tendon injury, ischaemia, arthritis, capsular fibrosis, scarring from burns and loss of soft tissue by injury fibrous contracture of the palmar fascia and congenital contracture.

The positions of deformity of the hand after nerve and tendon injury have already been described. These positions can be corrected passively, but unless movements are religiously performed, joints become stiff and eventually ankylosed by pericapsular fibrosis. Unless infection of soft tissues, tendons or joints of the hand is successfully treated, fingers may be left stiff and useless from fibrous adhesions. Fibrous ankylosis of interphalangeal and metacarpophalangeal joints is common in arthritis, especially pyogenic, rheumatoid and gouty arthritis. It is also common in burns and other soft-tissue injuries in which there has been loss of tissue and much scarring.

Dupuytren's Contracture

Fibrosis of the palmar fascia is common and begins with the appearance of hard nodules which are firmly attached to the skin composed of masses of vascular collagen in the palmar aponeurosis in its inner part. These nodules contract and pull the fourth and fifth fingers down into the palm with severe flexion of the metacarpophalangeal joints and full extension of the interphalangeal joints. Eventually these joints become fixed by pericapsular adhesions which prevent extension even if the fascial contracture is corrected. Other fingers, the thumb and even toes may be affected. It usually affects older people; occasionally there is a hereditary factor. The nature of work may be important, for constant gripping of a handle or certain tools may initiate this disease.

Treatment is difficult. In early cases with mobile joints simple subcutaneous division of the contracted bands is all that is necessary surgically, followed by physiotherapy and splintage in extension. Excision of nodules of fibrous tissue through small transverse incisions is a rather more radical procedure. Very rarely full excision of the palmar aponeurosis is carried out, an operation which often necessitates skin grafting because of the poor state of the skin overlying the contracted fascia. Occasionally all that can be done is amputation of a contracted finger which gets in the way.

Volkmann's Ischaemic Contracture

This is fortunately very rare. When it occurs it is usually a complicaton of a supracondylar fracture of the humerus associated with haematoma compressing the brachial artery, which goes into spasm. The artery may be contused, nipped or divided by the ends of the bones. If the arterial blood flow to the hand is not rapidly restored, fibrosis occurs in the flexor muscles of the forearm, with shortening that pulls the wrist into flexion and the fingers into hyperextension and clawing at the metacarpophalangeal joints and flexion of the interphalangeal joints. The cause of the deformity can be diagnosed if when the wrist is flexed the fingers can be extended. The importance of this condition is early recognition of the vascular injury and treatment for it (see p. 457). When contracture has occurred little can be done. Traction with elastic extension to the fingers may help them from becoming contracted. Sliding the origin of common flexor tendons from the medial epicondyle of the humerus down to the forearm may allow some extra length to be given to the flexor muscles, but these may be so fibrosed as to be mechanically useless. Occasionally improvement may follow excision of the infarcted muscles.

Congenital Contracture of the Little Finger

From birth the finger is occasionally partially contracted at the interphalangeal joints. Rarely is there any loss of function, all the soft tissues are shortened, and thus correction is impossible and in any case unnecessary. Usually both fifth fingers are affected.

FURTHER READING

Bunnell, S. (1964) *Surgery of the Hand*, Pitman, London.
Rank, B. K., and Wakefield, A. R. (1960), *Surgery of Repair as Applied to Hand Injuries*, 2nd ed. E. & S. Livingstone, Edinburgh.
Bailey, D. A. (1963) *The Infected Hand*. H. K. Lewis, London.
Ellis, M. (1962), *The Casualty Officer's Handbook*. Butterworths, London.

CHAPTER THIRTEEN

DISTURBANCES OF HORMONAL BALANCE AND THEIR TREATMENT

In the evolution of man the endocrine glands represent some of the oldest specialised tissues in the body and their action is slow compared with that of the central nervous system. They mediate changes by means of hormones, complex chemical compounds, which they discharge into the blood stream and which affect certain tissues only, their target organs. Hormones modify the speed of, rather than initiate, changes in the body. This chapter is concerned with dysfunction of the pituitary, thyroid, parathyroid and adrenal glands, but hormones are manufactured by many other tissues, in particular the gonads; the testis is discussed in Chapter Twenty-seven.

THE THYROID GLAND
GOITRE

The word goitre is used to describe any enlargement of the thyroid gland, but it most commonly refers to non-toxic or simple goitre. This condition is primarily due to an inadequate supply of iodine. The three reasons why the thyroid gland may enlarge in an effort to produce a normal amount of hormone are:

(1) not enough iodine in the diet;
(2) inborn errors of iodine metabolism; and
(3) ingestion of goitrogens, substances which prevent the normal use of iodine by the thyroid.

1. Iodine Deficiency

This is the most common cause of non-toxic goitre, and the World Health Organisation estimates that some two hundred million people in the world have a visible enlargement of the thyroid gland. The areas where goitre is endemic are usually mountainous, such as the Alps, Pyrenees, Himalayas and Andes. In such regions, soil and water contain very little iodine, and the daily intake falls below a hundred micrograms which is the minimal amount required for normal hormone production by the thyroid gland. When the circulating level of thyroid hormone falls, the anterior pituitary produces more thyrotropin or T.S.H. (thyroid-stimulating hormone), which in turn causes hyperplasia of the thyroid gland. Thus, all simple goitres represent in the first place hyperplasia of the thyroid, which is concentrating iodine more rapidly than the normal gland in order to make enough hormone from the diminished pool of iodide available in the body. Much of this iodide is recovered again when the hormone is broken down.

2. Inborn Errors of Iodine Metabolism

Normally the thyroid selectively concentrates iodine from the blood stream, combines it with tyrosine to form di-iodotyrosine, two molecules of which unite to form thyroxine. A deficiency of the enzymes necessary for any of these steps will lead to a lack of thyroid hormones, increased anterior pituitary activity and the development of a goitre. Absence of thyroid hormone production in the foetus results in a cretin, lesser degrees of upset iodine metabolism may be associated with mental deficiency and deafness (Pendred's syndrome).

3. Goitrogens

Many substances which occur naturally, such as calcium, and the oxazolidones, which are found in the cabbage family, interfere with the normal metabolism of iodine; but such substances are of no importance in man unless the intake of iodine is already at a critically low level.

Pathology

When the thyroid gland does not receive enough iodide it cannot produce a proper amount of thyroid hormones, and the anterior pituitary then secretes increased T.S.H., which stimulates the thyroid gland (Fig. 10). In

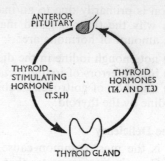

FIG. 10. Pituitary—thyroid axis

ANTERIOR PITUITARY

THYROID-STIMULATING HORMONE (T.S.H)

THYROID HORMONES (T4. AND T3)

THYROID GLAND

a *child* this results in uniform enlargement of the gland, which may become vascular, and reaches a maximum size at puberty. After this, in the female, the gland tends to enlarge before each menstrual period and continuously throughout pregnancy. In the male, however, there is often a tendency for the gland to diminish in size after puberty. The uniform hyperplasia of puberty becomes focal after the age of 30, so that nodules appear in the thyroid, nodules which initially are of increased activity. The great vascularity of these nodules may lead to their destruction by haemorrhage. Thus, with the passage of time a multinodular goitre is produced in which a careful search through the gland will always reveal a few nodules which are currently producing the body's requirement of hormone.

Symptom and Signs

The patient complains of a swelling in the neck and a choking sensation, which is worse in the pre-menstrual phase and during pregnancy. Pressure on the *neck veins* leads to their congestion, and the collateral circulation which develops can be seen as prominent veins running subcutaneously on the neck and upper chest. The trachea may be displaced to one side, so that breathing is difficult in certain positions and especially at night-time, when the patient may only be able to lie on one side, or require many pillows. The trachea may be narrowed by pressure from each side until little more than a slit remains, the so-called scabbard trachea. If there is a sudden haemorrhage into a nodule it may cause urgent dyspnoea or, by pressure on the sympathetic chain, a Horner's syndrome. Paralysis of a recurrent laryngeal nerve with hoarseness always indicates a malignant change in the goitre. Mild signs of hypothyroidism may be seen, but myxoedema is very rare in uncomplicated non-toxic goitre.

Tests

The use of the radio-active isotopes ^{131}I (half-life 8 days) or ^{132}I (half-life $2\frac{1}{2}$ hours) provide much information; it is better to use ^{132}I, as the patient receives less radiation. A tracer dose of about 10 micro-curies (mC_1) is usually given by mouth and the uptake in the thyroid gland measured at intervals during the next hours with ^{132}I, or days with ^{131}I. The urine can be collected over three periods 0–8, 8–24 and 24–48 hours, and the patient brings this to the hospital at the end of this period. Most patients take up between 40 and 50% of the dose in 36 hours and then discharge it slowly over subsequent days. In untreated non-toxic goitre the gland is often avid for iodine and so there is a high uptake, but the subsequent release of the isotope from the gland is very slow. Further information is provided by taking a sample of blood at 48 hours and measuring the amount of protein-bound radio-active iodine (P.B. ^{131}I) present; this is normally less than 0·5%, but is always lower in patients with non-toxic goitre. In addition, the neck area may be scanned using a well collimated, i.e., well shielded scintillation counter in order to show in which areas the radio-iodine is concentrated. Localised areas of in-creased activity are called 'hot' nodules, inactive areas are referred to as 'cold' nodules. When it is desired to assess the degree of hypothyroidism, the serum cholesterol is estimated (normally 160–240 mg. %), as it is usually a more reliable measure than radio-iodine in diminished thyroid hormone production. Estimation of protein bound iodine (PBI), normal level 3·5–7·5µg%, is an excellent measure of thyroid function.

Differential Diagnosis

A patient with a non-toxic goitre and an anxiety state may be mistaken for one with hyperthyroidism, but the radio-active iodine tests will differ-entiate between the two. A malignant change in the gland should be

F

suspected when there is rapid growth; the gland then feels hard and fixed, and later there may be involvement of local lymph nodes and hoarseness due to damage to a recurrent laryngeal nerve. Hypothyroidism and a firm enlargement of the thyroid may indicate thyroiditis.

Treatment

Non-toxic or simple goitre is one of the easiest diseases to prevent, since if everyone is provided with an adequate intake of iodine the condition practically vanishes. The addition of iodide or iodate (which is more stable) to salt used at table or in cooking is a good way of assuring a proper intake, and this method is used in many countries where goitre is endemic, e.g. Switzerland, New Zealand, United States, Argentina and Yugoslavia. In Switzerland 1 part of potassium iodide is used in 100,000 parts of salt, and in New Zealand 1 part in 20,000 parts. It is important that physiological and not pharmacological doses of iodide be used, as there is a slight risk of inducing hyperthyroidism if huge doses of iodine are given. In the British Isles salt is not iodised, and non-toxic goitre is fairly common.

If a child is seen with enlargement of the thyroid gland a proper intake of iodide should be arranged, and little more is necessary. By the time puberty is reached the addition of iodide to the diet no longer reduces the size of the gland. After puberty the patient should be given thyroid hormone by mouth, and this will shrink the gland, so long as it is not nodular. The giving of thyroid hormone by mouth can be done in a variety of ways, the original method was in the form of dried thyroid extract, full replacement being 180–240 mg. a day, i.e. 3–4 grains. Dried thyroid varies in potency according to the animal used, season and method of manufacture, it is not standardised biologically. Synthetic thyroxine (T4) is inexpensive and uniform in activity, given as the sodium-*l*-thyroxine the full daily replacement is 0·3–0·4 mg. Tri-iodothyronine (T3) is also available, it is about three times as potent weight for weight as T4, has an immediate effect on the body and is quite quickly metabolised; the daily dose is about 80–100 μg. In health the human thyroid produces mostly T4 and a small proportion of T3. It is possible to prescribe a similar mixture of the thyroid hormones T4 and T3 as Diotroxin (Glaxo), the full replacement dose being 0·3–0·4 mg. a day. The thyroxine or Diotroxin usually has to be continued indefinitely, since changes have taken place in the growing thyroid gland due to iodine deficiency, which appear irreversible. Finally, in adults with nodular non-toxic goitre only thyroidectomy will remove the nodules. After operation it is desirable to give thyroxine to make good the deficiency in the gland's own hormone production and prevent regrowth of the goitre.

HYPERTHYROIDISM

Overactivity of the thyroid gland in young people is usually referred to as Graves' disease in English-speaking countries and Basedow's disease on the continent of Europe. In older patients with nodular glands the symptoms and pathological findings in the thyroid often follow a different pattern, and are therefore more conveniently referred to as nodular toxic goitre. It is usual to consider the two groups separately, remembering that there is much overlap between the two.

GRAVES' DISEASE

Exophthalmic Goitre

Caleb Parry, a physician of Bath, gave the first description of hyperthyroidism in 1786, in 1835 Robert Graves of Dublin rediscovered it, and Basedow's account appeared in 1840. The cause of Graves' disease is not known; it is rare in childhood, common in adolescence and most common in young adults. It is less common with advancing age, except for a peak at the menopause. Women are more often affected than men in about the ratio of 8–1. The disease may follow a severe mental shock, and it has been suggested that it is hypothalamic in origin, activity in this part of the brain being supposed to stimulate increased secretion of T.S.H. by the anterior pituitary. However, the blood level of T.S.H. is not usually raised in patients with Graves' disease, but the feed-back mechanism from thyroid to pituitary which apparently controls T.S.H. secretion in health appears to be lost, and this fact is the basis of Werner's test (see p. 154). A long acting thyroid stimulator, L.A.T.S., is found in the serum of about 50% of these patients but its significance is not yet clear.

Pathology

The gland is uniformly enlarged to two or three times normal, and is smooth and not nodular. It is extremely vascular, cells lining the follicles are taller than normal and the follicles contain scant colloid. Lymphocytes are found throughout the gland, there may be collections of lymphoid tissue.

Symptoms and Signs

The patient is nervous, anxious, and fidgets; there is a smooth swelling in the neck, loss of weight, increased appetite, increased pulse rate, sweating of the palms and prominence of the eyes. Shakiness of the hands and palpitation on exertion, with dyspnoea and intolerance of hot weather, are common. There may be diarrhoea and oligomenorrhoea. Increased thirst is usual, with polydipsia and polyuria. Increased vascularity of the gland produces a thrill which can be felt over the main vessels and a bruit on auscultation. Tachycardia is present, even during sleep, the apex beat is thrusting and the increased blood flow may produce an apical systolic murmur. The diastolic blood pressure is low and the pulse pressure, i.e. difference between systolic and diastolic pressures therefore increased.

Exophthalmos, or increased prominence of the eyes, is common, and occasionally the first sign of the disease. The eyes have a stare, and both upper and lower lids are retracted so that a rim of white sclera is visible above and below the pupil when the patient looks straight ahead.

In hyperthyroidism there is a generalised myopathy which affects the eye muscles more severely than most of the other muscles in the body. There is poor co-ordination of eye and lid movements, so that if the patient is asked to follow the examiner's finger with her eyes the upper lid will be seen to lag behind the eyeball, especially in downward movement. The prominence of the eyes is due to lymphocytic infiltration, oedema and increased fat in the orbits. In severe exophthalmos the eye muscles become progressively paralysed, resulting in exophthalmic ophthalmoplegia. This always affects the superior eye muscles first, and the earliest sign of ophthalmoplegia is double vision (diplopia) when the patient looks up and to one side. The cause of exophthalmos is thought by some to be due to secretion of an exophthalmos-producing substance (E.P.S.), related to, but different from, T.S.H. produced in the anterior pituitary. Severity of exophthalmos is not related to the severity of hyperthyroidism, and the exophthalmos usually burns out in time, leaving a variable amount of deformity.

Tests of Thyroid Function

Radio-iodine is used to confirm the diagnosis (p. 151). Uptake of the isotope is faster than normal, rises to a higher peak and is discharged more rapidly from the gland. The protein-bound radio-iodine level in the

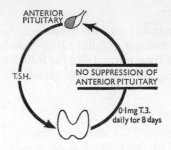

FIG. 11. Werner's suppression test

serum is raised. The basal metabolic rate (B.M.R.) is a measure of oxygen consumption by the cells of the body. For its performance the patient must be resting and starved, which has the disadvantage that a night in hospital is necessary. Anxiety, congestive cardiac failure, some blood diseases and perforated tympanic membranes all give false high readings. The best index of thyroid function is an estimation of protein-bound iodine (P.B.I.) in the serum, but the test is difficult and expensive, and therefore not performed routinely. The normal concentration is 3·5–7·5 μg./100 ml.

Patients who are doubtfully hyperthyroid often give equivocal laboratory results. Therefore further diagnostic tests are useful. The most difficult diagnostic problem is the patient with an anxiety state and an enlarged thyroid gland due to iodine deficiency. In Werner's suppression test (Fig. 11) the patient has a radio-iodine uptake test, and is then given 90 μg. of tri-iodothyronine (T3) daily for 1 week and the test is then repeated. Patients with non-toxic goitre and those with normal thyroid function show depression of the iodine uptake, but the increased uptake seen in hyperthyroidism is not suppressed.

Treatment

There are three methods of treating hyperthyroidism: (a) antithyroid drugs; (b) surgery; (c) radio-iodine. Combinations of two or more of these are often used.

(a) *Antithyroid Drugs.* Of all the antithyroid drugs carbimazole has the lowest incidence of toxic side effects; it acts by inhibiting the biosynthesis of thyroid hormones. Treatment consists of giving 10 mg. every eight hours for 18–24 months, when the dosage is gradually reduced in the hope that a remission of the disease will occur. More often the drug is used for a shorter period as preparation for surgery or radio-iodine treatment. All antithyroid drugs tend to increase the size of the thyroid gland, and the exophthalmos may worsen, therefore it is advisable to give thyroxine, 0·2–0·3 mg. a day at the same time. This suppresses pituitary secretion of T.S.H. and prevents further enlargement of the thyroid gland. Carbimazole may produce toxic effects: sore throat, fever and agranulocytosis. The patient should therefore be warned that if a sore throat occurs, to stop taking the drug and report immediately to a doctor. If agranulocytosis occurs, large doses of penicillin are given and fresh blood transfused.

In summary, carbimazole is most useful as sole treatment in young patients with mild hyperthyroidism, when it should be given for at least 2 years before the dose is tailed off. It is in addition supremely useful as pre-operative treatment for the hyperthyroid patient, when it should be given simultaneously with thyroxine for 4–8 weeks.

Potassium perchlorate is another antithyroid drug, it works by preventing concentration of iodide by the thyroid gland. The dose is 200 mg. four times a day. Unfortunately it occasionally produces toxic effects, including aplastic anaemia. Thyroxine (0·3 mg.) should be given concurrently to prevent increase in the size of the gland.

Thyroidectomy. Surgery is the most frequently performed treatment for hyperthyroidism in Great Britain. It is especially useful when the goitre is very large, unsightly or presses on the trachea and great veins; when treatment with antithyroid drugs is unsuccessful or unsuitable because of toxic effects, the patient's inability to take them regularly or because the patient lives a long way from regular medical care. Before thyroidectomy the patient is first prepared with carbimazole 10 mg. t.d.s. for 4–8 weeks and then when euthyroid, 10 drops of Lugol's iodine solution is given three times a day or 100 mg. potassium iodide. This is continued for 10–20 days until the thyroid gland has become firmer, smaller and less vascular. At partial thyroidectomy the isthmus and about seven-eighths of each lobe is removed, frequently with ligation of the inferior thyroid arteries. A small piece of thyroid, 4–8 g., is left on each side of the trachea to protect the parathyroid glands and recurrent laryngeal nerves. The wound is closed and two drainage tubes are left in for 24 hours. Clips or stitches in the skin are removed after 3–4 days. Thus, the patient's stay in hospital need be less than one week.

The complications are **tetany** due to damage or removal of parathyroid glands, and the serum calcium should always be determined after the operation. **Hoarseness** may result from damage to the recurrent laryngeal nerves, and the vocal cords should be inspected before operation and a week after operation. **Hypothyroidism** and, rarely, myxoedema results if too much thyroid tissue is removed, but it is readily corrected by giving thyroxine by mouth.

If the patient has not been properly prepared for the operation a **thyroid crisis** may occur during the subsequent 24 hours. This is due to excess thyroid hormone entering the circulation, it is characterised by hyperpyrexia, tachycardia, restlessness and air hunger, with delirium, collapse and death in severe cases. Thyroid crisis has been reported following other operations, such as tonsillectomy, in patients suffering from hyperthyroidism. Treatment of the crisis consists of sedation with intramuscular phenobarbitone or chlorpromazine, tepid sponging, administration of oxygen and intravenous saline. Propanolol a β-adrenergic blocking agent controls most of the symptoms. Potassium iodide and hydrocortisone are often prescribed, but their effect is not proven.

Radio-iodine Therapy. Treatment with ^{131}I is usually restricted to the treatment of patients over the age of 40 and for recurrent hyperthyroidism. It is never given therapeutically to children, or growing adults or to pregnant mothers, because the irradiation might lead to the development of thyroid cancer. However, it has never been known to produce thyroid cancer when administered to an adult, but the does of radiation which the ovaries receive will theoretically increase the mutation rate and might lead to abnormalities. The required dose is difficult to calculate, and is often decided empirically. The maximum effect is not obtained until 3 months have elapsed. The main drawback to radio-iodine therapy is the high incidence of hypothyroidism and myxoedema which continues to occur even 20 years after treatment and means that the patient must be followed up indefinitely. Radio-iodine is likely to be used much more extensively in the future.

Nodular Toxic Goitre

Patients past middle age with nodular goitre who develop hyperthyroidism often present a different clinical picture than the younger patients with Graves' disease.

Pathology

The gland shows multiple areas of involution and hyperplasia interspersed with fibrosis. Hyperplasia is often seen in the tissue between the nodules, rarely a single large area of hyperplasia is present. It is not possible to diagnose toxicity with certainty from the histological appearance.

Symptoms and Signs

This disease primarily affects the cardiovascular system and is of insidious onset. Therefore, the patient may present with congestive heart failure, swollen ankles and atrial fibrillation. There may be dyspnoea, tiredness and restlessness. Eye changes are rare, but there is usually weight loss.

Tests

Radio-iodine is most valuable, the B.M.R. may be misleading because of the cardiac failure. The chest is X-rayed to show cardiac enlargement and an electrocardiogram performed.

Treatment

The treatment of choice in this variety of hyperthyroidism is rest in bed, treatment of heart failure, Lugol's iodine by mouth and sub-total thyroidectomy. The patient's condition usually improves dramatically, and cardiac rhythm may revert spontaneously to normal. If the patient is gravely ill and cannot be made well enough for anaesthesia, radio-active iodine may be used, but relatively large doses of the isotope are required, and the response, compared with operation, is slow.

It is possible to summarise the use of the various kinds of therapy in the following table:

INDICATIONS

Antithyroid drugs	Thyroidectomy	Radio-active iodine
Children and young patients	Wage-earners and those who must return to work quickly	Adults, not pregnant, especially those over forty years
Mild hyperthyroidism	Long-term medical supervision not available or not desirable	Diffuse rather than nodular glandular enlargement
Ancillary to other forms of treatment, especially as pre-operative preparation	Bulky nodular glands with pressure symptoms	Recurrent hyperthyroidism because of risk to parathyroids and recurrent nerves
	Nodular toxic goitre	

THYROIDITIS

Infection of the thyroid gland with pyogenic organisms such as the streptococcus and staphylococcus, is extremely rare, and when it does occur, produces tenderness, pain on swallowing and fever. Occasionally typhoid infection occurs in the thyroid gland. The word thyroiditis has now come to be used for a group of diseases which present with fairly characteristic clinical patterns but whose aetiology is largely unknown. Because the cause of these diseases is not known, it is useful to name them after the individuals who first described them.

Hashimoto's Thyroiditis

Also called lymphadenoid goitre or struma lymphomatosa, was first described by a Japanese surgeon in 1912. The thyroid gland is only moderately enlarged, the histological changes are characteristic. The cells lining the follicles become plump and eosinophilic with granular cytoplasm, and are known as Askanazy or Hürthle cells. There is infiltration with lymphocytes, and the parenchyma of the gland is progressively replaced by lymphoid tissue and varying amounts of fibrosis. This is now considered to be an auto-immune disease in which the individual produces antibodies against the thyroid cells and thyroglobulin. The cause is unknown.

Symptoms and Signs

This disease occurs most commonly in women, usually between the ages of 30 and 50. The thyroid gland is moderately enlarged, non-painful, has a bossed surface and feels firm or rubbery with well-defined borders, and is often remarkably mobile. Initially there may be mild signs of hyperthyroidism, followed inevitably by increasing hypothyroidism, which in untreated patients progresses to myxoedema. It may be familial.

Tests

Thyroid precipitins can be readily demonstrated in at least 70% of these patients by mixing a little of the serum with a suspension of thyroglobulin-coated latex particles. The tanned red-cell agglutination reaction is a more sensitive test for thyroid antibodies. It is strongly positive in Hashimoto's disease, but also to a lesser degree in many other thyroid diseases, including hyperthyroidism and thyroid cancer. Uptake of radio-iodine is usually diminished in Hashimoto's thyroiditis, and following a brief initial rise in the P.B.I., this then falls to a low level. In addition, most patients show a raised level of gamma-globulin. Biopsy of the gland, which can be done with a split needle or drill, provides histological proof of the condition and is an excellent method for confirming the diagnosis.

Treatment

The patient requires full thyroid replacement therapy by mouth for the rest of her life, i.e. 0·3 mg. thyroxine daily or its equivalent. On this the patient feels better, the gland shrinks and becomes softer. Rarely, owing to fibrosis, partial thyroidectomy or removal of the isthmus is necessary in order to free the trachea.

De Quervain's Thyroiditis

This has been given many names and is sometimes called non-purulent thyroiditis, subacute, granulomatous, pseudo-tuberculous or giant-cell thyroiditis. It was first described in 1904 by the Swiss Surgeon de Quervain of Bern. The cause is unknown, but may be due to a virus, possibly that responsible for mumps, since an epidemic of this form of thyroiditis coincided with one of mumps in Israel in recent years. Histologically the cells forming the follicles swell up and burst, leaving only their nuclei; groups of these nuclei give an appearance similar to giant-cells. There is infiltration by plasma cells and lymphocytes and some increased fibrosis.

Symptoms and Signs

The onset is usually acute, often with a history of throat infection. Malaise, fever and a tender thyroid gland with pain radiating to the ears are the presenting features. There may be night sweats and a varying amount of weakness and lassitude.

Tests

The erythrocyte sedimentation rate (E.S.R.) is raised, but the white-cell count remains normal. Radio-iodine uptake is virtually nil and a biopsy obtained with a needle or drill is the most satisfactory method for confirming the diagnosis.

Treatment

Cortisone 50 mg. a day or prednisone 5–10 mg. a day for 3 weeks should be given after which the dose is gradually reduced over a week. If there is a relapse a further course of steroids is given, but the disease seldom lasts more than a few months, is self-limiting, and full recovery of thyroid function then occurs.

Riedel's Thyroiditis

This condition was described by Riedel in 1896 as a ligneous or woody thyroiditis. It is excessively rare, and few clinicians will see more than one example in a whole lifetime. The reported sex incidence is that it is twice as common in women as men and occurs in the 30–60 years age group.

Symptoms and Signs

The onset is insidious, with the gland becoming stony hard and bound to all the surrounding structures by fibrous tissue. There is surprisingly little evidence of hypothyroidism, but dyspnoea, dysphagia and hoarseness become progressively worse.

Tests

Thyroid precipitins have not been reported in this thyroiditis. Radio-iodine tests are usually normal. Removal of a piece of tissue when possible for pathological examination is the most helpful test, and differentiates it from carcinoma.

Treatment

It is not possible to perform a thyroidectomy on account of involvement of nearby structures in the neck. If the isthmus can be divided it relieves the pressure on the trachea.

HYPOTHYROIDISM

Hypothyroidism, or in its extreme form, myxoedema, does not call for treatment from the surgeon, since the giving of thyroxine by mouth will in most cases provide a satisfactory result, but hypothyroidism so often complicates other diseases that the surgeon should always keep it in mind. It is often overlooked.

Hypothyroidism produces general sluggishness of mind and body. There is increased weight, and typical fatty pads appear above the clavicles. Patients become difficult to manage, paranoid and hate the cold.

The bowels become progressively constipated, and patients may even present with the signs of intestinal obstruction, which on no account should be treated by laparotomy; intravenous infusion of small doses of tri-iodothyronine (10–20 mg.) and hydro cortisone hemi-succinate (50 mg.) being given every 8 hours.

Hypothyroidism is conveniently assessed by determining the level of serum cholesterol, which is normally 160–240 mg. % and rises in myxoedema to levels in excess of 300 mg. %.

THYROID CARCINOMA

Thyroid carcinoma is rare, only about 300 deaths being attributed to it each year in the Registrar General's returns for England and Wales, 45 million. It is seen more commonly in areas of endemic goitre, which suggests that prolonged stimulation of the gland by T.S.H. may be a factor in its aetiology. Ionising radiation may induce a malignant change during foetal life and childhood, and most examples of thyroid carcinoma in children follow irradiation of the neck.

Pathology

Thyroid carcinoma occurring in young patients is usually differentiated, that seen in the old is undifferentiated. The differentiated carcinomas can be subdivided into *papillary*, *follicular* and *medullary* according to the appearance under the microscope. It is convenient to consider these three main types of thyroid carcinoma separately, as each follows a different clinical course and requires different treatment.

Papillary Carcinoma

This occurs typically in those under 40, and accounts for almost all cases seen in childhood and adolescence. A small, hard, non-encapsulated slow-growing nodule occurs in one lobe of the thyroid, but careful microscopical examination of the gland will often show the tumour to be multicentric. Distant spread is via the lymphatics to nodes: immediately above the isthmus of the gland (Delphian nodes), in the groove between oesophagus and trachea, in the thymus, along both jugular chains and laterally above the clavicles. Histologically the metastases resemble thyroid tissue, but may show many papillary processes and varying amounts of colloid. So-called 'lateral aberrant thyroids' are metastases of differentiated thyroid carcinoma to lymph nodes in the neck.

Symptoms and Signs

A *solitary* firm nodule in the thyroid gland of a young patient should raise a suspicion of carcinoma. When enlarged lymph nodes can also be palpated the diagnosis is almost certain. Spread may also take place by the blood stream, and metastases occur in lungs and bones.

Tests

The best way to make certain of the diagnosis is to excise a lymph node which is examined microscopically. Ideally, this is done by frozen section, so that if cancer is found a suitable operation can follow at once. If a solitary nodule is present in the thyroid a total lobectomy should be done on that side, sparing the recurrent nerve and parathyroids.

Treatment

Total thyroidectomy is the correct treatment for papillary carcinoma of the thyroid if a previous biopsy of a lymph node has provided the diagnosis, since the disease is usually multicentric. One or more parathyroids must be preserved and both recurrent laryngeal nerves if possible. All the lymph nodes which appear on naked-eye inspection to be involved are excised at the same time, but a formal block dissection of the neck (p. 176) is not indicated and will not help in the removal of those nodes which are likely to be involved. Frequently, however, the correct diagnosis is only made by the pathologist when he examines sections of the lesion, therefore total lobectomy is recommended for solitary nodules, as it is in these that carcinomas are usually discovered. Following operation, full replacement therapy with 1-thyroxine or diotroxin 0·3–0·4 mg. is given daily for the rest of the patient's life. This ensures that the patient has a proper supply of thyroid hormone, but even more important, that the secretion of T.S.H. by the anterior pituitary is suppressed, so that there is no stimulus to the further growth of any thyroid cancer cells which remain in the neck or elsewhere.

Careful examination of the neck is done every 6 months and later at yearly intervals, for evidence of recurrent growth. Any suspicious node found on palpation is immediately excised. Prognosis is good, and the disease is compatible with long life.

Follicular Carcinoma

Typically, this type of tumour occurs in the middle years of life, but follicular areas are seen in most papillary carcinomas and, conversely, some degree of papillary change in most follicular carcinomas. The tumours referred to here are those showing a pure follicular pattern.

Pathology

The carcinoma reproduces in varying degree the follicular pattern of the thyroid, and the better differentiated it is, the better chance there is of eradicating the disease. Spread is more often by the blood stream rather than by the lymphatics, and therefore metastases are usually found in the lungs and skeleton, particularly the vertebrae, bony pelvis, ribs, skull and femora.

Tests

More than half these patients have noticed a nodule in the neck for some years, but latterly it has grown more quickly. About one-third of these patients present in the first place with signs due to metastasis, commonly a pathological fracture, or shortness of breath due to secondary deposits in the lungs. Hoarseness of voice is due to involvement of a recurrent laryngeal nerve. A radiograph of the lungs or skeleton will often help to confirm the diagnosis. If the metastases are well differentiated and the follicles contain colloid they may take up radio-iodine, it is then necessary to remove all normal thyroid tissue to augment this uptake as far as possible.

Treatment

Total thyroidectomy is done first in order to remove the primary tumour and all normal-functioning thyroid tissue. By this means the metastases are subjected to maximal stimulation by the anterior pituitary. The patient may be allowed to become myxoedematous, which takes 2 to 3 months, and at the end of this time a tracer dose of radio-iodine is given to see if the metastases will take it up. As this is time-consuming and may lead to rapid growth of the metastases, these patients are sometimes given 90 micrograms of tri-iodothyronine (T3) a day for a month, this is then stopped and is much more rapidly excreted than thyroxine. Two or three daily injections of 5 units of T.S.H. are then given, followed by a tracer dose of radio-iodine.

The metastases are mapped out by placing the patient on a table under which a well-screened tube passes along the whole length of the body.

By this means a 'profile' count is obtained, with peaks opposite those areas of maximum uptake. The uptake of radio-iodine by the metastases may be encouraged by giving carbimazole 10 mg. t.d.s. for a month and then stopping the treatment for 48 hours followed by the injection of T.S.H. intramuscularly, 5 units daily for 3 days. When a significant uptake of the tracer dose can be demonstrated in the metastases a large therapeutic dose of about 200 mC$_1$ is given in order to try and destroy the tumours. The patient's urine has to be stored for some time to allow decay of the radio-activity, since it is too active to discharge down the drain.

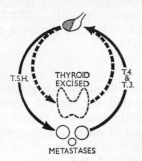

FIG. 12. Suppression of metastases of thyroid carcinoma by thyroid hormones

When metastases cannot be induced to take up radio-iodine they must be treated by conventional radiotherapy, which is unlikely to destroy them, but may provide palliation by reducing pain. The patient should be given full thyroid replacement therapy (thyroxine or diotroxin 0·3–0·4 mg. daily) with the object of suppressing any further growth of the metastases, as well as providing the patient with a normal supply of thyroid hormone and so giving them a sense of well-being (Fig. 12).

Medullary Carcinoma

This is a slow-growing tumour which spreads to lymph nodes and mediastinum often being calcified. A rare familial type is associated with neuromas and phaeochromocytomas.

Pathology. Appears microscopically to be more malignant than it is. Amyloid occurs in the stroma.

Symptoms and Signs. Slow growth with lymph-node and mediastinal involvement. Diarrhoea occurs with large tumours. After latent period of many years may show spurt of growth and metastasize.

Treatment. Surgical excision. Is unaffected by radio-iodine and radiotherapy.

Undifferentiated Carcinoma

Undifferentiated or anaplastic carcinoma of the thyroid usually occurs in patients over the age of 60, and is more common in women than men. The patient notices the fairly rapid increase of a swelling in the neck.

Pathology

These tumours are of two types: small cell and giant cell. The former, which are also described as carcinoma simplex, show masses of small cells packed together. Giant-cell carcinoma contains large irregular-looking cells, showing a great variety of shape and size. Sometimes the cells are spindle-shaped.

Symptoms and Signs

There is rapid painless growth of the thyroid gland, which may already be enlarged due to simple goitre. Hoarseness occurs early, and compression of the trachea leads to dyspnoea and stridor. Dysphagia due to involvement of the oesophagus occurs later.

Tests

The only disease from which this must be differentiated is Hashimoto's thyroiditis, and the blood is therefore tested for thyroid precipitins Diagnosis is confirmed by biopsy, conveniently done with needle or drill, thus allowing treatment to be started almost at once. Radiography and occasionally tomography of the neck will show the outline of the tumour and the extent to which the trachea is compressed or displaced.

Treatment

The treatment of undifferentiated thyroid carcinoma is radiotherapy. Using multiple fields, including the upper mediastinum, it is possible to give a total dose to the tumour of about 4,000 rads over a period of 3 weeks. If compression of the trachea becomes urgent, tracheostomy is performed and the radiotherapy continued. Thyroxine is given by mouth, since the gland is rapidly destroyed. The prognosis is usually poor, with maximum expectation of life of about 3 years for the small-cell lesions and considerably less, about 3 months, in the case of the giant-cell variety.

ADRENAL GLANDS (Fig. 13)

Cortex

The golden-coloured outer layer of the adrenal, which constitutes the cortex, secretes a large number of hormones which can be grouped together in three main categories: (1) *Glucocorticoids*, of which cortisol or hydrocortisone is the most important, regulate carbohydrate metabolism and help the tissues to deal with stress and infection. (2) *Mineral corticoids*, of which the chief is aldosterone, control transport of sodium across cell membranes and the excretion of potassium by the kidney. (3) *Androgens and oestrogens* are also secreted by the adrenal cortex.

The production of the glucocorticoids is controlled by adrenocorticotrophin (A.C.T.H.) from the anterior pituitary by a servo-mechanism, in which a reduction in the level of corticoids stimulates the pituitary to secrete more A.C.T.H. Thus, administration of cortisone or prednisone (which is a synthetic corticoid five times as potent as cortisone but with little affect on mineral metabolism) will suppress A.C.T.H. formation and

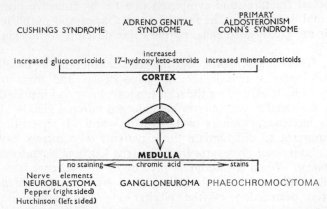

CUSHINGS SYNDROME   ADRENO GENITAL   PRIMARY
                              SYNDROME   ALDOSTERONISM
                                               CONN'S SYNDROME

increased glucocorticoids   increased   increased mineralocorticoids
                        17-hydroxy keto-steroids

CORTEX

MEDULLA
no staining ⟵ —— chromic acid —— ⟶ stains

Nerve   elements
NEUROBLASTOMA   GANGLIONEUROMA   PHAEOCHROMOCYTOMA
Pepper (right sided)
Hutchinson (left sided)

FIG. 13. Syndromes produced by hypersecretion of adrenal hormones and adrenal tumours

eventually lead to atrophy of the adrenal cortices. This is important to the surgeon, for if a major operation is contemplated in a patient who has been receiving cortisone, it will be necessary to provide additional cortisone, since the patient is not in a state to produce the necessary additional adrenal secretion on his own.

Pathology

Increased secretion of gluco-corticoids, mineral-corticoids and androgens may be due to hyperplasia of both adrenal cortices, one or more cortical adenomas or rarely a carcinoma. Often one type of cell predominates, but the pattern of cortical hormones produced is often a mixture of two or more elements.

Bilateral adrenal hyperplasia is treated by total adrenalectomy in the young and sub-total adrenalectomy in the older and the less severely affected; after total adrenalectomy the patient is maintained on daily cortisone. If a pituitary tumour is present it must be excised, and some success in treating this disease has followed implantation of radio-active gold grains or yttrium into the pituitary via a cannula inserted through the nose.

Cushing's Syndrome

This is due to excessive secretion of glucocorticoids, usually from bilateral hyperplasia of both adrenal cortices or an adenoma arising in the cortex of one adrenal. As Cushing originally pointed out, this is often due to overactivity of the anterior pituitary, which may be the site of a tumour. The tumour is rarely large enough to expand the sella turcica and be seen in radiographs of the skull.

Symptoms and Signs. Women are more commonly affected than men, most commonly in the age group 20–40. The onset is gradual, with obesity, hirsutism, amenorrhoea or impotence, muscle weakness, backache, pathological fractures and symptoms due to hypertensive heart disease and mental depression. The face is moon shaped and purplish, the face and hair are greasy with acne, purple striae develop in the skin over the flanks.

Tests. There is glycosuria, and the glucose tolerance is usually abnormal. Radiography reveals skeletal osteoporosis and there may be a pituitary tumour expanding the sella turcica. Presacral insufflation of air into the perirenal tissues may reveal enlarged adrenal glands. The urine contains increased amounts of 17-hydroxy- and 11-oxy-corticosteroids. It is important to differentiate those patients who merely have hypertension obesity and glycosuria from the true Cushing's syndrome.

Treatment. When a tumour is present in one adrenal it is removed surgically. Bilateral hyperplasia is treated by sub-total adrenalectomy or partial destruction of the pituitary by radio-active implant of yttrium.

Conn's Syndrome

This is produced by hyperaldosteronism due in 70% of cases to a solitary cortical adenoma of golden yellow colour and 3–5 g weight.

Symptoms and Signs. These are mainly due to potassium depletion and hypertension. Muscle weakness, cramps, polyuria and headache are common.

Treatment. Preliminary treatment is with an aldosterone inhibitor, spirolactone and potassium supplements, this is followed by excision of the adenoma.

Adrenogenital Syndrome

Excess secretion of androgens by the adrenals will produce virilism in the female and precocious sexual development in the male. Increased secretion of androgens in the foetus produces a female pseudo-hermaphrodite. The usual cause is an inborn error of adrenal metabolism, the patient being unable to synthesise cortisol. As a result, the adrenal cortex is stimulated by pituitary A.C.T.H. to produce large quantities of the precursor of cortisol, which is androgenic. A less common cause is an adrenal tumour, benign or malignant.

Symptoms and Signs. At birth a female child presents with signs of virilism, a big clitoris and potassium loss. Perirenal air insufflation may reveal an adrenal tumour.

Treatment. Excision of the tumour cures the condition; but irreversible damage to the kidneys may have already occurred from hypertension. Bilateral hyperplasia is treated by cortisone which must be continued for life.

Medulla

The adrenal medulla is composed of two kind of cells, one nervous in type, the other endocrine, usually differentiated by the ability of the latter to be stained brown with chromic acid (phaeochromocytes). The phaeochromocytes may form adenomas which secrete adrenaline and noradrenaline. The nerve cells may produce benign ganglioneuromas or highly malignant neuroblastomas.

Phaeochromocytoma

The chromaffin cells of the adrenal medulla secrete adrenaline and noradrenaline and tumours of these cells produce hypertension, which is typically paroxysmal, but may be continuous.

Symptoms and Signs

There are attacks of sudden increase in blood pressure, with blinding headache, anxiety, personality changes and convulsions. The patient goes pale in an attack, sweats and may suffer from dyspnoea and anginal pain. The B.M.R. is elevated.

Tests

The tumour may be demonstrated by an X-ray picture of the abdomen, intravenous pyelography and aortography. Pressure over the loin may start an attack of hypertension. The urine is assayed for vanillyl mandelic acid (V.M.A.). An injection of 5 mg. phentolamine will reduce the blood pressure.

Treatment

Preliminary treatment for one or two weeks is directed at minimizing the hypertension by giving α-adrenergic blocking agent, phentolamine and the β-blocker propanolol. The tumour with the adrenal gland is excised with great care, as handling releases nor-adrenaline and causes hypertension. After the operation hypotension is corrected by an intravenous infusion to which nor-adrenaline has been added.

THE PARATHYROIDS

The parathyroid glands were first described by the Swedish anatomist Sandstrom in 1880, and in 1925 the first operation for removal of a parathyroid tumour was performed in a patient with bone disease.

Hyperparathyroidism

This is a rare disease, and is probably often overlooked. Too much parathormone leads to a raised blood level of calcium and loss of calcium in the urine. It is usually due to an adenoma occurring in one of the parathyroid glands, occasionally there are two such tumours, and in about

10% of patients there is hyperplasia of all four glands. Carcinoma of the parathyroids is very rare. Secondary hyperparathyroidism resembles the primary disease clinically, all four parathyroids are enlarged and the cause is severe renal damage, hence it usually complicates renal failure.

Tertiary hyperparathyroidism is usually due to the chronic calcium loss of renal failure or steatorrhoea. All four parathyroids become hyperplastic and eventually adenomatous. The adenomas become autonomous and continue to secrete excess parathormone even if the cause of calcium loss is removed, e.g. by kidney transplant in renal failure.

Symptoms and Signs

These fall into four groups: (a) bone disease; (b) urinary-tract disease; (c) hypercalcaemic changes; (d) peptic ulcer and pancreatitis.

(a) *Bone disease.* The reason why some patients develop bone disease with hyperparathyroidism and some do not is unknown, but those with a good calcium intake are less likely to have skeletal changes. These changes are also called von Recklinghausen's disease or osteitis fibrosa cystica. There is generalised decalcification of the skeleton, cyst formation and the presence of tumour-like masses of osteoclasts. Cysts often occur in the jaws, and an epulis should raise a suspicion of parathyroid tumour. Vertebrae may collapse and a patient loses height, this being accentuated by the bowing of the femora. Bone pain, especially backache, is common. Pathological fractures may occur.

(b) *Urinary-tract Disease.* The commonest urinary tract finding is a calculus, and more patients are discovered in the genito-urinary department, where they present with renal-tract stones, than in any other part of the hospital. The stones are often bilateral and recur after removal. With advanced renal disease there may be polyuria and polydipsia (increased thirst), calcification of the renal tubules may be demonstrated by radiography and is called nephrocalcinosis.

(c) *Hypercalcaemia.* This leads to hypotonia of the muscles and generalised weakness. Deposition of calcium occurs in many tissues, and in the eye produces a band of keratitis adjacent to the limbus. The electro-cardiogram shows shortening of the Q–T interval.

(d) Chronic peptic ulcer and acute pancreatitis may also be presenting features of hyperparathyroidism.

Tests

Many patients escape diagnosis until late in the course of the disease when irreversible renal damage has occurred and therefore the possibility of a parathyroid tumour should always be kept in mind. The earliest sign is a raised level of serum calcium and lowered serum phosphate. These levels vary from day to day, and tests must be repeated frequently. No tourniquet should be used when obtaining the sample of venous blood. Radiographic examinations may show sub-periosteal erosion of phalanges, loss of lamina dura round the teeth, renal calculi and nephrocalcinosis.

Elevation of the level of serum calcium can be due to sarcoidosis, metastases and vitamin D, it can then be lowered with cortisone.

Treatment

The treatment of hyperparathyroidism is the removal of the parathyroid containing the adenoma, or sub-total parathyroidectomy if all the glands are involved by hyperplasia. The first operative attempt to find the parathyroid tumour is the most important one, and the search may have to include the thymus and upper mediastinum, where the glands may also occur. Formal exploration of the mediastinum by splitting the sternum is not done at the first exploration. After excision of the tumor there is usually postoperative tetany and mental changes due to hypocalcaemia. If severe, these are treated by intravenous calcium gluconate (10 ml. of 10% solution) calciferol 50,000–200,000 units daily and calcium by mouth (effervescent calcium Sandoz 8–24 g. a day). The hungry bones may take a year to replenish their calcium stores. The renal damage may be permanent.

PANCREAS

The bulk of the pancreas is concerned with its exocrine functions, producing a number of enzymes which enter the duodenum through the ampulla of Vater. In addition, its endocrine functions are performed by the islets of Langerhans, which consist of two kinds of cell—alpha and beta. The beta-cells produce insulin, the alpha-cells gastrin, which increases the volume and acidity of the gastric juice.

β-islet-cell Tumour (Nesidioblastoma)

A tumour of the beta-cells is rare, when it occurs it produces hyperinsulinism, and as a result, hypoglycaemia. Because it may go undiagnosed for many years, permanent mental changes may take place, and patients with this disease have been discovered in mental institutions.

Symptoms and Signs

These are mainly three, the 'Triad of Whipple': (1) When the patient fasts the blood sugar level falls to 50 mg. % or less. (2) This is accompanied by an aura, which may be a feeling of giddiness or apprehension, and there may be involuntary movements closely resembling an epileptiform fit. During the attack the patient may lose consciousness, sweat profusely and be incontinent. (3) The giving of sugar in any form during an attack brings it to an end. Intravenous glucose is the most dramatic way of doing this.

Tests

All patients who have epileptiform attacks should have a blood-sugar estimation, since a level under 50 mg. % is strongly suggestive of an insulinoma and demands further investigations to exclude other causes of hypoglycaemia.

Treatment

The pancreas is explored through a transverse abdominal incision and the tumour, which may be small, excised. If no tumour is discovered, subtotal pancreatectomy is performed in the hope of removing either a tumour or a sufficient number of hyperplastic islets.

α-islet-cell Tumour

Very rarely a tumour of α-cells occurs, and as a result there is a great increase in the acid and pepsin secretion of the stomach. Severe recurrent duodenal ulceration results, and there may also be ulcers in the jejunum. This pattern of symptoms is called the Zollinger–Ellison syndrome.

PITUITARY

Tumours in the pituitary produce symptoms in two different ways: (1) The raised intracranial pressure produces vomiting, headache and poor vision. Local pressure on the optic chiasma leads to reduction of the visual fields (bi-temporal hemianopia) and eventual blindness. (2) The hypersecretion of trophic hormones leads to endocrine changes.

Pituitary Tumours

There are three types of tumour arising from different types of cell in the anterior lobe of the pituitary: chromophobe, eosinophil and basophil. The *chromophobe* adenoma is the commonest, and grows to a large size, producing most of its changes by pressure on the surrounding structures and an increase in the general pressure inside the skull. Atrophy of the remainder of the pituitary produces a syndrome of hypopituitarism, with obesity, lowered basal metabolic rate, amenorrhoea in women, impotence in men, loss of hair and generalised weakness. An *eosinophil* adenoma is rare, and in childhood leads to gigantism and in an adult to acromegaly. A *basophil* adenoma is also rare and frequently very small, but it may produce large quantities of A.C.T.H. and Cushing's syndrome (*q.v.*).

Treatment

The treatment of tumours of the pituitary is usually surgical excision, hypophysectomy, if pressure symptoms are produced. If endocrine changes occur, and the tumour is not large, treatment is provided by the insertion of radio-active yttrium or gold into the pituitary fossa via a cannula passed through the nose or naso-labial fold via the sphenoidal sinus.

THYMUS

The thymus gland is composed of a mass of fatty tissue, with many thymocytes, lymphocytes and some lymphoid tissue, and lies immediately behind the sternum. It is relatively large at birth and until puberty, but it gradually becomes smaller in adults, and is often atrophic in the elderly. In the young it produces immunologically competent lymphocytes. It is occasionally enlarged in adults in hyperthyroidism and myasthenia gravis. Myasthenia gravis is a disease in which there is progressive weakness of the skeletal muscles, which may end in respiratory paralysis and death. The disease often progresses very slowly over many years, and is usually controlled by giving neostigmine in gradually increasing dosage.

Treatment

The operation of thymectomy has been used for myasthenia with somewhat unpredictable results. About a third of the patients are greatly improved, a third show some improvement and the remainder are quite unaffected. The gland is approached by splitting the sternum, and the postoperative complications are essentially pulmonary, because of the great muscle weakness and therefore the inability of the patient to cough up secretions.

FURTHER READING

Mason, A. S. (1957) *Introduction to Clinical Endocrinology*. Blackwell, Oxford.

Montgomery, D. A. D., and Welbourn, R. B. (1963) *Clinical Endocrinology for Surgeons*. Arnold, London.

The Thyroid Gland (1964) Edited by Pitt-Rivers, R., and Trotter, W. R. Vols. 1 and 2. Butterworths, London.

Means, J. H., De Groot, L. J., and Stanbury, J. B. (1963) *The Thyroid and its Diseases*. McGraw-Hill, New York.

Endemic Goitre (1960) W.H.O. Monograph. Geneva.

The Scientific Basis of Surgery (1965) cd. W. T. Irvine, chapters 7, 8, 17, 18, 19, 20. J. & A. Churchill, London.

Primary Hyperparathyroidism, A critical review (1966), Pyrah, L. N., Hodgkinson, A., and Anderson, C. K. *Brs. J. Surg.* **53**, 245.

Cope, C. L. (1965) *Adrenal Steroids and Disease*. Pitman, London.

CHAPTER FOURTEEN

FACE AND NECK

A great many conditions requiring surgical correction occur in the face and neck, and a convenient way of subdividing them is to consider those occurring in the young, which include many congenital lesions; and those occurring in adults, in whom infection and malignant disease play a much more prominent part. It is always helpful in diagnosis to remember which age group is likely to be affected by a particular disease. Since many more patients are seen in the adult group, these will be considered first.

LESIONS IN ADULTS

Swellings in the Neck

The majority of swellings in the neck are due to lymph nodes which are described in Chapter Ten and of the thyroid (see Chapter Thirteen). Branchial cyst is much less common (see p. 180).

Actinomycosis is a rare infection due to the actinomyces, but must always be thought of in any case of sepsis in the neck, especially if it follows dental extraction, and especially if induration is a prominent feature. Diagnosis is made by examination of pus for 'sulphur granules' by naked eye and by the recognition of mycelial masses in smears examined microscopically. Once recognised, the disease must be treated with penicillin in mega-unit doses over a period of 3–6 months. The disease used to kill, but since the use of penicillin a cure is invariable.

Ludwig's angina is the term given to infection deep to the floor of the mouth which, because it is limited by the mylohyoid muscle, tends to be confined and cause oedema to spread to involve the larynx, causing respiratory obstruction. The abscess must be drained, antibiotics given and, if necessary, tracheostomy performed.

Malignant Disease

Lymphatic metastasis usually causes painless enlargement of the lymph nodes in the neck. Carcinoma of the lip, tongue or mouth usually spreads to the submental and jugular lymph nodes, which then break down and fungate, becoming secondarily infected. The reticuloses also involve these nodes, which in Hodgkin's disease produce firm, rubbery and discrete nodes. In lymphatic leukaemia the nodes are usually soft.

Carotid Body Tumour

This is a rare tumour of chromaffin tissue arising between the internal and external carotid arteries. The tumour is ovoid (potato tumour) and is usually benign. Excision is difficult and dangerous, and may necessitate arterial reconstruction under hypothermia. Most surgeons prefer to leave these tumours alone unless they are causing symptoms or if there is a suspicion of malignancy. Metastasis may occur.

Salivary Glands

The diseases affecting the salivary glands are infection, stone, cysts, tumour and auto-immune disease.

Parotid Gland

Parotitis or infection of the gland is seen most often in mumps, but also occurs in patients after extensive operations who may become dehydrated, and if they have dirty mouths infection may ascend the parotid duct. If an abscess forms in the gland it should be drained, but preferably through the inner surface of the cheek, for a permanent salivary fistula is likely to arise after external drainage. Stone is uncommon in the parotid duct. Recurrent parotitis is common in children, in whom radiography shows extravasation through the duct terminals (sialectasis). Apparently the lesion is radiographically bilateral, though clinically unilateral. It usually resolves after one or two episodes of swelling, but occasionally antibiotics need to be given systemically or have to be injected into the duct.

Parotid Tumours (Salivary Adenomas) occur typically in adults and form mobile, apparently superficial swellings near the angle of the jaw. Pathologically they show a mixed picture, with areas of cartilaginous-like substance between masses of epithelial cells. They are well encapsulated and grow slowly. Treatment is excision of the tumour, together with a surrounding shell of healthy parotid to avoid recurrence from processes of growth that penetrate the capsule. When recurrence occurs it is invariably multinodular and much more difficult to excise. The problem of excision is made difficult by the branches of the facial nerve which pass through the gland, but it is possible to excise the more superficial part of the gland without damaging major branches. Occasionally the whole of the gland must be excised, with preservation of the facial nerve if the tumour goes deep to the nerve.

Soft swellings of the parotid gland or other salivary tissue may be due to cyst formation or occasionally to benign enlargement formed of masses of acinar and lymphoid epithelium, so called *adenolymphoma*. Cysts may also occur. Such swellings can be removed without fear of recurrence.

Carcinoma. Carcinoma of the parotid gland is a serious disease, difficult to eradicate and prone to local spread. Fixity to the masseter muscle, facial palsy and repeated recurrence after removal of apparently benign tumours are features of malignancy. Adenocarcinoma, squamous carcinoma and cylindroma are all seen. Metastasis occurs to lymph nodes in the neck, and late in the disease to lungs and liver. Treatment by total parotidectomy, with sacrifice of the facial nerve, offers hope of cure in the early stages. Block dissection of glands in the neck may be necessary.

Radiation therapy may be the only hope, but is often disappointing in its results, because these tumours are usually radio-resistant.

Submandibular Glands

Stone is common in the duct of the submandibular gland, causing pain and swelling in the floor of the mouth at meal times. It is usually possible to remove the stone under local anaesthetic through a small incision into the duct in the floor of the mouth. If the stone cannot be palpated in this position it is probably in the substance of the gland, which can be confirmed by X-rays. In this case excision of the submandibular gland is necessary. Tumours of the submandibular gland, adenoma and carcinoma, are rare, but when they occur the whole gland should be removed, as this leaves no disability and often prevents recurrence of the disease.

Mickulicz-Sjögren's Disease

This is a rare condition in which some or all four salivary glands and the lachrymal glands are enlarged and lose the power of secretion, so that the patient has dry eyes and a dry mouth. The disease is both disabling and unsightly. It is due to an auto-immune process occurring in the glands, which then develop a histological appearance comparable to that seen in Hashimoto's thyroiditis (see p. 158). There is no satisfactory treatment. Similar enlargement of the gland may occur in sarcoidosis, sometimes with fever and sometimes with uveitis.

Lips, Tongue and Mouth

Carcinoma of the Lip

Any chronic thickening of the lower lip should raise the suspicion of carcinoma, especially in elderly men. It is extremely rare on the upper lip. The growth is always a squamous-celled lesion, and may present as a fissure, warty growth or a thickened indurated mass. There may be a history of chronic irritation due to irregular teeth, rough pipe stem or other trauma. The carcinoma spreads locally and also via the lymphatics to the submental and submandibular lymph nodes and to those lying beside the jugular vein. If the growth is untreated death may follow fungation of secondary deposits in the neck with exhaustion from pain and sepsis. Secondary haemorrhage may occur from eroded vessels.

Treatment. Irradiation by low-voltage X-ray therapy (6,000 rads) gives excellent results if the growth is not extensive. Alternatively, the primary tumour is widely excised, followed by plastic repair of the lip when the mandible is involved—this is also resected. The patient is examined at monthly intervals thereafter, and if and when lymph nodes become palpably enlarged, block dissection of the cervical lymph nodes is carried out.

Molluscum Sebaceum

This is a benign condition which closely resembles carcinoma, producing a small raised tumour, which grows rapidly in a few weeks and then undergoes central necrosis and ulceration, followed by healing with minimal scarring. There is no evidence that it is premalignant. The diagnosis is clinical, and treatment involves curettage and cautery to the base. If there is any doubt about the lesion it should be excised for fear of malignancy.

Rodent Ulcer

This is the commonest malignant tumour of the skin, and occurs typically on the face, especially on the nose and lower eyelids though it may occur on the lip, commonly in those over 45 years. It is frequently seen in those with lightly pigmented skin who expose themselves to the intense sunlight of the tropics. It is often multifocal and appears as a semi-translucent firm nodule which breaks down at the centre. It scabs over with a honey-coloured crust, this may fall off and give the appearance of an ulcer that is healing centrally. Spread is local, and it is extremely rare for lymphatic or distal metastasis to occur. Extensive lesions may erode bone, expose the dura and destroy the eyes, causing hideous deformities.

Treatment. This is ideally provided by radiotherapy using a well-shielded X-ray beam. If the lesion is excised a healthy margin of surrounding skin must also be removed, or recurrence takes place. Excision is advised in cases of doubt, for lesions involving bone or cartilage and for those near the eye, since irradiation may cause necrosis of bone and cartilage and opacities in the lens.

Ulcers of the Tongue

Dyspeptic ulcers are small pimples, probably due to a herpetic virus. They break down on the tip and lateral border of the tongue, and produce extreme discomfort. They are called dyspeptic, although they are rarely associated with peptic ulceration.

Tuberculous ulcers are uncommon in Britain. They occur at the tip of the tongue, and are produced by tubercle bacilli, coughed up from open pulmonary disease. They are excessively painful, and an analgesic such as Benzocaine is applied locally as a palliative measure, while the primary disease in the lung is treated.

Syphilis of the tongue may occur in any of the three stages of the disease. A primary sore occurs as an indolent ulcer near the tip, with great induration and enlargement of the submental lymph nodes. Secondary syphilis produces superficial fissures and ulcers on the side and back of the tongue, said to resemble snail tracks. Tertiary syphilis may produce a diffuse gumma of the tongue, which is a large painless swelling which breaks down to form the typical indolent ulcer in the midline of the dorsum of the tongue.

Ulcers of the tongue may also be due to infection by many different organisms, including those of diphtheria, scarlet fever and the bacillus fusiformis of Vincent's angina. Ulceration also occurs in agranulocytosis and acute leukaemia.

Leukoplakia

This is more common in men than women, especially those over 40 years, and presents as an overgrowth of the epithelium of the tongue, which appears whitish, as if milk had been spilt on it. There may be fissures, and occasionally the thickened epithelium separates to leave a glazed red patch. It is commoner in those with a positive Wassermann reaction, and may be associated with infected and irregular teeth, smoking or any chronic irritation of the mouth. The importance of the condition is that it is premalignant, and whenever possible the thickened areas should be excised. The teeth should be attended to, irritants of all kinds avoided and antisyphilitic treatment given if the Wassermann reaction is positive.

Carcinoma of the Tongue and Mouth

This is much commoner in men than women, usually over 60 years of age. Carious teeth are often present, and leukoplakia, sometimes the result of syphilis, may precede the lesion. Most tumours are squamous celled and are often multifocal.

Symptoms and Signs. The tumour may present as a heaped-up or papilliferous growth, but more commonly as an indurated fissure or ulcer on the lateral border of the anterior two-thirds of the tongue. With ulceration there may be foetor oris, increased salivation, and, when the tongue becomes fixed, which occurs especially with lesions near the back of the tongue, speech is difficult. Pain may be a prominent feature and radiates to the ears. Later there is involvement of submental, submandibular and deep cervical lymph nodes. The Wassermann reaction may be positive.

Treatment. Diseased teeth are cleaned and if necessary extracted. Mouth washes and irrigations are used to clear up sepsis. If the primary lesion is small and on the anterior two-thirds of the tongue, cheek or floor of mouth it is widely excised with diathermy. All other lesions are treated by the insertion of radium needles as a *volume implant* which is superintended by a physicist. He is able to plan where the needles should be inserted in order to give an adequate dose of radiation to the whole tumour mass, hence the name, volume implant. Alternatively, high-voltage radiotherapy as a beam or from a source of radium or cobalt is used, especially for lesions near the back of the tongue, some of which are undifferentiated and are known as lympho-epitheliomata because of their histological picture of small round cells. When the regional lymph nodes are enlarged a block dissection of the cervical nodes is performed, once the primary lesion has been treated and it is obvious that the enlarged nodes are not due to sepsis from the primary focus. In a block dissection the sternomastoid muscle, the internal jugular vein and spinal accessory nerve are removed, together with cervical fascia and lymph nodes of the anterior and posterior triangles of the neck and the submandibular salivary gland. When lymph nodes are involved on both sides of the neck at least 2 weeks are allowed between the two operations, and it is preferable not to remove both internal jugular veins. When enlarged nodes are absent the patient must be seen at monthly intervals to watch for their appearance. After a year has passed without evidence of node involvement the interval between visits can be extended.

The Jaws

Teeth

Infection occurs in association with teeth either around the apex of a root, i.e. *apical abscess,* or at the junction of gum and tooth, *gingivitis.* Regular cleaning of the teeth after meals and visits to a dental surgeon will prevent most of these infections, but when they occur, radiography of the teeth and jaw is essential. Most of the cysts which are seen radiographically in the jaws are due to sepsis around the root of the tooth (dental cyst). Removal of the tooth allows drainage of the abscess.

Osteomyelitis of the jaws is rare, and almost always due to the staphylococcus. It occurs in infants in the upper jaw from spread of infection from the maxillary antrum. Osteomyelitis of the lower jaw is almost always due to blood-borne infection from a primary septic focus elsewhere in the body.

Odontomes

Tumours of the jaws derived from dental structures are called odontomes. Only three occur with any frequency. Dental or periodontal cysts are found around the apices of old infected roots. Diagnosis is by radiography which shows a round radio-lucent area usually in association with a root. Treatment is by removal of the tooth or marsupialisation. The *epithelial odontome* or *fibrocystic disease* is seen in young adults, usually in the lower jaw, and consists of a large multilocular swelling which is derived from remnants of the enamel organ. The whole tumour must be excised, and where necessary a bone graft used to repair the jaw. A *follicular odontome* or *dentigerous cyst* arises from an unerupted and often maldeveloped tooth and produces a cystic swelling with such thinned-out bone covering it that egg-shell crackling may be detected on palpation. In treatment the tooth remnants must be removed and the cyst curetted. There are many other forms of odontome, but all are very rare.

Malignant Disease

This is unusual in the jaws. A carcinoma may arise in the maxillary antrum and invade the upper jaw. It may cause pain in the face, bloody nasal discharge and diplopia if the orbit is involved. Examination by the otolaryngologist using specula and special mirrors may reveal invasion of the nose, nasopharynx or orbit. Radiographs may show bone invasion and opacity of the antrum. Histology may reveal a squamous lesion or an adenocarcinoma. Sarcoma is less common and requires radical excision if this is possible.

Treatment. If there is a carcinoma of the antrum this involves removal of the palate, curetting out the tumour and irradiating the cavity so formed with radium needles or beam radiation therapy. A dental obturator is then worn to cover the hole in the palate. Removal of the upper jaw and even the eye may be necessary in more extensive lesions. Osteogenic sarcoma occurs in the lower jaw of children and young adults, it is very malignant and very rare. Radiotherapy may be useful as palliation. Secondary deposits in the mandible of children are typical of Burkitt's lymphoma, which occurs in Central Africa and is treated with methotrexate.

Temporo-mandibular Joint

The articulation of the lower jaw with the skull is relatively inaccessible, and considering the amount these joints are used, they remain remarkably free from disease. The temporo-mandibular joint may click or lock due to displacement of the cartilaginous pad, or to malocclusion of the teeth. It may become ankylosed due to rheumatoid or gonococcal arthritis. Osteoarthritis may cause pain and clicking in the joint. Operations on the joint are rarely indicated, they are difficult to perform, and the results are often disappointing. Malocclusion of the teeth is a common cause of clicking jaw best treated by the dentist.

Nose

Epistaxis or Nose Bleed

This can occur at any age, and may be due to trauma. Other causes are sepsis, foreign body, hypertension and the blood dyscrasias, but many nose bleeds have no apparent cause, although they tend to occur during times of stress. Often the bleeding point can be seen on the septum quite near the anterior nares. Treatment consists of cold compresses to the nose and the back of the neck to produce reflex vasoconstriction and gentle packing of the nose with ribbon gauze, which may be soaked in 1 in 1,000 adrenaline. It may be necessary to cauterise the bleeding point, or even rarely it may be necessary to tie the ethmoidal arteries. Infection requires treatment by antibiotics, and in extreme cases blood transfusion is necessary. Underlying causes must be sought and, if possible, eradicated.

Rhinitis

Infection in the nose is extremely common, especially in the form of the *common cold.* It may be complicated by allergy as in *hay fever*, and when chronic leads to the growth of *polypi*, which require removal. Infection may spread from the nose to the maxillary antra, and radiography will show opacity of these, and transillumination confirm the presence of pus. The antrum is drained in chronic infection by the introduction of a trocar and cannula underneath the inferior turbinate using local anaesthesia. Acute infections are treated by antibiotics, inhalations and a vasoconstricting nasal spray.

Nasal Obstruction

This may be due to deflection of the nasal septum, which is often congenital, but may be acquired through injury. Difficulty in breathing through one nostril predisposes to infection. The obstruction is treated by correction of the deflection by removal of much of the cartilage of the septum from beneath its mucous covering, *submucous resection* (S.M.R.).

LESIONS IN THE YOUNG

Neck

Tonsils and Adenoids

The tonsil is composed of lymphoid tissue, and is particularly liable to inflammation. Acute *tonsillitis* is accompanied by a raised temperature, difficulty in swallowing and general malaise. The lymph nodes in the neck which drain the tonsil lie near the angle of the jaw. They may enlarge and be tender on palpation. The tonsils are bright red and often show spots of exudate in their crypts. Treatment in severe cases necessitates the use of penicillin and a sulphonamide and the use of a warm gargle, to which may be added aspirin to relieve the pain. The importance of treating the infection is that very occasionally it may predispose the individual to develop the much more serious conditions of rheumatic carditis and nephritis.

Quinsy or peritonsillar abscess typically forms behind the upper pole of the tonsil and causes great difficulty in swallowing. Acute pain, severe swelling and a high temperature are usual. The accompanying oedema may approximate the pillars of the fauces so that the patient feels that he is choking. The abscess is incised using local analgesia, achieved by swabbing the area with 5% cocaine. It is important that the patient is not allowed to aspirate the pus, which may flood the trachea and later cause lung abscess.

Chronic Tonsillitis is rather an ill-defined condition, but consists of enlarged infected tonsils which frequently undergo recurrent attacks of inflammation. Tonsils may, however, enlarge without being inflamed, it is only those that are hard and show chronic infection in the crypts, which need removal.

The Indications for Tonsillectomy are: repeated attacks of tonsillitis, especially when these are associated with very large tonsils; recurrently enlarged tender lymph nodes in the neck, whether or not these are also infected with the tubercle bacillus. Quinsy is another indication for tonsillectomy, but in this condition the operation should be deferred for 6 weeks—that is until after the acute symptoms have subsided. Enlargement of the tonsils is not of itself an indication for their removal, and indeed may cause harm by removing an important bacterial defence mechanism, especially in children.

The Adenoids. These comprise a pad of rather vascular lymphoid tissue on the posterior wall of the nasopharynx, which, when associated with chronically infected tonsils, may obstruct the airway and cause the child to breathe through the mouth. Adenoids predispose to attacks of infection in the middle ear by obstructing the openings of the Eustachian tubes. Removal of enlarged adenoids (adenoidectomy) is usually done at the same time as tonsillectomy.

Branchial Cyst

This occurs mainly deep to the upper third of the sterno-mastoid muscle and presents as an oval, lax or tense cystic swelling, sometimes lined by respiratory epithelium with much lymphoid tissue in its walls and filled by a clear fluid containing cholesterol crystals. It is derived from the second branchial cleft. Usually attention is first drawn to it when it becomes infected, but enlargement may occur at any age. It is often difficult to distinguish it from cervical adenitis, especially the tuberculous variety. Such cysts must be excised, for infection leads to an abscess and ultimately the formation of a fistula.

Branchial fistula or Cervical Sinus

This is seen as a small opening in the skin, occurring usually at the junction of the lower third and upper two-thirds of the sterno-mastoid muscle. It represents the opening of the branchial cleft formed by growth of the fourth branchial arch, which grows back and covers the second or third clefts. A viscid fluid exudes, and the track can be shown to pass upwards and inwards between the internal and external carotid arteries to end in the supra-tonsillar fossa. The condition may be unilateral or bilateral, and the fistula usually becomes infected. The fistula is excised through small step-ladder incisions in the neck. The condition is often familial, and may be associated with other congenital abnormalities, it also is derived from the second cleft. A persistent first branchial cleft produces a rare abnormality with an opening below the ear and another just inside the ear. The tract embraces the facial nerve.

Dermoids

Dermoids in the face and neck occur as cystic swellings lined by squamous epithelium, containing sebum and occurring at lines of junction between developmental blocks of tissue. The commonest is the—

External Angular Dermoid, which occurs at the upper and outer part of the eye just beneath the extremity of the eyebrow. There is often an underlying pit in the skull, rarely a defect in it communicating with an extradural dermoid, and very rarely indeed it may communicate with the meninges. The cyst should be excised for cosmetic reasons and also because it may enlarge greatly if left.

A *Submental Dermoid* occurs just beneath the chin in the midline, and usually lies in or superficial to the raphe which unites the two mylohyoid muscles. The differential diagnosis includes a thyroglossal cyst which differs in having a partly columnar-celled lining and by containing clear fluid.

A *Sublingual Dermoid* occurs beneath the tongue in the midline, projects into the floor of the mouth and may resemble a ranula, except that it does not transilluminate. All varieties of dermoid are treated by excision.

Sterno-mastoid Tumour

This is usually diagnosed in the second or third week of life as a solid oval swelling in the lower third of the sterno-mastoid muscle, which, because it is in the muscle, can only be moved laterally and not in the line of the muscle fibres. It is presumed to be due to trauma to the muscle or its blood supply during child-birth. If it is left untreated a fibrous contraction of the muscle ensues, and eventually wry-neck or torticollis. Under the supervision of a physiotherapist, the child's mother can be taught how to manipulate the neck each day so as to stretch the affected muscle. Treatment can usually be discontinued after 1 year of age. If the condition remains unrecognised and fibrous contraction of the muscle and cervical fascia occurs, it requires surgical correction by tenotomy, that is division of the tendon of the sterno-mastoid muscle. When the muscle is extremely fibrosed excision of the muscle and division of the contracted cervical fascia gives a more satisfactory result.

Cystic Hygroma

This presents as a brilliantly transilluminable swelling in the lateral or posterior aspect of the neck of a new-born baby. It is a form of lymphangioma and, being multilocular, cannot be completely aspirated by a needle. It is important that the lesion does not become infected, or severe toxaemia may result. Excision must be complete, or recurrence may occur. Skin grafting may be required to cover any defect left by the operation.

Cervical Rib

This is a fairly common deformity, which consists of an additional prefixed rib, is usually bilateral and arises from the transverse process of the seventh cervical vertebra or occasionally the sixth. It may be cartilaginous or bony. Its end may be free or continue as a fibrous band attached to the first rib. It produces symptoms by displacing the subclavian artery or the lower trunks of the brachial plexus upward. The arterial blood supply to the arm may be partially or completely interrupted by bracing back the arm, or forced dependency, and the radial pulse may only return when the arm is released. Pressure on the lower trunks of the brachial plexus (C8, T1, which form the ulnar nerve) may result in wasting of the small muscles of the hand. Compression of the subclavian artery by the rib may be followed by dilatation of the artery distal to the rib (post-stenotic dilatation). Thrombus in the aneurysm thus produced may fragment and the emboli sweep on in the blood stream to cause digital gangrene.

The neck should always be examined for the presence of an abnormal rib in any case of pain in the arm, vascular insufficiency and wasting of the small muscles of the hand. Radiography of the thoracic inlet may show a rib or presumptive evidence of a band from a 'beaked' seventh-cervical transverse process joining it to the first rib.

A cervical rib need only be removed if it causes pain or presses on nerves, artery or vein.

Lips, Tongue and Mouth

Cleft Lip

A knowledge of the embryological development of the face, mouth and neck makes it much easier to understand the various congenital defects which may occur. The fronto-nasal process develops into the forehead, nose and the small block of tissue below it which constitutes the central part of the upper lip. From each side the two maxillary processes grow in to produce the cheeks and the remainder of the upper lip on each side. The paired mandibular processes unite in the midline to form the chin and the lower lip. Lack of fusion of the fronto-nasal process with one of the maxillary processes will give rise to a cleft lip, and this is a little commoner on the right side than the left. Occasionally the cleft is bilateral. The commonest complication of a cleft lip is a cleft palate. In the condition of cleft lip the baby is still able to suck, and therefore thrives and is not more prone to infection than a normal baby. The deformity often occurs in families, but its inheritance may be difficult to trace. The nostril on the affected side is flattened, and other congenital deformities are often present.

Treatment is undertaken after the age of 3 months when the baby is thriving, free from infection and not anaemic. It is usual to admit the baby to hospital with her mother so as not to upset the baby's routine. They are housed in a separate room so as to minimise the risk of cross-infection. Bilateral clefts provide the biggest challenge to the surgeon, because the premaxilla, which is the block of tissue lying between the two clefts, projects and must be forced back into alignment with the lateral parts of the lip. If, after repair of the cleft, adjustment of the vermilion border of the lip is required it is deferred until the child is 5 or 6 years of age.

Cleft Palate

The palate, which is formed by a shelf of tissue growing in from each side, unites from before backwards, and the portion which last of all joins up, namely the uvula and soft palate, is the part which most frequently fails to fuse. Cleft palate is a severe disability, the baby cannot suck properly, feeds are taken with difficulty and often regurgitated through the nose, which frequently becomes chronically infected.

Treatment. Operation is a hazard in the neonatal period, and as time goes by the baby usually develops anaemia; therefore it is customary to defer definitive treatment until at least 1 year after birth. If operation is deferred later than two years of age it may be difficult to teach the child to speak properly. Wide relieving incisions are made laterally in the muco-periosteum covering the hard palate, in such a way as to allow the soft palate to be lengthened and its two halves brought together for suture in layers in the midline. It may also be necessary to reduce the diameter of the nasopharynx, and adequate mobility may not be obtained until the tonsils have been removed. More than one operation may be necessary, and speech therapy forms a necessary part of the after care.

Fraenum of the Upper Lip

A prominent fold of mucous membrane from the upper lip may pass between the two central incisors. This is disfiguring and tethers the lip so that it cannot be approximated properly to the lower one. Treatment is by excision of the fold through vertical incisions and suture of the defect horizontally so as to prevent recurrence.

Tongue-tie

Tongue-tie may be familial, is often blamed for delay in a child learning to speak, but is rarely if ever the cause of this. The fraenum beneath the tongue is unduly short, but wide and avascular. Correction is easily carried out in the very young without anaesthesia by cutting the fraenum with scissors, taking care to avoid the underlying blood vessels. The operation should only be done if the tongue cannot be protruded as far as the lower lip. An additional reason for freeing the tongue is to permit its important function of cleansing the back of the teeth and preventing caries.

Ranula

A ranula is a translucent cystic swelling which arises on one side of the under surface of the tongue, usually in a small child it contains a clear viscid fluid. Rarely, if it is very large, it may cause difficulty in speech. Some ranulas appear histologically to be ganglia, and others are probably derived from mucous glands in the floor of the mouth or from the sub-lingual gland. Ranula is treated by excision or marsupialisation, that is an unroofing of the cyst with suture of the cut edge to the mucosa of the floor of the mouth.

Micro- and Macro-stoma

Fusion of the maxillary and mandibular process on each side of the cheek may either proceed too far, so that a tiny mouth or microstoma is produced; or not proceed far enough, so that a very wide mouth or macro-stoma results. Both of these conditions are rare and are usually associated with severe congenital defects in other parts of the body. In addition, there may be extreme mobility of the tongue, which then falls back to obstruct the airway, and a cleft palate; a syndrome (Pierre Robin) usually associated with micrognathia and mental retardation.

G

The Ear

The external ear is formed by the fusion of the six tubercles of His and, considering the complexity of their development, it is surprising that more malformations are not seen. Absence of the pinna is very rare and associated with deafness. The commonest abnormality in this part of the body is an accessory auricle, which is a small tag of skin enclosing a rod of cartilage situated anterior to the ear. They are often multiple. Treatment is excision, which is best done in the first days of life, no anaesthetic being necessary. Blind pits are common towards the edge of the pinna, and represent failure of fusion between His's tubercles.

Pre-auricular fistula or Ear-pit

This is a blind opening situated just anterior to the external auditory meatus. The opening is frequently surrounded by scaly skin, and there may be an associated mass of cartilage. The pit frequently becomes infected and never heals, because it is lined with skin. It may be mistaken for an infected pre-auricular lymph node or recurrent boil. These fistulae may require excision, preferably before they become infected.

Branchial Remnants

The branchial clefts, which represent gill slits, usually disappear in early foetal life, two remnants may persist, the branchial cyst and the branchial fistula.

FURTHER READING

Moyer, C. A., Rhoads, J. E., Allen, J. G., and Harkins, H. N. (1965) *Surgery, Principles and Practice*, Ch. 46, 3rd ed., Pitman, London.
Aird, I. (1957) *A Companion in Surgical Studies*, 2nd ed., E. & S. Livingstone, Edinburgh.

CHAPTER FIFTEEN

BREAST

The most important diseases of the breast are carcinoma, hyperplastic cystic disease (fibroadenosis, chronic mastitis), benign tumours and acute inflammation. The chief symptoms produced by breast disease are few—lump in the breast, pain and sometimes discharge from the nipple.

The earliest physical sign of carcinoma of the breast is hardness. All other physical signs are signs of advanced and often incurable growth. A hard lump may be due to cyst, fibroadenoma, fat necrosis or carcinoma. These four entities are responsible for almost all the swellings seen in the breast apart from acute inflammation. Any of the four may be mimicked by the others, hence it is pointless to attempt to separate them.

It cannot be too strongly stressed that any woman with a firm discrete lump in the breast should be admitted urgently for its excision and, if necessary, immediate histological examination of the diseased breast tissue by rapid frozen section.

CARCINOMA OF THE BREAST

Carcinoma of the breast is one of the commonest malignant growths affecting women, equalled only in frequency by carcinoma of the uterus. In England and Wales some 8,000 women die of carcinoma of the breast each year. The mortality has remained constant over the last 30 years, a depressing fact in view of the publicity aimed at earlier diagnosis and more effective treatment.

It is estimated that in any year 18,000 women are likely to develop the disease. Perhaps in the future screening by mammography, that is routine soft-tissue radiography of the breast, in all women over the age of 45 may bring to light the earliest stage of carcinoma before it is clinically obvious.

Aetiology

The fundamental cause is unknown, but it is not uncommon to elicit a strong family history of carcinoma of the breast. Statistical support for a *hereditary* factor is lacking in women, but in animals it is possible to breed strains with a very high incidence of breast cancer.

Carcinoma of the breast is less common in women who have breast fed their children, and this fact may be linked to the observation that the progeny of mice allowed to suckle their mothers are more prone to carcinoma than those denied suckling. However, as yet no proof of a *milk factor* has been produced in man.

The results of hormone therapy for advanced carcinoma of the breast indicates that approximately 50% of breast cancers are dependent for growth on their endocrine environment. Such tumours are termed *hormone dependent*. Another fact indicating the importance of hormones is that the administration of oestrogens may sometimes activate a quiescent carcinoma. Carcinoma is more common near the age of the menopause than at other ages, and it is more common in nulliparous women. All these facts suggest a hormonal cause for some cases of cancer.

Natural History

Carcinoma of the breast is relatively slow growing. The average expectation of life of an untreated patient is 3 years, but it is not uncommon to see women who have had growths of the breast for 10 years or more. In view of the possibility of long survival without treatment, it is important only to consider 10-year survival rates in comparing the results of treatment by different methods.

Classification of Carcinoma of the Breast

The classification of carcinoma of the breast is confusing to the student, because a mixture of clinical and pathological terms is used. The names commonly used are listed below. They are separated either in terms of clinical behaviour or microscopical appearance.

1. *Clinical*

Scirrhous, Medullary, Inflammatory, Lactating, Pregnancy, Atrophic scirrhous, Duct carcinoma, Carcinoma male breast.

2. *Pathological*

Scirrhous (spheroidal-celled or carcinoma simplex), Medullary (encephaloid), Adenocarcinoma, Mucoid carcinoma, Squamous carcinoma, Duct carcinoma, Paget's disease of the nipple.

Scirrhous Carcinoma

1. *Clinical.* Scirrhous carcinoma is the commonest cancer of the breast, making up 60% of malignant disease in this organ. It presents as a swelling in the breast, which is usually painless. The age groups most commonly affected are those near to the menopause. The upper outer quadrant of the breast is the most common site, the lower inner quadrant the least common.

2. *Pathology.* When the swelling is incised it is hard and gritty. The cut surface is concave, unlike a benign tumour, of which the surface is convex because it is normally confined under tension within a capsule. The surface is greyish with flecks of yellow, and the tumour can often be seen to infiltrate surrounding fat. Histology shows columns of malignant cells, atypical in shape and chromatin, sandwiched between masses of fibrous

tissue. Around the growth there are often many lymphocytes, and there may be malignant cells in nearby lymphatics and capillaries. The degree of differentiation of the malignant cells is closely related to prognosis.

Other Types of Carcinoma of the Breast

1. *Medullary or Encephaloid Carcinoma.* This growth is softer and more rapidly growing than the scirrhous, and hence potentially is more dangerous. Histological section shows masses of malignant cells, with relatively little fibrous stroma.

2. *Inflammatory Carcinoma and Carcinoma of Pregnancy and Lactation.* These are tumours which may simulate a breast abscess. They are rapidly growing, hot and tender, and may show early fixation to the skin. Usually they present at a stage when radical treatment is impossible.

3. *Atrophic Scirrhous Carcinoma.* In elderly women the breast may be contracted and deformed by a very-slow-growing carcinoma which is often found accidentally during medical examination. Such growths may remain localised to the breast for several years.

4. *Duct Carcinoma.* Bleeding from the nipple of a postmenopausal woman suggests the possibility of duct carcinoma. If the growth obstructs a duct a swelling may be felt. Sometimes this swelling is a large cyst filled with blood-stained fluid and containing a papillary carcinoma. In other cases a solid growth is present which, when it is incised, presents a surface containing tiny ducts, from which exude minute solid cores of cells, the result of intraduct epithelial proliferation of such an intensity that the ducts are solid with cells. Abnormal mitoses and infiltration into the breast through the epithelium of the ducts indicates malignancy. Such a growth is called *comedo carcinoma* or *intraduct carcinoma*.

5. *Paget's Disease of the Nipple.* Eczema of the nipple is uncommon. If it persists for more than a month, then biopsy should be performed. In Paget's disease the nipple is first eczematous, later it may be ulcerated and destroyed. Much later a swelling may appear in the breast outside the nipple which microscopically has the appearance of an intraduct carcinoma.

Biopsy of the nipple shows downgrowths of the epidermis (acanthosis) and hydropic cells (Paget's cells) in these downgrowths, with lymphocytic infiltration in the dermis. Paget's cells are curious pale cells distended with oedema fluid. The nature of Paget's cells is unknown, but many regard them as a form of carcinoma *in situ* and part of an intraduct carcinoma which is almost always found in the breast after its removal.

6. *Carcinoma of the Male Breast.* Carcinoma of the male breast is uncommon, making up only 1% of all breast carcinomata. It has a bad prognosis usually, because local spread rapidly involves the chest wall and skin.

7. *Microscopical Variants of Carcinoma.* A well-differentiated carcinoma showing well-formed acini on microscopical examination is called *adenocarcinoma*. *Mucoid Carcinoma* is not uncommon. Occasionally a

growth may be composed almost entirely of mucoid degenerative material with only a few malignant cells. *Squamous Carcinoma* following squamous metaplasia of duct epithelium is rare.

Spread of Carcinoma of the Breast

Carcinoma of the breast may spread locally, by the lymphatics or by the blood stream.

1. *Skin Involvement*

Local invasion may result in fixation of the growth to the skin, the earliest sign of which is 'dimpling'. Dimpling is best demonstrated by elevating the patient's arm to put the elastic ligaments of the breast under tension and then sliding the skin over the swelling. The slightest adherence of the tumour to the skin is shown by tethering and a slight depression of the skin surface. This is a very important physical sign, as it indicates malignancy. Ulceration and fungation through the skin are late, and usually are signs of incurability. Peau d'orange is due to lymphoedema of the skin. The skin swells between its sebaceous and sweat glands, which, being tethered relatively deeply, remain depressed and more obvious than usual. Lymphoedema is a sign of extensive lymphatic obstruction.

Skin nodules are even more sinister. They result from extensive lymphatic permeation in the breast. Hard discrete nodules may arise at a distance from the primary growth.

Carcinoma en cuirasse is rarely seen nowadays. It arises from invasion of subepidermal lymphatics and capillaries. The skin is thickened, hard, infiltrated and discoloured. Ulcers and bossy tumours may appear. It denotes a hopeless outlook from the point of view of local surgery.

2. *Lymphatic Invasion*

The lymphatic drainage of the breast is to the axilla and to the mediastinum. The abdomen and the supraclavicular fossa are not involved directly. In the axilla the lymph nodes are arranged around veins. Four groups are usually described, though they are not clear-cut entities. The *anterior axillary* glands lie under the lower border of pectoralis major along the lateral thoracic vein. The *posterior axillary* nodes lie along the subscapular veins. The *apical* group is sited around the axillary vein as it crosses the first rib, and the *central* glands are scattered in the axillary fat.

Each of these groups can be examined systematically if the arm is first raised, allowing the fingers to be inserted gently into the apex of the axilla. When the arm is lowered to the side the muscles are relaxed and the axilla can be explored without discomfort to the patient.

The mediastinal glands which drain the breast follow the internal mammary vessels and drain mostly the medial quadrants of the breast. If the axillary nodes are involved by a growth in the lateral quadrants of the breast, then it can be expected that in 20% of patients the anterior mediastinal nodes will be involved; if the growth lies medially the internal mammary nodes can be expected to be involved in 60%. The pleura may be invaded by these lymph channels producing an effusion, but the lung is rarely directly involved. The supraclavicular nodes usually become invaded from the mediastinum and very rarely from the axilla.

Lymph node involvement is common. Sixty per cent of patients with carcinoma of the breast have involved glands when they are first seen. Palpation of axillary nodes carried a large observer error. In those judged clinically to be 'gland free' 25% can subsequently be shown to have microscopical involvement of lymph nodes.

Spread of carcinoma in the lymphatic system is mainly by tumour embolism. Lymphatic permeation may occur near to a growth or may be more widespread in late carcinoma.

3. *Blood-borne Spread*

Malignant cells can often be detected in the venous blood draining carcinoma of the breast. Most of such cells are probably destroyed, but some lodge and multiply. Spread to the pelvis and vertebrae is both by the arterial system and the paravertebral venous plexus. Lodgement at the metaphyses of long bones may arise because of the peculiar anatomy of the small arteries near the epiphyses, which are acutely looped.

Occasionally almost every bone in the body may contain metastases. The marrow may be replaced by growth to produce a leucoerythroblastic anaemia. Metastases in liver and lung occur late in the disease.

4. *Involvement of the Other Breast*

Most commonly this is due to the appearance of a second primary growth. Both breasts may be affected simultaneously, more often an interval of years elapses between the occurrence of the two growths. Less often the other breast is involved by spread of growth in lymphatics.

5. *Peritoneal Involvement*

Cystic ovarian metastases and peritoneal carcinomatosis are not uncommon in advanced carcinoma of the breast. The route of invasion is uncertain. Blood-borne spread, retrograde lymphatic spread and transcoelomic transplantion (in which malignant cells reach the peritoneum through the rectus muscle) have all been suggested. Probably all three take place.

Treatment of Carcinoma of the Breast

The treatment of carcinoma of the breast is a subject of continuous controversy. There exist a wide variety of opinions, ranging from those which advocate 'super-radical' surgery to those which maintain that treatment has no effect upon the course of the disease.

1. *Staging*

The most commonly used method of clinical staging divides women with breast cancer into four groups.

> *Stage I.* Growth only, no nodes.
> *Stage II.* Growth plus skin involvement or mobile axillary nodes.
> *Stage III.* Growth involves skin or is fixed to the pectoralis major. Axillary nodes if involved are still mobile.
> *Stage IV.* Widespread metastases.

This method of staging is simple, but does not take into account that in Stage I 25% of women will show axillary node involvement on microscopical examination though the glands were clinically impalpable. Most patients present in Stage II, a stage which includes a wide range of growth of different degrees of development. Growths in Stage II may be very small or very large, few or many axillary lymph nodes may be involved, skin invasion may be slight or have progressed to ulceration. In both Stages I and II internal mammary node involvement may have occurred without clinical sign.

It is very difficult to produce a more accurate system of staging. More complicated systems have been evolved, but their value has not been proved, and they have not been generally accepted.

2. *Surgery*

Opinions vary upon the extent of surgery needed for breast cancer. For many years the merits of radical mastectomy versus local mastectomy in Stages I and II have been argued. More and more it is being appreciated that radical mastectomy confers no extra benefit other than a lower incidence of local recurrence in skin and axillary lymph nodes. Most patients who die of this disease die of the effects of blood-borne metastases which appear clinically in the bones, brain and lungs. Many suspect that in a proportion of women, metastasis has already occurred by the time the patient presents for treatment though there may be no evidence of it. There is no proof that earlier diagnosis leads to a higher rate of cure. More surgeons now perform the minimum operatively, usually local removal of breast and obviously affected nodes. In Stage III if the growth can be removed with a good chance of primary wound healing, then local mastectomy should be performed and followed by radiotherapy.

The operation of radical mastectomy involves removal of the entire breast together with the pectoral muscles and the axillary lymph nodes and fat. In local mastectomy only the breast is removed with any easily accessible axillary lymph nodes. In 'super-radical' surgery dissection of the internal mammary and supraclavicular nodes is added to a conventional radical mastectomy.

3. *Radiotheraphy*

Radiotherapy is given after radical or local mastectomy if the axillary nodes are involved and for palliative treatment to extensive primary breast cancer. An ulcerated growth may heal following radiotherapy and permit simple mastectomy later. It is useful in dealing with secondary nodules in skin and for isolated painful secondary deposits in bone. For those who are unfit for surgery it is the treatment of choice. It is usually given by a 250-kilovolt machine in a dose of 6,000–9,000 rads, given over a period of 3–6 weeks. Radiation is directed particularly to the area of the wound, axilla, mediastinum and supraclavicular fossa.

4. *Endocrine Therapy*

Endocrine therapy is reserved for Stages III and IV, for widespread metastases and also for extensive local invasion, such as ulceration and fixation to deep structures.

Oral administration of *stilboestrol* is preferred for women well after the menopause in doses of 25–50 mg. per day. If stilboestrol has no effect, then an androgen may be tried. Stilboestrol may occasionally induce vaginal bleeding, testosterone may cause masculinisation, deepening of the voice, acne and increased libido. Testosterone has been replaced by synthetic androgens with predominantly anabolic effects. Nandrolone phenyl-propionate (Durabolin) 25–50 mg. weekly I.M. produces the same remission rate as testosterone with less side-effects. The results are very variable and often mainly subjective. Patients who have secondaries only in bone usually respond best.

In premenopausal women with recurrent breast cancer *bilateral oophorectomy* can be expected to produce regression of growths in 30% of cases for an average of 1 year, but occasionally for up to 3 years. It is usual to advise oophorectomy only for recurrent malignant disease and not as prophylaxis. Certainly pregnancy should be avoided, as it may induce recurrence of breast cancer.

Bilateral Total Adrenalectomy (with oophorectomy in premenopausal women) produces regression of recurrent breast cancer in approximately 40–50% of cases. The tumours that regress are said to be 'hormone dependent'. There is as yet no means of detecting which tumours are likely to be improved by adrenalectomy. Bony and cutaneous metastases respond best, brain and hepatic secondaries are less often affected. The remissions produced by adrenalectomy average 15 months, but may extend up to 4–5 years. The cause of relapse is unknown; either the tumour becomes independent of hormones or oestrogens synthesised by some unknown source reactivate it.

Statistically *hypophysectomy* gives slightly better results than adrenalectomy, but it is not so widely used, because the techniques involved are difficult and not always available. Hypophysectomy may be achieved by open operation or by implantation of radio-active yttrium rods into the pituitary through the sphenoidal sinus under direct radiographic control. *Pituitary stalk section* will infarct a large part of the pituitary, but is not often used. Adrenalectomy and hypophysectomy are being performed much less often now than a few years ago, because remissions are unpredictable and often short-lived. Only patients with intractable pain from bony metastases are considered or those who have previously shown a response to endrocrine therapy.

After both adrenalectomy and hypophysectomy lifelong maintenance therapy with cortisone is essential. Thyroxine (0·3 mg. daily) must be given in addition after hypophysectomy.

Patients undergoing adrenalectomy require careful pre- and post-operative attention. The operation is usually undertaken in two stages at an interval of 2–3 weeks. At the first operation bilateral oophorectomy and unilateral adrenalectomy, usually the right, is performed. Before the second adrenalectomy the patient must be given 300–400 mg. of cortisone over a period of 2 days to combat the possibility of postoperative adrenal failure. During and after the operation the blood pressure is measured every quarter of an hour and, if there is a marked fall, then hydrocortisone (100 mg. to the litre of normal saline) is given as fast as required to maintain the blood pressure. Rarely nor-adrenaline (2–8 mg./litre) must be given to keep the blood pressure at a reasonable level.

When the remission produced by adrenalectomy is ending complaints of malaise, tiredness and recurrence of bone pain are usual. Cortisone requirements are usually increased. Rarely does the growth recur in the original sites.

Reports of the use of cortisone alone or with oophorectomy or with cytotoxic drugs indicate that it may sometimes be effective in arresting the course of the disease. Rarely are remissions achieved as dramatic as those produced by adrenalectomy, but this course of treatment may be of use in those unfit for adrenalectomy or for those with extensive hepatic or intracranial metastases.

5. *Cytotoxic Therapy*

Cytotoxic drugs have proved disappointing in the control of breast cancer either as a 'cover' during operation or for metastatic disease.

Results of Treatment

The survival rates after treatment of carcinoma of the breast are summarised below. These figures indicate clearly the more favourable results when lymph nodes are not involved.

In Stage I—75% survival at 5 years
45% survival at 10 years
In Stage II—35% survival at 5 years
20% survival at 10 years

SARCOMA OF THE BREAST

Sarcoma of the breast is very rare. It is a rapidly growing, highly malignant and lethal tumour. Surgery is usually impossible because of advanced disease. Radiotherapy may offer useful palliation.

HYPERPLASTIC CYSTIC DISEASE OF THE BREAST

Definition and Nomenclature

Hyperplastic cystic disease of the breast is a painful nodular condition occurring within the reproductive age period. The histological features are fibrosis, epithelial hyperplasia and, often, cyst formation.

The disease is traditionally known by clinicians as chronic mastitis, a name which suggests an inflammatory cause and was given in the past because mononuclear 'inflammatory' cells were often conspicuous in the affected areas of the breast. Some prefer to call it fibroadenosis—a term that infers no cause but highlights the elements of the condition, fibrosis and glandular hyperplasia. Cyst formation is not invariable, so the term cystic hyperplasia is not always accurate.

Cause

The cause of hyperplastic disease of the breast is unknown, but it is presumed to be due to hormonal imbalance for the following reasons. It is restricted to the reproductive age period. In men and in animals the hyperplastic changes can be induced by the administration of oestrogens. Symptoms and signs are related to the menstrual cycle.

Pathology

Microscopy reveals fibrosis, epithelial hyperplasia and often cyst formation. Epithelial hyperplasia may present as adenosis (formation of new acini) or epitheliosis (proliferation of the duct lining). Cysts may be single or multiple. Lymphocytic infiltration is often prominent.

Symptoms

Women complain of pain and tension in the breasts, especially before periods. Nodules of variable size may appear in the breast, either single or multiple. Less often there may be discharge from the nipple, clear and serous or greenish or brown. Rarely men may be affected. The axillary lymph nodes may become enlarged and tender.

Physical Examination

The whole breast tissue may be firm and nodular, a sign best felt by picking up the breast between the fingers. Palpation with the flat of the hand may reveal no abnormality. Often there are discrete nodules which may be as hard as carcinoma or they may be obviously fluctuant. A tense cyst may be very hard. Hyperplastic disease should not be diagnosed after the menopause if a discrete lump is present in the breast.

Relation to Malignant Disease

It has never been proven that cystic hyperplasia progresses to carcinoma. Both diseases are common and often coexist. Many consider that the intense epitheliosis sometimes seen in hyperplastic disease with prominent intraduct proliferation is premalignant. This condition is rare, and can only be distinguished from carcinoma by absence of infiltration of cells through the basement membrane of the ducts.

Treatment

In most cases of diffuse hyperplastic disease all that is required is the reassurance that there is no growth and a well-supporting brassiere to relieve tension. Severe pain is rare, but when it occurs methyl testosterone is useful, either as an ointment ($\frac{1}{2}$–2%) or taken orally. If testosterone (5–10 mg. three times a day) is given by mouth it must only be taken for a short period, otherwise masculinisation may follow.

If a discrete firm lump is felt this must be excised as a matter of urgency, as carcinoma can only be excluded after histological examination. If a swelling is present there is no place for observation over a period of months. Urgent admission must be arranged for excision-biopsy of the swelling. Occasionally large swellings appear in the breast, often tender and often coincident with a period, which subside rapidly. In such cases of rapid recent onset a short period of observation for 2 or 3 weeks is permissible.

If biopsy shows intense epitheliosis with prominent intraduct proliferation, then local mastectomy should be advised. In all cases of operation for removal of isolated swellings in the breast arrangements should be made for a rapid frozen section to be performed, and the patient must be warned of the possibility of a more extensive operation.

BENIGN TUMOURS

Fibroadenoma

1. *Clinical*

Women who have a fibroadenoma present with a painless firm lump in the breast. There is usually evidence of a diffuse hyperplastic disease in the breasts, suggesting that fibroadenomata result from a hormonal stimulus which has acted upon fibrous tissue more than on glandular tissue.

Fibroadenoma usually occurs in young women from soon after puberty to 30 years, less often in women near the menopause. In the younger age group the tumours are hard and characteristically very mobile, slipping away from the examining fingers. They rarely grow to a large size, and never become malignant.

In older women fibroadenomata tend to be softer and often grow to a large size. Rarely, an enormous tumour may ulcerate through the skin and simulate malignancy. Very rarely these large fibroadenomata become sarcomatous.

2. Pathology

A fibroadenoma is made up of specialised periacinar fibrous tissue and acini. There is a well-defined capsule of compressed fibrous tissue and, because the tumour is under slight tension within its capsule, the cut surface tends to pout slightly and present a convex surface. The cut surface is white and homogeneous unless there is cystic degeneration. Tiny slit-like spaces can often be seen, evidence of dilated acini.

Microscopically there is great proliferation of fibrous tissue, within which there are many acini either compressed into stellate forms (intracanalicular fibroadenoma) or appearing as rounded dilated glands (pericanalicular fibroadenoma). The hard fibroadenoma of young women tends to be pericanalicular, the soft fibroadenoma of older women intracanalicular. However, the different types cannot be clearly separated, as both are often found in the same tumour.

3. Treatment

Treatment is that of any discrete firm lump in the breast. Urgent admission is advised for its excision and immediate histological examination by frozen section if there is doubt about the innocence of the tumour on examination of its cut surface. The tumour is enucleated from its capsule through a periareolar or inframammary incision. Recurrence is rare, though occasionally other tumours may appear elsewhere in the breast.

Duct Papilloma

Duct papilloma causes bleeding from the nipple. This is not a common complaint, but must always be treated seriously. Discharge from the nipple also occurs occasionally in hyperplastic disease if a cyst near the nipple communicates with a duct; such discharge is usually greenish or colourless. A milky discharge sometimes follows lactation, and usually ceases spontaneously unless a cyst (galactocele) is present which requires excision.

A discharge of fresh or altered blood usually comes from a papilloma or an area of intense epitheliosis near the areola. Pressure with the tip of a finger around the edge of the areola produces secretion from one or more of the duct openings on the summit of the nipple. The position of the abnormal ducts should be carefully noted.

Usually there are generalised changes in the breast typical of cystic hyperplasia, and hence it is likely that duct papilloma results from a hormonal stimulus which has produced intense localised epitheliosis rather than fibrosis.

Bleeding from the nipple is a complaint most commonly of young women, in whom it is almost always due to a benign condition. Bleeding from the nipple near the time of the menopause is much more likely to be due to carcinoma, certainly if there is a swelling in the breast. The duct may contain an isolated minute papilloma close to a lactiferous sinus or, more usually, there are several foci of intraduct epithelial proliferation. The true duct papilloma is formed on a stalk of areolar tissue and vessels covered by well-differentiated acinar epithelium.

In the treatment of duct papilloma the segment of breast from which blood can be expressed is localised. Under general anaesthesia a fine probe is passed up the abnormal duct and a small incision is made over it at the edge of the areola. The duct is identified and a segment of breast tissue around it is widely excised and sent for microscopy.

Lipoma

Lipoma of the breast is uncommon but to be expected in an organ mostly composed of fat. It is soft and characteristically lobulated, features which usually suffice to identify it. The tumour is encapsulated and is treated by enucleation.

Other Benign Tumours

Benign tumours of the skin occur on the breast, such as fibroma, haemangioma and melanoma. Local excision for diagnostic or cosmetic reasons may be necessary.

ACUTE INFLAMMATION

Breast Abscess

It is convenient to divide abscess of the breast into pre-, intra- and retro-mammary types. By far the commonest is the intramammary.

1. *Premammary Abscess*

Premammary abscess usually arises from infection of a sebaceous follicle (Montgomery tubercle) near the areola. Spontaneous discharge of pus is usual, but incision of a subcutaneous abscess may be necessary. Incision of a premammary abscess may rarely be followed by a persistent purulent discharge from a 'mammilliferous fistula'. Such a fistula communicates with a lactiferous duct, and hence with the nipple. Histology of the nipple shows squamous metaplasia of the epithelium of all or of several of the ducts. Treatment is as for fistula in ano, laying open of all the tracks into the nipple and allowing healing by granulation.

2. *Intramammary Abscess*

Abscess of the breast is a common complication of the puerperium. It is almost always associated with depressed, malformed and cracked nipples.

In the nulliparous woman abscess of the breast is a complication of depressed nipples. The infection is due to the *Staphylococcus aureus*, which produces cellulitis in the areolar tissue around the ducts, almost always going on to suppuration. The breast is first engorged and tender from difficulty in suckling. A firm tender area appears which becomes exquisitely painful and tense. If treatment is delayed fluctuation can be elicited. Fever and malaise are almost always associated.

Engorged breasts should be emptied by gentle manual expression. In most cases breast feeding must be abandoned because the nipples are malformed and because there is a risk of infecting the baby. If cellulitis is established tetracycline should be given (the majority of puerperal staphylococcal infections are resistant to penicillin, especially in hospital). Breast feeding is stopped and stilboestrol (5 mg. three times a day) is given. The breasts are manually expressed if and when they become tense.

If pus forms, as judged by the development of tension in the inflamed area, incision should be performed under general anaesthesia. A radial incision is made large enough to admit a finger. Because the abscess is usually loculated, it is essential to break down any septa with the finger; a drain should be inserted. Failure of rapid healing is usually due to inadequate incision. In such cases admission to hospital is necessary for further incision, rest and chemotherapy.

3. *Retromammary Abscess*

This is rare and is due to a breast abscess bursting through the posterior fascia, osteomyelitis of a rib complicated by a sub-periosteal abscess pointing through the breast, infection of a traumatic retromammary haematoma or from an empyema of the chest. Occasionally, tuberculous infection of a rib, cartilage or extra-pleural glands may flare up and present as an acute abscess near a costochondral junction. Treatment entails drainage of the abscess, identification of the cause and, later, treatment of the primary focus.

Non-Pyogenic Acute Mastitis

1. *Mastitis of the Newborn*

The breast of a newborn child may become red, hot and inflamed. This condition is thought to be due to the stimulus of maternal hormones upon the child's breast. Spontaneous resolution is usual, and no treatment is required. Rarely, secondary infection occurs, when an abscess may arise.

2. *Mastitis of Puberty*

In adolescent and pre-adolescent children, both boys and girls, one or both breasts may become tender and painful. A disc-like nodule forms deep to the nipple and represents the entire breast tissue. There may be asymmetrical breast enlargement. It is unlikely that irritation from straps or braces can play any part in its cause. Resolution is usual after 3–6 months, and no treatment is necessary other than reassuring the parents. The breasts later develop symmetrically and normally.

3. *Plasma-cell Mastitis*

Rarely, in postmenopausal women, a painful lump rapidly forms in the breast. The nipple is often retracted, and carcinoma is closely simulated. The condition is thought to be due to dilatation of mammary ducts, which fill with stagnant secretion. Rupture of one of these ducts provokes an intense plasma and giant-cell reaction. Biopsy and examination by frozen section is indicated to exclude carcinoma. Rarely a mammilliferous fistula is caused by plasma-cell mastitis.

Chronic Inflammation

1. *Unresolved Pyogenic Infection*

Slow healing, induration and purulent discharge may follow inadequate incision of a breast abscess. Hospitalisation, antibiotics and further incision suffice to clear up the infection. Biopsy should be performed at the time of incision to exclude carcinoma or tuberculosis.

2. *Fat Necrosis*

A hard lump may appear in the breast which may be indistinguishable from carcinoma. In only 40% of cases is there a clear history of trauma. Necrosis is usually an affection of the subcutaneous fat, and so skin fixation is a feature. Microscopy shows necrotic fat infiltrated with chronic inflammatory cells, including mononuclears, plasma cells and foamy macrophages full of fat. Syncytial giant cells are often present. Cyst formation and fibrosis may occur. Some lesions resolve spontaneously and some form large cysts. All should be treated as possibly malignant and examined histologically.

3. *Tuberculosis*

This is a rare infection of the breast, and usually arises from a retromammary abscess (*q.v.*). Treatment entails drainage of the abscess; the primary focus should be excised later and a prolonged course of tuberculostatic drugs administered.

Malformations

1. *Supernumerary Nipples*

These may be found anywhere along the 'milk line' from the axilla to the groin. They are very common, but are rarely affected by disease.

2. *Supernumerary Breast*

A rare occurrence. There may be a well-formed breast situated in the milk line or merely an area of breast tissue which may become apparent because of inflammation, cyst formation or growth.

3. *Hypertrophy*

Massive enlargement of one or both breasts may occur in young women. Reduction of the size of the breasts may be necessary by plastic surgery.

4. *Gynecomastia*

Enlargement of one or both breasts in young men may cause embarrassment. Gynecomastia is also common in older men taking stilboestrol for prostatic cancer, but in them treatment is unnecessary. It is occasionally seen complicating cirrhosis and chorionepithelioma of the testis. Treatment of gynecomastia for cosmetic reasons or to exclude carcinoma entails excision of the breast tissue through a periareolar incision with preservation of the nipple.

FURTHER READING

Cutler, M. (1961) *Tumours of the Breast.* Pitman, London.

Moyer, C. A., Rhoads, J. E., Allen, J. G., and Harkins, H. N. (1965) *Surgery, Principles and Practice*, Ch. 25, 3rd ed., Pitman, London.

Forrest, A. P. M. (1969) Carcinoma of the breast in *Recent Advances in Surgery*, 7th ed., J. & A. Churchill, London.

CHAPTER SIXTEEN

DISEASES OF THE CHEST

THORAX

In no branch of surgery in the last 25 years have there been such striking advances as in the thorax. This period has witnessed the introduction of partial and complete lung resection, excision and reconstruction of the oesophagus, and most spectacular of all, operations on every part of the heart with that organ cooled, by-passed or arrested. The stimulus for this particular progress probably came from the necessity of treating a large number of chest wounds during the Second World War, combined with the introduction of positive pressure anaesthesia using muscle relaxants, the establishment of blood banks and the use of antibiotics, especially penicillin. Yet even during this 25 years in Britain the pattern of chest surgery has completely changed, whereas originally most operations were for tuberculosis, later the accent was on the treatment of lung cancer, while more recently a great amount of time has been spent in dealing with heart lesions.

RESPIRATORY SYSTEM

Symptoms and Signs of Lung Disease

These are dealt with thoroughly in Chapter Five of the companion volume, *A Short Textbook of Medicine*, and that chapter can be read with advantage in conjunction with this one.

Anatomy of the Bronchial Tree

A proper knowledge of the anatomy of the bronchial tree is essential, in both the diagnosis and treatment of chest conditions, in understanding how infection and malignancy will spread, and for the proper planning of any operation on the lungs. Reference to the diagrams (Fig. 14) will best illustrate this anatomy; the names of the various segments should be memorised. The trachea, main bronchi and lobar divisions are usually examined by means of a bronchoscope, but visualisation of smaller bronchi (bronchography) is carried out by instilling iodised oil into the bronchial tree, either after puncture of the crico-thyroid membrane or after nasopharyngeal installation, and then positioning the patient so that the required part of the lung is filled with radiopaque contrast medium. Radiographs are then taken in two planes, and obstruction, narrowing or dilatation of the bronchi can be seen.

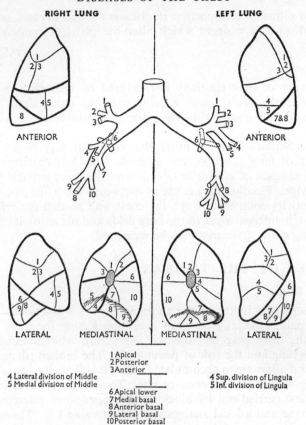

FIG. 14. Anatomy of the bronchial tree and segmental anatomy of the lungs

Tests of Respiratory Function

These tests are most important in the clinical assessment of a patient before lung surgery is undertaken. A full account can be found in Chapter Five of *A Short Textbook of Medicine*.

Blood Gas Analysis

This offers a direct assessment of the efficiency of intake of oxygen and output of carbon dioxide by the lungs. The normal partial pressure of alveolar carbon dioxide, pCO_2 is 40 mm. of mercury and the partial pressure of alveolar oxygen pO_2, 100 mm. of mercury. These estimations are made using samples of arterial blood.

Diffusion

Diffusion of gases across the membrane separating alveolus and capillary can be determined by using carbon monoxide and estimating how quickly and in what concentration it is taken up in the blood stream. This measure of diffusion is important in diseases such as fibrosis, sarcoidosis, carcinomatosis and oedema which alter the physical properties of the membrane.

Compliance

Compliance or lung elasticity is measured by recording the negative intrathoracic pressure through a catheter in the oesophagus during inspiration and at the same time recording the volume of air which is inspired.

Other techniques are even more elaborate, but may be useful in the assessment of lung function, for example *bronchospirometry*, in which individual samples of air are obtained from the main bronchi through a bronchoscope. Finally, there is use of *radio-active labelled gas*, which can have its activity counted through the chest wall so that the relative concentrations in different areas of the lung fields and the amount of exchange of gas going on in these areas can be measured.

INJURIES OF THE THORAX

Fractured Ribs

The commonest injury of the thoracic cage is a fractured rib, which produces pain, especially on deep breathing lasting for days or weeks. As a result, there may be impaired ventilation with atelectasis of the underlying lung and the risk of pneumonia. The broken rib may damage the lung and allow air to accumulate in the pleural cavity—*pneumothorax*, if bleeding occurs *haemothorax* results. Treatment is the relief of pain, which is best carried out by blocking the appropriate intercostal nerves with urethane and a local analgesic, e.g. lignocaine 1%. The application of adhesive strapping of the non-stretch variety gives the patient a feeling of security. All chest injuries must be radiographed. Often rib fractures cannot be seen, but signs of underlying damage may be revealed. If there is any evidence of lung contusion, or air or fluid in the pleural cavity, the patient must be admitted to hospital. Rib fractures in the bronchitic and elderly are especially dangerous in often being followed by pneumonia.

Crush Injuries

Multiple fractures of ribs and crush injuries of the thorax usually occur as a result of road and industrial accidents. The problems they present are either due to instability of the chest wall, and therefore difficulty in respiration, or as a result of local injuries caused by the broken ribs. When a number of ribs are doubly fractured and a segment of the chest wall cannot be used in respiration it is usually referred to as a *flail chest*. The injured part of the chest wall moves in the opposite direction to that which is engaged in active respiration, so-called *paradoxical movement*. Paradoxical movement is very serious. If it is allowed to continue anoxia increases, because air in the lung beneath the fractured ribs becomes progressively de-oxygenated as it oscillates to and fro over the tracheal bifurcation without being replenished by inspired air—*pendulum movement*. In addition, the mediastinal pleura is pushed away from the injuredside and the tension on it causes severe pain, distress and signs of shock. The emergency treatment is immobilisation of the flail segment, by a firm pad strapped into position by adhesive strapping. Tracheostomy is often necessary to reduce the dead space and it may also be necessary to use a respirator.

If the ventilatory capacity of the individual is not sufficiently improved by these measures the chest wall must be fixed. Some kind of traction, either by pins or wire around individual ribs, is attached to a light spring or weight so that the ribs are held out in a reasonable position while the patient is still able to move in bed and also use the remainder of the chest wall. Where fractured ribs need to be fixed this can be done with small pegs pushed into the intramedullary cavity, or by wire.

The likeliest complication of fractured ribs is injury to the pleura so that air enters the pleural cavity. If the opening is valvular a *tension pneumothorax* results, with increasing embarrassment to breathing, a condition which requires urgent relief; this is provided by a polyethylene catheter threaded through a cannula inserted between the third or fourth intercostal space anteriorly. The needle is then withdrawn, leaving the catheter in place, and this is then attached to an under-water seal. Alternatively, intermittent aspiration of the air with a syringe may be sufficient. If the rough end of the fractured rib allows air to enter the subcutaneous tissues *surgical emphysema* occurs, and can be felt as a crackling under the fingers. The air is usually absorbed without special treatment, but may spread widely. A fractured rib may lacerate the lung, which bleeds, and then there is not only a pneumothorax but also a *haemothorax*. The combination of air and fluid produces physical signs of dullness below and hyper-resonance above the fluid level. Under these circumstances the blood and air must be aspirated and an antibiotic given to prevent spread of infection. Breathing exercises assist expansion of the lung and help the patient regain normal chest function. Pain is relieved by *small* doses of morphia, insufficient to depress respiration, supplemented when necessary by intercostal nerve block.

Whenever there are extensive wounds of the thorax the possibility of damage to abdominal organs should not be forgotten, for a rib may transfix the diaphragm and lacerate liver, stomach, bowel and spleen. The chest symptoms and signs may mask those of *peritonitis*, which may advance insidiously and be fatal. Sometimes injury to the diaphragm results in herniation of abdominal contents into the chest months or years after the original injury, and the possibility of a *traumatic diaphragmatic hernia* must not be overlooked.

Traumatic Asphyxia

This is seen in severe crushing injuries of the chest when, because of a sudden increase in venous pressure, intense cyanosis and petechial haemorrhages appear in the skin of the head and neck, the upper limbs and over the chest wall to a variable extent. The lower level of the cyanosis is often sharply delineated. Subconjunctival haemorrhages are usually present. Rib fractures and serious contusion of the lung may be associated, but often no bony injuries are found and the patient is remarkably well, despite his bizarre appearance. The cyanosis rapidly fades, leaving the petechiae and bruises that disappear over a period of days. Treatment is not usually required, only if there are associated bony or lung injuries

(See p. 224 for injuries of the heart and pericardium.)

THE RIBS

Pectus excavatum

Funnel chest is a deformity in which the sternum is depressed and the adjacent ribs turn acutely in towards the midline. There is often an associated spinal deformity, a rounded kyphosis. The condition is present at birth but may become more severe as the child grows, leading occasionally to shortness of breath, because the volume of the lungs is restricted. A depressed sternum may also produce abnormal heart sounds, which may be mistaken for valvular disease. Minor degrees of this deformity require no treatment, but if it is severe small anterior segments of ribs are excised, near their junction with the cartilages, and the whole sternum elevated and held by a special metal bridge until it re-unites with the ribs. The cosmetic improvement is great, and respiratory function may be correspondingly enhanced.

Rib Tumours

Primary tumours of ribs are uncommon, and are often discovered only when radiographs are taken of the chest. Bony *exostoses* and *chondromas* are the commonest and, unless they increase in size or cause symptoms by pressure, may be left alone so long as the diagnosis is certain. Ribs, like all flat bones, are frequently the site of *secondary deposits* from a primary malignant tumour elsewhere in the body, the commonest primary site being the breast in women and the lung in men. The resultant destruction of bone may lead to a pathological fracture. Myelomatosis is a disease of the bone marrow (see p. 509). Primary malignant tumours of the rib are rare, but include *osteosarcoma* and *chondrosarcoma*.

Abscesses

A fluctuant swelling in the line of a rib is commonly due to tuberculous disease, the infection having tracked forward from an infected lymph node deep to a rib. Caseous pus follows the neurovascular bundle immediately under the rib, and may track a long way, even pointing at the sternal edge. Rarely the infection tracks forward from tuberculous disease of the thoracic spine. Once the diagnosis of tuberculosis has been made by examining pus, aspirated through a wide-bore needle, systemic treatment is started with streptomycin, P.A.S. and iso-niazid; the track may later be excised together with any dead tissue. A chronic empyema may eventually point between two ribs on the chest wall and discharge. This may follow any chronic infection of the lung or pleura. Tuberculosis, bronchiectasis, lung abscess, carcinoma blocking a bronchus or actinomycosis when infecting the lung may rarely present in this way; more often a sinus from the pleural cavity becomes chronic as a complication of thoracic surgery.

TRACHEOSTOMY

A tracheostomy is a temporary opening, usually made in the third or fourth cartilaginous rings of the trachea, through which the patient can breathe. Its obvious use is to relieve laryngeal obstruction, but during the last ten years it has acquired many uses other than by-passing an obstructed air-way. Its popularity dates from the great epidemics of poliomyelitis after the Second World War and the development of positive-pressure respirators. Briefly its advantages are as follows:

1. Relief of obstruction to the upper air-way.
2. Decrease of the dead space by 30–50%, with a corresponding increase in the respiratory efficiency.
3. Decrease in the air-way resistance due to the size of the air-way and by-passing the glottis.
4. Access to the bronchial tree.
5. The sucking out of secretion and occasionally the instillation of an anaesthetic or drug.
6. The insertion of a cuffed tracheostomy tube for the application of positive-pressure respiration.

Some of the indications for tracheostomy are listed in the table below:

Brain damage	Coma
	Cerebral haemorrhage
	Head injuries
	Barbiturate overdosage
Damage to motor nerve and end-plate	Poliomyelitis
	Cord lesions
	Muscular relaxants
	Myasthenia gravis
	Polyneuritis
	Tetanus
Bone and muscle damage	Fractured ribs
	Flail chest
Damage to air-way and lung	Carcinoma of larynx
	Carcinoma of thyroid
	Bronchitis and emphysema
	'Wet lungs'
	Postoperative pulmonary insufficiency
	Faciomaxillary injuries

If possible the trachea should be intubated before the operation, which can then be performed in the operating theatre in a good light and without hurry. Obviously in cases of urgency the operation must be performed on the spot with instruments that are available and without care for sterility.

A transverse or longitudinal incision is made through the skin in the midline. The strap muscles are separated to expose the thyroid isthmus, which is divided between two artery forceps. a U-incision is made in the cartilage of the third and fourth rings of the trachea and a small segment raised to leave an oval opening. At this the patient may cough uncontrollably and make for difficulty in insertion of the tracheostomy tube. If time permits a small volume, 1 ml., of lignocaine 4% injected into the trachea abolishes the coughing. A second difficulty is the venous congestion and cyanosis caused by respiratory distress. Usually a Durham's tracheostomy tube is inserted with the aid of its 'lobster tail' introducer. The introducer is replaced by an inner tube that can be easily cleaned without removal of the outer tube. A useful point of technique is to raise a small flap in the anterior tracheal wall, hinged below and stitched to the skin edge. By this means it is possible to slide the tube easily into the trachea and not have it slip anteriorly; the opening closes quickly if the tube is removed. The skin incision should not be sutured, but left to granulate. The tube is fastened to the neck by a tape.

The air should be humidified, since it no longer passes through the warm moist upper-air passages. A sucker and fine catheter should be available at the bedside to remove secretions which cannot be coughed up by the patient. Plastic cuffed tubes can be used where there is a danger of spillover of oesophageal contents. The pressure in the cuff should be released at regular intervals. When it is judged safe to remove the tube the effect of corking the opening should be tried. If no distress follows, then the tube may be removed. The fistula closes rapidly so long as the tracheostomy has only been established for a few days.

The main disadvantage of tracheostomy is that the indwelling tube may cause stenosis. If a cuffed tube is used, the cuff must be deflated every few hours.

PLEURA

The outer or parietal layer of pleura is separated from the inner or visceral by a small amount of fluid. An increase in this fluid is called a pleural effusion; the pleural space may also be filled by air, pus or blood.

Pneumothorax

The introduction of air into the pleural cavity by a needle was formerly often used in treating pulmonary tuberculosis in order to collapse the underlying lung. A pneumothorax may occur spontaneously from rupture of an emphysematous bulla or lung cyst. Tuberculosis and also a fractured rib may lead to pneumothorax. If the breathing is embarrassed the air should be aspirated, and if it continues to collect a fine plastic catheter is introduced and attached to a suction system. Pneumothorax due to underlying emphysematous bullae may be treated by *pleurodesis*, carried out by introducing a little talc or silver nitrate into the pleural cavity, which fuses the two layers by fibrosis. Lung cysts, if solitary and large, may be removed at thoracotomy.

Haemothorax

The commonest cause of a haemothorax is a fractured rib damaging the underlying lung. Following operations on the chest, haemothorax may also occur. Other causes are neoplasms of lung or pleura and a leaking aneurysm. Spontaneous pneumothorax may be associated with bleeding. Due to the movement of the lungs and heart, the blood is defibrinated and stays fluid for many days. Irritation of the pleura causes pain and the lung is pressed on. If left the blood eventually clots, leaving a layer of fibrin, like sugar icing, on the lung. This prevents full expansion.

The treatment of haemothorax is aspiration of the blood, which may have to be repeated. If infection occurs it is treated by a suitable antibiotic, and if the blood clots it can be liquefied by introducing the enzyme streptokinase in a dose of 200,000 units and then aspirating after 24 hours. Once the fibrin deposit has formed, decortication of the lung is necessary, an operation at which a thick layer of fibrous tissue is stripped off the lung so that it can re-expand.

Empyema

Pyothorax is commonly called an empyema, i.e. a collection of pus in the pleural cavity. This results from infection in the underlying lung due to pneumonia and lung abscess. Carcinoma, tuberculosis, bronchiectasis, foreign body, injuries or infections of the ribs, following chest operations and from perforations of the oesophagus or hollow viscera below the diaphragm are all important causes now that lung infection can be cured by antibiotics. Empyema due to pneumonia is now a rarity, so an underlying cause must always be looked for. The pus is often localised and the empyema then described as *basal, apical, mediastinal, diaphragmatic, interlobar* or *encysted*. A *total* empyema is rare and associated with collapse of the lung. The infecting organisms in order of frequency are: pneumococcus, streptococcus, staphylococcus, tubercle bacillus. The diagnosis is confirmed by aspirating pus with a needle and culturing it.

Treatment

Most empyemas respond to repeated aspiration of the pus with a needle and syringe and the use of an appropriate antibiotic, intrapleurally and systemically. Drainage is necessary if the pus cannot be aspirated completely and increases in amount. So long as there are dense adhesions between lung and chest wall, it is safe to drain the abscess cavity. Streptococcal pus is thin and forms adhesions late—therefore it should be aspirated daily and the empyema not drained until on standing the pus is three parts solid; too early drainage may cause total empyema, lung collapse and overwhelming infection.

The site of the empyema is first determined radiographically. The patient is sat up and, under local or general anaesthetic, about 2 inches of a rib overlying the lowest part of the empyema is excised. A finger is introduced to break down adhesions between loculi, pus is mopped out and a large drainage tube sewn in place and connected to an underwater-seal drainage bottle. A biopsy of the pleura is usually performed. Often bronchoscopy is indicated to exclude a bronchial cause. The appropriate antibiotic is given and breathing exercises vigorously encouraged to help to expand the lung, obliterate the abscess cavity and prevent deformity of the chest and spine. The tube is removed when drainage ceases, and when a sinogram shows the cavity is obliterated. Some empyemas become sterile with antibiotics, but do not absorb. It is then necessary to excise the empyema as a sac of pus at the same time decorticating the surface of the lung.

BRONCHI

Foreign Bodies

Nuts, bones, teeth and all manner of strange foreign bodies can be inhaled into the air passages, where they may cause wheezing, cyanosis and cough. A bronchus may be blocked, producing atelectasis and a lung abscess. Even if the object is not radiopaque, the site of the segments of collapsed lung as shown in radiographs may reveal its position. Sometimes the appearance of compensatory emphysema in the unobstructed segments of the lung may be more obvious in a radiograph than the signs of collapse.

Treatment

Bronchoscopy under general anaesthesia allows many foreign bodies to be removed and may allow drainage of an abscess. Rarely is drainage of an abscess through the chest wall required. A peripherally sited foreign body may cause a chronic abscess that may only be treatable by excision of part of the lung. Such radical treatment is usually only necessary where the foreign body lies so far down the bronchial tree as to be inaccessible to the bronchoscope.

Bronchiectasis

Dilatation of the bronchial tree, either in a fusiform or saccular pattern may occur as a congenital abnormality and then become secondarily infected. More commonly, dilatation of the bronchi is secondary to collapse followed by infection of segments of the lung, especially after measles or whooping cough in childhood. Now that antibiotics are so commonly effective in the treatment of chest infection in childhood, bronchiectasis is becoming rare. Upper-respiratory-tract infection, especially sinusitis, is commonly associated with bronchiectasis, and may cause recurrence of disease after surgical treatment. Bronchiectasis may also be secondary to tuberculosis, carcinoma of the lung or a foreign body. In some children the entire respiratory tract from the para-nasal sinuses to the bronchi appears to secrete an excessive amount of mucus, infection is common, and in such cases recurrence of bronchiectasis even after surgical treatment is likely.

Symptoms and Signs

Usually there is a cough which may be paroxysmal, producing copious foul sputum. Occasionally the condition presents as haemoptysis with no history of a cough—dry bronchiectasis. Fever and malaise with toxaemia and often malnutrition and stunting of growth occurs. There may be loss of resonance over the affected lung segments and moist sounds in the chest. The fingers may be clubbed, a condition called pulmonary osteoarthropathy. The most serious complication is a cerebral abscess, other complications are haemoptysis, pleurisy, empyema and recurrent pneumonia.

Diagnosis

Bronchography shows dilatation of the bronchi, usually of the basal segments. Often the lingula and middle lobe are affected.

Treatment

Postural drainage is the mainstay of treatment, especially when several lung segments or lobes are affected. The patient is tipped head down for an increasing time each day in a position that drains the affected bronchi. He is helped to expectorate sputum by the physiotherapist, who also instructs in breathing exercises. If the disease is confined to a segment or a lobe, *segmental resection* or lobectomy is carried out after a full course of chemotherapy and postural drainage so that the lungs are as dry as possible. Any cause that can be discovered is treated before operation, such as infected paranasal sinuses. Long convalescence away from town air is part of the treatment. Surgery for bronchiectasis is not often necessary nowadays, it is mostly treated by postural drainage and antibiotics.

Carcinoma of the Bronchus

Deaths due to lung cancer have increased far more than those due to any other malignant disease during the last 25 years. At the present time almost 30,000 deaths a year occur in England and Wales due to carcinoma of the bronchus, in a population of about 50 million. It is almost ten times as common in men as women, and reaches a peak of incidence during the fifth decade. Heavy cigarette smoking over many years predisposes to its development, and workers in the chromate industry also show a high incidence of lung cancer.

Pathology

The disease usually arises in the bronchial mucosa of one of the main or segmental bronchi, rarely does it arise in the periphery of the lung or in the alveoli. The histological types are squamous (56%), adenocarcinoma (11%), undifferentiated (28%) and oat-cell (5%) (London Chest Hospital). Spread occurs by lymphatics and by the blood stream, especially to bones, brain and liver. Bronchi become obstructed, causing atelectasis and abscess formation beyond the obstruction. If the pleura is involved an effusion (often bloodstained) or empyema may result. The recurrent laryngeal and phrenic nerves may become paralysed. Ribs and vertebrae may be eroded and the oesophagus involved.

Symptoms and Signs

Cough, haemoptysis and dyspnoea occurring in a middle-aged male should suggest carcinoma of the bronchus. Recurrent or unresolved pneumonia, empyema and laryngeal palsy, bone pain and brachial neuritis may also be presenting features. Rarely peripheral neuritis or even a Cushing's syndrome may occur. An enlarged lymph node in the neck, axilla or groin, a pathological fracture or cerebral metastasis may be the first evidence of the disease.

Diagnosis

The early diagnosis of carcinoma of the lung is made by radiography of the chest, and thus mass-radiography is particularly useful. The tumour may be mediastinal or peripheral, the latter usually having a better prognosis. Bronchoscopy may show widening of the carina at the bifurcation of the two main bronchi because of enlarged sub-carinal lymph nodes; if the growth is seen in a bronchus a biopsy is taken. An involved lymph node may be available for biopsy, especially in the supra-clavicular region. Malignant cells may be seen in sputum or a pleural effusion.

Treatment

Treatment is wide removal of the tumour with surrounding healthy lung and any affected lymph nodes.

Lobectomy may suffice, but *pneumonectomy* may be required. Approximately three out of four patients are unsuitable for surgery when first seen because of widespread local disease, distant metastases or poor respiratory reserve. Of those explored four out of five are suitable for excision. A 5-year survival rate of about 25% of those resected is usual. An intensive course of radiotherapy may make an otherwise inoperable tumour amenable to resection. Radiotherapy also plays a useful part in the palliative treatment of lung cancer, either teletherapy or insertion of radio-active gold grains into the tumour via a bronchoscope.

LUNGS

Tuberculosis

Until 20 years ago pulmonary tuberculosis was one of the most serious diseases afflicting mankind, but since the introduction of adequate chemotherapy the whole picture has altered, and certainly in Great Britain and North America the disease is becoming rare. However, it is still extremely prevalent in many parts of the world, being aided by poor living conditions, under-nutrition and lack of facilities for diagnosis and control. Immigrants to Britain from India, Pakistan and the West Indies are often found suffering from tuberculosis and present a serious problem in the control of the disease.

Pathology

A small pneumonic lesion, the primary lesion or Ghon focus, may occur in any part of the lungs. Lymphatic spread follows and the local lymph nodes enlarge. The radiographic appearances of a small shadow and hilar adenopathy is called a *primary complex*. There is little upset in health, and in most people healing takes place, with fibrosis and calcification. Sometimes, however, the lung lesion increases in size and spreads through the lobe, where it may cavitate. There may be an accompanying pleural effusion. The hilar nodes may in children compress a bronchus and cause segmental collapse, which radiographically produces a 'hilar flare'. A lymph node may caseate and, rupturing into a bronchus, cause widespread tuberculous bronchopneumonia. Blood spread produces multiple small lesions throughout the body—miliary tuberculosis.

Secondary infection with tuberculosis occurs at any time, most often in the upper lobes. There is infiltration often with central caseation. The sputum may contain tubercle bacilli, and blood may be present from erosion of blood vessels—haemoptysis. The rate of progress is variable, but is usually slow, with, in some, spontaneous arrest by fibrosis and calcification. The disease may be active and yet not progress for years, though flares of increased activity are possible at any time. A persistent cavity is always a danger, especially if tubercle bacilli persist in the sputum. The elderly bronchitic who has perhaps for years had tuberculosis may appear well and yet infect children or adults by droplet infection.

Treatment

The general principles of treatment are rest, which may be local for the affected part, and general for the individual as a whole. Good food, fresh air and chemotherapy are essential. Pus when it forms must be drained. Excision of diseased lung segments is rarely needed nowadays because chemotherapy is so effective. Collapse therapy in the form of an artificial pneumothorax, pneumoperitoneum and phrenic nerve crush are seldom used now.

Chemotherapy

The three main tuberculostatic drugs are usually used simultaneously. Streptomycin is injected in ½-g. doses twice a day, or 1 g. may be given each day. In any case it is important to determine first that renal function is good, or dangerously high levels will occur in the blood stream followed by damage to the eighth nerve with deafness or vertigo. Para-amino-salicylic acid (P.A.S.) is often given in cachets, and 15–20 g. are swallowed daily. Iso-nicotinic acid hydrazide (I.N.A.H.) up to 400 mg. daily are given by mouth. In a course of treatment up to a total of 60–70 g. of streptomycin is given with P.A.S. and I.N.A.H. The latter two drugs are administered alone for 18 months. Newer drugs are always being introduced as some tubercle bacilli become resistant to the therapy, but none has proved equal to the original three 'main line' drugs.

Operation

This is never contemplated until 6 or more months after beginning chemotherapy, and then is only used for lesions where residual disease or scars are considered to be unstable or where medical treatment has failed to control the disease completely, especially when the sputum persistently contains tubercle bacilli. Thus, lobes already completely destroyed, abscesses, tuberculomata and bronchiectatic lesions are all suitable for resection. The lesion should show radiographic evidence of healing, such as fibrosis and calcification. The general condition of the patient should be satisfactory, and there should be no fever and the E.S.R. should be normal. The removal of a segment or a lobe of a lung may be carried out. Thoracoplasty, that is the removal of a series of ribs to collapse the underlying lung, may be necessary for long-standing fibrocaseous disease of the upper lobe.

Lung Abscess

The commonest cause of lung abscess is inhalation of infected material, including vomit, blood or a foreign body, which first results in an 'inhalation' or 'aspiration' pneumonia. Occasionally carcinoma of the bronchus causes atelectasis, which goes on to abscess formation, rarely multiple abscesses may follow blood-stream infection due to pyaemia. Pneumonia and bronchiectasis may be complicated by abscess formation. Carcinoma of the oesophagus may involve the lung and there form an abscess. Solitary abscesses are commoner on the right and in the lower lobe.

Symptoms and Signs

The patient has a high swinging temperature, radiography reveals an opacity which may show a fluid level and there are physical signs of local consolidation. The abscess may erupt into a bronchus and be coughed up as foul-smelling pus, or very rarely point and discharge through the chest wall, *empyema necessitatis*. Chemotherapy is started, antibiotic being chosen according to the organisms found in the sputum. Intensive breathing exercises and posturing to drain the abscess are encouraged, and bronchoscopy can be carried out to remove a foreign body or find the underlying cause such as a carcinoma.

The majority of lung abscesses resolve with chemotherapy. External drainage is rarely needed nowadays, and in any case is dangerous owing to the risk of secondary haemorrhage and empyema. Cerebral abscess is a complication of lung suppuration. Incomplete resolution is best treated by lobectomy.

Hydatid Cyst

Hydatid disease is rare in the British Isles except for south Wales, but is commonly seen in the Middle East and Australia, New Zealand and South America, especially where sheep, dogs and humans are found in close proximity. The disease is due to infestation by the cystic stage of *taenia echinococcus* (see p. 70). The worm lives in the intestine of a dog, and the ova are excreted in the faeces, to be swallowed by the intermediate host, which is commonly a sheep but may rarely be man.

Symptoms and Signs

Hydatid cysts in the lungs often produce no symptoms, but when they enlarge there may be cough and haemoptysis. The cyst may rupture into a bronchus and the contents be coughed up ('grape-skin' sputum). Long-standing cysts may become calcified. Diagnosis is assisted by finding an eosinophilia and a positive Casoni intradermal test.

Treatment

At thoracotomy the cyst is carefully shelled out without rupture, formalin having first been injected to kill the daughter cysts within. Alternatively, lobectomy may be preferred in order to remove the lesion intact. Any spillage is likely to be followed by the growth of more cysts.

THE DIAPHRAGM

Congenital Hernial Openings

Occasionally the diaphragm fails to develop properly during foetal life and is replaced by a thin fibrous sheet, lying high in the chest. Failure of diaphragmatic descent (eventration) is usually only recognised at radiography, since it does not produce symptoms. The stomach may herniate through the oesophagal opening (hiatus hernia) soon after birth, and symptoms of reflux of gastric contents into the oesophagus occur.

There is usually marked oesophagitis, with loss of blood and pronounced anaemia. There is often continuous dribbling from the mouth, regurgitation of feeds and a failure to gain weight. All the symptoms are relieved by sitting the baby up in a so-called sentry box.

Occasionally part of the diaphragm fails to develop, usually postero-laterally and more often on the left side, the foramen of Bochdalek. Abdominal contents herniate through the opening in foetal life, the lung does not expand and the baby is distressed and cyanotic at birth, with displacement of the heart to the right. Rarely an opening persists immediately behind the sternum, the foramen of Morgagni, through which the colon may herniate.

Trauma

As a result of trauma, the diaphragm may be split or weakened and abdominal organs herniate through it at any time after an injury, from hours to many years. Hiatus hernia of adults is described below.

THE OESOPHAGUS

Dysphagia is a cardinal symptom of all oesophageal disorders. A barium-swallow examination and oesophagoscopy (which must be carried out under general anaesthesia and is not without risk) are the essential investigations. In a newborn infant a cyanotic attack, especially when the baby is being fed, should indicate a diagnosis of atresia of the oesophagus until proved otherwise (see Chapter Twenty-eight).

Reflux Oesophagitis

Painful dysphagia or heartburn is usually due to the reflux of gastric juice into the oesophagus. It is often associated with a hiatus hernia, but not necessarily so.

Symptoms and Signs

Heartburn, waterbrash, pain, dysphagia and anaemia are the presenting features. The patient is often overweight, usually over 40 and complains of most discomfort when stooping down and when lying flat in bed at night. The differential diagnosis lies between peptic ulcer, gall-bladder disease, pancreatitis and ischaemia of the myocardium. It is surprising how often pain due to oesophagitis, cholelithiasis and angina are associated in the same patient, and the presence of any one of these makes it necessary to investigate the possibility of the other two. The treatment of reflux oesophagitis will be considered jointly with that of hiatus hernia below.

Hiatus Hernia (Fig. 15)

Herniation of the stomach through the oesophageal hiatus in the diaphragm is typically seen at the extremes of life. In young babies it may be associated with what appears to be a short oesophagus and, on the other hand, it is seen in old patients who are obese, and it may be aggravated by anything raising intra-abdominal pressure, such as an ovarian tumour or pregnancy. In health there is a distinct differential of pressure from the oesophagus to the stomach. This is partly due to the acute angle between the oesophagus and stomach, partly to the walls of the hiatus formed by the decussation of the muscle fibres of the right crus of the diaphragm and also sphincteric action at the junction of oesophagus and stomach. The commonest kind of hiatus hernia is described as *sliding*, in so far as the stomach passes straight up into the chest. A rarer form is the *rolling* hernia, in which part of the stomach passes up between the

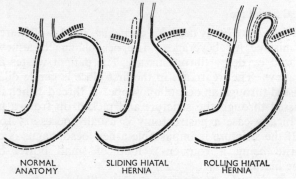

NORMAL   SLIDING HIATAL   ROLLING HIATAL
ANATOMY   HERNIA   HERNIA

FIG. 15. Hiatus Hernia

oesophagus and hiatus, often being nipped in this position. The complications of hiatus hernia and reflux oesophagitis are increasing loss of blood from erosion of the mucosa and fibrosis of the oesophagus, leading to stricture and dysphagia. In extreme cases the patient becomes progressively more emaciated. Rarely incarceration or strangulation may occur, of the stomach or other viscera.

Treatment

In the first place there should be correction of any factor which appears to be causative. The patient, if obese, should lose weight. Tight belts and corsets should not be worn. The patient should place blocks under the head of the bed at night-time and avoid stooping at all times. An alkali mixture, preferably taken dry and washed down with a minimum of fluid, will coat the walls of the oesophagus and protect it from acid. When all these measures fail, operation may be considered necessary, the hiatus being approached either from the abdomen or the chest, according to the build of the patient and the technique favoured by the surgeon. The oesophagus is thoroughly freed and brought down to the diaphragm, being secured there by sutures through the phrenico-oesophageal ligaments. The stomach is stitched to the underside of the diaphragm and an acute angle made between it and the oesophagus. Finally, the hiatus is closed with sutures either in front or behind the oesophagus so that it is a snug fit. The results of this operation are not uniformly successful.

In infancy the babe should be sat up day and night in a sentry box, as the symptoms often resolve spontaneously as the child grows up; the oesophagus later descending to the abdomen, rather as the testis descends. If postural treatment is not successful a thoracic incision is made, the
H

oesophago-gastric junction freed and placed in its proper position and the hiatus closed around it. When the oesophagus is narrowed by a long stricture it must be excised and a length of bowel brought up to replace it. In older patients, vagotomy and pyloroplasty, by reducing the acid content of gastric secretion, may help relieve symptoms.

Oesophageal Stricture

In countries where lye is used for cleansing, bottles of it are sometimes drunk in mistake for beverages. The oesophagus becomes narrowed, being replaced by dense fibrous tissue. The patient wastes away, as he cannot swallow. The treatment in the first place is gentle dilatation with bougies passed through an oesophagoscope. A thread which is swallowed may be passed through the stricture and picked up from a gastrostomy opening. In any case a gastrostomy is usually necessary to feed these patients. If the stricture is impassable a new oesophagus is constructed, the favourite being a roux-en-Y loop of small bowel brought up through the hiatus.

Cardiospasm

Another name for this condition is achalasia of the cardia. Its cause is unknown. Typically young adults of either sex are affected, and it may follow toxaemia of pregnancy. The lower end of the oesophagus fails to relax and radiologically there is an appearance of spasm immediately above the diaphragm. Dysphagia, vomiting and loss of weight occurs. At night the oesophagus fills with secretion, which may spill over into the lungs to cause cough and pneumonia. In minor degrees of cardiospasm dilatation by means of a mercury bougie (Hurst bougie) is sufficient if it is passed just before a meal. A special bag (Negus bag) may be inserted under general anaesthesia through an oesophagoscope and the cardia stretched by inflation of the bag with water. By far the best results are obtained as a result of Heller's operation or cardiomyotomy. This can be done via the chest or abdomen. The oesophago-gastric junction is exposed and the muscle layers of oesophagus and stomach over a distance of about 12 cm. are incised, leaving the mucosa intact. The best results are achieved in the earlier cases. When the oesophagus is greatly dilated it may never regain its tone. Oesophagitis may follow Heller's operation.

Carcinoma

Carcinoma of the oesophagus is typically a disease of old age. Common sites are the lower end of the oesophagus in men and in the post-cricoid region (strictly the hypopharynx) in women, in whom it may be associated with hypochromic anaemia. The mid oesophagus at the level of the aortic arch may also be affected. The tumour is much commoner in certain countries, such as Japan. In type it may be ulcerating or fungating.

Pathology

Almost all oesophageal carcinomata are squamous in type. Occasionally at the lower end an adenocarcinoma may be found either from spread from a gastric lesion or in gastric mucosa that sometimes lines the oesophagus in its lower part to a variable extent. Oesophageal growths are slow growing, but unfortunately only cause dysphagia late. At the lower end spread may occur locally to involve the diaphragm and aorta. Lymph nodes along the lesser curve of the stomach are often invaded. In the mid oesophagus adherence or involvement of the pleura commonly makes operative excision impossible. Empyema or lung abscess may follow perforation of the growth. The recurrent nerve may be involved on the left side. Apart from local spread, nearby lymph nodes are often involved, though blood-borne spread is uncommon. At the upper end the larynx or trachea, recurrent nerves and sympathetic chain may be invaded.

Benign growths are rare, but occasionally a submucosal lipoma or leiomyoma may obstruct the oesophagus and can be cured by excision of the tumour.

Symptoms and Signs

Painless dysphagia and rapid loss of weight are typical of carcinoma of the oesophagus. The patient can often localise the site of obstruction. Often medical advice is only called for when the dysphagia is severe and when saliva can no longer be swallowed. As the volume of saliva is about 1 litre in 24 hours, those affected find themselves continually expectorating saliva and sputum.

Diagnosis

A barium swallow reveals an irregular narrowing of the oesophagus and oesophagoscopy allows a biopsy of the tumour to be obtained. Both investigations are essential in any case of dysphagia.

Treatment

Many patients with oesophageal cancer are old and frail and would not stand an extensive operation. Others show evidence of spread into the abdomen or involved lymph nodes in the neck or paralysis of nerves, all suggesting inoperability. Treatment by insertion of tubes of the Souttar or Celestin type provide excellent palliation by allowing the passage of saliva and fluids. Occasionally teletherapy or implantation of gold seeds into a growth through an oesophagoscope may be of value.

Operation is most often performed for lower oesophageal growths. A period of intensive feeding before operation allows improvement of nutrition. A fluid diet is given with a high protein and carbohydrate content (see p. 23). The oesophagus is approached through an incision that opens both abdomen and chest on the left side. Mid-oesophageal growths are approached through the right chest. If possible the growth is excised widely and continuity restored by bringing either the distal part of the stomach or the jejunum into the chest, where it is joined to the oesophagus. If the growth cannot be removed obstruction can be relieved by by-passing it with a loop of jejunum. Success, especially in Japan, has attended intensive radiotherapy of the oesophageal lesion following gastrostomy, the tumour being later excised and a short circuit operation performed.

HEART AND GREAT VESSELS

CONGENITAL LESIONS

Patent Ductus Arteriosus

In foetal life the lungs are not aerated and the blood in the pulmonary artery is shunted into the aorta via the ductus arteriosus. Shortly after

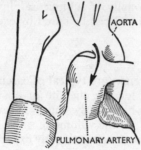

FIG. 16. Patent ductus arteriosus

birth the ductus closes, separating the two circulations, pulmonary and systemic. The commonest congenital heart lesion follows failure of closure, the patent ductus arteriosus (Fig. 16), which allows shunting of some of the systemic blood from the aorta into the pulmonary circulation. The arterio-venous shunt from the left to the right side of the heart adds an extra load to the left ventricle, the severity of which depends on the size of the ductus.

Symptoms and Signs

Often the baby or child presents with no obvious abnormality until a stethoscope is placed over the second left intercostal space, where a continuous machinery-like murmur, the Gibson murmur, is heard throughout the cardiac cycle. Cyanosis is not a feature unless there is reversal of the circulation through the ductus, a rare and usually terminal event. When the patent ductus is large symptoms may become obvious in childhood or early adult life. The commonest findings are failure to grow at the normal rate, increased liability to chest infection, dyspnoea and palpitations. Cardiac failure is a late occurrence, but it must be remembered that the average age at death in patients in whom the ductus has not closed is 35 years. Bacterial endocarditis is more likely to occur in a patient with a patent ductus. Antibiotics are necessary to control the infection, but are unlikely to provide a permanent cure until the ductus has been closed. A radiograph of the chest may show a prominent pulmonary artery; under the fluorescent screen the pulmonary arteries in the hila of the lungs are seen to be prominent and pulsatile. Cardiac catheterisation may be successful in demonstrating the ductus by revealing a high pressure and high oxygen saturation in the pulmonary artery.

Treatment

Surgical exposure of the patent ductus is carried out through a left thoracotomy incision. The ductus may either be doubly tied or may be

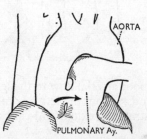

Fig. 17. Aortic window

divided, the two ends being oversewn. The operation can be done at any age, but is often delayed until the child is about five years old, as this is a suitable age for admission to hospital. Children often grow more rapidly after the operation.

A rare variant of the above condition is the aortic window or patent aortic–pulmonary septum (Fig. 17). It is difficult to differentiate from a patent ductus clinically, a large shunt being present at the root of the aorta and pulmonary artery. Symptoms are much more severe than with a patent ductus. The defect can only be repaired at open-heart surgery.

Coarctation of the Aorta

In this congenital abnormality there is stenosis or atresia of the descending aorta in the neighbourhood of the ligamentum arteriosus (Fig. 18). In about 20% of patients there is also a patent ductus proximal to the narrowing, and rarely the length of the coarctation is considerable. Occasionally an aneurysm may lie in the aorta distal to the stenosis.

Symptoms and Signs

It is rare for coarctation to produce symptoms or signs before adolescence, and then the diagnosis is often made accidentally by the discovery that the femoral pulses are absent or that hypertension is present only in the upper half of the body. Occasionally the patient complains of headache or nose bleed and palpitations due to the hypertension proximal to the narrowing. The diagnosis is confirmed by finding an elevated blood pressure in the arms and absent or greatly diminished femoral pulses. A radiograph of the chest may show an unusual-looking aortic arch, and there may be notching of the ribs brought about by the greatly hypertrophied intercostal vessels, which act as anastomotic channels. Abnormal pulsation of anastomotic arteries around the scapulae may be easily visible. Intermittent claudication rarely occurs

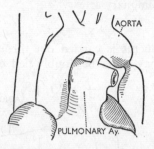

Fig. 18. Coarctation of aorta

from a poor arterial flow to the legs. The right subclavian artery may arise anomalously from the left side of the aortic arch. Angiocardiography will demonstrate the extent and calibre of the narrowing.

Treatment

If left untreated the average life expectancy of patients with coarctation is greatly diminished, and is probably about 35 years. Death is usually due to rupture of the aorta, cerebral haemorrhage or left ventricular failure. These complications are more likely to occur when an extra load is placed on the heart, as in pregnancy. The lesion is occasionally the site of bacterial endocarditis. Treatment is excision of the narrow segment and anastomosis of the two ends of the aorta; when the narrow segment is lengthy it may be necessary to insert a prosthesis such as a Teflon graft.

Pulmonary Stenosis and Atresia

Pure stenosis of the pulmonary valve may be either valvular or, more rarely, infundibular. In either case there is a greatly diminished blood flow through the lungs, which appear radiographically as starved of blood. Pulmonary stenosis may be an isolated abnormality or associated with other congenital defects, the commonest group being known as the tetralogy of Fallot: a syndrome of pulmonary stenosis, ventricular septal defect, over-riding of the aorta and right ventricular hypertrophy. Abnormalities associated with pulmonary stenosis account for most of the cyanotic heart conditions of childhood, producing the so-called blue babies, although pure pulmonic stenosis does not cause cyanosis.

Symptoms and Signs

The pulmonary arterial narrowing leads to a loud pulmonary systolic murmur, which is often conducted over most of the precordium. The heart is enlarged and, if there is an associated septal defect or over-riding aorta, cyanosis and finger clubbing. The child may adopt a squatting position and may fail to thrive. Repeated pulmonary infections occur, and death in early life is common. The blood shows polycythaemia, and an electrocardiogram shows evidence of right-axis deviation with right ventricular hypertrophy. The diagnosis is confirmed by cardiac catheter studies and angiocardiography.

Treatment

Pure pulmonary stenosis of the valvular type was first treated by Lord Brock by dilatation with a valvotome passed through the right ventricular wall, which split the fused valve cusps. The infundibular variety was cored out by rongeurs. More recently open-heart surgery has permitted a direct attack on the lesion with full correction.

The first successful treatment of the tetralogy of Fallot was introduced by Taussig and Blalock, who anastomosed the left subclavian artery to the pulmonary artery, thus by-passing the lesion and rerouting some systemic blood through the lungs, in effect creating an artificial ductus arteriosus. Today, complete correction of the defect can be carried out if the child is cooled and the heart by-passed so that the pulmonary outlet can be opened and corrected and the other lesions dealt with at the same time.

Atrial Septal Defect

A defect in the interatrial septum results in a left-to-right shunt of blood and is often associated with other cardiac abnormalities. A big load is put on the right ventricle, which often shows hypertrophy. There are two different congenital varieties of the defect.

(a) *The ostium secundum defect* lies centrally or high up in the atrial septum and is the common lesion.

(b) *The ostium primum defect* lies low in the septum and is often also associated with defects of the atrio-ventricular canal, so there may be an abnormal mitral or tricuspid valve and an associated ventricular septal defect.

Symptoms and Signs

There are few symptoms which point conclusively to an atrial septal defect in the child, especially if the opening is not large. The patient may fail to thrive. A blowing systolic murmur will be heard to the left of the sternum. The second sound over the pulmonary area is split and does not vary with respiration. Cyanosis only occurs if the shunt of blood is reversed, as for example in pneumonia. The diagnosis is confirmed by catheter studies, and the extent of the lesion can be estimated by dye dilution and blood-gas analysis.

Treatment

Many techniques have been devised in the past to deal with this lesion such as operating through a well attached to the atrial wall or invaginating the redundant atrial wall so that it can be sutured to the edges of the septum. At the present time the technique favoured is a direct attack to close the defect using hypothermia or a temporary by-pass with the heart–lung machine. The septum primum defects, which may be associated with abnormalities of the bundle of His, are more complicated and complete correction may not be possible.

Ventricular Septal Defects

Defects of the ventricular septum are fairly common and are often associated with other abnormalities of the heart. An isolated defect produces few symptoms or signs, and may be compatible with long and healthy life, though there is always a risk of endocarditis, cardiac failure or heart block.

Symptoms and Signs

If the opening is large there may be failure to grow properly, and a very loud systolic murmur is heard to the left of the sternum, often accompanied by a thrill. The lesion may be complicated by pulmonary hypertension. If there is reversal of blood flow from right to left cyanosis results, the *Eisenmenger syndrome*. Cardiac catheterisation reveals the shunt and may give a good idea of its size.

Treatment

Most ventricular septal defects should be corrected by open-heart surgery using a heart–lung machine. The operative risk is somewhere around 5%. Once decompensation has occurred with a right-to-left shunt of blood, surgery has little to offer.

ACQUIRED CARDIAC DEFECTS

Mitral Stenosis

Mitral stenosis occurs as a result of rheumatic fever, often contracted in childhood, though occasionally there is no history of rheumatic infection. Mitral stenosis is much commoner in women than men, and the symptoms are made worse during pregnancy. The leaflets of the mitral valve become thickened, fibrotic and adhere at the commissures. As there is shortening of the chordae tendinae, the final condition of the valve is a fibrotic funnel-shaped opening rather like a fish's mouth. The valve may be stenosed and yet allow reflux, mitral incompetence.

Symptoms and Signs

Narrowing of the mitral valve raises the pressure in the pulmonary system and leads to lung changes, increased fibrosis, raised pulmonary artery pressure and impaired gaseous exchange in the alveoli. Narrowing of the valve also leads to starving of the left ventricle of blood, and therefore a poor output from the heart. The patient becomes short of breath on exertion, needs an increasing number of pillows at night-time and fatigues easily. Haemoptysis results from the pulmonary hypertension, and when this is severe there is pulmonary congestion and finally attacks of right ventricular failure. There may be thrombosis of blood in the atrial appendage, and clots may break off and produce emboli in any part of the body. At some stage atrial fibrillation occurs and increases the risk of congestive heart failure.

Auscultation reveals a characteristic rumbling diastolic murmur, often with presystolic accentuation, all of which is best heard near the apex of the heart, especially with the patient leaning forward and lying to the left side. The second pulmonary sound is augmented and there may be an 'opening snap' heard over the mitral valve. A radiograph of the chest shows an enlarged pulmonary artery, right ventricular enlargement and a large left atrium. Calcification in the region of the mitral valve may also be seen.

Treatment

In clear-cut mitral stenosis a closed operation to split the mitral valve at each commissure will usually produce a good result. The finger is inserted through the left atrial appendage and guides a two-bladed dilator introduced through the left ventricular wall. The valve cusps are then forced apart and, if they are still flexible, a good result can be expected. If the disease is not treated until late the valve leaflets may themselves be rigid and unable to close properly, and the lungs will be fibrotic and stiff. If mitral regurgitation complicates the stenosis valvotomy has much less to offer, although in the early stages it may allow more efficient closing of the valves if the cusps are flexible. At the present time severe mitral regurgitation is treated at open-heart surgery by the introduction of an artificial valve of ball or flap type.

. The indication for valvotomy in mitral stenosis is increasing breathlessness in a patient who has not recently had rheumatic fever and who by reason of the disease is not able to carry on a normal life. It may be needed as an emergency, late in pregnancy.

Aortic Stenosis and Aortic Regurgitation

Aortic Stenosis

This is fusion of the aortic leaflets, and frequently follows rheumatic disease, as in the case of mitral stenosis; indeed, the two valve lesions often co-exist. However, there are many examples of aortic stenosis with no history of rheumatic fever, and congenital bicuspid aortic valves may be stenosed. Unlike patients with mitral disease, those with aortic stenosis are often little affected for many years until angina presents when the prognosis is bad. Death is usually sudden and follows an attack of congestive failure.

Aortic Regurgitation

This follows a similar natural history to aortic stenosis, and the two conditions may be associated in greater or lesser degree. There is often a loud rough diastolic murmur over the aortic valve, which has a blowing character if there is much regurgitation. Aortic regurgitation due to syphilis is much less often seen today than that due to rheumatic infection.

Treatment

By the time that patients with aortic valve lesions present with angina or dyspnoea the prognosis is poor. Dilatation of the valve, as is done for mitral disease, has yielded poor results. Open-heart surgery allows the replacement of damaged aortic valves by various prostheses or healthy aortic valves taken from a body within a few hours of death.

Tumours of the Heart

Primary cardiac tumours are very rare, but there is one seen much more commonly than any other—the myxoma, most often arising in the left atrium. Severe and sudden symptoms of unconsciousness or convulsions may occur due to acute blocking off of the flow of blood as the tumour plugs the mitral valve. The only method of much help in diagnosis is angiocardiography. By open-heart surgery the tumour which often arises from the atrial septum can be removed. The prognosis is excellent after surgical treatment.

PERICARDIUM

Trauma

Road accidents, stab wounds and bullet wounds can often lead to njuries of the pericardium and underlying myocardium. Blood accumulates in the pericardial sac and embarrasses the action of the heart, a condition known as *tamponade*. The pulse becomes less and less easy to feel, and radiography of the chest reveals a greatly increased heart shadow.

Treatment

If the haemopericardium is embarrassing the heart, treatment is urgently needed by aspiration of the fluid in the pericardial sac through a widebore needle inserted through an intercostal space. As soon as possible the patient is taken to the operating theatre and the chest opened and the pericardium explored, since there is probably a bleeding point on the surface of the heart, or there may be a hole in the myocardium which needs closure. Small effusions may need no treatment, but close observation is essential.

Constrictive Pericarditis

The pericardium becomes thickened and inelastic so that the heart cannot fill properly in diastole, and there is therefore a poor cardiac output. Tuberculosis is the major cause of this condition, but may not be the sole aetiological factor.

Symptoms and Signs

The history is usually a long one, with progressive fatigue, dyspnoea and palpitations. The peripheral veins are congested and there may be great oedema of the lower limbs, ascites and hepatomegaly. The systolic blood pressure is usually low. Radiography may show a small heart shadow, and there may be evidence of calcification of the pericardium. Screening of the heart under the fluorescent screen shows greatly diminished heart movements.

Treatment

Pericardiectomy is the treatment of choice, and is best done through a vertical incision splitting the sternum, which affords excellent exposure. As the usual cause is tuberculosis, pre- and post-operative tuberculostatic drugs must be given.

AORTA

Aneurysms

Aneurysms of the thoracic aorta may be saccular or fusiform, and the aetiological factor is atherosclerosis or syphilis. Aneurysms are typically seen in men after the age of 50. For many years there may be few symptoms or signs, but, as the aneurysm increases in size, pain, which can be dull or intermittent and sharp, is caused by erosion of nearby structures, especially bone. There may be hoarseness from involvement of the recurrent laryngeal nerve, Horner's syndrome from pressure on the sympathetic chain and a distinctive wheezing and stridor due to pressure on the trachea. Compression of the superior vena cava may produce distended veins in the upper part of the body. A systolic murmur may be heard over the aortic area, and a tracheal tug can be elicited when the aneurysm involves the arch of the aorta. Angiocardiography will reveal the extent of the lesion.

Treatment

Aneurysms of the thoracic aorta have a poor prognosis and are extremely difficult to treat successfully. A few successes have attended excision assisted by the use of by-pass techniques and the insertion of Teflon tubes.

Dissecting Aneurysm

A dissecting aneurysm almost always starts from a small tear in the intima of the thoracic aorta which allows blood to penetrate into the diseased media and strip the intima from the underlying media over a progressively large area (see Chapter Eight). The tear usually starts in the arch of the aorta, immediately distal to the sinuses of Valsalva, the extravasated blood may pass down the abdominal aorta to the lower limb arteries or may track up subclavian and even carotid vessels.

Symptoms and Signs

The patient, who is typically a robust man of middle age, suddenly, after exercise, has a violent pain in the chest which may radiate to neck and arm. The pain typically goes through to the back. Shock occurs and there is dyspnoea. The resultant signs are related to obstruction of various branches of the aorta, which may involve the blood supply to the spinal cord, renal and gastro-intestinal organs.

Treatment

Since the condition is usually fatal if untreated, a surgical attack should be made, so long as the patient is fit enough to withstand it and the renal arteries are not affected. Angiography performed by the retrograde route through the femoral artery may demonstrate the origin of the dissection (see Chapter Eight). The lower part of the descending aorta is doubly clamped and divided. The inner and outer layers of the distal segment are attached circumferentially with a fine continuous suture, the distal segment is re-anastomosed to the proximal one and an opening is made in the intima above the anastomosis, the so-called fenestration operation. By this means the new lumen which the blood has stripped up between intima and media is re-anastomosed to the main lumen of the aorta. Often the aneurysm must be excised in the thorax and replaced by a plastic graft. The aortic valve may need repair.

Cardio-Pulmonary By-Pass

Many of the cardiac operations described above can only be performed on a bloodless arrested heart. Blood is led from the right atrium by two plastic carnulae passed through its wall or via the appendage and threaded into the S.V.C. and I.V.C. The blood is taken to a machine where gas exchange can take place, oxygen being added and carbon dioxide lost, and returned to the body via a femoral or iliac artery. Under general anaesthesia an adult needs a blood-flow of about 2–4 litres per sq. metre of body surface. In addition the body may be cooled or the blood passed through a heat exchanger. Oxygenators are of 3 types; bubble, screen or disc according to the technique of exposing blood to gas. Recently attempts have been made to perfect a membrane oxygenator. The blood is usually propelled by roller pumps in which rubber tubing is squeezed by rotating cams since this does least damage to the red cells.

FURTHER READING

Belcher, J. R., and Sturridge, M. F. (1962) *Thoracic Surgical Management.* Baillière Tindall & Cox, London.

Flavell, G. (1963) *The Oesophagus*, Butterworths, London.

Wood, P. (1968) *Diseases of the Heart and Circulation.* 3rd Ed. Eyre & Spottiswoode, London.

Cooley, D. A. (1966) *Surgical Treatment of Congenital Heart Disease.* Kimpton, London.

Milstein, B. B. (1963) *Cardiac Arrest and Resuscitation.* Lloyd-Luke, London.

CHAPTER SEVENTEEN

HERNIA

A hernia is the protrusion of a viscus from its normal situation through an opening in the walls of the cavity within which it is contained. In this chapter we are concerned with abdominal hernias (Fig. 19), the walls of which consist of peritoneum, which are far the commonest and the most important hernias in surgery. It has been estimated that approximately one in every hundred of the population has a hernia at one of the common sites at which they occur, inguinal, femoral or umbilical. Inguinal hernia is much the commonest, constituting about three-quarters of the whole, femoral is next and umbilical hernias account for only 10%. There are in

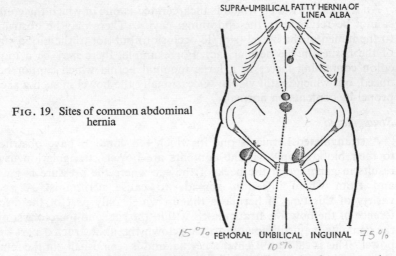

SUPRA-UMBILICAL FATTY HERNIA OF LINEA ALBA

FIG. 19. Sites of common abdominal hernia

15% FEMORAL UMBILICAL INGUINAL 75%
10%

addition many rare types of hernia, and it should not be forgotten that abdominal incisions of all kinds made by the surgeon may give way and lead to man-made hernias. Hernia through the diaphragm is considered on p. 213. Hernia through the pelvic diaphragm may give rise to vaginal or rectal prolapse.

Hernias may be congenital or acquired; most of them result from a congenital weakness which is aggravated by increase in intra-abdominal pressure, so that the precipitating factors to remember are coughing, constipation, difficulty in micturition, pregnancy and unusually severe muscular effort. Acquired hernias often develop from muscle weakness, especially in middle age, when the muscles of the abdominal wall bulge and at operation show infiltration with fat.

Classification

All hernias, no matter where they occur or what size they are, can be usefully classified in the following way, since treatment will depend on the class into which the hernia falls.

Reducible

This means that the contents can be milked back into the abdominal cavity. There may be bowel, omentum or one of the other abdominal viscera present.

Irreducible

In this case the contents cannot be returned to the abdominal cavity, and the condition is therefore more serious. Irreducible hernias are of two types: incarcerated and strangulated.

Incarcerated

An irreducible hernia which is incarcerated is one in which the contents cannot be returned to the abdominal cavity. There may be obstruction to the lumen of the bowel (simple occlusion) but not to the blood supply of the tissues in the hernial sac. For example, there may be a loop of colon containing faeces in a large inguinal hernia which cannot be reduced, but which is still viable. Occasionally the bowel in such a sac can propel its contents on normally.

Strangulated

A strangulated hernia is one in which the contents have obstruction to their blood supply. If the contents are bowel, strangulation usually results in gangrene at the neck of the sac where the pressure is greatest and from where infection spreads to cause peritonitis. A special variety of this type of hernia is that in which only part of the circumference of the bowel is strangulated within the sac, and therefore some of the contents may still be able to pass down the unobstructed part of the bowel. This is called a Richter's hernia, and is seen usually in the femoral region. The symptoms and signs which these different types of hernia produce will be discussed under the regional headings.

INGUINAL HERNIA

The commonest type of hernia is an indirect inguinal hernia in a man. Most are due to a congenital defect in which the processus vaginalis, which accompanies the testis into the scrotum, remains patent, providing a preformed peritoneal sac extending throughout the length of the inguinal canal. Inguinal hernia is much commoner in the male than in the female, and is commoner on the right side than the left, a fact probably associated with the later and less complete descent of the right testis during foetal

life. In the female a peritoneal sac may pass through the inguinal canal
and enter the labium accompanying the round ligament.

Anatomy

The anatomy of inguinal hernia is that the sac enters the deep inguinal ring and passes downwards and medially, lateral to the inferior
epigastric vessels. The external oblique aponeurosis is in the front of it,
and some of the fibres of the internal oblique muscle in the lateral part.
Posteriorly there is the fascia transversalis and the conjoined tendon.
The floor of the canal is the inguinal ligament, and the roof is made up of
the fibres of the internal oblique as they arch over the cord. The sac
comes out through the superficial inguinal ring, often on the lateral and
anterior aspect of the spermatic cord, and may then pass downwards,
clothed at this level by the fibres of the cremaster muscle, until it may
eventually reach the upper pole of the testis in the scrotum.

A direct inguinal hernia is a condition more likely to be acquired
than congenital, due to weakness of the abdominal muscles. The sac
passes out directly through the layers of the abdominal wall to appear
at the superficial inguinal ring. To do this it must pass medial to the
inferior epigastric vessels, and anatomically this is the differentiation
between an indirect and direct hernia. Clinically it may be very difficult
to differentiate between the two, and in practice it matters very little,
because treatment of a similar nature is required in either case.

Symptoms and Signs

An inguinal hernia often causes no symptoms, though an ache at the
end of the day is not uncommon. In its early stage pain in the groin may
arise, often referred to the testis. A swelling may be seen in the groin
when the patient strains or coughs, becoming more prominent due to the
expansile impulse imparted to it by increased intra-abdominal pressure.
A hernia is best seen with the patient standing. When the swelling is large
enough to reach down into the scrotum or labium it should be gently
reduced with the fingers so that the direction it takes during reduction can
be followed. In a baby it is not possible to obtain this co-operation, but
it is then only necessary to roll the structures in the spermatic cord under
gentle pressure from the fingers and compare the two sides, when thickening will often be felt on the side where a sac exists. This resembles a layer
of silk between the fingers and the cord. In the case of bilateral inguinal
hernia in infants it is usually by observing the swellings when the baby
strains that the diagnosis is made.

In differential diagnosis it is important first of all to determine that the
swelling comes from above, because collections of fluid or tumours in the
scrotum may extend up towards the abdominal cavity. A femoral hernia
appears below the inguinal ligament and, if a finger palpates the pubic
tubercle, it will be appreciated that the hernia is lateral and below this
point.

Complications

The most important complication of an inguinal hernia is strangulation which can occur at any age and at any time of life, although it more often occurs when the hernia first appears. An indirect hernia is more likely to strangulate than a direct one, small bowel is usually involved. The diagnosis is made when the swelling is *tense, tender, irreducible and shows no impulse on coughing.* Auscultation of the abdomen usually reveals increased bowel sounds because peristalsis is trying to force the contents past the obstruction. The patient complains of colicky pain, inability to pass a motion or flatus, and the abdomen may be distended. If the obstruction is left unrelieved, nausea is followed by vomiting, and the patient rapidly becomes dehydrated, toxic and ill. When the abdomen is silent, peritonitis has occurred and the outlook is grave.

Treatment

The treatment of hernia is almost always best carried out by operation. An indirect hernia in a baby, child or young adult is presumed to be due to a congenital sac and therefore the removal of this sac should cure the condition. Such an operation is described as *herniotomy,* and is carried out through a small crease incision over the inguinal region. The fibres of the external oblique are split and the sac is dissected away from the spermatic cord as far as the internal ring. The sac is opened and any contents replaced in the general peritoneal cavity, the sac is then trans-fixed at its neck, tied off and the excess removed. The weakness in the transversalis fascia is closed and the external oblique repaired. In a baby under 1 year of age it is unnecessary to incise the aponeurosis of the external oblique, as the superficial and deep inguinal rings are so close that traction on the sac will bring the neck into view at the superficial ring.

When an indirect hernia is seen in an older patient or when there is weakness of the abdominal wall it becomes necessary to strengthen the posterior wall of the canal in addition to herniotomy. The basis of all operations for this is a technique first described by Bassini, which consists of stitching the conjoined tendon to the inguinal ligament behind the spermatic cord with some non-absorbable suture. There are many varia-tions on this theme. Meticulous attention to detail in this operation, with the avoidance of any haematoma or infection in the postoperative period and adequate closure of the external oblique so that the superficial ring is neither too small nor too large, results in a long-term cure of some 90% of patients, even when the patients are the subjects of chronic cough or constipation or difficulties of micturition. Causes of recurrence of a hernia are haematoma formation and infection in the wound. Postoperative chest complications with their accompanying coughing may also spoil a repair.

When the muscles of the abdominal wall are weak or atrophied the problem of hernial repair is very much greater. The object of the many operations which have been devised is to try to strengthen the posterior wall of the inguinal canal. Most of these operations are based on the principle of swinging healthy tissue into the area from near by, or using non-absorbable sutures, or fascia from the patient, to close the gap. The success of this special technique appears to depend more upon the skill of the individual operator rather than the materials or the operation which he adopts.

In the case of direct inguinal hernia, the hernial sac is not removed but invaginated; some kind of repair is necessary in every case, since the walls of the canal must be weak to have allowed the hernial sac to pass directly out through the superficial inguinal ring. The operation for repairing the canal is referred to as a *herniorrhaphy*. When both indirect and direct sacs occur at the same time it is usual to attempt as far as possible to pull the whole sac through into the indirect position and deal with it there, since this will lead to a stronger repair being carried out. A sliding hernia or hernia en glissade is an inguinal hernia in which the caecum on the right and the sigmoid colon on the left form the posterior wall of the hernia, having slipped down from the posterior abdominal wall. Such a hernia is difficult to treat operatively, and should be suspected in an old man with a large scrotal hernia. Repair is easiest after orchidectomy, permission for which should always be obtained before hernia operation in the old or in those with large inguinal herniae.

When for some reason a patient is unfit for operative repair of a hernia, a truss is supplied. This consists of a suitable pad which is attached by a belt round the waist, and sometimes in addition a light strap under the perineum to hold it in place. In older patients it is necessary to have a light steel spring in the waist band in order to keep up the pressure, and the waist band should lie about halfway between the iliac crest and the great trochanter. It is usually convenient to have it made with a pad over each inguinal region, since by this means it is more easily held in place. In an infant, if for some reason operation cannot be undertaken, a small rubber truss is provided. It is essential that whatever kind of truss is used that it is applied after the sac has been reduced, or it may press on the contents and cause obstruction to them. Thus, a truss is best put on by the patient before rising in the morning and not taken off until he goes to bed at night.

Treatment of Strangulated Hernia

Whenever an acute abdominal condition is suspected it is essential that the hernial orifices are examined, for strangulated hernia is by far the commonest cause of intestinal obstruction. If a patient is seen with a hernia which has become irreducible but without causing evidence of intestinal obstruction during the previous 2 or 3 hours an attempt may be made to reduce its contents. The patient is placed flat on his back with the foot of the bed raised on 12-inch blocks. It is best to have the thighs a little flexed, and a pillow may be placed under the knees to do this. An ice bag is placed over the swelling, and if necessary morphia is given by injection. At the end of 1 hour an attempt is made to reduce the contents manually by gentle pressure over the swelling. The thighs should be internally rotated and flexed and occasionally it is possible to return the contents to the abdomen. No force should be used and if gentle pressure does not succeed the patient requires an emergency operation.

When a hernia is strangulated the condition is one of bowel obstruction. Treatment should follow the plan set out in Chapter Three. The stomach contents are aspirated by naso-gastric suction, fluid is replaced intravenously, premedication is given and the patient taken to the operating theatre as soon as possible. No time should be lost for any reason at all, as a successful outcome depends entirely on early treatment. An incision is made over the most prominent part of the swelling, the inguinal canal is opened and the neck of the sac first investigated, since this is the most likely site at which the bowel will be damaged. A small relieving incision is made in the sac to allow the bowel to be lifted out of it. If it seems possible that it may survive it is wrapped in a warm saline pack and again inspected after 5 minutes. A change in colour indicates that circulation is still present and that the bowel can probably be returned safely to the peritoneal cavity. Other signs of viability include peristalsis crossing the damaged segment and palpation of arterial pulsation in the mesentery. If, however, the bowel is still a bad colour and shows no signs of return of circulation it must be resected. The hernia is repaired and the patient returned to bed and continued on naso-gastric suction and intravenous fluids until bowel sounds return and flatus is passed.

FEMORAL HERNIA

Femoral hernia is seen much more commonly in women than in men, but inguinal hernia still remains the commonest hernia seen in women. Femoral hernia is commoner in those who have borne children. Its particular importance is that it is the most common of all hernias to become strangulated and because a strangulated hernia may be so easily missed. Richter's type of hernia may be particularly sinister, since strangulation of part of the circumference of the bowel occurs without signs of intestinal obstruction until perhaps days have elapsed.

Anatomy

The femoral canal is the medial part of the femoral sheath, and lies on the pectineus muscle, being covered by the inguinal ligament. On its lateral side lies the femoral vein and on the medial the pectineal part of the inguinal ligament (Gimbernat's ligament). The femoral canal opens in the thigh at the fossa ovalis or saphenous opening, which is normally covered by cribriform fascia. In health the canal contains a little loose fatty tissue and a fairly prominent lymph node.

Symptoms and Signs

A typical femoral hernia is a small irreducible and symptom-free swelling in the groin which appears lateral and inferior to the pubic spine. This distinguishes it from inguinal hernia, which will be above and to the medial side of the spine. As it enlarges it turns upwards and backwards on itself so that it may eventually overlie the inguinal ligament, and thus be difficult to distinguish from an inguinal hernia. It is usually difficult to reduce a femoral hernia, and it is for this reason that the contents often become strangulated. Occasionally the sac becomes shut off by a plug of omentum from the general peritoneal cavity and may distend with fluid, so that it provides all the physical signs of a cyst in this area. The differential diagnosis is first of all from inguinal hernia, then from a saphena varix, an enlarged and inflamed lymph node, or extremely rarely, a psoas abscess.

Treatment

Since a femoral hernia cannot be controlled by a truss, and since it is so often the site of strangulation, it should whenever possible be repaired surgically. It can be approached in a number of ways, but it is usual nowadays to make the incision above the inguinal ligament. In Lotheissen's operation the fibres of the external oblique are split lengthways and the femoral sac drawn through the transversalis fascia into the inguinal canal. Repair is carried out by stitching the conjoined tendon to Cooper's ligament, a condensation of fascia along the rim of the pubis. Two or three mattress sutures of thread are usually all that are required. McEvedy's operation consists of opening the lower part of the posterior wall of the rectus sheath, which gives excellent exposure of the neck of the sac without disturbing the contents of the inguinal canal. Many surgeons prefer to approach the sac from below the inguinal ligament, mobilising it down to the neck which is then stretched to allow the intestine to be drawn out. If gangrenous or irreducible bowel is found in a femoral hernial sac the neck should be freed by incising medially into Gimbernat's ligament, since the femoral vein lies on the lateral side. Relief of strangulation carries a low mortality unless bowel has to be resected.

UMBILICAL HERNIA

True umbilical hernia, that is herniation directly through the umbilical scar is usually only seen in infants and in most cases closes spontaneously. Details of this and exomphalos will be found in the chapter on paediatric surgery. However, the term umbilical hernia is also applied to what are really para-umbilical hernias seen at the two extremes of life, in childhood and in older patients.

Para-umbilical hernia of children is usually a supra-umbilical hernia due to a hole in the lower part of the linea alba just above the umbilical scar. It is not uncommon to find a small triangular defect at this site which allows herniation, typically in young girls, especially over the age of one year. As it enlarges, the hernia tends to hang downwards like a little elephant's trunk, and therefore requires repair. Since it is never the site of strangulation, repair can be delayed until the child is old enough to be admitted to hospital without too much upset, i.e., over 4 years of age. If for any reason there is urgency in having the hernia repaired it is better that the mother should be admitted with the child. The operation consists of making a small curved incision just below the umbilicus and, after excising the sac and inverting its stump, bringing together the two edges of the linea alba with sutures. The scar obtained by this approach is invisible.

Para-umbilical hernia in adults is typically seen in the obese patient with a chronic cough. Women are affected much more often than men, and the hernia may eventually reach a great size and hang down below the pubis. These hernias are extremely difficult to reduce, and are often complicated by strangulation of the loops of small bowel which are usually found within.

Treatment

The treatment of this condition usually consists in first persuading the patient to lose weight. Next the chronic cough must be dealt with and, when the patient is fit for operation, the sac is excised through a wide horizontal incision. After the contents have been returned to the abdomen the layers of the rectus sheath are overlapped from above downwards by mattress sutures so that the abdominal wall is now two layers thick where previously there was a gap. If strangulation of bowel occurs, then operation must be performed as an emergency. Recurrence is common because of a high incidence of infection in the wound, because of the haematoma that is likely to collect in the dead space left after dissection and removal of the sac. Other causes of recurrence are the common occurrence of coughing and straining after operation in the obese person.

EPIGASTRIC HERNIA

An epigastric hernia consists almost always of the herniation of fatty tissues through a defect in the linea alba, and therefore appears as a small tender swelling somewhere between the xiphisternum and the umbilicus. It may occur at any age, is usually quite small and occasionally causes considerable pain. It may emerge a little to one side of the midline. The School Medical Officer notices it in routine examination of children, for the swelling is often most prominent when the child is standing. Occasionally, though rarely, not only extra-peritoneal fat but also a portion of great omentum or one of the abdominal viscera enters the sac. Because the swelling may be almost impalpable epigastric pain caused by the hernia may lead to a diagnosis of peptic ulceration. Therefore an extremely careful palpation of the anterior abdominal wall should be carried out in a patient suspected of this condition. Treatment is relatively simple, in that a direct incision is made over the swelling, the hernia reduced and the dense fibrous aponeurosis repaired by sutures which overlap it.

INCISIONAL HERNIA

Some of the most severe and grotesque hernias seen are those which follow weakening or disruption of an abdominal incision. Especially if the patient puts on much weight and if the muscles are of poor tone, the hernial sac is likely to continue to increase in size until a considerable part of the abdominal contents is contained within it. If in addition there is chronic cough, constipation or straining at micturition the problem is even greater.

Treatment of these patients is sometimes impossible surgically, but every endeavour should be made to carry out surgical repair if it is at all feasible. The patient should be put on a strict reducing diet and cough and any other related condition, such as constipation, treated vigorously. Great ingenuity may be needed in reducing the contents back into the abdominal cavity and repairing the attenuated abdominal wall. Non-absorbable sutures, such as steel wire, are particularly useful for this, and the insertion of wire mesh, nylon or other non-absorbable materials and occasionally skin grafts has been advocated. If such measures are unsuccessful, then a firm abdominal belt must be prescribed, since this will control the hernia during waking hours and prevent strangulation of bowel within the sac.

FURTHER READING

Aird, I. (1957) *A Companion in Surgical Studies*, Chap. 31. Livingstone, Edinburgh.
Ogilvie, Sir H., (1959) *Hernia*, Arnold, London.
Nyhus, L. M. and Harkins, H. N. (1964) *Hernia*. Pitman, London.

CHAPTER EIGHTEEN

THE ACUTE ABDOMEN AND THE PERITONEUM

THE ACUTE ABDOMEN

The diagnosis of acute abdominal conditions is often difficult because of the many variations of presentation and the large number of diseases that must be considered. The most important decision to be made is whether to operate or not, especially when such a decision may make the difference between death and possible recovery. In clinical diagnosis the two pathological states to be differentiated are *inflammation* (including peritonitis) and *obstruction*. Peritonitis may be the result of bacterial inflammation or leakage of irritant fluid into the peritoneum—blood, bile, urine, gastric juice or pancreatic enzymes. Obstruction may be of a viscus, such as the gall bladder or some hollow tube, e.g., the intestine or the ureter. When a clinical diagnosis is being made it should first be thought of in terms of inflammation or obstruction. Other features may indicate the likelihood of a particular viscus being involved, but often the symptoms and signs may indicate only spreading peritonitis or complete obstruction.

Pain

Pain is a prominent symptom in almost all acute abdominal conditions. In inflammation it is continuous, aching and throbbing in nature. The onset may be sudden, for example, the pain due to a perforated peptic ulcer or ruptured ectopic gestation. In appendicitis pain becomes progressively more intense over a period of hours. The patient characteristically lies still, and may experience pain on movement and on breathing. Colic due to obstruction is usually sudden in onset, and comes in spasms of increased intensity, though between these episodes there is some pain. Colicky pain is often associated with sweating and vomiting. The patient usually cannot lie still, but rolls about, is doubled up or walks about restlessly.

The pain of local peritonitis is due to inflammation of the parietal peritoneum over the anatomical site of the affected organ, the right iliac fossa in appendicitis and the right hypochondrium in cholecystitis. Spread of the inflammation may follow, causing diffuse peritonitis with generalised continuous abdominal pain.

The site of pain may lie over the diseased organ or be referred to some place remote from it. When pain is referred, its site corresponds to the dermatome segment from which the involved organ developed embryonically. For example, central abdominal pain in the early phase of appendicitis reflects the midline origin of the appendix from the mid-gut and is due to tension on the visceral peritoneum caused by swelling or obstruc-tion. Only later does the inflammation spread to the parietal peritoneum, and then the pain shifts to the right iliac fossa. In inflammation of the gall bladder there may be hyperaesthesia below the right scapula in the region supplied by the ninth, tenth and eleventh intercostal nerves—the same seg-ments as those from which the biliary apparatus develops. If the dia-phragm becomes inflamed from cholecystitis, leakage of gastric juice or extravasation of blood, then pain may be referred to the tip of the shoulder in the segments supplied by cervical nerves three, four and five, the same segments that make up the phrenic nerve. Small-bowel colic is commonly referred to the midline because the mid-gut is embryonically a midline organ. Renal colic is commonly referred to the distribution of the first lumbar nerve in the groin, inner thigh and scrotum.

Vomiting

Vomiting may be due to the severity of the pain or the toxaemia of inflammation. Obstruction of the intestinal tract, may be due either to a mechanical factor or the paralysis of the bowel (paralytic ileus) that is commonly associated with inflammation. The patient with localised inflammation (such as in early appendicitis) rarely vomits more than once or twice. Vomiting of bile in a newborn child may indicate duodenal or small-bowel obstruction; persistent vomiting of fluid which is free of bile should suggest the possibility of stenosis of the pylorus, especially in a child when it is forcibly expelled—projectile vomiting. In adult pyloric stenosis the vomit is offensive and large in volume, and often contains recognisable food taken more than 24 hours previously.

When the gut is obstructed the vomit consists at first of food or bile, but with the passage of time the volume of vomit increases and its colour changes from yellow to brown. 'Faecal vomiting' is a serious symptom, in which the vomit is thick, brown and offensive and indicates advanced obstruction. These changes are not due to the presence of true faeces but to the formation of degradation products of blood exuded into obstructed or strangulated bowel. True faecal vomiting only occurs from a fistulous communication between the stomach and transverse colon. Vomiting in cases of peritonitis usually occurs only once or twice unless the inflammation is diffuse, when the bowel is bathed in inflammatory exudate causing paralysis of peristalsis. Paralytic ileus is really a form of obstruc-tion, and may be indistinguishable from other forms of intestinal obstruction.

Bowel Function

Constipation is a common feature of acute abdominal conditions. In intestinal obstruction neither faeces nor flatus can be passed; it is the failure of passage of wind that is more significant, especially if none is released by an enema. In most acute inflammatory conditions constipa-tion is usual from the start, though diarrhoea may occur due to irritation of the colon or rectum by pelvic peritonitis or an abscess. Diarrhoea may also be a feature of incomplete obstruction.

Gastro-intestinal Bleeding

Blood may be seen in the faeces when bleeding has occurred into the gastro-intestinal tract. Bright blood of normal colour indicates rectal or anal bleeding, tarry motions (melaena) indicate high intestinal, duodenal or gastric bleeding; dark blood usually comes from the upper rectum or colon. Occasionally blood can only be detected by chemical means— occult blood. Pale putty-coloured stools may give contributory evidence of obstructive jaundice. When a stool cannot be passed it may be possible to obtain a specimen by rectal examination and inspection of any traces of faeces on the finger stall.

Genito-urinary Symptoms

Urinary infection (pyelitis, cystitis) often gives rise to acute abdominal symptoms, therefore enquiry should always be made about frequency of micturition, dysuria or haematuria. In women inflammation, rupture, twisting (torsion) or haemorrhage from the genital organs may occur. The menstrual history must be obtained, particularly details of the frequency and regularity of the periods, the date of the last period and whether it was normal in duration and amount. The occurrence of a purulent vaginal discharge indicates inflammation in the genital tract.

Age

The patient's age gives some help in diagnosis, for certain conditions are more common within a particular age range. Large bowel obstruction due to cancer is unusual before middle age; obstruction due to agenesis of nerve plexuses in the bowel wall is most likely to present in the newborn. Perforation of a peptic ulcer is uncommon under the age of 20 years, though perforation of the small bowel may occur in newborn infants, due to obstruction by masses of inspissated meconium associated with pancreatic fibrosis. Conditions such as cholecystitis or twisted ovarian cyst only occur very rarely in childhood. Acute appendicitis may arise at any age.

Past History

The previous medical history may give some assistance in diagnosis. Before perforation of a peptic ulcer there may be a story of indigestion, though in many this is limited to a complaint of vague discomfort spread over a few weeks. Flatulent dyspepsia or attacks of biliary colic may precede an episode of acute cholecystitis. Progressively increasing constipation or intermittent attacks of diarrhoea may terminate in acute obstruction of the colon. Acute appendicitis may be preceded by bouts of pain and tenderness in the right iliac fossa. Loss of appetite and weight before the onset of an acute abdominal condition are sinister and suggestive of some malignant cause.

Physical Examination

Perhaps one of the most important and difficult assessments to be made in clinical medicine is the elementary decision as to whether someone is ill or not. The general appearance of the patient gives important clues as to the seriousness of the condition.

The 'Hippocratic facies' of ashen countenance, drawn features and sunken eyes denotes a state of toxaemia and dehydration which may well terminate fatally unless treatment is begun at once. The high respiratory rate or the dilated alae nasi of an infant may give evidence of pneumonia or a severe upper respiratory tract infection, even when examination of the lungs reveals no physical signs. High fever and rigors suggest the possibility of urinary infection. On the other hand, a normal state of hydration and a normal pulse, temperature and respiratory rate by no means rule out a serious abdominal condition.

Abdominal Examination

It is important that the whole abdomen be included in the physical examination. Hernial orifices must not be forgotten, and a rectal or vaginal examination always concludes examination of the abdomen for an acute condition.

Inspection of the abdomen may reveal distension, resonant to percussion if it is due to gas, or dull if it is due to fluid. Distension of the small bowel is usually centred around the umbilicus or supra-pubic region. Distension of the colon causes fullness in the flanks. Peristalsis due to small-bowel obstruction may be visible, giving an appearance of 'laddering', with movements that tend to pass towards the right iliac fossa. The respiratory excursion of the abdominal wall is likely to be restricted in peritonitis by the rigidity of its muscles.

Palpation is performed gently with the flat of the hand to estimate slight degrees of tenderness and muscle guarding. The quadrants farthest away from the painful area should be examined first, pressure being finally applied over the site where pain is expected. The elicitation of tenderness and muscle guarding is good evidence of local peritonitis due to inflammation of the parietal peritoneum over an affected organ. Hyperaesthesia and release tenderness are supportive signs of peritonitis. The sign of rebound or release tenderness is demonstrated by sudden release of pressure over the tender area causing greater pain than pressure itself. Rebound tenderness should never be ignored, for almost always it indicates the need for operation.

Deep palpation can rarely be carried out where there is tenderness and rigidity, but in obstruction it may reveal the presence of a mass. Often, when an inflammatory mass is covered and protected by rigid abdominal muscles, its presence can only be suspected by a vague sense of resistance to deep palpation. This can only be confirmed when the muscles have been relaxed by anaesthesia or by the fuller development of the swelling, which is often due to suppuration. In diffuse peritonitis the whole abdominal wall is rigid, board-like and intensely tender.

Percussion is useful in the detection of fluid or gas and, in the case of ascites, of shifting dullness. In perforated peptic ulcer there may be diminution of the normal area of hepatic dullness over the lower thorax. Percussion of the rigid tender abdomen is painful and rarely provides useful information.

Auscultation of the abdomen with a stethoscope must always be carried out, and is imperative in all acute abdominal conditions. Auscultation of the abdomen will often provide the surgeon with more important information than auscultation of the chest, because the consequences of altered bowel sounds may be disastrous in a matter of hours. A silent abdomen indicates peritonitis and paralysis of the bowel. Increased bowel sounds often suggest intestinal obstruction and, when they have a characteristic tinkling quality, are diagnostic of obstruction.

Special Investigations

In any hospital there are three special examinations that can always be obtained night and day—microscopy of urine, a white-cell count and a plain radiograph of the abdomen. The urine should be tested for albumen and sugar. Microscopy of the sediment obtained after centrifuging may reveal leucocytes and organisms. A white-cell count may be useful in indicating infection, though a normal count does not rule this out. Serial white-cell counts are very useful in following the course of inflammation, especially postoperatively when a residual abscess is suspected.

A plain radiograph of the abdomen is essential where obstruction or perforation of a viscus is suspected. It may also reveal opaque gall stones or renal stones. Views must be taken of the patient in the recumbent and erect position; recumbent to show the distribution of gas in the bowel, erect to show the presence of fluid levels. Absence of gas in the large bowel supports the diagnosis of small-bowel obstruction. A 'ground glass' appearance in the pelvis in the erect view suggests the presence of intraperitoneal fluid—a common feature of obstruction. Generalised gaseous distension of the large and small bowel may confirm the diagnosis of paralytic ileus. A gas bubble immediately under the diaphragm is diagnostic of perforation of a peptic ulcer. Radiographs of the chest may be useful to exclude conditions such as pneumonia and pneumothorax that may cause abdominal pain; widening of the aortic shadow may suggest dissection of the aorta.

Other special investigations may be necessary in an emergency, such as measurement of the serum electrolytes if the patient is dehydrated due to vomiting or diarrhoea. The haemocrit and level of serum proteins give useful information of haemoconcentration, as also does the urine specific gravity and the urea concentration. Elevation of the serum amylase is diagnostic of pancreatitis. An electrocardiogram can be extremely helpful when coronary thrombosis is suspected and the patient's symptoms are mainly abdominal.

Indications for Operation

Exact diagnosis of acute abdominal conditions is often not possible. The vital decision is whether an operation is necessary to remove an inflamed or necrotic organ, to close a leak, to relieve obstruction or to drain pus or an irritant fluid. Only the accumulated experience of dealing with numerous abdominal crises can provide the answer as to when to operate. Certain symptoms and signs are particularly ominous and should never be disregarded. Among these are evidence of strangulation in intestinal obstruction (see p. 244), evidence of generalised or generalising peritonitis and any suggestion of perforation. A 'silent abdomen' is particularly dangerous. Sometimes operation must be carried out, if only to exclude the possibility of some potentially fatal condition, for example, after abdominal injury when a ruptured spleen is suspected.

In some cases a period of close observation is reasonable. During this phase no analgesics are given for fear of masking signs. The pulse rate is recorded hourly, a rising pulse rate being suggestive of increasing severity of some pathological process. The temperature and respiratory rate are recorded 4-hourly. The abdomen is frequently examined for increasing tenderness and rigidity and for any change in the quality and number of bowel sounds. Failure to relieve distension by an enema, or persistent vomiting, may indicate completeness of intestinal obstruction. Most patients who reach hospital with abdominal pain should be admitted for urgent surgical treatment or for a short period of observation. Certainly none should be sent home before being examined by a surgeon. This rule applies particularly to children, where the difficulties of diagnosis will often be beyond the experience of junior medical officers.

ACUTE PERITONITIS

Inflammation of the peritoneum may be due to inflammation, perforation or vascular insufficiency of an intra-abdominal organ. Infarction or strangulation may follow arterial embolism and venous thrombosis or mechanical pressure on the vessels of the intestine, such as occurs in obstruction, volvulus or intussusception. In ischaemic tissues bacterial proliferation is rapid and may cause generalised peritonitis and fatal toxaemia. Irritation of the peritoneum may follow leakage from a viscus of urine, bile, blood, gastric and pancreatic enzymes. Such irritation is rapidly followed by the development of bacterial infection. Peritonitis is either local or diffuse, but not all local peritonitis progresses to become diffuse.

Symptoms and Signs

In the early phase of peritonitis the patient lies motionless in bed. The main symptom is intense, continuous, burning pain, usually beginning in a localised area over the affected viscus and often spreading rapidly over the whole abdomen. The pulse and temperature may be little raised. Vomiting may occur of fluid which eventually becomes dark and 'faecal' in quality; constipation is a constant accompaniment.

Later

Later there are signs of dehydration and toxaemia, going on to collapse with pallor, clamminess of skin, low blood pressure, a rapid pulse and quick, shallow respirations. In the terminal phases of peritonitis the patient becomes confused and plucks fitfully at the bedclothes. In children and uraemic patients twitching and convulsions may occur.

Terminal

Examination of the abdomen reveals tenderness, at first localised, but later becoming generalised if the disease process progresses. Tenderness is accompanied by rigidity of the abdominal muscles. The respiratory excursion of the abdominal muscles is restricted by pain, so that respiration is carried on predominantly by the thoracic muscles. After a variable period of time, hours or days, the rigidity may relax when the abdomen becomes distended as paralytic ileus becomes established. Auscultation of the abdomen reveals few or no bowel sounds.

Treatment

When it is considered that operation is indicated it must be performed as a matter of urgency, for a delay of a few hours may make all the difference to the possibility of recovery. In some cases the patient may be so ill that a period of resuscitation may be necessary, but this should not be prolonged, and should only be instituted to make the patient fit for anaesthesia.

Once a diagnosis has been made pain should be relieved by morphia. The blood volume should be restored by the intravenous infusion of normal saline, plasma or blood, depending on what it is considered that the patient has lost. Time rarely permits for complete correction of electrolyte losses and replacement of blood volume. Once the patient is fit for anaesthesia, further correction of hydration can be provided during the operation itself and after it. An intravenous antibiotic of the broad-spectrum type, for example, ampicillin, should be given during this period. At the same time the stomach should be emptied through a large-bore plastic oesophageal catheter passed through the nose, through which continuous suction is maintained to keep the stomach empty.

Progress is assessed by the improvement in the patient's well-being, correction of the signs of dehydration, improvement in the colour of the skin, a rise in the level of blood pressure and loss of the clammy quality of the skin.

Emergency operations are usually performed through a midline or paramedian laparotomy incision. The inflamed organ may be removed, perforations closed and exudate aspirated from the peritoneum. Obstruction of small bowel may be relieved by division of adhesions, removal of foreign bodies, untwisting of bowel or resection if it is infarcted or gangrenous. Large-bowel obstruction or perforated diverticulitis may necessitate the performance of a colostomy. Occasionally, in ulcerative colitis, when the large intestine is severely ulcerated extensive colonic resection may be needed. The distended small bowel proximal to a point of obstruction should be emptied through a long metal tube attached to a sucker inserted through a stab wound in the bowel wall. This removes a large volume of heavily contaminated fluid, relieving distension and making wound closure easier and the postoperative convalescence more comfortable.

The volume of fluid aspirated from the peritoneum and the gut must be replaced by an equal volume of normal saline. If blood is removed from the peritoneum an equal volume should be replaced by intravenous infusion. Occasionally, at operation for peritonitis, only drainage of pus is necessary. The drains most commonly used to release secretions or pus are of corrugated rubber or tubes of plastic or rubber. The drainage tube is brought out through the original laparotomy wound. A sump drain, a small tube inside a larger perforated tube, may be placed in the pelvis.

Postoperatively, close observation must be maintained and treatment prolonged until there is evidence of subsidence of peritonitis or relief of obstruction. Signs of a satisfactory outcome are the improved state of the general health of the patient and maintenance of normal hydration, with a progressive fall in the pulse rate and temperature. A soft abdomen free of tenderness is comforting to both the patient and the surgeon. The return of bowel sounds is the first landmark in recovery, and the passage of flatus or a stool suggests that any crisis is over. Aspiration of stomach contents is maintained continuously until a marked decrease in the volume of aspirate indicates that gastro-intestinal secretions are passing along the bowel by peristalsis. Aspirations are then performed at lengthening intervals, at first hourly, later 2 hourly and eventually 4 hourly. If after 4 hours only 20–50 ml. of aspirate is obtained it is safe to remove the naso-gastric tube. A change in the quality of the fluid removed heralds improvement: offensive odour should be lost, and the colour should change from brown to the greenish-yellow of normal bile. Oral fluids are given, once the volume of aspirate diminishes, cautiously at the rate of 30 ml. per hour. So long as less is aspirated than is being given by mouth, it is assumed that the ileus is diminishing.

In recent years many surgeons have preferred to make a temporary gastrostomy after operations likely to be followed by ileus, rather than use a naso-gastric tube for a long period. A fine-calibre plastic tube is stitched into the stomach and led out through a tiny stab wound in the abdominal wall. An indwelling tube in the oesophagus is most unpleasant and, by limiting coughing, may predispose to lung complications. The oesophagus may become irritated and eventually ulcerated if a tube is left within it for a long time; even fibrous stenosis may occur.

During the period of postoperative ileus fluids must be given intravenously to keep the patient in a state of normal hydration. The maintenance volume of fluid (see p. 20) is given, supplemented by a volume of normal saline equal to any gastric aspirate or fistulous discharge from the gut. Accurate fluid-balance charts must be kept. The secretion of urine must be carefully measured: a sign of satisfactory progress is an increasing volume of urine of specific gravity greater than 1·008.

Pain and apprehension must be relieved by regular, small doses of morphia. Adequate periods for sleep must be allowed, especialiy when many observations are being made and so much treatment is being given. The patient should lie comfortably, sitting up a little to assist coughing and breathing. Regular breathing exercises and help in coughing up sputum is given by the physiotherapist at daily visits and whenever respiratory distress occurs or is feared. An antibiotic is given in the intravenous infusion if there is peritonitis. It may have to be changed if the result of culture of fluid obtained at operation shows that the organisms are insensitive to it.

INTESTINAL OBSTRUCTION

The intestine may become obstructed by occlusion of its lumen by a foreign body, disease of the intestinal wall itself and by pressure from outside. If its vascular supply is impaired, either by venous or arterial obstruction, the bowel is said to be strangulated. The commonest cause of intestinal obstruction is incarceration of bowel in an external hernia (usually inguinal or femoral); the second commonest cause is fibrous adhesions, usually the result of a previous operation. For these reasons every patient presenting with an acute abdominal condition must be examined for evidence of a hernia or the scar of a previous abdominal operation. In the absence of a hernia or a history of previous operation, the possibility of neoplasm of the intestine should be considered.

Small-bowel obstruction is usually sudden in onset. In ileal obstruction pain is sited in the peri-umbilical region or in the lower abdomen. In jejunal obstruction the site of pain may be higher. The intensity and frequency of intestinal colic depends upon the completeness of the obstruction. Early copious vomiting is a feature of jejunal obstruction with profound losses of water and electrolyte that rapidly cause collapse. The reason for the massive volume of vomit in high intestinal obstruction is that 7–8 litres of secretions enter the small bowel every day from the stomach, liver and pancreas, of which a large proportion may be lost. In ileal obstruction vomiting occurs later, being first bilious and later faecal; the speed of change in the character of the vomit depends upon the severity and rapidity of the obstruction.

Distension of the abdomen is minimal or absent in high small-bowel obstruction. In ileal obstruction central abdominal distension is a feature and, through a thin abdominal wall, distended loops of bowel may be seen and felt. Intermittent or incomplete ileal obstruction causes hypertrophy of the intestine, with visible peristalsis. In the early phase of obstruction tenderness of the abdomen is absent, whereas tenderness and rigidity are typical of peritonitis. If intestinal obstruction remains unrelieved the signs of peritonitis supervene, especially if there is any degree of strangulation.

In obstruction constipation is usually complete and flatus cannot be passed even after an enema. Tenderness, rigidity and the palpation of a tender mass may all suggest the possibility of strangulation. Coincident with colicky spasms of pain, borborygmi may be audible to the patient or bystanders. Through the stethoscope runs of noisy peristaltic sounds can be heard of a typical high-pitched quality. If strangulation and peritonitis occur, then gangrene supervenes. It must be stressed that in intestinal obstruction, especially in hernial obstruction, an element of strangulation can rarely be excluded clinically with any confidence, so that operation must almost always be performed as a matter of urgency.

Obstruction of the colon is most often due to a lesion in the sigmoid. There may be painless distension of the abdomen of slow onset, associated with increasing severity of constipation. Intermittent attacks of diarrhoea may occur and blood and mucus be passed. Often, however, colicky abdominal pain may occur over days, weeks or months at an increasing tempo until complete obstruction occurs. Occasionally the onset is acute, resembling small-bowel obstruction with pain, vomiting and distension, except that the distension is most obvious in the flanks. Volvulus of the sigmoid colon is an acute emergency, with sudden severe pain, gross abdominal distension and the rapid onset of signs of strangulation if the obstruction is not relieved. True faecal vomiting may occur as a rare and usually terminal event if the ileocaecal valve becomes incompetent following gross distension of the colon.

Obstruction in the right side of the colon, anywhere to the right of the splenic flexure, may present with the symptoms and signs of ileal obstruction; visible small-bowel peristalsis is then common.

Plain radiographs of the abdomen, with the patient erect, show fluid levels in ileal obstruction with absence of gas in the colon. In jejunal obstruction one or two distended loops may be seen in the upper abdomen, with absence of gas more distally. Right-sided colonic obstruction may show ileal fluid levels and distension of the caecum, this will be especially gross in the rare cases of volvulus of the caecum. Obstruction of the sigmoid is characterised by considerable distension of the colon proximal to it. In volvulus of the sigmoid colon the abdomen is filled by enormously distended redundant loops of colon.

Treatment

The principles of treatment are as for peritonitis: gastric aspiration, intravenous fluid replacement and operation. Only if the obstruction appears incomplete may a period of expectant treatment be allowed, and then only under close observation. If an enema releases flatus, then operation may be deferred so long as distension is relieved, pain dies down and vomiting or the volume of gastric aspirate decreases. If strangulation is suspected operation must be carried out urgently.

Obstruction in a hernia is relieved locally. In all other cases laparotomy is performed. If the caecum is found collapsed, then the small bowel must be obstructed. The site of obstruction is found where collapsed and distended gut meet. Postoperative adhesions are the commonest intra-abdominal cause of small bowel obstruction, especially the isolated bands which so often form after surgery. Sometimes several loops of intestine are matted with adhesions often inaccessibly placed in the pelvis. To free all these loops of adhesions may be dangerous, because the bowel may be so easily perforated. A short-circuit may then be performed by side-to-side entero-anastomosis proximal to the matted loops, care being taken that the blind loop of excluded bowel is not too long. Exclusion of small intestine may be followed in later years by such complications as anaemia and steatorrhoea with malnutrition (see p. 299).

Obstruction of the caecum or ascending colon is by-passed by anastomosing the ileum side by side with the transverse colon, an operation called ileo-transverse colostomy. Sigmoid obstruction is relieved by transverse colostomy so long as the lesion is thought to be resectable; iliac colostomy is performed if the condition is considered inoperable. Caecostomy may be performed for an obstruction in the transverse colon or at the splenic flexure; it is also useful to fix the caecum after untwisting a volvulus so as to prevent recurrence.

Strangulated intestine is plum-coloured or black, with a loss of sheen on its surface and poor or absent arterial pulsation in its mesentery, which may be thickened with oedema. Resection of bowel is a considerable hazard to the patient already suffering from intestinal obstruction, and so the surgeon must be sure that the bowel cannot recover before deciding to remove it. Recovery is judged after the affected gut has been wrapped in a warm saline pack for 5 minutes or so. Viability is assessed by watching for a change in colour of the bowel, seeing peristalsis crossing the damaged segment and the recovery of arterial pulsation in the mesentery. Small patches of gangrene can be invaginated by catgut sutures. Extensive gangrene always requires resection.

PARALYTIC ILEUS

Paralysis of the myenteric nerve plexuses of the bowel is most often due to peritonitis, where the gut is bathed in pus, exudate, secretions (urine, bile, gastric or pancreatic juice) or blood. Paralysis of the intestine allows localisation of infection, which would be spread if peristalsis continued. Less often ileus may be associated with a retroperitoneal haematoma after abdominal or spinal injury. Immobilisation on a plaster bed or in a plaster hip spica may precipitate a neurogenic obstruction. Prolonged mechanical obstruction may eventually result in a state of paralysis. Ileus may be prolonged in states of hypoproteinaemia and hypokalaemia.

The symptoms of ileus are distension and vomiting. Pain is usually inconspicuous (unlike mechanical obstruction) and bowel sounds are absent. The abdomen may be free of tenderness or rigidity so long as there is no peritonitis. After any abdominal operation normal bowel sounds disappear for about 48 hours, but should return about the third to fourth day. Persistent distension, profuse gastric aspirate and a silent abdomen lead to a diagnosis of paralytic ileus. The possibility of mechanical obstruction must be considered, and the possibility of leakage from a suture line or formation of pus must be suspected. It must be stressed that the diagnosis of obstruction and ileus following surgery can be extremely difficult, and can usually only be made by someone particularly experienced in the management of postoperative abdominal conditions. Radiography of the abdomen shows generalised distension of both the small and large intestine in paralytic ileus, fluid levels in the small bowel suggest mechanical obstruction.

Treatment

In ileus due to peritonitis prolonged gastric aspiration keeps the stomach empty of fluid and gas. Ideally a tube should be passed long enough to travel through the entire length of the small bowel. The Miller Abbott tube is 6 feet in length and has a balloon at its end that, when inflated by air or air and mercury, can act as a bolus that will pass the length of the intestine. It is, however, swallowed with difficulty in the very ill, and is being used less and less. Most often a tube is passed into the stomach and aspiration is carried out through it continuously. Not only are secretions removed but swallowed air, which is responsible for a large part of the distension of the bowel, is prevented from passing into the intestine. Hydration and electrolyte balance are maintained by intravenous infusion. Small regular doses of morphia enhance bowel tone and relieve anxiety. Chemotherapy is essential, usually one of the broad-spectrum antibiotics is given intravenously. If obstruction or leakage of a viscus is suspected operation may be needed, a difficult decision which only an experienced surgeon can make. There is no place for the administration of drugs such as pituitrin and physostigmine, which cause the gut to contract. Intestinal movement can be stimulated pharmacologically, but the effect is transitory and usually leaves the patient worse after the effect of the drug has worn off.

Improvement in the patient's condition is measured by decrease in abdominal distension and decrease of the volume of gastric aspirate, passage of flatus and the return of bowel sounds. With all these signs the patient's well-being is improved.

INJURIES OF THE ABDOMEN

Most abdominal injuries are contusions causing bruising and local haematomata, more severe injuries may be very serious if intraperitoneal

I

haemorrhage or damage to a viscus occurs. Diagnosis may be extremely difficult, and a period of close observation is essential to exclude severe injury. Therefore it must be a rule that anyone who has suffered an abdominal injury is admitted to hospital and kept there until fully recovered. Operation must be performed in any case of doubt, and it is always preferable to perform an unnecessary laparotomy than miss an injured bowel or other viscus.

Abdominal Wall

Haematomata in the muscles of the abdominal wall may cause symptoms and signs of intraperitoneal disease. Bruising of the muscles is followed by tenderness and rigidity. A mass may appear if a large haematoma collects, this is superficial and made more obvious and more painful by tensing the abdominal muscles. So long as the signs remain localised and so long as the bowel sounds are preserved, observation may be continued, but in any case of doubt, laparotomy must be performed.

Occasionally the rectus abdominis muscle may be ruptured by severe trauma, or it may occur during labour or in a bronchitic person after a spasm of coughing. Occasionally a massive haematoma may collect within the rectus sheath after rupture of an epigastric artery in an aged arteriosclerotic patient. So long as the diagnosis is clear, careful watch may be kept until the haematoma absorbs. Rarely the rectus sheath must be opened, the haematoma evacuated and the muscle repaired.

Intraperitoneal Haemorrhage

When this occurs there may be obvious signs of bleeding, with pallor, sweating, thirst, abnormal temperature, faintness and a rapid low-tension pulse. The patient may feel excessively cold. The abdomen may be guarded and tender and bowel sounds are absent. An important symptom is pain in the shoulder due to irritation of the diaphragm by blood. This sign may be produced by elevating the feet above the level of the heart, and is strong confirmation of bleeding.

Usually the development of the signs of bleeding may be very insidious in onset, and indeed, there may be a period after the initial injury when the patient appears quite normal and shows no abnormal physical signs. This feature is particularly characteristic of a rupture of the spleen, when hours or days may elapse before the full development of the signs of intraperitoneal haemorrhage. Suspicious signs are increasing anaemia, high pulse rate and persistent tenderness in the abdomen.

The abdominal viscera most likely to be damaged by injury are the spleen, liver, small intestine and bladder, in that order. The pancreas may be crushed and produce the signs of pancreatitis. Abdominal injury may easily be missed in the unconscious patient or the patient who has suffered multiple injuries. It is essential in such patients for an examination of the whole body to be undertaken.

Penetrating Wounds

Penetrating wounds of the abdomen must always be explored, no matter how superficial they may appear to be. A small puncture wound may conceal intraperitoneal damage that can be fatal. The track must be followed down to and if necessary into the peritoneum. It must also not be forgotten that thoracic wounds often involve abdominal organs.

Abdominal injuries due to blast are particularly misleading, in that there may be no external evidence of injury, while there are multiple ruptures of small and large bowel. This applies particularly to those who may be swimming at the time of an underwater explosion.

CHRONIC PERITONEAL DISEASE

Tuberculous Peritonitis

This is typically a disease of children and young adults which tends to disappear with improved standards of living, so that it is rarely seen in Britain today. Usually the disease is secondary to a focus elsewhere, and there may be active tuberculosis in the mesenteric lymph nodes, the ileocaecal region or involving a fallopian tube. The onset of the condition is insidious, and often the child is brought to the doctor because of enlargement of the abdomen, general ill-health and wasting in the rest of the body. On examination dilated veins are often to be seen under the skin of the abdominal wall, and the omentum may be palpable as a knobbly mass. Diagnosis is confirmed at laparotomy when the abdomen is found full of a clear yellow fluid and the bowel and viscera are studded with small tubercles. If there is an obvious lesion, such as a tuberculous pyosalpinx, this is excised, but otherwise the fluid is sucked out and the abdomen closed. A full course of streptomycin, P.A.S. and isoniazid is given. For the first few weeks the patient will require rest in bed with the opportunity of having an excellent diet and plenty of fresh air. Erythrocyte sedimentation rate is a good guide to progress, as is also the body weight. Chemotherapy can usually be concluded at the end of 6 months, but a follow-up should be carried out for some years in case of relapse. There are two rare variants of tuberculous peritonitis which cause the abdominal surgeon particular trouble. In the encysted form, fluid is found encapsulated within the peritoneal cavity and requires aspiration at laparotomy, intestinal obstruction may occur if this is not done. In the fibrous form there are widespread adhesions which lead to repeated attacks of subacute and later acute intestinal obstruction. There may be severe wasting, colicky abdominal pain and malabsorption, leading to frequent, pale, bulky stools. Obstruction is relieved at operation, and chemotherapy will usually bring the disease under control.

ASCITES

A collection of fluid in the peritoneal cavity is a common finding, and a thorough investigation must be made of the patient in order to discover the cause, which may be cardiac disease, as in right-sided heart failure, renal disease or portal hypertension. A description of the latter and its treatment will be found on p. 342. A further differential diagnosis is ovarian cyst, which may be so enlarged as apparently to fill the abdominal cavity and be indistinguishable from ascites. Malignant ascites is described below.

Malignant Disease of the Peritoneum

The common cause of a malignant effusion in the peritoneal cavity is the spread of carcinoma from one of the abdominal viscera, especially stomach, colon and ovary, which seeds throughout the peritoneum, and the ascites is then a terminal event. The primary lesion may be found in some distant organ, such as the breast. Treatment can only be palliative, but it is often to the patient's advantage to have the fluid removed through a needle in order to relieve pressure on the diaphragm and so make breathing more easy. The introduction of radio-active colloidal gold or anti-mitotic agents, such as cyclophosphamide, is sometimes effective in reducing the formation of ascitic fluid. This is particularly useful in the malignant ascites which accompanies ovarian tumours in young women.

Another cause of ascites is pseudomyxoma peritonei, in which the peritoneal cavity is filled with a jelly-like material. This usually follows rupture of a pseudo-mucinous cyst of the ovary or less often by a muco-coele of the appendix or gall bladder. The removal of the offending organ does not cure the condition, and it is impossible to remove all the mucinous material. Careful histological examination will reveal occasional malignant cells scattered through the mass, and the condition must be considered as one of low-grade malignancy.

RETROPERITONEAL DISEASE

The retroperitoneal space is not often involved by disease, but when it is, symptoms and signs are produced which are difficult to interpret. The most puzzling is retroperitoneal fibrosis, in which dense fibrous tissue in the retroperitoneal space may eventually obstruct the ureters and cause anuria (see p. 380). Retroperitoneal tumours and swellings may become very large before they are noticed or cause symptoms. They usually appear to be fixed, not moving with respiration. There is always some difficulty in diagnosis, especially to differentiate lesions of the kidney, adrenals, spleen, liver and pancreas from those in the retroperitoneal space itself.

Diagnosis is aided by intravenous pyelography, which may show the kidney to be displaced downwards or pushed to one side. Air insufflated into the retroperitoneal tissues via a needle inserted in front of the sacrum may outline the adrenal glands, greater accuracy is achieved if tomography is used with air insufflation. Visualisation of the gastro-intestinal tract with barium may give indirect evidence of a retroperitoneal swelling. A tumour on the right side may displace the duodenum to the left, a left-sided tumour may deform or compress the stomach. A swelling arising from the pancreas often opens out the curve of the duodenum.

Cysts occasionally develop in the retroperitoneal tissues, and may reach an enormous size. They are often developmental in origin from mesonephric and Wolffian duct remnants. True pancreatic cysts and pseudo-cysts of the pancreas (see p. 350) may also be very large. Malignant tumours are uncommon, they frequently reach a considerable size. Apparent encapsulation may make removal fairly simple, but most recur, and few can be cured. A massive growth of the adrenal may simulate a sarcoma. Fibrosarcoma, and most rarely of all liposarcoma, occur retroperitoneally. Such tumours are either radio-resistant or only temporarily radio-sensitive. Surgical removal is attempted, followed by radiotherapy. Benign tumours are rarer than the malignant; leiomyoma and ganglioneuroma may be found—the latter may have a 'dumb-bell' extension into the neural canal, causing compression of nerve roots or the spinal cord. Large retroperitoneal tumours may best be approached by a thoraco-lumbar incision.

FURTHER READING

Cope, Sir Z. (1963) *The Early Diagnosis of the Acute Abdomen.* 12th ed. Oxford University Press, London.
Shepherd, J. A. (1960) *Surgery of the Acute Abdomen,* E. & S. Livingstone, Edinburgh.

CHAPTER NINETEEN

THE APPENDIX

ACUTE APPENDICITIS

Between the ages of 10 and 30 years acute appendicitis accounts for more than half of all abdominal emergencies. Appendicitis is a potentially dangerous condition, causing the deaths of more than 600 persons in England and Wales each year. Most of these deaths could have been avoided by early diagnosis and treatment, for when inflammation is limited to the appendix and appendicectomy is carried out early, the fatality rate is minimal—less than 0·1%. In cases where the inflammation has spread from the appendix to cause peritonitis the mortality is much higher, especially in the very young and the very old.

Appendicitis is a relatively recently diagnosed condition. Until the beginning of this century inflammation of the bowel in the right iliac fossa was called perityphlitis (typhlon = caecum) and was treated conservatively by physicians. The coronation of King Edward VII in 1902 was postponed because he developed an appendix abscess, and only after this time was appendicitis frequently diagnosed and treated by operation. It is not known why appendicitis should now be so common, but racial and environmental factors and dietary habits may well be involved. Appendicitis is still less often seen in India, Africa and the West Indies, and when it does occur, tends to follow a benign course.

Pathology

The cause of appendicitis is not entirely understood. The appendix is a blind sac or diverticulum containing virulent organisms; it is commonly obstructed. Its wall contains much lymphoid tissue, the presence of which, as in the tonsil, seems to be a factor in the localisation of infection especially in the relatively young. The pathway of infection may be from the lumen of the bowel or from a transient bacteraemia, and is usually due to coliform organisms.

Two types of appendicitis are recognised.

1. Catarrhal Appendicitis

In this the mucous membrane is swollen, oedematous and congested, the sub-mucous lymphoid tissue contains areas of inflammation and, later, suppuration. Externally the appendix is reddened and turgid with flakes of organised fibrin. In many instances this form of appendicitis takes a mild course and, if left untreated, may resolve in 1 or 2 weeks.

2. *Obstructive Appendicitis*

A faecal concretion, stricture, kink, foreign body or oedematous area of the appendix are the usual obstructing factors. Inflammatory changes are swifter, and faecal pus under tension causes ulceration of the mucosa. Gangrene of the whole wall may occur within a few hours of the onset of symptoms.

The natural history of appendicitis is either resolution or progress to perforation, abscess formation or diffuse peritonitis. Resolution may be complete, but more commonly the appendix is damaged and rendered prone to repeated attacks of inflammation, *recurrent appendicitis*. There is no true granuloma that can be called *chronic appendicitis*; this term is loosely applied to patients with recurrent appendicitis, and less happily to those with recurrent pains in the right iliac fossa or even chronic dyspepsia, in whom the appendix is removed after exclusion of all other causes for the symptoms.

An *appendix abscess* represents the attempt of the body to wall off inflammation. The appendix, often perforated, lies bathed in pus in a cavity walled off by bowel, omentum and parietal peritoneum, all intensely inflamed. There is an associated high swinging fever and leucocytosis. A small abscess may decrease in size with treatment or resolve spontaneously, mainly due to subsidence of oedema and absorption of the small volume of pus. A large abscess may rupture into the peritoneal cavity, into the bowel or be discharged via the abdominal wall, rectum or vagina. An appendix abscess (see p. 255) usually takes several days to form, but earlier than this an *appendix mass* may be felt (in a child often within 24 hours of the onset of symptoms), formed by omentum wrapping round the inflamed organ.

Perforation of the appendix usually occurs distal to some obstruction, and is due to tension in the organ or thrombosis of its arterial supply caused by inflammation. A sudden discharge of highly infective material into the free peritoneal cavity may lead to a sudden crisis; more often the perforation is walled off by the surrounding viscera forming an abscess or mass. Faecoliths are often found, having been discharged through a perforation, and must be removed at operation, or a sinus may form discharging on to the abdominal wall.

The most serious complication is *diffuse peritonitis*. Pockets of foul-smelling pus are found throughout the abdomen, with much fibrinous exudate on the bowel, which is itself dilated and paralysed by the infection. Diffuse peritonitis is most often seen at the extremes of life, in the young and the old, in whom the powers of localisation of infection seem reduced, and in whom the diagnosis may be difficult and delayed.

Clinical Features

The disease may present in many ways, and it is not possible to describe all of them. However, the following are the most significant and typical features. The attack may start without warning, or may be preceded by vague abdominal discomfort, indigestion, constipation, diarrhoea or a sore throat. *Pain* is usually the first symptom, and is of gradual onset and rarely severe. Anorexia and nausea follow, a single vomit is common. Frequently there is fetor oris, with a typical 'alimentary' smell of the breath and furring of the tongue. The temperature may be normal, but more usually there is a slight rise to, say, 99° or 100° F. The pulse rate may be normal or slightly raised.

The initial pain is usually diffuse, and the patient indicates the peri-umbilical region as its centre. Occasionally there are spasms of colic. The painful impulses arising from the inflamed appendix pass along afferent sympathetic nerves to the region of the tenth and eleventh thoracic segments of the cord, where they are interpreted as coming from that part of the abdominal wall supplied by those segments. Since the appendix is part of the mid-gut, which is embryologically a median viscus, the pain is referred to the midline.

Usually after a few hours the pain shifts to the right side of the abdomen; however, the initial pain may be of very short duration or even absent, and then the first symptom is pain in the right iliac fossa. This localised pain is due to extension of inflammation to the sensitive parietal peritoneum over the appendix. The pain is more constant and becomes increasingly severe. The position of the pain may be some guide to the site of the inflamed appendix, which is most commonly in the region of McBurney's point, one-third of the distance from the anterior superior iliac spine to the umbilicus.

However, if the appendix is low in the pelvis the pain may be sited just above the pubis; if it is retrocaecal pain may occur in the flank. Rarely, in the case of maldescent of the caecum, the pain may be in the right upper quadrant of the abdomen; extremely rarely, if there is mal-rotation of the gut, the caecum lies on the left side and pain is felt in the left iliac fossa.

Tenderness and *muscle guarding* over the inflamed appendix are the two most important physical signs. Tenderness is more marked if the appendix is in contact with the parietal peritoneum, and then is usually localised to the right iliac fossa. Less often, when the appendix is situated deeply behind the caecum, the loin is tender. If the appendix is buried within coils of small intestine in the pelvis tenderness may only be elicited by rectal or vaginal examination. Rectal examination should therefore never be omitted in any patient with abdominal pain.

Muscle guarding is due to reflex spasm of the abdominal muscles over the inflamed peritoneum adjacent to the appendix. It is variable in extent and may, by its intensity, mask the presence of a mass of inflamed tissue or an abscess deep to it.

Rarely the patient presents with spurious diarrhoea, passing many small motions containing little faecal matter but a lot of mucus. The inflamed appendix will then be found in contact with the rectum or lower sigmoid colon. Sometimes the patient has pain in the lower abdomen at the end of micturition and may also have frequency, the inflamed appendix is then usually adherent to the urinary bladder.

APPENDIX ABSCESS

The formation of an abscess is indicated by the development of the signs of suppuration, usually some days after the onset of acute appendicitis. The temperature remains high, and may be irregular and swinging. The pulse rate is raised; there is sweating and the leucocyte count is increased. On abdominal or rectal examination, a *tender mass* is revealed. Often there is some abdominal distension, and even symptoms and signs of incomplete intestinal obstruction. In the case of a pelvic abscess there may be little tenderness except on pelvic examination, but symptoms of diarrhoea, passage of mucus per rectum and dysuria indicate the possibility. In epidemics of gastro-enteritis it is common to see examples of pelvic appendicitis missed until an abscess becomes obvious.

DIFFUSE PERITONITIS

Perforation is a serious complication which may occur at any phase of appendicitis. The initial pain, which was aching in character, suddenly becomes much more severe, spreading over the remainder of the abdomen as diffuse peritonitis develops. The general condition of the patient deteriorates rapidly. The pulse rate increases and the temperature rises, perhaps to 102° to 103° F. or more. Within a few hours there may be signs of peripheral circulatory failure. The patient looks ill, dehydrated, hollow-eyed and toxic and has a rapid, weak pulse. The face is pale and the skin cold and clammy. Death may follow from toxaemia and dehydration from infection, ileus and vomiting.

On abdominal examination, the area of tenderness is widespread, and often there is a board-like rigidity of the abdominal muscles. Later there is some distension of the abdomen with less rigidity. The abdomen is silent on auscultation.

DIFFERENTIAL DIAGNOSIS

A variety of conditions mimic acute appendicitis. In the initial phase of the disease it may be legitimate to observe the patient for a few hours, re-examining him at intervals in an effort to confirm the diagnosis. It is very dangerous to delay operative treatment too long, for the patient may run the risk of possible perforation of the appendix, with consequent increased mortality and incidence of complications. On occasions, the stage is reached where the diagnosis of acute appendicitis can only be made by laparotomy. The timing of this is a matter of experience and judgement— usually it must be done within 24 hours from the onset of symptoms, or even earlier in children.

Initial Stage

Because of the vagueness of the abdominal pain in the early phase of appendicitis, it may not be possible to distinguish such simple conditions as constipation, mild food poisoning or stomach-ache due to dietary indiscretion. Under these circumstances it is advisable to observe the patient for a few hours. If local tenderness and guarding in the position of the position of the appendix appears, then appendicectomy should be performed.

Definitive Stage

When localised pain has developed there are a number of common conditions which mimic acute appendicitis. Each position occupied by the inflamed organ offers its own peculiar difficulties in diagnosis.

Appendix in the Iliac Fossa

The symptoms and signs of acute appendicitis are really those of peritonitis in the right iliac fossa. Although the appendix is the organ most likely to be affected, there are others which may give rise to identical clinical features.

Mesenteric Lymph Nodes

Acute non-specific mesenteric adenitis (see p. 298) is most common in children. Tenderness is unusual, but if it can be elicited it is usually periumbilical in situation. Attacks of pain are severe and short-lived, with freedom between them. If there is any tenderness in the right iliac fossa, any doubt in the diagnosis or if symptoms persist for more than 12–16 hours, then the appendix should be removed. There is far less danger in operating than in leaving an inflamed appendix.

Tuberculous infection of lymph nodes in the abdomen is rare nowadays in this country; suppurative adenitis also occurs rarely, both may only be diagnosed at operation.

Ileum

Acute inflammation of the terminal ileum may be a feature of regional ileitis (see p. 293), and can rarely be diagnosed before operation. Meckel's diverticulum (see p. 296) and the appendix are both blind diverticula of the midgut, and so inflammation in either causes similar features. Occasionally intussusception (see p. 288) causes recurrent attacks of pain in the right iliac fossa, but there are other features which make the diagnosis obvious. Occasionally a mass in the right iliac fossa caused by intussusception may simulate an appendix abscess or mass.

Caecum

Inflammation of the caecum may be a specific infection due to actinomycosis or non-specific, as in the inflammation around a carcinoma,

Crohn's disease, a diverticulum or an ulcer of the caecum. At operation induration is felt in and around the caecum, which must often be removed if a growth is suspected.

Because these conditions present like appendicitis and can rarely be diagnosed before operation, it is essential, if the appendix is found to be uninflamed, for the mesentery, terminal ileum and caecum to be examined.

Retrocaecal Appendix

Pyelitis, pyonephrosis and a stone in the kidney usually give rise to pain, tenderness and muscle-guarding in the loin, but there may also be pain and tenderness in the right iliac fossa. Frequency of micturition and dysuria may be minimal in the early phase. Pyelitis is usually accompanied by a high temperature (102–103° F.), and shivering attacks (rigors) are very suggestive of it. The urine usually contains pus cells and organisms, usually *Esch. coli*. In pyonephrosis the kidney may be enlarged and tender. With a stone, pain is often sudden in onset, colicky in nature and may be severe. There may be haematuria obvious to the naked eye, or only on microscopy.

A calculus in the right ureter may give rise to pain, tenderness and rigidity in the right iliac fossa with or without urinary symptoms. The urine usually contains red blood cells, and a radiograph of the abdomen reveals the shadow of a stone, which must be differentiated from phleboliths in pelvic veins or a faecolith in the appendix.

Pelvic Appendix

Diseases of the pelvic organs frequently cause difficulty in the diagnosis of appendicitis. Many require emergency operation in any case, and can only be diagnosed at laparotomy. A vaginal or rectal examination is essential. Important evidence on vaginal examination is the presence of a purulent discharge, increase in size of the uterus, fullness or swelling in the fornices and tenderness on pressure on the cervix and in the fornices. It is uncommon to see acute appendicitis in the menstruating woman. Vaginal bleeding and iliac pain may suggest a ruptured ovarian follicle, salpingitis, ectopic gestation or endometriosis.

Ovary

The commonest ovarian cause of pain in the right iliac fossa is a ruptured follicle, often at the midpoint of the cycle. Signs may simulate appendicitis closely, but all that is found at operation is a little blood around a burst follicle in the ovary and in the pelvis. An ovarian cyst may twist, rupture, be infected or cause internal haemorrhage. All these complications of an ovarian cyst may cause pain in the right iliac fossa, but the diagnosis is usually obvious at the time of examination.

Tube

The site of pain and tenderness caused by salpingitis is usually immediately above the pubis on either side, but it may occur in one or both iliac fossae. There may be a purulent vaginal discharge or a history of it. The period may be prolonged, or there may be a history of heavy, irregular periods, miscarriage or recent delivery. Often there is frequency of micturition. On examination, vaginal discharge, tenderness of the cervix or fornices or a mass in a fornix may help in the diagnosis.

Ruptured ectopic gestation occurs when the fertilised ovum develops in the Fallopian tube instead of in the uterus. Symptoms usually occur about the second month of pregnancy, and there is often a history of a missed period. A large blood clot may form in the pelvis, or massive haemorrhage may occur into the peritoneum. The onset is marked by a sudden stabbing pain in the lower abdomen on the side of the tube which is affected. If considerable bleeding has occurred the patient rapidly becomes pale and shocked with air hunger. The area of tenderness and rigidity depends on the volume and rapidity of the bleeding. Vaginal examination may reveal a swelling on one side of the pelvis. Culdoscopy, the insertion of an endoscope, through the posterior fornix may be of great help to the gynaecologist in differentiating ectopic gestation from a small ovarian cyst in pregnancy.

The Uterus

Pregnancy may cause pain in the right iliac fossa, but can easily be diagnosed, so long as it is thought of. Uterine fibroids may twist or degenerate, especially in pregnancy.

The Bladder

Cystitis usually causes obvious symptoms and signs (see p. 381), but may simulate pelvic appendicitis. Microscopy of the urine and pelvic examination usually suffices to make the diagnosis clear.

The 'High' Appendix

If the caecum is maldescended or if the appendix is long and lying behind the caecum appendicitis may cause tenderness and guarding in the right hypochondrium or in the right loin. In such circumstances appendicitis must be distinguished from pyelitis, acute cholecystitis and basal pneumonia and pleurisy.

Respiratory Infection Simulating Appendicitis

Abdominal pain is common, especially in infancy, in cases of pneumonia, bronchitis or severe upper respiratory-tract infection. In some, pain is due to inflammation of the diaphragm, and is referred to the abdominal wall. In most, pain is probably the result of swollen mesenteric lymph nodes associated with a severe infection. Usually there are no physical or radiological signs in the chest, but an increased respiratory rate, dilated alae nasi in a child and a high temperature suffice to make the diagnosis especially when pallor around the mouth is seen. Tenderness and guarding are minimal in the abdomen, but it must not be forgotten that appendicitis may coincide occasionally with a respiratory infection, and in any case of doubt operation should be performed if the patient does not rapidly improve after admission to hospital.

Diffuse Peritonitis

When appendicitis has progressed to diffuse peritonitis it may be impossible to identify it from other causes, such as perforation of a peptic ulcer or diverticulitis. The history of the disease and occurrence of maximal tenderness in the lower abdomen may suggest appendicitis. In any case operation is indicated in all such patients after resuscitation.

TREATMENT

Acute Appendicitis

The treatment of acute appendicitis is removal of the appendix at the earliest possible time. Any evidence of 'acuteness' merits appendicectomy, for example, tenderness, guarding, fever, leucocytosis and oral fetor should indicate operation. Indications for conservative treatment have been overstressed in the past, the only indications for delay should be improvement in symptoms and signs, diagnosis of an abscess or inadequate surgical facilities, such as may be found on board ship. The time interval from the onset of symptoms is irrelevant, because appendicitis may become acute at any time from the onset of symptoms, even after several days.

The commonest incision for appendicectomy is a small grid-iron incision centred over McBurney's point in a line at right angles to that joining the umbilicus to the anterior superior iliac spine. The incision should be enlarged without hesitation if there is any difficulty in removing the appendix. A retrocaecal appendix may demand extension of the incision postero-superiorly, cutting through the oblique muscles of the abdominal wall. A pelvic appendix may require the incision to be enlarged downwards and medially, retracting, the lateral border of the rectus sheath inwards to increase exposure. If there is doubt about the diagnosis and the intention is to explore the lower abdomen a right paramedian incision is needed. After removal of the appendix a drain is usually unnecessary, but if there is much pus it is safer to insert one. Postoperative chemotherapy need not be given if the inflammation is confined to the appendix and peritoneum of the right iliac fossa.

Appendix Abscess

When an appendix abscess has been diagnosed it is usual to wait for it to subside spontaneously or for it to come to a surface to allow surgical drainage. The appendix is then removed after an interval of 3 months, when all inflammation has subsided and adhesions are minimal.

During the period of expectant treatment the patient is nursed in bed in any position of comfort (Fowler's position and the use of a pillow or 'donkey' under the knee are never used now). Fluids are given by mouth, and if there is a suspicion of ileus or intestinal obstruction the stomach should be kept empty by continuous aspiration through a naso-gastric tube, and fluids must be given intravenously. Antibiotics such as streptomycin and penicillin given together by intramuscular injection are often prescribed. In the less acute cases, however, spontaneous disappearance of a mass in the right iliac fossa may follow without any antibiotics being given.

Operation is dangerous and difficult during the formation and localisation of an abscess. It is usually difficult to find the appendix if operation is performed early, and infection may be spread into the free peritoneum. However, operation may be essential if signs of peritonitis develop, so a careful watch must be kept on the pulse by hourly recording, on the temperature chart and for evidence of spreading tenderness or muscular rigidity over the mass or increase in its size.

If the abscess enlarges or comes to a surface, then it must be drained, especially if fever and leucocytosis are high. Drainage is usually done through the abdominal wall or per rectum. Occasionally a large abscess is found at the first presentation of the patient; on such an occasion, drainage is the primary treatment.

Perforated Appendicitis

When the appendix has perforated every hour's delay results in more extensive peritonitis with an increased mortality. Operation is therefore urgently required, after a short period of resuscitation by intravenous fluid replacement therapy and gastric suction, to prevent vomiting during anaesthesia. A broad-spectrum antibiotic, such as ampicillin, should be given intravenously during this period of pre-operative treatment. After the appendix has been removed pus and exudate is aspirated from the peritoneum and a drain is inserted. Ileus and toxaemia are to be expected after the operation, so continuous gastric suction is continued until the volume of aspirate decreases and the fluid becomes inoffensive and clear. Intravenous fluids are given to restore and maintain the blood volume and electrolytes (see p. 23), and antibiotics are continued. Pain and distress are relieved by regular small doses of morphia.

Acute Appendicitis in the Young and Aged

In infants under three years of age the incidence of perforation and peritonitis is greater than in adults. Diagnosis is difficult, because only an incomplete history can be obtained from the parents, and usually the picture is one of a miserable toxic child who resents abdominal examination. Guarding of muscles is very difficult to elicit in a child who is crying and holding the abdominal wall taut. Localisation of infection is poor, possibly because the great omentum is comparatively short and under-developed and does not assist as readily as in adults in walling off the infected area. It is very common to see diffuse peritonitis in small children which may develop very rapidly.

In patients over the age of 60 years, and especially the elderly, the liability to diffuse peritonitis is also greater, usually due to delay in diagnosis, because symptoms tend to be disregarded by older people.

In both the very young and the very old there should be no hesitation in removing the appendix as a matter of urgency when doubt as to the diagnosis exists.

Acute Appendicitis in Pregnancy

The appendix is displaced laterally and upwards as the uterus increases in size, and the position of tenderness and guarding in appendicitis follows suit. Pyelitis occurs frequently in pregnancy, and it is unfortunately common for the diagnosis of appendicitis to be delayed because the symptoms are so like those of renal-tract infection. If the urine shows no evidence of infection, then appendicectomy should be performed urgently on any pregnant woman presenting with signs of inflammation in the right iliac fossa. Peritonitis following perforation of an appendix is associated with a high risk of abortion and premature labour, and so operation should be carried out particularly gently. Miscarriage is most likely to occur during the first three months of pregnancy, and so morphia should be given before and after operation in the early months of pregnancy.

POSTOPERATIVE COMPLICATIONS

Appendicectomy may be followed by any of the complications common to other operations. Among the more frequent and important are collapse of part or whole of the lung following the anaesthetic, pneumonia, wound infection and deep-vein thrombosis in the leg, with the possibility of subsequent pulmonary embolism.

More closely associated with the operation of appendicectomy are:

1. Residual Abscess

The occurrence of fever in the postoperative course of acute appendicitis is common, because residual infection in the peritoneum persists after removal of the appendix. In severe cases fever and toxaemia may be worse immediately after operation than before it. Recurrent abscesses may develop and persist for several weeks. These abscesses must be treated by drainage and antibiotics when the need arises. Drainage is usually carried out through the abdominal wall or through the rectum. Serial white-cell counts are invaluable in following subsidence of infection as well as the daily record of pulse rate and temperature. The patient should not leave hospital until the white-cell count and the pulse rate have returned to normal.

Pyrexia after appendicitis demands inspection of the wound and gentle palpation of it for deep infection. Passage of mucus per rectum, especially when a finger in the rectum feels induration, oedema or a swelling in the rectal wall, indicates the development of a pelvic abscess. If the wound and pelvis reveal no evidence of inflammation and the urine and chest are free of infection, then subphrenic abscess should be suspected.

2. Paralytic Ileus (p. 246)

3. Pylephlebitis

This is now rare.

4. Faecal Fistula

This is an uncommon complication which may occur when there has been necrosis of the caecal wall. Often the immediate postoperative period has been difficult, and discharge of pus and faeces from the wound results in an improvement. The fistula usually heals spontaneously, but if it persists for a few weeks some other disease in the region of the appendix should be suspected, such as Crohn's disease, actinomycosis, carcinoma or a foreign body, such as a faecolith. If mucous membrane comes to line the fistula and pouts on to the abdominal wall, then it must be formally closed by operation.

5. Intestinal Obstruction

This is due to adhesions, may occur months or years after operation and is more common after a paramedian than after a grid-iron incision. Occasionally it is seen in the early postoperative phase from the effect of numerous small pockets of pus in the peritoneum with associated plastic fibrinous adhesions. Many of these cases of intestinal obstruction are incomplete and resolve with conservative therapy (see p. 245), but operation should not be delayed if there is a fear of strangulation or complete obstruction.

RECURRENT AND CHRONIC APPENDICITIS

Recurrent Attacks of Subacute Appendicitis

The attacks are like those of mild catarrhal appendicitis. The signs and symptoms are usually typical and the diagnosis not in doubt.

Chronic 'Grumbling Appendix'

In this condition there is usually a dragging, aching pain in the right lower quadrant of the abdomen. The pain is never severe. Attacks may be repeated over months or years without causing any general upset.

Occasionally the symptoms may resemble those of dyspepsia due to a peptic ulcer or sigmoid diverticulitis. The appendix is thickened and fleshy with increased lymphoid tissue and has been the seat of repeated attacks of subacute infection. Very rarely there may be a mucocele of the appendix.

It is important to make the diagnosis of grumbling appendix only after all other lesions which cause pain in the right iliac fossa have been excluded. At operation the appendix is removed and careful examination made of the terminal ileum, caecum, mesentery, uterus tubes and ovaries, all of which can be palpated or seen through a small grid-iron incision. If nothing abnormal is found the last 3 feet of ileum is withdrawn through the wound to look for Meckel's diverticulum. In young girls many who complain of attacks of pain in the right iliac fossa have emotional problems which may possibly cause pain by abnormal motility of an irritable caecum. Such cases are, however, very difficult to distinguish from true appendicitis, and in any case of real doubt the appendix must be removed.

X-ray Examination

Radiography is rarely necessary for the diagnosis of appendicular disease. When it is needed it is performed to exclude other diseases that may be suggested by the history, for example, carcinoma of the colon and diverticulitis, which may be revealed by a barium enema. A barium meal followed through to the terminal ileum may help exclude peptic ulcer and Crohn's disease. Radiography is rarely of help in diagnosing appendicitis, the appendix is often not filled and tenderness in the caecal area elicited by the radiologist is not a very valuable sign. Radiographs should be used to exclude other diseases rather than to diagnose appendicitis.

NEOPLASMS

Tumours of the appendix are rare.

Carcinoid Tumour (p. 298)

This is the commonest tumour of the appendix, although it is only found in 1 in 300 of appendices removed at operation. It forms a discrete, hard, yellowish nodule in the submucosa of the tip of the appendix. Microscopically, masses of rounded cells with large deeply stained nuclei are seen, they derive from the Kulschitzky cells of the intestinal glands These cells have a selective affinity for silver stains. Appendicular carcinoids are usually benign. Malignant carcinoid in the appendix is extremely rare, but when it does occur it metastasises to the lymph nodes lying along the right colic and ileo colic vessels and to the liver. Symptoms due to the secretion of serotonin by these cells are only seen in patients with large metastatic deposits; they include flushing of the face, noisy borborygmi and a pulmonary systolic murmur.

Carcinoma of the Appendix

This is very rare as a primary condition. Occasionally carcinoma of the caecum may spread into the appendix or obstruct it, and may cause appendicitis from this obstruction. It is treated as for any adenocarcinoma in the large bowel.

FURTHER READING

Cope, Sir Z. (1963) *The Early Diagnosis of the Acute Abdomen*, 12th ed. Oxford University Press, London.

CHAPTER TWENTY

DISEASES OF THE STOMACH AND DUODENUM

Diseases of the stomach and duodenum are common, the commonest being peptic ulcer, which affects about 10% of all men and many women in Britain between the ages of 45 and 55 years. The cause of peptic ulcer is unknown, but the one fact that stands out from the results of the vast amount of research on the stomach is that ulceration is connected with the secretion of hydrochloric acid. For this reason the physiology of gastric secretion has been intensively investigated in recent years, both in man and animals.

Gastric Secretion

The gastric glands that secrete hydrochloric acid occupy more than two-thirds of the stomach (body mucosa), only the cardia and pyloric antrum being devoid of acid-secreting cells. The gastric glands of body mucosa

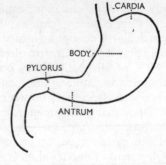

FIG. 20. Anatomy of the stomach

contain oxyntic or parietal cells that form hydrochloric acid, cells that secrete pepsin and cells secreting mucus (see Fig. 20). Mucus-secreting cells are also found in the cardiac and pyloric mucosa, where the secretion is weakly alkaline.

Much of our knowledge of the natural control of gastric secretion is due to the pioneering work of Pavlov. Pavlov found that gastric secretion continues at a slow rate during fasting or rest and is greatly augmented by feeding. The response to food can be divided into three phases which overlap in time. The first or *cephalic* phase of gastric secretion (appetite, nervous or vagal phase) occurs in response to the smell, sight and taste of food, and results from impulses passing down the vagus nerves to the stomach from the hypothalamus. The second and more important phase in man is the *gastric* or humoral phase, in which a hormone, gastrin, is released from the pyloric antrum when it is in contact with food. Gastrin is also secreted in response to other stimuli, such as an increase of pressure in the antrum. The nervous and humoral phases are interdependent, for the flow of gastric secretion produced by the presence of food in the antrum is reduced by vagal denervation of the stomach. The third or *intestinal* phase begins when food reaches the intestine, where it probably causes the release of a gastrin-like hormone from the intestinal wall. Fat in the stomach leads to an inhibition of gastric secretion, but an even greater inhibition results when fat enters the duodenum. This inhibitory effect of fat is thought to be due to the release of the hormone enterogastrone. Gastric secretion during the cephalic phase is rich in acid and pepsin, whereas in the humoral and intestinal phases less pepsin is produced.

PEPTIC ULCER

The cause of peptic ulcer is unknown. Because ulceration is connected with acid secretion, the aim of most surgical procedures for the cure of peptic ulcer is the reduction of acid secretion, an empirical approach, but one that is successful in most cases.

Aetiology

Duodenal ulcer is about 5–10 times more frequent than gastric ulcer. A family history is common, especially in those affected when young. Duodenal ulcer is widely scattered throughout all social strata, but it seems to be particularly common in business executives and doctors, in whom stress may play a part. Gastric ulcer is commoner among manual workers. About 80% of all peptic ulcers occur in men; gastric ulcer is relatively more common in women than men.

There is an association between peptic ulceration and certain blood groups. Duodenal ulcers are more common in group O. Substances related to the blood groups, mucopolysaccharides, are present in the saliva, gastric mucosa and gastric juice, which may have some protective action against the development of duodenal ulcer. Not all persons have these mucopolysaccharides (non-secretors). Non-secretors in group O are more liable to duodenal ulcer than are secretors. Benign gastric ulcer is not related to blood groups, but there is a connection between carcinoma of the stomach and the blood group A.

There is good evidence that nervous factors, presumably mediated through the vagus, may lead to hypersecretion of acid in the stomach, with consequent development of duodenal ulcer. Exacerbations of an ulcer are frequently associated with periods of anxiety and mental stress. Peptic ulcer may rarely be associated with lesions of the hypothalamus and following spinal-cord injuries. Severe burns, particularly if they become infected, may be associated with acute peptic ulceration.

It appears that hypersecretion of acid and pepsin are responsible for the persistence of peptic ulcers. It may well be that most people have ulcers at some time, but in most cases healing occurs and is permanent. An ulcer has a natural tendency to healing, but in the presence of hypersecretion of acid it is likely to recur.

The initiating cause of ulceration is not known. Spasm or thrombosis of local vessels or trauma due to food, mainly on the lesser curve of the stomach, have all been suggested. A foreign body, such as a hair ball, is often associated with a gastric ulcer. It is not only acid but also peptic activity which causes persistence of an ulcer. The rate of pepsin secretion shows peaks of activity through the day. The greater the acidity of the gastric juice, the greater is the peptic activity. A layer of mucus normally lines the stomach and duodenum, which may protect against ulceration. The protective activity of mucus may be related to the presence of muco-polysaccharides, hence the possible relation of duodenal ulcers to blood group O.

In the Zollinger–Ellison syndrome an islet-cell tumour of the pancreas (α-cell and non-insulin secreting) liberates a hormone resembling gastrin which produces continuous secretion of gastric juice large in volume and high in acid content, which gives rise to duodenal and even jejunal ulceration. Following gastrectomy or vagotomy for the ulcer found in the Zollinger–Ellison syndrome, recurrence is likely to occur due to the high acid secretion, which persists until the tumour is removed from the pancreas, or after total gastrectomy, when the tendency for recurrent ulceration is removed. Peptic ulcer may complicate hyperparathyroidism (p. 168).

In the majority of patients with duodenal ulcer the level of acid and pepsin secretion is high, but in one-third of patients the secretory pattern falls within the normal range. The majority of those suffering from gastric ulcer have either a normal or low acid output. It is reasonable therefore to assume that different factors are involved in the causation of duodenal and gastric ulcers.

Pathology

The majority of gastric ulcers occur in the midpart of the lesser curve, and they vary considerably in size. Ulcers near the cardia or near the pylorus, and certainly those on the greater curve, should be suspected of malignancy. Usually gastric ulcers are single, but multiple ulcers can occur, especially acute ulcers. The edge of the ulcer crater is punched out, slightly rounded and oedematous, in contrast to the heaped-up, more shelving and irregular edge of a malignant ulcer. It is often difficult, however, to distinguish naked-eye between a simple and a malignant ulcer. The muscle coat of the stomach may be penetrated to a variable depth, eventually to involve structures such as the pancreas and liver. The lesser omentum is usually oedematous and infiltrated by inflammatory tissue; lymph nodes are enlarged because of reactive hyperplasia. Occasionally the stomach mucosa is extensively affected by shallow ulcers that penetrate only the mucosal membrane, often with an associated hyperaemia and purpuric haemorrhages, a condition called acute erosive gastritis which has a great tendency to cause massive bleeding. In most cases the cause is unknown, but drugs such as aspirin, butazolidine and phenindione may cause it, as may the severe toxaemia that occurs in uraemia or septicaemia. The onset may be sudden with severe and repeated haematemesis.

Duodenal ulcers nearly always occur within 2–3 cm. of the pylorus where the jet of gastric secretion impinges on the duodenal wall as it comes through the pylorus, a point well above the entrance of the alkaline pancreatic juice and bile. The ulcer is usually solitary, lying on the anterior or posterior wall. The overlying peritoneum is thickened and shows a characteristic haemorrhagic stippling when it is rubbed. The duodenum may be adherent to nearby organs, such as the gall bladder and pancreas.

Gastric and duodenal ulcers co-exist in a small number of patients. Usually the duodenal ulcer is the primary lesion, the gastric ulcer may arise as a result of stasis and gastritis due to fibrous stenosis or spasm of the pylorus.

Symptoms and Signs

Although distinctive symptoms are attributed to duodenal and gastric ulcer, it may be difficult in practice to distinguish between them. Symptoms of peptic ulcer often mimic other conditions, such as cholecystitis, pancreatitis, hiatus hernia and coronary disease.

Attacks of epigastric pain occur after food. Characteristically there is freedom between the periods of dyspepsia. Usually the pain is felt in the epigastrium or just below the xiphisternum. Radiation of pain through to the back suggests penetration of an ulcer into the pancreas. Occasionally, during an acute phase, pain may be severe enough to suggest a perforation that has been localised.

The following facts may be used to help distinguish duodenal from gastric ulcer, but no symptoms are absolutely diagnostic of either. Most gastric ulcers occur over the age of 50 years, most duodenal ulcers arise at a much younger age. The pain of duodenal ulcer occurs 2–3 hours after food, in the case of gastric ulcer the interval is shorter. The pain of duodenal ulcer is usually relieved by food or alkalis, that of gastric ulcer by vomiting. The patient with a duodenal ulcer has a good appetite, but is afraid to eat; in the presence of a gastric ulcer the appetite is frequently poor, due to an associated gastritis. In duodenal ulcer vomiting is infrequent unless there is stenosis of the pylorus or the ulcer is in an acute phase. Vomiting may be associated with gastric ulcer, and some patients can only gain relief of pain by making themselves sick. Weight loss is usually minimal in patients suffering from duodenal ulcer unless the pylorus is stenosed, but it may be considerable with gastric ulcers. The tenderness overlying a duodenal ulcer is usually elicited in the epigastrium or slightly to the right of midline; over a gastric ulcer tenderness may be found in the mid-epigastrium or to the left of it.

Symptoms of peptic ulcer occur in bouts, usually in the spring or autumn. Each attack may last up to several weeks at a time and is followed by a remission lasting up to several months. This history of periodic attacks of dyspepsia may last for years, but commonly those coming to surgery have experienced more and more prolonged attacks until the symptoms become continuous and unrelieved by any measures.

Investigations

Barium Meal. The patient swallows a creamy suspension of barium sulphate so that the oesophagus, stomach and duodenum can be visualised. The examination is carried out with the subject standing, supine and finally supine slightly tipped head downwards to demonstrate the fundus and cardia of the stomach. In the tipped position a hiatus hernia or incompetent cardia can be recognised when there is regurgitation of stomach contents into the oesophagus. Radiographs are taken of the stomach and duodenum to provide pictures of the changes seen on the fluorescent screen. The radiologist who has seen the outline of the alimentary tract on the screen has a much better opportunity than the clinician of judging structural changes in the stomach and duodenum, for the radiologist sees the stomach and duodenum in action, whereas the surgeon is only given representative snap shots to look at.

An ulcer in the stomach is seen as a crater; often opposite to the ulcer there is an indentation of the greater curve due to spasm or fibrosis. Only constant deformities are significant. Inconstant changes in contour may well be due to peristalsis. The emptying rate of barium from the stomach is normally 3–4 hours. Delayed emptying indicates pyloric spasm or stenosis.

The duodenal cap is normally triangular in shape, ulceration or spasm causes a persistent deformity. A series of radiographic exposures of the duodenum is taken by the radiologist to demonstrate persistent deformities. Often the actual ulcer itself cannot be seen, only deformity of the duodenal cap. Radiographic diagnosis of duodenal ulcer is accurate in over 90% of cases. If symptoms strongly suggest duodenal ulceration they should be treated as if an ulcer were present, even if a barium meal fails to reveal it. Occasionally it may be several years before radiography confirms the presence of an ulcer.

Gastroscopy. A gastric ulcer may be visualised directly with a gastroscope, a long, narrow, flexile telescope that can be passed into the stomach. Gastroscopy may help decide if a gastric ulcer is simple or malignant. It will also demonstrate the healing of an ulcer, and is occasionally useful in confirming the presence of a gastric ulcer which has not been demonstrated radiographically. Recently a new instrument, the fiberscope, has been introduced which by its flexibility permits visualisation and even photography of not only the stomach but also the duodenum. Both gastroscopy and the use of the fiberscope may be helpful in the diagnosis of an ulcer at the stoma of a previous gastric resection. Unfortunately the entire stomach is not always accessible to endoscopy, so a negative inspection does not exclude the presence of an ulcer.

Tests of Gastric Function. Test meals can be performed by measuring the stimulation of gastric acidity produced by a meal of gruel, a volume of alcohol or an injection of histamine. As a measure of gastric function such test meals have been found unsatisfactory because, when repeated on the same patient, they may give widely differing results. A more recent technique which gives reproducible results, *the maximal histamine test meal*, measures the maximal secretory capacity of the stomach. In this test a very large dose of histamine is given by injection so large that *all* the gastric glands are stimulated. The unpleasant side effects of histamine, such as flushing, headache and a fall in blood pressure, are prevented by the prior administration of an antihistamine. For some unknown reason antihistamines do not prevent the stimulus to gastric secretion. The stomach is continuously aspirated for an hour, to provide a measure of basal secretion, through a naso-gastric tube carefully placed in the pyloric antrum by radiographic control. An injection of mepyramine maleate (anthisan) is given intramuscularly, followed by an injection of histamine. Following these injections, the aspirate obtained in a subsequent hour is collected— the maximal acid secretion. The amount of hydrochloric acid normally secreted in the basal period is between 2 and 3 mEq/litre/hour, and during maximal secretion about 18 mEq/litre/hour. The average amount secreted basally by a patient with a duodenal ulcer is about 6 or more mEq/litre/ hour, whereas during stimulation with histamine it is about 36 mEq/litre hour. A high level of acid secretion makes the diagnosis of duodenal ulcer likely, but it must not be forgotten that one-third of patients with duodenal ulcer show a normal secretory pattern. Another method of measuring acid secretion is the *all-night secretion test* in which gastric secretion is aspirated over-night. In duodenal ulcer it is usual to find acid and pepsin to be secreted in high concentration in a large volume. In the Zollinger–Ellison syndrome the night secretion is raised in volume and acidity.

The *insulin test meal* can be used in investigation of patients suffering from duodenal ulcer. A dose of insulin sufficient to cause hypoglycaemia is given intravenously. Hypoglycaemia stimulates acid and pepsin secretion, an effect mediated by the vagus nerve. The test is particularly useful following the operation of vagotomy when there is doubt as to whether the vagus nerves have been completely divided or whether nerve regeneration has occurred.

Treatment of Peptic Ulcer
Medical

The initial treatment for peptic ulcer is rest, gastric diet, sedatives and alkalis unless complications have arisen necessitating surgery. A gastric diet means regular and frequent small meals, so that food is constantly in the stomach neutralising acid. The food should be planned so as not to stimulate acid secretion. Attractive foods cause the stomach to secrete, so the diet is monotonous and usually is restricted to variations of milk, fish and eggs. Tasty foods, alcohol and cigarettes should be avoided. When symptoms are acute, frequent milk feeds taken every 2 hours and rest in bed are usually effective in the relief of symptoms. Although such a diet may help in speeding the healing of an ulcer, there is no guarantee that it will prevent the recurrence of dyspepsia. It is usual to continue the diet for 1 or 2 months after the symptoms are relieved. Vitamins and iron should be included in the diet. Antacids help to neutralise the hyperacidity and are taken after meals. Many patients with peptic ulcer are under stress, and for them a sedative is helpful especially to ensure sleep. Antispasmodics such as probanthine may be helpful in reducing acid secretion and relieving pain due to hypermotility and spasm. Carbenoxolone (Biogastrone) a steroid derived from liquorice, is claimed to have a specific effect in healing gastric ulcers but none on duodenal ulcers.

The most effective treatment for peptic ulcer is bed rest, best of all in hospital away from the home environment. When symptoms are very acute they almost invariably disappear after a period of rest in bed. Very severe symptoms sometimes necessitate a continuous infusion of milk given through a naso-gastric tube.

Most duodenal ulcers can be healed and relapses kept to the minimum by medical therapy. Patients are often seen who have had mild dyspeptic symptoms for 20 or 30 years. Most sufferers from duodenal ulcers are only inconvenienced during one or two episodes a year, lasting 2 or 3 weeks at a time. Gastric ulcers more commonly become intractable than duodenal and more often need surgical treatment.

Surgical

The following are the main indications for surgical treatment of peptic ulcer:

(i) *Failure of Medical Treatment to Relieve Symptoms.* Adequate medical treatment must have been tried before surgery is indicated. The best results of surgery are usually obtained in those who have suffered considerable pain and inconvenience from their ulcers. On the whole it is wiser to delay operating on those patients who are psychologically unstable. Strong indications for operation are symptoms which prevent the patient earning his livelihood or are causing loss of time at work or the enjoyment of normal activities.

(ii) *Complications.* The complications of perforation and stenosis warrant operation. Haemorrhage may necessitate surgery sometimes as an emergency.

(iii) *Malignancy.* The possibility of malignancy must be considered in gastric ulcers, especially if the duration of symptoms is brief, the pain continuous and if dyspeptic symptoms arise for the first time in patients over 40 years of age.

Pre-operative Preparation

Dehydration, electrolyte deficiencies and anaemia are corrected. Carious teeth should be removed if time allows and chest infection is treated. A plastic naso-gastric tube is passed immediately pre-operatively. A series of daily stomach wash-outs is needed in cases of pyloric stenosis to remove food residues and allow gastritis to settle.

Operation

Partial gastrectomy (Fig. 21) is the operation of choice for gastric ulcer. The essential feature of the operation is removal of the ulcer. The stomach is divided immediately proximal to the ulcer and just distal to the pylorus; usually about two-thirds of the stomach is removed. The stomach remnant is partly closed to leave an opening the size of the duodenum to which it is anastomosed—gastro-duodenostomy (Billroth I operation). The advantage of this operation is that gastric contents pass along the intestinal tract

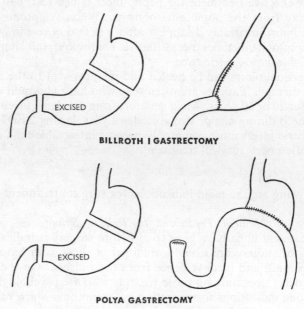

BILLROTH I GASTRECTOMY

POLYA GASTRECTOMY

Fig. 21. Types of partial gastrectomy

in the normal way from the stomach to the duodenum, the only loss being the pylorus and part of the stomach. The complications following the Billroth I operation are less than those seen after a gastric resection with restoration of continuity by gastro-jejunostomy in which the distal two-thirds of the stomach is excised, the duodenal stump closed and a loop of jejunum near the duodeno-jejunal junction anastomosed to the stomach pouch (Billroth II or Polya operation).

Ulceration at the stoma following partial gastrectomy for gastric ulcer is rare, largely due to the fact that the secretion of acid and pepsin is normal or low in these patients and very low after gastric resection. Partial gastrectomy is still the most commonly performed operation for duodenal ulcer, the Polya type of operation being employed. The Billroth I or gastro-duodenostomy type of operation is definitely contra-indicated for duodenal ulcer, as it is followed by very high rate of stomal ulceration.

Vagotomy and a drainage procedure (Fig. 22) is being performed more frequently for a duodenal ulcer. Both partial gastrectomy and vagotomy decrease output of acid by about two-thirds. Vagotomy delays emptying of the stomach, so it must be combined with a drainage procedure—either gastro-enterostomy or pyloroplasty. A pyloroplasty widens the pylorus by a 10-cm. longitudinal incision centred on the pyloric sphincter which divides the muscle coats and the mucosa. The opening is closed at right angles to the line of incision, thus greatly widening the region of the pylorus. The ulcer can be inspected when the duodenum is opened.

Gastro-enterostomy was commonly performed for duodenal ulcer

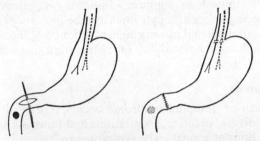

FIG. 22. Vagotomy and pyloroplasty

before the Second World War, but has been abandoned largely because stomal ulcer arises in some 30–50% of patients within 10 years of the operation. Nowadays gastro-enterostomy is reserved for old patients who are unfit for major surgery and who have long-standing pyloric stenosis.

Gastrectomy and Vagotomy Sequelae

Any operation on the stomach or duodenum may be followed by symptoms due to interference with normal function. About 15% of patients suffer minor sequelae; 5–10% have more serious complications. Loss of a major part of the stomach or of the pylorus probably causes some symptoms in all subjects, but complications are uncommon except in the psychologically unstable or those who are particularly sensitive. For these reasons the selection of patients for gastric surgery must be made with great care. The longer the history and the more the patient has suffered, usually the better the result. Patients treated for duodenal ulcer fare worse than those treated for gastric ulcer. Before operation a warning should be given that surgery can guarantee relief of pain in the vast majority of cases, but that mild dyspeptic symptoms may persist. Often records reveal that symptoms described after operation were present before it and were unrelated to the peptic ulcer.

Mortality Following Operation

Following partial gastrectomy the mortality is around 3%. Vagotomy and a drainage operation has a lower mortality—under 1%. The higher mortality after gastric resection is due to the operation being more extensive and because of the possibility of duodenal leakage, which is always a serious complication.

Anastomotic or Stomal Ulcer

Anastomotic ulceration is rarely seen following partial gastrectomy for gastric ulcer, but for duodenal ulcer the incidence of anastomotic ulcer is about 3%. The commonest site for a stomal ulcer is within the first 2 inches of the efferent loop of the jejunum; less frequently it may be at the anastomosis of stomach to jejunum. Following vagotomy and gastro-enterostomy or vagotomy and pyloroplasty, the incidence of anastomotic ulcer or recurrent duodenal ulcer is higher—about 5%, because of incomplete denervation and the possibility of regeneration that incomplete vagal section allows.

Dumping Syndrome

Small stomach or dumping syndrome occurs shortly after the patient eats food. Giddiness, sweating, palpitations and faintness are experienced within half an hour of a meal. The symptoms are relieved by recumbency and tend to lessen or disappear completely with the passage of time, so no surgical treatment should be contemplated for at least 2 years for symptoms following a gastric operation. The syndrome may be due to the osmotic effect of food entering the jejunum, which by extracting water from the circulation may cause rapid distension of the jejunum. The patient should be reassured of a good chance of relief of symptoms with the elapse of time. Small dry meals should be taken of high-protein, low-carbohydrate content. Sugary drinks should be avoided. The patient should if possible rest flat after meals for about ½ hour.

Another complication of gastrectomy is hypoglycaemia. Carbohydrate is rapidly absorbed from the jejunum to hyperglycaemic levels, followed by a rapid fall due to the action of insulin secreted during the phase of hyperglycaemia. The glucose-tolerance curve of such patients is of the 'lag-storage type'. Symptoms of hypoglycaemia are giddiness, blurring of vision, sweating and a feeling of hunger. Sugary foods must be avoided after gastrectomy, and the patient assured that hypoglycaemic symptoms when they occur usually disappear with time.

Bilious Vomiting

Patients occasionally give a history that occasionally, perhaps once a week or once a month after gastrectomy, they may vomit pure green bile of small or large volume. Up to ½ litre at a time may occasionally be vomited. The cause is obscure, but may be due to afferent loop stasis or kinking of the small bowel at the stoma. If it is troublesome, persistent or frequent, operation may be necessary.

Anaemia

Microcytic hypochromic anaemia is common after partial gastrectomy, but may not be noticeable for many years. It is due to decreased iron absorption, and is more likely after the Polya type of partial gastrectomy. It is easily cured by giving the patient iron by mouth. Vagotomy is not often followed by anaemia and its occurrence suggests another ulcer.

Weight Loss

It is rare for a patient after partial gastrectomy to regain his pre-operative weight, and weight loss may be severe enough to prevent a patient undertaking hard manual labour. The cause of loss of weight after gastric operations is not entirely known, but suggestions have been made that it is due to malabsorption from rapid emptying of the stomach, hypermotility of the intestine and steatorrhoea. Vagotomy is not usually followed by loss of weight to the same extent as after partial gastrectomy.

Diarrhoea

Diarrhoea is relatively rare following partial gastrectomy, but is a serious complication after vagotomy and a drainage procedure. In a small number of people following vagotomy it may prove to be a serious inconvenience, especially as it is episodic and may be so severe as to cause occasional incontinence. Whether a selective vagotomy that only denervates the stomach diminishes the incidence of diarrhoea has not been established.

Malabsorption Syndrome

As a result of long-term studies of patients after partial gastrectomy, particularly of the Polya type, it is now clear that deficient absorption may occur from the small intestine of vitamins A and B, iron and calcium. Patients after vagotomy are less likely to suffer from these defects.

Other Complications

Intestinal obstruction due to intra-peritoneal adhesions and other complications common to any abdominal operation may occur. Occasionally after a Polya operation loops of jejunum may become ensnared between the jejunum below the site of anastomosis and the colon.

Perhaps the most serious complication after gastric resection is the development of a duodenal fistula. A breakdown at the site of closure of the duodenal stump at or the site of an anastomosis may cause leakage of duodenal secretion which is intensely irritant and erosive. If it is liberated into the peritoneum general peritonitis and death may follow. If external drainage can be provided life may be saved, but the duodenal secretion may cause severe erosion of the skin and deeper tissues. If the volume of leakage is large it may be difficult to keep the patient in a state of reasonable hydration and nutrition, and death may follow from losses of water and salts.

Treatment of Post-gastrectomy Sequelae

Acute obstruction from adhesions or the ensnaring of a loop of bowel deep to an antecolic gastro-enterostomy may demand urgent operation for its relief. Small stomach sequelae and episodes of afferent loop-obstruction may be treated by a variety of ways. Operations are done to convert a Polya to a Billroth I type of gastrectomy. Another method is to anastomose the afferent and efferent loops below the site of their anastomosis to the stomach in the hope of preventing bilious vomiting. The pantaloon operation of Steinberg increases stomach capacity and relieves obstruction at the stoma. Interposition of a loop of jejunum between the gastric remnant and the duodenum increases the size of the 'stomach' and slows gastric emptying.

Many patients who develop post-gastrectomy sequelae are psychologically unstable, and may not be helped by further operation. The number and variety of the operations advocated for the cure of post-gastrectomy symptoms is a fair index of the difficulty of their cure.

COMPLICATIONS OF CHRONIC PEPTIC ULCER

PERFORATION

Perforation of a peptic ulcer is usually a sudden event leading to diffuse peritonitis. Less often a small leak through a tiny perforation is walled off by omentum and nearby viscera, resulting in localised peritonitis and sometimes a subphrenic abscess.

Duodenal ulcers perforate much more often than gastric ulcers, and men are more commonly affected than women. The perforation that causes diffuse peritonitis lies on the anterior wall of the duodenum or stomach. Posterior perforations are more often subacute or chronic, burrowing into the pancreas, or in the case of a gastric ulcer into the liver, lesser sac and pancreas. Often there is a long history of dyspepsia before the perforation, but many perforations, especially those of duodenal ulcer, occur without any previous history of dyspepsia or with only symptoms of mild degree.

Symptoms and Signs

Pain is sudden and excruciating, starting in the epigastrium and spreading throughout the abdomen. Referred pain may be felt in the shoulder due to irritation of the diaphragm. There is usually shock and collapse, but initially the pulse is characteristically slow. Vomiting may occur once or twice, but rarely more often. The abdomen is exquisitely tender with rigidity that starts in the epigastrium and spreads over the abdomen. The most intense muscular rigidity is seen in perforation of a viscus—'board-like rigidity'. Bowel sounds are absent due to peritonitis and ileus. The patient lies still, for every movement causes pain. The knees are flexed in an attempt to relieve the spasm of abdominal muscles. If the perforation is small and the leakage localised tenderness and rigidity may be confined to the upper abdomen. Abnormal physical signs may occasionally be maximal in the right iliac fossa, so simulating appendicitis and peritonitis, because of gastric contents reaching the right iliac fossa via the right paracolic gutter.

Diagnosis

The history of a sudden onset of epigastric pain followed by board-like rigidity and a 'silent' abdomen renders the diagnosis easy in the majority of cases. The presence of air under the diaphragm can be confirmed by radiographic examination of the abdomen in the upright position. The differential diagnosis includes any cause of generalised peritonitis, chole-cystitis, pancreatitis, coronary infarct, pneumothorax and dissecting aneurysms.

Treatment

Once the diagnosis has been made an injection of morphia is given to relieve pain. The stomach is emptied via a naso-gastric tube and an intravenous infusion of normal saline is set up. The patient is taken to the operating theatre, where laparotomy is performed through an upper abdominal incision. The perforation is closed with catgut sutures, fluid is sucked out of the peritoneal cavity and the abdomen closed, usually without drainage unless pus has formed or the perforation has occurred more than 12 hours before operation.

Partial gastrectomy or vagotomy and gastro-enterostomy has been recommended in the treatment of perforation, particularly where a history of dyspepsia over several years has been given, suggesting that the ulcer is likely to cause further trouble. However, major operations are unwise unless the interval between perforation and surgery is short and infection is minimal. Patients may be seen who are too ill for any operation, particularly if the diagnosis has been long delayed. Conservative treatment may then be tried, gastric suction, intravenous fluids and chemotherapy.

Prognosis

The overall mortality following operation for perforation is about 8%. This may seem a high figure, but it must be remembered that a small number of patients who present with perforation are very seriously ill, either because the diagnosis has been long delayed or because of senility or other diseases, such as cardiac failure and bronchopneumonia. The mortality very largely depends on how quickly the ulcer is sutured after perforation. Operation performed within a few hours has virtually no mortality. The mortality after repair of a perforated gastric ulcer is higher than that after repair of a duodenal ulcer because patients with gastric ulcer are often old and their perforations often large, allowing considerable peritoneal contamination. Following closure of a perforated duodenal ulcer, it is likely that ulcer symptoms will recur in about half of those treated. It must be remembered that an appreciable number of perforated gastric ulcers are carcinomatous, so there is a stronger case for immediate partial gastrectomy to be performed for perforated gastric than perforated duodenal ulcer. Immediate gastrectomy is indicated if a perforated duodenal ulcer is complicated by pyloric stenosis or haemorrhage.

PENETRATION OF AN ULCER

Sometimes a duodenal or gastric ulcer may extend into the pancreas, liver or other neighbouring viscera. Invasion of the pancreas is suggested by the change in the character of the pain, which becomes more constant and often radiates to the back. It may be difficult clinically to distinguish carcinoma of the stomach from a benign ulcer. Gastrectomy is necessary; often the base of the ulcer may have to be left on the pancreas, but this causes no complications.

HAEMORRHAGE

Haemorrhage from a duodenal or gastric ulcer may present as haematemesis or melaena or sometimes both. There are many causes of bleeding from the upper gastro-intestinal tract, and it is important to remember them in the approximate order of their frequency of occurrence.

Peptic Ulcer accounts for about 90% of gastro-duodenal bleeding. It may be due to an acute ulcer in the stomach or duodenum, multiple gastric erosions or a chronic ulcer. Occasionally bleeding occurs from a stomal ulcer following gastrectomy or gastro-enterostomy and more rarely from hiatus hernia or an ulcer associated with it.

Portal Hypertension leads to bleeding from oesophageal varices.

Drug Sensitivity. Aspirin, butazolidine, phenindione and other drugs may cause acute erosions with bleeding. Corticosteroids, by inhibiting normal healing, may precipitate haemorrhage from an existing ulcer.

Tumours of the Stomach may cause bleeding. Benign tumours, such as leiomyoma and angioma may bleed profusely. Bleeding from a malignant tumour is small in quantity and of altered blood—'coffee ground vomit'.

Blood Dyscrasias. Haemophilia, thrombocytopaenia and the reticuloses may all cause bleeding from the stomach.

Toxaemia and Septicaemia may give rise to ulceration and bleeding, especially following uraemia and burns.

Vessel-wall defects such as von Willebrand's disease and pseudoxanthoma elasticum.

Investigation of Haemorrhage

It is necessary to enquire about the possibility of haemoptysis and of bleeding from the mouth, nose and pharynx. Swallowed blood may be vomited, simulating haematemesis. Bleeding from an ulcer must be distinguished from that due to portal hypertension. There may be a history of chronic ulcer, perhaps confirmed by radiography. Signs of portal hypertension include splenomegaly, hepatomegaly, spider naevi in the skin and, with severe liver failure, hepatic coma, foetor oris and encephalopathy (see p. 343). It must be remembered that patients with portal hypertension are often affected by peptic ulcer, and bleeding may in fact come from an ulcer rather than from oesophageal varices.

Examination of the blood may reveal a dyscrasia. Radiography of the stomach with a small volume of barium and gastroscopy give valuable information in an interval when bleeding has ceased.

Treatment of Haemorrhage

The patient is usually admitted to hospital under the care of a physician. All cases should be seen by a surgeon for his early assessment. The patient is reassured and sedated with morphia. The foot of the bed is raised, and a blood transfusion is commenced if the haemorrhage has been massive and the blood pressure is low. Massive haemorrhage is defined as bleeding gross enough to cause a fall in blood pressure or faintness or blackouts. A careful watch is kept on the pulse rate, blood pressure, haemoglobin, haematocrit, electrolytes, blood urea and urinary output. If no further bleeding occurs, early feeding of milk every 2 hours is started as soon as possible, followed by semi-solids given frequently with the intention of keeping the stomach full and thus relatively inactive. In most cases bleeding stops spontaneously. A barium meal is deferred for 10–14 days.

Operation

The mortality from haematemesis treated by non-surgical measures is approximately 10%. Most of those who die are people over 50 years of age, in whom bleeding is less likely to stop spontaneously, possibly because of their sclerotic vessels. Operation should be seriously considered in any patient over the age of 50 years, especially in those who bleed for a second time and are known to have a chronic ulcer confirmed by radiography. The usual operation is partial gastrectomy, as described for chronic duodenal ulcer and gastric ulcer. A bleeding vessel in a duodenal ulcer may be underrun by a suture and recurrence prevented by vagotomy and pyloroplasty. Occasionally no ulcer can be found at operation, though the stomach and duodenum may be full of blood. If there has been haematemesis the hiatus must be examined for hernia or evidence of oesophageal varices. If there is melaena the whole alimentary tract below the stomach must be examined for any focus that might cause bleeding. If none is found and it is certain that bleeding has come from the stomach the viscus

K

is widely opened and a search made for a shallow acute ulcer which is then treated by suture. If a diffuse erosive gastritis is found, a partial gastrectomy is performed.

If portal hypertension can be diagnosed before operation the passage of a Sengstaken tube (see p. 344) may arrest haemorrhage. Later, after bleeding has been arrested, portacaval anastomosis can be performed to lower the pressure in the portal venous system. If operation becomes imperative because bleeding cannot be controlled, then the veins on the lesser and greater curvatures of the stomach are divided up to the hiatus. with division of the stomach just below the cardia followed by re-anastomosis. By this means the portal and azygos venous systems can be separated, thus relieving the congestion in oesophageal varices. A more rapid and simpler operation is to open the chest on the left side, open the oesophagus and under-run the varices by continuous sutures.

PYLORIC STENOSIS

Fibrosis and narrowing may occur in the duodenum due to duodenal ulceration near the pylorus. Spasm of the pyloric muscle is often marked in acute exacerbations of duodenal ulcer which usually relaxes with medical treatment. Pyloric stenosis may also be due to carcinoma in the pyloric antrum, and occasionally an ulcer in the pyloric canal may cause obstruction. Hypertrophic pyloric stenosis occurs in infants (see p. 429), rarely in adults.

Clinical Feature

There is usually a long history of periodic attacks of dyspepsia, the attacks becoming progressively longer, until eventually bouts of vomiting supervene. Occasionally in old people the onset may be painless, the presenting symptom being vomiting. Vomiting is the cardinal sign of pyloric stenosis occurring at infrequent intervals, perhaps once a day or every 2 days. The vomitus is large in amount, contains undigested food and is offensive in odour. Often the contents of several meals are brought up. Starvation causes a rapid loss of weight, perhaps 5–10 kg. in a month. Visible gastric peristalsis may be seen when the stomach is full, the hypertrophied stomach can then be seen contracting through the abdominal wall. Waves of peristalsis pass from left to right across the epigastrium. Splashing may be elicited by sudden pressure over the distended stomach— succussion splash. Examination by barium meal shows a marked delay in gastric emptying, but is rarely useful in distinguishing duodenal ulcer from carcinoma. As vomiting becomes more persistent the patient loses weight, becomes dehydrated and, as sodium, potassium and chloride ions are lost, a state of hypochloraemic alkalosis with pre-renal uraemia results. The level of ionised calcium falls in alkalosis, so tetany may occur. After deficiencies of salts and water have been corrected operation can be undertaken with safety.

Treatment

Dehydration and losses of salts must be corrected. The stomach is emptied and washed out. A large-bore stomach tube is passed, the stomach is aspirated and then washed out by passing normal saline through a funnel attached to the tube. The washout is performed by siphonage. Often several litres of normal saline must be used until the fluid returning from the stomach is clear of food residues. The usual surgical procedure is that of partial gastrectomy, but alternatively, vagotomy and pyloroplasty may be carried out where duodenal ulcer is the cause. In elderly and unfit patients gastro-enterostomy is all that may be possible.

Hour-glass Constriction of the Stomach

Stenosis of the mid-part of the stomach is almost entirely confined to women; it is very rare nowadays. An ulcer on the middle of the lesser curve may cause fibrosis and scarring, dividing the stomach into two sacs. Rarely the cause is carcinoma. The symptoms and signs are those of pyloric stenosis. Hour-glass constriction is treated by partial gastrectomy.

CARCINOMA OF THE STOMACH

Carcinoma of the stomach is relatively common—about 8,000 people die of it in England and Wales every year. Men are more often affected than women at an age usually between 40 and 70 years. Occasionally much younger persons are affected. Carcinoma of the stomach is associated more commonly with blood group A than with other groups. It is relatively rare in Jews and Asiatics. Persons suffering from pernicious anaemia are three times more likely to develop carcinoma of the stomach than normal people.

Pathology

The regions of the stomach affected by carcinoma are mainly the pyloric antrum (50%), lesser curve (25%) and cardia (10%). Carcinoma of the stomach may present as a malignant ulcer with rolled everted edges, a proliferating polypoid mass or a thickening that may be localised or diffusely involves the whole stomach ('leather-bottle stomach').

Histologically most carcinomata of the stomach are spheroidal-celled, if there is much fibrous tissue they are called scirrhous. In the more differentiated growths acini of columnar cells are seen. Mucoid change is common, squamous metaplasia is rare, except when a squamous carcinoma extends from the oesophagus into the stomach.

Carcinoma of the stomach spreads to lymph nodes along the lesser and greater curves and eventually to those around the coeliac axis. Nodes in the portal fissure of the liver may become involved causing jaundice from pressure on the hepatic ducts. Occasionally, at a late stage, there may be spread to the left supraclavicular lymph nodes (Troisier's sign). Spread also occurs by the portal veins to give rise to metastases in the liver, lungs and elsewhere. Widespread implantation of cancer cells throughout the peritoneum may be associated with ascites. Occasionally cancer cells grow in the ovaries, producing large cysts or solid tumours—Krukenberg's tumours. Lastly, carcinoma of the stomach may directly invade surrounding structures, such as the pancreas and transverse colon. A gastro-colic fistula may be produced with distressing vomiting of faeces. ✳

Symptoms

Often the onset of carcinoma of stomach is insidious, with increasing weakness, loss of energy, loss of weight and anorexia. Later there may be symptoms referable to the stomach, such as nausea and vomiting. There may be no definite symptoms until secondary deposits, particularly in the glands in the porta hepatis, press on the bile ducts and cause jaundice. There may be little or no pain but simply discomfort referred to the region of the epigastrium, particularly after meals. Pain may be similar in periodicity to peptic ulcer or may have no relation to food.

Carcinoma arising in a benign gastric ulcer is extremely rare—less than <1% of all carcinomas of the stomach. Nevertheless, there are well-authenticated case histories in which, following a long period of gastric symptoms from a confirmed gastric ulcer, the pain has changed in character with loss of periodicity. 'Ulcer cancer' can only be diagnosed with certainty histologically if malignant cells are seen infiltrating the scarred base of a benign ulcer in which there is a complete breach of the muscle coats, filled by fibrous tissue. A benign ulcer always shows fusion of the muscularis mucosa with the edge of the muscle coat where it is breached in the base of the ulcer.

When a growth obstructs the pylorus vomiting is an early symptom. There may be visible peristalsis and a succussion splash. Dysphagia suggests a lesion at the cardia. Because the onset may be insidious with general malaise, tiredness, loss of weight and perhaps anaemia, it may be impossible clinically to distinguish carcinoma of the stomach from carcinoma of the caecum.

Occasionally both barium meal and enema must be performed to make the distinction. ✳

Physical Signs

A tumour in the epigastric region usually indicates carcinoma in the pylorus or the lower part of a leather-bottle stomach. Ascites may be detected. Weight loss and anaemia may be obvious. Lymph nodes may be enlarged in the left supraclavicular fossa. If the vomit is examined altered blood may be found either with the naked eye or by testing for occult blood. In the later stages the patient shows gross physical changes— cachexia and emaciation. There may be obstructive jaundice due to enlargement of nodes in the porta hepatis.

Diagnosis

Any patient who has dyspepsia for more than a month should be examined by barium meal. Radiography may show impaired motility of the stomach wall or a filling defect at the site of the growth. Radiography of the stomach may show no abnormality, and yet the clinical condition strongly suggests carcinoma. Laparotomy may then be indicated. Gastroscopy is sometimes helpful in diagnosis. Surgery should be considered in all cases of gastric ulcer that lie near the pylorus, near the cardia or on the greater curve. Dyspepsia beginning after the age of 40 years is suspicious, especially where the history is brief.

Treatment

It must be admitted that operative treatment of carcinoma of the stomach gives poor results, but equally it must be realised that surgical excision is the only treatment for gastric carcinoma, for these growths are insensitive to radiation and cytotoxic drugs. The primary growth is removed wherever possible unless there are widespread secondaries. In cases in which the growth is apparently confined to the stomach wide resection with the omenta and regional lymph nodes is performed. Palliative resection of the growth or gastro-enterostomy is performed if there is vomiting. Narcotic drugs, diet and gastric lavage all have a place in making the patient more comfortable in advanced stages of the disease.

At laparotomy about 50% of patients are incurable because of secondary deposits in the liver or spread through the peritoneum or penetration into viscera which cannot be removed. Of the remaining 50% which are deemed possibly curable the operation of choice is partial gastrectomy for all growths at the pyloric end of the stomach. When the cardia is affected total gastrectomy may be carried out, usually together with the greater omentum and the spleen. Restoration of continuity is performed by anastomosing jejunum to the oesophagus. The pyloric end of the stomach may be retained, fashioned into a tube and anastomosed to the oesophagus. The long-term results of surgery for carcinoma of the stomach are poor, perhaps only 10% of those who have resection survive for more than 5 years. The prognosis is certainly better if lymph nodes have not been involved.

SIMPLE TUMOURS OF THE STOMACH

Benign gastric tumours are rare. Adenomata occur as single or multiple polypi. Leiomyomas are liable to ulceration and haemorrhage, occasionally they become malignant. Neurofibromas and neurogenic sarcomas rarely occur in the stomach.

FOREIGN BODIES IN THE STOMACH

Most foreign bodies are swallowed by children, many must never be noticed. The objects swallowed are of infinite variety, including whistles, nails, pins and dentures. Patients in mental hospitals, hysterical women and prisoners commonly swallow foreign bodies. If hair is swallowed over a period of years a hairball (trichobezoar) may form in the stomach, giving rise to a large mass the shape of the stomach. Usually foreign bodies cause no symptoms, because the vast majority pass spontaneously. Warning symptoms are pain and vomiting, very rarely perforation may occur.

If a foreign body passes the cardia it is likely to pass through the pylorus and eventually the rectum. The only foreign bodies that require removal are open safety pins, nails and needles and very large bodies, such as spoons, which can never pass through the pylorus.

So long as there are no symptoms and the shape of the object and its size suggests that it will pass, no treatment is required. Radiographs should not be performed too frequently, perhaps at weekly or fortnightly intervals, and a careful watch should be kept on the faeces for signs of the foreign body. If it remains in the stomach after several weeks, then it should then be removed at operation after opening the stomach.

INJURIES OF THE STOMACH

The stomach is rarely injured by external trauma, except perhaps in stab wounds. Occasionally the stomach may be injured from within by foreign bodies or during examination with the gastroscope or oesophagoscope. It is extremely rare for spontaneous rupture to occur following severe vomiting. Symptoms and signs are those of peritonitis, and laparotomy or thoracotomy is required for the damage to be repaired.

ACUTE DILATATION OF THE STOMACH

Acute dilatation of the stomach used to be a common complication of abdominal operations, but is extremely rare nowadays. It may follow any operation, the application of a hip spica ('plaster ileus') or immobilisation on an orthopaedic bed. The cause is not known, but at post mortem (this condition used to be highly fatal) not only is the stomach dilated but also the duodenum up to its third part. This fact has suggested that perhaps there is some degree of duodenal ileus from pressure on the mesenteric vessels. Dilatation of the stomach causes severe pain and discomfort in the epigastrium and vomiting of large volumes of brown offensive fluid. The abdomen becomes distended by the enlarged stomach. As soon as the condition is suspected the stomach should be emptied and kept empty by continuous aspiration, fluid and salts are replaced by intravenous infusion.

FURTHER READING

The Scientific Basis of Surgery. (1965) Edited by Irvine, W. T. J. & A. Churchill, London.
Avery Jones, F., and Gummer, J. W. P. (1960) Clinical Gastroenterology. Blackwell, Oxford.
Wells, C., and Kyle, J. (1960) Peptic Ulceration. E. & S. Livingstone, London.
Shackelford, R. T. (1955) Surgery of the Alimentary Tract. Vols 1-3. Saunders, Philadelphia.

CHAPTER TWENTY-ONE

THE SMALL INTESTINE

The commonest lesion of the small intestine is obstruction. Congenital anomalies are rare but important, because, if recognised early, they can usually be corrected by operation. Tumours are excessively rare, granulomata (Crohn's disease) are becoming more common. As the methods of investigation of the function of the small bowel become more refined, the importance and frequency of intestinal malabsorption is being more and more appreciated.

INTESTINAL OBSTRUCTION

Obstruction of the small bowel may be due to paralysis of peristalsis (ileus), mechanical occlusion of the bowel lumen or disease of the bowel wall itself. Simple occlusion means blockage of the intestine from causes in the lumen itself, in the bowel wall or outside it. Strangulation results when the blood supply of the intestine is impaired either by arterial or venous occlusion; strangulation may occur with or without obstruction of the bowel lumen.

There arc many causes of intestinal obstruction; they can be conveniently summarised as below, although it must be appreciated that they are not listed in order of their frequency of occurrence:

Adynamic Obstruction (Paralytic ileus)

Toxic—due to peritonitis, uraemia and typhoid.

Reflex—injuries of the spine, plaster of Paris spica, retroperitoneal haematoma, and fractured spine.

Dynamic or Mechanical Obstruction

Lesions in the lumen—foreign bodies, gall stones, 'bolus obstruction', enteroliths, meconium ileus.

Lesions in the bowel wall—Crohn's disease, tuberculosis, tumour, atresia.

Lesions outside the bowel wall—adhesions, external hernia, enlarged lymph nodes, pressure of tumours.

Additional lesions—intussusception, volvulus, mesenteric thrombosis and embolism—all lesions that may cause bleeding per rectum and obstruction.

Pathology

The intestine below the site of obstruction is empty and contracted. Proximally it is dilated and thinned unless the onset has been slow, when the gut wall will show muscular hypertrophy. The mucous membrane may be ulcerated. Within the dilated bowel, gas and fluid accumulate and, if the distension becomes gross, the vessels supplying the gut may be compressed, leading to a state of strangulation. Rarely, perforation may occur, causing peritonitis.

In strangulation the vessels supplying the bowel may become compressed and occluded, leading to congestion and exudation into the lumen and into the mesentery. If the arteries are compressed, thrombosis of them eventually occurs. The infarcted segment is dark red, matted and stiff with exudate. The affected segment is clearly demarcated from the normal bowel adjacent to it. Recovery after relief of strangulation is judged by a change in colour of the bowel (which means that there must be an intact circulation), seeing peristalsis crossing the damaged segment or by feeling pulsation in the mesentery.

Strangulation carries a high mortality, even after the affected segment of the damaged intestine has been excised. Water and electrolytes may be lost from vomiting and in exudate in the bowel lumen; severe losses of blood may also occur into the bowel. Death may follow from hypovolaemic shock. Absorption of toxins, products of bacterial proliferation in the strangulated segment, may cause death from prolonged hypotension and toxaemia. Experimentally it appears that strangulation of bowel sterilised by antibiotics does not cause death so long as fluids and salts are replaced intravenously.

VARIETIES OF INTESTINAL OBSTRUCTION

The commonest causes of intestinal obstruction are external hernias and postoperative adhesions.

Obstructed hernia

In any case of intestinal obstruction the hernial orifices must be carefully examined. If a hernia is *tense, tender, irreducible and without an impulse on coughing* it is certainly strangulated. Mere irreducibility and pain may denote only a simple occlusion, but it is safer to assume that in any case of hernia causing discomfort strangulation may be present. All such patients should be operated on as an emergency. Special difficulty may be encountered in Richter's hernia, in which only part of the bowel circumference is trapped in a hernial sac so that the signs of strangulation are present in the absence of signs of intestinal obstruction. This type of hernia is particularly common in the femoral canal. Diagnosis is often late, and so the condition carries a high mortality, even after intestinal resection has been performed.

Adhesions and Internal Hernia

Most intraperitoneal adhesions form after an abdominal operation, though some appear after inflammation, such as a previous attack of peritonitis or due to adherence of bowel to a tuberculous lymph node. The flat multiple filmy bands that mat the intestines together after peritonitis are less often the site of obstruction than single cords or bands. Volvulus or twisting of the bowel may occur around a single band. A remnant of the vitello-intestinal duct attached to a Meckel's diverticulum may cause intestinal obstruction from adhesion to bowel or volvulus around a band. Sometimes a congenital aperture in a mesentery or following operation may lead to obstruction when a loop of intestine slips through the defect. Adhesions are thought to be less common since talc has been abandoned for glove powder. Talc is very irritating and causes granulomata and intense adhesions if spilt in the peritoneum, it has been replaced by starch powder.

Very rarely bowel may be obstructed in an internal hernia; these arise in pouches of developmental origin in the mesenteries or adjacent to bowel. Several lie near the duodenum, the duodeno-jejunal flexure, below the inferior mesenteric vein and near the caecum. Very rarely herniation may occur into the foramen of Winslow.

Intra-luminal Causes of Obstruction

Swallowed foreign bodies rarely obstruct in the small bowel. Once the pyloric sphincter is passed most foreign bodies are spontaneously evacuated per rectum. Lodgement may occur in the duodenum, duodeno-jejunal flexure or in the terminal ileum. They very rarely cause obstruction. 'Bolus obstruction' is the commonest cause of intestinal obstruction due to a foreign body. It is common after a gastric operation in edentulous patients and is due to masses of pith from swallowed fruits, such as oranges and dried fruits, that pass rapidly into the jejunum, where they swell and cause obstruction. Operation is often necessary to remove this cause of obstruction, but occasionally the mass may pass spontaneously. A large gall stone may pass silently from the gall bladder through a cholecyst-duodenal fistula to enter the duodenum. Impaction of the stone usually occurs in the terminal ileum. The diagnosis is often difficult because the patient is usually obese and has often had earlier attacks of abdominal pain and vomiting due to cholecystitis. The stone is almost always radiolucent, so does not show in a plain radiograph. Gas shadows may be seen in the course of the bile ducts, evidence of a biliary fistula. Once gall-stone ileus has been diagnosed, operation must be performed and the stone removed.

Meconium ileus occurs in the neonatal period, and is due to obstruction of the bowel by masses of meconium that are viscous and inspissated because of a deficiency of pancreatic enzymes. The condition is very rare and affects infants born with fibrocystic disease of the pancreas. The signs of intestinal obstruction may be associated with intestinal perforation and intraperitoneal calcification seen in radiographs. At operation the damaged loops of small bowel must be excised and a temporary loop-ileostomy performed. Through the ileostomy pancreatin, an extract containing pancreatic enzymes can be instilled to dissolve any masses of meconium that may have to be left.

Lesions in the Wall of the Intestine

Lesions in the intestinal wall that cause obstruction are uncommon. They include non-specific granulomata such as Crohn's disease, strictures that may be of unknown cause or due to the healing of a tuberculous ulcer. Tumours are rare, benign tumours are more common than malignant ones.

In Crohn's disease obstruction is rarely complete and usually settles with a conservative non-surgical régime. Tumours and strictures must be excised or by-passed.

Lesions Outside the Wall

Most extrinsic lesions are the result of adhesions or external hernias, and can readily be relieved by operation. Tumours involving bowel or compressing it can be removed or by-passed by entero-anastomosis.

INTUSSUSCEPTION

Intussusception is the invagination of one part of the intestine into another part. It occurs most commonly in infants under the age of 2 years, the maximal incidence being between 4 and 9 months. An intussusception has three layers of bowel—the entering, returning and ensheathing layers. An intussusception tends to progress distally, the apex or caput remaining constant and progress taking place at the expense of the outer layer of bowel. As the apex of the intussusception progresses distally the vessels in the invaginated mesentery become more and more stretched and compressed, until finally the bowel is strangulated. Eventually gangrene and sloughing may occur. An intussusception may pass through the whole colon and present at the anus. A mass is commonly felt in the abdomen which is formed by the oedematous strangulated bowel.

No cause is known for intussusception, but it is commonly thought that it arises from abnormal peristalsis set up from swelling of lymphatic tissue in the gut in Peyer's patches. The mesenteric lymph nodes adjacent to an intussusception are considerably swollen and very similar to the enlarged nodes often seen in mesenteric adenitis (see p. 298). This has suggested the possibility that some infection causes swelling of lymphatic tissue that initiates the intussusception.

A Meckel's diverticulum or a tumour may initiate an intussusception. In adults there is almost always a primary cause, usually a benign tumour, occasionally a malignant one. The commonest variety of intussusception is the ileocolic, in which the ileo-caecal valve forms the apex of the intussusception. Intussusception may begin also in the terminal ileum—the ileo-ileal type, which later passes through the ileo-caecal valve. Colic

Colic

intussusceptions occur in the sigmoid colon, usually secondary to a carcinoma at the apex. Retrograde intussusception is rarely seen in a gastroenterostomy, where the jejunum becomes invaginated into the stomach.

Redcurrant jelly + Sausage mass

Symptoms and Signs

Typically the onset of intussusception is sudden. A child becomes pale, screams with pain and draws up the knees. Vomiting may occur and a normal stool be passed. Between the spasms of colicky pain the child may appear perfectly well and show no abnormal physical signs. At some time a stool is passed containing mucus and blood of a typical appearance —redcurrant jelly stool.

The important physical sign is a mass anywhere in the course of the colon, but most often in the right hypochondrium under the right costal margin. The mass is typically sausage-shaped, and slightly curved because of its attachment to the mesentery, which restricts the development of the intussusception on one side. The mass is tender and may be felt to contract and harden if there is a spasm of colic. In the most extreme cases an intussusception may present at the anus. Bowel sounds may be augmented, but only during the phases of colic. Plain radiographs of the abdomen may be unhelpful, for in the early stages of an intussusception intestinal obstruction is incomplete and fluid levels may not be seen. If the intussusception is left unreduced, then strangulation occurs, with gangrene of the bowel and death from peritonitis.

Any child with a history of spasms of colicky abdominal pain must be admitted to hospital for observation. If a mass is felt or if blood or mucus are passed per rectum, then operation must be performed. The diagnosis may be very difficult because the spasms of pain may be infrequent, the mass may be difficult to feel in a small crying child and blood may not be passed. Occasionally laparotomy must be done because of a strong suspicion that intussusception has occurred. Other conditions may only with difficulty be distinguished from intussusception—gastro-enteritis, Henoch-Schönlein purpura (where bleeding occurs into the bowel that may itself initiate intussusception) and non-specific acute mesenteric adenitis.

Treatment

The mortality of intussusception depends entirely upon the interval between the onset of symptoms and operation. Delay in diagnosis may allow strangulation and gangrene of the bowel to occur. Resection of strangulated bowel in infants carries a high mortality. Within the first 12 hours operative treatment should not be followed by any complications. For some reason recurrence is almost unknown, so no attempt should be made at operation to fix the bowel; only reduction of the intussusception is necessary.

A vertical abdominal incision is made to the right of the midline centred over the umbilicus. The intussusception is reduced by pressure on its head and not by pulling it out by traction on the small bowel. Traction may cause rupture of the bowel, especially if it is damaged by strangulation. Difficulty may be encountered in achieving complete reduction because the oedematous caput of the intussusception has to pass through the ileo-caecal valve. With gentle coaxing reduction can be achieved unless gangrene is established. The mesentery is often oedematous and the lymph nodes greatly enlarged and hyperplastic.

Small patches of gangrene can be invaginated by seromuscular sutures. Extensive gangrene necessitates a major resection of bowel. Great care must be taken pre- and post-operatively with the fluid and electrolyte balance, which must be controlled by someone who is experienced in the handling of the hydration of small babies.

The reduction of intussusception by barium enema has been extensively used, but not in Britain, where most surgeons and physicians recommend operation. An enema may certainly reduce an intussusception, but there is always doubt as to completeness of the reduction.

After reduction of the intussusception the apex must be carefully examined for any tumour or polyp that may have initiated the invagination. Such causes are rarely found in children.

Chronic intussusception occurs in adults, especially in the left side of the colon initiated by a tumour such as a carcinoma or polyp at the caput of the invagination. The symptoms are those of attacks of intestinal obstruction. Sometimes the apex of the intussusception can be felt per rectum. Such patients are treated by colonic resection.

VOLVULUS

Volvulus or twisting may occur when a long, mobile loop of bowel revolves around its own mesentery or where the apex of a loop is attached to some viscus or the abdominal wall by adhesions that provide a fixed point around which volvulus may occur. In many cases of intestinal obstruction an element of volvulus precipitates an acute crisis at the junction of collapsed and distended bowel. As the distended loop becomes larger and heavier it tends to fall over and finally cause a complete obstruction.

Volvulus of the Colon

Volvulus of the colon is an uncommon complication. Usually old people with a long redundant sigmoid colon are affected. There may be a lengthy history of constipation and purgation, during which the sigmoid has become greatly increased in size and length. Patients in mental institutions are commonly affected. It is a common emergency in West Africa.

The sigmoid loop twists around its mesentery, and unless the obstruction is rapidly relieved, strangulation may occur, with gangrene and even perforation of the bowel because of the rapid and massive distension with gas.

The onset is sudden, with severe colicky pain, later the pain becomes enormously Vomiting may occur. The abdomen becomes rapidly and continuous. distended, with tenderness and rigidity overlying the distended colon. A plain radiograph is diagnostic in showing the abdomen to be filled by an enormous loop of pelvic colon filled with gas, the size of a motor-car tyre.

Treatment

If the patient is not too ill the passage of a flatus tube in the knee elbow position may occasionally produce a dramatic and offensive deflation. Occasionally successful reduction follows the introduction of a tube through a sigmoidoscope. If this fails operation should be performed with a flatus tube in the rectum so that, after the bowel has been untwisted, it can be decompressed. A long incision is made to allow the colon to be exteriorised. It is untwisted and decompressed. Recurrence may be prevented by performing a temporary colostomy that fixes the bowel. If gangrene has occurred the sigmoid colon is exteriorised and resected by the Paul–Mickulicz manoeuvre (see p. 308).

Volvulus of the caecum is rare, and occurs when the caecum and ascending colon have a mesentery. Pain and distension are prominent, together with the signs of small-bowel obstruction. A plain radiograph shows small-bowel fluid levels and a large caecum distended by gas. At operation the bowel is untwisted and fixed by a temporary caecostomy. Right hemicolectomy may be needed if gangrene has occurred.

Volvulus Neonatorum

In the neonatal period, within 2–3 days of birth, a history of bilious vomiting is strongly suggestive of volvulus neonatorum often associated with duodenal stenosis. Other conditions to be considered are Hirschsprung's disease, intestinal atresia, imperforate anus and meconium ileus.

Bilious vomiting is the prominent feature; there may be little distension, as the level of small-bowel obstruction is high. Usually meconium has not been passed. A plain radiograph is diagnostic, showing a large gas bubble in the stomach but no intestinal gas shadows beyond.

In children who suffer volvulus neonatorum there has been a failure of intestinal rotation, so that the mid-gut still hangs on a mesentery and twists around the duodeno-colic isthmus.

An urgent operation must be performed to untwist the bowel and to divide the band of adhesions which is found stretching across the duodenum from the colon to the right paracolic gutter. If there is an associated duodenal atresia this must also be relieved by duodeno-duodenostomy (see p. 426).

Volvulus of Small Bowel

The small bowel may undergo volvulus around a focus of adhesion formed after an operation, or sometimes by adhesion to a chronically infected lymph node. Operation is indicated to relieve the obstruction.

MESENTERIC VASCULAR OCCLUSION

Ischaemia of bowel may follow atherosclerotic narrowing, thrombosis or embolism of mesenteric arteries or thrombosis of mesenteric veins. Thrombosis of mesenteric arteries is secondary to atherosclerosis that may previously have narrowed them, especially at their origin, from the aorta. Arterial emboli come from the heart or from atherosclerotic plaques in the aorta. The cause of venous thrombosis is unknown, occasionally it is associated with portal hypertension, blood dyscrasias, hypertension and pressure on the veins by tumours. Rarely nowadays it may be due to septic thrombosis following intraperitoneal suppuration such as appendicitis.

Acute mesenteric vascular occlusion is a highly fatal condition. Pain is sudden in onset, severe and often generalised. Signs of obstruction develop rapidly, going on to those of peritonitis. The diagnosis can be very difficult. Many patients who suffer mesenteric vascular occlusion have other diseases and are very unfit. The decision to operate to confirm the diagnosis is often a difficult one. Occasionally blood may be passed per rectum, supporting the diagnosis.

Where the superior mesenteric artery is narrowed by atherosclerotic disease at its origin the rare condition of intestinal claudication may result, in which pain comes on shortly after meals and a systolic murmur may be heard in the epigastrium. Malnutrition and steatorrhoea may arise. If intestinal ischaemia can be diagnosed clinically aortography may help to confirm the diagnosis. In some cases the narrowing can be by-passed by an arterial graft, or the narrowing itself may be removed by thrombo-end arterectomy.

Treatment

After resuscitation, laparotomy is performed. Gangrenous bowel must be resected. When resection is needed the mortality is high. Occasionally very extensive resections leave only a small length of intestine. With less than 100 cm. of small bowel it is very difficult to preserve normal nutrition.

If the diagnosis is clear and made in a few hours from the onset of symptoms heparin may allow recovery of the bowel by preventing spread of thrombus distal to the initial site of occlusion. The infusion of dextran (Rheomacrodex) has occasionally been dramatically effective. In some cases early operation permits removal of an embolus from the origin of the superior mesenteric artery or by-pass of the block by a graft.

REGIONAL ILEITIS (CROHN'S DISEASE)

Non-specific granulomata occur in any part of the alimentary tract, but are most common in the terminal ileum, where the lesion may occasionally extend into the right side of the colon. Non-specific inflammation means that no particular cause is known, though the histological appearances are constant and suggest an inflammatory cause, being similar to those seen in tuberculosis but without caseation.

Aetiology

The cause of Crohn's disease is unknown. The sexes are equally affected and at any age, though the peak incidence is between 10 and 40 years. Occasionally there is a familial history. Many attempts have been made to relate ileitis to tuberculosis, but although the histology is very similar, caseation never occurs and acid-fast bacilli cannot be cultured from the ileum or mesenteric nodes. The Mantoux reaction is often negative. A relationship to ulcerative colitis has been suggested, but the latter disease is a disease of the mucosa, whereas Crohn's disease is a disease of all the coats of the bowel. The microscopical appearance of Crohn's disease is very similar to that of sarcoidosis, but there is no clinical association between the two diseases. In addition, the Kveim test for sarcoid is negative in ileitis. The non-caseating giant-cell systems seen in Crohn's disease are apparently a non-specific reaction to some foreign irritant, for a similar picture is found in the granulomata produced by some metallic poisons, leishmaniasis and leprosy. Experimental production of lesions similar to ileitis is said to be possible in animals if mesenteric lymphatics are obstructed by sclerosants.

Pathology

The affected bowel is thickened and rubbery, with oedema over a very variable extent. In 30% of patients the colon is also involved, the appendix rarely. Lesions may extend in continuity or as 'skip' lesions which are clearly separated from each other.

Histology shows oedema throughout the coats of the bowel, permeated by inflammatory cells, including plasma cells, leucocytes and eosinophils. Lymphoid follicles are prominent containing giant cells like those of tuberculosis, except that caseation is not associated. A chronic phase is also met in which the prominent feature is fibrosis of the bowel wall, perhaps with ulceration of the mucosa. The mesenteric lymph nodes are always greatly enlarged—histology shows reactive hyperplasia of the sinus endothelium and occasionally non-caseating giant-cell systems.

Ulceration of the mucous membrane occurs, and at a later stage fibrosis with narrowing of the intestinal lumen. Diseased loops may adhere to each other or to other viscera to become part of an inflammatory mass, often with fistula formation into another viscus, such as the bladder, or externally through the abdominal wall.

Symptoms and Signs

Most often the diagnosis of Crohn's disease can only be made at operation. Acute appendicitis is commonly mimicked, and only when the appendix is found to be normal is the terminal ileum examined and seen to be reddened, with all the appearances of an acute inflammation. Repeated attacks of colicky pain and diarrhoea may suggest ulceration of the bowel, which may be confirmed radiologically if a barium meal is followed through to the ileo-caecal region. More often than not, however, radiography is negative unless the intestinal lumen is rigid or narrowed (Kantor's string sign). Crohn's disease is next in frequency to appendicitis in causing an inflammatory mass in the right iliac fossa in young people. Peri-anal fistulae may complicate long-standing cases. Extensive bowel replacement by Crohn's disease may cause severe diarrhoea and malnutrition from steatorrhoea. A faecal fistula following appendicectomy is strongly suggestive of regional ileitis.

Spontaneous resolution has frequently been reported in active phases of the disease, but in most patients the disease progresses continuously or in episodes separated by months or years.

Treatment

Long-term surveys of the history of this disease show that the longer the follow-up period, the greater is the recurrence rate, irrespective of whether or not surgery has been undertaken. After a 10–15-year period 80% of patients have been shown to have recurrences. The present view is that initially the disease should be treated medically. Surgery is reserved for failure of conservative treatment, to relieve symptoms and complications, the onset of intestinal obstruction and abscess formation and fistula.

In the acute phase of ileitis it is sound practice not to remove the appendix for fear of provoking a faecal fistula. A mesenteric node may be excised which if it shows non-caseating tubercle follicles provides useful confirmation of the diagnosis. A long period of rest and convalescence may be followed by spontaneous resolution.

Medical treatment for the established disease includes rest in bed and a high-protein, high-carbohydrate diet with vitamins and iron. Cortisone may help produce a remission. The effect of treatment is followed by improvement in symptoms and well-being, a gain in weight and a fall in the E.S.R.

If symptoms persist or worsen or if fistula or obstruction occur, operation is performed. The diseased bowel is excised, usually a right hemicolectomy is performed. Another method is to exclude the diseased bowel by dividing the ileum proximal to the disease, burying the distal end and anastomosing the proximal end to the transverse colon. Which operation is best is still the subject or controversy; both carry a high recurrence rate.

When recurrence after surgery was first met it was thought due to an inadequate primary excision. A more conservative attitude now prevails

with the realisation that extensive bowel resection does not guarantee
against recurrence and may be harmful in leaving the patient with dangerously little small bowel. Malabsorption syndrome and malnutrition may
be the effect of either extensive bowel replacement by disease or resection
leaving too little small intestine. Perhaps it is better to consider the results
of treatment in terms of relief of symptoms and control of the disease
rather than of radical cure.

TUBERCULOSIS OF THE SMALL INTESTINE

Tuberculous Ulceration of the small bowel is usually secondary to
pulmonary tuberculosis from swallowed bacilli which infect the gut.
Because pulmonary tuberculosis has become rare in Britain, and certainly
advanced tuberculous disease has become even rarer, tuberculous ulceration of the intestine has almost disappeared in this country. Nowadays
almost the only tuberculous ulcers seen in the bowel are those in a pathological museum. The ulcers tend to encircle the bowel following the course
of the lymphatics; as they heal, stricture formation may follow. Tubercles
may be seen on the peritoneal surface, the edges of the ulcer are typically
undermined. Fistula formation between viscera occurs, and a faecal
fistula may appear at the umbilicus. Cold abscesses may form.

Hyperplastic Ileocaecal Tuberculosis is rarely diagnosed in Great
Britain, but is still common in India. As the diagnosis of tuberculosis
of the ileocaecal region has become less frequent in this country, so the
diagnosis of Crohn's disease has become more common. The description
of hyperplastic tuberculosis is often identical to that of regional enteritis
and colitis. Tuberculosis can only be diagnosed if acid-fast bacilli are seen
in the specimen or can be cultured from it or the mesenteric lymph nodes.
If caseation occurs tuberculosis must be the cause, the diagnosis being
made after resection of the inflamed bowel.

TYPHOID ULCERATION

The intestinal complications that the surgeon may meet in typhoid
fever are perforation and haemorrhage, both occurring in the third week
after the onset of the infection. The ulcers run longitudinally following
the course of Peyer's patches.

ACTINOMYCOSIS

Actinomycosis (see p. 64) is a rare disease most often seen in the
cervico-facial region, next often in the ileo-caecal angle. The appendix
and caecum are involved. A massive induration of structures in the right
iliac fossa results, with sinuses burrowing widely in the abdominal wall
discharging the characteristic pus containing sulphur-coloured granules.
A faecal fistula may follow appendicectomy. Portal infection with honey-
comb liver abscesses is a rare complication. The diagnosis is made when

the actinomycetes are seen in pus obtained from sinuses. Actinomycosis is treated by a prolonged course of penicillin (see p. 65). Iodides are not used nowadays. Other antibiotics, such as tetracycline, may be necessary if penicillin is not entirely effective or if the disease recurs.

ENDOMETRIOSIS

Deposits of endometrial tissue may rarely be seeded on to the small bowel, where they may cause scarring and stricture formation from haemorrhage. These endometrial deposits bleed because they undergo the cyclical changes of menstruation. Abdominal pain occurs, and there are usually gynaecological symptoms, menorrhagia, dysmenorrhoea and sterility.

Endometrioma may also present as an ovarian cyst (chocolate cyst) or as a mass in the recto-vaginal septum, at the umbilicus or in the groin. Swellings appear that vary in size with menstruation and may cause bleeding.

Intestinal obstruction may need operative relief by a short-circuit. Progesterone-like hormones may suppress symptoms. An artificial menopause may be indicated.

MECKEL'S DIVERTICULUM

Meckel's diverticulum (Fig. 23) is a remnant of the vitello-intestinal duct that in the embryonic life joined the midgut to the umbilicus and the

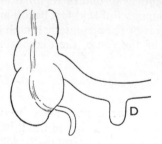

FIG. 23. Meckel's diverticulum, D

yolk sac. Normally the duct from the umbilicus to the gut is obliterated before birth. Rarely it remains wholly patent, causing a faecal fistula at the umbilicus. If only the mid-part is patent a cyst forms. Most commonly the proximal part remains open, forming a diverticulum of variable length. Occasionally a fibrous band joins the umbilicus to the tip of the diverticulum or lies free in the peritoneum, where it may ensnare small bowel and cause obstruction. Meckel's diverticulum is rare (found in 0·5% of post mortems) and even more rarely causes symptoms.

The diverticulum lies about 50 cm. from the ileo-caecal valve, projects from the antimesenteric border and averages 5 cm. in length. It is lined by intestinal mucosa, sometimes with islands of ectopic acid-secreting cells identical to those found in the stomach. A peptic ulcer may arise in the intestinal mucosa adjacent to one of these islands of acid-secreting cells. Nodules of pancreatic tissue may also be found.

Symptoms arise from the complications to which a diverticulum of the intestine is subject—inflammation which closely mimics appendicitis, perforation or haemorrhage from a peptic ulcer and intestinal obstruction from volvulus around the fibrous remnant of the duct or adhesion to nearby viscera. Rarely the diverticulum acts as the apex of an intussusception.

The diagnosis is almost always made at operation. In cases explored because of a presumed diagnosis of acute appendicitis, if the appendix appears normal, the terminal ileum should always be examined for Meckel's diverticulum. The presence of a diverticulum does not mean that it is necessarily the cause of symptoms. It must be removed if it is inflamed, causing haemorrhage or obstruction or containing a nodule suggesting a peptic ulcer or pancreatic tissue.

DUPLICATION

Duplication of the intestine is a rare congenital anomaly in which segments of bowel may be double-barrelled. Extensive lengths may be involved, or the duplication may be restricted to a large diverticulum on the mesenteric border or even a cyst in the mesentery clearly separated from the intestine. There may be no symptoms, or there may be pain, diarrhoea or bleeding. A mass may occasionally be felt, especially where a large mesenteric cyst forms. The condition can usually only be diagnosed at operation. Usually some form of gut resection is necessary for its cure.

TUMOURS OF THE SMALL BOWEL

Tumours of the small bowel are all rare. *Benign tumours* include adenomatous polyps, leiomyoma or fibroma, lipoma, angioma, neurofibroma and carcinoid. In the Peutz–Jegher's syndrome polyposis of the small intestine is associated with pigmentation of the face, buccal mucosa and lips. It is an inherited defect. Usually there are repeated attacks of obstruction or intussusception; malignant change does not occur. Most small-bowel tumours present with bleeding, diarrhoea, obstruction or intussusception.

Malignant Tumours include adenocarcinoma, sarcoma and malignant carcinoid. Sarcomas of the reticuloendothelial system are prone to arise in the small bowel. Such growths cause bleeding and obstruction. Wide excision is necessary at operation, both of the primary growth and of the regional lymph nodes. Postoperative radiotherapy is given for sarcomata.

Carcinoid Tumours

Most carcinoid tumours are benign and arise in the appendix. Carcinoid tumour is found in 1:300 appendices that are removed at operation. Carcinoids that are found in the small intestine are often malignant; rarely they are found in the colon or rectum. Many carcinoid tumours secrete 5-HT (serotonin, or 5-hydroxytryptamine), a potent vasoconstrictor and stimulator of smooth muscle. When a malignant carcinoid metastasises to lymph nodes and liver the secretion of 5-HT may cause attacks of flushing of the skin and bouts of diarrhoea with audible borborygmi. Asthmatic attacks follow spasm of the bronchi. Pulmonary stenosis is common, and is due to fibrosis of the pulmonary valve.

In the appendix a carcinoid is usually an accidental finding. A small yellow nodule is seen under the mucosa near the tip of the organ. In the terminal ileum malignant tumours frequently metastasise to the lymph nodes and liver. Carcinoid tumours derive from the Kulschitsky cells, which are sited at the bottom of intestinal glands. They stain typically with silver stains and chromic acid. The tumour shows a uniform picture of sheets of round cells with very large hyperchromatic nuclei.

Investigations

5-hydroxyindolacetic acid (5-HIAA), a breakdown product of 5-hydroxytryptamine, may be found in the urine.

Treatment

Benign tumours are found only after appendicectomy. Malignant tumours must be widely excised, usually by right hemicolectomy. Serotonin antagonists may be of help in the relief of symptoms.

MESENTERIC ADENITIS

Non-specific Adenitis

Children very commonly complain of the sudden onset of acute abdominal pain centred around the umbilicus which comes in severe colicky spasms. The pain lasts usually only a few seconds or a few minutes at a time, during which period the child is doubled up and pale. He or she may vomit. All grades of severity of these attacks occur. Sometimes the child is pyrexial, sometimes there is an associated upper respiratory infection or sore throat, sometimes the periods of pain precede an infective fever or otitis media. Physical signs are usually restricted to slight tenderness around the umbilicus. It is often difficult to be certain that the child is not going to develop appendicitis, and certainly if the pain shifts to the right iliac fossa, then operation should be performed.

At operation the lymph nodes in the mesentery are found to be enlarged, swollen and oedematous. No bacterial cause has been found to account for the adenitis, but recent work incriminates a group of adenoviruses. All children who have abdominal pain suggestive of adenitis should be admitted to hospital for a period of observation. In the vast majority of cases the symptoms subside within a few hours, and nothing need be done. If there is any tenderness in the right iliac fossa or if the pain does not settle within 16 hours, then an operation should be performed and the appendix removed. A leucocytosis, especially if polymorphs predominate, is suggestive of appendicitis. It is much more dangerous to leave an acutely inflamed appendix than to make a wrong diagnosis and remove a normal appendix.

Tuberculous Adenitis

Tuberculous adenitis is uncommon nowadays because of the rapidly falling incidence of tuberculosis, especially of the bovine type. Many adults, however, are seen with calcified lymph nodes in the mesentery who must in childhood have had some tuberculous infection. Tuberculous mesenteric adenitis may give rise to attacks of vague abdominal pain, diarrhoea or constipation and fever. Rarely is there any indication for treatment. Very occasionally there is a caseating lymph node which may cause abdominal pain or adhesion to bowel, causing obstruction.

MESENTERIC CYSTS

Mesenteric cysts are rare and usually congenital in origin. Dermoids and teratomata are occasionally discovered, and very rarely cysts may follow trauma. A rounded, tense swelling is found in the region of the umbilicus, mobile in a direction at right angles to the line of attachment of the mesentery. Treatment is by excision, when it is often necessary to remove an attached segment of small bowel because the mesentery must be removed.

STEATORRHOEA

Steatorrhoea is defined as the excretion of more than 6 g. of fat in a 24-hour stool on a diet restricted to 50–100 g. of fat per day. It is characterised by an increase in volume of stool from the normal of about 100–200 g. to 500–1000 g. per day. The stools are pale and offensive, bulky and light in weight, floating in the lavatory pan and requiring repeated flushing to remove them.

Causes

1. *Defects of Digestion*

(a) There may be a deficiency of bile due to jaundice or cirrhosis of the liver.

(b) A deficiency of pancreatic secretion, perhaps due to cystic fibrosis of the pancreas, chronic pancreatitis, carcinoma of the pancreas or where the pancreas has been removed surgically.

(c) Post-gastrectomy steatorrhoea due to intestinal hurry and short-circuit of the duodenum.

2. Defects of Intestinal Absorption

(a) *Anatomical Lesions.* Here much of the small intestine may have been resected at operation or a blind loop formed at operation in which the intestinal flora changes resulting in defects of absorption of vitamins and fat. Occasionally diverticula of the small bowel may have the same effect as the 'blind-loop' syndrome.

(b) *Lesions of the Intestinal Mucosa* localised, in regional ileitis or jejunitis; generalised, in idiopathic steatorrhoea, coeliac disease and tropical sprue.

Other diseases may infiltrate the mucosa, such as Hodgkin's disease, lymphosarcoma and intestinal lipodystrophy (Whipple's disease) an anomaly of lymphatics.

Symptoms and Signs

The stools are frequent, massive, bulky and pale. The effects of steatorrhoea are nutritional, loss of weight, malnutrition, tetany, osteomalacia, macrocytic anaemia, vitamin deficiencies, electrolyte loss and sometimes haemorrhages due to prothrombin deficiency.

Investigations

Faecal fat is estimated in 24-hour periods over 3 days. A full blood count is carried out, a xylose tolerance test usually gives a flat curve, plasma proteins are measured. Serum calcium and plasma electrolytes are estimated. A jejunal biopsy of the mucosa can be obtained with the use of a special instrument, the Crosby capsule. An atrophic mucosa suggests idiopathic steatorrhoea, a normal biopsy suggests that steatorrhoea is a secondary effect. The glucose tolerance curve may be abnormal in pancreatic disease.

Treatment

The treatment is usually non-surgical. Operations may be performed for the relief of jaundice and in some cases of pancreatic disease. Oral administration of pancreatic enzymes ('Pancreatin') is useful in pancreatic insufficiency.

It is important that massive resections of small bowel be avoided as far as possible, and operations should not allow intestine to be excluded by short-circuit or anastomosis. In stagnant loops of bowel, bacterial proliferation may interfere with absorption of food from the gut. If steatorrhoea is caused by blind loops of intestine these may have to be undone to restore normal anatomy and function. Long-term administration of antibiotics can be given to change intestinal flora. Iron and vitamins, including B_{12}, are given.

FURTHER READING

Shackelford, R. T. (1955) *Surgery of the Alimentary Tract.* Saunders, Philadelphia.

Hawkins, C. F. (1963) *Diseases of the Alimentary Tract.* Heinemann, London.

Recent Advances in Gastroenterology (1965) edited by Badenoch, J., and Brooke, B. N. J. & A. Churchill, London.

CHAPTER TWENTY-TWO

COLON

Anatomy and Physiology

The main functions of the colon in man are to act as a reservoir for faecal material from which a great deal of water can be reabsorbed. The bacterial action which takes place in this milieu allows the elaboration of a number of substances, including vitamins, which are also absorbed. Alterations in the colonic flora due to the introduction of pathogenic organisms or the effects of antibiotics may disturb the balance and lead to inflammation of the mucosa and vitamin-B deficiency.

The small-bowel contents are relatively sterile and fluid, and the ileo-caecal valve allows them to run through into the large bowel, where the consistence gradually thickens as the contents pass, often taking 12 or 18 hours to traverse the full length of the large bowel. The smooth and regular flow of peristaltic waves down the small bowel is replaced in large measure by mass peristalsis in the large bowel, which aids its emptying.

The surface marking of various parts of the large bowel are useful not only in clinical surgery but also in studying radiographs, which are usually prepared after the introduction of a barium mixture per rectum. The caecum lies in the right iliac fossa, where it can often be palpated near McBurney's point. It may, however, not descend properly in adult life, and is then tucked up under the right lobe of the liver. The hepatic flexure usually lies well below the right rib margin; the transverse colon is the most variable part of the large gut, and may hang down into the pelvis, lie over to one side or rarely be found above the umbilicus. The splenic flexure is the highest point which the colon reaches and, being under the rib margin, is not often palpable. The sigmoid colon is of very variable length, and in some people forms a long redundant loop which may undergo volvulus.

Bowel Preparation for Rectal or Colonic Surgery

Prior to an operation on the anus or rectum it is essential to empty the rectum of faeces. Evacuation is best avoided after surgery for 2–3 days, so for comfort it is important to have the bowel empty before operation, especially as many people undergoing operations on the large bowel suffer from constipation. Before a rectal or anal operation a simple enema is given the night before and a colon wash-out on the morning of the operation. When colonic resection is to be performed the entire large bowel is washed out daily for several days, using a tube and funnel. Large volumes of *saline* may be needed before the fluid that is returned is free of faecal masses. If scybali are found in the bowel at operation despite pre-operative wash-outs, a preliminary colostomy may be necessary through which the bowel may be cleared. It must be appreciated that the removal of faecal accumulation is more important than the lowering of the bacterial count by sulphonamide or antibiotic.

It is usual to start the patient on one of the non-absorbed sulphonamides in order that its bacteriostatic action may be exerted in the colon. Phthalyl-sulphathiazole is the safest preparation, and can be given in 1- or 2-g. doses by mouth every 6 hours for 3–4 days. Reduction of the bacterial count of the colon is safe, but complete sterilisation can be harmful by increasing the liability to staphylococcal enterocolitis (see p. 317). If less time is available, the risk must be taken and ¼ g. of neomycin given by mouth four times in the 24 hours before operation to sterilise the gut. Streptomycin can be given by mouth in the 2 days before operation, in ½ g. doses twice a day, this is especially useful where the gut has been pre-pared on a previous occasion with sulphonamide when sulphonamide resistant organisms can be anticipated.

CARCINOMA OF THE COLON

Carcinoma of the colon is most often seen in the sigmoid colon between the ages of 55 and 70. It is a little commoner in women than men, although rectal carcinoma is much commoner in men than women. The Registrar General's figures for England and Wales record about 15,000 deaths per year from carcinoma of the large bowel, including the rectum. This figure is second only to that of carcinoma of the bronchus. If the rectum is excluded, then 50% of all cancers in the colon occur in the pelvic or sig-moid colon, 25% occur in the caecum and ascending colon, 5% in the splenic flexure, 10% in transverse colon, 5% in the hepatic flexure and 5% in the descending colon.

Pathology

The tumour is always a columnar-celled adenocarcinoma. Several clinical types may be recognised: *annular*, which chiefly occurs on the left side, particularly in the pelvic colon and rectosigmoid region. It gives rise to a stricture and obstruction which often leads to early diagnosis. *Papilli-ferous*, which projects into the lumen of the bowel and occurs especially in the caecum. It is likely to become ulcerated and may bleed, but rarely causes obstruction until late, as the bowel contents in this region are fluid. *Malignant Ulcer* takes the form of a deep indurated depression with fungating margins, more likely to be found in the distal pelvic colon and resembling the type of tumour often seen in the rectum. Colloid degenera-tion may occur in any of these lesions, and usually indicates a high degree of malignancy. More than one growth may be found in the colon, so it is important to palpate the whole large bowel and carry out sigmoidoscopy.

The disease arises first in the mucosa, spreads through the muscle coats and then circumferentially around the bowel. Passing into the lymphatic channels, it reaches the lymph nodes in the mesentery. Malignant cells may also enter the portal venous system, and are the cause of secondaries in the liver. The disease also spreads by direct extension and may infiltrate nearby viscera or the peritoneum lining the abdominal wall. Multiple deposits in the peritoneum and omentum, often associated with ascites, are to be seen in the late stages of any bowel carcinoma. Perforation of a carcinoma of the colon usually gives rise to a localised abscess near the tumour, but sometimes results in widespread faecal soiling of the whole peritoneal cavity and generalised peritonitis, a condition which usually ends fatally.

The prognosis is at its best when it is found that the tumour has not penetrated the whole thickness of the bowel wall and has not yet spread to the regional lymph nodes. The prognosis is hopeless when there is secondary spread to the liver and other distant sites, but this does not always mean that excision of the primary tumour should not be done. Distressing symptoms and the fear of obstruction may be removed and a sense of well-being imparted to the patient if the growth in the colon is removed. The degree of differentiation of the tumour and the local reaction of the tissues are no less important in assessing prognosis.

Symptoms and Signs

The onset of symptoms is almost always slow and usually insidious. The carcinoma may remain latent for one of two years unless intestinal obstruction supervenes, the patient only complaining of a lack of energy and a loss of well-being. The most important early symptoms are change of bowel habit, rectal bleeding and passage of mucus. The blood is usually bright red if the growth is low down, but is dark in colour and mixed with faeces if the carcinoma is sited more proximally.

Later the main symptoms are vague abdominal discomfort, flatulent dyspepsia (which may be mistaken for peptic ulcer) and a change of bowel habit, including increasing constipation, bouts of diarrhoea and blood and slime in the motion. The diarrhoea is of the false type resulting from bacterial decomposition of faeces above an obstruction. The stools are therefore often offensive, watery and small in amount. As the disease progresses, the clinical features tend to vary according to the position and the type of growth, loss of weight comes late, often the complexion is sallow and there is a general feeling of ill health.

The Proximal Colon. In the caecum the symptoms caused by a growth are particularly likely to be vague. There is sometimes flatulence, with occasional vomiting. There may be diarrhoea or sometimes constipation. Anaemia is a feature owing to toxic absorption from the inflamed, ulcerated area and loss of blood from it. There may be a palpable tumour in the right side of the abdomen. Dyspepsia and anaemia may simulate gastric carcinoma. Anaemia and occult blood in the faeces should always be investigated by sigmoidoscopy and barium enema. Frequently it is only in the later stages of the disease that intestinal obstruction occurs. The symptoms may suggest subacute appendicitis in an older patient.

A growth of the caecum may actually cause acute appendicitis by obstructing the opening of the appendix. Suspicion of carcinoma may be roused by the development of a pericaecal abscess or a faecal fistula after appendicectomy for appendicitis. All 'appendix abscesses' in the older patient should be examined by barium enema when the acute phase is over.

The Distal Colon. Here obstructive symptoms predominate and tend to occur at an earlier stage than in the proximal part of the large bowel. There is usually increasing constipation, which alternates with spurious or false diarrhoea. The stools sometimes contain an excess of mucus and occasionally blood. The abdomen slowly becomes distended, and colicky pain is a common complaint. If the narrowed bowel is completely occluded by faeces the symptoms and signs of acute obstruction are superimposed on the existing condition.

The Recto-sigmoid Region. Annular and ulcerating growths usually attract notice by the onset of intestinal obstruction. Papilliferous growths may give rise to excessive mucous secretion, diarrhoea and bleeding. Haemorrhoids are commonly diagnosed. So much mucus may be lost as to produce electrolyte imbalance, especially hypokalaemia.

Diagnosis

It should be remembered that in the early stages of carcinoma of the colon the symptoms and signs may appear insidiously and be vague.

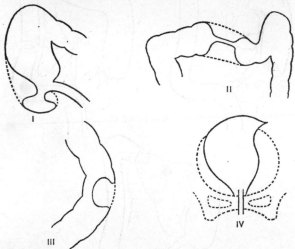

FIG. 24. Radiographic appearance of carcinoma of the colon: (i) caecum; (ii) transverse colon; (iii) sigmoid colon; (iv) recto-sigmoid junction

The possibility of carcinoma of the colon should be kept in mind when any adult complains of general malaise, loss of appetite and loss of weight. All patients who present with a recent change in bowel habit or rectal bleeding should be investigated for the presence of carcinoma of the colon.

PR

Although the presenting symptom of bleeding may suggest haemorrhoids, digital examination of the rectum followed by sigmoidoscopy should always be performed to rule out the possibility of a tumour in rectum or lower colon. Digital examination, proctoscopy, sigmoidoscopy and a barium enema examination may all be required before a tumour of the colon or rectosigmoid junction can be excluded. A barium enema may show a filling defect, narrowing or complete obstruction (Fig. 24). Many innocent neoplasms of the colon tend to undergo malignant change, and therefore any lesion, such as an ulcer, induration or infiltration, calls for immediate biopsy if it can be seen through a sigmoidoscope. If reasonable doubt still exists after all investigations have been carried out, a laparotomy should be performed.

The two conditions which cause particular difficulty in the differential diagnosis are an appendicular mass on the right side and diverticulitis on the left side of the abdomen. Many other conditions may mimic carcinoma of the colon, such as an amoeboma or Crohn's disease, but these are uncommon.

Treatment

The ideal is to perform a radical excision of the affected portion of the gut, including about 10 cm. above and below the tumour, together with

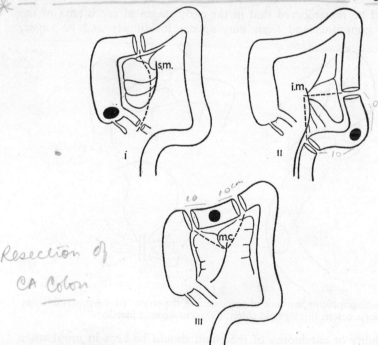

Resection of CA Colon

FIG. 25. Extent of resection for carcinoma of colon: (i) caecum; (ii) sigmoid colon; (iii) transverse colon; s.m., superior mesenteric; i.m., inferior mesenteric; m.c., middle colic arteries.

a fan-shaped area of mesocolon having its apex at the root of the mesentery (Fig. 25). This will include all the lymphatic vessels and nodes which drain the area of the carcinoma. Unless acute intestinal obstruction is present, the bowel is prepared by wash-outs and a non-absorbable sulphonamide. Subacute obstruction can often be relieved by enemata and colonic wash-outs.

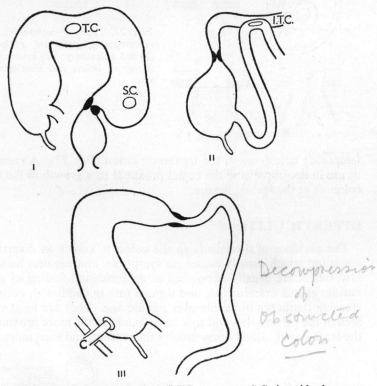

Decompression of Obstructed Colon.

FIG. 26. Decompression of obstructed colon: (i) TC, transverse, S.C. sigmoid colostomy; (ii) ITC, ileo transverse colostomy; (iii) C, caecostomy

When a patient presents with acute intestinal obstruction it is imperative to perform immediate colostomy (Fig. 26) proximal to the tumour in order to allow the patient to recover from the effects of obstruction. In the case of carcinoma in the caecal region, an ileo-transverse colostomy short-circuiting the obstruction can be made. At a later date the tumour, together with its lymphatic drainage, should be removed should it be considered resectable. If there is only minimal intestinal obstruction some surgeons perform primary excision with restoration of continuity of the bowel. If a permanent colostomy is fashioned because the tumour is apparently inoperable it is important to perform a biopsy either of the carcinoma itself or of an affected lymph node to confirm the diagnosis. Even

Colostomy proximal to tumour

when it is impossible to remove all affected nodes, it is well worth while excising the tumour and anastomosing the bowel, since such palliative surgery avoids a colostomy, although life may not necessarily be prolonged. A permanent colostomy is best fashioned in the pelvic colon, a

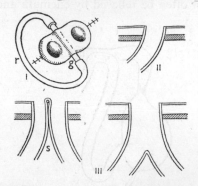

FIG. 27. Types of colostomy: (i) loop colostomy g, glass rod, rubber tube; (ii) end colostomy; (iii) spur colostomy (S, spur), before and after crushing of spur

temporary colostomy in the transverse colon (Fig. 27). A caecostomy is of use in decompressing the bowel proximal to a growth in the transverse colon or at the splenic flexure.

DIVERTICULITIS

The presence of diverticula in the colon is known as diverticulosis, a condition which usually causes no symptoms and requires no treatment. Diverticula are usually discovered as an incidental finding as a result of barium enema examination, and though rare in childhood, occur with increasing frequency in people over middle age. They are most commonly seen in the pelvic colon and to a lesser extent in the more proximal part of the large bowel. Rarely they involve the rectum, and even more rarely the

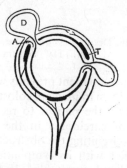

FIG. 28. Diverticulosis, mucosal pouches (D) herniating between taeniae coli (T) at sites of penetration of arteries (A)

appendix. Each diverticulum consists of a little protrusion of mucous membrane through the muscle wall of the gut and commonly occurs at a weak spot, which is where the wall is pierced by a blood vessel on either side of a taenia coli (Fig. 28).

Etiology

Diverticulosis coli is seen more commonly in men than women, and though rare before the age of 40, is seen with increasing frequency after this time. It is more often seen in fat people. It has often been said that constipation is a factor in the development of diverticula, but there is no evidence for this. Recent experimental work has suggested that incoordination in the muscular contractions of the lower colon and upper rectum result in abnormally high pressures in these organs, and this provides a more plausible theory for the development of diverticula by pulsion.

Pathology and Complications

The diverticula are pouches of mucous membrane not covered by muscle, and therefore do not have the power of emptying themselves. The stasis of faecal material within leads to pathological changes, the commonest of which is inflammation. Diverticulitis may involve a single diverticulum, or a whole segment of the bowel, usually in the sigmoid colon, may be converted into an inflamed tender mass. The recurrent attacks of inflammation lead to fibrosis and hypertrophy of the circular muscle, and the gut wall becomes thickened, rigid and narrowed. The mucosal lining is usually unaffected except for occasional ulceration of a single diverticulum. In its extreme form it resembles a scirrhous carcinoma. If a diverticulum perforates the result is either a localised abscess or generalised peritonitis. Localised perforation to an adherent viscus is likely to be followed by fistula formation most commonly into the bladder —vesico-colic fistula. Rarely severe haemorrhage may occur from diverticulosis, a cause which can only be diagnosed by exclusion of all other possible causes of rectal bleeding.

Symptoms and Signs

These can be conveniently grouped according to the way in which the disease presents.

1. *Pain and Change of Bowel Habit.* Perhaps the commonest presentation of diverticulitis is recurrent attacks of pain in the left iliac fossa, often associated with constipation and bouts of diarrhoea. Often the history may extend over months or years. The symptoms are very much like those of carcinoma of the colon, which must be carefully excluded by barium enema and sigmoidoscopy. Urinary infection, spinal and gynaecological disorders must also be excluded.

2. *Inflammation.* When a patient suffers from an attack of acute diverticulitis of the pelvic colon there is usually colicky pain, local tenderness and some rigidity in the left iliac fossa, a mass may be palpable through the abdominal wall or per rectum. The disease has been called 'left sided appendicitis'. If a diverticulum perforates there will be signs

of localised peritonitis with a high fever and leucocytosis and often inhibition of bowel movements. General peritonitis is very serious and presents with board-like rigidity of the abdominal muscles, absent bowel sounds and signs of severe toxaemia. The differential diagnosis will include a perforated inflamed appendix or perforation of a peptic ulcer.

3. *Obstruction.* Recurrent attacks of diverticulitis may lead to much narrowing and fibrosis of the colon, and eventually inflammation, with its attendant oedema, may produce almost complete obstruction to the lumen of the bowel. There is usually a long history of recurrent attacks of minor bowel upset, with constipation and occasionally diarrhoea and the passage of mucus.

4. *Abdominal Mass.* When an inflamed segment of large bowel is wrapped round with great omentum it may be palpated in the pelvis or left iliac fossa as a tender mass. In the female salpingitis may be simulated. It may also be confused with a carcinoma of the large bowel, even at operation. Sometimes it is only after the bowel has been opened that a growth can be excluded. As both diverticulitis and growths are common in the colon, they may co-exist.

5. *Fistula.* A well-recognised complication of diverticulitis is the formation of fistulae between the colon and other abdominal organs due to inflammatory attacks. The bladder is most commonly involved, and the patient then passes flatus or faecal material in the urine—pneumaturia—but never urine per rectum. Vesico-colic fistula is rare in women, because the uterus intervenes between the bladder and rectum. A fistula may form to another part of the gut, such as the small bowel, and very rarely the vagina or uterus is involved. Drainage of an abscess in the left iliac fossa may be followed by a faecal fistula.

6. *Haemorrhage.* Diverticulitis of the colon often produces constipation and occasionally spurious diarrhoea with the passage of mucus; sometimes, however, blood is passed, much less often, however, than is the case with carcinoma of the colon. Occasionally, in a small percentage of patients, a very large haemorrhage per rectum occurs as a complication of diverticulosis. Such a haemorrhage is usually much larger than is seen with malignant disease of the large bowel. Bleeding from diverticulitis should always rouse the suspicion of a coincident growth or polyp.

Diagnosis

The diagnosis of diverticulitis of the colon is usually made on the history of recurrent attacks of left-sided abdominal pain and bowel upset. During an attack a tender mass may be palpable, and the white-cell count is raised and there is usually some fever. Sigmoidoscopic examination is rarely successful in demonstrating the disease, though an oedematous mucosa may be seen, but a barium enema examination is almost always diagnostic. Between attacks the diverticula are clearly shown as small pouches along the bowel edge, and during inflammation the bowel is narrowed and has a saw-tooth edge (Fig. 29). In long-standing cases there is much narrowing and the bowel demonstrates rigidity of its wall due to fibrosis. When diagnosis is in doubt, and the differential diagnosis is always likely to be carcinoma of the colon, laparotomy should be performed.

Treatment

Diverticulosis of the colon requires no treatment apart from small doses of liquid paraffin by mouth and a diet from which indigestible elements are excluded, such as pips, seeds and skins. If acute attacks are severe, then the patient must go to bed and be given a fluid diet and a course of antibiotics such as streptomycin 0·5 g. intramuscularly twice a day for 6 days;

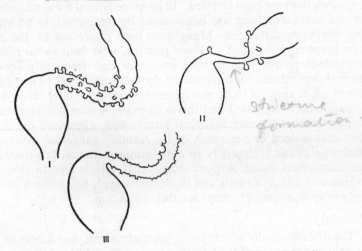

stricture formation

FIG. 29. Radiographic appearances of diverticulitis; (i) multiple pouches in segment; (ii) stricture formation simulating carcinoma; (iii) 'saw-tooth' pattern

heat is applied to the abdomen to relieve pain. If the attacks are frequent and crippling or if there is haemorrhage or any doubt as to whether the lesion is malignant or not, then operation is advised and the bowel prepared as for all operations on the colon. The segment of involved bowel almost always the sigmoid colon, is excised and the two ends anastomosed. If obstruction occurs, then a proximal colostomy in the transverse colon must be carried out, followed by resection of the diseased bowel; the colostomy can be closed later. If acute perforation occurs with abscess formation the affected loop of bowel can sometimes be exteriorised and used as a colostomy, if the lesion is circumscribed drainage alone may suffice. If an abscess occurs, then it must be drained. If a fistula occurs to another part of the abdominal cavity the bowel should be prepared and a formal operation performed to excise the diseased loop. A preliminary cystoscopy with biopsy of the edge of a vesico-colic fistula helps to exclude carcinoma of the bladder or colon. The adhesions and the changes in the

L

bowel wall may make such an operation an extremely difficult undertaking, and often it can only be performed after a preliminary colostomy. In an old man, if it is certain that carcinoma is not responsible, a vesico-colic fistula may be accepted by the patient without discomfort, and may even heal. A longitudinal extramucosal myotomy of the affected segment (like a Ramstedt operation) may relieve the symptoms but its safety and value have yet to be assessed.

ULCERATIVE COLITIS

The cause of this serious and chronic disease of the colon is unknown. In its fulminating form it resembles bacillary dysentery, but no specific organism has ever been isolated. In its more typical form relapses of more or less acute diarrhoea are interspersed by remissions, in which most of the symptoms disappear. Many have been impressed by the character-istic personality of most of these patients, who tend to be rather fussy, meticulous people, emotionally immature and frequently showing ab-normal dependence on a parent or another individual. The onset of the illness often appears to be precipitated by an emotional crisis, and it has therefore been suggested that this is an example of psychosomatic disease. It may be that the psychological factors only aggravate the disease, or they may indeed be the result of it. Another suggested explanation for ulcerative colitis is that it is an auto-immune disease, but there has been no clear proof by serological testing that this is so. In some patients evidence of allergy to milk can be demonstrated, and in such cases avoid-ance of milk appears to improve their condition.

Pathology

The disease usually affects the colon and rectum, but it may be confined to only one segment of the bowel or involve the whole of the large gut and spill over into the terminal ileum. The inflammation predominantly in-volves the mucosa, which is the site of many shallow ulcers. Between the ulcers the mucosa becomes heaped up with oedema, and in time becomes hyperplastic and polypoid. Hundreds of these so-called pseudo-polyps may be found lining the bowel, a condition which may be pre-malignant. The muscle coat is not directly involved in the ulcerative process, but the inflammation leads to fibrosis, and eventually the bowel is converted to a narrow and rather rigid tube, without any sign of haustration.

Symptoms and Signs

The disease usually starts in early adult life, being slightly more common in women than men. The principal symptom is diarrhoea, which continues with varying severity throughout the illness, while during an acute relapse the stools are greatly increased in number and contain blood, pus and mucus. During a relapse abdominal pain may be severe and colicky, the temperature raised and the patient becomes weak, anaemic and eventu-ally emaciated. The intensity of the attacks varies greatly not only from patient to patient but also according to the severity of the disease. In its most acute form the patient becomes gravely ill in a few days, with extreme dehydration due to the fluid lost by the bowel and he or she may die during such an attack. During a remission the patient may return almost to normal, but is always at risk of developing another severe attack. In some patients a low-grade colitis may persist for many years, only occasionally flaring up.

There is usually tenderness over the affected part of the colon. The patient looks anaemic, and the haemoglobin may fall to 40 or 50% quite

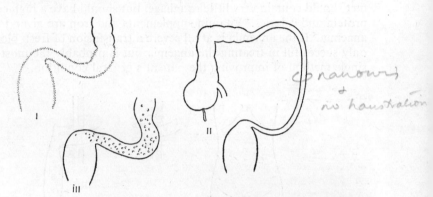

FIG. 30. Radiographic appearances in ulcerative colitis: (i) blurring of outline of rectum and sigmoid; (ii) narrowing and lack of haustration in distal colon; (iii) pseudo-polyp formation

quickly during an attack. At sigmoidoscopy, the mucosa of the rectum is seen to be red, granular, bleeds easily and presents superficial ulcers and an excess of mucus and pus mixed with a fluid stool. A barium enema examination in the early stages shows a rather fuzzy outline (Fig. 30), and in the later stages the bowel is shorter, narrower and lacks normal haustration. In radiographs taken after evacuation of the barium, pseudo-polyps may be seen.

Complications

Stricture of the bowel, peri-anal abscess and perforation of the colon, leading to localised abscess or generalised peritonitis, may all occur. Distension of the abdomen, tenderness or a change in the character of the bowel sounds suggest the possibility of perforation of the colon. The severity of the symptoms and signs may be suppressed if the patient is being treated with steroids. There may be severe haemorrhage and also the loss of large volumes of fluid from the bowel during an acute attack. In patients in whom the disease has been present for 10 years or more and in whom the whole of the large bowel is involved there is a real risk of the development of malignant change, which has been assessed as high as 10%. Arthritis, iritis and hepatitis may be associated with colitis. A curious skin condition, pyoderma gangrenosum, is occasionally seen. These associated conditions may only clear up if the colon is removed.

↳ pyoderma gangrenosum

Treatment

There is no specific therapy for ulcerative colitis. In the first place treatment is largely symptomatic, aimed at replacing losses and maintaining nutrition. The patient is given a period of complete rest in bed. The diet should contain very little roughage, but should have a high content of protein and calories. Vitamin supplements and iron are given to combat anaemia. If the anaemia is at all severe a transfusion of fresh blood is not only successful in treating the anaemia but is probably the most effective single method of improving the patient's general condition.

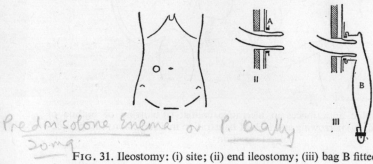

Prednisolone Enema or P. orally
20mg

FIG. 31. Ileostomy: (i) site; (ii) end ileostomy; (iii) bag B fitted to ileostomy

Patients who do not obtain a remission with the above treatment are given a course of corticosteroids. The simplest method is for the patient to administer an enema containing prednisolone 20 mg., and this can be supplied in a plastic pack which the patient can introduce. The enema is inserted into the rectum at night-time, when the patient lies prone and retains it for as long as possible; many are able to retain it all night. Three weeks is a reasonable time to continue such therapy. A more effective way of giving the prednisolone is by mouth 10–40 mg. daily, reducing the dose after 2 weeks. Many patients will have a remission after such treatment, which may be prolonged. There are many side effects to such therapy, and the most serious is the possibility of perforation of the bowel or some other hollow viscus. Salazopyrin, a sulphonamide derivative, which is given by mouth in doses of 1 g. four to six times a day for several weeks is often effective in controlling colitis. A maintenance dose of 0·5 g. daily may be given for several months but watch must be kept for rare instances of blood dyscrasias. When used in conjunction with the corticosteroids it may help in prolonging remission.

The surgical treatment of ulcerative colitis has entirely changed the

3 wks

S
1 g
4–6
times a day
for
several wks.

picture of this disease during the last 20 years. The complete colon and
rectum is excised, usually in two stages, and the terminal ileum brought
out in the right iliac fossa, where, by use of an adhesive disc, a very neat
bag can be fitted so that the patient leads an almost normal life (Fig. 31).
In about 20% of patients the rectum may be little affected, and it is then
possible to anastomose the terminal ileum to the rectum so that the patient
is continent. Failure of conservative treatment is the most important
indication for colectomy in ulcerative colitis, perforation, fulminating
disease and severe haemorrhage are others. When there is arthritis or pyoderma, then surgery is almost the only treatment which will clear them up.
The preoperative preparation of the patient by correction of anaemia and
water and electrolyte depletion is most important. The dose of prednisolone or other corticosteroid must be increased to cover the operation period,
and a non-absorbable sulphonamide, such as phthalysulphathiazole, is
useful to minimise the risk of infection. The choice of the best time to perform colectomy may be very difficult in a patient with a severe exacerbation, as it is important not to allow the patient to become too ill to withstand
the major surgery necessary, but, on the other hand, it may be worth waiting
a while in order for a remission to occur. There are dangers in prolonging
steroid therapy if a rapid onset of remission does not occur. The bowel
may perforate or even disintegrate, and severe haemorrhage may occur.
The usual procedure in an acute phase of the disease is to give steroids for
about 7–10 days only. If a remission is not induced, then operation
should follow as an emergency. In pregnancy the relapse rate is low, a
flare up may however follow delivery. The disease still carries a high
mortality unless treated in centres where the best medical and surgical
treatment is available.

Complications

In addition to the complications already mentioned of narrowing and
shortening of the bowel and the occurrence of a malignant change, there
are two other rare but important complications. Arthritis may occur,
which is severe and crippling often affecting single joints and only clearing
up when the offending bowel is removed. The other complication is
pyoderma, which may go on to ulceration, especially on the legs. Jaundice
due to hepatitis is also seen occasionally in this condition.

The Ileostomy Patient

The idea of an ileostomy is usually revolting to the patient, but careful
preparation and showing the patient others who have been successfully
treated in this way will often reassure and convert them. Follow-up
studies in clinics where the disease has been especially treated show that
over 90% are eventually entirely satisfied with their ileostomy, and
manage with only minor restrictions in their diet. Most can swim, dance
and play tennis. Women marry and produce normal children, and they
are not barred from life assurance.

OTHER ULCERATIVE LESIONS OF THE COLON

Crohn's Disease

This is commonly seen in the terminal ileum, but may also present in the colon, either as a solitary lesion or as a complication of ileal disease. There may be diarrhoea and colic, loss of blood and mucus in the stools, and intermittent attacks of subacute obstruction. Fistulae may arise in the perineal region or from the colon to adjacent viscera, usually to small bowel. A barium enema examination reveals a narrowed segment in the colon, and the diagnosis is usually made at laparotomy. Regional colitis may present with symptoms and signs indistinguishable from ulcerative colitis. The diagnosis may be made by rectal biopsy or histology of bowel removed at operation.

Amoebiasis

Infection with the entamoeba histolytica produces no typical clinical picture apart from that of dysentery, and the onset of the disease is almost always insidious. Usually the patient has lived in an area where the disease is endemic. Eventually there is the passage of blood and mucus in the stools, and the tell-tale cysts and amoebae may be identified in a warm specimen examined under the microscope. A localised tumour, which is a granuloma or amoeboma, may arise in the colon. It is most often seen in the caecum and rectum, but may occur in any part of the large bowel. Clinically it is almost always diagnosed as carcinoma because of a palpable mass and the narrowing seen in a barium enema. The treatment of amoebic disease is described in Chapter Six.

Solitary Ulcer of the Caecum

This benign condition, which is almost always confused with carcinoma of the caecum, is of unknown aetiology. A large perforating ulcer with heaped-up edges occurs in the caecum, usually on the posterior wall, and may ulcerate into adjoining tissues. There is vague pain in the right iliac fossa, sometimes a palpable mass and loss of blood in the stools. Diagnosis is usually made by barium enema and a hemi-colectomy performed in the mistaken impression that the lesion is malignant. The symptoms and signs of appendicitis are simulated.

Solitary Diverticulum of the Caecum

Diverticulitis of the caecum presents like acute appendicitis, but at operation the appendix is found uninflamed. The inflamed diverticulum may be seen projecting from the caecal wall or may be buried in a mass of inflammatory tissue. An isolated diverticulum can be excised like an appendix. An inflammatory mass in the caecal wall may be left to resolve or more often right hemi-colectomy is performed for fear of malignancy.

Necrotising Enterocolitis

This alarming condition is typically seen in a patient who has undergone major surgery and been given a course of antibiotics. There is acute fulminating diarrhoea, in which not only is there a great loss of fluid but the mucous membrane of the bowel sloughs and is passed as a cast. The cause appears to be staphylococci which colonise the bowel following the suppression of other more susceptible organisms by antibiotics. The more potent the antibiotic, the more likely is enterocolitis to occur. If unrecognised the condition may be fatal, but rapid restoration of blood volume and the use of antibiotics such as erythromycin and ampicillin is often followed by complete recovery and apparently regeneration of normal bowel mucosa. Cocci may be seen in direct smears taken from the stool, enabling an immediate diagnosis to be made.

POLYPOSIS COLI

Multiple polyposis of the colon is a familial condition inherited from a Mendelian dominant gene. The polyps develop as adult life is reached, and symptoms usually occur in the second or third decade, with the passage of blood and mucus. Sigmoidoscopy may demonstrate polyps, and a barium enema will show those which are situated in the colon. These polyps invariably undergo malignant change, and therefore colectomy is indicated. Since it is possible to inspect the rectum regularly, anastomosis of the ileum to the rectal stump is justifiable. Any polyps which occur later in the rectum can be removed using diathermy.

Solitary polyps or multiples of two or three may occur in any part of the large bowel. They are typically seen in the rectum in children, when they bleed and finally separate, or they may be removed with a snare. In adults rectal or colonic polyps should always be treated with suspicion, since they may undergo malignant change. Polyps that are accessible and can be seen through a sigmoidoscope can be removed with a diathermy snare. Some, low down in the rectum, can be prolapsed digitally through the anus and removed. The specimens must be carefully examined histologically for malignant change. Carcinoma *in situ* and carcinomatous changes that do not involve the pedicle or base of the tumour may be treated as if benign, though sigmoidoscopy must be performed 3 monthly for at least 2 years. If the pedicle or base of the tumour shows malignant change, then bowel resection must be performed.

Benign polyps may be smooth or covered by villous fronds, they may be sessile or on a stalk. Villous papillomata may be enormous, the bowel being filled by soft fronds of tumour. Such tumours secrete large amounts of mucus, so much as to cause hypokalaemia. Large villous tumours in the rectum can be removed piecemeal in several sessions with a careful follow up for recurrence. Polyps in the colon may be difficult to show up by barium enema. Air contrast studies may be of use, in which a barium enema is performed, the barium evacuated and the bowel distended by air to show the mucosal pattern.

MEGACOLON

Megacolon in children may be either of the acquired variety due to habit or anal stenosis or, on the other hand, it may be of the Hirschsprung variety, in which there is lack of the normal innervation of the bowel musculature affecting the rectum and distal colon. These conditions are dealt with in Chapter Twenty-eight.

Megacolon may also be seen in adults, and it is then first necessary to exclude the possibility of its being of the Hirschsprung or aganglionic type, and the best method of doing this is to perform a rectal biopsy. In Brazil acquired megacolon is one of the commonest surgical diseases of the rectum and sigmoid, and is due to the late results of infection with the South American trypanosome, so-called Chagas' disease.

FURTHER READING

Goligher, J. C. (1968) *Surgery of the Anus, Rectum and Colon*. Cassell, London.
Muir, E. G. (1961) *Carcinoma of the Colon*. Arnold, London.

CHAPTER TWENTY-THREE

DISEASES OF THE RECTUM AND ANUS

HAEMORRHOIDS OR PILES

Haemorrhoids or piles are due to varicosity of the submucous veins of the anal canal. The commonest that require treatment are *internal haemorrhoids*. Here the veins are covered with mucous membrane and arise initially at the junction of the lower rectum and anal canal. The symptoms due to haemorrhoids are not constant but typically intermittent, the patient complaining every few months of 'an attack of the piles'. *External haemorrhoids*, are veins covered by squamous epithelium; this term includes dilated perianal veins and redundant folds of perianal skin. Sometimes there is thrombosis within one of these dilated veins at the anal margin. It usually arises suddenly, and the swelling is very painful, tense and bluish. If left it shrinks to form an anal skin tag.

Pathology

The cause of piles, as with varicose veins which they resemble, is unknown. Certainly, in many patients, there is an hereditary factor. In normal defaecation there is congestion of the rectal veins, but when the act is completed the rectum should be empty, the muscles relaxed and circulation in the veins returned to normal. However, prolonged congestion may be brought about by chronic constipation, anxiety, the habit of straining at stool and the use of powerful purges. Piles often become worse during pregnancy. Any condition, such as a tumour of the colon or rectum or one arising outside the bowel, such as an ovarian tumour, enlarged prostate inflammation of the lower bowel and rectum, such as ulcerative colitis or proctitis, indeed anything which results in congestion may aggravate or possibly cause haemorrhoids. Portal hypertension may result in varicosities at the site of anastomosis between the portal and systemic systems of veins, and this includes, on rare occasions, the lower rectum.

The longitudinal mucosal folds in the lower rectum (columns of Morgagni) contain the terminal branches of the superior rectal (haemorrhoidal) artery surrounded by thin-walled valveless veins. The enlargement of these veins gives rise to *primary piles*. The artery divides into right and left branches, the former dividing again into anterior and posterior divisions. This anatomical arrangement localises the position of the primary piles; on proctoscopic examination with the patient in the lithotomy position these are at three, seven and eleven o'clock. As the condition advances the areas between these primary sites may also be affected by varicosity, and these are called *secondary piles*.

Piles are usually classified by degree, and this is convenient in planning treatment. When they only bleed, and there is no other complication, they are classified as *first degree*. Often there is a loss of elasticity of the sub-mucosa and the piles prolapse outside the anus. If such piles return spontaneously after defaecation they are classified as *second degree*. Piles which prolapse, but remain outside the anal margin after defaecation and require replacement manually, are called *third degree*. All degrees are liable to complications, thrombosis and strangulation are particularly liable to occur in prolapsing piles, and may be followed by sloughing, ulceration and infection.

Symptoms and Signs

The first symptom is usually bleeding on defaecation. Sometimes there is a sense of fullness or local irritation. Later, if untreated, piles prolapse with rectal discomfort, a feeling of incomplete evacuation, mucoid discharge and pruritis ani. Pain is not associated with uncomplicated piles, but may appear later, and then indicates thrombosis, strangulation or suppuration.

On inspection with first-degree piles there may be no obvious abnormality at the anus. With second- and third-degree piles, one or more dark red swellings present which are prolapsing internal piles. During an 'attack' they may be large and dark in colour. In extreme circumstances they may appear as swollen ulcerated and sloughing masses, indicating strangulation. The final result of fibrosis and thrombosis of an internal pile is a small pale polypoid swelling.

The patient is next asked to strain, and internal piles, which were previously not seen, may prolapse. Laxity of the anal musculature may also be obvious. Digital examination is next done to feel if there is an ulcer or tumour in the rectum and to judge the size of the anus and the tone of the sphincter. Internal piles cannot be palpated normally, but only when there has been thrombosis or fibrosis. Proctoscopy is the most important examination, and allows a clear view of the number, position, size and to some extent the degree of the piles. When examining the anal region other simple conditions may be found, such as a fissure, sentinel pile or fistula.

Care must be taken to exclude other lesions, especially carcinoma of the rectum. In all patients a general examination of the abdomen is carried out, followed by proctoscopy and sigmoidoscopy in order to discover if there is a carcinoma higher up in the rectum. This is particularly important in older patients with a history of recent onset of haemorrhoids.

Treatment

In early and uncomplicated cases the treatment may be conservative. This consists in attempting to regulate bowel habits, with the use of liquid

Isogel, Celevac.

paraffin, methyl cellulose (Isogel, Celevac) and perhaps a mild aperient. Astringent ointments such as ung. hamamelidis, and anaesthetic creams, such as those containing Nupercaine may also help. These simple measures are especially useful during pregnancy, since haemorrhoids frequently disappear after delivery.

When internal piles are of first or second degree and the main complaint is bleeding the treatment of choice is injection of a sclerosant. The object is to produce submucous fibrosis in the region of the base of the pile, with subsequent venous obliteration and adhesion of the mucous membrane to the underlying muscle. 2–3 ml. of 5% phenol in almond oil is injected into the submucosa at the base of each primary pile under direct vision through a proctoscope. This usually requires several sessions, and many hospitals provide special clinics for treating piles.

2-3 ml
5%
PAO

In third-degree piles or when injection therapy fails to control the condition, haemorrhoidectomy is indicated. The patient is given a general anaesthetic after suitable purging and bowel wash-out. The primary piles are identified and pulled down with forceps. The mucocutaneous junction is incised and dissected upwards towards the base of the primary pile until the lower margin of the internal sphincter is seen. The base of the pile is then transfixed and ligatured. The excess of the pile mass is excised. Care must be taken to leave a bridge of mucous membrane and skin between each of the dissected areas to avoid the possibility of a stricture developing.

Strangulated prolapsed piles may sometimes be reduced digitally. In most cases the foot of the bed must be raised and cold compresses applied to the anal region. The piles then shrink and can be reduced; operation should be carried out later when all infection has subsided usually after three or four weeks.

CARCINOMA OF THE RECTUM

This is the commonest carcinoma of the gastro-intestinal tract. It generally occurs after middle life, but may occur in the young. It typically starts as a malignant ulcer, but occasionally a polyp undergoes neoplastic change. *Three quarters of rectal growths can be felt by digital examination of the rectum.*

Pathology

It is always a columnar-cell carcinoma of varying degrees of differentiation, and sometimes shows colloid degeneration. There is an ulcer with a hard, raised margin or a *fungating friable mass* which projects into the bowel; more rarely a fibrous annular constriction with comparatively little new growth or ulceration is found in the upper rectum. The tumour arises from the mucosa and gradually extends through muscle wall. It spreads via the lymphatics to the para-rectal lymph nodes, and thence to the nodes along the inferior mesenteric artery. It only spreads to the inguinal nodes when the anal canal is involved. In addition, there may be a direct spread to involve structures near the rectum, including the sacrum, vagina and uterus, bladder and ureters and other nearby viscera. Blood spread is usually by the portal veins, and the liver is the most commonly involved organ. There may be multiple metastases throughout the peritoneal cavity in the late stages, sometimes associated with ascites.

Stages of Growth (Dukes)

The staging of the growth is important from the point of view of prognosis. About 50% of patients when first seen have some degree of spread beyond the primary site.

1. Confined to the mucous membrane—15%.
2. Penetration through the bowel wall but no lymphatic involvement—35%.
3. Lymphatic involvement—50%.
4. Venous spread—17%.

Symptoms and Signs

This condition may present insidiously. Bleeding is often the first sign, and a diagnosis of haemorrhoids may well be made. *It is important in all cases of rectal bleeding to rule out the possibility of carcinoma of the rectum.*

The earliest symptoms and signs may include a change of bowel habit, sometimes increasing constipation punctuated by bouts of diarrhoea. There may be a dull dragging pain, with the feeling that the rectum has not been completely emptied after defaecation. The stool may be accompanied with bloodstained and offensive mucus. Pain is usually slight until the wall of the bowel has been penetrated, and then it becomes more constant and throbbing.

In the late stages of the disease the patient is anaemic, with loss of appetite and loss of weight. There may be attacks of intestinal obstruction which are partially relieved by offensive diarrhoea, only to recur. Later still, with the extension of the growth, there may be invasion of nearby viscera, including the bladder, prostate and vagina, resulting in distressing symptoms. The sacral plexus of nerves may be involved, causing severe and constant pain. Later still there may be ascites, jaundice and oedema of the lower limbs.

Diagnosis

This is usually easy provided a full rectal examination is carried out, with digital palpation followed by sigmoidoscopy. Biopsy should always be carried out at this stage, and then treatment can be planned.

Treatment

The pre-operative preparation of the bowel is the same as for operations on the colon; a full blood count and chest radiograph is obtained. Anaemia is corrected and breathing exercises instituted.

Abdomino-perineal excision is the operation of choice for most growths, particularly those below the peritoneal reflection and for many above. The iliac colon is brought out as a terminal colostomy in the left iliac fossa. Most of the pelvic colon, including the meso-colon with its lymph nodes, the rectum, meso-rectum and pelvic cellular tissue, and an area of the pelvic peritoneum, are removed. The perineal wound is largely closed and the remaining cavity drained.

There are variations in technique in the operation, such as the *perineo-abdominal*, where the dissection is started first in the perineum, or *synchronous combined excision*, where two surgeons work together, one from the abdomen and one from the perineum.

The *anterior resection* type of operation can be carried out for well-differentiated growths which have not spread far and are above the peritoneal reflection, i.e. more than 10–12 cm. from the anal margin. Here the growth, with at least 5 cm. of the rectum distally and the pelvic colon proximally, is removed. The same lymphatic field is removed as in an abdomino-perineal operation, but the iliac colon is anastomosed directly to the stump of the rectum so that no colostomy is necessary. The whole operation is carried out through the abdomen.

A *perineal excision* of the rectum may be carried out in very old and fragile patients. A colostomy is made at the first operation, and the operability of the lesion assessed. Later the rectum is excised by the perineal approach.

Inoperable Tumours

A colostomy may have to be carried out as a palliative measure when the growth cannot be removed because it has spread so extensively or is causing obstruction. Carcinoma of the rectum grows slowly and so it is always better to carry out a palliative resection of the growth if at all possible, because, despite a proximal colostomy, the patient suffers severe pain and disability in the later stages of the disease. Diathermy or teletherapy of an inoperable growth may reduce mucous discharge. For intractable pain due to involvement of nerves, the intrathecal injection of alcohol or cordotomy may be employed, that is section of the spinothalamic tracts in the spinal cord.

Results of Operation

There is about a 5% operative mortality. In general, about 90% of growths are removed, but this includes a proportion of palliative resections. About 60% survive for 3 years or longer following operation. Tumours restricted to the rectum which have not penetrated the wall allow approximately 80% 5-year survival.

MALIGNANT DISEASE OF THE ANUS

This is a much rarer condition than rectal carcinoma. It is usually squamous-celled carcinoma arising from the anus or anal canal, and the lymphatic drainage is to the inguinal nodes. Carcinoma of the rectum may spread downwards to involve the upper part of the anal canal. Biopsy of the tumour may be the only way to decide whether the primary site was anal or rectal.

Symptoms and Signs

They are similar to those of carcinoma of the rectum, except that pain and irritation occur at a much earlier stage and the pain is much more severe.

Treatment

An early squamous epithelioma is best treated by wide local excision, but few tumours when first seen are suitable for this, so that an abdomino-perineal excision of the rectum is usually required. When the inguinal lymph nodes are involved block dissection is performed. The results of treatment are much poorer than with carcinoma of the rectum, and the 5-year survival rate is very low.

BENIGN GROWTH OF THE ANUS AND RECTUM

Adenoma

An adenoma shows a well marked acinar pattern in a solid tumour covered by rectal mucosa.

In adults this is usually sessile and is prone to malignant change. In children it is often pedunculated, bright red, smooth or lobulated and never turns malignant. The treatment in either case is excision or removal by diathermy, and all the tissue removed must be sectioned, so that if a malignant change has occurred a more radical excision can be done forthwith.

Villous Papilloma

A villous papilloma shows fronds of epithelium on a connective tissue core.

This only occurs in adults, and may be localised or very extensive, filling the rectum. It often results in bleeding or a mucous discharge per rectum. Malignant change may occur. The treatment consists initially in biopsy. If it is benign, then a local removal by diathermy via a sigmoidoscope or if high up by anterior resection of the rectum and sigmoid colon is carried out. Even if early malignant changes are present, it is still reasonable to remove the growth locally so long as the tumour has not invaded the wall of the bowel at the base of the polyp. If the growth is enormous, then an abdomino-perineal resection may be necessary. Occasionally patients lose so much potassium containing fluid from villous tumours that they present signs of hypokalaemia; muscle weakness, depression, E.C.G. changes.

Familial Polyposis of the Rectum

This has already been mentioned in the chapter on the colon, and presents in the same way as isolated polyps. Sigmoidoscopy is necessary, and in addition barium enema to confirm the widespread involvement of the colon with polyps. Because these polyps invariably undergo malignant change, treatment is extensive, involving total colectomy and ileo-rectal anastomosis. Polyps which arise in the rectum can be destroyed by diathermy and kept under surveyance every 3 months with a sigmoidoscope to discover if a malignant change supervenes. All members of a family prone to familial polyposis should be carefully examined for evidence of polyps and the children examined by sigmoidoscopy from puberty onwards. At 15 years total colectomy and ileorectal anastomosis should be performed if polyps have appeared.

ABSCESS AND FISTULA

Peri-anal and Peri-rectal Abscesses

The lower rectum and anal canal are prone to infection. The organisms responsible are usually staphylococci, streptococci, *E. coli* and *B. proteus*. Sometimes infection with tubercle bacilli or involvement by Crohn's disease may present in the rectum. The peri-anal and peri-rectal cellular planes contain much fat and present a favourable nidus for infection. This tends to track in many directions until a free surface for discharge is found. The following types of abscesses are found:

Peri-anal

This is a small collection of pus situated subcutaneously and superficially at the side of the anal verge. Apocrine glands around the anus are prone to become infected.

Ischio-rectal

This is the commonest type of abscess, and is situated in the ischio-rectal fossa between the anus, anal canal and the levator ani on the medial side and the pelvic wall on the lateral side. The abscess is situated deeply within the fat of the ischio-rectal fossa. It is usually secondary to some source of infection such as piles or fissure. It starts in one side, and the pus may track towards the skin superficially on the medial side of the buttock. It may track towards the bowel superficial or deep to the external sphincter, to the opposite ischio-rectal fossa posteriorly by way of the anococcygeal route or most infrequently penetrates the levator ani and reaches the pelvirectal space above that muscle.

Submucous

This starts at the lower part of the rectum or anal canal beneath the mucous membrane. The abscess tracks laterally and downwards to the anal margin and, having ruptured, leaves a submucous fistula.

Pelvi-rectal

This is a rare type of abscess arising above the level of the levator ani. It is usually due to pelvic cellulitis, and may arise from inflammation of the female organs in that region, or from prostatic and vesicular disease in the male. Sometimes it may arise from conditions in the rectum, such as neoplasm, trauma or ulceration. Diseases of the colon, such as ulcerative colitis, or of the small bowel, such as Crohn's disease, may be complicated by a high abscess or fistula.

Symptoms and Signs

The main feature is throbbing pain in the buttock or perineum, which may be intense. The pain is usually aggravated by sitting, walking or defaecation. As the condition progresses there is pyrexia and associated toxaemia. Tenderness is very often extreme, and with abscesses that are deeply situated this may be in contrast to the lack of signs of swelling or inflammation superficially. At a later date brawny induration and deepseated fluctuation may become apparent.

When the abscess is chronic in type, then the discomfort may be relatively slight. Chronicity should suggest an underlying complication, such as an associated fistula, tuberculosis, actinomycosis, Crohn's disease or ulcerative colitis.

Treatment

In the acute case of ischio-rectal abscess the treatment is free and early incision. Drainage is of the greatest importance if the complication of fistula is to be avoided, though this may have been established if the abscess has already opened into the anal canal. In peri-anal and ischio-rectal types of abscesses the incision should be planned so that the edges retract widely and healing takes place from the bottom of the cavity outwards. Submucous abscesses need opening at their lowest point in the rectal wall. As a general rule, drainage should be performed before the classical signs of suppuration are detectable. If a fistula already exists, then the abscess is first drained and the fistula treated later at a second operation. However, if the fistula is low in the anal region, then the cavity and fistula can be laid widely open at one and the same time. If there is underlying chronic disease, then it is important to biopsy the wall. Tuberculosis requires no surgery or a very limited operation, but streptomycin and P.A.S. must be given for many months. Crohn's disease and ulcerative colitis require treatment first, if there is to be any hope of clearing up an abscess which is secondary to them.

FISTULA-IN-ANO

A fistula-in-ano is a track leading from the skin near the anus to some part of the anal canal or rectum. This is always discharging mucus and pus, and will never heal without operation. It is secondary to a peri-anal or peri-rectal abscess, and there are several types. A *complete* fistula opens both on the skin and the mucous surface of the rectum or anus. An *incomplete* one (and therefore not a true fistula) is a blind track or sinus which opens either on to the skin or into the rectum. Fistula-in-ano may have several openings both externally and internally and the external opening is always a guide to the position of the internal opening. A transverse line across the anus at its midpoint divides the region into two segments. If the external opening is behind this line, no matter how many external openings may exist, then the internal opening is single and in the midline posteriorly, if in front of the transverse line, then the track passes radially to the bowel (Goodsall's law). These tracks may be reasonably straight or extremely tortuous, with many off-shoots, and may even surround part of the anus like a horseshoe.

Symptoms and Signs

The patient complains of pain at defaecation and a constant discharge of pus and mucus from the opening or openings. Recurrent peri-anal sepsis

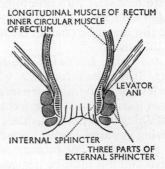

LONGITUDINAL MUSCLE OF RECTUM
INNER CIRCULAR MUSCLE OF RECTUM

LEVATOR ANI

INTERNAL SPHINCTER
THREE PARTS OF EXTERNAL SPHINCTER

FIG. 32. The musculature of the ano-rectal region. Continence depends on preservation of the ano-rectal ring—the deep part of the internal and external sphincter and the levator ani

should always suggest the diagnosis of fistula. A minority are associated with some other disease; ischio-rectal abscess and fibrous rectal stricture due to operation, lymphogranuloma inguinale, gonorrhoea, tuberculous and malignant disease. There may be ulcerative colitis, diverticulitis or Crohn's disease.

Treatment

The treatment consists essentially of laying open the track together with all its ramifications. Of great importance, however, is to know the relationship of the track to the anal musculature. The reason for this is that *incontinence* may result in excising anal fistulas from injury to the sphincters. Continence depends on the integrity of the ano-rectal ring. This consists of the deep parts of the external and internal sphincters and the puborectalis muscle. The accompanying diagram gives an outline of the relationship (Fig. 32).

The following types of fistula are described:

Subcutaneous. This lies superficial to the external sphincter, and is often associated with a fissure. The external opening is small and within an inch of the anal margin. The track is usually palpable as an indurated cord, and it is relatively easy to insert a probe and lay the track widely open.

Submucous. The track is in the submucous coat and runs from the lower rectum towards the anal margin. It is usually single, but bilateral fistulae may occur following an abscess in the posterior wall of the rectum which tracks towards both sides. This type of fistula may be complete or may open only internally or externally. Whenever possible, the fistula should be laid open into the lumen of the bowel.

Anal

A *low anal fistula* has its internal opening between the subcutaneous and superficial parts of the external sphincter. This type can be laid open freely. A *high anal fistula* has its internal opening between the ano-rectal ring and the superficial part of the external sphincter. Here division of the sphincter may lead to incontinence, the operation is carried out in *two* stages, division of the higher part of the internal opening being performed later with care to preserve the ano-rectal ring.

Intramuscular. This is a very rare type, in which the track lies between the two muscular coats of the rectum. It should be opened into the lumen of the bowel.

Ano-rectal. In this type the track extends above the level of the ano-rectal ring. It may be incomplete, with the internal opening above the level of the levator ani or may open internally at a lower level or externally. Sometimes it passes round the rectum in a horseshoe fashion. Since the ano-rectal ring must not be divided, treatment consists in coring out the fistula, leaving a conical-shaped wound which heals from the depths of the wound to the surface. The primary cause is usually inflammatory disease in the pelvis and this must be treated.

FISSURE-IN-ANO

This is a common condition in which there is a longitudinal ulcer of the anal verge, usually situated in the midline posteriorly, but anterior fissures may be seen in women, especially after parturition. An anal fissure results from a tear of the mucosa, usually from the passage of hard faeces. Fibrosis occurs around the base and margins of the fissure, and oedema may be present. At the lower end of the fissure there is usually a tag of mucous membrane called a 'sentinel' pile which was torn down at the original injury. A fissure is a source of infection in the anal region. Occasionally they are multiple and superficial.

Symptoms and Signs

The outstanding feature is a sharp, stabbing pain in the anal region during and after defaecation. It may be so painful that the patient avoids defaecation, with resulting constipation. Slight bleeding is common, and there may be some discharge. In addition, there is frequently pruritus. Inspection of the anal region reveals the sentinel tag, and gentle retraction exposes the lower end of the fissure. A finger or proctoscope should not be inserted into the anal canal because of the pain caused by sphincteric spasm. Gentle palpation with the gloved finger identifies the position and lower extent of the fissure and makes it possible to estimate if fibrosis is present. In addition, the degree of spasm of the sphincter can often be judged.

Analgesic ointment on anal dilator
Suppositories (Nupercainol)

Treatment

With recent fissures spasm of the sphincter is the main factor in preventing healing. In mild cases the daily use of an analgesic ointment smeared on an anal dilator or suppositories (Nupercainol, Duncaine) will often result in relief of spasm and permit healing. It is important to advise the patient on how to keep the stools soft and regular. Fissure is quite common in children, in whom it is the commonest cause of rectal bleeding, and almost always responds to these simple measures.

When the fissure is more chronic and indurated internal sphincterotomy is performed under local analgesia. A piece of cotton-wool dipped in 2% lignocaine is tucked into the anus and 2 ml. of the same solution is injected subcutaneously around the fissure. A small incision is made beside the fissure, the lower edge of the internal sphincter is pulled down and about 0·5 cm. divided. Relief of pain is immediate, but healing may take many weeks.

More chronic fissures, particularly where fibrosis is prominent, require excision. The indurated and fibrous tissue around the fissure is excised, leaving a triangular wound widely open, with its apex in the anal canal. This is combined with a division of the fibroid lower edge of the internal sphincter. Healing takes at least 2 weeks, and the patient is encouraged to sit in a warm bath after each daily bowel action. Each day a lubricated anal dilator is passed. A simple procedure for recent fissures is forcible dilation of the anal canal, under general anaesthesia.

PRURITUS ANI

The anal region is usually moist, and if toilet in that region is inefficient there is irritation from faeces. Because the area is so sensitive, irritation occurs readily, and it may be scratched excessively, even during sleep, with resulting excoriation and subsequent minor infections. Fibrosis of the skin and subcutaneous tissues may follow, so that the region tends to become rather rigid. This loss of elasticity predisposes to cracks and fissures. Often an anxiety state in a patient seems to be reflected in the condition of the anal region. In others pruritus may be associated with specific lesions of the rectum, anal canal or vulva, such as piles, fissures and carcinoma. There may be primary infection of the skin, especially with fungi. Thread worms may cause great irritation. Pruritus ani is occasionally seen in diabetes. In most cases an anxious temperament seems associated with an excessively moist anus.

Treatment

In the first instance attention to any obvious disease, such as diabetes, threadworm infestation or colitis, should be dealt with. Next, any local anal abnormality, no matter how minor, should be corrected, e.g. haemorrhoids injected, anal fissure treated. Then the general health should be checked, and sedatives may be used if there is a background of anxiety. With regard to the local condition, extreme care should be taken in toilet of the region, and after defaecation the anal region should be washed gently in soap and water and dried. A lotion containing zinc oxide, calamine, phenol and magnesium hydroxide (St Marks lotion) is very often useful. An ointment containing hydrocortisone may be effective. The patient must be instructed to avoid scratching the area.

PROLAPSE OF RECTUM

This condition may be *partial or mucosal*—and occurs when the mucous membrane alone prolapses from the anus. If the whole thickness of the rectal wall is affected, then it is called *complete*. In children mucosal prolapse is the usual type, only seen during straining at stool. In adults it is quite common to have partial prolapse associated with haemorrhoids, or sometimes in old age, when there is loss of sphincteric tone; less frequently it may be associated with an enlarged prostate. A complete prolapse is typically seen in the elderly, especially women and is associated with weakness of the pelvic and anal muscles. A history of nervous disease, mental deficiency or loss of cortical control in old age is common.

Symptoms and Signs

The main symptoms are discomfort in the anal region and, on occasions, a thin bloodstained discharge. In partial prolapse the mucosa projects from the anal margin for an inch or so and appears smooth. A complete prolapse may be several inches long, and the mucosa is raised in circular folds. A complete prolapse is much bulkier, since it includes all layers of the rectal wall and is best regarded as a sliding hernia of the pouch of Douglas. The sphincters are dilated and patulous, and this may result in incontinence.

Treatment

Children. In children the prolapse is usually partial. The condition is treated conservatively, the parents being reassured that the condition always rights itself within a year or two, even without treatment. The child is taught to defaecate without prolonging the act. The motions should be regular and the stools soft; a mixture of liquid paraffin and milk of magnesia may be necessary. The mother is taught to reduce the prolapse after each motion. There is no advantage in strapping the buttocks together.

Most children who suffer from rectal prolapse are finicky over food, take an ill-balanced diet and suffer from constipation. Often the home background is poor. A period of 'pot-training' in hospital and a generous diet helps to cure the prolapse.

If the child or the parents are much distressed by the prolapse it can be corrected in one of two ways. A solution of 5% phenol in oil is injected into the submucous layer high in the rectum, and the resulting fibrosis anchors the mucosa. Alternatively, a chromic catgut ligature is inserted subcutaneously around the anus and tied to leave a small anal opening, adequate for defaecation but not big enough to permit prolapse. The catgut disappears completely in a month or so, and the prolapse is often cured. Whenever prolapse is seen in a child, tests should be made to see if there is pancreatic fibrosis, since this rare familial condition occasionally presents in this way.

Adults. Adults suffering from partial prolapse require an operation similar but more extensive to that carried out for internal haemorrhoids, since this is satisfactory in fixing the mucosa of the rectum.

Complete prolapse is really a sliding hernia of the pouch of Douglas and requires a different approach. In those patients who are fit an abdominal approach is used. The sac of the hernia is excised and the puborectalis muscles sutured together and the rectum fixed in the hollow of the sacrum. Anterior resection of the rectum down to the level of the levator ani may prove effective.

Another method of fixing the bowel to the hollow of the sacrum is to mobilise it completely, as if for anterior resection, and then attach a circumferential sheet of Ivalon sponge, which can be secured to the sacrum.

For those who are not fit for an abdominal operation, Thiersch's method is suitable. This can be done under local analgesia in the old and infirm, but is more conveniently done under general anaesthesia with the patient in the lithotomy position. A silver wire or heavy nylon suture is threaded deeply around the anus, using a tiny posterior incision and a curved needle. The ligature is tightened around the little finger introduced into the anal canal, and the knot is then turned in deeply and the skin wound requires no suture. The only complication is faecal impaction, or the ligature may break or ulcerate into the rectum.

PROCTITIS AND RECTAL STRICTURE

In proctitis the mucous membrane of the rectum is oedematous and velvety in appearance, with mucus, pus and fibrin on its surface. In its severest form there are multiple ulcers, and the condition may progress to peri-rectal suppuration or stricture. Symptoms are tenesmus with frequent passage of blood and mucus. There is rectal pain and pruritus ani. A variety of causes may result in proctitis, and a few of them go on to scarring, fibrosis and rectal stricture.

Non-specific

Sigmoidoscopy shows the condition to be limited to the rectum. This can be confirmed by barium enema, which rules out a generalised condition of the colon. A rectal swab produces non-specific bacterial flora. The course is usually episodic, with occasionally long, or rarely permanent, remission. A few patients later develop ulcerative colitis.

Treatment

Anaemia is corrected. The diet should be of the high-caloric but low-residue type. Treatment with salazopyrin by mouth over a period of several months may help, a course of retention enemas or suppositories of prednisolone may be effective.

Specific Causes

Tuberculous. This is now very rare and occurs usually in association with pulmonary or intestinal lesions. It leads to ulceration, ischio-rectal abscesses and fistulae.

Crohn's Disease. This occasionally presents as proctitis, and a biopsy may be necessary in addition to a full investigation of the ileum and colon to see if there are any other areas involved. Crohn's disease and ulcerative colitis are the commonest specific causes of proctitis.

Dysenteric. This may be bacillary or amoebic in type, and is part of a generalised colitis.

Ulcerative Colitis. In the majority of cases of ulcerative colitis the rectum is involved. In proctitis, barium enema shows no abnormality in the colon.

Venereal. Gumma is rare, but may be followed by stricture. Gonorrhoea is more frequent in women than in men. Lymphogranuloma venereum may also result in stricture in women.

Pyogenic. This usually follows operations, injection of piles or injections using oily analgesic preparations.

Bilharzia. This is seen in Africa, especially Egypt, and some parts of the East. The bladder is the organ commonly affected, but the rectum may be involved, with papillomata and induration of its wall. Ova can be identified in the stools.

Post-radiation. This follows the use of radium in treatment of carcinoma of the cervix typically or radiotherapy for pelvic tumours of any kind. Proctitis, induration and stricture may be mistaken for neoplasm.

STRICTURE OF THE RECTUM

Rectal stricture is a common sequel to operative correction of imperforate anus, and a careful enquiry as to surgical treatment in the first year of life is important. Carcinoma of the rectum is perhaps the most serious cause of narrowing in this organ, and is fully dealt with earlier in this chapter. Lymphogranuloma venereum commonly causes stricture of the rectum. Syphilis and gonorrhoea should be suspected.

PILONIDAL SINUS

This presents as a neat little opening, occasionally multiple and situated in the midline usually 2–3 cm. behind the anus. Pilonidal means nest of hairs, and hairs often protrude from the sinus. It is very liable to infection and abscess formation, and usually first becomes troublesome in the early twenties.

Controversy has raged in the past as to whether this condition is congenital or acquired. It seems likely that most of these sinuses result from hairs perforating the skin, since only dead hairs and no hair follicles are ever found in sections of excised specimens. A similar lesion rarely occurs in the clefts between the fingers of barbers due to customers' hair. Also rare examples have been described in the umbilicus and axilla and in amputation stumps. The post-anal pit seen in children in the midline appears to be of quite different aetiology, and no hairs are seen in it. Pilonidal sinus is never seen before the growth of body hair at puberty.

Treatment

When an abscess forms in a pilonidal lesion it should be drained and the condition left to become quiescent. Later the sinus is excised widely to include all the side tracks. The track will be found to go right down to the sacrococcygeal fascia, and all the involved tissue is removed *en bloc*. If infection is still present the wound is left open to granulate from the bottom. If the wound is relatively clean primary suture is carried out, and a number heal by first intention.

SACROCOCCYGEAL TUMOURS

These are rare tumours which arise in the hollow of the sacrum behind the rectum. They include dermoid cyst, teratoma, benign and malignant and chordoma arising from neurogenic tissue. A malignant chordoma can rarely be excised. It is a slow growing tumour that may respond to radiotherapy but the prospect of cure is poor.

The treatment in all these is excision as soon as possible. In a child the best approach is from the perineum, with the child on its face and the legs abducted. A horseshoe incision is used behind the anus, detaching the anal sphincter from the coccyx.

FURTHER READING

Gabriel, W. B. (1963) *The Principles and Practice of Rectal Surgery*. H. K. Lewis, London.
Goligher, J. C. (1968) *Surgery of the Anus, Rectum and Colon*. Cassell, London.

CHAPTER TWENTY-FOUR

THE BILIARY AND PORTAL SYSTEMS

The major part of a surgeon's work on the biliary system is concerned with gall stones and their complications. Cholecystitis or inflammation of the gall bladder is so often associated with gall stones that it is difficult to deal separately with the two conditions. Cholelithiasis or gall stones reflect very faithfully the dietary and, indirectly, the economic conditions prevailing in a country. For example, Sweden, the United States and Holland, which all enjoy a high standard of living and a high fat content in the diet also enjoy a high incidence of gall-bladder disease. On the other hand, the number of patients with gall-bladder symptoms in Holland fell almost to vanishing point in the last war, when there was strict rationing of food, and especially fats. In recent years there has been a great increase in gall stone disease.

THE GALL BLADDER

CHOLECYSTITIS

Inflammation of the gall bladder is usually associated with gall stones, although a great many people have gall stones who never show any sign of them at all. The inflammation is frequently, but not always, due to the growth of bacteria, the common organisms being: *Escherichia coli, streptococci, Cl. Welchii,* and where typhoid is endemic, *B. typhosus.* Acute and chronic cholecystitis are virtually two different diseases, and will be considered separately.

Acute Cholecystitis

Many patients have a long history of flatulent dyspepsia preceding the acute attack, which is often precipitated by a meal containing much fat. There is acute pain of rapid onset in the right subcostal region, the pain radiates to the right infrascapular area and sometimes the shoulder tip, occasionally it is agonising. The patient is nauseated and vomits. The abdomen is often a little distended, bowel sounds much diminished or absent, no flatus is passed and there is constipation. On palpation there is marked tenderness in the right upper quadrant, which is made worse when the patient takes a deep breath: Murphy's sign. The inflammation may be catarrhal or obstructive, and in the latter case the gall bladder distends and may then be palpable. Slight jaundice, even in the absence of common duct obstruction, is occasionally seen. Few laboratory tests are of any help, the white-cell count is elevated, with increased polymorphs, cholecystography shows failure of concentration of contrast medium.

Treatment

The aim of treatment should always be to allow resolution of the acute attack, cholecystectomy being performed 3–6 weeks later. The patient is put to bed and given pethidine 50–100 mg. for pain or morphine 10–15 mg. Only clear fluids are allowed by mouth. It is doubtful if anti-biotics help resolution, but they may prevent complications, therefore tetracycline 250 mg. six hourly is given by mouth. The indications for operation are recurrent severe attacks of pain in a patient fit enough to undergo surgery, or complications such as jaundice. A rising temperature and white-cell count and increasing tenderness and rigidity of the abdom-inal wall indicate impending perforation of the gall bladder, and although this is rare, it is imperative that emergency cholecystectomy be done, for bile peritonitis is often fatal.

Chronic Cholecystitis

This is an extremely common condition, especially in obese women. There are two main groups of symptoms:

1. Chronic flatulent dyspepsia, with nausea, belching and abdominal distension, especially marked after eating fatty food.

2. Repeated attacks of colicky pain in the right subcostal area radiat-ing to the subscapular region and shoulder tip, with nausea and vomiting, again usually following a heavy meal. No physical signs are found apart from subcostal tenderness. No test is diagnostic, the white-cell count is normal, but radiographs may reveal opaque calculi in the gall-bladder area, oral cholecystography may show impaired or absent concentration of dye, or non-opaque stones may be seen if the gall bladder is visualised.

Cholecystography is carried out orally in the first place. The patient takes an organic compound that contains iodine responsible for radio-pacity (Telepaque) by mouth in the evening. Next morning no breakfast is eaten and the gall-bladder area is X-rayed. If the contrast medium is concentrated the patient is given a fatty meal by mouth, such as olive oil or a fried egg, and more pictures taken to demonstrate if the gall bladder is capable of contracting in response to such a stimulus. Stones are usually shown as filling defects. Failure to visualise the gall bladder is good evidence of cholecystitis and hence stones. Only 10% of stones are radio-paque. If the gall bladder is not visualised an intravenous injection of Biligrafin may be given, a radiopaque substance concentrated in the liver, and therefore capable of outlining the bile ducts. This may show dilatation of the common bile duct or the presence of calculi as negative shadows in the ducts.

Treatment

A low-fat diet will usually relieve the patient of symptoms, it is unusual to have symptoms of chronic cholecystitis when losing weight. A cure is provided by removing the gall bladder together with any stones it may contain. At the time of cholecystectomy the common bile duct should be explored if it appears enlarged, thick walled, contains stones or the patient has had attacks of jaundice, indicating that a stone has obstructed the duct. An operative cholangiogram is often performed to detect or exclude the presence of stones in the ducts (see p. 338).

CHOLELITHIASIS

Aetiology

The immediate cause of gall stones is unknown, *but* there are many factors which may contribute to their formation. Tiny solid particles are constantly produced in the liver and can be found in the bile, where they may form the nuclei for stones. The concentration of bile salts which keep cholesterol in solution may fall in liver disease, or in the presence of infection, which is typically blood borne. Stagnation of bile can cause precipitation of solids. The healthy gall bladder concentrates the liver bile by removing water, adds mucus, and the stored bile is discharged under the stimulus of cholecystokynin, which is secreted in response to fat or other cholagogue, like magnesium sulphate, entering the duodenum.

Pathology

There are three types of gall stone:

1. Mixed: calcium bilirubinate, and cholesterol, usually associated with infection. The commonest.

2. Cholesterol: Often solitary, may become very large. Fairly common.

3. Pigment: Soft, crumbly and multiple. Seen in haemolytic disease. Rare.

Symptoms and Signs

The history is usually suggestive of chronic cholecystitis, while the presenting symptoms depend on the site of the gall stone (Fig. 33), whether it is stationary or moving and if infection is superadded. *Biliary colic* occurs when a stone moves in a duct. There is intense pain for minutes up to a few hours and the patient rolls about in agony. The pain begins in the upper abdomen and radiates to the right scapula and shoulder tip. The face is pale, the extremities cold and clammy, pulse fast, and there may be vomiting, often of bile. *Jaundice* results when a stone blocks the common bile duct or hepatic duct, the commonest place is the ampulla of Vater. The yellow discoloration of skin and sclera appears a day after the colic, and often passes off in 2 or 3 days. The urine is dark with bile pigments, the stools pale due to lack of them, and there may be itching of the skin, especially the palms and soles of the feet. Many gall stones impact in the ducts and cause jaundice, without any preceding pain—this silent jaundice must be distinguished from that caused by carcinoma of the ampulla or head of pancreas. *Courvoisier's Law* tries to do this, it states that in the jaundiced subject if the common duct is obstructed by a stone the gall bladder will not be palpable, because previous attacks of inflammation will have rendered its wall fibrous. On the other hand, the jaundiced patient with a palpable gall bladder probably has a malignant obstruction of the bile ducts. Although Courvoisier's Law is a useful generalisation, there are

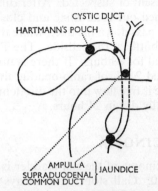

CYSTIC DUCT
HARTMANN'S POUCH

FIG. 33. Sites where a gall stone may obstruct in the biliary tree

AMPULLA
SUPRADUODENAL } JAUNDICE
COMMON DUCT

many exceptions to it, for example, stone and ampullary carcinoma occasionally occur in the same patient. Also a mucocele of the gall bladder due to a stone in the cystic duct will wrongly suggest carcinoma.

Complications

Blockage to the bile ducts may cause infection to ascend, cholangitis, in which there are rigors and fever with drenching sweats (Charcot's intermittent fever). If the cystic duct is blocked and the gall bladder is infected it may be converted into a bag of pus—empyema of the gall bladder. If the patient is not operated upon urgently the gall-bladder wall becomes gangrenous and perforates, causing biliary peritonitis.

Treatment

Biliary colic is treated with pethidine, 50–100 mg. injected intramuscularly or morphine 10–15 mg. Rest in bed and clear fluids only by mouth usually allow the acute symptoms to subside. Fever and cholangitis will not subside until the obstruction in the biliary system is relieved, and surgery is also indicated if a mass forms and increases in size in the gall-bladder area and if the fever and pain worsen.

Any patient who is fit enough for operation and who has symptoms due to gall stones should have them removed. Cholecystography is essential in confirming biliary disease, but should not be done in the presence of jaundice. If operation has to be carried out in a jaundiced patient vitamin K should be injected intramuscularly in 10-mg. doses daily, since the depressed prothrombin formation in the obstructed liver leads to excessive bleeding.

Cholecystectomy is performed, the cystic duct being tied off nearly flush with the common bile duct (C.B.D.). At operation a cannula is introduced into the stump of the cystic duct and contrast medium injected for operative cholangiography. Radiographs are taken on the operating table, and will show if bile flows freely into the duodenum and if stones remain in the C.B.D. The C.B.D. is opened and the stones removed if they are present or suspected. After dilating the ampulla with bougies the duct is flushed out with saline and closed round a T-tube, which allows some bile to pass down the duct, while the remainder (about 500 ml. daily) flows into a bottle at the bedside. The T-tube is left in for 7 to 10 days and then clamped for 8 hours. If there is no pain or gush of bile when the clamp is removed 2 ml. of radio-opaque fluid is injected and a radiograph taken. If there is free flow into the duodenum the tube is pulled out and the wound is usually dry in 24 hours.

CARCINOMA

Carcinoma of the gall bladder is a rare disease, seen typically in women over 50. Gall stones are always present, and are considered to be an aetiological factor. There is usually a history of chronic cholecystitis, with pain in the gall-bladder area which becomes continuous. A palpable mass is present, and jaundice is a late complication. Ideally treatment is cholecystectomy and partial hepatectomy—an operation that is rarely possible, since the tumour spreads to the liver and bile ducts. The prognosis is extremely poor.

BILE DUCTS AND JAUNDICE

BILE DUCTS

Infection

The cause of ascending infection is usually inadequate drainage resulting from stones or operative stricture of the bile ducts. Obstruction at the ampulla in the duodenum due to fibrosis, spasm or tumor are very rare causes of ascending cholargitis. It may follow cholecyst-jejunal anastomosis performed for carcinoma of the pancreas. Foreign bodies in the ducts, such as parasites, are rare causes. Once bile salts start to be precipitated, a vicious circle occurs, with further silting up of the duct system.

Symptoms and Signs

Cholangitis presents as Charcot's intermittent fever. The temperature chart shows alarming peaks every 1 or 2 days, and the patient has rigors, sweating attacks and prostration. There is usually jaundice, which also varies in intensity, a furred tongue, nausea and vomiting. The urine is dark and scanty, the stools pale. The liver is enlarged and tender on palpation.

Treatment

This consists of combating dehydration by giving adequate fluids by mouth or intravenously. An antibiotic such as chloramphenicol, which is secreted in the bile, is given for a total of 1 g. a day. As soon as the patient is fit enough laparotomy is performed, the common bile duct is opened and cleared of all débris so that provision can be made for good drainage of bile into the bowel. The C.B.D. is drained, often with a T-tube. If the gall bladder is infected it is removed or drained. Prognosis depends mainly on removal of the cause but also on how much liver damage has already occurred and how efficiently the bile is drained and infection controlled.

Trauma

The bile ducts are rarely damaged except by gunshot wound, stabbing or most commonly as a complication of a surgical operation. The outcome will depend on whether the escape of bile is slow or rapid. A slow leak is usually walled off by omentum, and a pool of bile gradually accumulates, which often later presses on the C.B.D. to produce jaundice. Symptoms may be difficult to assess, but when it is clear that there is an encysted collection of bile it should be drained.

A rapid leak of bile produces peritonitis, often of a particularly severe kind. Immediate laparotomy is performed to repair the leak and drain the bile.

Strictures of the bile ducts, most of which result from accidental injury to the ducts during cholecystectomy, constitute a particularly crippling form of iatrogenic disease. The patient presents with jaundice, a biliary fistula or a combination of the two. The abdomen is opened and a search made for the two ends of the duct. The head of the pancreas is reflected forward by Kocher's manoeuvre in which the peritoneum is divided on the outer side of the duodenum. The distal end is sought. The proximal end is usually embedded in dense adhesions, or may even be buried in liver substance, when it must be found by needling. Ideally the two ends are brought together and anastomosed over a T-tube drain, but this is rarely possible. A Roux-en-Y loop may be brought up and anastomosed to the stump of the C.B.D., a tube of plastic or metal only sets up fibrosis. In the absence of any patent proximal bile duct, the left lobe of the liver may be amputated and a loop of small bowel anastomosed to the transected stump of left intra-hepatic duct. Whatever the anastomosis performed, it is likely to stenose and the patient suffer from cholangitis.

CHOLANGIOHEPATITIS

This is a particularly severe form of bile-duct infection seen in the Far East, especially Malaya and China. It is caused by the eating of raw freshwater fish infected with clonorchis. The parasites, which are visible to the naked eye, collect in the common bile duct, and together with precipitated bile salts obstruct it, allowing infection to follow. Primary malignancy of the liver may occur.

MALIGNANT DISEASE

Tumours of the bile ducts are almost always carcinomatous and cause painless jaundice, which rapidly deepens. Laparotomy may allow a loop of bowel to be anastomosed to the bile ducts proximal to the carcinoma. The prognosis is hopeless.

JAUNDICE

Physiology

The normal level of bilirubin in the serum is 0·4–1·0 mg./100 ml. Above this level the tissues, especially the sclera, are tinged yellow and the patient is said to be jaundiced (*jaune*, French for yellow). The bilirubin is derived from the breakdown products of haemoglobin, which are conjugated in the liver with glucuronic acid and enter the duodenum in the bile. Most of the bilirubin in the gut is excreted in the faeces as stercobilin, but a small amount is reabsorbed and excreted as urobilinogen in the urine.

Types of Jaundice

There are three main types of jaundice:

(i) *Hepatocellular* (Hepatic) follows damage to liver cells as occurs in virus hepatitis, Weil's disease and poisoning by substances like carbon tetrachloride and chlorpromazine. The damaged liver cells cannot conjugate bilirubin, the level of which rises in blood and urine. In extreme liver damage urobilinogen disappears from the urine, as it does when the bile ducts are completely obstructed. Early in hepatic disease there may be an excess of urobilinogen in urine.

(ii) *Obstructive* (Post-Hepatic) is due to obstruction to the bile ducts from stones, tumours of the pancreas and bile ducts and in babies born with atresia of the bile ducts. Secondary tumours cause jaundice because of the pressure of malignant lymph nodes on the bile ducts. As bile cannot enter the gut, the level of serum bilirubin rises, there is plenty of bilirubin in the urine but no urobilinogen.

(iii) *Haemolytic* (Pre-Hepatic) is due to the increased destruction of red cells that occurs in spherocytosis (fragile red cells), sickle-cell anaemia and mismatched transfusion. The increased amounts of bilirubin pass down the bile ducts into the gut, but there is none in the urine, hence the name acholuric jaundice.

Diagnosis

The history may suggest the possibility of exposure to infective hepatitis, previous transfusion, carbon tetrachloride, chlorpromazine (Largactil), testosterone, Weil's disease. Pain suggests stone. Painless jaundice with a palpable gall bladder suggests pancreatic carcinoma (Courvoisier's Law). However, hepatitis and pancreatic carcinoma can be very painful.

The urine should be tested for bilirubin and urobilinogen. The stools for stercobilin. Serum is examined for bilirubin (total) and direct and indirect Van den Bergh test. The direct is positive early in obstructive jaundice, the indirect in hepatocellular jaundice. Alkaline phosphatase, normally up to 15 K.A. units, is raised, and high levels—over 35 units— are diagnostic of obstructive jaundice. Flocculation tests, e.g. cephalin and thymol, are positive early with hepatocellular disease, late if at all with obstructive jaundice. Glutamic pyruvic transaminase is high in hepatitis, as it reflects liver damage. Red cells are examined for fragility and sickling. Radiographs may show opaque gall stones, cholecystography is never done in the presence of jaundice as the gall bladder is not visualised. There remain many cases in which the distinction between hepatic and obstructive jaundice can only be made at laparotomy.

THE LIVER

The liver is not often a target for the surgeon, which is fortunate, since it is highly vascular and friable and does not hold sutures well.

Trauma

The liver is largely protected by the ribs, but may be lacerated in road accidents or by stabbing and gunshot. The diaphragm, pleural cavities and lungs are likely also to be involved. The signs are those of shock and intra-peritoneal bleeding; pain, especially on taking a deep breath, rigidity of the abdominal wall and a rising pulse rate. Radiographs are taken of both abdomen and thorax. The treatment is transfusion and immediate laparotomy, which may have to be done by the thoraco-abdominal approach. The liver is sutured or packed, the pack being removed 3 or 4 days later; the abdomen and chest are drained and a wide-spectrum antibiotic is given, e.g. tetracycline.

Abscesses

Infection may reach the liver by three different routes:

1. Ascending the bile ducts, i.e. cholangitis, it may produce multiple small green (bile-stained) cholangitic abscesses, commonly due to *E. coli*, occasionally due to typhoid.

2. Blood-borne infection via the hepatic artery produces multiple *pyaemic* abscesses, which are best treated by antibiotics. There is a high swinging fever, and abscesses are usually to be found in other parts of the body.

3. Blood-borne infection via the portal vein results in two major conditions: amoebic abscess and hydatid cyst, very rarely a non-specific infection ascends from inflamed bowel, e.g. appendicitis, to produce portal pyaemia.

Amoebic Abscess

This is seen in tropical countries as a complication of amoebic dysentery. A large abscess, often solitary, develops, usually in the right lobe of the liver. There is a tender enlargement of the liver, with pain referred to the back and shoulder. Loss of weight, anorexia, general malaise and a sallow complexion are so non-specific that the diagnosis is often missed until late in the disease. There is fever, leucocytosis due to secondary infection of the abscess and often a small effusion in the right pleural cavity. Amoebae are only found in the stools of about 25% of these patients.

Treatment is the daily injection of 0·9 g. hydroxychloroquine for 10 days and, if improvement follows, a further 20 daily injections of 0·6 g. to produce a cure. If there is no response emetine hydrochloride 65 mg. is injected daily for a week. If neither drug is effective the liver is needled, and when pus is obtained, a trocar and cannula is used to drain the anchovy-sauce-like pus. Penicillin or tetracycline is given concurrently to deal with secondary infection.

Hydatid Cyst

Hydatid disease is due to *Taenia echinococcus* a tape worm infesting the gut of dogs. Eggs are passed in the dog's faeces, and usually complete their life cycle in their intermediate host, the sheep. Man may take the place of the sheep, and thus the disease is common in sheep-rearing countries like Australia, it is sometimes seen in south Wales. The eggs are digested in the gut, and the parasite passes up the portal vein to the liver, where a cyst is formed with a dense fibrous capsule; the germinal layer produces daughter cysts. Symptoms are due to a space-occupying lesion which may press on the bile ducts, become infected or rarely rupture. There is eosinophilia and a positive Casoni intradermal test.

Treatment

This consists of exposing the cyst, injecting 2% formalin to kill the daughter cysts and shelling out the intact cyst or marsupialising it if this is not possible.

PORTAL HYPERTENSION

The normal portal venous pressure measured on the operating table is 120–140 mm. of water. This pressure is greatly raised in conditions which obstruct the flow of portal-vein blood leading to a distinctive pattern of symptoms: bleeding oesophageal varices, ascites, hypersplenism, jaundice and liver failure. The possibility of portal hypertension should always be considered in any patient who presents with severe haematemesis and melaena.

Site   *Intra H* : 75%
                          Extra H : 25%

Pathology

The site of obstruction to the portal vein is within the liver in more than 75% of those suffering from portal hypertension, and in the extrahepatic circulation in the remaining 25%. This distinction is important, because it determines the method of treatment.

Intrahepatic Causes

Cirrhosis of the liver, usually of unknown aetiology such as Laennec's cirrhosis, is by far the commonest. Occasionally there is a history of hepatititis and jaundice, or rarely of bile-duct stricture, gall stones, pancreatitis, injections of heavy metals and syphilis. In all of them the portal vein is patent and available for decompression. The site of venous obstruction is in the intralobular tributaries of the hepatic veins.

Extrahepatic Causes

The commonest is replacement of the vein by a cavernomatous mass of small vessels which is presumed to occur following thrombosis of the vein by extension of clot up the umbilical vein at birth. The portal vein may also thrombose as a result of trauma, cirrhosis or malignant invasion. Rarely the portal vein is occluded, but the umbilical vein in the abdominal wall remains patent, then the unusual flow of blood from portal to systemic circulation can be heard with a stethoscope as a hum at the umbilicus, this is the Cruveilhier–Baumgarten syndrome—portal hypertension with a patent umbilical vein.

Symptoms and Signs

Anastomoses between the portal and systemic venous circulation produce varices which may lead to bleeding at the lower end of the oesophagus and in the upper part of the stomach. Oesophageal varices produce painless haematemesis and melaena, which is often severe and is the cause of death in most patients if the bleeding cannot be arrested. Other sites of portal systemic anastomosis are a 'caput medusae' at the umbilicus and haemorrhoids in the anal canal, both very rare in portal hypertension. The spleen may be enlarged and may cause 'hypersplenism' interfering with the release of red and white cells and platelets from the bone marrow, causing anaemia and leucopenia. The term Banti's syndrome was applied to the triad of bleeding, splenomegaly and leucopaenia before it was appreciated that portal hypertension was the cause. Ascites is common in the late stages, and is associated with a low level of serum albumen, coupled with salt retention due to secondary hyperaldosteronism. Jaundice may be slight and fluctuate; if it becomes severe, terminal liver failure is indicated. The inability of the cirrhotic liver to handle ammonia produces the picture of ammonia intoxication and hepatic failure, especially when the protein load is increased due to the presence of blood in the gut that has come from bleeding varices. In hepatic failure there is a flapping tremor of the

M

hands, mental confusion and irrational behaviour, leading to lethargy, stupor and finally coma. There may be twitching of the muscles, and the tendon reflexes are increased, there may be frank convulsions. The same pattern of symptoms occurs in patients after successful porta-caval shunts if the blood ammonia level rises, as may happen after a heavy meal of protein or taking ammonium salts.

Special Tests

The blood is examined for anaemia and leucopenia. The prothrombin time is measured. Operative treatment is contra-indicated if liver-function tests indicate severe cellular damage and if the level of serum bilirubin is over 3 mg./100 ml. or the serum albumin level is below 3 g. %. Radiographs of abdomen may show hepatomegaly and splenomegaly, a barium swallow should demonstrate oesophageal varices, though occasionally oesophagoscopy is necessary to confirm their presence. Liver biopsy by needle may be helpful, but is dangerous if the patient is jaundiced, for bleeding may result.

Treatment

This depends whether the patient is bleeding or shows signs of liver failure and ascites, if both are present the treatment of the bleeding must take precedence.

Haemorrhage

The patient is given immediate replacement of blood, massive transfusion may be called for. A Sengstaken triple-lumen tube is passed nasally; it has one lumen through which the stomach contents are aspirated, another through which a small balloon in the stomach is inflated. Traction on the tube arrests the gastric balloon at the oesophago-gastric junction. A third lumen in the tube allows inflation of a sausage-shaped balloon to a pressure of 25 mm. of mercury, which lies in the lower oesophagus, presses on the veins and stops bleeding. The stomach tube is aspirated hourly, and a purge such as milk of magnesia given through it to clear the gut of blood, and so lessen the absorption of nitrogen. Neomycin is similarly introduced in 1-g. doses 4 hourly to reduce the bacterial flora of the intestines and minimise nitrogen absorption. The oesophageal balloon must be deflated every 24 hours to avoid ulceration of the oesophagus, and the whole tube is removed gently as soon as bleeding stops. Vasopressin (20 units in 5% dextrose) may be given cautiously intravenously over a period of 10 minutes to reduce portal venous pressure.

If bleeding is not controlled by the Sengstaken tube the patient is taken to the operating theatre and thoracotomy performed through the bed of the left 8th rib, the oesophagus is opened vertically and the columns of veins underrun with catgut (Crile's operation). If this is not successful, or if the abdomen has been opened in the expectation of finding a bleeding peptic ulcer, the vessels of the greater and lesser curvature are divided between ligatures from the hiatus down to half-way along the stomach. The stomach is then divided near the cardia and resutured to interrupt the submucosal veins—portal azygos disconnection.

Portacaval Shunt

Any patient who has been successfully treated for bleeding due to portal hypertension should be prepared for a shunt operation (Fig. 34).

The patient is given a low-sodium, high-calorie diet; if ammonia intoxication is present the amount of protein taken is also kept to the minimum. Vitamin K is injected to shorten the prothrombin time, anaemia corrected and additional vitamins B and C administered. Operation is performed when there are no overt signs of liver failure or ascites, the serum albumin is over 3 g. % and the serum bilirubin below 3 mg. %. When the patient is anaesthetised and on the operating table portal phlebography is performed by introducing a needle through the abdominal wall into the en-

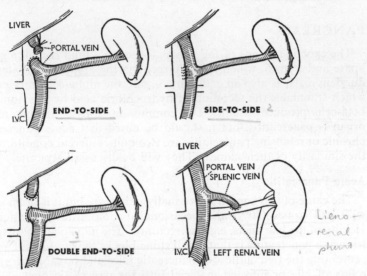

Fig. 34. Types of operation performed for portal hypertension to make a portal systemic anastomosis

larged spleen. When blood is freely withdrawn breathing is arrested and 30 ml. of 70% diodone injected as quickly as possible. A film in a cassette under the patient is exposed immediately after injection and another, 2 seconds later. If the portal vein is seen to be patent a portacaval shunt is performed through a right thoraco-abdominal approach through the bed of the 9th rib. The portal venous pressure is measured to confirm the existence of hypertension. There are three ways of performing the shunt: in all of them a curved clamp is put on the inferior vena cava so that only part of its lumen is occluded: (1) the portal vein is tied at its bifurcation and the distal end anastomosed to the I.V.C.; (2) the portal vein and I.V.C. are anastomosed side to side; (3) the portal vein is divided and both ends are anastomosed end-to-side with the I.V.C. Postoperatively the patient is warned against taking too much protein in the diet.

If phlebography shows that the portal vein is not patent the portal and systemic venous systems can be anastomosed by a lieno-renal shunt. Intravenous pyelography is first done to demonstrate the presence of normal kidneys. The spleen is excised, and all the splenic vein preserved; this is then sutured end-to-side with the renal vein.

When hypersplenism dominates the clinical picture, i.e. splenomegaly, anaemia and leucopaenia, splenectomy is performed and may cause a long remission of symptoms.

A shunt operation is indicated particularly for the prevention of hae-matemesis. Ascites is an indication of a more severe degree of liver disease and is best treated with salt restriction, diuretics and spirolactone (aldo-sterone antagonist).

PANCREAS

The exocrine glands of the pancreas secrete a fluid containing amylase, lipase and trypsin, which is discharged via the ampulla of Vater into the duodenum. It is also an endocrine organ, the alpha-cells produce gastrin which stimulates the secretion of hydrochloric acid by the stomach. The beta-cells produce insulin. The commonest disease encountered in this organ is pancreatitis, but it should be noted that acute pancreatitis and chronic or relapsing pancreatitis are two quite different conditions, despite the similarity of their names. They will be discussed separately here.

Acute Pancreatitis

The cause of this condition is usually unknown, but it is often associated with gall stones (30%) and occasionally complicates operations in the vicinity of the bile ducts, e.g. gastrectomy. The most plausible explanation for acute pancreatitis is that a gall stone blocks the ampulla of Vater, thus preventing the free outflow of pancreatic juice and possibly permitting the reflux of bile or infected material into the pancreatic ducts. When the common bile duct is free of stones the cause is disputed. Pancreatitis is very rarely seen complicating mumps and even more rarely in hyperpara-thyroidism. Often there is a history of alcoholism.

Symptoms and Signs

An obese patient, often a woman with a past history of chronic chole-cystitis, has a sudden severe epigastric pain which radiates to the back. The pain may be overwhelming and suggestive of peptic perforation, it is accompanied by varying degrees of shock: pallor, cold damp extremities, fast pulse and low blood pressure. There is moderate rigidity and guard-ing of the abdominal wall, less than would be found with a perforation of a peptic ulcer; indeed, it may be so slight that an abdominal condition is not suspected and the patient is diagnosed as having a coronary occlusion. The lips often have a bluish cyanotic look. Fortunately there is an immediate rise in the level of serum amylase which can easily be estimated in the laboratory as an emergency and is diagnostic of pancreatitis.

* Amylase ↑ *

Treatment

If any doubt remains about the diagnosis it is better to 'look and see' rather than 'wait and see', and immediate laparotomy is performed. In pancreatitis there is peritoneal effusion, sometimes bloodstained. Patches of fat necrosis are typical, and the pancreas is swollen with oedema, and in very severe cases is gangrenous. Treatment is merely drainage of the peritoneal cavity and closure; if the gall bladder is inflamed and contains stones it should be emptied and cholecystostomy performed by tying a drainage tube into it. When the diagnosis of acute pancreatitis can be made with certainty the treatment should always be expectant. The patient is given pethidine for pain and for theoretical reasons propantheline (Probanthine), since it relieves spasm of smooth muscle and presumably relaxes the sphincter of Oddi. The stomach is kept empty, with continuous suction applied to a naso-gastric tube, since some degree of ileus always occurs. Fluid replacement is achieved intravenously. If tetany occurs due to lowering of the serum calcium 10 ml. of 10% calcium gluconate is given *slowly* in the intravenous drip. Because of the signs of inflammation, tetracycline is also given via the infusion, up to 1 g. in 24 hours. If the patient is shocked it has become usual in recent years to give hydrocortisone, but there is no certain evidence that it is of any value. An inactivator of trypsin, Trasylol, is used but its effectiveness is uncertain. Peritoneal lavage also has advocates, it certainly removes large amounts of enzymes. The prognosis in those who are operated on is about 50%, with those treated expectantly about 75% survive. Haemorrhagic pancreatitis with sloughing carries a high mortality.

In those who recover, cholecystography should be performed, and if any abnormality is found, such as poor opacification or evidence of stones, the patient should have cholecystectomy performed, and if necessary exploration of the common bile duct several weeks after the acute episode. The urine should be tested for sugar, as severe pancreatitis may produce diabetes. Grey Turner's sign is rarely seen about 2 weeks after a patient has recovered from severe pancreatitis as a livid discoloration of the left loin; it is very rare.

Chronic Relapsing Pancreatitis

This disease has a geographical distribution, being seen more commonly in the United States and on the continent of Europe than it is in Great Britain. It is much commoner in males than females, and about a third of the patients involved are chronic alcoholics, though it is not at all clear which comes first, the alcoholism or the pancreatitis. A number of these patients also become drug addicts.

Symptoms and Signs

There are recurrent attacks of epigastric pain which radiate to the left loin, associated with nausea, vomiting, flatulence and constipation. Each attack is associated with varying degrees of ileus, and the repeated damage to the pancreas results eventually in steatorrhoea and diabetes. Serum amylase rises in each attack, and may remain elevated between attacks in the absence of symptoms.

Radiographs of the abdomen may show a stippled calcification of the pancreas and stones in the pancreatic ducts. Cholecystography may reveal evidence of poor concentration in the gall bladder and calculi, which may also be demonstrated in the bile ducts. At operation radiography of the pancreas may reveal stricture in the duct system, solitary or multiple.

Treatment

During an acute exacerbation treatment is the same as for acute pancreatitis. A uniformly successful surgical treatment for this condition has not been discovered. If the gall bladder is diseased and if gall stones are present cholecystectomy is performed and the common bile duct explored and drained. Since it is believed that stenosis of the ampulla may be responsible, the duodenum is opened and the ampullary sphincter divided over a grooved director introduced through the common bile duct. If the pancreatic ducts are full of stones they are scooped out through the tail of the pancreas, which may be amputated so that the exposed pancreatic duct may be anastomosed to a Roux-en-Y loop of jejunum: retrograde pancreatico-jejunostomy. When all else fails and the patient is crippled by pain, partial or sub-total pancreatectomy is done. However, since these patients are often mentally sick and addicts to alcohol or drugs, the success rate is low. Fortunately recurrent pancreatitis is a rare disease in Great Britain.

Carcinoma of the Pancreas

Pancreatic carcinoma is not common. It usually occurs after 50 years of age, and is seen twice as frequently in men as women. About 75% occur in the ampulla and head of the pancreas, and are grouped together, since they are clinically indistinguishable. The remainder are found in the body and tail of the pancreas or involve the whole organ. Pancreatic growths are adenocarcinomata, highly malignant and showing little differentiation. Growths of the lower end of the common bile duct are better differentiated and offer greater chances of cure after radical excision. Spread is usually to lymphatic glands along the upper border of the pancreas and around the inferior mesenteric vessels. Peritoneal spread is common, eventually causing ascites.

Symptoms and Signs

Jaundice with or without pain, dyspepsia, loss of weight and a palpable gall bladder are the most frequent findings. Obstruction to the bile duct causes jaundice. Obstruction to the pancreatic duct may cause steatorrhoea and sometimes chronic pancreatitis or rarely pancreatic cysts. Diabetes may be a presenting feature. Laboratory tests show obstructive jaundice, which, with a palpable gall bladder, suggests malignancy (Courvoisier's Law). There is usually occult blood in the faeces and occasionally frank melaena. Barium-meal examination may show widening of the duodenal loop by the tumour.

Tumours of the distal part of the body and tail of the pancreas present differently. Diagnosis is difficult and sometimes impossible, since jaundice, if it occurs at all, is late. Usually the tumour grows rapidly, with distant metastases that cause peritoneal carcinomatosis, the patient succumbing in a few months. The onset of such a tumour may be heralded by a totally non-specific thrombophlebitis which flits from site to site. In such cases the primary growth may never be palpable and only discovered at post-mortem examination. Often there is only malaise, loss of weight and appetite, suggesting carcinoma of the stomach. The diagnosis may only be made at laparotomy.

Treatment

The jaundiced patient is given vitamin K by subcutaneous injection to shorten the prothrombin time 2–3 days before laparotomy is performed. A large hard mass in the head of the pancreas is typical of carcinoma, chronic pancreatitis causing jaundice is rare, and more often than not conceals a centrally placed growth. The differential diagnosis of carcinoma of the ampulla from stone in the common bile duct and simple stenosis of the ampulla may be difficult. Biopsy is best avoided, as it often causes a fistula unless it is performed through the duodenum. Early growths of the ampulla and head of the pancreas may be excised by pancreatico-duodenectomy, continuity being restored by anastomosing the stomach remnant, common bile duct and cut pancreas with a Roux-en-Y loop of jejunum. Unfortunately this operation carries a serious mortality, and the recurrence rate is high, so that there are very few patients who are suitable for it, and few are likely to survive a long period. Occasionally a minute Vaterian tumour can be excised via the duodenum. Most patients at laparotomy are only suitable for palliative surgery, and the best operation is anastomosis of a loop of jejunum to the gall bladder and entero-anastomosis between afferent and efferent limbs of the loop. Alternatively, a Roux loop is brought up to the gall bladder.

After such a short-circuit operation the jaundice usually clears, but the patient may still be troubled by steatorrhoea. Occasionally long survival results, and it must be assumed that the original diagnosis of carcinoma was wrong and the condition was a form of pancreatitis or fibrous stenosis of the ampulla.

Pancreatic Cysts

The commonest cyst of the pancreas is the pseudocyst, which may follow trauma to the gland by a crushing injury, the result of trauma during a surgical operation or most often as a sequel of pancreatitis. Any part of the pancreas may be involved, but the body is the usual site. A cyst may fill the lesser sac or lie in the mesocolon. Other rare causes of pancreatic cyst are hydatid disease and fibrocystic disease.

Symptoms and Signs

A swelling appears in the epigastrium, which, since it arises from a retroperitoneal organ, is resonant to percussion because of the stomach and colon overlying it. An intraperitoneal tumour is dull to percussion, as bowel is pushed aside by it. A pancreatic cyst may enlarge in any direction, and eventually may come to fill the abdomen. Radiographs often show calcification in the wall of the cyst. The contents are fairly thick and contain pancreatic ferments and sloughs of pancreas.

Treatment

External drainage with a wide-bore tube relieves the symptoms, but almost always creates a permanent fistula, the fluid from which excoriates the surrounding skin. The ideal operation is one of internal drainage, anastomosing the cyst to some part of the bowel; no attempt should be made to excise a pancreatic cyst. Some cysts are best drained into the duodenum by division of the ampullary sphincter, because the duct system of the pancreas communicates with the cyst.

Pancreatic Islet-cell Tumours

These are dealt with in Chapter Thirteen.

Trauma

The pancreas is so well protected that it is not often traumatised. Occasionally crushing injuries, as with the tail-board of a reversing truck, will split it—also gunshot wounds and stabs. Other organs are certain to be injured at the same time. Treatment is immediate laparotomy, at which bloodstained free fluid and fat necrosis will point to pancreatic damage. The peritoneal cavity is drained, and the ileus, which inevitably complicates recovery, is treated by gastric suction and intravenous infusion. Abdominal wounds under such circumstances are particularly liable to burst.

SPLEEN

The only operation performed on the spleen is its removal, for which the two main indications are injuries and certain blood diseases.

Trauma ✳

The spleen is well protected by the overlying ribs, and lies in contact with stomach and diaphragm. Direct blows, gunshot wounds and stab wounds, especially if a rib is fractured, may cause rupture. If the spleen is enlarged and friable, as it is in malaria, it is much more easily damaged. Splenic rupture may be a complication of a chest injury. The spleen may often undergo delayed rupture; there is an initial silent period of 7–14 days following injury, and then haemorrhage suddenly occurs, perhaps while the patient is at rest. It is presumed that the original injury caused a subcapsular haematoma which later burst.

Symptoms and Signs

Pain and tenderness occurs in the left upper abdomen and loin, with radiation to the left shoulder tip as the diaphragm is involved. Tenderness on the left side increases and is followed by rigidity, which eventually spreads over the whole abdominal wall. As the blood clots first on the left side there may rarely be shifting dullness in the right flank and fixed dullness on the left. The patient is restless, pale, shocked and sweating. Radiographs of the abdomen may show a diffuse haziness and absence of splenic shadow in the left upper quadrant.

Treatment

Shock and blood loss are treated by immediate infusion of blood followed by laparotomy. The splenic pedicle is secured and splenectomy performed. Convalescence is often complicated, first by ileus and later by wound dehiscence.

Blood Dyscrasias ✳

Haemolytic Anaemia

Spherocytosis or acholuric jaundice as it is also called, is a congenital, familial condition in which the red cells are unduly fragile. They are destroyed by the spleen, which enlarges. There is mild fluctuating jaundice and a great tendency to the formation of pigment stones in the gall bladder and bile ducts. Splenectomy, carried out during a remission, produces a permanent disappearance of the symptoms. There is a much rarer acquired form of the disease, for which splenectomy is only sometimes of value and only tried where cortisone has failed to achieve a remission.

Thrombocytopoenic Purpura

This is a bleeding disease in which the number of circulating platelets falls below the normal 200,000 per cu. mm. to 20–50,000 per cu. mm. The disease is subject to acute flare-ups which can be controlled by cortisone. Splenectomy, by reducing platelet destruction, may result in a long remission of symptoms.

Hypersplenism

There is a group of patients in whom the spleen enlarges and is so active that there is a reduction in the circulating white cells (polymorphs) and sometimes a pancytopenia. In Felty's syndrome rheumatoid arthritis is associated with a large spleen and a neutropenia. Splenectomy is occasionally of benefit in both these conditions, more especially if the marrow shows increased activity.

Splenomegaly

In many tropical countries enlargement of the spleen is endemic. It may be due to malaria or to other parasites. If the organ is so big that it displaces the other abdominal organs and raises the diaphragm it may be removed for mechanical reasons. The operation itself may be very difficult because of vascular adhesions. Ileus may follow due to decompression of the peritoneal cavity, with attendant collapse of left lower lobe of lung due to disturbance of the diaphragm.

FURTHER READING

Rains, A. J. H. (1964) *Gallstones.* Heinemann, London.

Smith, R., and Sherlock, S. (1964) *Surgery of the Gall Bladder and Bile Ducts.* Butterworths, London.

Sherlock, S. (1963) *Diseases of the Liver and Biliary System,* 3rd ed. Blackwell, Oxford.

Hunt, A. (1958) *Portal Hypertension,* Livingstone, Edinburgh.

Howard, J. H., and Jordan, S. N. (1960) *Surgical Diseases of the Pancreas.* Pitman, London.

Cattell, R. B. and Warren K. W. (1953) *Surgery of the Pancreas.* Saunders Philadelphia.

CHAPTER TWENTY-FIVE

DISEASES OF THE GENITO-URINARY SYSTEM

SYMPTOMS

The symptoms most commonly complained of in disease of the urinary tract are pain, frequency of micturition, difficulty in passing urine and haematuria.

Pain

Fixed Renal Pain is a dull ache in the loin occasionally radiating anteriorly to the right upper quadrant of the abdomen; such so-called fixed pain usually denotes distension or inflammation of the kidney. *Renal colic* is much more severe, intermittent in character and radiates from the loin or abdomen to the groin, testicle or upper thigh. Renal colic is usually of such severity as to cause vomiting, sweating and restlessness. *Ureteric pain* may also be fixed or colicky. Its localisation is often related to the site of disease, upper ureter—loin, lower ureter—iliac fossa. Often ureteric pain radiates to the groin or testis. *Vesical pain* is suprapubic and associated with pain during micturition, especially at the end of the act. *Strangury* is a very unpleasant pain referred to the external urethral meatus accompanied by a desire to micturate, a desire which is frustrated by the passage of only a few drops of urine. *Dysuria* or *urethral pain* is scalding and occurs during micturition.

Frequency of Micturition

Nocturnal frequency of micturition is often of more significance than diurnal frequency. The number of times a person has to get up at night to pass water and the length of time he can hold it during the day is usually recorded in his case notes thus:

$$\frac{D}{N} = \frac{4 \text{ hourly}}{2}$$

Frequency due to infection is often associated with a burning sensation on micturition (dysuria).

Difficulty

Difficulty in passing urine usually denotes obstruction at the bladder neck or in the urethra. The urinary stream is thin and cannot be projected far. In prostatic obstruction there is difficulty in initiating micturition (hesitancy), the stream is slow, and straining does not help. Urethral stricture can only be overcome by straining.

Haematuria

The presence of blood in urine is always a very important sign even if it occurs only once, and demands full investigation to find out the cause. The volume of blood passed may vary from frank haematuria, in which the urine is red, to a smoky urine, which indicates that it contains only a very small quantity; sometimes haematuria can only be recognised by finding red blood cells microscopically. Bright red blood in urine obviously indicates fresh bleeding, but soon after haemorrhage blood in urine is altered, becoming darker. *Initial* haematuria, in which blood is passed at the beginning of micturition, suggests a urethral cause. *Terminal* haematuria suggests a vesical cause. The passage of clots indicates considerable haemorrhage, and passage of worm-like casts of the ureter suggests a renal cause. The association of bleeding with pain is most likely due to inflammation or calculus; painless haematuria is more suggestive of tumour.

PHYSICAL EXAMINATION

Dryness of the tongue may indicate uraemia. The lumbar regions are examined for evidence of enlargement of the kidneys or for tenderness or rigidity over them. Tenderness may be felt over the course of the ureters. The bladder may be felt to be distended suprapubically, or there may be tenderness over it. The penis must be examined for congenital deformity, stenosis or inflammation of the external urethral meatus, urethral discharge and induration suggesting a urethral stricture. The scrotum may reveal swellings of the testis or epididymis or a collection of fluid in the tunica vaginalis. The spermatic cord should be palpated for thickening. Rectal examination should always be performed so that in men the prostate gland and seminal vesicles can be felt. The nervous system should be examined, especially pupillary and ankle reflexes to exclude a neurological cause of the symptoms.

INVESTIGATIONS

There are a wide range of techniques available for the investigation of urological disorders. Indeed, the diagnosis of disease of the urinary tract is one of the most precise in any part of the body.

Urine Examination

Specimens of urine are examined for protein, sugar and pH. For microscopy, specimens of urine free of contaminants are taken either in midstream (M.S.U.) or by catheter (C.S.U.). Such specimens are centrifuged, and the sediment examined for red and white cells, organisms, and casts. Cultures are made for organisms and tested for sensitivity to antibiotics. The average urinary output in 24 hours is about 1,500 ml., and the specific gravity varies from 1·008 to 1·020.

Tests of Renal Function

Because so much renal tissue is normally held in reserve, there has to be considerable damage before evidence of renal failure becomes apparent. Information given by detailed tests of renal function are often of no more practical value than impressions gained from clinical examination and simple biochemical tests.

Blood Urea

The normal level of blood urea lies between 20 and 40 mg./100 ml. of blood. A level above 50 mg. suggests renal impairment, and above 100 mg. renal function is so reduced that pyelography fails to reveal any concentration of radiographic contrast medium, and therefore should not be done. The overall renal function must be reduced by over 50% for a rise in the level of blood urea.

Specific Gravity the capacity of the kidneys to concentrate urine is a guide to renal function especially in extra-renal uraemia due to electrolyte and acid base balance disorders (see p. 19). Often, after operations, there is diminished excretion of urine and in seriously ill patients it may be difficult to know if this oliguria is due to dehydration or renal impairment. Passage of urine with a specific gravity of around 1·010 (the specific gravity of glomerular filtrate) is suggestive of renal failure, especially if the concentration of urea in the urine is low. It is permissive, when in doubt, to give a water load of 1 litre and to measure the urine volume, its urea content and its specific gravity before and after this infusion. Failure to increase the output of urine and a low urea concentration in the urine are good evidence of renal impairment. In the routine assessment of a patient, if random specimens of urine have a specific gravity exceeding 1·020 it is usually unnecessary to perform a *concentration test*; this test requires water restriction (500 ml.) for 36 hours, but is a good guide to the ability of the kidneys to concentrate urine. Urea concentration and urea clearance tests are rarely of value in the assessment of renal function before surgery.

Excretion Tests

Often the problem in surgery is the detection of unilateral renal disease. The most useful guide to this is given by *intravenous pyelography* (I.V.P.).

Divided Renal Studies

Simultaneous collection of urine from both kidneys via ureteric catheters is the most precise excretion test for disordered function of one kidney. If the blood supply of one kidney is poorer than its opposite usually due to stenosis of the renal artery, then the urine volume and its sodium and chloride content is lower and its urea content higher. Such specimens may also be examined for the presence of organisms and cells. The test is time consuming and subject to technical errors.

The radioisotope renogram is an elaborate technique which is used to measure the function of each kidney separately. Shielded scintillation counters, placed over both loins, detect the uptake of isotope (I^{125}-labelled hippuran). The apparatus is very expensive and requires the services of a physicist. The test is of value in the diagnosis of the causes of hypertension due to unilateral renal disease and to demonstrate the results of obstruction.

RADIOLOGY OF THE URINARY TRACT

Plain radiographs, that is, those taken without the use of contrast medium, are invaluable in showing the shape and size of the kidneys, the presence of calculi (90% of which are radiopaque) and the presence of psoas shadows, which may be obscured in perinephric inflammation. Abnormalities of bone such as secondary deposits from carcinoma of prostate and osteoporosis from hyperparathyroidism may also be revealed.

Intravenous pyelography affords the most valuable routine information in urology. The urinary tract is outlined following the intravenous injection of a contrast medium that is selectively excreted by the kidneys. The medium owes its radiopacity to the high concentration of iodine that it contains. Preliminary plain radiographs are taken of the abdomen and pelvis. After an intravenous injection of 40 ml. of 45% urografin, radiographs are taken of the abdomen at 5, 10, 15 and 30 minutes and of the pelvis after micturition. These radiographs display not only the anatomy of the urinary tract but also are of use in assessing renal function, for a poor renal shadow is correlated with poor renal function. The bladder radiographs may show pouches or diverticula, filling defects due to growths and enlargement of the prostate. The persistence of contrast medium in the bladder after micturition is a guide to incomplete emptying; residual urine is a common feature of enlargement of the prostate.

When the I.V.P. is not clear more precise demonstration of renal and ureteric anatomy can be achieved by *retrograde pyelography*. A cystoscope is passed and one or both ureters catheterised. With the patient conscious, to avoid painful over-distension of the renal pelvis, contrast medium is injected through the catheter to display the renal pelvis and ureter.

The bladder can be outlined by *cystography*, in which radiopaque fluid is injected through a catheter; the urethra can be similarly demonstrated by *urethrography*. A very refined form of investigation of the neuro-muscular process of micturition, the *micturating cystogram* is undertaken using an image intensifier and a ciné-camera, by which the passage of radiopaque medium from the bladder during micturition can be followed on moving pictures.

Occasionally it is necessary to outline the arterial system of the kidneys, and this is done by *aortography* (renal angiogram) performed either by injection of contrast medium through a fine polyethylene catheter passed up the iliac artery after percutaneous puncture of the femoral artery. The catheter is passed to a point in the aorta corresponding to the level of the renal arteries, and contrast medium is very rapidly injected. Serial films are swiftly exposed within the time that blood flows through the kidney, about 2 seconds. Selective angiograms are obtained by catheterising one renal artery with a special catheter.

Air Insufflation

Occasionally it is desirable to outline the kidneys and suprarenal glands, and to do this, air is injected presacrally. The patient is allowed up, and the air rises deep to Gerota's fascia in the perinephric tissues, revealing the outlines of psoas muscles, kidneys and adrenals. Combined with tomography this technique can give more precise information.

Endoscopy

Instruments are available for inspection of the bladder and urethra by special illuminated telescopes. The *cystoscope* is used for the bladder, the *panendoscope* and *urethroscope* for the urethra. Through these endoscopes, catheters, diathermy electrodes and biopsy forceps can be passed. With a special form of cystoscope, a *resectoscope*, some types of prostatic enlargement can be removed piecemeal via the urethra, an operation called trans-urethral resection (T.U.R.) of the prostate.

AFFECTIONS OF THE KIDNEYS AND URETERS

Infections of the Kidney

Pyelonephritis

Pyelonephritis, as its name indicates, is an inflammation and suppuration of the kidney parenchyma and renal pelvis. Usually the renal pelvis and calyces are mainly involved, sometimes the ureter is affected as well. The epithelial lining of the urinary tract is swollen and red, sometimes it shows purpuric haemorrhages and often a mucopurulent discharge. Although this condition is sometimes called 'acute pyelitis', nevertheless the renal substance itself is always involved to a greater or lesser extent. In severe acute pyelonephritis the kidney is swollen and the cut surface shows cortical abscesses and yellow streaks of pus radiating into the medulla due to infection in the collecting tubules of the kidney. In chronic pyelonephritis the capsule of the kidney becomes adherent and its surface scarred. The cortex is thinned, and microscopy shows fibrosed, hyalinised glomeruli and atrophic tubules containing colloid casts.

The common organism in urinary tract infection is *Esch. coli*. Numerous other organisms may be involved including staphylococci, streptococci, *B. Proteus* and *B. Pyocyanea*. The route of infection is from the blood stream during episodes of transient bacteraemia or from spread of ascending infection from, for example, the bladder to the kidneys. Infection may also spread through subepithelial lymphatics. The commonest predisposing factors in urinary infection are obstruction and stasis in the urinary tract, and the likeliest causes are: the enlarged prostate, stone, a congenital abnormality of the renal tract, ureteric reflux or the gravid uterus.

Symptoms and Signs. 1. *Acute Pyelonephritis* begins with *fever* and *malaise* and sometimes shivering or a *rigor*. There is frequency of micturition, very often with scalding. Pain and tenderness in the loin are typical, though occasionally the signs are more obvious in the iliac fossae. Microscopy of the urine reveals pus cells and organisms.

Treatment. A clean specimen of urine is collected (in women, by catheter or more often by a special 'catch technique', in men, midstream) and examined microscopically; cultures are set up with tests for sensitivity to antibiotics. A course of a soluble sulphonamide such as sulphadimidine (0·5 g. 6 hourly) is started. If the disease is not controlled within 48 hours an appropriate antibiotic is given, depending upon the results of the sensitivity tests, but as the majority of infections are sensitive to sulphonamide, this drug may be started immediately. Rest in bed, copious fluids and analgesics are prescribed. Administration of potassium citrate is important when sulphonamides are being taken, and sufficient should be given to alkalinise the urine for the growth of *Esch. coli* is inhibited in an alkaline medium. After the acute attack has subsided, intravenous pyelography should be undertaken to find out any predisposing cause such as a calculus, hydronephrosis or a congenital anomaly. Vaginal examination may reveal pregnancy or pelvic infection; rectal examination may reveal prostatic enlargement.

2. *Chronic Pyelonephritis.* Recurrent attacks of subacute infection may result in severe renal damage, the kidney finally becoming small, scarred and contracted. This process can occur without clinical symptoms, or may be found in patients with hypertension or those who die of uraemia due to chronic renal failure. It is sometimes associated with ureteric reflux.

Treatment. In many cases it is impossible to arrest the course of pyelonephritis unless there is a predisposing cause which can be treated. The long-term use of antibiotics for recurrent subacute attacks may be of value. From the surgical point of view it is important to find the cause if that is possible. In cases of unilateral pyelonephritis nephrectomy may dramatically cure hypertension.

Pyonephrosis

Invariably pyonephrosis is secondary to ureteral obstruction causing distension of the renal pelvis and calyces with pus. In unilateral disease there is usually a pre-existing hydronephrosis due to a congenital lesion or stone; bilateral pyonephrosis follows obstruction in the bladder or urethra. The infection may be tuberculous, and in renal tuberculosis the obstruction may be due to healing by fibrosis.

Pathology. The kidney becomes converted into a pus-filled sac. Pus cells or organisms may be few or absent in the urine, if the ureter is blocked by, for example, a stone. The kidney becomes fixed to nearby structures by inflammatory adhesions, which may make nephrectomy difficult.

Symptoms and Signs. Generally pyonephrosis is preceded by attacks of pyelonephritis or cystitis with rigors, a high swinging temperature and leucocytosis. There is pain in the loin and the kidney is enlarged and tender. The urine contains pus cells and organisms, and sometimes red blood cells unless the pyonephrosis is a closed one, i.e. shut off by obstruction in the ureter. Pyelography may show a cause, such as a stone, and usually absence of function in the affected kidney. Cystoscopy is necessary to exclude obstruction, for example in the lower end of the ureters.

Treatment. In most cases the kidney is so damaged that nephrectomy is the only course. If the patient is too ill for a major operation nephrostomy or drainage of the kidney only may be possible, with secondary nephrectomy later, a very difficult operation. If function in the other kidney is poor, then every effort is made to preserve any functioning renal tissue by nephrostomy. Antibiotics are used in the acute phase. Bilateral pyonephrosis is usually a terminal event, the result of infection ascending from bladder or urethral disease. Antibiotics and treatment of ureteral, vesical or urethral obstruction in such patients offer the only hope of improvement.

Perinephric Abscess

Diffuse cellulitis of the fibro-fatty tissue around the kidney almost always goes on to abscess formation, *perinephric abscess*, requiring a drainage operation. The infection may be blood borne, and often there is a history of a staphylococcal lesion, a boil or some other septic focus 2 or 3 weeks before perinephric infection. In such cases organisms probably lodge in the kidney to form a small sub-cortical abscess from which spread to the perinephric tissues occurs. Rarely a large solitary *cortical abscess* forms, and equally rarely a *renal carbuncle* may arise, a staphylococcal lesion of the kidney characterised by an area of necrosis and acute inflammation lying near its surface. Renal carbuncle is notoriously difficult to diagnose; it should be kept in mind as a cause of unexplained fever.

Perinephric abscess also occurs secondary to gross inflammatory disease of the kidney. Probably the commonest underlying disease is renal calculus, but any inflammation in the kidney may go on to perinephric abscess: acute—such as infected hydronephrosis; chronic—such as tuberculosis.

Symptoms and Signs. Perinephric abscess is very painful, causing increasing aching in the affected loin associated with fever. The loin is tender and, as the infection develops, swelling can be detected. Because the infection is deep and under tension, swelling is slight and best seen by looking down over the patient's back when he is sitting forward. A slight change in contour of the affected loin can then usually be seen. A swinging fever and high leucocytosis indicate abscess formation. In plain radiographs the psoas shadow may be obscured, calculi revealed and scoliosis be present, concave to the affected side. Intravenous pyelography often shows no renal disease, but the ureter may be displaced by the abscess. The urine commonly shows no abnormality in early cases. With renal carbuncle and cortical abscess the symptoms and signs are very similar, except that swelling does not occur, but there is likely to be tenderness in the loin, with high fever and leucocytosis.

Treatment. Development of a perinephric abscess can rarely be aborted by antibiotics. By the time the diagnosis is made drainage is usually necessary through an incision in the loin. Investigations must be undertaken to allow underlying diseases to be eradicated and to prevent recurrence of infection.

Often a renal carbuncle can only be cured by nephrectomy, occasionally it will heal with antibiotics. Sometimes, at an operation for exploration of a suspected perinephric abscess, a cortical abscess is found which should be drained.

Renal Tuberculosis

Tuberculosis of the kidney is always secondary to disease elsewhere, usually from a primary lesion sited in the lung or in a lymph node from which the infection has spread via the blood stream. Occasionally there is long-standing disease elsewhere, perhaps in bone or in lung. It is a disease typically of young adults.

Pathology. In the early phase of infection tubercle follicles appear in the kidneys, usually in the region of the cortex, most of which heal. Occasionally one or more grow and become caseous. Spread occurs from the cortex to the medulla along the tubules, and the earliest radiological detectable focus of disease is an ulcer at the apex of a pyramid projecting into a calyx. Later, caseation and ulceration progress (ulcerocavernous disease) leading to greater involvement and destruction of the kidneys. If the pelvi-ureteric junction becomes stenosed the kidney becomes hydronephrotic and if infected a pyonephrosis may form. Calcification commonly occurs and denotes an attempt at healing. Rarely a tuberculous pyonephrosis calcifies and is apparently inactive, and the kidney is destroyed (so-called auto-nephrectomy). However, in such foci of infection tuberculous organisms lie dormant and may at any time be responsible for recrudescence of the disease.

The ureter is commonly involved, both from infected urine and from periureteral lymphatic spread. It becomes thickened and ulcerated, with regions of stenosis that cause back pressure on the kidney. The bladder is commonly infected from the kidney; tubercles and ulcers can often be seen at cystoscopy on the lips of the ureteric orifices. In the late stages of ureteric disease the ureteric orifice is enlarged, stiff and gaping (golf-hole ureter). If healing takes place, fibrosis narrows the vesico-ureteric junction and leads to hydronephrosis.

Though in the early phase of disease both kidneys always contain tubercle follicles, established disease of both kidneys is unusual. The presence of tubercle bacilli in urine secreted by an apparently radio-logically normal kidney (tuberculous bacilluria) does not necessarily mean that progressive disease in that kidney will arise. Contralateral infection is usually late in the disease and follows infection ascending from the bladder in infected urine or from retrograde lymphatic spread around the ureter.

Symptoms and Signs. The first symptom may be polyuria. Later there is frequency of micturition, particularly at night; micturition is usually both frequent and painful. Haematuria may occur, being usually slight in amount. There is usually pain in the loin, and colic may occur from the passage of clots or of caseous material. Tenderness may be found in the loin, but renal enlargement is not a feature unless hydronephrosis or pyonephrosis occur. Early in the disease the general health is not affected, but later there is fever, malaise, night sweats and exhaustion from painful frequency, especially when the bladder is contracted and small.

Diagnosis. The urine is acid in reaction, contains pus cells and is sterile by ordinary cultural methods. *Sterile acid pyuria* demands full bacterial examination, and should indicate tuberculosis until proved otherwise. At least three specimens of urine taken first thing in the morning (early morning urine, E.M.U.) should be examined microscopically for acid-fast bacilli, cultures prepared and if there is any doubt, guinea-pigs inoculated with the sediment after centrifugation. Treatment should not begin until acid-fast bacilli have been identified. They take about 6 weeks to grow on Lowenstein-Jensen medium.

The intravenous pyelogram may show no abnormality in the early phase of the disease, and must be repeated after a month or so if the clinical condition and the findings in the urine indicate the possibility of tuber-culosis. The earliest pyelographic finding is 'fluffiness' of a calyx or a loss of definition in its outline. Other findings are distortion or absence of one or more of the calyces. When the disease is more advanced the pelvis of the kidney and its calyces may be deformed and ureteric dilatation and stenosis are seen.

Cystoscopy may be necessary to identify bladder involvement. A ureteric catheter is passed to define any pyelographic changes in the pelvis and ureter and also to collect urine from the affected kidney for microscopy and culture. Catheterisation of the contralateral kidney could theoretically transfer infection, and so is rarely done or indeed indicated.

Careful examination of the whole body should be made for evidence of any other foci of disease, for example in the lungs, bones and joints, the genitalia and prostate. The erythrocyte sedimentation rate (E.S.R.) is a useful guide to activity of the disease, but is not of diagnostic value.

Treatment. The results of treatment of urogenital tuberculosis have been immensely improved by the use of tuberculostatic drugs. In most cases surgery can be avoided in the stage of active infection. Surgery has a place when healing causes fibrosis and stenosis of the renal pelvis and ureters.

The results of treatment are better if patients are admitted for a period of

6 months to a sanatorium, where adequate rest can be assured and, most important, where administration of antibiotics can be supervised. At the same time the general health can be improved by a well-balanced diet, with iron and vitamins. The usual régime of administration (see p. 63) of streptomycin, para-aminosalicylic acid (P.A.S.) and isoniazid hydrazide (I.N.A.H.) is continued for 6 months, during which time the urine should become free of tubercule bacilli. Thereafter P.A.S. and I.N.A.H. are continued for a further 18 months.

Surgery is required to drain an abscess in the kidney; in 'cavernotomy' the cortex overlying the abscess is removed and caseous tissue sucked out. A tuberculous pyonephrosis or hydronephrosis may necessitate nephrectomy, usually with removal of the ureter down to the bladder (nephro-ureterectomy). Stricture of a calyx may rarely indicate the need for partial nephrectomy. Contraction of the bladder, a serious sequel to antibiotic therapy, may require special operations to increase bladder capacity.

Renal and Ureteric Calculi

Calculi are found in the kidney, ureter, bladder and urethra. Those in the ureter come from the kidney, those in the urethra come from the bladder. Stone is commoner in the tropics than in temperate climates. Urine contains both crystalloid and colloid substances, which are normally kept in solution by buffer systems. An excess of colloid or of crystalloid may upset this equilibrium and lead to deposition of calculi. Although a list of numerous factors contributing to calculus formation can be drawn up, it must be admitted that, in the vast majority of cases, no cause can be found. The following causes must always be excluded:

1. *Inborn Errors of Metabolism.* Although a strong familial history of stone formation is common, in most patients no metabolic error can be found. However, some people excrete abnormally large amounts of cystine, oxalates (oxalosis) or uric acid and may continually develop calculi composed of one of these substances. Xanthinuria or cystinuria is a very rare cause of stones.

2. *Abnormality of Calcium Metabolism.* The best-known abnormality of calcium metabolism is hyperparathyroidism, and all patients suffering from renal calculus should have serum calcium and phosphorus estimations performed, if necessary, on several occasions, specimens of blood being obtained *without a tourniquet*. Hypercalcaemia, hypophosphataemia and a raised level of serum alkaline phosphatase are indications of hyperparathyroidism. In patients with recurrent calculi more elaborate calcium excretion tests must be performed, in which the amount of calcium excreted in 24 hours is measured. Normally, on a hospital ward diet, a patient should not excrete more than 300 mg. of calcium in 24 hours. Renal calcification (nephrocalcinosis) is also seen in overdosage with vitamin D, sarcoidosis and scleroderma.

3. *Stasis and Concentration of Urine.* Prolonged recumbency of patients

being treated, for example for tuberculosis of the spine or for poliomyelitis, is very likely to be followed by stone formation in the kidneys, especially in the lower poles, where stagnant urine is likely to collect. Stasis due to obstruction to urinary flow at the pelvi-calyceal, pelvi-ureteric or uretero-vesical junction or lower at the vesical outlet is also very liable to be complicated by stone formation. In all cases the chances are greatly increased if infection has supervened or has been the cause of the obstruction.

In the tropics stone formation is common, presumably because of sweating and excretion of concentrated urine. In the Second World War the incidence of stone in troops in desert areas was much higher than in Great Britain.

4. *Infection.* Urinary infection is a potent factor in the causation of stone, especially when it is associated with an element of obstruction to urinary flow. Persistence of urinary infection favours recurrence of stone formation after treatment. In only about 10% of patients suffering from calculi is the urine sterile. Organisms such as *Staphylococcus albus* and *B. proteus* are capable of splitting urea, forming an alkaline urine in which phosphatic calculi are prone to form.

5. *Diet.* There is reputed to be an association between vitamin A deficiency and stone formation. It is also known that excessive administration of vitamin D may cause calculi and calcification within the kidney substance (nephrocalcinosis), the latter is also seen in hyperparathyroidism.

6. *Congenital Causes.* Any congenital anomaly of the kidney and urinary system may be associated with stasis and possibly stone formation.

7. *Foreign body.* A foreign body in the bladder, e.g. a piece of catheter, a suture or self-introduced material may all become coated with phosphates.

Types of Calculi

In children the nucleus of a stone is often ammonium urate; in young adults, uric acid and in older persons, calcium oxalate. Stones formed of phosphatic salts and calcium carbonate are common and occur as a secondary change, usually on some nucleus, such as a tumour, foreign body or calculus, especially following infection. It is unusual to have a stone of a pure chemical substance, one component may predominate but almost always there are at least traces of others.

Calcium Oxalate stones are small, hard and dark in colour, with an irregular spiky surface ('mulberry' stones).

Uric Acid stones are hard, smooth and brownish in colour.

Phosphatic and Carbonate stones are grey-white in colour and often very large. Calcium phosphate stones are white and hard, mixed phosphatic calculi are softer and paler.

Ammonium and sodium urate stones occur. Oxalate, uric acid and urate stones occur in acid urine, phosphatic stones arise in alkaline urine.

Renal calculus is usually unilateral. Calculi in the ureters originate in the kidney, most pass spontaneously, but if the stone sticks the most likely places where it may be arrested are the pelvi-ureteric junction, the pelvic brim and the lower end of the ureter. Usually the obstruction is incomplete, but often some degree of temporary hydronephrosis can be detected on pyelography. Occasionally, when obstruction is complete suppression of urine from the affected kidney occurs and may be permanent unless the obstruction can be relieved. When there are stones in both kidneys one may have had its function destroyed, so that obstruction of the sole functioning kidney may cause uraemia and death.

Symptoms and Signs. Pain and haematuria are the most prominent symptoms, though neither is invariable. Usually there are no other abnormal physical signs unless renal enlargement occurs due to hydronephrosis or if there are signs of renal infection or failure.

Often the first warning of the presence of a calculus is an attack of renal colic (see p. 353) due to the passage of a stone into or down the ureter. Colic may last for minutes or hours, may never recur, or there may be a variable number of attacks lasting until the stone is passed into the bladder or per urethram. Colic may continue until the kidney ceases to function or the obstruction caused by the stone is spontaneously relieved by subsidence of oedema at the site of impaction. Frequency of micturition often accompanies colic. If infection supervenes, the symptoms and signs of pyelitis or even pyonephrosis or perinephric abscess may occur. Renal pain, fixed in the loin, may persist after the colic has subsided or may be a presenting feature of calculus in the kidney itself, especially if there is associated infection. Such pain is typically made worse by movement and is relieved by rest. Occasionally it is only felt in the hypochondrium and not in the loin. Stones which fill the renal pelvis and calyces (staghorn calculi) may be quite painless, even when both kidneys are involved, and may only be discovered accidentally in radiographs of the abdomen or in the investigation of renal failure and anuria.

Haematuria may be obvious to the naked eye, or may only be revealed microscopically. It usually follows an attack of colic, and rarely lasts more than a day or two. Sometimes it is the complications of calculi that lead to their detection, such as hydronephrosis, pyonephrosis, perinephric abscess and very rarely squamous carcinoma of the renal pelvis.

Diagnosis. Because most calculi are opaque to X-rays, plain radiographs of the abdomen and pelvis will usually reveal them. Cystine stones are the least opaque and may be missed. Uric acid stones are radio-lucent and can only be identified as filling defects in the pyelogram. The presence of a calcified shadow in the loin may have to be distinguished from a stone in the gall bladder. A lateral view is of great value, for gall stones lie anterior to the paravertebral gutter in which renal calculi are situated. A lateral view will also distinguish calcification in costal cartilages, a common feature of ageing. In the abdomen calcified mesenteric lymph nodes and calcification in the aorta and its branches may be confusing. In the pelvis calcified phleboliths in pelvic veins are often confused with ureteric calculi, and can only be distinguished from them by intravenous pyelography or occasionally by the passage of a ureteric catheter which will show if the stone lies in the course of the ureter. If a stone is impacted at the ureteric orifice the opening is reddened and oedematous; indeed, the calculus may be seen protruding from it at cystoscopy.

Treatment. Treatment for calculus includes the treatment of renal colic, impacted calculi, operative removal of calculi, the complications of calculus and any underlying cause.

Renal Colic

This is extremely painful. Once the diagnosis is made in adults morphia (15 mg.) and atropine (0·6 mg.) are given intramuscularly; children may require Nepenthe, in doses related to body weight. Thereafter the patient is encouraged to drink copious fluids and to be active. Spasmolytic drugs (Probanthine 15 mg. t.d.s.) should be given. The majority of ureteric calculi pass spontaneously, and the patient should keep a close watch for the passage of a stone per urethram—an incident usually painful, but not always so. Intravenous pyelography and microscopy and bacteriological investigation of the urine are essential. Detection of any underlying cause is important if recurrence is to be avoided (see below).

Impaction of Calculus

Stones usually impact in the lower end of the ureter, but no part is free from this hazard, especially the pelvi-ureteric junction and the part at the level of the fourth lumbar vertebra. Most calculi of less than 0·5 cm. diameter can pass naturally. Cystoscopy, and if possible ureteric catheterisation past a stone, will often dislodge it and be followed by its passage within 10 days of this manoeuvre. There are special instruments (corkscrews, wire baskets) which can be passed around the stone for its mechanical removal, and success with these is appreciated by the patient. A stone impacted at or near the ureteric orifice can often be eased in its passage by slitting the ureteric orifice with a diathermy electrode, *meatotome*, which can be passed through a cystoscope.

Operative Removal of Calculi

Stones may need to be removed by operation if they lie in the kidney, fail to pass into the bladder from the ureter and especially when they are causing complications. Stones in the renal pelvis are approached through a loin incision and removed by opening the renal pelvis, *pyelolithotomy*. It is important to be sure that all the stones are removed and, if necessary, radiographs may be taken on the operating table. Stones in a calyx or embedded in the kidney substance may be approached by an incision through the convex border of the kidney, *nephrolithotomy*, an operation not lightly to be undertaken. Not only may there be considerable blood loss and kidney damage but the operation may be followed by secondary haemorrhage requiring nephrectomy for its arrest. Small calculi in the kidney substance are usually left and watched radiographically for growth or movement into the renal pelvis. Very large calculi, such as staghorn calculi, are very difficult to remove without irreparable damage to the kidney, and are usually left, especially if both kidneys are involved. If only one kidney is affected, then nephrectomy may be indicated, particularly if the kidney is functionless.

Stones in the upper ureter can be reached extra-peritoneally through a loin incision; in the lower ureter through a subumbilical or oblique incision in the iliac fossa. The stone is more easily removed if it is dislodged proximally rather than from the point at which it is stuck, where the ureter will be found to be inflamed and oedematous.

The treatment when stones occur in both kidneys presents a difficult problem. If the calculi are very large and seriously interfering with renal function often nothing can be done for fear of jeopardising the remaining renal tissue. In less severe cases operation is performed first on the side showing better function, or on the side in which symptoms have been felt most recently, in the hope of preserving as much renal function as possible.

Complications of Calculus

Calculi commonly cause serious infection and obstruction. Stones may have to be removed to relieve hydronephrosis. Pyonephrosis may require nephrostomy (that is drainage of the renal pelvis through the kidney) if renal function is poor or if a solitary kidney is involved or if nephrectomy is technically impossible because of severe peri-renal inflammation. Suppression of urine is the most serious complication of stones, and usually arises when one kidney has been removed or its function destroyed and when a calculus obstructs the sole remaining kidney. Pyelography or a history of recent pain indicates the better-functioning kidney. A catheter is passed up the ureter, which may relieve the obstruction, if not, a nephrostomy is usually necessary with or without removal of the stone.

Underlying Causes of Calculus

The underlying cause of calculus formation in most patients is never discovered. Patients should be advised to take large volumes of fluids, three litres daily, and to alter the pH of the urine from alkaline to acid by ingesting acid sodium phosphate. Aluminium hydroxide gel may help prevent the recurrence of stones by decreasing phosphate absorption in the gut, where it forms insoluble aluminium phosphate.

All patients should have serum calcium estimations performed, if necessary on several occasions. If hypercalcaemia is found it is possible that a parathyroid tumour is present and can be removed. In cases of cystinuria a large fluid intake will help prevent further stone formation. Penicillamine is a specific drug in the prevention of cystine stones; for uric acid stones and oxalate stones there are no satisfactory methods for prevention.

Congenital abnormalities of the kidney and ureter must be corrected when possible; for example, double pelvis or double ureter when stones may form in one of the reduplicated structures. Where stones repeatedly form in damaged calyces (usually in the lower pole of the kidney) calculus formation may only be cured by partial nephrectomy.

Renal Failure

Acute Renal Failure

In acute renal failure there is oliguria or complete cessation of renal function, *anuria*. This must be distinguished from failure to pass urine or retention of urine, and the distinction is usually made by passage of a catheter to ascertain if the bladder contains urine and how much. *Oliguria* is defined as an output of urine of less than 700 ml. of a specific gravity of 1·008–1·014. Normally at least 1,500 ml. of urine is excreted of specific gravity 1·010–1·020. Renal failure may ensue from a variety of causes, which are usually classified in three main groups, *pre-renal*, when there is arterial hypotension and decreased perfusion pressure in the kidney; *renal*, where the kidney itself is damaged, and *post-renal*, when there is obstruction to urinary flow beyond the kidney.

1. *Pre-renal*. In any condition of severe and prolonged hypotension or decreased blood volume, the glomerular filtration rate is greatly decreased. An arterial pressure of at least 70 mm. Hg is required for the secretion of urine. Hypotension or hypovolaemia soon lead to renal damage, so that pre-renal uraemia may be associated with renal failure unless the causes are rapidly corrected. Pre-renal uraemia is usually a feature of hypovolaemia and dehydration due to plasma loss in burns, fluid and electrolyte loss in vomiting, gastro-intestinal fistula or severe diarrhoea.

2. *Renal*. Renal failure from glomerular damage is a feature of glomerulo-nephritis; necrosis of the cortex of the kidneys is a complication of pregnancy usually associated with concealed accidental haemorrhage and abortion. These may require treatment with the artificial kidney. Both may be recoverable if the phase of acute renal damage can be tided over.

The renal tubules may be damaged in poisoning due to mercury, carbon tetrachloride, phenol and phosphorus. Lower nephron necrosis, that is damage to the tubules below the second convoluted tubule, is usually due to diminished blood supply to the tubules. The same factors that may cause pre-renal uraemia may go on to produce lower nephron-necrosis. Other causes are intra-vascular haemolysis from mismatched blood transfusion and haemolytic poisons. A neurogenic effect can also occur, and a strong stimulus to a peripheral nerve may cause ischaemia of the renal cortex and diversion of blood to the medulla of the kidney. This reflex may explain some of the anurias met following abortion, burns and the irreversible shock of severe injury.

3. *Post-renal*. Obstruction to urinary flow at any point beyond the kidney may cause renal failure, the commonest being the enlarged prostate in men and pelvic neoplasm in women. Bilateral obstruction in the renal pelvis or ureters, for example by calculi or tumour or disease, such

as growth in the bladder, prostatic enlargement or stricture of the urethra, may cause renal failure. Below the ureteric orifices there has to be a considerable degree of retention of urine before renal failure occurs.

Recognition of Renal Failure

It is often surprisingly long before renal failure is recognised. In surgical patients uraemia may arise insidiously in the postoperative period, and it is most important for careful observation to be kept in order to recognise it in its earliest phases. Careful records must be kept of postoperative blood pressure and of the fluid balance of patients whenever severe changes might be expected. Patients who have had serious blood, plasma or electrolyte loss and patients who are hypotensive for any length of time are at risk of developing renal failure. Meticulous charting of all fluids given and all excreted, plus those lost by aspiration or fistulae, must be carried out. Daily serum electrolyte and urea estimations should be made when the possibility of renal failure exists, together with tests for haemo-concentration—blood haematocrit, serum protein estimation and urine urea concentration and specific gravity. A technique for measuring the osmolality of the urine is also valuable in distinguishing oliguria due to haemoconcentration from that due to renal failure.

In established uraemia a dry, furred tongue, hiccoughing, mental clouding and muscle twitching are all serious signs. Coma and convulsions usually indicate a terminal state. Air hunger and other signs of acidosis may also indicate the presence of uraemia.

Treatment. Pre-renal uraemia is best prevented by avoiding hypotension and hypovolaemia by accurate blood-volume replacement and correction of fluid and electrolyte deficiencies as and when they occur. The passage of small volumes of urine of high specific gravity and urea content, a raised level of serum proteins and a raised haematocrit all indicate the need for additional intravenous fluids, the nature of which will depend upon the level of serum sodium and potassium and the alkali reserve. Often there is doubt whether failure is pre-renal or renal; under such circumstances it is reasonable to give a litre of fluid intravenously to see if there is an increase in urine output.

Renal Failure

Once renal failure is diagnosed a régime is instituted whereby endogenous catabolism of tissue is depressed by the administration of carbohydrate, and protein intake is stopped. The fluid intake is restricted to 500 ml. per day plus a volume equal to any losses from vomiting, intestinal fistula and the volume of urine excreted during the preceding 24 hours. Intravenous feeding (see p. 23) can provide calories and fluid if oral feeding is impossible. By such means the rise of blood urea can be slowed, but even more important, over-hydration can be prevented. Most uraemic patients in the past have been given too much fluid and have died from pulmonary oedema and bronchopneumonia. The volume of fluid of 500 ml. water per day represents unavoidable fluid losses that cannot be measured. It is best given by mouth, when possible, as sweet fluids. The amount of sodium and chloride to be given depends upon the results of frequent serum electrolyte estimations. In uraemia, acidosis and depression of the serum alkali reserve may indicate the need for sodium rather than chloride, best met by the administration of $\frac{1}{6}$ molar sodium lactate. A common cause of death in renal failure is hyperkalaemia (raised potassium) and a level of potassium of 7 m.eq./l. is regarded as critical, for above this level cardiac arrest may occur. The use of a potassium exchange resin (resonium) given by mouth or by enema will slow the rise of potassium. Electrocardiograms may give evidence of intracellular potassium retention, even when serum levels are within normal limits.

Uraemic patients are very susceptible to infection, and during their treatment they should be nursed under barrier conditions. Antibiotics should be restricted to proven infections, and because of the reduced excretion, they need only be given in small doses.

Dialysis may be carried out either by the artificial kidney (haemodialysis) or by peritoneal dialysis. The indications are based on both biochemical and clinical assessment.

Post-renal Failure

The initial treatment of post-renal failure is the relief of obstruction to the urinary outflow. The bladder is catheterised in obstruction due to enlarged prostate or stricture of the urethra; ureteric catheterisation may relieve calculous anuria; lavage of the renal pelvis may clear obstruction due to sulphonamide crystals; finally, nephrostomy may have to be performed, sometimes on both sides.

Once the recovery from post-renal obstruction has been achieved, correction of the underlying cause must be carried out as soon as renal function returns to normal or near normal. If severe impairment persists it may be necessary for the patient to have permanent catheter drainage; for example, urethral catheter, suprapubic tube or nephrostomy drain.

Chronic Renal Failure

Chronic renal failure may be due purely to renal causes, as in chronic nephritis or to post-renal obstruction which, by its slow onset, has insidiously destroyed kidney function. When not severe, chronic renal failure can be managed conservatively by reducing the dietary intake of protein and increasing the intake of fluids. In severe cases two main methods can be used first, long-term haemodialysis with an artificial kidney, second by renal transplantation either from related donors or cadaveric kidneys. Haemodialysis is performed as often as necessary, usually two to three times a week. A silastic tube inserted into a peripheral artery and a vein forms an arteriovenous shunt that can simply be uncoupled and connected to the artificial kidney.

Hydronephrosis

Intermittent or partial obstruction to the outflow of urine from the kidney leads to distension first of the renal pelvis, then the calyces, later, thinning of the renal parenchyma leads to reduction of renal function. Eventually the kidney may be converted into a thin-walled functionless sac in which infection and stone formation are common sequels. Bilateral hydronephrosis may lead to renal failure and death unless the cause can be treated. In *renal hydronephrosis* the distension may mainly affect the calyces and renal substance, especially if most of the pelvis lies in the kidney itself (intra-renal pelvis). In *pelvic hydronephrosis*, as might be expected, the pelvis is mainly extra-renal and more dilated than the calyces. *Calycine hydronephrosis* is distension limited to one or more calcyces. In some patients dilatation of part or all of the ureter, *hydro-ureter*, is associated.

Pathology

The cause of most hydronephroses is not known. It is postulated in such cases that there is a congenital defect of neuromuscular transmission along the ureter or at the pelvi-ureteric junction, although no mechanical barrier exists; such hydronephroses are sometimes called *primary* or idiopathic. *Secondary* hydronephrosis follows mechanical obstruction. If the block is in the bladder or urethra the hydronephrosis will be bilateral. There are many causes of secondary hydronephrosis, including:

Renal. Calculus, tuberculosis, neoplasm of the renal pelvis. An aberrant renal artery to the lower pole of the kidney may constrict the pelvi-ureteric junction or be associated with a primary hydronephrosis.

Ureteric. Calculus, neoplasm, tuberculosis, external pressure by tumour, retroperitoneal fibrosis (p. 380).

Vesical. Neoplasm, diverticulum, calculus, ureterocoele (see p. 371), bladder contraction due to tuberculosis, irradiation or interstitial cystitis (see p. 381). Benign or malignant enlargement of the prostate, tumour of the bladder and obstruction at the bladder neck.

Urethral. Stricture, calculus, neoplasm and congenital valves (see p. 408).

Symptoms and Signs

Renal pain fixed in the loin or colicky is the usual presenting symptom of primary hydronephrosis. Attacks of nausea and vomiting may be confusing by suggesting a gastro-intestinal lesion. Haematuria and infection are common. Occasionally there are no symptoms, and during abdominal examination a large painless tumour is felt in the loin. The features of secondary hydronephrosis are those of the causative process, the kidney is unlikely to be palpable except in unilateral cases.

Investigations

Intravenous pyelography will demonstrate the degree of distension and the function of the kidneys. In primary hydronephrosis it may show established pelvic dilatation on one side and early pelvi-ureteric obstruction on the other. In advanced hydronephrosis no contrast medium may be excreted or poorly defined rounded calyces may be revealed after any time up to 2 hours. Where no shadow is seen in the affected kidney, or where the outline of the renal pelvis is poor, cystoscopy and retrograde catheterisation of the ureter is carried out. It is very important to use a scrupulous aseptic technique, for infection produces pyonephrosis, which may necessitate nephrectomy. Cystoscopy and pyelography may indicate the cause of secondary hydronephrosis. The urine should be examined for infection.

Treatment

The treatment of secondary hydronephrosis is obviously treatment of the cause of the condition. In primary hydronephrosis it is vital to preserve renal function as much as possible, because both sides are likely to become affected. Nephrectomy is only performed for the grossly diseased kidney with absent function. The ideal operation is partial resection of the renal pelvis and anastomosis of it to the ureter by a very wide stoma, an operation (Anderson–Hynes) which is extremely effective and carries a low failure rate. Eventually it may be necessary to operate on the other side; in all unilateral cases the apparently normal kidney should be observed carefully for the development of dilatation.

Ureterocoele and Mega-ureter

Ureterocoele

Ureterocoele is a congenital anomaly in which the ureteric orifices are stenosed and project into the bladder on the summit of an eminence of redundant mucous membrane. The ureter and renal pelvis may become dilated (hydroureter and hydronephrosis). The condition may be recognised in intravenous pyelograms, since it produces a typical filling defect in the vesical shadow. Cystoscopy confirms the diagnosis. The condition is very simply cured by slitting the meatus with a diathermy knife (meatotomc) to form a larger ureteric meatus.

Mega-ureter

Massive dilatation of the ureter is often bilateral and due to some neuromuscular defect in the lower end of the ureter or to ureteric reflux. It is often associated with stenosis of the bladder neck and occasionally urethral valves which require treatment. The ureters become very wide and tortuous, with associated hydronephrosis. Less often mega-ureter is an isolated defect of one ureter, with little dilation of the kidney. Mega-ureter is usually congenital, and often gives rise to symptoms in early childhood, for example infection, frequency, haematuria and enuresis. If the condition is bilateral it is usual to divide the ureters and re-implant them in the bladder, at the same time taking a wedge of muscle out of the bladder neck. In unilateral megaureter, re-implantation should be tried, but nephrectomy is necessary if there is gross disorganisation of the kidney. Mega-ureter is occasionally, though rarely, associated with Hirschsprung's disease (see p. 428).

Tumours of the Kidney

Renal-cell Carcinoma, Hypernephroma (Grawitz Tumour)

Renal-cell carcinoma is the commonest malignant tumour of the kidney. The term hypernephroma was given because the cells of the tumour resemble adrenal cells in being polygonal, clear and, on special staining, show much lipid in their cytoplasm. These cells are in fact renal tubular cells. Adults aged 50 and over are most commonly affected—men more often than women.

Pathology. The cut surface of the kidney shows a rounded and apparently encapsulated tumour, usually in the upper pole. It is typically golden yellow in colour, with areas of haemorrhage. It rarely invades the renal pelvis, but may compress it or splay out its calyces. The growth is very vascular, and processes of it may invade veins and even project from the renal vein into the inferior vena cava, from where tumour emboli may sometimes break off.

The tumour spreads locally and may invade the perinephric fat; lymph nodes in the fat and around the great vessels may be involved. Hypernephroma owes its poor prognosis to venous involvement and embolism, especially to the lungs, where it gives rise to typically rounded shadow in radiographs ('cannon-ball' secondaries). The liver and bones may be involved, metastasis may also appear in the supraclavicular lymph nodes from spread via the thoracic duct. Isolated secondary deposits in lung or bone sometimes appear years after the primary has been treated, and their removal is then well justified.

Microscopically a renal carcinoma consists of sheets of pale polygonal cells with small central nuclei. Attempts at tubule formation are seen in some areas, and occasionally a well-differentiated adenocarcinoma is found which can only be distinguished with difficulty from a benign adenoma.

Symptoms and Signs. Painless haematuria is a common presenting symptom, and demands full investigation; clots may give rise to colic. Pain in the loin also occurs, presumably the result of distension of the renal capsule. Very large tumours may be discovered by the patient himself before any other symptoms are produced. Usually the enlarged kidney can be palpated. The sudden appearance of a left-sided varicocoele is said to be a mode of presentation of hypernephroma, but it must be very rare, and indeed indicates that the tumour has invaded the left renal vein and obstructed the spermatic vein which joins it. The appearance of metastases in bone which are osteolytic and prone to undergo pathological fracture is an indication for pyelography in a search for a primary tumour. Renal-cell carcinoma commonly causes fever and may present as a 'fever of unknown origin'. Anaemia, loss of weight and malaise are often associated. Polycythaemia, due to erythropoitin secreted by the tumour, may be the *Plain XR* presenting feature, but disappears as soon as the tumour has been removed.

Diagnosis. Radiographs may show an unusual soft tissue mass in the loin, *IVP* occasionally with calcification. Intravenous pyelograms usually show a characteristic deformity of the calyces, which are pushed aside in the region of the growth. Filling defects in the calyceal pattern may be shown. Retrograde pyelography may be needed to confirm an abnormality *Aortography* shown in the intravenous pyelograms. To confirm the diagnosis, delineation of the renal vasculature by aortography shows the arteries feeding the *venous* tumour to be numerous and splayed out; characteristically there is pooling *lakes* of contrast medium in venous 'lakes' in the tumour. A cyst may give pyelographic abnormalities resembling a tumour, but aortography shows *cf.* that the cyst is avascular without venous pooling. *cyst*

Treatment. The kidney is removed through a loin incision unless the tumour is large, in which case either a transabdominal or a thoraco-abdominal approach is employed. Whichever route is used, wide exposure is essential for adequate removal. As soon as possible, the renal vessels are clamped to prevent tumour embolism. As much perinephric fat as possible is removed, together with any enlarged lymph nodes around the renal pedicle. If lymph nodes are involved it is usual to give a course of radiotherapy to the tumour site. Rarely an isolated distant metastasis may be removed with the prospect of long survival, especially if the interval between treatment of the tumour and appearance of the secondary deposit is protracted.

Most renal-cell tumours are highly malignant, and only one-third of those affected survive 5 years after surgical treatment. Venous and lymphatic involvement seriously decrease the chances of survival.

Nephroblastoma, Embryoma (Wilm's Tumour)

Nephroblastoma of the kidney is one of the few malignant tumours of children. It very rarely occurs over the age of 7 years. Very rarely it is bilateral.

Pathology. The origin of an embryoma of the kidney is undecided, but it very probably arises from mesonephric tissue. The kidney is enlarged, sometimes massive, and completely replaced by white tumour tissue in which there may be haemorrhage or cystic degeneration. It is very adherent to perinephric tissue and may cause ascites. Microscopically an embryoma appears to be a tumour of mesenchyme, with disordered masses of spindle cells, degeneration and haemorrhage. It is unlike a teratoma in not having elements of all three basic embryonic layers. The tumour grows rapidly and, in a small child, may become as large as its host. Tumour spread occurs early, both locally and by the blood stream.

Symptoms and Signs. Haematuria is a common presenting symptom, or the mother may feel a mass in the loin when bathing the child. Enlargement of the abdomen from a rapidly growing tumour may occur. The child soon becomes wasted and anaemic, often with high fever. Diagnosis is made by feeling the mass and the intravenous pyelogram which shows a large filling defect or absence of function on the side of the swelling.

Treatment. Treatment is nephrectomy; there is now evidence that if this is carried out as an emergency as soon as the diagnosis is made and followed by radiotherapy, the results of treatment are greatly improved. If the tumour is very large a pre-operative course of radiotherapy must be given to reduce the size of the tumour and to improve the general health of the child. The outlook in general is poor, but the introduction of Actinomycin D for the treatment of metastases has improved results in recent years.

Transitional-cell Papillary Tumours of the Renal Pelvis and Ureter

Papilliferous growths are found most commonly in the bladder but these tumours also occur in the renal pelvis and ureter. Those in the renal pelvis are very prone to spread by 'seeding' in the ureter and bladder. These transitional-celled tumours show all gradations from the frankly malignant to the purely benign; indeed, it may be difficult to say that a papilloma is benign. As in the bladder, all papilliferous tumours should be regarded as potentially malignant. It is possible, though not proven, that carcinogenic agents in urine may be responsible for papillomata in the kidney as they are in the bladder (see p. 384).

Haematuria is the commonest symptom. Pyelography shows a filling defect in the renal pelvis or hydronephrosis; sometimes defects in the ureter may be seen. Cystoscopy may show papillomata protruding from the ureteric orifice or in the bladder near to it. Nephro-ureterectomy is required, that is removal of the kidney, the whole of the ureter and occasionally diathermy of any papillomata in the bladder.

Squamous-celled Carcinoma of the Renal Pelvis

The presence of calculi in the renal pelvis for many years may induce first metaplasia of transitional to squamous epithelium, leukoplakia and, finally, the development of squamous carcinoma. The prognosis is poor because of local and distal spread. The kidney must, if possible, be removed and radiotherapy given postoperatively.

Benign Tumour of the Kidney

Benign tumours are rare and usually found at post mortem. Adenomas sometimes grow to large size and show cystic formation. They may be difficult to distinguish from carcinomas. Lipomas and fibromas rarely cause symptoms. Angiomas are rare, they may cause haematuria and often offer great difficulty in diagnosis, for there may be no pyelographic signs. Aortography may be of help. Cystoscopy at the time of bleeding is important in the hope of locating the side from which bleeding is occurring. When bleeding is severe or persistent nephrectomy should be performed.

Cysts

Polycystic Kidney

The cause of cyst development in the kidney is not really known, but it is suggested that in embryonic life there is a failure of fusion of the mesonephros and the duct system that grows up from the urogenital sinus. Both kidneys are affected, often asymmetrically. Massive enlargement of the kidneys at birth may cause difficulty in delivery. Usually the condition is not recognised until adult life, and cysts tend to grow progressively in size between areas of apparently normal-looking renal tissue. The cysts are lined by cubical epithelium and contain clear or bloodstained fluid. The spleen, pancreas and liver may also be affected.

Symptoms and Signs. Apart from severe renal impairment in childhood, most people with polycystic kidneys are unaware of them till adult life. In some, the condition is compatible with normal longevity and may only be found at post mortem. Common presentations are the discovery of large swellings in the abdomen, haematuria, hypertension and renal failure with uraemia.

Pyelograms show elongated spidery calyces, which are splayed out and narrow; sometimes rounded indentations of the renal pelvis and calyces can be seen. If renal function is poor, and especially if the blood urea is raised, retrograde pyelography may be necessary for the diagnosis.

Treatment. Nothing can be done to correct the condition. Puncture of the cysts at operation, Rovsing's Operation, has been practised in the past, but is of doubtful value, except in relieving pain. When chronic renal failure occurs, the protein intake should be restricted and fluid intake increased.

Solitary Cysts

Solitary cysts may reach a great size and be mistaken for tumours. The cysts are lined by flattened epithelium and are filled with clear fluid. They may cause aching pain or present without symptoms as an abdominal tumour. Pyelography may show a rounded filling defect in the calycine system or only a soft tissue shadow. Aortography is of great value in distinguishing a cyst from a tumour (see p. 357). Solitary cysts may be left, aspirated or excised, leaving that part of the cyst wall that is attached to the kidney.

Injuries of the Kidney

The kidney is usually injured by a blow in the loin or by crushing. Other viscera may be damaged, especially the liver and spleen. Penetrating wounds by a knife or bullet are likely to involve other organs as well as the kidney. The kidney may be bruised or contused, torn or even completely avulsed from its pedicle. If a tear goes into the calyces or renal pelvis haematuria will result. A large subcapsular peri-renal haematoma may produce a mass in the loin. If the peritoneum is injured blood in the peritoneal cavity may produce the signs of peritonitis.

N

Symptoms and Signs

Haematuria is the commonest symptom, it may be minimal or so severe as to require transfusion, or it may be intermittent over a period of 2 or 3 weeks. There is pain and tenderness in the loin, and if haemorrhage or extravasation or urine has occurred around the kidney a swelling may result in the loin. Shock and signs of internal haemorrhage may arise with severe bleeding. Evidence of other visceral injury must be sought for very carefully.

Treatment

Relatively few renal injuries require operative treatment. The patient is put to bed, carefully examined for associated injuries, including injuries to abdominal and thoracic viscera and to the spine and thoracic cage. The pulse and blood pressure are charted repeatedly and the urine observed for haematuria and consecutive specimens retained for comparison to see if bleeding is increasing or decreasing. Transfusion with blood is indicated if the blood pressure falls. As soon as possible an intravenous pyelogram is performed, not only to reveal the state of the injured kidney but also to establish that there is another functioning kidney without congenital anomalies. In minor injuries the pyelogram may be normal; in more severe injuries the calycine pattern may be distorted and in very severe injuries no contrast medium may be secreted on the affected side. Blurring of the psoas shadow may indicate a perinephric haematoma.

With rest and analgesics most patients show decreasing haematuria. Rest must be continued for 10–12 days, depending on the severity of the injury. Early rising is likely to be followed by recurrence of bleeding. Operation is indicated for suspicion of associated visceral injury. Persistent bleeding is an indication for transfusion. In most patients requiring operation bleeding is so severe and renal damage so great that nephrectomy is required. The approach is through the loin if the kidney alone is thought damaged, or through the abdomen if other visceral injury is suspected. It is wiser to operate and find no other injured organ than to leave a ruptured spleen or jejunum that will cause death. The intravenous pyelogram is repeated 2 or 3 months after the accident to assess the state of the kidney, as occasionally hydronephrosis may result.

Renal Hypertension

The commonest renal cause of hypertension is chronic pyelonephritis affecting both kidneys, for which no surgical procedure is of any avail. Hence the investigation of hypertension has as it main aim the detection of unilateral renal disease. Unilateral pyelonephritis produces a small contracted scarred kidney; often the kidney appears hypoplastic. Hypertension may follow long-standing hydronephrosis or calculous disease. It is also met in polycystic disease and radiation nephritis.

Among the many causes of hypertension, the part played by renal ischaemia has been increasingly appreciated in recent years. In animals constriction of the arterial supply to one kidney causes the release of an enzyme renin that activates plasma hypertensinogen to hypertensin, a substance that causes hypertension. This sequence of events has not been demonstrated in man, but there is no doubt that ischaemic kidneys cause hypertension in man and that in many cases removal of the kidney in cases of unilateral renal ischaemia or other disease reduces the blood pressure to normal. Stenosis of the renal artery is caused by atherosclerosis, and hyperplasia of the smooth muscle of the media.

Investigation

Any person developing hypertension under the age of 45 years should be fully investigated for a renal cause. Blood pressure should be recorded twice daily at rest to test the constancy or lability of the hypertension. General evaluation of the state of the cardiovascular system with electrocardiograms and retinoscopy is important. The urine should be repeatedly examined for cells, casts and protein. The blood-urea level is only raised when there is severe renal damage, and should be normal in those patients suitable for surgical treatment.

Intravenous pyelograms are important in showing structural lesions in the kidney, especially asymmetry in size and thinning or scars in the renal cortex. A diminution of only 1 cm. of vertical length of a kidney merits further investigation for ischaemia. Pyelograms of a kidney affected by renal artery stenosis also show differences in function: the excreted contrast medium on the affected side may be denser than its opposite, because an ischaemic kidney reabsorbs more water than normally. Its function is protected from the high blood pressure by the arterial stenosis.

Measurement of the volume of urine excreted by both kidneys and its electrolyte and urea content is performed by obtaining specimens of urine from both ureters after bilateral ureteric catheterisation. In unilateral renal ischaemia the volume of urine excreted is small, and its content of sodium and chloride lower, its urea content is higher.

When these investigations indicate the possibility of renal artery stenosis aortography should be performed to delineate the renal arterial supply. The radioisotope renogram may be a useful screening test because of its simplicity in the detection of asymmetrical renal function.

Treatment

Nephrectomy is employed for unilateral renal disease and reconstructive arterial surgery for renal artery stenosis, either by removal of the stenosis (endarterectomy) and vein patch or by-passing of it (spleno-renal anastomosis) or the use of a graft from the aorta to the right renal artery. At operation, biopsies of both kidneys are usually taken so that assessment of the degree of hypertensive changes or pyelonephritis can be measured. The results of operations for renal artery stenosis have not proved so long lasting as was originally expected. It is often difficult to be sure if the stenosis is an effect of hypertension or the cause of it. What is needed is a refined method of detecting pyelonephritis.

Congenital Abnormalities

Hydronephrosis (see p. 370)

Polycystic Kidneys (see p. 375)

Renal Ectopia

The kidney may be arrested at any phase of its ascent during foetal life from the pelvis to its final lumbar position. Such ectopic kidneys are often poorly developed and prone to complications, such as infection or stone. Ectopic kidneys often have short ureters and an abnormal arterial supply. In crossed ectopia both kidneys lie on one side.

Malformations

The commonest malformation is persistence of foetal lobulation; it is of no significance. One or both kidneys may be divided to a varying extent into two halves, for example there may be completely separate halves, or only the pelvis may be double. The ureters may be double joining at any point along their course or entering the bladder at separate places, usually the ureter of the upper half entering the bladder lower than the lower half. Occasionally a ureter may open ectopically, in the male as far down as the prostatic urethra and in the female in the vagina, where it may cause incontinence of urine.

Solitary kidney is uncommon. Usually there is another kidney, but it may be very rudimentary with or without a ureter. Hypoplasia may occur with deficient parenchyma; such kidneys are prone to infection and stone formation, and may be a cause of hypertension.

Fusion of the kidneys by their lower poles across the midline is called *horseshoe kidney*. Such kidneys lie low, their ascent being arrested at the level of the inferior mesenteric artery. Their ureters are often duplicated and the blood supply abnormal. In pyelograms horseshoe kidneys are seen to be low and their pelves point forwards and inwards. Occasionally one-half of a horseshoe kidney must be removed because of infection, hydronephrosis or stone. A discoid kidney is one in which both kidneys lie on one side fused in one single mass.

Supernumerary Vessels

The commonest supernumerary artery is an extra vessel that passes from the aorta to the lower pole of the kidney, often associated with hydro-nephrosis from pelvi-ureteric obstruction. Division of the artery is dangerous, because it is an end-artery and supplies a large segment of renal tissue. Usually a plastic operation on the renal pelvis is necessary to relieve obstruction (see p. 371).

Many congenital anomalies of the renal tract cause no trouble and can be left. Often, however, they are responsible for infection, obstruction and stone formation when, if possible, surgical correction should be carried out.

Moveable Kidney (Floating Kidney)

The kidney normally moves with respiration, and its mobility and position vary considerably in different individuals. In women, especially with advancing age, the right kidney can often be felt and even held down by its upper pole. In the past, fixation of the kidney (nephropexy) was performed for such symptoms as aching in the loins, nausea, vomiting and constipation. It is now recognised that such symptoms are unlikely to be due to hypermobility of the kidney, which is simply part of a generalised visceroptosis. Occasionally, however, obstructive symptoms do arise when the kidney intermittently falls and kinks the pelvi-ureteric junction. The renal pain due to this obstruction is relieved by rest and the passage of large volumes of urine (Dietl's crisis). In such rare cases nephropexy and denervation of the kidney pedicle to relieve pain is justifiable, though the results are unpredictable.

DISEASES OF THE URETER

Congenital lesions of the ureter have already been described on p. 371.

Trauma

The ureter may rarely be damaged by severe crushing injury. The most common injury is that caused accidentally by surgery. The ureter is particularly at risk in the operation of hysterectomy, especially where the ureter lies close to the vault of the vagina and is liable to be caught in ligature of the uterine artery. Injury from external trauma may cause haematuria or signs of urinary extravasation, extra-peritoneal or intra-peritoneal. If there are signs of peritonitis, then the abdomen must be explored and the ureter repaired if possible. Injury due to operation causes pain in the loin due to swelling of the kidney or the late development of a uretero-vaginal fistula. Pyelography is performed, followed by attempted passage of a ureteric catheter. By these means the diagnosis of injury to the ureter is established, and the level of obstruction.

If the injury is low in the pelvis, then the ureter may be divided and implanted into the bladder; at a higher level the ureter may be divided and anastomosed. Infection is a serious hazard in ureteric obstruction and, where the kidney is severely damaged, nephrectomy may be unavoidable. If both ureters are obstructed anuria results, requiring urgent laparotomy and bilateral implantation of the ureters into the bladder (ureteroneocystostomy). If the patient is seriously ill with uraemia emergency bilateral nephrostomy may have to be done.

Infection

Ureteritis may be part of a generalised urinary infection in which the ureter becomes dilated, especially in pregnancy. Tuberculosis causes a chronic infection that may persist until the ureter is removed. For this reason, when nephrectomy is performed for tuberculosis it is usual to remove the ureter as well (nephro-ureterectomy). Calculi may form in a chronically infected dilated ureter, which may reach a considerable size.

Tumours

Tumours of the ureter are usually papillomata or carcinomata seeded from a primary tumour in the kidney. Rarely primary tumours occur in the ureter. Because of the possibility of seeding of tumour cells, it is usual to perform nephro-ureterectomy for papillomata or carcinomata of the renal pelvis.

Retroperitoneal Fibrosis (Peri-ureteric Fibrosis)

The cause of retroperitoneal fibrosis is uncertain. It must be differentiated from infiltration by malignant disease in the retroperitoneal tissues. There is some evidence that retroperitoneal fibrosis is the result of an auto-immune reaction. Recently cases have been linked with the administration of a drug methysergide used for migraine. The ureters are gradually obstructed, so that a patient may present with unexplained uraemia and even anuria. Sometimes there is a history of back pain. An intravenous pyelogram may show hydronephrosis or non-function in the later stages. Retrograde ureteric catheters pass easily to the kidneys, but the pyelogram and ureterogram show functional obstruction, usually at the pelvic brim. The E.S.R. is often raised.

Idiopathic retroperitoneal fibrosis is amenable to surgery because the dense fibrosis surrounds, but does not adhere to, the ureter, which can therefore be dissected free. Recurrences have been recorded.

FURTHER READING

Textbook of Genito-urinary Surgery, (1961) edited by Winsbury-White, H. P., assisted by Fergusson, J. D., 2nd ed. Livingstone, London.

Chapman, T. L. (1959) *Urology in Outline*, E. & S. Livingstone.

Bergman, H. (1967) *The Ureter*, Hoeber, New York.

de Wardener, H. E. (1963) *The Kidney*, 2nd ed. Churchill, London.

Symposium on Renal Failure (1966) Brit. J. Urol., pp 605–684.

Gow, J. G. (1963) *Genito-urinary Tuberculosis*, Lancet, ii, 261.

Anderson, J. C. & Hynes, W. (1949) *Retrocaval Ureter*, 21, 209.

Williams, D. I. & Karlaftir, C. M. (1966) *Hydronephrosis Due to Pelvi-ureteric Obstruction in the Newborn*, Brit. J. Urol., **38**, 138.

Tumours of the Kidney and Ureter (1964) Vol IV of Neoplastic Diseases at Various Sites, ed. Sir Eric Richer, Livingstone, London.

CHAPTER TWENTY-SIX

BLADDER AND PROSTATE

THE BLADDER

CYSTITIS

Inflammation of the bladder occurs much more often in women than men, because it is so often associated with pregnancy and gynaecological disorders; in addition the female urethra is shorter and the urethral meatus more liable to trauma.

Pathology

The organisms most commonly responsible for cystitis are *Esch. coli*, streptococci, staphylococci, *B. proteus* and *B. pyocyaneus*, which may reach the bladder from infected urine excreted by the kidney, by blood-borne infection or by lymphatic spread from nearby organs. Sometimes they are introduced by the surgeon during instrumentation.

In acute cystitis the mucosa of the bladder is congested with scattered haemorrhages in the mucosa, with, in the most severe cases, ulceration and sloughing. Threads of mucus, pus and fibrin are seen adhering to the bladder wall. In chronic cystitis the mucosa is inflamed, and oedema may be seen with blebs and bullae, phosphatic deposits may be attached to the wall of the bladder. The urine may be opaque with pus. Chronic or recurrent cystitis is often secondary to causes such as stone, tumour, enlarged prostate or stricture of the urethra or some neurogenic defect affecting the bladder; a common cause in women is trauma, as in 'honeymoon cystitis'. In women also, cystitis may be associated with minor degrees of bladder-neck obstruction, chronic cervicitis and cystocele associated with vaginal prolapse, but in many cases no primary cause can be found. *Cystitis cystica* is a form of chronic cystitis in which there are multiple small cysts scattered throughout the mucosa of the bladder.

Chronic Interstitial Cystitis (Hunner's Ulcer)

This is a rare condition, virtually confined to women, in which the urine is usually sterile, but there is ulceration of the bladder mucosa and fibrosis of the muscle wall, leading eventually to contraction in the size of the bladder. The ulcers are small and very slow to heal. If they heal they cause more fibrosis and then tend to break down again. Other types of chronic cystitis include tuberculosis and bilharziasis.

Symptoms and Signs

In *acute cystitis* there is severe frequency of micturition and very often a constant urge to pass water. There may be strangury, that is a frequent desire to pass water, with only small amounts being painfully expelled. Pain and tenderness occur in the suprapubic region. Haematuria is common. The temperature may be raised. The urine contains pus cells, red blood cells and organisms. Complications such as retention of urine may occur should there be an associated obstructive condition, such as an enlarged prostate.

In *chronic cystitis* the main symptom is frequency of micturition. Pain and tenderness may be slight. In such conditions as Hunner's ulcer or tuberculosis, frequency is due to contraction of the bladder, which may eventually hold only 20–30 ml. or so of urine and lead to exhaustion of the patient from the constant need to pass water.

Treatment

Rest in bed is advised if the patient is febrile. Copious fluids should be taken with a mixture of potassium citrate to alkalinise the urine, traditionally hyoscyamus is given for spasm. A specimen of urine must be taken for identification of the causative organism and its sensitivity to antibiotics. Until the sensitivity tests are available, usually 24–48 hours after the urine has been cultured, a soluble sulphonamide such as sulphadimidine (0·5 g. 6 hourly), which is free of the danger of crystalluria or anuria, may be given and may be effective by itself. If symptoms persist, an antibiotic should be given, the choice depending upon the results of the sensitivity tests. The drugs commonly used for cystitis include ampicillin, nalidixic acid and nitrofurazone because cystitis is most commonly due to gram-negative bacilli which are penicillin resistant.

In chronic or recurrent cystitis the aim should be to treat the underlying cause if this can be ascertained, though acute flares of cystitis must be treated as described above. Interstitial cystitis may be treated by fulguration of ulcers by diathermy through a cystoscope and by gentle distension of the bladder to increase its capacity. If there is severe contraction and rigidity of the bladder its capacity may have to be increased by transplanting part of the sigmoid colon with its blood supply preserved to the fundus of the bladder (colocystoplasty). Alternatively, to relieve the severe frequency, both ureters may be transplanted into an isolated segment of ileum which opens as an ileostomy (ileal conduit).

Tuberculous Cystitis

The early and successful treatment of tuberculosis has reduced the incidence of this distressing condition. It is usually secondary to renal tuberculosis, but occasionally spread may occur from the epididymis or prostate. Severe bladder contraction may be a complication of the treatment of vesical tuberculosis, because the use of streptomycin may produce rapid healing with a great deal of fibrosis.

Pathology

Tubercles form under the vesical mucosa, usually first on or near the ureteric orifices. These tubercles may break down to form ulcers, and if the ulceration is extensive it is associated with fibrosis, which causes the bladder to become contracted and its capacity small, resulting in intense frequency of micturition, with pain and strangury. Tubercle bacilli and pus cells are found in the urine. Cystoscopy will reveal tubercles, very often around the ureters, and small ulcers in the bladder wall. In the early stages the ureteric orifices are oedematous, and small tubercles may be seen breaking down later to form ulcers. Later still the orifices become rigid, retracted and gaping—the so called 'golf-hole' ureters.

Treatment

The initial treatment of tuberculous cystitis is the same as that for renal tuberculosis (see p. 361). If as the bladder heals it becomes severely contracted with a small capacity, then plastic operations to increase bladder volume may be necessary. Such operations should only be performed when it is certain that active disease has been arrested.

Bilharziasis

Parasitic infestation by the *Schistostoma haematobium* occurs in the Middle East and in Africa, particularly in the Nile delta. The infection is water-borne by cisterciae, which swim in water and penetrate the skin, to pass into the portal and pelvic veins. Eventually eggs are formed which have a characteristic terminal spine. These lodge in the wall of the bladder, where they cause intense inflammatory changes, bulky granulation tissue and eventually malignant change. The earliest symptom is haematuria associated with increasing frequency of micturition, pyogenic infection and fistula formation into the colon.

The ova can often be seen on microscopy of the urine. Cystoscopy reveals chronic cystitis, with excessive granulations and bullous oedema. Where the *Schistostoma mansoni* is the cause of infestation, inflammation of the rectum and lower colon may also be found.

Treatment

Bilharziasis may be difficult to eradicate, but good results have been achieved with recent preparations of antimony, given intramuscularly. Operation to transplant the ureters may be necessary for chronic cystitis and also for the treatment of malignant disease of the bladder.

TUMOURS OF THE BLADDER

Transitional-celled tumours of the bladder mucosa are very common. Occasionally carcinoma may spread from the rectum or uterus to involve the bladder. There is an association between primary bladder tumours and certain carcinogens secreted in urine, especially in those who work with some aniline dyes (β-naphthol). Because of this association, certain chemicals are no longer synthesised in this country, including benzidine, which was once used medically to detect occult blood in faeces, is no longer available because of the dangers to those who make it. Those working with raw rubber, and in the manufacture of cables are especially at risk and must be warned to report haematuria and other urinary symptoms. The urine must be screened periodically for neoplastic cells.

Pathology

Most primary tumours of the bladder are papillomata or carcinomata. Papillomata show all degrees of differentiation; benign and malignant growths merge imperceptibly one into the other, so much so that many regard all papillomata as potentially malignant, especially if they are left to grow for any length of time, or if they recur after treatment. However, at the ends of the spectrum of growths there are many tumours which appear to be truly benign and others which are obviously malignant Microscopically, bladder tumours are either *papillary* or *solid*. Papillary tumours tend to be well differentiated, solid tumours are usually anaplastic. Occasionally squamous metaplasia may occur, giving rise to leukoplakia and squamous-cell carcinoma. Malignant growths at the base of the bladder are very rarely adenocarcinomata arising from the sub-mucosal tubular glands found in that region.

Papilloma

Papillomata are very common tumours, villous in appearance, with a delicate branching of fronds arising from a narrow stalk. The commonest site for a papilloma is immediately above and lateral to one of the ureteric orifices. They are often multiple and show a strong tendency to recurrence after removal. The microscopical structure is of transitional epithelium in branching fronds with a fine central connective tissue core.

Papillary Carcinoma

Carcinomata have a broader base with fronds that are shorter and thicker. Microscopy shows several layers of transitional epithelium with cells varying in size. With increasing malignancy there is an increasing degree of anaplasia on microscopy and appearance of mitotic figures. These tumours eventually infiltrate the bladder-muscle coat and involve the perivesical tissues and adjacent organs. More distant spread is slow and death from ascending urinary infection and haemorrhage occurs before organs such as the liver are involved.

Solid Carcinoma

Solid carcinoma is a nodular, often ulcerated, tumour with a surface frequently encrusted with phosphates. The edges of a malignant ulcer are rolled and everted. Growth is rapid, with early infiltration of the muscle coat, the perivesical tissues and structures on the pelvic wall, especially nerves; thus severe pain is a feature. Lymph nodes are involved, and blood-borne metastases in this type of tumour are more often seen than in the case of papillary carcinoma. Cystitis is more common, with solid tumours, and appears earlier in the disease than with the papilliferous type.

Tumours, particularly infiltrating tumours near the ureteric orifices, may lead to obstruction and hydronephrosis. Tumours near the internal meatus may cause retention of urine.

Sarcoma

This is extremely rare and is only amenable to treatment by radiotherapy after diagnostic biopsy.

Symptoms and Signs of Bladder Tumours

The earliest sign of bladder tumour is painless, intermittent, sometimes profuse, haematuria. Later, infection and spread of the malignant tumour cause frequency and pain. If pelvic nerves are involved pain may be severe and intractable. In the final stages anaemia and exhaustion arise from bleeding, constant pain and strangury.

Diagnosis

The earlier that tumours are diagnosed the more successful is their treatment. It is imperative that anyone complaining of haematuria should

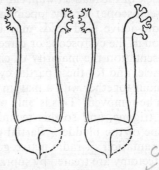

FIG. 35. Pyelographic picture of bladder neoplasm showing filling defect in bladder outline, complicated by left hydronephrosis.

Cystoscope

be examined with a cystoscope unless acute infection is present, when cystoscopy should be delayed until the acute phase has subsided. If a neoplasm is seen, its appearance is noted and a biopsy performed with special forceps or with a resectotome. A bimanual examination under anaesthesia is made with one hand on the bladder and a finger in the rectum or vagina to assess the extent of infiltration. Only malignant tumours can be felt. The urine is examined for evidence of infection. Intravenous pyelography is performed to assess renal function, to detect hydronephrosis and to reveal filling defects in the 'bladder shadow' (Fig. 35); occasionally a papilloma of the renal pelvis may be demonstrated.

BUA

IUP

Treatment

Bladder tumours can be excised, the operation being local, partial or total cystectomy. Bladder tumours may also be coagulated by diathermy or treated by irradiation with isotopes placed in the bladder or by external sources of radiation. Often two methods are used in combination.

Benign Papillomata

In the majority of cases papillomata can be treated by diathermy fulguration through a cystoscope; large tumours require several treatments at monthly intervals. Repeated cystoscopy must be performed later at increasing intervals. The patient can only be considered cured if free of tumour for at least ten years. Further fulgurations are carried out if the tumour recurs. If papillomata are too large for diathermy, or if there are several of them, it may be necessary to carry out suprapubic cystotomy and excise the growths down to the base with diathermy. Radioactive gold seeds or radioactive tantalum wires are then implanted into the wall of the bladder in the region of the base of the tumour. Diffuse papillomatosis involving the bladder wall can be treated either by instilling a cytotoxic drug such as thiotepa into the bladder lumen, 60 mg. once a week for about six weeks, or by total cystectomy.

Papillary Carcinoma

Papillary carcinoma in its earliest stages, when it has not infiltrated the muscle of the bladder wall, can be resected through an operating cystoscope (resectoscope) or by opening the bladder by suprapubic cystotomy. Radio-active gold seeds may be implanted into the tumour base either through the cystoscope or directly at open operation. At the time of their presentation the majority of carcinomata are already infiltrating bladder muscle, and for these partial cystectomy may be performed so long as the tumour together with a margin of at least 2 cm. of normal tissue around it can be removed. This is only possible if the tumour does not encroach on the trigone, and so this technique is usually reserved for growths in the dome of the bladder. Partial cystectomy is sometimes supplemented by implantation of radio-active gold seeds. Tumours unsuitable for partial cystectomy are treated by suprapubic cystotomy, diathermy excision of the tumour down to its base and, under the supervision of a physicist, a dose of radon or radio-active gold equivalent to 6,000–7,000 rads given by the use of a special gun which places the radio-active seeds at specified intervals. Alternatively, external irradiation may be given. Good results have followed this method of treatment with up to 50% of patients free of tumour for 5 years. When the growth has spread to perivesical tissues the treatment of choice, although only palliative, is irradiation by super-voltage X-rays. Total cystectomy is indicated for diffuse papillomatosis, for large tumours which are too large for excision and implantation of gold seeds and sometimes for deeply infiltrating tumours, often combined with pre- and post-operative external radiotherapy. Cystectomy may be needed for post-irradiation cystitis. The ureters are transplanted into a loop of ileum as a conduit or into the sigmoid colon. Lastly, palliative transplantation of ureters into the colon may be indicated in patients with severe symptoms and inoperable disease. In adults transplantation has the serious disadvantage of causing hyperchloraemic acidosis due to absorption of chloride from the urine by the colonic mucous membrane.

Solid Carcinoma

Solid carcinomata are treated in much the same way as the papillary type, except that resection through a cystoscope in early cases is not feasible. The prognosis for this type of growth is worse than for papillary carcinoma because of the early local spread of solid carcinoma, to lymph nodes and sometimes by the blood stream. When a patient has been treated for a bladder neoplasm it is essential that he should attend for regular cystoscopic examination so that any recurrence can be treated at the earliest possible time.

INCONTINENCE OF URINE

Incontinence of urine may be defined as involuntary micturition due either to abnormal detrusor action or defective sphincter function.

1. Active Incontinence

In bed-wetting or nocturnal enuresis there is abnormal detrusor activity. Boys are mainly affected, especially deep sleepers, who seem to have polyuria at night. The majority become continent spontaneously, but enuresis may continue until the early twenties. It is presumably due to some failure of neuromuscular co-ordination or development, and there may be psychological problems. Diurnal enuresis is less common and more suggestive of a urogenital lesion.

Treatment

A full physical examination must be made to exclude any abnormality of the genitalia, a palpable bladder or kidney, spina bifida or talipes equinus. The urine should be examined microscopically. If any abnormality is found, a rare event, pyelography and cystoscopy must be performed. The lumbar spine and sacrum should be radiographed to reveal any congenital abnormality.

Parents usually bring their children for treatment for bed-wetting round about the age of 5-6 years. Fluids should be restricted at night, and the child should be wakened at specific hours and trained to empty his bladder before it becomes too full. An alarm clock can be supplied which rings when the bed is wetted and produces a conditioned reflex associating a full bladder with an unpleasant noise. Dextro-amphetamine and ephedrine administered to prevent the child sleeping too deeply may occasionally help in the training. Imipramine (25 mg. at night) is often effective.

2. Passive Incontinence Due to Defective Sphincter Action

(a) *Paralytic*. Damage to the cauda equina from trauma, neurological disease, prolapsed intervertebral disc, spina bifida, inflammation and transverse myelitis may cause paralysis of the sphincter of the bladder. Urine constantly dribbles away, the bladder remaining empty and contracted. Paralytic incontinence must be distinguished from overflow continence (see below), in which the bladder is distended.

(b) *Mechanical*. A stone or growth at the neck of the bladder may rarely interfere with its function. An ectopic ureter may open directly into the vagina or prostatic urethra distal to the vesical sphincter.

(c) *Traumatic*. Damage to the urethral sphincter may follow operations for removal of the prostate gland and very occasionally after difficult labour. In most cases recovery occurs after a few weeks, during which there is partial continence. Vesical, urethral and ureteric fistulae are rare causes of incontinence. Such fistulae may be caused by injury from operation, parturition, tumour or granuloma.

Treatment

(*a*) Incontinence due to disease of the cauda equina or spinal cord, in which there is some hope of recovery (for example, fractured spine) is treated by insertion of a plastic indwelling catheter under the strictest aseptic conditions (see p. 487). Operation on the spine may be indicated urgently for relief of pressure on the cord, e.g. haematoma, tumour, abscess, disc protrusion or fracture dislocation. Where the damage is irrevocable or untreatable, as in some neurological diseases, most effects of trauma and in spina bifida, an incontinence appliance must be worn in which urine collects through a funnel into a bag strapped to the thigh. Occasionally in children a tube is inserted suprapubically and, to stop urine leaking from the urethra, the urethra itself is excised.

In lesions of the spinal cord which are irreversible a state of 'automatic bladder' should arise after a few weeks, in which the bladder can be stimulated to evacuate by some stimulus such as stroking the thigh or pressure above the pubis. So long as the lesion of the cord lies above the sacral segments, bladder reflexes are intact, and so is the sympathetic supply of the sphincter muscles, which may show increased tone out of balance with the detrusor. In such cases resection of part of the vesical sphincter by a perurethral operation may, paradoxically, improve micturition and automatism. In a minority of patients permanent catheterisation or suprapubic cystomy may be necessary.

(*b*) Mechanical incontinence is treated by removing the cause, for example excision of an ectopic ureter, with if necessary removal of part of a double kidney.

(*c*) Traumatic incontinence following prostatectomy usually improves spontaneously, recovery being aided by exercises and faradic stimulation of the sphincter. Rarely, however, it may be permanent, and an incontinence bag is then required. Stress incontinence associated with uterine prolapse may be treated by anterior colporrhaphy, a bladder sling or bladder-fixation operation. Urethral and vesical fistulae can be closed by operation; ureteric fistulae can be dealt with by transplantation of the affected ureter into the bladder or by removal of the kidney if it is grossly infected.

3. False Incontinence

When the bladder is chronically distended, large and atonic, urine dribbles away, a state called overflow incontinence. Enlargement of the prostate, stricture of the urethra and injury or disease of the spinal cord are common causes. The obstruction is slow and bladder distension painless and often unnoticed by the patient. The danger is deterioration of renal function to the point of severe uraemia; infection is especially likely if a catheter is passed.

Treatment

The cause must be treated, paying particular attention to strict asepsis and slow decompression of the bladder to prevent deterioration of renal function and haemorrhage.

RETENTION OF URINE

Retention of urine is inability to evacuate the bladder, and must be distinguished from suppression of urine or anuria when the bladder is empty.

1. Mechanical Obstruction

Bladder-neck obstruction due to benign or malignant prostatic enlargement and Marion's disease (fibromuscular hyperplasia of the bladder neck) are common causes. Rarely stone, growth or blood clot within the bladder may result in retention of urine. Urethral causes include a stricture, urethritis, stone or foreign body. Pressure outside the bladder may result in retention, the commonest cause being the retroverted gravid uterus; occasionally uterine fibroids, or an ovarian cyst may be responsible.

2. Neurological Causes

Spasm of the bladder sphincter after operation is a very common cause of acute retention after such operations as haemorrhoidectomy, hernia, pelvic and perineal operations. The spasm is frequently associated with pain; and if pain can be relieved micturition can usually be established. Chronic retention is often associated with diseases of the spinal cord such as tabes dorsalis, disseminated sclerosis, injury, inflammation and neoplastic deposits in the vertebrae. Occasionally hysteria may be associated with acute or chronic retention.

3. Atony of the Bladder

In aged persons the bladder may become distended probably from loss of function of the brain cortex and hence awareness of the distension. It is common in such persons after operation or severe illness and in men is often associated with some degree of enlargement of the prostate.

Symptoms and Signs

Acute Retention is rapid in onset and, except where a spinal cord lesion is the cause, is very painful. The distended bladder is easily felt and is very tender. In the elderly the commonest cause is prostatic enlargement, in the middle aged urethral stricture or fibrosis of the bladder neck; in young men urethritis or prostatic abscess may rarely be a cause. In women a retroverted gravid uterus or a fibroid impacted in the pelvis are the usual causes. In children balanitis may be associated with retention. Acute retention following an operation is probably the most common cause of all.

Chronic Retention is gradual in onset and is usually painless, though acute retention may supervene on a state of chonic retention and be very painful. The bladder is less tense than in acute retention; it is usually easily felt, and on occasions may reach above the umbilicus. When the bladder is greatly distended back pressure on the ureter and pelvis of the kidney may result in hydronephrosis and hydroureter, eventually leading to uraemia.

Treatment

It is always important to differentiate retention from oliguria and anuria; this is easily done by feeling an enlarged bladder or in its absence by passing a catheter. Where it is thought that retention is due to pain, as in postoperative retention, urethral or prostatic inflammation, balanitis, acute retention from prostatic obstruction without previous urinary symptoms, simple measures are worth trying, such as relief of pain by analgesics and a hot bath. Where no obstructive lesion is suspected the intramuscular injection of a cholinergic drug such as carbachol (0·25 mg. intramuscularly) should be tried.

(a) *Prostatic Enlargement.* Acute retention must usually be relieved by passing a Foley catheter, preferably of the polyethylene type, as a preliminary to prostatectomy within 48 hours. Strict aseptic precautions must be observed to avoid infection in the urinary tract. Some surgeons prefer to operate as an emergency to avoid infecting the bladder by catheter drainage, but only if renal function is unimpaired (as shown by good secretion of contrast medium in the pyelogram and a normal blood-urea level) and in the absence of any signs or symptoms of infection of the urine. If, for technical reasons, a catheter cannot be passed drainage can be established most conveniently and safely by suprapubic cystostomy performed under local analgesia using the Riches' type of tube and introducer (Fig. 36) or by insertion of a plastic catheter (Supracath). Sometimes, when retention has occurred as an isolated incident without previous urinary symptoms, a single catheterisation may re-establish micturition and delay the decision for operation for months or even years. When acute retention has supervened on chronic retention with uraemia prolonged catheter drainage, using either a polyethylene catheter or suprapubic drain, is required until the patient's general condition has recovered. This improvement may take weeks or months before the prostate or other cause of obstruction can be removed. In the very old and very unfit the patient may never become well enough for operation. In such

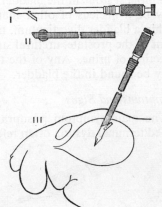

FIG. 36. Suprapubic cystostomy by Riches' method. (i) Riches' introducer; (ii) Self-retaining catheter; (iii) catheter and introducer inserted into bladder

patients suprapubic drainage may rarely have to be permanent with the wearing of a special appliance and the need for weekly bladder washouts to reduce the severity of infection.

(b) *Urethral Stricture.* Strictures can generally be dilated with bougies made of steel or gum elastic; sometimes only very fine filiform gum-elastic bougies can be passed, on to which can be screwed larger instruments. Rarely it may not be possible to pass a bougie, and then suprapubic drainage may be required; later when inflammation around the stricture has subsided it is usually possible to dilate the stricture or perform urethroplasty.

(c) *Acute Urethritis or Prostatic Inflammation.* Retention due to acute inflammation usually responds rapidly to antibiotics and analgesics. If the retention is very painful and passage of a catheter contra-indicated the bladder may be emptied once by suprapubic aspiration, using a lumbar-puncture needle.

(d) *Following Spinal Cord Injury*, retention is best treated with a fine polyethylene catheter of the Gibbon type attached to a closed drainage system.

It is safe to decompress the bladder suddenly in acute retention, but some surgeons still believe that in chronic retention decompression should be slow to avoid sudden deterioration in renal function and haemorrhage into the urinary tract.

STONE

Stone in the bladder is now rarer than in years gone by. It is still common in tropical countries. It occurs more often in men than women. In most instances the stone forms in the bladder itself, usually as a result of stasis from obstruction and infection; sometimes a foreign body forms the nucleus. Stones formed in the kidney may lodge in the bladder. The commonest stone in the bladder is made of phosphates, occasionally there may be a nucleus of other material such as oxalate. A stone may form within a bladder diverticulum, more often it is associated with an enlargement of the prostate, urethral stricture or other condition causing stasis or infection of urine. Any of the types of renal calculi mentioned on p. 363 may be found in the bladder.

Symptoms and Signs

The main symptom is suprapubic pain at the end of micturition, so-called terminal dysuria often referred to the tip of the penis, when the stone

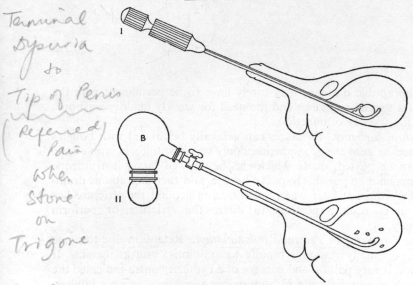

FIG. 37. Lithotrity; (i) stone grasped in lithotrite for crushing; (ii) Bigelow evacuator used to remove fragments of stone after crushing

presses on the sensitive trigone. Occasionally the flow of urine is intermittent, stopping and starting as the stone plugs the internal meatus. Terminal haematuria occurs in many patients. Frequency of micturition is worst during the day, but, when infection develops, occurs both day and night. Movement disturbs the stone, and so aggravates the symptoms, which therefore tend to be worse during the day than during the night. If the volume of residual urine is large the stone lies out of the main urinary stream, causing few or no symptoms. Rarely, retention of urine may result from impaction of the stone at the internal meatus.

Most bladder stones are radiopaque. At cystoscopy the number, size and the probable consistency of the stone can be determined. Pyelography and examination of the urine for infection must be performed.

Treatment

The best means of treatment is to crush the stone by a lithotrite passed into the bladder and to evacuate the fragments through a cannula by means of an evacuator (Fig. 37). Lithotrity cannot be performed if the stone is more than 4 cm. in diameter or if it is too hard or too soft. If the prostate is enlarged or a diverticulum or neoplasm of the bladder present, then the stone is removed at the time of operation for the primary cause. If the stone is not suitable for crushing, then it should be removed by suprapubic lithotomy.

Foreign Bodies in the Bladder

An astonishing variety of objects have been found in the bladder, ranging from candle wax to lead pencils. Around them stones rapidly form by the incrustation of phosphates. The symptoms are those of persistent severe cystitis, and the object may be seen in radiographs or at cystoscopy. Smaller foreign bodies may sometimes be removed through an operating systoscope, but often suprapubic cystotomy has to be performed.

DIVERTICULA

1. Acquired

By far the commonest type of diverticulum follows chronic obstruction to the bladder outlet by an enlarged prostate. A large, solitary diverticulum is usually associated with bladder-neck stenosis (Marion's disease). The wall of an acquired diverticulum consists of mucosa and fibrous tissue with a few muscle fibres. Usually it lies near one of the ureteric orifices; occasionally there may be several. Diverticula may be found at any age, but usually give rise to symptoms in adult life; they are rare in women. The bladder may become distended because of obstruction to its outlet, and there may be evidence of back pressure on the kidneys and ureters. Occasionally a single large diverticulum may obstruct a ureter.

Diverticula may cause no symptoms and only be found by chance. Usually they lead to chronic infection and even stone formation because of stasis of urine in the sac. Persistent pyuria suggests the possibility of a diverticulum, especially if it occurs after operation for removal of the prostate. Rarely, carcinoma or papilloma may grow in a diverticulum.

Intravenous pyelography and cystoscopy reveal the position and usually the cause of the diverticulum. If the bladder is filled with a radiopaque substance and radiographed in different planes (cystography) the size of the diverticulum can be gauged. Sacculation and trabeculation occurs in long-standing obstructions due to enlargement of the prostate, and one or more of the saccules may grow to a very large size, even bigger than the bladder itself.

Treatment

The cause of bladder-neck obstruction must be removed. Large diverticula should be excised, because they form a constant source of infection.

2. Traction Diverticulum

The bladder may extend alongside an inguinal or femoral hernia, where it may easily be damaged at operation for these conditions unless the surgeon takes care to avoid the inner aspect of the base of the sac.

3. Congenital Diverticulum

This is very rare. The wall of such a diverticulum contains muscle fibres in addition to mucous membrane and arises near a ureteric orifice. It is treated by excision.

INJURIES TO THE BLADDER

Injury to the bladder is uncommon but very dangerous because of infection due to extravasation of urine. The bladder may be involved by penetrating wounds or more often from direct violence to the lower abdomen, especially when the bladder is full. The commonest injuries are associated with fractures of the pelvis. Occasionally the bladder may be ruptured by instrumentation or by over-distension during cystoscopy. The rupture may be intra-peritoneal or extra-peritoneal.

Intra-peritoneal Rupture

This usually follows a blow on the lower abdomen when the bladder is full. Urine escapes into the peritoneum, causing severe peritonitis, which has a high mortality because the diagnosis is often delayed. There is shock, hypogastric pain, abdominal tenderness in the suprapubic region and signs of spreading peritonitis. Catheterisation may reveal little or no urine, and what is obtained is bloodstained. A cystogram is of especial value in aiding diagnosis. Treatment consists of urgent laparotomy, with suture of the tear and drainage of the bladder either suprapubically or by a catheter in the urethra.

Extra-peritoneal Rupture

This is almost always associated with major trauma, usually fracture of the pelvis. The tear is either on the anterior wall of the bladder or near its base. Urine escapes into the pelvic cellular tissues, where it causes severe cellulitis and suppuration. Symptoms and signs are the same as those of rupture of the intra-pelvic part of the urethra (see p. 406), shock, hypogastric pain and tenderness, but without evidence of peritonitis. Again, passage of a catheter may produce a little bloodstained urine or none. The danger here is from spreading pelvic cellulitis and suppuration. Treatment consists in exploration of the bladder, with suture of the tear if it is accessible. The bladder is drained, per urethram, by means of a catheter. The extra-peritoneal tissues are aspirated and drained. Broad-spectrum antibiotics (e.g. tetracycline) are given in the intravenous infusion and later by mouth.

VESICAL FISTULA

External Fistula

A suprapubic fistula may follow cystotomy, usually for removal of the prostate. Should it persist, the causes may be either scarring obstruction at the bladder neck or persistent urinary infection. Infection may fail to clear because of residual obstruction or the presence of a foreign body, e.g. a stone, or a new growth that may not have been found before operation. Once the track has become epithelialised, it will not close, except after formal excision of the track and closure of the bladder. A perineal fistula from the bladder may arise following perineal prostatectomy or after discharge or incision of a peri-urethral abscess. A fistula between the bladder and vagina may be a sequel to operations on the genital tract, or injuries sustained during parturition. It may complicate malignant disease or necrosis following excessive radium treatment for carcinoma of the cervix.

Internal Fistula

An internal fistula involving the bladder may be due to adherence of inflammatory granulomata or neoplasms of the gastro-intestinal tract, such as sigmoid diverticulitis, regional ileitis or carcinoma. The commonest fistula is one between the bladder and pelvic colon following diverticulitis or carcinoma. Symptoms of cystitis may be surprisingly absent, although gas and faeces are passed in the urine (pneumaturia). At cystoscopy there is severe cystitis, and it may be difficult to see the opening of the fistula, which is usually in the dome of the bladder; a cystogram may define the opening more clearly. If possible a biopsy should be taken from the edge of the fistulous opening at cystoscopy to establish the diagnosis.

Treatment

It is important to discover and treat the primary cause. Many patients with vesicocolic fistula due to diverticulitis have little trouble and can be left with it if they are old and frail so long as there is no chance of malignancy. Many are aged and unfit for operation. When operation is undertaken it may be performed in one stage or in two, the first being a transverse colostomy, the second closure of the fistula. In cases of diverticulitis the colon may be separated from the bladder, the bladder closed and the diseased segment of bowel removed. Where carcinoma of the colon is the cause, sigmoid colectomy and partial cystectomy is performed. If a growth has extensively invaded the bladder total cystectomy and uretero-colic anastomosis may be considered.

CONGENITAL ABNORMALITIES

Ectopia Vesicae

In this condition the anterior wall of the lower abdomen and bladder are deficient. Sometimes the pubic bones are widely separated and the posterior wall of the bladder bulges forward into the gap, exposing mucosa, from which urine constantly dribbles. The exposed vesical mucosa is subject to constant irritation and friction, it is vascular and ulcerates readily. Malignant change is a likely complication after many years of irritation. Boys are more commonly affected than girls, and the child walks with a characteristic waddle. Associated with this condition is epispadias, a congenital deformity of the penis, wherein the urethra is malformed, being split on the dorsal surface (see p. 408), the testes are usually undescended. Urinary infection is surprisingly uncommon, and the condition is compatible with long life although untreated.

Treatment

It is usual to wait until the child is four years old before transplanting the ureters into the pelvic colon. At a later date the remnant of the bladder is excised and the gap in the abdominal wall closed, the epispadias being repaired by a plastic operation. Children who have ureteric transplants into the colon tolerate the procedure much better than when the operation is done in adult life, when biochemical upsets are much more likely to occur (see p. 387). Attempts have also been made to reconstruct the bladder, when the shape of the defect is suitable, using flaps raised from the abdominal wall. Some of these patients are continent.

Persistent Urachus

Usually the allantois is converted into a solid cord stretching from the bladder at its apex to the umbilicus. It may, however, fail to close off in varying degrees. Complete failure results in urine escaping in the region of the umbilicus. If the lower end of the track remains patent, then a diverticulum of the bladder forms. If the intermediate portion remains patent a urachal cyst results. Suppuration may occur, and an abscess may form. Treatment involves excision of the allantoic remnant.

THE PROSTATE

Hyperplasia of glandular? muscular?

BENIGN ENLARGEMENT OF THE PROSTATE

Adenoma

The cause of benign enlargement of the prostate is unknown. Hyperplasia of glandular and muscular tissue in the prostate forms an adenoma, which, as it increases in size, compresses the surrounding normal glandular tissue into a false capsule. When the adenoma is enucleated surgically it is removed within this plane of compressed normal glandular tissue. The lateral lobes of the prostate enlarge in a postero-lateral direction, bulging into the rectum and compressing the urethra from side to side. In addition, the direction of the urethra becomes more convex posteriorly. As the middle lobe of the prostate enlarges it grows upwards into the bladder between the internal sphincter and the internal meatus. Middle-lobe enlargement without lateral-lobe enlargement may occur.

The prostatic urethra becomes elongated and distorted. The act of micturition is interfered with, so that there is difficulty in emptying the bladder. The bladder muscle first becomes hypertrophied, later there is trabeculation and sacculation. As the prostate grows upwards into the bladder a pouch forms behind it, interfering with the mechanism of the bladder neck and leading to incomplete emptying of the bladder. The voluntary effort of bladder emptying leaves a volume of urine, *residual urine*, which cannot be voided because of the intravesical projection of the prostate. In this stagnant pool of urine infection frequently occurs and stones may form. Prostatic obstruction causes bladder enlargement and ureteric obstruction going on to hydro-ureter and hydro-nephrosis, eventually leading to renal failure.

Symptoms and Signs

The first symptom is usually difficulty in micturition, especially in starting the act. The stream is poor in calibre, and there may be terminal dribbling. Frequency of micturition occurs and, as time passes, those affected have to get up during the night to pass water. As the difficulty increases, so the residual urine accumulates, until a state of chronic retention, with overflow and dribbling incontinence, arises. Acute retention may occur, often provoked by alcohol, cold or inability to pass water for some social reason. Haematuria rarely occurs; it is profuse. Infection may be followed by increasing frequency of micturition both by day and by night. Occasionally stones may form in the bladder. In advanced cases there is increasing back pressure on the kidney, with symptoms and signs of uraemia.

Diagnosis

Enlargement of the lateral and posterior lobes of the prostate is felt by rectal examination, when a firm, smooth and usually symmetrically enlarged gland can be felt. The size of the prostate can only be assessed when the bladder is empty. A distended bladder pushes the prostate back and gives a false impression of its size. It is important to remember that if enlargement of the prostate is confined to the middle lobe rectal examination may disclose no abnormality. Cystoscopy under such conditions is essential to disclose middle-lobe enlargement and such complications as stone, diverticulum and neoplasm. Cystoscopy is usually only performed immediately prior to prostatectomy to avoid the risk of introducing infection and of causing oedema leading to acute retention.

The investigations which must be performed in suspected prostatism include microscopy and culture of the urine, radiographs of the spine and pelvis (to show neoplastic involvement) and intravenous pyelography to reveal the anatomy and function of the kidneys and to detect stones in the kidney or bladder. The volume of residual urine is assessed roughly by the amount of contrast medium left in the bladder during intravenous pyelography after the patient has tried to empty his bladder. The level of blood urea is estimated and serum acid phosphatase measured for the detection of carcinoma of the prostate. Cystoscopy is carried out immediately prior to operation.

Treatment

Operation is indicated for increasing difficulty in passing urine, a large volume of residual urine and impairment of renal function as judged by a raised blood urea or poor renal secretion in the intravenous pyelogram or hydronephrosis. One or more attacks of acute retention necessitate operation, especially if there is a previous history of difficulty in micturition, urinary infection, haematuria or epididymitis.

In acute retention the bladder is usually emptied by means of an indwelling urethral catheter; a Riches' suprapubic cystostomy (see Fig. 36) may be necessary if this fails. The urine is examined for infection, the blood urea measured and intravenous pyelography performed before operation. The optimum conditions for prostatectomy are a sterile urine, a normal level of blood urea and a pyelogram revealing good renal function without hydronephrosis. Under such conditions, if the patient's general condition is satisfactory, prostatectomy should be carried out within 24–48 hours, for the longer the interval after catheterisation, the greater is the danger of infection. If there are clinical signs of renal failure, including a level of blood urea of more than 50 mg. % or poor renal secretion or urinary-tract dilatation in the intravenous pyelogram, then a period of urethral or suprapubic drainage is indicated before an operation. Improvement is accompanied by fall in the level of blood urea and amelioration of the general condition. Infection must be treated and prevented by the administration of sulphonamides or antibiotics. If renal function is severely impaired, then vesical drainage may be prolonged for weeks or months until the patient's condition has improved. Occasionally the blood urea falls, but never reaches the normal level. In such cases if the general condition is satisfactory, then operation may be performed accepting the extra risk. In a small number of patients suprapubic cystostomy may be necessary, and in this group a few may never become fit enough for removal of the prostate because of uraemia, cardiovascular or pulmonary disease. However, in the great majority of patients prostatectomy in one stage can be performed successfully even in the very old.

Types of Prostatectomy

Retropubic Prostatectomy

The prostate is approached extraperitoneally via a suprapubic incision through the cave of Retzius, the potential space between the back of the pubis and the bladder. The capsule of the prostate is incised transversely and the adenoma enucleated from within the false capsule. A V-shaped wedge is cut from the bladder base between the ureteric orifices to prevent the formation of a stricture at the bladder neck. A self-retaining urethral catheter is then passed into the bladder and the capsule of the prostate closed. A drain is inserted into the retropubic space. Catheter drainage is maintained for 3–4 days until the urine is free of blood.

Transvesical Prostatectomy

In Freyer's operation the bladder is exposed extraperitoneally through a suprapubic incision. The bladder is opened and a finger inserted to burrow through the mucosa of the bladder neck to shell out the prostatic adenoma from its false capsule. The bladder is drained by a urethral catheter for 7–10 days. In Harris' modification of this operation the bladder is more widely opened. Bleeding from the prostatic bed is controlled under direct vision by diathermy and by the insertion of haemostatic sutures at the bladder neck, for which a special instrument, the 'boomerang needle', is used. The bladder is closed and drained by a urethral catheter. In all these operations a wedge is removed from the posterior lip of the prostatic cavity to avoid obstruction developing due to subsequent fibrosis. When there is urinary infection or severe renal damage a suprapubic drainage operation may be necessary before removal of the prostate as a secondary operation.

Trans-urethral Resection

Trans-urethral operations are usually performed for moderate enlargement of the middle and lateral lobes of the prostate, fibromuscular bladder-neck obstruction, carcinoma of the prostate and the calculous prostate. Special operating cystoscopes are used with which the hypertrophied gland can be removed piecemeal with a diathermy 'hot' loop or a 'cold punch'.

Postoperative Complications

The mortality of prostatectomy varies from 5 to 10%, depending on the age and the general health of the patients treated and the skill of both surgeons and nurses in the postoperative period. Most important is the postoperative nursing care in dealing with reactionary and secondary haemorrhage, retention of urine due to blood clot in the bladder and infection. Many patients are partially incontinent for a few weeks after the operation, but very rarely is this incontinence permanent. Incontinence is due to traction on the membranous urethra during the removal of the prostate and interference with the sphincter of the bladder.

Ligation of the vasa deferentia is often performed before starting the prostatectomy because this decreases the risk of epididymitis caused by infected urine passing up the vas from the bladder, a very painful and unpleasant postoperative complication.

CARCINOMA OF THE PROSTATE

The incidence of carcinoma of the prostate increases with age, but some prostatic carcinomata occur at an earlier age than it is usual to see benign hypertrophy of prostate. It may be occult and only found in specimens removed at prostatectomy or post mortem. Carcinoma is the cause in about 20% of patients suffering from prostatic obstruction.

Pathology

Carcinoma arises in the "posterior lobe" of the prostate, that is in the part below and behind the level of the ejaculatory ducts. The disease spreads directly through the capsule of the prostate and involves surrounding structures, including the rectum. It spreads readily via the pelvic veins, particularly to the pelvic bones and to the vertebrae. Iliac and sometimes even the inguinal lymph nodes may be involved. Microscopically adenocarcinoma may be found with well-formed acini. Usually the growth is less well differentiated and may contain a great deal of fibrous tissue.

Symptoms and Signs

The symptoms are the same as those of benign hypertrophy of the prostate. Rectal examination reveals a hard nodular gland which may be fixed to the overlying rectal mucosa. Radiographs of the spine and pelvis may reveal metastases which have not given rise to symptoms; pathological fracture may be the first indication of prostatic carcinoma. Bone pain or sciatica may arise when the pelvis and vertebrae are involved. Carcinoma may only be diagnosed at operation for benign hypertrophy when difficulty is experienced in removal of the gland. Occasionally it is only on histological examination of a prostate gland removed by operation that a latent focus of malignant disease is found. The serum acid phosphatase is diagnostic of carcinoma if it is raised above the normal value of three King–Armstrong units. Sometimes the diagnosis can be confirmed by prostatic massage and examining prostatic secretion thus expressed from the urethra for malignant cells. A prostatic biopsy should be obtained whenever the rectal findings are suspicious (resectoscopic or needle biopsy). Secondary deposits in bone from carcinoma of the prostate must be differentiated (in radiographs) from Paget's disease of bone and deposits from other carcinomas that spread to the skeleton, i.e. breast, lung, thyroid, adrenal and kidney.

Treatment

In many cases those affected are aged and unfit, and in the vast majority of patients the disease is too advanced for radical cure by total prostatectomy. Such patients are treated with oestrogens. Most tumours regress or are arrested by administration of stilboestrol in doses of 100 mg. a day; occasionally larger doses may be required. Subcapsular removal of the testes is of value when the disease appears to be resistant to stilboestrol. With hormone treatment the prostate becomes softer and may revert to a normal size, secondary deposits become painless and may heal. In many patients there is definite prolongation of life, but in most the growth eventually escapes hormonal control and grows again.

If urinary retention is present, then the patient is catheterised and every precaution taken to prevent infection of the urine. Under treatment with large doses of oestrogens the majority of patients are able to pass their urine successfully after some weeks as the prostate shrinks in size. However, if the obstruction persists, transurethral resection of the prostate is indicated.

BLADDER-NECK OBSTRUCTION

Occasionally the symptoms of prostatism occur without enlargement of the prostate ('prostatisme sans prostate'). Marion's disease, or obstruction of the bladder neck, affects relatively young men and is due to hypertrophy of muscle and fibrosis of the posterior lip of the internal meatus, a change that is possibly congenital in origin. In some there is hypertrophy of glandular tissue deep to the mucosa of the bladder neck. At cystoscopy prostatic enlargement is absent, but the bladder neck is narrowed, and there may be a prominent bar of tissue in the bed of the internal meatus. Obstruction may also be due to fibrosis and calculus formation in the prostate.

Symptoms and Signs

In the congenital form there is often a long history of difficulty in micturition identical to prostatism, except that it occurs in a rather younger age group and occasionally in women. Diverticulum of the bladder is commonly associated and, with the passage of time, dilatation of the upper urinary tract.

Diagnosis

The association of symptoms of urinary obstruction in the absence of enlargement of the prostate and the absence of the enlargement of the middle lobe of the prostate on cystoscopy are diagnostic of bladder-neck obstruction.

Treatment

Resection of the posterior part of the internal meatus may be performed transurethrally or by open operation, at which the bladder is opened and a wedge of the posterior lip of the internal meatus is excised.

ACUTE PROSTATITIS

Prostatitis may be a complication of urethritis, follow instrumentation or arise for no known reason, possibly by blood-borne infection. Among the causative organisms are *N. gonorrhea*, *Esch. coli* and *Staphylococcus aureus*. Staphylococcal infection may be complicated by abscess formation.

Symptoms and Signs

Prostatitis causes pain in the perineum, frequency of micturition and pain on defaecation. Occasionally, if there is gross swelling of the prostate, difficulty in micturition or even acute retention may occur. Rectal examination reveals the prostate to be enlarged and very tender with softening if suppuration has occurred.

Treatment

The urine and any urethral discharge should be examined microscopically and bacteriologically. Chemotherapy is commenced using penicillin and streptomycin until the organism is found and its sensitivity to antibiotics ascertained. Hot baths and morphine are comforting, especially if there is difficulty in passing urine. Should an abscess form, then it may be drained into the posterior urethra using a urethroscope, or through a perineal incision.

CHRONIC PROSTATITIS

Chronic prostatitis is often a sequel of urethritis. The symptoms are aching pain in the perineum and frequency of micturition, sometimes with recurrent urinary infection. The prostate is enlarged, firm and often tender. Calculi may form in the prostate and be revealed in radiographs. The urine may contain mucous threads, and there may be a glairy discharge from the urethra. Fluid obtained by prostatic massage should be examined for pus cells and organisms.

Treatment

Appropriate chemotherapy is given. Prostatic massage and short-wave diathermy may be of help. Sometimes the condition is resistant to treatment and may continue for a long time.

TUBERCULOUS PROSTATITIS

Tuberculous prostatitis is almost always associated with tuberculosis elsewhere in the genito-urinary tract, and so a full investigation for urogenital tuberculosis must be carried out in any case of chronic prostatic disease. It is usually found in association with disease of the epididymis and seminal vesicles. The prostate becomes nodular and firm, exceptionally a cold abscess forms. The treatment is that for any form of urogenital tuberculosis (see p. 361).

PROSTATIC CALCULI

Prostatic calculi are usually associated with chronic prostatitis, in which deposits of calcium carbonate form in the follicles of the gland. There may be no symptoms, and calculi may only be found accidentally in radiographs. The calculous prostate is usually diagnosed during the investigation of symptoms of prostatism which they may cause. The prostate is speckled with calcification, which can be seen in plain radiographs. Treatment is usually required for symptoms of bladder-neck obstruction, and the best treatment is perurethral resection of the prostate. Occasionally the gland is best dealt with at open operation, when a wedge of the bladder neck is removed and any calculi scraped out.

URETHRA

URETHRITIS

Urethritis is usually due to gonorrhoea (see p. 68), instrumentation of the urethra or non-specific causes (see p. 69). Probably the commonest cause of urethritis nowadays is the presence of an indwelling catheter for the relief of retention of urine. To avoid it the catheter should not be too large, should be made of non-irritating plastic and inserted under scupulous aseptic conditions. It is largely with the complications of urethritis that the surgeon has to deal.

STRICTURE

Stricture of the urethra follows trauma, inflammation or congenital meatal stenosis. Strictures in women are very rare.

Pathology

Inflammatory Stricture follows gonoccocal urethritis or urethritis due to the presence of an indwelling catheter in the treatment of retention. A stricture may occur anywhere in the urethra, but common sites are the fossa navicularis, the penile urethra and the membranous urethra.

Traumatic Stricture follows healing of a ruptured urethra either in the bulb or in its intrapelvic part (see p. 406). Sometimes it occurs following damage due to the passage of a large instrument such as a resectoscope. The commonest form now seen in surgical practice is that following prostatectomy where damage to the membranous urethra has occurred.

Congenital Stricture or stenosis occurs at the external urethral meatus, and is cured by dilatation or urethoplasty.

Congenital or traumatic strictures are usually short. Inflammatory strictures are usually tortuous, and may often be multiple. The urethra proximal to a stricture becomes dilated, and the dilatation may extend to the bladder, ureters and kidneys; urinary infection is very likely to complicate obstruction. A peri-urethral abscess may form around a stricture and, discharging into the perineum, cause a urinary fistula. Such fistulae may be multiple and extensive, forming the so-called 'watering-can perineum'.

Symptoms and Signs

The main symptom of stricture is difficulty in passing urine; infection causes pain and frequency. Acute retention may occur particularly after exposure to cold or alcoholic excess. Chronic retention is unusual unless there has been long-standing obstruction.

The diagnosis is made from the history and by feeling the stricture in the perineum or with a sound. When a sound is passed it is gripped by the narrowed urethra, on which it grates in a characteristic fashion. With skill most strictures can be passed, but some are impassable. Force must be avoided in bouginage, or false passages, or even rupture of the urethra with urinary extravasation, may be caused.

Treatment

Dilatation. Most strictures can be dilated by passing graduated steel sounds of the Lister type; if there is difficulty, then flexible gum-elastic bougies are tried. Filiform bougies may be all that can be passed; on these fine instruments larger gum-elastic bougies can be screwed to allow the stricture to be dilated, the filiform acting as a guide. The stricture is gradually dilated until a size 14–16 English sound can be passed. Subsequently, the patient attends regularly at intervals for dilatation; these intervals are progressively increased from weeks to months. The frequency of dilation varies from patient to patient, depending upon how resilient the stricture is and how fast it contracts. Most dilatations can be carried out under local analgesia in the Out-patient Department. Occasionally flares of urinary infection and even septicaemia may follow dilatation.

Urethrotomy. If the stricture contracts rapidly after dilatation a grooved guide can be passed through the stricture and, within the groove, a guarded knife to cut it—*internal urethrotomy.*

If the stricture is impassable, then a sound is passed as far as the stricture and an incision in the perineum made down to its tip just anterior to the stricture. A probe-pointed director is then passed through the stricture under direct vision so that it can be divided—*external urethrotomy*. A soft indwelling catheter is then left in the urethra and the perineal wound allowed to heal by granulation. Regular dilatations are then carried out.

In a few cases where the stricture is very short it may be possible to excise it and to approximate the urethral ends. Usually only the roof of the urethra is repaired, and the wound is left open to fill in gradually by granulation tissue and epithelium from the adjacent urethral mucosa. Unfortunately operations for stricture are liable to be followed by recurrence.

Urethroplasty is employed for intractable and multiple penile strictures. In the first stage of the operation the urethra is opened through the perineum proximal to the stricture to allow a perineal urethrostomy to be formed. Three months later the stricture is excised and a roof to the urethra formed by a strip of skin which is buried and grows to line the new urethra. This operation is similar to that performed for hypospadias in children (Denis Browne).

PERI-URETHRAL ABSCESS AND FISTULA

A peri-urethral abscess may discharge or require incision and drainage. In either case a urinary fistula may form. Once the inflammation has settled, then the stricture associated with it must be regularly dilated or treated by urethroplasty. If acute retention occurs, then suprapubic cystotomy may be necessary.

RUPTURE OF THE URETHRA

The danger of rupture of the urethra is in the first instance due to extravasation of urine and later due to urethral stricture. Rupture practically never occurs in women.

Rupture of the Anterior Urethra

This occurs usually in the bulbous urethra and follows an injury to the perineum after a fall astride an object or a kick in the perineum. There is perineal haematoma, discharge of blood from the urethra and usually retention of urine. Extravasation of urine occurs if the patient attempts to pass water. Extravasation is limited posteriorly by the attachment of the triangular ligament to the perineal body, and so urine passes forward into the scrotum and penis and upward on to the anterior abdominal wall. Laterally it is prevented from passing into the thigh by the attachment of the superficial to the deep fascia in the thigh lateral to the pubic tubercle.

Treatment

Bleeding from the urethra following injury necessitates an attempt at passage of a catheter, but only in an operating theatre where preparations have been made for an operation should the catheter not pass. If the catheter passes, incomplete rupture is diagnosed and the catheter is left in for 5 days; infection being guarded against by use of sulphonamides and antibiotics. If there is a large perineal haematoma this must be drained and the wound left open to granulate. If the catheter does not pass, the perineum is explored and suprapubic cystotomy performed. In the perineum the two ends of the urethra are identified if necessary by passing two catheters, one from the urethral meatus and one retrogradely from the bladder. The two ends of the urethra are approximated in the roof by catgut sutures and a catheter left in the urethra while the bladder is drained suprapubically. The perineum is then left open to granulate. Some degree of urethral stricture must be anticipated and treated by regular urethral dilatation.

Intrapelvic Rupture of the Urethra

Rupture of the membranous urethra is usually associated with fractured pelvis, rarely with instrumentation. In any fracture of the pelvis the urine should be examined for blood and, if the patient cannot pass water, a catheter should be introduced in the operating theatre. In intrapelvic urethral rupture the signs and symptoms are as for extraperitoneal rupture of the bladder (see p. 394).

Treatment

A catheter should be passed under sterile conditions in the operating theatre. If the catheter does not pass into the bladder a suprapubic cystotomy is performed and a sound is passed through the internal meatus until it meets a sound passed from the urethral meatus. When the tips of the instruments are approximated the urethral sound can be threaded into the bladder and a rubber catheter attached to it. The catheter is then pulled retrogradely from the bladder into the urethra, where it acts as a splint and approximates the torn ends of the urethra. Continuous traction is exerted on the catheter to keep the two ends of the ruptured urethra as close together as possible. Vesical and retropubic drainage is established. Once the urethral damage is repaired the fractured pelvis must be treated (see p. 488). Following rupture of the urethra a stricture of some degree must be expected, so it is essential to carry out dilatation with sounds at increasing intervals.

STONE AND FOREIGN BODIES

A stone or foreign body may become impacted in the urethra, sometimes behind a stricture, causing pain, difficulty or even retention of urine. A stone in the posterior urethra can often be pushed into the bladder, where it can be treated by crushing. If the stone is in the anterior part of the urethra, then it may be extracted by means of forceps after enlargement of the external meatus. Removal by external urethrotomy may have to be performed if the former methods are unsuccessful.

TUMOURS OF THE URETHRA

Tumours of the urethra are rare. They cause pain and bleeding, and sometimes a swelling or hardness can be palpated along the course of the urethra.

Papilloma

This may arise secondary to papilloma in the bladder. *Carcinoma* is rare, and may occur in association with a stricture of the urethra. Secondary deposits from bladder carcinoma may seed in the urethra.

Treatment

Urethroscopy and sometimes urethrography may help in the diagnosis. A biopsy must be taken. Papillomata can be fulgurated, but for carcinoma partial or total amputation of the penis must be performed. In women it may be necessary to carry out cystectomy with excision of the urethra. Many of these growths are inoperable, and palliation with radiation is all that can be offered.

CONGENITAL ABNORMALITIES

Hypospadias

If the genital folds fail to fuse normally the urethral orifice may come to lie proximal to its normal situation, most commonly at the base of the glans penis, but it may lie anywhere along the undersurface of the shaft, and may be as far back as the root of the penis. In the grossest degrees of failure of fusion there may be a bifid scrotum, and it may be difficult to decide the sex of the child, so-called female pseudo-hermaphroditism. The prepuce is characteristically hooded, being deficient on the under surface, so that when it is picked up and stretched it forms a large roughly quadrilateral sheet. In the grosser types of hypospadias the testes may be undescended. The penis in hypospadias frequently shows ventral curvature due to fibrosis of the corpus spongiosum, which, if untreated, may cause chordee in adult life, that is curvature of the erect penis.

Treatment

Most operations on the penis are best deferred until the child is 3 or 4 years of age, as the tissues are then easier to handle, the patient more co-operative and likely to be continent both by day and night. If chordee is present this is treated first by dividing all the tissues on the ventral surface transversely just in front of the urethral opening, wherever that may be. The wound is closed longitudinally and the urethral opening displaced even farther backwards.

o

If the opening of the urethra is on the glans it is slit open to make it into a common opening with the blind fovea at the tip. This simple operation, is completed by securing the cut urethral lining to the skin surface on each side to prevent subsequent stenosis of the opening. A good forward stream is obtained by this technique.

If the opening of the urethra is on the distal part of the shaft of the penis, Ombrédanne's method of raising a purse of skin is employed, and the hooded prepuce then mobilised to cover the raw area. When the opening of the urethra lies proximal to the glans penis Denis Browne's operation is used. First, the urinary stream is diverted by means of a perineal urethrostomy. Secondly, a strip of skin is buried beneath lateral skin flaps. The buried skin grows to form a new urethra. Lastly, the perineal urethrostomy is allowed to close.

Epispadias

Episadias is the reverse of hypospadias, for the urethral orifice opens on the upper surface of the glans penis, which is usually split longitudinally. The urethral orifice may lie just behind the glans or in the body of the penis. Often there is simply a wide gutter along the whole of the length of the penis associated with ectopia vesicae and agenesis of the pubic bones, which are widely separated.

Treatment

Minor degrees of epispadias can be helped by plastic operations using skin tunnels. When the condition is associated with ectopia vesicae, as it often is, the treatment is usually carried out in two stages. In the first the ureters are transplanted into the colon, and in the second the defect in the anterior abdominal wall is repaired after excising the bladder.

Posterior Urethral Valves

This rare congenital abnormality of males produces a huge thick-walled bladder, bilateral hydroureters and hydronephrosis in the new-born. Treatment consists of decompressing the bladder and then excising the valves. The latter may be possible through a urethroscope, but good results have followed a direct attack on the bladder neck and urethra after dividing the symphysis pubis.

FURTHER READING

Swinney, J. and Hammersley, O. P. (1963) *Operative Urological Surgery*. Livingstone, Edinburgh.

Riches, E. (1960) *Modern Trends in Urology*. Butterworth, London.

Tumours of the Bladder (1959) Vol. II Neoplastic Diseases at Various Sites, ed. Wallace, D. M., Livingstone, London.

Fergusson, J. D. (1958) *The Treatment of Prostatic Cancer*, Ann. R.C.S., **22**, 237.

Miller, T. (1947) *Retropubic Urinary Surgery*, Livingstone, Edinburgh.

Sir Denis Browne (1949) *Hypospadias*, Postgrad. med. J., **25**, 367.

CHAPTER TWENTY-SEVEN

THE MALE GENITALIA

TESTICLE

Epididymo-orchitis

Epididymitis or epididymo-orchitis may be acute or chronic. Acute inflammation may be due to gonorrhoea or a non-specific pyogenic urinary-tract infection, with the latter there is often underlying bladder-neck obstruction or prostatitis. Epididymo-orchitis may also follow operations on the bladder or instrumentation of the urethra. Often in young men no cause can be found. In such cases it has been suggested that, during severe exertion, sterile urine may be forced up the vas, exciting a chemical inflammation in the epididymis. Chronic epididymitis may follow acute inflammation, tuberculosis is a common cause.

Symptoms and Signs

The epididymis becomes very swollen and tender in acute inflammation. The scrotum is so reddened and oedematous that it may be difficult to determine if the inflammation is limited to the epididymis or if it has spread to the testis; a collection of fluid in the tunica vaginalis may further obscure what is felt in the scrotum. The cord is often thickened and tender. In the acute phase epididymo-orchitis may be very painful and there may be general effects, fever and malaise. Occasionally suppuration occurs with discharge of pus and, if severe disorganisation has occurred, then suppuration of the testis may be followed by extrusion of seminiferous tubules in strands—hernia testis. The signs of epididymo-orchitis are closely similar to those of an acute torsion of the testis (see p. 413). Subacute and chronic inflammation of the epididymis is accompanied by a variable degree of inflammation affecting all or only part of the epididymis.

Investigations

Careful examination must be made of the genitals, prostate and seminal vesicles for hardness, thickening and tenderness. Any urethral discharge is examined microscopically and by culture. The urine is often infected, and must similarly be examined. Wassermann and gonococcal fixation tests are performed. To diagnose bladder-neck obstruction, prostatitis or tuberculous disease, intravenous pyelography must be performed. Epididymo-orchitis is so often a secondary manifestation that it cannot be stressed too strongly that a primary cause must always be sought.

Treatment

The patient should be put to bed and his pain relieved by analgesics; a suspensory bandage or scrotal support of strapping between the thighs is worn. Ampicillin 500 mg. eight hourly is started after a specimen of urine has been taken for microscopy and culture. If the causative organism is resistant to the drug the appropriate antibiotic is then given.

Gonococcal Epididymitis

Epididymitis is the commonest complication of gonococcal urethritis occurring in the 2nd to 4th week after the urethral infection. The organism spreads along the vas deferens, often with other pyogenic organisms to cause pain, swelling and tenderness of the epididymis with redness and swelling of the skin of the scrotum and thickening of the cord. A small lax hydrocele is often associated.

Treatment

Treatment should be instituted as for gonococcal urethritis (see p. 69).

Tuberculous Epididymitis

Spread of tuberculous infection to the epididymis may occur from infected urine passing up the vas or by blood-borne infection. It is always an infection secondary to the disease elsewhere, almost always in the urogenital tract and most commonly from the kidney. The vas, seminal vesicles and prostate often show evidence of disease at the time when the epididymal infection becomes obvious. Bilateral infection is not uncommon. The course is usually slow, but occasionally a cold abscess forms involving the testis and discharging through the back of the scrotum. Sterility is inevitable.

Symptoms and Signs

Epididymitis occurs at a relatively young age, from about 20 to 40 years. A painless nodule forms in the epididymis, usually at the lower pole, where the vas joins it. Spread may occur into the testis, tunica vaginalis, and eventually the scrotal skin is involved posteriorly with sinus formation. Characteristically, any hydrocele that is formed is small and lax. The vas is thickened, often with beading which is diagnostic of tuberculosis. Rectal examination may reveal a thickened seminal vesicle or hardness of the prostate. Tuberculous epididymitis must be distinguished from new growths and syphilis of the testis and in cases with an acute presentation from other causes of epididymitis and torsion of the testis.

Investigations

Where tuberculous epididymitis is suspected a careful search must be made for the organism and the primary focus, which may not only be in the genito-urinary tract but also in the lung, spine or in any bone or joint.

In all cases, at some phase in the disease, tuberculous lesions are found in the kidney or bladder. Early morning urine specimens must be examined repeatedly for acid-fast bacilli, and intravenous pyelograms and cystoscopy are performed.

Treatment

As soon as the tubercle bacillus has been demonstrated a course of tuberculostatic drugs is given (see p. 63). Epididymectomy or epididymo-orchidectomy may be necessary, and to clear up a persisting sinus part of the diseased scrotum must be excised. Chemotherapy is maintained as in treatment of renal tuberculosis (see p. 361).

Orchitis

Orchitis without epididymitis is rare and usually due to the virus of mumps affecting adolescents or young adults. The inflammation is extremely painful and liable to be followed by testicular atrophy and, in bilateral infection, sterility. Typhoid is a rare cause of orchitis; syphilis may affect the testis (see below).

Syphilis of the Testis

Syphilitic infection of the testis is very rare. In the secondary stage there may be a painless epididymitis, in the tertiary stage diffuse fibrosis may occur, going on to atrophy or the formation of a gumma. Gumma of the testis is extremely rare, if it ulcerates the ulcer has punched-out edges and a wash-leather slough in its base and is sited on the anterior surface of the scrotum. Syphilis of the testis produces a characteristic heaviness, shared only by tumour or haematocele. The testis is also insensitive to pressure, as are many tumours. Orchitis may be seen in congenital syphilis. Evidence of syphilis should be sought elsewhere and the Wassermann and Kahn tests performed. Treatment is that for tertiary syphilis (see p. 67). Occasionally orchidectomy must be performed if the possibility of neoplasm cannot otherwise be excluded.

TUMOURS OF THE TESTIS

Most tumours of the testis are malignant. Fibroma, adenoma, lipoma and dermoid cyst occur, but are extremely rare. Malignant tumours are usually either seminomas, tumours of the seminiferous tubules or teratomas, tumours of totipotent cells in the testis or a combination of these two tumours. Very rarely a trophoblastic teratoma (previously called a chorionepithelioma) is found and even rarer a malignant tumour of the interstitial cells of Leydig, which are normally found scattered between the seminiferous tubules.

Seminomas occur in a rather older group than teratomas, which are commonest in the second or third decades. The imperfectly descended testis is more likely to undergo malignant change than the fully descended organ. Testicular tumours may manufacture hormones, which can be detected in the urine by performing the Ascheim–Zondek test for pregnancy; trophoblastic teratoma (chorionepithelioma) is most active—seminoma less so and teratoma least of all. Secondary tumours may also produce positive hormone reactions.

Symptoms and Signs

The testis becomes enlarged, hard, insensitive and heavy, and there may be a small hydrocele containing bloodstained fluid. Early in the disease the testis may be felt separate from the epididymis, but in most cases all that can be felt is a large tumour in the scrotum. Metastatic deposits may be felt in enlarged para-aortic glands or as far distant as the supraclavicular lymph nodes. A radiograph of the chest may demonstrate widening of the mediastinum or metastases in the lung fields. Blood-borne metastases may appear in the lungs, causing haemoptysis or lead to enlargement of the liver. Sometimes a tumour may produce obvious secondary deposits and yet the primary be so small as to escape notice. Tapping a hydrocele may allow palpation of an underlying tumour of testis which would otherwise escape notice. In a small proportion the presentation is acute and closely resembles the signs of epididymo-orchitis or torsion of the testis.

Differential Diagnosis

Heavy insensitive tumours in the testis must be differentiated from gumma and haematocele. A common difficulty is distinction between a tumour of the testis and chronic epididymo-orchitis, especially that due to tuberculosis. Usually the diagnosis is obvious.

Pathology

The cut surface of a testis affected by seminoma shows it to be enlarged and wholly or partially replaced by a solid, white, homogeneous tumour. Histology shows spheroidal cells arising from spermatocytes in the germinal layer of the seminiferous tubules. The tumour spreads by lymphatics to the spermatic cord and the para-aortic lymph nodes and by blood stream to the liver and lung.

Teratomata contain structures derived from all three germinal layers—ectoderm, mesoderm and endoderm. Elements such as bone, nerve tissue, fragments of gut and squamous epithelium may all be present in a chaotic arrangement. In addition, there are the histological signs of malignancy, anaplasia and abnormal mitoses. Spread of malignant teratoma occurs more often by the blood stream than by lymphatics. Cyst formation is common in many teratomata—fibrocystic disease. Rarely in the very young, a benign teratoma may be found; dermoid cyst of the testis is a benign variant of teratoma in which only squamous epithelium occurs.

Trophoblastic teratoma (chorionepithelioma) is a tumour derived from syncytial trophoblastic epithelium. It occurs very rarely and can only be diagnosed when the tumour has been removed and examined histologically. Some malignant lymphomas, such as lymphosarcoma, may arise in the testis or present there as metastatic deposits. Tumours of the interstitial cells of Leydig may rarely cause hormonal effects such as gynecomastia.

Treatment of Testicular Tumours

Orchidectomy is performed with division of the spermatic cord at the internal ring. Following operation a course of radiotherapy is given to the para-aortic region. Treated this way 5-year survival can be expected in 80% of patients who have seminoma, the results for teratoma are less satisfactory; chorionepithelioma and malignant lymphoma carry the worst prognosis. Chorionepithelioma of the uterus and testis has been found to respond to the antimetabolite aminopterin and it has been also used for disseminated teratoma of testis. Dramatic cures have been reported.

SPERMATOCELE AND CYSTS OF THE EPIDIDYMIS

Cysts commonly form in the epididymis on one or both sides. Men around 40–60 years of age may develop these cysts, though younger and older persons may be affected. Small cysts in the head of the epididymis may be tense and painful. Multilocular cysts may replace the major part of the epididymis. Large cysts may resemble hydroceles, except that in a hydrocele the testis is enveloped by the tunica vaginalis and cannot easily be felt, whereas below a spermatocele the testis can be felt distinctly. The fluid in a spermatocele is milky, contains little protein, and microscopy shows the remains of sperms. Epididymal cysts contain crystal clear fluid containing little protein. Hydrocele fluid is yellow and so full of protein that it solidifies on boiling.

Epididymal cysts or spermatoceles require removal if they are large or cause pain. Sometimes cysts near the epididymis arise from congenital remnants of the Mullerian system (hydatids); these cause no symptoms unless they become tense, or undergo torsion, as they may in children.

TORSION OF THE TESTIS

Torsion of the testis usually occurs in the young child or adolescent, though it may occasionally be seen in older men up to 25 or 30 years. The testis may be incompletely descended, and usually shows some congenital abnormalities, such as a mesentery (mesorchium) between the testis and epididymis, horizontal lie of the testis (hanging like a bell clapper), anteversion of the testis and high reflection of the tunica vaginalis off the cord so that part of the cord is intravaginal. The twist almost always occurs within the tunica vaginalis. Torsion may be precipitated by sudden strains but equally well may occur at rest in bed. There may be several incomplete episodes before the final crisis occurs. Torsion is the commoner cause of a painful scrotal swelling in a boy under the age of 15 years. Epididymitis is rare at this age.

Symptoms and Signs

There is sudden severe pain in the lower abdomen, often accompanied by vomiting. The scrotum becomes acutely tender, and the testis swollen and painful. If the testis is undescended a tender swelling in the groin may simulate a strangulated hernia, but is distinguished by the absence of the testis from the scrotum. The swollen, painful testis closely resembles the state seen in epididymo-orchitis, but the age of the patient, the suddenness of onset of symptoms and the absence of a history of urethritis or venereal contact usually enables the diagnosis to be made. Symptoms may be less severe, especially in cases of recurrent partial torsion, where spontaneous untwisting may occur and nothing abnormal may be found on examination after the acute symptoms have subsided.

Treatment

Torsion causes ischaemia, gangrene and finally atrophy of the testis, sometimes followed by testicular neuralgia. In the first few hours the twist may be undone at operation with survival of the testis. In most cases gangrene is established at the time of operation, and all that can be done is orchidectomy. It must be stressed that any young person developing pain and swelling in the testis of sudden onset without the signs of urethritis should have the scrotum explored. If the twist can be undone with survival of the testis the testis should be anchored to the scrotum to prevent recurrence. At the same time or at a later date the opposite testis should similarly be fixed.

Signs similar to those of torsion of the testis may be met in torsion of its appendages. Occasionally, thrombosis of veins in the pampiniform plexus may give similar signs. Idiopathic scrotal oedema may resemble torsion. It is safer to explore the scrotum in any case of doubt whenever the symptoms suggest torsion; the tunica vaginalis must be opened to expose the testis and its appendages.

IMPERFECT DESCENT OF THE TESTIS

The testis may be incompletely descended, that is arrested at some point in the path it takes from the abdomen to the scrotum; it may also stray and become ectopic.

Incomplete Descent

The testis arises embryonically in the region of the kidney in the genital folds which lie medial to the mesonephros. It descends later through the retroperitoneal tissues into the inguinal canal and scrotum. About the first month of intra-uterine life a fibro-muscular band called the gubernaculum, which is attached to the lower pole of the testis, grows downwards through the abdominal wall to the subcutaneous tissue of the skin that later forms the scrotum. The testis carries with it a funnel-shaped extrusion of peritoneum, the processus vaginalis. During the last months of foetal life the testis normally passes through the inguinal canal into the scrotum.

Arrest of testicular descent may occur at any stage—within the abdomen, in the inguinal canal or at the superficial inguinal ring. It is important to remember that spontaneous descent rarely occurs after a few weeks after birth. When the testis is retained within the abdomen, or in the inguinal canal, it is usually impalpable. In bilateral testicular maldescent the penis and scrotum may be very small, and occasionally the boy is overweight. In unilateral maldescent the genitals are normally developed and the body appearance is within normal limits. In maldescent the testis is usually smaller than normal, whereas ectopic testes are normally developed in size.

It is important to distinguish a *retractile testis* from incomplete descent. In most children the testes are mobile and easily and rapidly withdrawn by the cremaster muscles into the inguinal canal. Stimuli such as fear, examination by a doctor or a cold hand may cause retraction. By careful and gentle examination in warm surroundings the testes can usually be stroked by the examiner downwards and medially into the bottom of the scrotum. Retractile testes do not require any treatment, and the parents can be reassured that if a testis can be brought to the bottom of the scrotum it will stay there after puberty.

The hazards of incomplete descent include atrophy of the testis, which cannot function unless it is lying in the scrotum. This failure to develop and function is usually attributed to the higher temperature that exists within the abdomen or inguinal canal as compared with that in the scrotum. An inguinal hernia is associated in most cases of maldescent. Torsion is much more likely to occur in the maldescended than in the normal testis. The testis in an abnormal position is more liable to injury and may be painful. There is an increased liability to malignant change. If the condition is bilateral, then sterility may follow.

Treatment

The aim of treatment of maldescent must be to bring the testis into the scrotum before the age of five years for after this age the process of atrophy begins and if the testis is left undescended until puberty, sterility may result. Hormone treatment is reserved for a few patients seen near puberty with bilateral incomplete descent associated with immature development of the genitals, often with obesity. Overweight boys always appear to have small genitals, because the penis is swallowed up in the fat of the abdominal wall and the scrotum appears relatively smaller than it is; parents should be reassured about this. Chorionic gonadotropin extracted from pregnant mare's serum (Pregnyl), or obtained from pituitaries, is given at about the age of 11–12 years when the first signs of puberty are manifest. The hormone is given in doses of 500 units intramuscularly twice a week for twelve injections or until the testes descend; rarely is it necessary to operate to bring them down.

Operation is performed in the majority of cases of maldescent of the testis and in all cases of ectopic testis. The operation of orchidopexy is usually carried out on boys aged about 5 years. Earlier the structures are so small that operation may damage the arterial supply of the testis. After puberty, even if the testis can be brought down, it is unlikely to function. After puberty it may be impossible to lengthen the spermatic cord and bring the testis into the scrotum.

At operation any hernia is excised and the spermatic cord and testicular vessels mobilised so that the testis can be brought into the scrotum with minimal tension. This may be difficult if the spermatic vessels are short. It is usual to fix the testis within the scrotum so that it cannot retract upwards, commonly this is done by a suture through the tunica albuginea passing through the scrotum and attached to the thigh by a light elastic band. Even if the testis cannot be brought down fully, it may still grow and function, although lying a little higher than normal. An intra-abdominal testis must usually be excised for fear of malignancy and because it cannot function.

Ectopic Testis

The testis may descend through the inguinal canal as usual, but after emerging through the external ring may pass upward and laterally to become ectopic in situation, parallel to and above the inguinal ligament. Other rare sites for an ectopic testis are superficial to the external ring, the femoral triangle, the perineum and the root of the penis. Signs suggestive of ectopic testis are a normal-sized testis lying very superficially. A hernial sac is often associated, and the external genitals, like the testis itself, are usually fully developed.

Treatment

Operation is carried out as soon as the condition is suspected. The testis after being freed can easily be placed in the scrotum because its cord is of normal length or even longer than normal.

THE TUNICA AND CORD

Hydrocele

A collection of fluid in the tunica vaginalis is called a hydrocele. Usually the cause is unknown—*primary or idiopathic hydrocele*. A few are due to underlying disease of the testis, including inflammation, growth or torsion —*secondary hydrocele*.

Usually elderly men are affected by the idiopathic variety, but hydrocele may occur at any age. The scrotum enlarges slowly without pain or tenderness unless haemorrhage or infection has occurred. The swelling is smooth, globular and distinguished from a hernia because the upper limit of the hydrocele can easily be defined; the spermatic cord is clearly palpable above it, and there is no impulse on coughing. A hydrocele is elastic, fluctuant and translucent to a bright light; it is dull to percussion, whereas a large hernia is usually resonant. Translucency may be lost if the wall is thick or if haemorrhage has occurred.

Acute secondary hydrocele follows trauma, torsion or inflammation. Chronic secondary hydrocele is associated with tuberculosis, syphilis and neoplasm. Secondary hydroceles are typically lax and of small volume. They are most easily demonstrated by transillumination and are easily missed unless this simple test is used. Rarely it may be necessary to aspirate a secondary hydrocele in order to palpate the testis and epididymis beneath it for diagnostic purposes.

Idiopathic vaginal hydrocele is the commonest form of hydrocele (see Fig. 38). The tunica vaginalis becomes filled with straw-coloured fluid; up to several litres may collect, but more usually only 100–500 ml. is

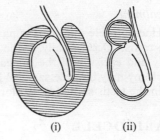

FIG. 38. (i) Vaginal hydrocele, testis enveloped by distended tunica vaginalis. (ii) spermatocele, testis clearly defined below cyst of epididymis

(i)   (ii)

found. If bleeding has occurred the fluid may be brown in colour or contain cholesterol crystals. The swelling surrounds the testis, which cannot be felt and is often compressed and flattened.

Hydrocele is commonly seen in infants in the first year of life; most infantile hydroceles disappear spontaneously. After 1 year hydroceles in children are usually *communicating hydroceles*. In these there is a patent processus vaginalis of such fine calibre that only fluid from the peritoneal cavity passes down it. Such hydroceles decrease in size during the night and enlarge by day.

Treatment

Excision of the sac of the hydrocele is performed so long as the patient is not too old and is in good general condition. In the very elderly or unfit, aspiration by means of a wide-bore needle and syringe is carried out. It is important to avoid the testis before inserting the trocar; the testis lies posterior to the hydrocele, and often its shadow can be seen by transillumination. Tapping usually has to be repeated every few months.

Treatment of communicating hydrocele involves division of the patent processus vaginalis or removal of a hernial sac and evagination of the tunica vaginalis around the testis.

A hydrocele of the spermatic cord is formed when fluid collects in the intermediate part of the processus vaginalis. A cystic swelling appears in the cord or in the canal of Nuck in a woman. Such swellings are treated by excision and removal of any hernial sac.

Haematocele

Bleeding into the tunica vaginalis usually follows tapping of a hydrocele or an injury to the testis. The fluid in a secondary hydrocele around a tumour of the testis may be bloodstained. Rarely, haematocele may arise spontaneously in blood diseases. The signs are those of hydrocele, but with absence of translucency to a strong light, heaviness and loss of elasticity. In the acute phase there may be severe pain and tenderness, with oedema in the overlying scrotal skin. Aspiration may produce old blood unless the effusion is completely clotted. In long-standing haematocele atrophy of the testis may occur. Tumour and syphilis must be excluded.

Treatment

Haematocele due to trauma usually subsides with rest and support to the testis. Occasionally, if the swelling persists, aspiration may be necessary and excision of the tunica if fluid collects again; occasionally orchidectomy may be necessary. Whenever there is doubt about the diagnosis then the testis should be explored.

VARICOCELE

Varicosity of the veins in the pampiniform plexus surrounding the testis extending to the internal ring is common, though the cause is not known. The left side is more commonly affected than the right. Very rarely, acute development of a varicocele may be a sign of malignant disease in the left kidney with obstruction of the spermatic vein on that side.

Most commonly a varicocele causes no symptoms, and may only be brought to light during a routine medical examination. Sometimes aching pain is complained of, but usually it is obvious that there is a psychogenic basis for the pain. Varicocele most commonly occurs in young men. It may cause infertility due to its thermal insulating effect causing a rise in the scrotal and testicular temperature.

Treatment

In the vast majority of cases the patient should be reassured that no disease is present and no treatment is required. If there is some discomfort a suspensory bandage can be worn. In a few cases operation may be advised, in which segments of the main veins in the pampiniform plexus in front of the vas are excised and the spermatic cord shortened, with careful preservation of the arterial supply to the testis.

PENIS AND SCROTUM

Phimosis

Inability to reflect the prepuce over the glans penis is most often due to adhesions between the prepuce and the glans. At birth the prepuce is adherent to the glans by fine fibrous tissue, but during the first 3 or 4 years it becomes free. Inability to retract the prepuce over the glans during this period is not an abnormality. Narrowing of the orifice in the prepuce may rarely be congenital in origin. Sometimes the prepuce is very long and narrow, occasionally the preputial orifice is minute is size.

Mothers often complain that their infants scream or strain when they pass urine, but this is normal in many babies, and is usually unrelated to any abnormality of the prepuce. If the orifice of the prepuce is narrow or if the prepuce itself is long, then, when the baby passes urine, the prepuce may be seen to swell, causing discomfort or eventually infection (balanitis). If the prepuce remains adherent to the glans longer than normally concretions of smegma accumulate under it and may cause infection. Mothers often bring their babies with what appears to be balanitis, but this is part of a napkin rash due to ammoniacal dermatitis. Such infection may cause narrowing of the preputial orifice from scarring.

Treatment

Circumcision is only required medically for organic narrowing of the preputial orifice or for infection of the preputial skin. There may be racial or religious reasons for the operation, and some mothers are convinced that hygiene cannot be maintained without circumcision. It is possible that carcinoma of the cervix is more prevalent in the partners of the uncircumcised. Carcinoma of the penis is never seen in the circumcised.

The prepuce is usually adherent to the glans penis but in nine out of ten little boys the prepuce becomes free by the age of 3 to 4 years. Attempts at retraction should be avoided. Occasionally it is convenient to free the prepuce from the glans by passing a probe between the two structures. Circumcision is only needed after the age of 3–4 years if the prepuce does not become free of if there is balanitis or narrowing of the preputial orifice.

In the operation of circumcision the prepuce is freed from the glans and cleaned with cetrimide under general anaesthesia. The excess of prepuce is excised, but enough should be left to cover at least the margin of the glans penis. The cut end of the mucous membrane and skin are approximated with interrupted catgut sutures. Complete haemostasis is essential, for haemorrhage of quite a small amount may be serious in a baby.

Ammoniacal dermatitis is the commonest cause of soreness of the prepuce, and is associated with rashes on the genitals and buttocks. Circumcision under these circumstances may expose the penis to further irritation and cause a sore place at the external urethral meatus, which with healing may produce scarring and even meatal stenosis. Ammoniacal dermatitis is due to proliferation of organisms in the napkins which break down urea and release ammonia. A satisfactory method of treatment is to tell the mother to rinse the napkins in a non-irritating mild antiseptic such as boracic acid (1 tablespoonful to the breakfast cup of hot water).

Adult balanitis may follow pyogenic or venereal infection or a tight prepuce. Occasionally squamous carcinoma may be concealed under a tight prepuce and be obscured by the infection and swelling. The diagnosis of carcinoma can only then be made after freeing the prepuce under anaesthesia, usually by slitting it along its dorsal aspect (dorsal slit).

Circumcision in adults may be indicated for inability to retract the prepuce, causing discomfort in intercourse, balanitis or difficulty in passing urine. Balanitis in adults may be a sign of diabetes.

Paraphimosis

If a tight prepuce is drawn back the penis may become constricted at the corona, and the prepuce is then irreducible. Swelling distal to the constricting band becomes intense, with severe pain and difficulty in passing urine. Infection follows later.

Treatment

Reduction of the paraphimosis may be effected by gradual compression on the glans so as to diminish its size and allow the tight prepuce to be drawn over the corona. Injection of hyalase into the tight band may assist to relieve the constriction. If these measures fail a general anaesthetic will be necessary so that the constricting band and the prepuce can be divided dorsally. Circumcision is usually performed later when oedema and inflammation have subsided.

CARCINOMA OF THE PENIS

Carcinoma of the penis is usually a squamous lesion. Usually phimosis is associated, often there is a long history of balanitis. Carcinoma of the penis is almost never seen in the circumcised. It is often preceded by leukoplakia or a papilloma on the glans or in the sulcus beyond the glans. At first the lesion is superficial, but later it grows deeply to involve the body of the penis. The inguinal nodes are involved early in the disease.

Symptoms and Signs

Carcinoma of the penis usually occurs in elderly men. A bloodstained or purulent discharge from the prepuce in an adult is suspicious of carcinoma. A dorsal slit of the prepuce must usually be performed before malignancy can be excluded. Sometimes carcinoma produces diffuse swelling of the skin of the penis with great oedema.

Treatment

A dorsal slit or circumcision must be performed, followed by biopsy of any ulcer or suspiciously indurated area. Small localised superficial carcinomata can be treated by super-voltage radiation, locally by insertion of radio-active gold grains or in some patients by radical circumcision. When the disease is more advanced, but still limited to the glans, amputation through the body of the penis is performed. For more extensive involvement total amputation of the penis and excision of the testes and scrotum is performed, leaving the urethral opening in the perineum. If the inguinal lymph nodes are involved, then their removal by block dissection is indicated. The prognosis for such extensive disease, requiring as it does a mutilating operation, is very poor.

BENIGN GROWTHS OF THE PENIS

Sebaceous cysts and other tumours may occur on the penis. Papillomata may be found growing inside the prepuce or from the glans. They are soft, friable and often become infected. Many are virus warts, but some are condylomata due to venereal disease. Papillomata are treated under anaesthesia by removal with scissors and touching their bases with a cautery. All tumours should be examined histologically. A dorsal slit of the prepuce or circumcision is usually required, if only to expose the lesion for diagnosis.

SCROTAL TUMOURS

Chronic irritation of the scrotum by tar is called 'chimney sweep's cancer'. It is nowadays very rare. An indurated ulcer with rolled, everted edges appears on the scrotal skin, and is treated by wide excision, together with the inguinal nodes if they are involved.

Sebaceous cysts, lipoma and other simple tumours may occur in the skin of the scrotum. They are removed if they are causing symptoms.

INFECTIVE CONDITIONS OF THE SCROTUM AND PENIS

Primary Chancre

This occurs on the glans or corona as an ulcer with an indurated base. The diagnosis is confirmed by demonstrating the treponema pallidum in scrapings from the base of the ulcer. The lymphatics become cord-like and the lymph nodes in the groins enlarged, painless and shotty. A chancre may resemble carcinoma of the penis, and biopsy may be necessary in some cases to exclude it. Wassermann and Kahn reactions are performed. A chancre must be distinguished from chancroid and lymphogranuloma.

Elephantiasis

This may be due to infection with *Filaria bancrofti* (see p. 72), which gives rise to enormous enlargement of the scrotal skin. Recurrent attacks of inflammation due to streptococci and other pyogenic organisms are common. Oedema of the penis and scrotum may also be due to venous thrombosis in the pelvis, ascites, lymphatic obstruction and cardiac failure.

CHAPTER TWENTY-EIGHT

PAEDIATRIC SURGERY

Most of the special departments in surgery are devoted to particular regions of the body, such as cranial, thoracic and genito-urinary. Paediatric surgery, however, is concerned with the whole child, and this should serve to draw attention to the fact that it is much more than the surgical care of small patients. A whole group of conditions is peculiar to the early days or years of life, and this includes the congenital deformities.

Patience, gentleness and a meticulous respect for not losing blood are the prime requirements of the paediatric surgeon, who also has to learn afresh his knowledge of fluid and electrolyte balance, which is so different in babies than in adults. It is also especially important that the surgeon should be responsible for the fluid and electrolyte balance of his own patients and not expect this to be carried out by the paediatrician; experience has shown that this kind of delegation is not usually successful, and may even end in disaster. Some of those diseases which are common to both adults and children will be found discussed in other parts of this book, for example, acute appendicitis in Chapter Seventeen.

Admission to hospital can be a most upsetting experience for a young child, but if he is acutely ill and operation necessary this is something that has to be faced, and skilled nursing and sympathy overcome most of the problems. However, when an operation is not urgent its timing is most important. After the age of 1 and up till about the age of 5 most children stand separation from their parents poorly, and therefore it is better if mother and child can be admitted to hospital together. More satisfactory is to delay the operation until the child is of such an age that he can understand what is going on; over the age of 5 years children make excellent patients. The choice of pre-medication and anaesthesia is extremely important, but cannot be dealt with here. It should be remembered that the child's stomach empties much more quickly than the adult, and therefore it is rarely necessary to wait 4 hours for the stomach to empty; indeed, the resulting hypoglycaemia may in itself be harmful. As far as possible skin stitches are best avoided, as they are difficult and painful to remove. Subcuticular wound closure with absorbable sutures is preferable, and an acceptable alternative is the use of butterfly-shaped adhesive dressings which hold the wound edges together.

BIRTHMARKS

The commonest tumour of childhood is the *haemangioma*, which often grows rapidly in the first 10 months of life and then regresses over the next few years. The lesion is either flat and mainly composed of capillaries or heaped-up and called a strawberry birthmark, with cavernous spaces within. As soon as the lesion stops growing a pale patch appears at the centre, looking rather like a little milk which has been spilt on it. So long as the parent can be encouraged to be patient, by far the best cosmetic result is obtained by doing nothing. Occasionally very aggressive lesions may grow so exuberantly as, for example, to dislocate the eye from the orbit or in other ways imperil other organs, and then it may be necessary to inject a sclerosant or reduce the blood supply to the region by tying vessels. The use of radiotherapy is to be avoided if at all possible in childhood, as the long-term result is a papery scar with a definite tendency to undergo malignant change.

Port wine stains do not follow this natural history, but remain much the same throughout life, and can be treated at any age by multiple diathermy puncture. *Hairy pigmented moles* also never improve and are unsightly, they require excision and repair of the defect. This is often better left until the child is 5 years old.

HERNIA

Umbilical and inguinal hernias are extremely common in babies, and good judgement is necessary in deciding the correct treatment.

Umbilical Hernia

Umbilical hernias have a great tendency to close spontaneously, and do not require treatment before the age of 1 year. If they are very unsightly or distress the parent it is only necessary to provide a small rubber belt which will mould the navel in place. Supra-umbilical hernias, especially in girls, do not resolve, and often enlarge after the age of 3 years. Operation is never urgently required, and can be delayed until the age of 5 when the patients will be quite happy to come into hospital.

Inguinal Hernia

Inguinal hernia is commoner in boys than in girls, and much commoner on the right than on the left side. It is not possible to ask a baby to strain like an adult and produce a swelling in the groin, but it is easy to recognise if a hernia is present by rolling the spermatic cord under the fingers, when the walls of the sac give the impression of two layers of silk lying deep to the surface. Inguinal hernia is treated by herniotomy, removal of the sac, no kind of repair is necessary. It is very conveniently done in a small baby, since it is only necessary for the child to be in hospital for one or two nights, and if subcuticular stitches are used there is no problem with removing skin stitches. In some clinics the operation is done on an outpatient basis. Occasionally a hernia becomes incarcerated in a child (i.e. the contents become irreducible), and when this happens the child should be supported with the legs in the air attached to a small overhead bar by adhesive strapping. In this position the hernia almost always spon-taneously reduces within an hour, and if it does not do so, then immediate operation is indicated. Hydrocele is also common in babies, and tends to absorb during the first year of life. More about this subject is found in Chapter Twenty-seven.

EXOMPHALOS

When the central part of the abdominal wall fails to develop properly it is replaced by a semi-transparent sheet of tissue from which the umbilical cord projects. This condition, called exomphalos or omphalocele, is one that requires immediate treatment, and it is said that the best results are obtained when the midwife hands the baby to the surgeon. Any or all of the abdominal contents can be found in the thin-walled sac, which may rupture during the birth of the baby. It is necessary to tie off the umbilical vessels, for they may not be entirely thrombosed, and then excise the wall of the sac and bring together the abdominal wall to repair the defect. If the rectus muscles cannot be brought together without much tension the skin of the abdominal wall is closed over the defect and at a later date the muscles are dealt with. The important thing is to cover up the intestines and liver securely, if the baby is to survive.

OESOPHAGUS

Oesophageal Atresia

Oesophageal atresia or tracheo-oesophageal fistula (Fig. 39) is a common developmental abnormality. Any newborn baby who vomits and becomes

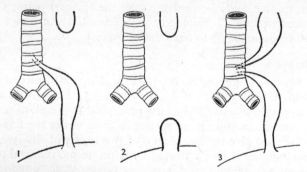

FIG. 39. Tracheo-oesophageal fistula. (i) commonest type oesophageal fistula into the trachea near bifurcation; (ii) Defect of oesophagus; (iii) Double fistula

cyanosed when fed should be assumed to have this defect until proved otherwise. The diagnosis is readily confirmed by passing a fine lubricated catheter down the baby's nose and seeing if it is arrested in the upper oesophagus. Further confirmation is obtained by injecting not more than

1·0 ml. of lipiodol and taking radiographs of the baby, when a blind sac will be seen in the upper thorax. It is important to include the abdomen in the picture, for if gas is seen in the bowel it demonstrates that the distal oesophageal segment is in continuity with the trachea. If no gas is seen in the gut it means that the distal end of the oesophagus is blind and it is likely that reconstruction will be more difficult.

The common variety of atresia of the oesophagus is a blind proximal loop and a distal one connecting with the bifurcation of the trachea, as shown in the diagram. More rarely the other varieties illustrated will be encountered. The baby should be very carefully nursed before operation, and there is no advantage in operating during the first 24 hours of life, when it is better to give an antibiotic, aspirate the excess mucus at $\frac{1}{2}$-hourly intervals and turn the baby from side to side in the cot, preferably with the head lower than the rest of the body so that there is good aeration of the lungs and any secretions are easily extracted. The child is then taken to the operating theatre and under a general anaesthetic the right chest is opened through the third or fourth inter-space, the azygos vein divided between ligatures and the proximal blind oesophageal pouch dissected free. The distal oesophagus is then detached from the trachea, the hole closed and the two ends of the oesophagus anastomosed over a fine catheter. It is convenient to leave a small-bore polyethylene tube passing through the anastomosis into the stomach for early feeding of the baby. Postoperative care consists of careful fluid balance, always remembering that more babies are lost during the first days of life through over-hydration than through dehydration. Milk can be introduced through the fine catheter, and it is often most convenient to nurse the baby in an incubator. The complications of the operation are a leak from the suture line, which need not be fatal if a gastrostomy is performed, or the catheter can be used to introduce fluid into the stomach. Stricture formation may occur later at the anastomosis, and this will often require only gentle dilatation with bougies on a few occasions. The condition may be associated with other congenital abnormalities, such as imperforate anus, and therefore a careful search should be made for any other lesion.

Oesophageal Hiatus Hernia

Occasionally a baby feeds well but regurgitates much or all that has been taken, the vomit never being projectile nor bile stained. Often the baby drools saliva, and the chin then becomes excoriated. The condition is usually associated with a lax oesophageal hiatus, and often a hiatus hernia, part of the stomach lying in the chest. Free reflux of stomach contents occurs into the oesophagus, and the resulting oesophagitis leads to loss of blood and severe anaemia. Treatment in the first place is always conservative, with the baby sat up in a 'sentry box'; often as time passes the condition resolves spontaneously. Occasionally the symptoms do not improve, and then it is necessary to open the chest and carry out the repair described in Chapter Sixteen.

Dysphagia Lusoria

Compression of the trachea and oesophagus may occur due to the great vessels arising in an anomalous pattern from the arch of the aorta in such a way as to produce a vascular ring. The baby often has crowing respiration, hyperextension of the neck and attacks of obvious respiratory difficulty. The diagnosis is made by careful radiography of the chest and thoracic inlet. Treatment consists in dividing one of the anomalous vessels where it presses on the trachea. Lusoria is Latin for deceitful, and was first used by the English surgeon Bayford in 1794 to describe difficulty in swallowing due to an abnormal subclavian artery.

INTESTINAL OBSTRUCTION OF THE NEWBORN

Every newborn baby whose vomit is bile stained should be suspected of intestinal obstruction. It is true that many babies regurgitate a little of their feed, but if this is not bile stained it is not significant. If the obstruction is in the large bowel the onset of vomiting may be delayed for some days. A newborn baby can survive for many days without the ingestion of food or fluid, but when obstruction of the bowel is present dehydration occurs quite rapidly. The baby acquires a wizened old-man look, the anterior fontanelle is depressed and the urine scanty and highly concentrated, so that it marks the napkin. The skin is inelastic.

Obstruction of the bowel is accompanied by abdominal distension, which may be gross. Obstruction near the pylorus often allows visible peristalsis of the stomach to be seen through the abdominal wall; in a baby it looks as if a golf ball were being passed from left to right just under the surface. Auscultation of the abdomen with a stethoscope usually reveals increased bowel sounds, but in the presence of peritonitis there will be a quiet abdomen with only an occasional tinkling sound.

A normal baby can be expected to pass meconium during the first 18 hours of life. Meconium is a dark-green sticky substance containing desquamated cells, bile, enzymes and epithelial cells which have been swallowed with the liquor amnii in utero. If there is obstruction to the alimentary tract these squamous cells will not appear in the meconium, and this constitutes Farber's test, in which meconium is stained and the squames looked for on a microscope slide. The anus should be carefully inspected and a rectal examination performed. The most important single investigation is the taking of good radiographs of the abdomen, which should be obtained with the baby horizontal and vertical. The position of gas and fluid in the bowel is an excellent guide to the site of the obstruction. Some of the common causes of intestinal obstruction will now be listed:

Duodenal Stenosis

Stenosis of the duodenum always occurs distal to the ampulla of Vater, so that the vomit is bile stained and the upper abdomen distended. A radiograph of the abdomen is diagnostic, since gas is confined to stomach and duodenum, and little or none is seen in the remainder of the bowel. Malrotation of the mid-gut can present similarly. Of babies with duodenal stenosis, one-third are mentally defective or have mongolism. Treatment is operative. After the stomach contents have been aspirated a duodeno-duodenostomy is performed.

Ileal Atresia

In contrast to lesions in the proximal gut, which are usually those of stenosis or narrowing, in the distal small bowel the commonest lesion is atresia or lack of development. The atretic areas may be multiple, and therefore a thorough search has to be made at operation along the whole length of the bowel. The surgical problem here is anastomosing the grossly distended proximal loop to the tiny empty distal loop. It is important that the anastomosis should be end-to-end rather than side-to-side, since peristalsis works so much better if the former is done.

Malrotation of the Mid-gut

Between the 6th and 10th weeks of intra-uterine life the bowel grows more rapidly than the coelomic cavity, and the bowel therefore is extruded into the umbilical cord, later returning to the abdomen in an orderly and anti-clockwise fashion. The caecum passes from left to right and descends into the right iliac fossa, the mesentery of the small bowel gains attachment near the midline, and if there is any hold-up in this process the bowel will be found to be rotated about a central axis, producing a mid-gut volvulus. On opening the abdomen the caecum will be found high up and usually on the left side, and there is often a band passing across from this to the right paracolic gutter. This band presses on the duodenum and causes a high-gut obstruction. It is only necessary to divide this band and untwist the volvulus to allow the bowel contents to pass on; nothing further is necessary. Sometimes this condition is not diagnosed for many years, the gut twisting and untwisting on a long mesentery about a central axis, and the physical development of the child often being delayed.

Meckel's Diverticulum and Omphalomesenteric Abnormalities

Meckel's diverticulum is a blind pouch found on the anti-mesenteric border of the distal ileum in about 1% of people. It occasionally contains ectopic gastric mucosa and islands of pancreatic tissue. Blood vessels run from the gut to its tip, and there may be a fibrous cord joining it to the umbilicus. Acute inflammation may occur in the diverticulum in much the same way as it does in the appendix, and the correct diagnosis can only be made at operation. Volvulus may occur around the fibrous band leading to the umbilicus, and finally the diverticulum may act as the apex of an intussusception. Very rarely the tip of a Meckel's diverticulum communicates with the umbilicus to produce a faecal fistula, it must be excised. A small mass of moist red tissue may be seen at the umbilicus, looking like a raspberry, this umbilical polyp is a remnant of the cord; it should be tied off with a ligature and will soon separate. Alternatively, it can be cauterized with silver nitrate.

Hirschsprung's Disease

This may produce intestinal obstruction in the newborn, and is occasionally associated with mental deficiency. The child has a distended abdomen, and may pass very small amounts of flatus, especially after rectal examination. The large bowel is distended, and the cause of the condition is absence of a normal myenteric plexus in the distal large bowel. If the defect extends only into the sigmoid colon it is referred to as a short segment, but the abnormality may extend throughout most or all of the colon in rare cases. Once the diagnosis has been made, a colostomy is performed proximal to the abnormal bowel, and the baby then develops normally. At the age of about 1 year the aganglionic segment is excised and continuity restored by a pull-through operation in which the colon is anastomosed to a tiny stump of anal canal. Hirschsprung's disease is often recognised only after a few months or even years have elapsed, when failure to thrive, intractable constipation and a distended abdomen are associated with a rectum of normal calibre containing a few pellets of dried faeces.

Imperforate Anus

This is a common congenital abnormality, and it is surprising how often it is overlooked in the first days of life. Three degrees of the condition

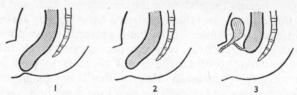

1   2   3

FIG. 40. Imperforate anus; (i) Membrane between anus and hind-gut; (ii) More extreme degree of (i); (iii) Deficiency of hind-gut with fistula into posterior urethra

can be recognised (Fig. 40), and the treatment is different in each. In the first a tiny speck of meconium may be seen in the perineum, and if a slit is made posteriorly from this microscopical opening, a fairly normal anus can be expected, with good muscle control. This condition is probably best described as a covered anus rather than an imperforate one. When no opening at all is present the baby is held upside down and the abdomen and perineum X-rayed. The distance between the perineum, upon which a radio-opaque marker can be placed, and the blind rectum can be estimated. Gas normally reaches the distal gut in about 18 hours. If the gap is 2 cm. or less a perineal operation is justified, in which the bowel is mobilised and brought down, its edges being stitched to the skin. Many of these babies have a fistula between rectum and urethra or bladder, which must be divided before the bowel can be adequately mobilised. If the gap is longer than 2 cm. it is advisable to perform a transverse colostomy and then at the age of about a year carry out a pull-through operation into the perineum. Occasionally this is successful, but there appear to be a number of children in whom a proper sphincter does not exist, and they really are then provided with a perineal colostomy, which is less easy to control than an abdominal one. Some of these children will be better off with a good abdominal colostomy. In female babies the anus may occur in the posterior vaginal wall, and with this abnormality it is necessary to transplant the anus to its normal place in the perineum.

HYPERTROPHIC PYLORIC STENOSIS

The cause of this condition is unknown, and symptoms do not usually present until 2 weeks of age. Pyloric stenosis is much commoner in males, and appears to be inherited as a recessive character. The baby usually

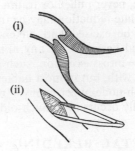

FIG. 41. (i) Hypertrophic pyloric stenosis;
(ii) Splitting of the hypertrophied pyloric
smooth muscle

appears normal for the first 2–6 weeks, and then starts to regurgitate feeds, finally vomiting them forcibly, a condition aptly described as projectile vomiting. Visible peristalsis of the stomach may be seen, and the baby loses weight and becomes dehydrated. If the abdomen is carefully palpated, during a feed or just after the baby has vomited, the pyloric tumour can be felt just below the right costal margin. Treatment consists of irrigating the stomach through a fine nasal catheter, using water or saline to remove the stale milk curds. Subcutaneous or intravenous half normal saline is given to correct dehydration and electrolyte depletion, normal saline if there is great salt depletion. No child should be submitted to operation unless dehydration and losses of sodium and potassium have been corrected. Under general anaesthesia the abdomen is opened through a small transverse incision and the pylorus inspected. A Ramstedt's operation (Fig. 41) is then done, which consists of splitting the pyloric muscle fibres longitudinally, first with a knife and then with blunt dissection until the mucosa pouts into the wound. The child can be fed within a few hours of operation, and the condition does not recur. Complications of the operation are inadequate division of the pyloric muscle fibres, wound infection and, very rarely, gastro-enteritis.

INTUSSUSCEPTION

In this condition the bowel, usually the distal ileum, telescopes, and this if unrelieved produces intestinal obstruction and eventual gangrene of the bowel. Typically an overweight male baby about weaning time screams with pain, draws up his knees and, perhaps, vomits. For a short while he appears pale and shocked. The attack soon passes off, and the child then appears fairly well. A stool composed of blood and mucus, 'redcurrant jelly', may be passed, and if a rectal examination is made there is usually no faecal content and only a little blood on the examining finger. It may be possible to feel the intussuscepted bowel as a sausage-shaped mass lying in the line of the colon. Since these fat babies are more dehydrated than they would appear, it is essential to give them subcutaneous or intravenous fluid before operation is undertaken, but surgery is urgently necessary, since if treated within the first 24 hours recovery is almost certain. The abdomen is opened, the intussuscepted bowel milked back into place, never pulled or traumatised; it is rare for the condition to recur. If seen late reduction may be impossible and the bowel gangrenous. It must then be excised and an end-to-end anastomosis performed. A search should be made for any abnormality which might have caused the start of the intussusception, such as a Meckel's diverticulum, and this must be dealt with, but in most babies no cause is found, although there is marked lymph-node hypertrophy. Intussusception due to a diverticulum or polyp usually occurs in a much older child.

RECTAL BLEEDING

The commonest cause of bleeding is an anal fissure; which usually occurs posteriorly at six o'clock. It is due to the passage of a hard stool, and if the fissure is gently smeared with a little anaesthetic cream morning and evening and the baby given a mild aperient, such as magnesia and liquid paraffin, to keep the motions soft the fissure will heal. If this is unsuccessful the patient is given an anaesthetic and the sphincter dilated with two or three fingers in order to overstretch it, and thus overcome the spasm which prevents healing. The second commonest cause of bleeding is a rectal polyp, which may be single or occasionally multiple. It can often be felt with a finger in the rectum, but is best identified at proctoscopy. It is removed with a wire snare and, unlike the rectal polyp of the adult, is not a premalignant condition.

CONGENITAL DISLOCATION OF THE HIP

Congenital dislocation of the hip is uncommon in Great Britain, but is much more common in Northern Italy and in parts of Central Europe. There is often a strong familial history. The acetabulum is shallow and ill-developed. The head of the femur is small and the neck anteverted with coxa valga, that is the angle between the neck and femoral shaft is greater than normal. The capsule of the joint is lengthened and may show a constriction between the head and the acetabulum that prevents replacement of the head in the acetabulum. The condition may affect one or both joints.

Treatment is most satisfactory when the diagnosis can be made soon after birth. At birth all infants should be examined for any limitation of

FIG. 42. Congenital dislocation of the hip; (i) Radiography shows head of femur outside the joint; (ii) 'Frog-type' plaster

abduction at the hip and for a characteristic click on abducting the flexed hip—Ortolani's sign. It may be noticed that a limb is short, or asymmetry of the groin creases or widening of the perineum may be seen. When the child walks a limp and a characteristic waddling gait is obvious. A typical physical sign is telescoping. When the hip is flexed, pulling on the leg shows that the femur can be slid up and down the side of the ilium. The trochanters are felt above Nélaton's line (a line joining the anterior superior iliac spine to the tuberosity of the ischium). Trendelenburg's sign is positive, that is the buttock crease falls on standing, a sign of instability of the hip joint either from dislocation of its head or from muscle paralysis particularly affecting the glutei.

In adult life the head of the femur may be associated with a false joint on the side of the ilium. The pelvis is often deformed and hypoplastic on one or both sides, leading to difficulties in parturition. Radiographs (Fig. 42) show the epiphysis of the head of the femur outside and above the acetabulum, the neck of the femur anteverted and there is coxa valga. The acetabular slope is more vertical than normal and there is delay in ossification of the femoral head.

The earlier treatment is instituted, the better the result. Ideally treatment should be begun before the child walks. In tiny babies abduction of the legs by malleable metal splints is all that is needed, with observation to see that the head of the femur remains and develops in the acetabulum. In older babies reduction is achieved by gradual traction on an abduction frame. After this, by traction and external rotation, the head is negotiated into the acetabulum. Immobilisation is achieved in a 'frog plaster' in 90° abduction and external rotation, a position which is maintained for 6–9 months (Fig. 42). Young children from 1 to 10 years may need operative treatment to reduce the dislocation. An arthrogram is performed by injection of opaque medium into the joint, which may show an hour-glass constriction of the capsule that can be relieved operatively, followed by reduction and plaster immobilisation. The acetabular cavity can be deepened by a shelf operation in which the dorsal lip of the acetabulum is fractured, levered down and held in place by a bone graft. A rotation osteotomy of the femur and osteotomy of the pelvis may be needed to correct extreme anteversion of the neck of the femur. In adults who have had no treatment the condition is best accepted until, and if, osteoarthritis develops, when osteotomy or arthroplasty or arthrodesis may be indicated.

MALIGNANT TUMOURS OF CHILDHOOD

Leukaemia is by far the commonest malignant disease encountered in childhood, others are Hodgkin's disease, malignant tumours of the brain and those of the genito-urinary system. Malignant tumours of the soft issues tend to be sarcomas, and not carcinomas as in adults, and do not carry quite such a bad prognosis as was previously thought. Reference to tumours of particular organs will be found in other chapters of the book.

FURTHER READING

Mason Brown, J. J. (1962) *Surgery of Childhood.* Arnold, London.
Gross, R. E. (1953) *The Surgery of Infancy and Childhood.* Saunders, Philadelphia.
Stephens, F. D. et. al. (1963) *Congenital Malformations of the Rectum, Anus, and Genito-Urinary Tracts.* Livingstone, Edinburgh.
Nixon, H. H., and O'Donnell, B. (1961). *The Essentials of Paediatric Surgery.* Heinemann.
Twistington Higgins, T., Williams, D. I. and Nash, D. F. E. (1951) *The Urology of Childhood.* Butterworth.

CHAPTER TWENTY-NINE

ORTHOPAEDIC AND ACCIDENT SURGERY

Orthopaedics, as the name implies, was originally concerned with treating deformities in children; today it embraces not only all ages but also all kinds of injury. It may be defined as the surgery of repair of the locomotor system of the body when this has been rendered abnormal by developmental anomaly, disease or injury. The locomotor system comprises not only bones, joints, muscle, and tendons but also nerves and blood vessels. Many different tissues are involved in this branch of surgery, and widely differing techniques are necessary in their repair. The orthopaedic surgeon uses methods akin to carpentry in operating on bones and joints, but in operations such as a tendon graft or nerve suture in the hand, fine dexterity is necessary, with accurate knowledge of anatomy, physiology and the processes of healing. It is particularly easy for the surgeon to become too concerned with mechanical problems and to forget that it is function that is to be conserved or restored. Treatment should not be ordered merely to correct some radiographic abnormality; the main reason for treatment is to improve or conserve function.

METHODS OF EXAMINATION AND INVESTIGATION

Diagnosis is achieved by following the usual clinical sequence of history, physical examination and special investigations. The *history* is particularly important, for though the complaint itself may be diagnostic—for example, a twisted spine in scoliosis or a displaced fracture of the forearm with marked angulation—it is easy for attention to be focused on this, neglecting important clues to diagnosis, such as a history of a carcinoma of the breast prior to a pathological fracture.

Examination

This must include the body as a whole, as well as detailed examination of the affected part, unless the condition is of a very minor nature. A methodical system of examination must be followed, otherwise signs may be overlooked. *Inspection* yields most information, and comparison with the normal side is of paramount importance. Skin colour, the presence of operative or other scars, the soft tissue and bony contours, posture and the range of movement of the affected part should all be studied. *Palpation* confirms or excludes impressions gained from inspection and also provides information about local temperature, induration, fluctuation, muscle tone, soft tissue or bony swelling, passive range of movement, tendon and joint crepitus and abnormal joint mobility. *Measurements* are recorded in the case notes for an accurate assessment of differing lengths or circumferences of the limbs providing a 'baseline' from which future changes may be judged. Accurate records are important medico-legally when claims for industrial compensation or damages are being assessed.

Diagrams are helpful and, however simple, convey much better than words the situation found at the time of examination. *Muscle power* may be charted according to the following scheme.

> *Grade.* 5 Full power
> 　　　　 4 Movement against gravity and resistance
> 　　　　 3 Movement against gravity alone
> 　　　　 2 Movement with gravity excluded
> 　　　　 1 Evidence of muscle contraction but no movement
> 　　　　 0 No evidence of any muscle contraction

Investigations

Radiography is the most valuable single investigation in orthopaedic and accident surgery. All the relevant parts must be included. In radiographs taken to diagnose a fracture the joint above and the joint below the involved bone must be included. Serious errors may arise if this rule is forgotten.

The film must be orientated correctly. Conventionally it is arranged that the film of the part in question is in the anatomical position—as if the observer was facing the patient. The patient's left side will then be on the right of the film, great care must be taken that the 'left' or 'right' side markers are not accidentlly placed on the wrong side. If possible, their position should always be checked against asymmetrical features, such as the liver or heart, or with the clinical records.

The outlines of the soft tissues should be studied for alterations in contour, density or the presence of foreign bodies. Gas or fluid may be seen in tissue planes in surgical emphysema or clostridial infection. The bones should be carefully studied by the observer, following both the outer and inner lines of the cortex, the direction and form of the trabeculae, the bony density in various parts, the epiphyseal lines and the so-called 'joint-space' (really the thickness of cartilage between opposing bony surfaces). All bones or parts of bones on the film must be carefully examined. Important lesions are often overlooked because a bone is affected which is not in the centre of the film. The importance of comparison between the suspected abnormal and the normal side cannot be over-emphasised.

The diagnosis of some nervous or muscular conditions is sometimes aided by electrical methods of investigation. *Nerve conduction times* may be measured by following the electrical nerve impulse after stimulation, and may be of use, for example, in diagnosing ulnar- and median-nerve lesions by providing accurate evidence of the site of a block in nerve conduction.

In *electromyography* electrical potentials from skeletal muscle are recorded by surface or intramuscular electrodes, which provide information of the state of innervation of the muscle.

Biochemical investigations include estimation of serum calcium and phosphorus and measurement of phosphatase, alkaline and acid.

TECHNIQUES AND MATERIALS

Infection complicating an orthopaedic operation is so disastrous that special techniques are used to minimise its possibility. The importance of preventing infection in orthopaedic operations is largely due to the serious results of infection of bone and joint. Bone infection tends to become chronic, persisting for many years despite treatment. Loss of function, ugly scars and deformity result; amputation may be necessary. The *'no-touch technique'* is a method of operating in which the tissues or the parts of the instrument which handle tissue and all ligatures and swabs are never touched by hand. Despite meticulous scrubbing of the hands with bactericidal agents and despite the wearing of sterilised gloves, it has been known for some time that the longer the operation, the greater is the chance that bacteria from the surgeon's hands pass through small holes in the gloves. These perforations result from unnoticed damage during operation and allow any tissues touched by the surgeon's fingers to become infected. Further advances in reducing the incidence of wound infection will probably come from better methods of sterilising the air in the operating theatre.

Orthopaedic surgeons prefer to operate in a *'bloodless field'*. The limbs can be exsanguinated by elevation for a few minutes, followed by tight wrapping with an Esmarch's rubber bandage. This is followed by arrest of arterial blood flow by the pressure of an inflated pneumatic tourniquet wrapped around the proximal part of the limb. A tourniquet may safely be left in place for up to $1\frac{1}{2}$ hours; it must then be released, but can be replaced after a few minutes. The duration of its application must be carefully measured. Surveillance in the operating theatre should be such as to make it impossible for a patient to leave the theatre with a tourniquet still applied. The system of the bloodless field greatly facilitates dissection, the identification of structures and neat reconstructive surgery. Vessels which are divided are ligated before the tourniquet is released to prevent haematoma formation in the wound postoperatively. A firm pressure bandage must also always be applied. Suction drainage of the 'Redivac' type has proved to be a great advance in preventing haematoma.

Orthopaedic operations, particularly those on the hip and thigh, are often carried out on a special table on which the patient is only supported by the upper thorax, pelvis and heels, and the position of the legs relative to the trunk may be held firmly in any position—for example, while a pin is being inserted to hold a fractured neck of femur.

Special materials are often used in orthopaedic operations. *Bone grafts* may be autogenous (from the same patient), homologous (from another patient or cadaver) or heterologous (from another species such as beef bone). Autogenous grafts 'take' most readily. All forms of transplanted bone provide an inorganic bone structure, a framework into which the host tissue osteoblasts can grow. No living cells survive the transfer of the graft from donor to recipient site. The bone grafts may be applied in the form of chips or cortical slabs.

Various forms of metal and sometimes plastic are used in plates, screws and various types of nails used for holding long bones. Such materials must produce the minimum reaction in human tissues if infection is to be avoided and the strength of the prosthesis is to be preserved. The most commonly used metal is 'Vitallium', the trade name for a strong, light and non-corroding alloy. It is also used as a replacement for some joint surfaces—for example, as a prosthesis to replace the necrotic head of the femur after fracture, or after destruction of a joint surface by osteoarthritis. Sutures of stainless-steel wire are used for tendon and nerve repair; specially fine sutures for nerve approximation can be made from human hair. All these materials act in the tissues as a foreign body, never become incorporated but merely become surrounded by a fibrous tissue shell. Infection may be disastrous in the presence of a large foreign body, resulting in total failure of the operation and months of serious disability. The infection cannot be eradicated until the foreign material has been removed.

PHYSIOTHERAPY AND REHABILITATION

Rest is essential to recovery and healing processes after an injury or surgical operation, both for the whole body and for the part involved. Rest must not be too prolonged, or the patient becomes lethargic, muscles atrophy and joints stiffen so that the normal activity, power and range of movement may never be regained. The older the patient, the more likely this is. Furthermore, there is little doubt that prolonged recumbency predisposes to a greater incidence of deep-vein thrombosis, pulmonary embolism and bronchopneumonia.

Within the limits of any splint or plaster, the patient is encouraged to move as soon as possible and as much as possible. The physiotherapist assists by exercising different muscle groups and encouraging deep breathing and coughing. Even when a limb is encased in plaster for months, its muscle groups should be exercised vigorously by static contractions. In this way the muscles are kept 'in tone', and when the plaster is removed are able to begin powerful movements at once. Joint stiffness after injury or operation is due largely to intramuscular and intermuscular adhesions and to fibrotic changes in the joint capsule. Adhesions are overcome by graduated *active* exercises encouraged to the limit of pain. Passive exercises are of far less value and sometimes may be dangerous, since they may cause further injury, leading to the formation of even more fibrous tissue.

Patients in hospital for long periods must be kept busy. Occupational therapy fills this need, and can also be used for assessment of the physical abilities and limitations of the patient. A well-equipped workshop offers a wide range of activities to test and exercise different muscle groups and facilities. Training for a new job can begin in the occupational-therapy department. Rehabilitation should continue after discharge from hospital, helping towards returning the patient to his previous job or resettlement in another.

MULTIPLE INJURIES

The number of persons coming to hospital with multiple injuries is now reaching epidemic proportions because of the increase in numbers of vehicles on the roads and the increasing mechanisation of industry, agriculture and work in the home. Much could be done to reduce the toll by preventive measures. In industry, in the mines and in agriculture more stringent safety precautions need to be applied. On the roads safer driving methods must be instilled, and manufacturers must be persuaded to incorporate proven safety features in vehicles as standard fittings. Padded panels, recessed controls, collapsible steering wheels, anti-roll bars and safety belts are at present found on only a minority of cars. Perhaps the most important factor of all in accident prevention is the improvement of existing designs of roads and raising of the standard of driving.

Treatment

In the patient with multiple injuries systems may be involved besides those strictly within the province of the orthopaedic surgeon. Despite the ready availability of neuro-surgeons, thoracic surgeons and other specialists for advice and specialised measures, it is of the utmost importance that the care of the patient and the ultimate responsibility for all decisions taken should rest with one man, who will usually be the orthopaedic surgeon. Multiple responsibility may result in confusion and sometimes in disaster. The most efficient treatment is provided where all injured patients from a large area are segregated in an Accident Service in part of a comprehensive, well-formed general hospital.

Initial Diagnosis

The patient usually arrives amid scenes of great excitement and, while no time must be lost, a calm approach to the initial assessment of the problem must be made before any action is taken. A brief history (usually a sentence or two from an ambulance man is enough) is essential, and will often give a lead as to the type of injury to be expected. Thus, a man injured by a falling wall and released only with some difficulty may be expected to have crush injuries of his chest and abdominal viscera—ruptured spleen, liver and kidneys being likely possibilities. A miner caught by a roof fall is likely to have spinal injuries, in addition to any obvious external injuries. Passengers in the rear seat of a stationary car struck from behind are likely to have cervical 'whip-lash' injuries.

The next stage is a rapid examination of the whole body, during which obvious injuries are detected and priorities for treatment are established. A well-designed accident chart on which the findings can be quickly recorded saves much time. *First the air passages must be clear* and the patient breathing without obstruction. If the tongue is falling back an airway should be inserted. If there is intra-oral bleeding, clots must be removed by suction. Respiratory distress, with cyanosis of the tongue and lips, indicates the need for oxygen either given by mask or, better still, via an endotracheal tube connected to an anaesthetic machine.

The degree of shock due to blood loss must be estimated. The volume of haemorrhage is partly judged by the patient's general condition, the colour and temperature of the skin, the pulse rate and the blood pressure, and also by the amount of blood that might be expected to have been lost from the known injuries. Three stages of haemorrhagic shock may be distinguished, a rough classification, which has relevance to the urgency of treatment.

The most severely shocked patients have probably lost at least half their blood volume, and may be unconscious from blood loss alone. The skin is extremely pale, and the extremities are cold, damp and cyanosed. 'Air hunger' is often marked, and the pulse at the wrist is almost impalpable, with the blood pressure unrecordable. Severe injuries may also be obvious. For such patients Group O Rh negative blood must be immediately available. A transfusion is begun—usually by inserting a large-bore cannula through an incision over the long saphenous vein just above and in front of the medial malleolus. Other veins will be collapsed, and time should not be wasted in attempting 'stab' drips or in using narrow-bore polyethylene cannulae. While the transfusion is being set up, blood should be taken for grouping and cross-matching and 2 pints of O negative blood sent for. The first of these should be transfused under pressure, using Martin's pump, while the patient's response is observed. Usually an immediate improvement is obvious, and transfusion can then be continued later with cross-matched blood of the correct group. Meanwhile, any obvious external bleeding is stopped by firm pressure with a large pad of dressings and bandaging. Tourniquets are seldom if ever necessary. If a spurting artery is seen, forceps should be applied and the vessel tied.

Moderately shocked patients are pale, cold and clammy, but have a pulse of fair volume and a systolic blood pressure of about 90 mm. Hg. Here more time is available and after the 'drip' is set up plasma or a plasma substitute (dextraven) may be transfused until blood of the correct group is available—usually after about 15–20 minutes.

The third group of patients are pale, but obviously less ill than those previously described—the pulse rate is above 100 per minute, and the systolic blood pressure around 100–110 mm. Hg. The injuries sustained, however, make it likely that about 2–3 pints of blood have been lost. Thus, blood should be cross-matched and transfused without delay, as further bleeding may occur.

At this point it is worth mentioning that the amount of blood lost from a particular fracture has been estimated by measuring the amount of swelling of the limb or trunk and correlating this with the measured fall in blood volume. The amounts lost for common closed fractures are as follows:

Tibia and fibula   1–2 pints
Shaft of femur   1–4 pints or more
Forearm   1–1½ pints
Arm and shoulder   2–4 pints
Pelvis   2–6 pints or more
Spine   1–2 pints
Multiple ribs   2–4 pints

If the expected loss for the known injuries has been replaced by transfusion, and yet the patient remains shocked and obviously has a diminished blood volume, there may be bleeding from another lesion, for example a ruptured spleen or liver, with intraperitoneal bleeding.

The amount lost depends on the severity of the injury, the associated soft-tissue injury and the degree of comminution of the fracture. Open fractures bleed more than closed fractures. The severity of the injury and the amount lost in a given fracture can be judged by the degree of swelling. Thus, using the above table, it will be seen that a combination of a severe fracture of the tibia and a fractured shaft of femur may be associated with haemorrhage of up to 6 pints—which is half the blood volume of an average adult. The patient who sustains a fractured pelvis or ruptured spleen additional to a fractured femur may lose the whole of his blood volume unless replacement is begun energetically and immediately.

FURTHER MANAGEMENT OF MULTIPLE INJURIES

After initial diagnosis and resuscitation a more careful and detailed examination is made. The patient's body surface should be examined from head to toe for lacerations, bruises, swelling or tenderness. All bones should be palpated for contour and joints put through a normal range of movement if possible. The chest and pelvis should be 'sprung' to elicit tenderness from an otherwise unsuspected fracture.

The chest should then be examined, in particular the position of the mediastinum is important, and air or blood in the pleural cavity may be detected by percussion and auscultation. The abdomen should be examined for localised tenderness, dullness to percussion, distension and the presence or absence of bowel sounds. A rectal examination should be performed if there is a pelvic fracture or any possibility of pelvic visceral injury. A tear in the rectal wall may be felt, or the prostate may be found widely displaced if the membranous urethra is ruptured. A specimen of urine must always be seen before excluding renal-tract injury to the urinary system. Finally, a full neurological examination must be performed, with particular attention to the level of consciousness, size and reaction of the pupils and the state of the reflexes at the time of examination. At

P

this stage radiographic examination of all parts suspected to be the site of injury should be undertaken. Often this may mean radiography of almost the entire body. The radiographs are best taken on a special trolley without moving the patient.

All the positive findings should be recorded in the notes, preferably on a specially prepared major accident chart. The further progress of the patient must be charted every 10–15 minutes; pulse, blood pressure, respirations, size of pupils and level of consciousness being the minimum observations required. All treatment must be noted, with the time of administration, in particular a careful count of intravenous fluids must be recorded on a fluid-balance chart.

In the treatment of multiple injuries it is important to establish priorities. Obstruction to the airway is the most urgent problem, and severe blood loss the next. Surgical operation must not be delayed beyond resuscitation and partial restoration of the blood volume. Injury to abdominal viscera demands early surgery, whereas fractures of the limbs need only a temporary splint for their control, and any operation may be deferred for days or even a week or two if a more serious lesion is present. Open fractures must be closed within a few hours if infection is to be avoided. Arterial injuries must be treated at once to prevent gangrene. Immediate surgery is vital for the relief of an extradural haematoma causing progressively increasing pressure on the brain. Burr holes and evacuation of blood should be performed without delay, as the patient may succumb at any moment.

A recent advance in the treatment of major injury is the use of hyperbaric oxygen for limbs in which the vascular supply is precarious or for the treatment of gas gangrene. The patient is placed in a pressure chamber filled with oxygen at a pressure of 2 atmospheres; under these conditions the amount of oxygen in solution in plasma is greatly augmented. Dramatic results have been reported in the treatment of anaerobic infections.

After a major injury, especially one in which a limb has been crushed, the urine output must be measured carefully, watching for oliguria or anuria. Injection of 500 ml. of 10–20% mannitol intravenously has a protective effect on kidney function, and may be given prophylactically. If anuria becomes established the use of haemodialysis (artificial kidney) may be life saving.

Further advances in the accurate restoration of blood volume after injury will come with the wider use of methods of measuring the blood volume by isotopes and estimation of the central venous pressure via a catheter placed in the right atrium of the heart.

FURTHER READING

Plews, L. W. (1966) *Accident Service, Pitman, London.*

London, P. S. (1967) *Care of the Injured*, Livingstone, Edinburgh.

Clarke, R., Badger, F. G., and Sevitt, S. (1959) *Modern Trends in Accident Surgery and in Medicine.* Butterworth, London.

Matthews, D. N. (1963) *Recent Advances in the Surgery of Trauma*, Churchill, London.

CHAPTER THIRTY

FRACTURES AND DISLOCATIONS

Now that it is recognised that all injuries should come into the ambit of an Accident Service closely supervised by orthopaedic surgeons, it is more important for the student to know of the presentation, mode of healing and complications of bone and joint injuries than of the detailed management of all fractures. In this chapter the general principles of fractures will be described, and later on the treatment of only the very common fractures will be given in any great detail.

TYPES OF FRACTURES

Fractures are usually the result of a severe injury, but in some cases the trauma may be trivial or even unappreciated. *Stress* or *fatigue fractures* are fractures which usually follow excessive activity but without any definite incident of injury. The best example is a fracture of the neck of the second metatarsal, in which pain is felt in the forefoot and tenderness elicited over the head of the metatarsal. Radiography may show no abnormality until perhaps 2 or 3 weeks have elapsed, when a cuff of subperiosteal ossification is seen around the neck of the second metatarsal and the fracture line, only a crack, becomes visible. A *pathological fracture* (see p. 449) is a fracture of a bone that is previously diseased, usually without any history of injury.

Fractures may be *open* (compound) or *closed*. If open, the skin may have been broken by external injury or from a jagged piece of bone lacerating the skin from within. Open fractures are very serious because of the likelihood of infection and the development of osteomyelitis. Infection delays healing, and thus solid union. The infection is likely to become chronic, with persistent purulent discharge and sequestrum formation. Fractures which become compound from within are less likely to become infected, so long as they are early and efficiently closed. The most serious fractures are those that are compound with loss of skin or with severe contamination by dirt and foreign bodies or where there is crushing of soft tissues.

The line of a fracture is important to its stability after reduction. Transverse fractures are stable if they can be reduced in such a way that at least part of their ends are hitched together. Oblique or spiral fractures tend to be unstable because the pull of nearby muscles makes the bone ends slide. Shearing strains on a fracture may impair its healing. The bones involved in a fracture may be mobile or impacted. If they are impacted in good position, as is usual, no treatment may be necessary apart from physiotherapy to preserve the function of nearby joints. A fracture is said to be comminuted if there are several fragments. Compression or crush fractures occur in such bones as the vertebrae, os calcis or talus. In children the bones are very flexible, and partial fractures (greenstick fractures) are typical.

CLINICAL PRESENTATION

Usually it is obvious that a person has sustained a broken bone, but it cannot be stressed too strongly that any person who comes to hospital having sustained an injury and complains of pain must be radiographed. Apart from the welfare of the patient, it is legally inexcusable not to have had radiographs performed of the bones, although in many results will be negative. A particular pitfall is the fracture of the scaphoid bone, in which the break may not be revealed for some time, and so a radiograph should be repeated after 2–3 weeks, during which time treatment for a possible fracture should be carried out. Many 'sprained' ankles reveal a crack in the fibula or evidence of a severe ligamentous tear shown by sub-luxation. Fractured ribs may be revealed in a chest radiograph or, more important, underlying lung or pleural damage. Occasionally radiography may reveal some other cause for pain, for example, a loose body in a joint or evidence of an old fracture, a crushed vertebra or arthritis. Underlying bone disease may be found, such as Paget's disease or secondary malignant deposits. It is important that not only the tender area in the bone is shown but also the joint above and below it.

The symptoms of a fracture are obvious—pain, loss of function, swelling and bruising. Examination may reveal an obvious deformity and tenderness localised to the affected bone. Movement of the fracture to elicit bone crepitus or abnormal mobility is rarely justified and likely to cause increased pain. Some fractures are likely to be complicated by injuries to nerves and vessels, and the relation of these structures to bones should always be remembered. It is important to record in the case notes that nerves and vessels adjacent to the fracture have been tested before and after any manipulative procedure, if only to prove that the treatment has not caused or aggravated any further damage. Nearby viscera may be injured, for example, the bladder in fractured pelvis and the lung or spleen in fractured ribs. Awareness of these possibilities ensures that serious and potentially fatal complications are not missed.

HEALING OF FRACTURES

The healing of a fracture is a complicated process in which several phases can be described. A haematoma forms between the bone ends and extends into the surrounding soft tissues. The extent of the haematoma will obviously depend upon the degree of violence sustained and the efficiency of early treatment in limiting bleeding. Bleeding and swelling may continue for up to 12–36 hours and cause late complications. External pressure efficiently applied may decrease the size of the swelling around the fracture. The periosteum is stripped up by haemorrhage, and osteoblasts from the periosteum and bone marrow proliferate to form callus—a mass of osteoblasts, fibroblasts and blood cells that becomes partly calcified to form a structure called *woven bone*. The callus gives the fracture rigidity and forms a structure on which the future lamellae of bone can form. The first radiological evidence of healing of a fracture is the appearance of calcification around the bone ends in the subperiosteal zone. Calcification, and hence radiopacity, usually takes 3–4 weeks to appear. The amount of the callus will depend upon the size of the fracture haematoma and the degree of comminution of the bones. A transverse fracture may show little callus if it is accurately reduced. If several bone fragments are present, then much more may be produced. The degree of vascularity will also vary the amount of callus. The callus or woven bone lies not entirely external to the bone ends but also between them and in the marrow cavity.

In the next phase the callus becomes consolidated and toughened by deposits of bone lamellae; when this phase is complete the bone is usually united. Finally, the bone becomes remodelled, the swelling around the fracture decreases and bone trabeculae are seen radiologically traversing the fracture. Bone remodelling is seen at its best in the infant, in whom angulation can be spontaneously corrected and in whom after a lapse of 1–2 years often no radiographic evidence of an earlier fracture can be seen.

TREATMENT OF FRACTURES

The first-aid treatment of a fracture includes the simple measures that allow the subject to be taken to hospital as quickly and as comfortably as possible. Limb fractures are splinted, in the upper limb by binding the arm to one side or in a sling. In the lower limb the ankles should be tied together so that the unaffected limb can be used as a splint. The patient with a suspected fracture of the spine should not be allowed to flex, and so should be carried face down. The patient with fractured ribs is best sat up to allow easy breathing. Only if a long journey must be made to hospital should morphia be given to injured patients and more elaborate splintage applied before arrival at hospital. Morphia should certainly not be given in cases of head, abdominal or chest injuries.

The case of the patient who has suffered a major accident is discussed on p. 437. Once a fracture is diagnosed appropriate radiographs are taken and a decision made as to whether reduction is necessary and when it is to be performed. Reduction is usually achieved by manipulation of the affected part under general anaesthesia. If the fracture is unstable, for example, an oblique fracture of the femur, a decision is made as to whether traction should be added to maintain reduction or whether operative fixation is required.

Most fractures require immobilisation to permit union and relieve pain, which is dramatically relieved by preventing movement. Immobilisation is achieved in a plaster of Paris cast or by traction on a frame or by operative fixation. Traction is usually applied to a metal pin passed through a bone. Operative fixation may be performed with metal plates, screws, nails, circumferential wires or bone grafts.

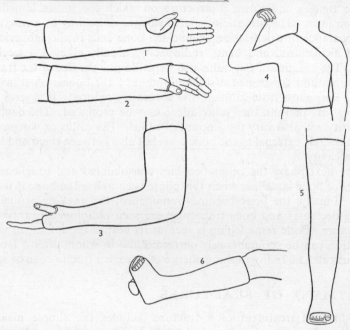

FIG. 43. Standard plasters for immobilisation of fractures; (1) Colles' fracture. (2) Scaphoid fracture. (3) Fracture forearm bones. (4) Shoulder spica. (5) Full thigh plaster. (6) Below knee plaster

A plaster cast should effectively immobilise the fracture and in most cases the joint above and below it. The fracture is usually lightly padded by a thin layer of cellular bandage, bony points must also be padded, and the upper and lower limits of plaster where they are likely to cut the skin. A plaster slab is first prepared of 6–12 thicknesses of plaster bandages of appropriate length. Heavier plasters are needed for the lower limb than for the upper. The plaster is completed by winding wet plaster bandage around the limb until a shell of sufficient strength has been made. It is important that joints that are not included in the plaster should be able to move freely, especially fingers and toes. A number of standard plasters can be described (see Fig. 43).

Forearm

Extending from the ante cubital fossa to the knuckles. The elbow is free to move, as are the fingers. The wrist is dorsiflexed and the hand held in the position of function with the thumb well forward of the palm. A bar of plaster is carried from the dorsum of the knuckles across the palm, leaving the thumb free, except in a fracture of the scaphoid, when the thumb is included up to but not including its terminal joint.

The wrist is slightly palmar flexed after reduction of Colles' fracture and dorsiflexed for Smith's fracture (see p. 462).

Elbow

Extending from the insertion of deltoid to the knuckles, the elbow at 90° and the forearm in the mid-position between pronation and supination, except in some forearm fractures. The wrist is dorsiflexed and a bar is carried across the palm.

Shoulder

A shoulder spica is rarely used for fractures around the shoulder joint. The arm is abducted to 90° and flexed and externally rotated so the hand lies in front of the mouth. The thorax and the whole of the arm to the knuckles is included in the plaster.

Ankle

Extending from the tibial tubercle to the root of the toes, leaving knee and toe movements free. The foot must be at 90° to the lower leg and plantigrade that is neither inverted nor everted.

Knee

Extending from the upper thigh to the ankle, the knee slightly flexed.

Hip

A hip spica immobilises the hip joint with the leg slightly abducted and flexed at the hip and knee. The plaster includes the pelvis up to the nipples and the whole leg down to the root of the toes.

Spinal Jacket

To immobilise the thoraco-lumbar spine. The plaster extends from the manubrium sterni to the pubis, both bony points being padded with adhesive rubber pads. The iliac crests and vertebral spines are also padded. The plaster extends down under the arms to the lower dorsal spine.

Before and after reduction of a fracture it is vitally important to test for evidence of vessel and nerve damage. Close observation is essential to watch for the effects of swelling that follow injury and manipulation. Toes and fingers must be watched carefully. Anaesthesia, pain, deadness, duskiness and whiteness are all warning signs, and may necessitate the splitting of a plaster to relieve tension. If these symptoms are ignored severe tension may be set up with vascular and nerve impairment and finally, in the worst cases the end result may be a useless limb. Any complaint of soreness under the plaster must be taken seriously, for an ulcer may easily form from rubbing, especially over bony points. The plaster must be removed or a window cut to find the cause of pain.

In the next phase, once pain and swelling have subsided, physiotherapy is encouraged to exercise joints that are not immobilised and to strengthen muscles immobilised in plaster. For example, the quadriceps muscle wastes rapidly unless active contractions are performed within the plaster. Energetic activity by the patient can offset the stiffness and weakness that is felt when mobility is allowed.

In the upper limb clinical signs of solidity precede radiographic signs of bone union. As the limb does not bear weight, immobilisation is usually of shorter duration than in the lower limb, except perhaps in fractures of the waist of the scaphoid, where union is notoriously slow. Freedom of tenderness over the fracture and absence of pain on gentle springing of the bones is good evidence of clinical union. In the lower limb the clinical signs of union are important, but evidence of solid callus formation in radiographs is awaited before weight-bearing is permitted. Mobilisation is allowed only when the radiographs show good evidence of fusion, such as the disappearance of the fracture line.

Finally, in the all-important phases of rehabilitation every effort is made by the physiotherapist to regain active movement. The occupational therapist gives treatment which will eventually restore the patient to his former job. In a major fracture of a bone such as the femur this may be a long process, for it may be a year before a man can return to full work in a heavy job.

COMPLICATIONS OF FRACTURE

Non-union and Delayed Union

The most serious complication of a fracture is non-union. Many fractures show delayed union, being slow to unite, but eventually join, so long as immobilisation is prolonged. Radiographically non-union is diagnosed when the bone ends are sclerosed, there is little or no surrounding callus and, very rarely, a false joint (pseudarthrosis) is formed.

The causes of non-union are many. Infection of a compound fracture commonly leads to failure of union. The anatomy of the blood supply may be such that a fracture may lead to avascular necrosis of one of the bones, for example the proximal fragment of a fracture through the waist of the scaphoid or the head of the femur in a sub-capital fracture. Poor blood supply is held to be the cause of slow union of fractures in the lower third of the tibia.

Imperfect immobilisation may be a factor in non-union. The bone ends may be over-distracted and held apart by excessive traction, or soft tissues such as muscle may be interposed between the bone ends. Fractures into joints are slow to heal, and it is thought that synovial fluid has some inhibiting influence. Paradoxically operative fixation may slow the process of healing, though it is not often followed by non-union. An underlying disease of bone may be a factor, for example, secondary carcinoma.

The deformity that may result from malunion is called malalignment. In many cases accurate restoration of the shape of bones does not matter, but malalignment may be responsible for the development of osteoarthritis in nearby joints due to a shift in the normal lines of weight bearing. Shortening of a limb may follow incomplete reduction of a fracture of the femur or tibia.

Joint stiffness is one of the commonest complications of fractures. It may be inevitable if the fracture line goes into the joint, especially if a good deal of blood becomes extravasated into it (haemarthrosis). Every attempt should be made to obtain a smooth joint outline, if necessary by operative fixation, as otherwise a roughened articular surface predisposes to osteo-arthritis.

Haemorrhage at the time of injury and subsequent fibrosis around a joint may limit its function. The shoulder joint is particularly liable to become stiff, resulting in a so-called 'frozen shoulder'. If muscles become stuck to the site of a fracture movement of a joint may be limited, for example, the quadriceps, by adhering to a fracture of the lower part of the femur, may prevent full flexion of the knee joint.

When there is extensive haemorrhage into muscle or where the perio-steum is disturbed a mass of bone may form in the haematoma—myositis ossificans. It is not clear how osteoblasts migrate into the muscle to form bone. The commonest and most serious site of myositis ossificans is in the antecubital fossa, following a supracondylar fracture of the humerus. With rest the bony mass may resolve spontaneously. It is thought that forced passive movements of the joint to overcome its stiffness may aggravate the condition. Very rarely the bone may persist and may need excision, but the results of this operation are not uniformly successful.

Injuries to arteries associated with fractures are most serious because a limb may be lost or at best digits may become seriously contracted. The peripheral pulses must always be felt in any case of limb fracture. If they are absent and do not return after reduction of the fracture and if signs of ischaemia are present, the artery must be exposed. Release of tension due to haematoma by incision of the fascial sheath of a limb is often effective. If persistent spasm is found the artery is painted with a solution of papa-verine; if this is ineffective the lumen is forcibly distended with ligno-caine. If the artery is contused or divided it must be reconstructed by excision and suture or the interposition of an autogenous vein graft.

Where nerves are injured at the time of fracture the lesion is usually in continuity (see p. 589) and recovery can be expected after a few weeks. If function does not return then the nerve must be explored. If it is found divided or crushed the damaged part must be excised and the nerve recon-structed by suture and occasionally by nerve grafting. In some fractures immediate operation must be performed to relieve pressure on the nerve, for example, in fractures of the medial epicondyle of the humerus the bone fragment may have been dragged with the ulnar nerve into the joint. Dislocation of the head of the femur is commonly accompanied by paralysis of the sciatic nerve. Replacement and fixation of the epicondyle of the humerus or reduction of a dislocated femur is usually followed by rapid recovery of nerve function.

Occasionally, despite satisfactory union of a fracture, the patient complains of pain in the hand and foot, the skin of the toes or fingers is shiny, red and extremely tender to touch. Radiographs show extreme osteoporosis of the bones. The cause of this condition is unknown, it is known as Sudeck's atropy. Recovery from it is slow and treatment purely symptomatic.

A complication unique to fractures is that of fat embolism. The condition is rare and prone to occur in only the most serious injuries. Small particles of fat from the bone marrow gain entry into the blood stream and embolise, particularly into the lungs, brain, skin and kidneys. The patient becomes very ill, febrile, toxic and confused. Signs depend upon the organs mainly affected. Dyspnoea, haemoptysis and a febrile, pneumonic illness indicate lung involvement. A purpuric rash may appear on the skin. The sputum may contain fat globules. Confusion and coma occur if the brain is affected, haematuria denotes renal embolism. The urine may also contain fat globules. The condition is highly fatal, and at post mortem fat emboli may be seen in the small arteries of the lungs, kidneys and brain, with purpuric haemorrhages around them. Fortunately fat embolism is rare. There is no specific treatment, the prognosis is very bad.

Open Fractures

It has previously been mentioned that fractures may be compound from within or without and that the great fear is of infection of the bone. An open fracture is an acute emergency. At all costs, the bones must be covered by skin and all effort aimed at first-intention healing for infection may at best mean prolonged invalidism, non-union and chronic osteomyelitis and at the worst amputation. Operation must be undertaken at the earliest opportunity, certainly within 8–12 hours of injury. Tetanus prophylaxis must not be forgotten. At operation all damaged tissues are carefully excised. The edges of the skin wound are trimmed, any foreign bodies are removed and the wound irrigated with saline and hydrogen peroxide. Often the skin can only be closed by rotation of a flap of skin, often with the use of relieving incisions and grafting of any defects. Skin cover is the primary consideration, the fracture is reduced, but a perfect position is secondary in importance to rapid healing of the skin. Internal fixation by screws or plates is avoided unless the wound is small and uncontaminated.

Neglected compound fractures seen 24 hours after wounding are rare except in war-time. Excision of the wound is carried out, but no attempt is made to close the skin. The limb is immobilised in plaster, and 4 days later, if there is no evidence of gross infection, the wound is closed by delayed primary suture. Seriously infected wounds must be left to heal by granulation with plaster immobilisation.

2ⁿ CA
Pagers.

Pathological Fracture

In many cases pathological fracture is the first evidence of underlying bone disease. The commonest cause is a malignant tumour, most often secondary carcinoma, next in frequency comes Paget's disease. Other bone tumours, including enchondroma, osteoclastoma, osteogenic sarcoma, Ewing's tumour and myeloma, may be complicated by pathological fracture. Chronic pyogenic or syphilitic osteomyelitis or bone cyst are rare causes.

Among the general disorders of bone liable to cause fracture are fragilitas ossium, hyperparathyroidism, rickets, the rare lipoid storage diseases and osteomalacia.

Treatment includes diagnosis and treatment of the cause, with immobilisation by internal fixation of the fracture if that is feasible.

DISLOCATIONS AND SUBLUXATION

Joints are said to be dislocated if their surfaces are completely separated and subluxated if part of the joint surfaces are still in contact. Pathological dislocations are due to underlying diseases, usually infection or neuropathy. Fractures associated with a dislocation are complicated by effusion of blood into a joint (haemarthrosis). A haemarthrosis is very painful and develops so rapidly that the joint is tense and exquisitely tender. The blood must be released by aspiration, as it may become infected or organised and lead to stiffness and arthritis from intra-articular adhesions.

Dislocations are treated by manipulation, and occasionally, where there is a tendency for recurrence, by traction. For example, dislocation of the cervical spine is often treated by traction to the skull with special calipers to prevent recurrence. Open reduction at operation may be necessary if manipulation fails, for example, if a dislocated phalanx has buttonholed the extensor expansion. Recurrent dislocation, as in the case of the shoulder joint, demands special operations to limit movement.

Dislocations have many complications in common with fractures. There may be pressure on nerves or vessels, joint stiffness may follow neglect or failure to reduce dislocations. Avascular necrosis may occur if the vessels to part of a bone are damaged. Arthritis may follow, especially if there are many incidents of dislocation.

FURTHER READING

Watson-Jones, Sir R. (1952) *Fractures and Joint Injuries*, 4th ed. Livingstone, London.

Adams, J. C. (1964) *Outline of Fractures Including Joint Injuries*, 4th ed. Livingstone, Edinburgh.

CHAPTER THIRTY-ONE

FRACTURES AND DISLOCATIONS OF THE UPPER LIMB

Most injuries to bones and joints of the upper limb are due to a fall on the outstretched hand, a few are due to direct violence or some twisting strain.

CLAVICLE

The usual cause of a fracture of a clavicle is a fall on the outstretched hand or point of the shoulder. It is a common injury, often suffered in games such as rugby. The site of fracture (Fig. 44) is most usually at the

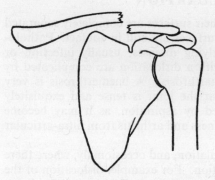

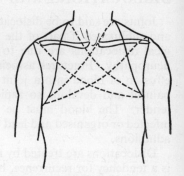

FIG. 44. Fracture of outer third of clavicle

FIG. 45. Figure-of-eight bandage applied to reduce a fracture of the clavicle

junction of the middle and outer thirds, occasionally the outer end is fractured. Deformity is caused by the weight of the shoulder which pulls the outer fragment downwards and medially. Clinically there is pain over the site of the fracture, with swelling and tenderness and inability to move the shoulder.

Almost all fractures of the clavicle unite, whatever the degree of malalignment. For a time a prominent mass of callus round the fracture may be unsightly, and its size may be minimised by reduction, achieved by a figure-of-eight bandage (Fig. 45) applied with a pad of wool in each axilla. By tightening the bandage the shoulders are braced back. A sling is worn so long as there is any pain. Active exercises to the shoulder can be begun in a week and the bandage abandoned in 2–3 weeks. There are no complications of this fracture, except that at the site of union there may be an obvious projection.

Dislocation of the Acromio-clavicular Joint

The cause is a fall on the hand or on the point of the shoulder, which may subluxate or dislocate the joint. Because the capsule is torn, the shoulder tends to drop, widening the joint space (Fig. 46). If the injury is severe the conoid and trapezoid ligaments may be torn with a greater drop of the level of the shoulder. Examination reveals tenderness over the point of the shoulder, and often a step can be felt between the clavicle and the acromion.

Minor injuries are best treated by a sling and active exercises as soon as

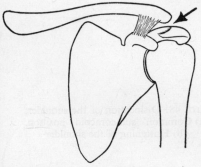

FIG. 46. Dislocation of the acromio-clavicular joint

FIG. 47. Fracture of the scapula: (1) blade; (2) neck; (3) coracoid process

pain subsides. In the more severe dislocations, with ligamentous injury, the joint can be reduced under anaesthesia and transfixed by a wire drilled through the acromion and the clavicle, which is left *in situ* for about 6 weeks, or a screw may be used inserted between the clavicle and coracoid process.

Dislocation of the Sterno-clavicular Joint

Dislocation of this joint is rare. Most commonly it occurs anteriorly; posterior dislocation is a severe injury that may compress and damage vessels in the neck. Treatment is by a sling and a pad over the dislocated joint attempting to press it back.

SCAPULA

Fractures of the scapula (Fig. 47) are uncommon, and are usually the result of direct violence. Fissured fracture lines may be seen in the blade of the scapula, or the neck or acromion process may be fractured. The only treatment necessary is a sling and active exercises when pain has subsided. Union is invariable, and the fracture rarely shows any serious displacement or causes dysfunction.

DISLOCATION OF THE SHOULDER

A <u>fall on the outstretched</u> hand or a fall backwards on to the hand may result in a dislocation of the shoulder, an injury to which rugby players are prone. The commonest displacement is the sub-coracoid (Fig. 48), in which the head of the humerus comes to lie beneath the coracoid process. Very rarely the humeral head may lie beneath the glenoid cavity or posterior to it. There is <u>severe pain over the shoulder, which is flattened.</u> <u>Movements at the shoulder are resisted,</u> and it is impossible to place the

Ant.

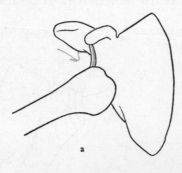

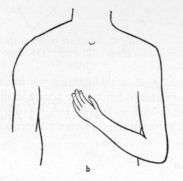

FIG. 48. Dislocation of the shoulder.
(a) Common sub-coracoid position.
(b) Flattening of the shoulder

hand on the unaffected shoulder. The head of the humerus may be felt in the axilla in its sub-coracoid position. <u>If the axillary (circumflex) nerve is</u> <u>damaged, then there is paralysis of the deltoid muscle,</u> detected by asking the patient to initiate the first few degrees of abduction; at the same time the examiner feels the muscle fibres contract under his hand unless there is paralysis. There may also be a small area of anaesthesia over the lower posterior margin of the deltoid muscle.

Kocher's manoeuvre (Fig. 49) is employed to reduce a dislocated shoulder under general anaesthesia. There is no place for immediate reduction without anaesthesia, because it is extremely painful. The elbow is flexed and the arm externally rotated to stretch the subscapularis muscles; the point of the elbow is adducted across the chest, at the same time the arm is pulled down. Finally, the arm is internally rotated. If the hand can now be placed on the point of the unaffected shoulder the head of the humerus is reduced. Occasionally, when Kocher's manoeuvre fails, traction on the slightly abducted arm against the counter-pressure of the surgeon's unshod foot in the axilla is effective.

The position of the humeral head is checked by radiography before and after manipulation. A sling is worn until pain has subsided sufficient to permit active exercises, which must be energetically pursued, for severe and intractable stiffness may follow any injury to the shoulder, especially in the old.

In old people a dislocation of the shoulder may be unappreciated and perhaps not presented for diagnosis for several days. One attempt at

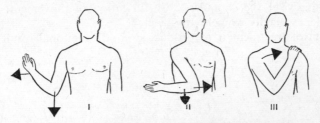

FIG. 49. Kocher's manoeuvre. (i) External rotation. (ii) Adduction of elbow and downward traction. (iii) internal rotation

reduction is permitted: if it is impossible to reduce the dislocation, then failure must be accepted and active exercises prescribed. Surprisingly good function may be achieved by strengthening scapulo-humeral movements.

The function of the axillary nerve must be tested before and after reduction of a dislocation and the findings recorded in the case notes. Most deltoid paralyses recover spontaneously after an interval in which the function of the shoulder must be aided by physiotherapy. It is no longer thought necessary to splint the arm in abduction to prevent lengthening of the muscle. The radial pulse must be felt before and after reduction. Injury to the axillary artery is rare, but can occur, especially in the elderly if the artery is atherosclerotic. Dislocation of the shoulder may be complicated by fracture of the greater tuberosity of the humerus or the neck of the humerus.

Recurrent Dislocation of the Shoulder

This is fairly common. The head of the humerus slips out of the glenoid fossa increasingly frequently and with less and less effort, reduction becoming increasingly simple. The cause is a defect in the labrum glenoidale, which has been stripped up anteriorly in the original injury. There is also commonly a depression in the postero-lateral part of the head of the humerus where it was damaged by impact with the glenoid labrum.

Many operations for this condition have been described. Their common effect is to limit lateral rotation at the shoulder joint by fibrosis induced by operation. The labrum can be sutured or stapled back to the margin of the glenoid fossa (Bankart's operation), or the subscapularis muscle can be divided and overlapped (Putti-Platt operation).

HUMERUS

Neck of the Humerus

A fall on the hand or on the point of the shoulder may result in a fracture of the anatomical neck of the humerus (Fig. 50A). The upper fragment may be adducted or abducted, impacted or mobile. There is pain and swelling over the shoulder, with limitation of movement. Usually old people, especially women, are affected.

The aim of treatment is to produce a good functional result without

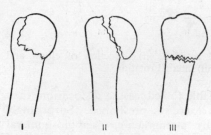

FIG. 50A. Fracture of neck of humerus. (i) Adducted and impacted. (ii) Adducted unimpacted. (iii) Fracture through anatomical neck

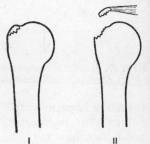

FIG. 50B. Fracture of greater tuberosity of humerus. (i) Without separation. (ii) With separation

necessarily producing a good radiological position. The shoulder becomes stiff very rapidly after injury, especially if it is splinted or held immobile for any length of time. If the fracture is impacted early movements are practised so soon as pain permits. Not only is the shoulder exercised but also the fingers and elbow in all fractures of the humerus. If the fracture is mobile a sling is worn over a bandage, splinting the humerus to the chest for 2–3 weeks, then exercises are allowed. Rarely in the young or where there is gross anatomical deformity the fracture must be reduced and fixed at open operation. Immobilisation in a shoulder spica with the arm abducted to 90° may then be necessary for some weeks. In children the fracture line may run immediately distal to the epiphysial line. Treatment is as for fractures of the neck of the humerus in adults. Complications of fractures in this region are stiffness of the shoulder and, more rarely, axillary nerve damage.

Greater Tuberosity of the Humerus

A fall on the shoulder may result in a fracture of the greater tuberosity across the base of the tuberosity (Fig. 50B). There may be no displacement, or there may be considerable separation due to the pull of the supraspinatus muscle. Pain and tenderness are felt over the point of the shoulder, with inability to initiate abduction if the separation is considerable, because the supraspinatus acts to achieve the first 15° of abduction, after which the deltoid muscle takes over.

A crack fracture or minor degree of separation necessitates only a sling until pain has subsided, followed by active exercises. If there is considerable separation an attempt at reduction should be made under general anaesthesia by pressing the fragment back into its anatomical position when the arm is abducted. If this manoeuvre fails operative reduction should be performed, except in the old, in whom operations on the shoulder are best avoided because of the fear of subsequent stiffness. With exercises a remarkable compensation can be achieved for severe anatomical and functional damage to the shoulder.

Fracture Dislocation of the Head of the Humerus

This is an uncommon accident. The dislocation is reduced in the usual way (see p. 452) and the fracture of the humerus treated as previously described. If there are difficulties in reduction, then open operation may be needed.

Shaft of the Humerus

The fracture may run transversely or obliquely (Fig. 51). Damage to the radial nerve must be looked for, and will be revealed as a wrist drop. Crack fractures and spiral fractures heal uneventfully. It is customary to protect the arm by a U-shaped plaster slab, extending from the point of

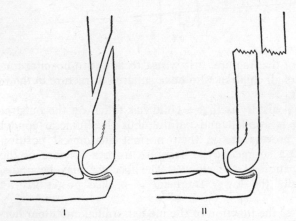

FIG. 51. Fracture of shaft of humerus. (i) Oblique. (ii) Transverse

the shoulder round the elbow and up to the axilla, which is bandaged on to the arm. The hand is supported by a collar and cuff sling. Transverse fractures must be 'hitched' by manipulation so that some part of the ends of the bone fragments are in apposition. As soon as pain permits exercises to the fingers and elbow are encouraged. Most fractures of the humeral shaft unite in about six to eight weeks, occasionally non-union or delayed union may occur.

Non-union must be treated by bone grafting. There is a place for insertion of an intramedullary nail in some cases. If the radial nerve has been injured and fails to recover within a few weeks it must be explored. The damaged segment may have to be excised and the ends resutured. If recovery does not occur a tendon transplant operation can be performed in which certain flexor tendons in the forearm are inserted into paralysed extensor tendons.

Supracondylar Fracture of the Humerus

This fracture is of extreme importance because of the possibility of arterial damage that may end in the development of Volkmann's ischaemic contracture of the forearm muscles. Because this complication can follow

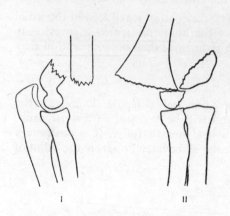

FIG. 52. Supracondylar fracture of humerus. (i) Posterior displacement. (ii) Lateral displacement

reduction of the fracture, it is wisest to admit to hospital for a period of 24–48 hours all children who have suffered a fracture in the region of the elbow joint.

The usual history is that a child has fallen on the outstretched hand. The elbow is swollen and painful, but the humeral condyles and the olecranon process are in their normal anatomical position, thus distinguishing a supracondylar fracture from a fracture of the olecranon or a dislocation of the elbow. The fracture may be undisplaced, but more usually the lower fragment is pushed posteriorly and laterally (Fig. 52).

In all cases the function of the median, radial and ulnar nerves must be examined and the presence of the radial pulse confirmed. Displaced fractures are reduced under general anaesthesia by pulling the flexed arm downwards and forwards. It is particularly important to reduce the lateral displacement to prevent the late development of ulnar neuritis from a valgus deformity of the elbow. After reduction the position of the bones is checked radiographically and the arm supported by a collar and cuff sling. Union takes place usually is about 3–4 weeks, when active exercises of the elbow can be permitted. Throughout the period after reduction, exercises of the shoulder and fingers are encouraged.

Complications

Injury to the brachial artery is the most serious complication. The brachial artery may be compressed by haematoma, contused or in spasm or even divided, lying crushed between the bone ends. Absence of the radial pulse may be noted after a child has sustained a supracondylar fracture of the humerus, but the pulse may return after reduction of the fracture. After reduction, flexion of the elbow may cause the radial pulse to disappear, and occasionally supracondylar fractures may have to be immobilised in extension, because any degree of flexion causes disappearance of the radial pulse. More often when flexion of the elbow is reduced the pulse may return.

The radial pulse may not return after reduction of the fracture or after decreasing the angle of flexion at the elbow. If signs of ischaemia develop in the fingers or if there is pain in the forearm, then the brachial artery must be explored under general anaesthesia. Incision of the fascia overlying the antecubital fossa may release blood and oedema and, by reducing tension, allow the return of pulsation. If the artery is in spasm, painting it with $2\frac{1}{2}\%$ solution of papaverine sulphate may relieve the contracture. Forcible distension of the vessel by injection with saline or lignocaine may also be effective. If the artery is severed or thrombosed following contusion the damaged segment of the vessel must be removed and if possible reconstituted by direct suture or by interposition of an autogenous vein graft.

The sequel of unrelieved arterial injury is ischaemia of the forearm flexor muscles, leading to a contracture of a hand called Volkmann's ischaemic contracture. Because of fibrosis of the flexor muscles the wrist becomes flexed and the fingers clawed. The earliest sign of a developing contracture is pain elicited by extension of the fingers. If a contracture becomes established some improvement may be given to the function of the hand by splinting that does not restrict active exercises and allows extension of the fingers and wrist. Where fibrosis is established, sliding the origin of the flexor muscles from the medial epicondyle down the forearm, may improve function. Widely infarcted and ischaemic muscle may need excision. Transplants from extensor tendons can help restore flexor control of the fingers.

It is imperative that close observation be maintained in all cases of fractures around the elbow for the earliest realisation of the development of ischaemia. Pain elicited by passive extension of the fingers is the earliest sign.

Median, radial and ulnar nerve palsy may be due to ischaemia following vascular injury. Occasionally it may follow contusion or the effects of the tension produced by the fracture haematoma. Most nerve lesions recover spontaneously and completely; it is important to encourage the patient to practise physiotherapy to keep joints mobile and assist muscles until recovery is complete.

Myositis ossificans is not common, but is a serious complication, causing loss of movement and pain at the elbow. It is thought to be aggravated by passive movements, which must never be allowed. Radiographs show a mass of callus deep to the brachialis muscle. With rest in a sling and *active exercises* the bone usually becomes smaller and eventually disappears. Rarely a residual bony mass must be excised.

Malunion is serious, for if the lateral displacement of the lower fragment persists, then the carrying angle is increased and, many years later, the signs of ulnar palsy may develop—delayed ulnar neuritis. Angulation may need correction by osteotomy.

Other Fractures of the Humerus near the Elbow Joint

The lower humeral epiphysis may rarely be separated and displaced posteriorly and laterally in the young up to the age of 15 years. Fracture of the medial epicondyle may be associated with trauma to the ulnar nerve, especially if the condyle has been drawn into the joint. Fractures of the lateral epicondyle, perhaps involving part of the capitellum, may be complicated by delayed ulnar neuritis, perhaps many years later, unless reduction is achieved accurately. T-shaped fractures into the elbow joint are complicated by haemarthrosis.

Reduction is achieved by manipulation and pressure on the displaced bone under general anaesthesia, followed by rest to the arm in a sling with the elbow in flexion. Most fractures which involve the articular surfaces of the elbow joint need operative reduction and internal fixation of the displaced fragment by a nail or screw.

ULNA

Olecranon

Fractures of the *olecranon* follow a fall on the point of the elbow. The fracture may be undisplaced, or a bone fragment of variable size may show a varying degree of separation (Fig. 53). If the fragment is large, i.e. involving a large part of the elbow joint and the gap between the bone ends wide, then union can only occur by fibrous tissue, with the certainty of an irregular joint line. In addition, the ulnar nerve may be damaged. A fracture of the olecranon may be associated with forward dislocation of the elbow. If the fracture is undisplaced it is immobilised in plaster of

Paris at 90° of flexion of the elbow, the cast extending from the axilla to the knuckles. If the fracture shows separation the fragments are approximated and fixed by a vitallium screw inserted through the olecranon.

Fractures of the *coronoid* process may complicate posterior dislocation

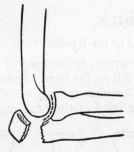

FIG. 53. Fracture of the olecranon with separation

of the elbow but cause no complications. After reduction of the dislocation the elbow is flexed to 90° in plaster of Paris for 3 weeks.

Fractures of the shaft of the ulna are often associated with fractures of the radius (see below). In the Monteggia fracture the ulna is broken and the head of the radius is dislocated. Most fractures of the shaft of the ulna need operative reduction and internal fixation.

Dislocation of the Elbow

The elbow may be dislocated by a fall on the hand. The displacement is posterior and sometimes lateral (Fig. 54). The diagnosis is easily made by finding the olecranon process displaced posteriorly. Pain, tenderness, swelling and immobility are features; the function of the median and ulnar nerves must be tested and the radial pulse felt before and after reduction. Radiographs are essential to exclude a concomitant fracture. Reduction is achieved under general anaesthesia by flexing the elbow and by traction on the forearm. The arm is rested in a collar and cuff sling and active movements permitted when pain subsides, usually in a week or two.

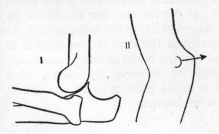

FIG. 54. (i) Posterior dislocation of elbow.
(ii) Deformity of elbow

An associated fracture of the coronoid process requires no treatment. If the head of the radius is fractured it may have to be excised a few weeks after the dislocation has been reduced. Fracture of the medial epicondyle may be associated with damage to the ulnar nerve, necessitating reduction of the elbow, followed by operative fixation of the medial epicondyle and anterior transplantation of the ulnar nerve. Fracture of the olecranon process may require fixation by a screw after the dislocation of the elbow has been reduced.

RADIUS

Head of the Radius

Fractures of the head of the radius (Fig. 55) are common and are due to a fall on the hand. There may be a crack without displacement, which only requires resting in a sling for 2–3 weeks. A vertical fracture of the outer third of the head may show downward displacement of the loose

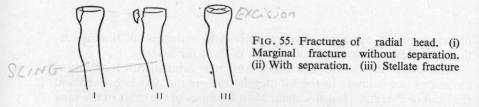

EXcision

SLING

FIG. 55. Fractures of radial head. (i) Marginal fracture without separation. (ii) With separation. (iii) Stellate fracture

fragment. Only a sling is needed. If the head is extensively comminuted it should be excised, for irregularity of the joint surfaces will cause osteo-arthritis. Occasionally a greenstick fracture of the neck of the radius occurs in children.

Shaft of the Radius

The treatment of fractures of the shaft of the radius depends on the relation of the fracture line to the insertion of pronator teres. If the fracture lies above the insertion of pronator teres, then the upper fragment is supinated by biceps and the supinator muscle, the lower fragment is pronated. The fracture is manipulated under general anaesthesia and the forearm immobilised in the supinated position in a full elbow plaster with 90° flexion of the elbow. If the fracture line lies below the insertion of pronator teres the upper fragment lies in the mid-position, the lower is fully pronated. After manipulation the limb is immobilised in the mid-position. It is very important that the bones should be accurately reduced anatomically. If this cannot be achieved by manipulation operative reduction and fixation by a metal plate must be performed, especially if both bones of the forearm are broken.

Colles' Fracture

One of the commonest fractures of the radius is of the distal third (Colles' fracture), in which the bone is broken within 2·5 cm. of the wrist joint (Fig. 56). Typically this fracture is sustained by an old lady who has fallen on her hand. The diagnosis is made from the appearance of the characteristic 'dinner-fork' deformity of the wrist due to the prominence made by the posterior displacement of the distal fragment of the radius. Examination of the wrist also reveals that the radial styloid is displaced proximally, so that the styloid processes of ulna and radius lie approximately at the same level. Radiography shows the radial fragment to be *displaced and rotated posteriorly, impacted to the radial side and supinated.*

The fracture must be reduced under general anaesthesia. Occasionally in very unfit people it is preferable to reduce the fracture under local analgesia, using a brachial plexus block or, alternatively, after injection of local analgesic into the fracture haematoma. The important components of reduction are correction of the posterior rotation of the lower fragment

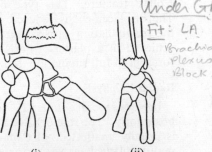

FIG. 56. Colles' fracture showing: (i) lateral, and (ii) posterior displacement

Under GA

Fit: LA.
Brachial
Plexus
Block.

and correction of radial impaction that if left will limit flexion of the hand.

In reduction the forearm is held with the elbow flexed at 90°, an assistant providing counter-traction against the upper arm. The wrist is grasped and hyperextended to increase the deformity, with traction the bone fragments are disimpacted. The wrist is then flexed, pressure on the distal fragment manipulating it anteriorly and towards the ulna side and finally pronating it. A slab of plaster of Paris is applied to the back of the hand and forearm with the wrist in slight palmar flexion extending from just below the elbow crease to the knuckles. The back slab is bandaged on by a crêpe bandage so that the position of the fracture can easily be confirmed clinically, for it is possible for the distal fragment to slip posteriorly after reduction.

Following reduction, radiography is used to check the position of the fracture at 10–14 days. Usually immobilisation is maintained for about 4–6 weeks until the signs of clinical union are manifest, that is absence of pain on pressure over the fracture and a feeling of solidity on springing it. During the period of immobilisation it is important that the fingers, elbow and shoulder should be exercised. Stiffness of the shoulder is probably the commonest complication of a Colles' fracture. Patients should attend a Fracture Clinic following reduction, daily for a few days and thereafter at fortnightly intervals.

A late complication is spontaneous rupture of the extensor pollicis longus tendon, due to roughening of the groove on the radius or to

Complication → ① Shoulder stiffness

" — Late → Rupture of Extensor P.
② longus tendon

avascular necrosis of the tendon. Repair is effected by tendon graft or tendon transplant from the extensor indicis. Another complication is the carpal tunnel syndrome due to irritation or pressure on the median nerve where it passes deep to the flexor retinaculum (see p. 591).

Fracture of the radial styloid may follow a back-fire injury in starting a car or following a fall on the hand. Usually there is no displacement. The fracture is immobilised as for Colles' fracture. There are no complications.

Smith's Fracture

A fall on the back of the flexed wrist may result in a fracture of the radius, but with forward displacement—the Smith's or reversed Colles' fracture. This type of fracture often involves the wrist joint. The displacement is reduced under general anaesthesia by reversal of the manipulation carried out for a Colles' fracture. Immobilisation is achieved in a plaster-of-Paris cast extending above the elbow with the forearm in full supination and with dorsiflexion of the wrist.

Radial Epiphysis

In young people under 20 years the radial epiphysis may be displaced posteriorly. The fracture line runs through the diaphysis, so the epiphysis is usually unaffected. If damage to the epiphysis does occur deformity may result in later years, for example, the radial epiphysis may become prematurely fused, but, as the ulna goes on growing, dislocation of the wrist occurs to the radial side. The radius is short, and the ulnar styloid projects on the dorsum of the wrist—Madelung's deformity. This deformity more commonly is congenital in origin due to failure of growth of the radius. Osteotomy may be needed to correct deformity due to trauma or excision of the lower end of the ulna.

Ulna and Radius

The ulna and radius may be fractured at the same level when there is direct violence or at different levels as a result of a twisting strain. Accurate reduction of these bones is essential for full function to be restored after union. If reduction cannot be achieved by manipulation under general anaesthesia, then open reduction and fixation by a metal plate of one or both bones must be performed. After reduction the arm is immobilised in plaster of Paris, usually for 8–10 weeks. The plaster should extend from the deltoid insertion to the knuckles. Non-union is a hazard for which a bone graft may be needed. Cross-union between the two bones is a rare complication after open reduction, best avoided by making a separate incision for each bone. Unless accurate reduction is achieved, there may be a limitation of pronation and supination.

Monteggia Fracture

In the Monteggia fracture the head of the radius is usually dislocated forwards, sometimes posteriorly, and the upper third of the ulna fractured with anterior angulation. It follows a fall on the outstretched hand, often with a twist pronating the hand. This is a difficult fracture to treat because of the difficulty of reducing both the ulna and the radius and keeping them both reduced. Healing may be prolonged, and stiffness of the elbow is likely unless accurate reduction can be maintained.

Under general anaesthesia traction is applied to the forearm with the elbow in 90° flexion and the forearm fully supinated. An assistant presses firmly on the head of the radius, pushing it backwards into place. If reduction is successful, then the arm is immobilised in plaster of Paris with the elbow in 90° flexion and the forearm in full supination, the plaster extending from below the axilla to the knuckles of the hand. Manipulative reduction often fails.

More often operative reduction is needed. The fracture of the ulna is exposed and reduced and held reduced by either a plate and screws or an intramedullary nail. The head of the radius is manipulated into its normal position. After operation the arm is immobilised in a sling until movements are regained, and then plaster of Paris is applied in a full-length arm plaster with 90° of flexion of the elbow until union is complete. If the head of the radius cannot be reduced, then it must be excised or the annular ligament is repaired. Non-union of the ulna may necessitate bone grafting.

SCAPHOID

Fractures of the scaphoid are particularly important, first because of the difficulty in diagnosis, and secondly, because of the possibility of non-union due to avascular necrosis of the proximal part of the scaphoid. The injury may follow a fall upon the hand or a backfire injury in which the starting-handle of a car is driven against the thenar eminence. There may be little swelling and only pain and tenderness related to the 'anatomical snuff box' of the hand that overlies the scaphoid. Any sprained wrist or any injury leading to tenderness over the scaphoid requires a radiograph of the wrist in three planes *antero-posterior*, *lateral* and *oblique*. The fracture may only be a fine crack and may show up only in dry films examined under a strong light and with a magnifying glass. If no abnormality is seen and yet the physical signs strongly suggest a fracture the wrist should be immobilised in plaster and radiographed again in 2–3 weeks, when decalcification around the fracture line makes it obvious.

Fractures may occur through the waist, proximal pole or tubercle of the scaphoid (Fig. 57). As the vessels to the proximal part of the scaphoid enter through the tubercle, fractures of the waist or proximal pole are likely to lead to avascular necrosis of the proximal fragment, followed by osteoarthritis of the wrist, causing severe pain and disability.

The fracture is rarely displaced, so manipulative reduction is not required. A fractured scaphoid is immobilised in a plaster cast extending from just below the elbow to the heads of the metacarpals. The wrist is fully dorsiflexed and the thumb is included in the plaster up to but excluding its interphalangeal joint; the thumb is held in the position of opposition well forward of the palm. Immobilisation must be prolonged until the fracture line in the scaphoid has disappeared. This usually takes 6–12 weeks, but may take months if the proximal pole

FIG. 57. Fracture of the scaphoid: (1) tubercle; (2) waist; (3) proximal pole

becomes avascular. A fracture of the tubercle of the scaphoid fuses rapidly and causes no complications.

If non-union of the scaphoid occurs, bone grafting or drilling of the fracture can be tried. The proximal avascular part of the scaphoid or sometimes the whole of the bone may be excised. Occasionally a painful wrist due to osteoarthritis following an old fracture of the scaphoid must be arthrodesed.

OTHER CARPAL BONES, THE METACARPUS AND PHALANGES

Carpus

A flake of bone may be chipped off the triquetrum. Strapping or a short period of plaster immobilisation suffices while the wrist is painful. Dislocation of the lunate is a serious injury, because it causes pressure on the median nerve. Manipulation or operative reduction is urgently needed. The bone may undergo avascular necrosis.

Metacarpals

A common boxing injury (Fig. 58) is a fracture of the base of the first metacarpal, which may involve the metacarpo-trapezoid joint (Bennett's fracture). Many of such fractures are impacted, but some, especially those involving the joint, may be unstable. Reduction is achieved by traction under general anaesthesia and immobilisation of the thumb in the type of plaster used for a fracture of the scaphoid. If the fracture is unstable, open reduction and fixation of the fragment with a metal pin may be needed. Another method of stabilising the fracture is to apply traction attached to adhesive tape wrapped round the thumb. The means of traction is an elastic band or tape tied to a wire loop embedded in the plaster around the thumb. Immobilisation for 4–6 weeks is usually necessary.

Any metacarpal may be fractured, fracture through the neck of the fifth is a common injury. Several bones may be broken in a crushing injury. Displacement is slight and no reduction is needed. Pain is relieved

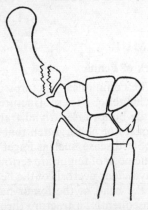

Fig. 58. Bennett's fracture dislocation of the base of the first metacarpal

by application of a slab of plaster bandaged on to the back of the hand and forearm. Active movements are begun as soon as pain subsides.

Phalanges

Fractures of the shafts of phalanges are reduced by traction and immobilisation over a splint of aluminium wire or by strapping the affected finger to its neighbour. The terminal phalanx may be comminuted by a crushing injury, often with loss of the nail or skin rendering the fracture compound. Dislocations of interphalangeal or metacarpo-phalangeal joints are usually easily reduced by traction under general anaesthesia. Occasionally the head of a phalanx or metacarpal may buttonhole the extensor expansion or joint capsule and require operative reduction.

FURTHER READING

Aston, J. N. (1967) *A Short Textbook of Orthopaedics and Traumatology.* English Universities Press, London.

Bankart, A. S. B. (1938) *The Pathology and Treatment of Recurrent Dislocation of the Shoulder Joint,* Brit. J. Surg. **26**, 23.

Seddon, H. J. (1956) *Treatment of Volkmann's Contracture by Excision of the Infarct,* J. Bone & Joint Surg., **38B**, 152.

Thomas, F. B. (1957) *Reduction of Smith's Fracture,* J. Bone & Joint Surg., **39B**, 463.

London, P. S. (1961) *The Broken Scaphoid Bone,* J. Bone & Joint Surg., **42B**, 239.

CHAPTER THIRTY-TWO

FRACTURES AND DISLOCATIONS OF THE LOWER LIMB

FEMUR

Neck of Femur

The commonest fractures of the neck of the femur are subcapital and trochanteric. These fractures usually occur in old people who have fragile bones after trivial trauma, such as a trip when crossing the road. It must not be forgotten that a fracture in this region is a common sequel of bone disease, such as Paget's disease or secondary carcinoma. Fractures of the neck of femur are serious because of the likelihood of non-union due to avascular necrosis of the head of the femur. Most of the arteries supplying the head of the femur pass up the neck of femur to reach the head. Consequently, a fracture through the neck of the femur is likely to interrupt most of the blood supply that comes to the head except that which passes through the ligamentum teres.

The treatment of fractures of the neck of the femur has been revolutionised by operative means of reduction and fixation that avoids prolonged immobilisation in bed with traction or in plaster. Old people put to bed for any length of time with their legs immobilised are likely to suffer serious complications, such as pneumonia, urinary infection, uraemia and pulmonary embolism.

A person who has suffered a fracture of the neck of the femur will be in great pain and show a characteristic deformity of external rotation of the leg due to the weight of the limb. The amount of shortening of the limb is greater in trochanteric fractures. Many of the patients who sustain these fractures are old and have severe disabilities, such as heart disease, severe bronchitis and hypertension. Nevertheless, there are few that cannot be treated by operative means.

After preliminary assessment and resuscitation radiographs are taken. Subcapital fractures (Fig. 59) are usually unimpacted adduction fractures, the fracture line passing almost vertically immediately below the head. A few are abduction fractures likely to be impacted with a fracture line that runs almost horizontally. In trochanteric fractures (Fig. 59) the fracture line runs either between the trochanters (intertrochanteric) or through them (pertrochanteric). There may be a severe degree of comminution, with several bony fragments in trochanteric fractures.

Impacted subcapital fractures require no operative fixation and only a period of rest until pain subsides to allow active exercises to be commenced. Weight bearing is permitted after six weeks. Subcapital unimpacted fractures are reduced under general anaesthesia by traction and internal rotation. The position is checked radiographically in both the antero-posterior and lateral planes, and the limb is held in position on a special orthopaedic table. Through a small incision over the base of the greater trochanter a special metal guide wire is inserted up the centre of the neck of the femur into the head. When the position of the guide wire is thought satisfactory a special trifin nail (Smith–Petersen nail) is hammered into position around the guide wire, which can then be removed. The pin must be accurately placed and extend to just below the

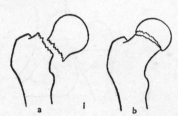

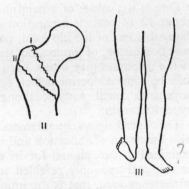

FIG. 59. Fractures neck of femur. (i) *a*, Unimpacted adducted fracture; *b*, impacted, abducted fracture. (ii) i, Pertrochanteric; ii, intertrochanteric fractures. (iii) Position of limb rolled externally

articular cartilage of the head of the femur. It must hold the fragments tightly impacted. The next day following operation active exercises are begun and the patient moved out of bed. Weight bearing may be permitted early after the first week. Intensive physiotherapy and assistance to the patient in the home may allow rapid discharge from hospital.

In over 60% of cases the result is satisfactory union, with a good hip joint. Avascular necrosis of the head of the femur may occur, the nail may break or be extruded; sepsis is a rare complication. If any of these complications occurs it is usually necessary to remove the nail and perform some operation to relieve pain or improve stability of the hip. The head may be replaced by a metal prosthesis (Austin Moore) or an osteotomy can be performed just below the lesser trochanter, the femur being displaced towards the acetabulum (Fig. 60). Occasionally the joint must be excised to leave an unstable but painless limb. The choice of operation depends upon the fitness of the subject, the condition of the bones and the preference of the surgeon. Some advocate primary arthroplasty with insertion of an Austin Moore prosthesis in patients over the age of 65 who have grossly displaced sub-capital fractures.

Trochanteric fractures are treated similarly, except that the appliance used for fixation of the fracture is a trifin nail attached to a long metal plate that extends down the femur. The postoperative course is as for subcapital fractures.

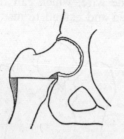

FIG. 60. Displacement osteotomy

Slipped Epiphysis

One of the causes of a painful limp occurring in a young person aged about 12–14 years is separation of the upper femoral epiphysis. As in many diseases of the hip joint, pain may be referred to the knee. There may be a history of trauma, but this is often only trivial. Bilateral slipping of the epiphyses may occur, even without any history of trauma. There may be some endocrine defect, for many of those affected are rather fat boys with small gonads, though rarely is there evidence of frank hypopituitarism.

The clinical signs are tenderness and muscle spasm around the hip joint, with limitation of abduction and internal rotation. Radiographs must be examined in two planes, for in the early cases the degree of slip may be minimal and only revealed in a lateral film. If left the condition causes coxa vara, that is diminution of the angle between the neck and shaft of the femur. In addition, the neck of the femur becomes absorbed and the head deformed in shape. The late consequence of these changes is osteoarthritis in adult life. Avascular necrosis of the head of the femur may occur.

In early cases, before the head has slipped far, progress can be prevented by the insertion of a Smith–Petersen nail or Moore's pins. If the degree of slipping is gross subtrochanteric osteotomy may be performed. Manipulative reduction has been abandoned because of the high incidence of avascular necrosis of the femoral head it may cause. Operation such as arthrodesis may be needed for the late appearance of osteoarthritis.

Shaft of Femur

A fracture of the shaft of the femur is a major injury, caused either by direct or indirect violence. If the proximal third is fractured the

proximal 1/3 : uppa Flexed, Lower Adducted
middle 1/3 : sag posteriorly
Lower 1/3 : Flexed — lower.

FRACTURES AND DISLOCATIONS OF THE LOWER LIMB   469

upper fragment tends to be flexed by psoas and the lower adducted. Fractures of the middle third tend to sag posteriorly because of the weight of the limb. The lower fragment of a fracture of the lower third of the femur is flexed posteriorly by the gastrocnemius muscles. The direction of the fracture line is important for its stability after reduction. Transverse fractures are stable, oblique and spiral fractures are unstable. Fractures of the lower third of the femur may extend into the knee joint, being associated with haemarthrosis. The fracture line may be T-shaped into the joint, or a condyle may be separated. Rarely injury to the popliteal artery may be associated, a serious injury that may result in amputation or development of ischaemic contracture of the toes.

The first-aid treatment is to bind the legs together and move the patient to hospital as quickly as possible. If a Thomas' splint is available this can be applied and traction to the heel maintained with a special clip that goes on to the boot or shoe. In hospital resuscitation is carried out and radiographs taken. Most cases are treated by traction following insertion of a Steinmann's pin through the upper part of the tibia immediately below the tibial tubercle under general anaesthesia. To the pin a Böhler's stirrup is attached, from which a cord passes to the end of a Thomas' splint to which it is tied (fixed traction). Thomas' splint has a knee attachment to allow bending of the knee. The splint itself is supported from an overhead beam. The cord from the splint passes over a pulley to a weight, and the end of the bed is raised to reduce pressure of the splint on the perineum. The weight should be only so much as to maintain reduction—say 10–15 lb. It is most important to reduce the fracture sufficient to prevent shortening of the limb and angulation of the fracture. Over-distraction may be serious in allowing interposition of muscle between the bone ends, causing non-union. The splint must be well padded to prevent deformity, especially in those midshaft fractures which tend to sag posteriorly and lower-third fractures in which the distal fragment is flexed. By flexing the knee in the splint the flexion deformity of lower-third fractures can be corrected. In the early phase after reduction radiographs are taken weekly for the first month.

Exercises to the knee are important, and the patient is encouraged to move about in bed as much as possible and to lift himself up and down by hanging on a support from the overhead beam. Once pain has subsided, quadriceps exercises can be started. Immobilisation is maintained until there are signs of clinical and radiological union, usually after about 8–12 weeks. A walking caliper should then be fitted and worn for about 6 months, during which more and more weight bearing is permitted. It may take 9 months to a year before a heavy worker is able to return to his job.

Operative reduction and fixation is indicated for fractures that are difficult to reduce or maintain reduced, especially when it is suspected that muscle is interposed between the fractured ends. Fractures involving the knee joint, for example, separation of a condyle, may need operation.

If it is suspected that arterial damage has occurred urgent exploration of the affected vessel is indicated. Open fractures must be treated as a surgical emergency. Blood must be aspirated from the knee joint if a fracture line runs into it and has caused haemarthrosis.

After operative reduction fixation by screws or plates is suitable for a spiral fracture. Transverse fractures may be immobilised by an intramedullary nail of the Kuntscher type. The fracture is exposed and a guide wire passed from it to emerge from the trochanteric fossa. The fracture is reduced and an intramedullary nail hammered over the guide wire across the fracture long enough to extend the length of the femur but short of the knee joint. The advantages of open operation and fixation are that accurate reduction is achieved, movements are freer because external splinting is unnecessary. The great danger is infection leading to osteomyelitis and even eventually amputation. Union is not hastened and may even be delayed. An intramedullary nail may break or penetrate the knee joint and may be difficult to remove.

In young children fractures of the shaft of the femur are best treated by traction on a 'gallows'. Adhesive one-way stretch plaster is applied to the whole length of both limbs, after which crêpe bandages are applied. Spreaders are attached to the strapping, from which cords run just clear of the bed. In this position reduction is excellent. Defaecation and micturition are easy, and the child accepts the position readily. Occasionally, in young adults, the lower femoral epiphysis may be displaced by a violent hyperextension injury. The displacement must be reduced by traction.

The commonest complication of a fractured femur is stiffness of the knee joint with limitation of flexion, especially in fractures of the lower third. Much of this stiffness is due to adhesion of the quadriceps femoris to the site of the fracture. Energetic physiotherapy must be encouraged from the beginning. Occasionally, gentle manipulation of the knee under general anaesthesia may help improve movement. Forcible manipulation, however, may cause fracture of the patella. Other complications should be avoidable, for example, shortening of the leg and angulation of the femur. Occasionally non-union may necessitate bone grafting.

DISLOCATED HIP JOINT

Dislocation of the hip joint may be congenital, traumatic or pathological. Traumatic dislocation is a severe injury and not often seen.

Congenital (See Chapter Twenty-eight)

Traumatic

Traumatic dislocation of the hip is rare. Usually the dislocated head lies posteriorly on the ilium. The limb lies in a characteristic posture, with shortening, slight flexion, adduction and internal rotation. There may be signs of pressure on the sciatic nerve. In anterior dislocation the limb lies abducted, flexed and externally rotated. It is important for radiographs to be taken in both anterior and lateral views, both to confirm the dislocation and its position and also the possibility of an associated fracture (Fig. 61). It is convenient to reduce the dislocation by laying the anaesthetised patient on the floor. Posterior dislocation is reduced by traction and by flexing the knee and hip. The limb is then abducted and externally rotated until the dislocation is reduced and the limb can be straightened. Traction is maintained for a period of six weeks.

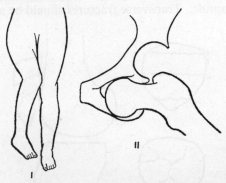

FIG. 61. Dislocation of the hip. (i) Typical position of limb in posterior dislocation. (ii) Anterior dislocation of the hip

Fractures may be associated with a dislocation, such as a fracture of the shaft of the femur or the acetabular rim, the latter, if large, permits redislocation unless it is screwed back into place. Central dislocation occurs when the head of the femur is driven into the pelvis through a fracture of the acetabulum. It is reduced by traction, which must be maintained for several weeks. Operative reduction of the acetabulum may be necessary to restore a smooth joint cavity. Accurate reduction is essential to prevent shortening of the limb and minimise the late development of arthritis.

Pathological

Pathological dislocation of the hip joint is a complication of septic arthritis or osteomyelitis of bones within the joint. It is rarely seen now these conditions can be treated so efficiently.

PATELLA

Fracture of the Patella

The patella may be fractured by a fall on the knee or by indirect violence due to the action of the quadriceps in resisting a violent flexion movement. In comminuted or stellate fractures (Fig. 62) the bone may be shattered

Q

into many fragments, so that the articular surface may be grossly malaligned and liable to cause osteoarthritis in later years. The fracture may run transversely across the middle of the patella or near to either the upper or lower poles (polar fracture). Separation of the bony fragments leads to union by fibrous tissue, with loss of full extension. Separation indicates a wide tear of the quadriceps expansion on either side of the patella and haemarthrosis into the joint. Such fractures must be explored, blood evacuated and the quadriceps expansion sutured on either side of the bone. Polar fractures are best treated by excision of the smaller fragment and resuture of the capsule. Transverse fractures should be accurately reduced

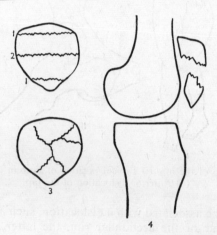

FIG. 62. Fracture of patella: 1 polar and 2 waist fractures; 3 stellate fracture; 4 waist fracture with separation

and held together by a screw or in older patients excised. Immobilisation in plaster of Paris in a full leg plaster from just below the groin to the ankle is maintained for 4–6 weeks, followed by active exercises to regain knee movement. If there is gross comminution of the patella and if its posterior surface shows considerable irregularity, then the patella must be excised, as otherwise osteoarthritis may occur. Complications are stiffness, osteoarthritis of the knee and hyperextensibility of the knee, genu recurvatum.

Dislocation of the Patella

Dislocation of the patella is prone to occur where there is a varus or valgus deformity of the knee or hypoplasia of the lateral femoral condyle. Recurrence is very likely, and if it happens many times over many years, then osteoarthritis of the knee is likely to develop. The patella is reduced by pressure and the knee is extended. Anaesthesia may be needed, but in recurrent cases spontaneous reduction may occur or the bone may be replaced without pain.

Recurrent dislocation can be treated by a variety of surgical methods. A common procedure is to transplant the patellar tendon more medially and distally. If osteoarthritis is feared or is developing, then the patella must be excised.

DISLOCATION OF THE KNEE

The knee can only be dislocated by great violence involving severe ligamentous damage and, frequently, damage to the popliteal nerves and the popliteal artery. Reduction is achieved by manipulation. An associated fracture of the femur may require operative fixation. Haemarthrosis must be dealt with by aspiration. After the reduction prolonged immobilisation may be needed. Instability or stiffness of the knee is likely.

TIBIA AND FIBULA

Fractures of the tibia, especially if there is displacement, are often accompanied by fractures of the fibula, so it is important that radiographs should show the whole extent of both bones in case the fractures lie at

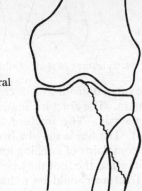

FIG. 63. Depressed fracture of lateral condyle of tibia

different levels. Fibular fractures require no particular attention unless the ankle joint is involved, for the fibula is reduced when the tibia is reduced.

At the upper end of the tibia the condyles may be fractured, depressed and impacted by varus or valgus strains (Fig. 63). T-shaped fractures into the joint with fracture of the neck of the fibula may be complicated by haemarthrosis. The popliteal artery may be damaged irrecoverably, leading to amputation. The lateral popliteal nerve may be injured. In the treatment of such fractures it is important to deal with the haemarthrosis by aspiration and as far as possible restore an even joint surface to prevent the late onset of osteoarthritis. If there is much depression the fragments may be elevated and fixed by a screw, but on the whole operative methods of reduction are unsatisfactory, and it is better to attempt to regain movements early than to strive to regain an accurate anatomical reduction. Immobilisation is carried out by enclosing the leg in a full-length plaster for about 3 months without weight bearing or by traction for 6 weeks and early movements.

Occasionally the tubercle of the tibia may be separated in the young before the epiphysis has fused. Plaster immobilisation is indicated. Only if there is much separation of the fragment may operative fixation be necessary.

Fractures of the shaft of the tibia are common and important because

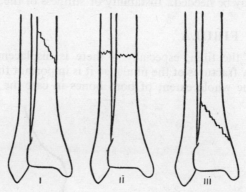

FIG. 64. Fractures of shaft of tibia: (i) and (iii) oblique; (ii) transverse fractures

they are often difficult to reduce and because delayed union and non-union is common. The fracture may follow direct violence or a sudden severe twisting strain. The fracture line may be transverse, spiral or oblique (Fig. 64). The fibula may be broken at the same or at a higher level. The patient complains of swelling and pain over the site of the fracture and, in severe injuries, the foot may be rolled externally.

The fracture should be reduced under anaesthesia. If it is transverse and the fragments can be hitched together immobilisation in a full-length plaster from the thigh to the toes suffices. Oblique and spiral fractures are usually unstable and often need prolonged traction or operative fixation. Traction is applied to a Böhler stirrup attached to a Steinmann pin inserted through the calcaneum. The limb is encased in plaster, the knee in 45° of flexion and rested on a Braun's frame. Operative reduction is maintained by fixation with screws or a metal plate. Operation is obligatory for failed reduction or where the reduction proves unstable and the fracture surfaces slip even with traction.

Whether traction or operative reduction should be performed is a matter of choice of the surgeon concerned. In recent years the tendency has been more and more towards operative intervention and the use of plates rather than screws for fixation. Occasionally it is possible to immobilise the fracture by the insertion of an intramedullary nail. The advantages of operation are accurate reduction with restoration of limb length. Prolonged traction may still result in inadequate reduction and stiffness of the ankle and knee. The major fear of operation is infection, osteomyelitis, non-union and even amputation.

Operations using special plates that compress the fracture allow early weight bearing in plaster after three weeks. In plaster the knee must be slightly flexed and the foot held at an angle of 90° at the ankle joint. In the early phase great swelling may occur, necessitating splitting of the plaster if the toes become blue, painful or swollen. The fracture and prominent bony points must be padded. As soon as pain subsides energetic physiotherapy is encouraged, with static exercises to the quadriceps muscle, which wastes rapidly in plaster.

Non-union of the tibia is the great fear, especially in the lower third fractures, where vascularity appears to be poor. Delayed union is common and weight bearing must not be permitted until there is good evidence of radiological union, such as fading of the fracture line and the appearance of well-calcified callus. Clinically the fracture must be free of tenderness, and there should be a sense of solidity on gentle springing of it. Nonunion is diagnosed by the appearance of sclerosis and the possibility of some movement clinically at the site of fracture. Non-union necessitates operation, freshening of the sclerosed bone ends and bone grafting using a sliding graft of cortical bone from the tibia or packing round it of bone chips derived from the iliac crest. Union is slow, and may fail to occur, necessitating further operation.

Compound fractures of the tibia are common. Those that are compound from within, when the skin is punctured by a spike of bone, are not as serious as those in which the skin is lacerated from without. The wound is excised and closed. The fracture is manipulated into a good position and immobilised if necessary with traction. Where there is skin loss, contusion or contamination of the wound by dirt and foreign bodies, full débridement must be carried out. Primary skin cover is vital, more important than position of the fracture, because the development of infection is so serious. Flaps of skin of full thickness may be rotated from a nearby area or from the opposite leg (cross leg flap). Occasionally the wound edges may only be approximated after a relieving incision has been made in the calf. The defect left by the relieving incision is covered by a partial thickness skin graft.

FRACTURES AND DISLOCATIONS OF THE ANKLE JOINT

Fractures of the ankle are commonly associated with some degree of dislocation of the talus from the ankle joint. The commonest mechanism of injury is a stumble, followed by a fall with a twisting strain at the ankle of either external rotation, abduction or adduction. Fractures and fracture dislocations of the ankle are called Pott's fractures. Occasionally the ankle may be fractured following a fall from a height, when the talus is driven up between the tibia and fibula. Minor injuries are often diagnosed as strains or sprains. All ankle injuries must be radiographed.

A sprained ankle is an inversion injury, in which there is tenderness localised to the anterior part of the lateral ligament of the ankle near its insertion, in which radiographs are negative. Ligamentous injuries may

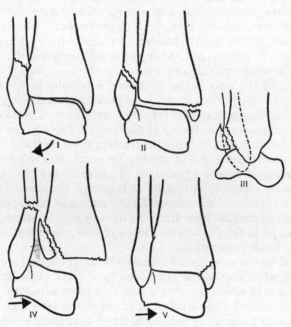

FIG. 65. Fracture dislocation of the ankle joint. (i) External rotation injury. (ii) Abduction injury. (iii) Third degree injury with chip off posterior edge of tibia. (iv) Diastasis of inferior tibio-fibular joint. (v) Adduction injury

be more painful and take longer to heal than a fracture, especially if the ligamentous tear is so severe as to allow hypermobility of the ankle joint and a tendency to recurrent inversion with subluxation. If a fracture has been sustained the ankle may be very swollen, tender and bruised. Movements are restricted and painful. The site of the fracture may be localised by palpation or the appearance of an obvious deformity.

An external rotation injury causes fracture of the lower fibula in its lowest 7–10 cm., the fracture line passing downwards and obliquely forwards (Fig. 65). A more severe force avulses in addition the medial malleolus. More violence avulses a fragment off the posterior margin of the inferior articular surface of the tibia.

In a fracture due to abduction the fibula is fractured transversely about 5 cm. above the joint. A greater force avulses the tip of the medial malleolus. More severe injuries may cause separation (diastasis) of the tibia and fibula following rupture of the inferior tibio-fibular ligaments.

Fractures due to forces adducting the ankle cause a fracture of the medial malleolus in a line passing almost vertically; the tip of the fibula may also be avulsed.

Less common fractures include fractures extending from the ankle joint into the shaft of the tibia, chips off the lower end of the tibia and separation of the lower tibial epiphysis in adolescents.

Treatment

Fractures of the fibula that are undisplaced are treated by immobilisation for 3–4 weeks in plaster of Paris from just below the knee to the toes, the foot at a right angle and plantigrade, that is neither inverted nor everted. If there is no great tenderness or swelling an undisplaced fracture may only require support in an adhesive plaster, though if pain is complained of it is kind to apply a plaster cast. Fractures with displacement must be treated by manipulation under general anaesthesia. It is important to inspect the radiographs and ascertain that the gap between the talus and each malleolus is equal in width, for any difference suggests subluxation, which must be treated by reduction under anaesthesia.

The anaesthetised patient lies with his knee flexed over the end of the table and supported behind the knee to relax the calf muscles. The manipulator sits and grasps the heel. Traction is applied downward, followed by pressure and movements aimed at reversing the displacement. Accurate reduction is essential. The foot is held in the reduced position and a plaster-of-Paris cast applied from below the knee to the toes, with padding over the fracture site and the bony points. If there is great swelling the leg should be elevated in bed and, if the toes become painful, swollen or discoloured, the plaster must be split. Operative reduction may be needed for a malleolus that cannot be accurately replaced, usually the medial. Periosteum or fascia may be interposed between the fractured surfaces, this is removed and the fracture is fixed by a screw. Diastasis of the tibia and fibula is corrected by a screw inserted transversely between them above the ankle joint. For injuries of any severity immobilisation in plaster of Paris must be maintained for 8–12 weeks. After the plaster is removed intensive physiotherapy must be encouraged to restore joint mobility. A crêpe bandage or adhesive strapping must be worn, for some degree of swelling of the leg lasting over several weeks is inevitable after removal of a plaster.

The most serious complication of a fracture around the ankle joint is osteoarthritis, best avoided by accurate reduction. Occasionally the joint must be fused for severe pain and stiffness. Mal-union may follow damage to the epiphysis in a child, and may later require osteotomy for its correction. Non-union is very rare.

Talus

Fractures of the talus are rare and are caused by a violent inversion injury with plantar flexion that dislocates the sub-taloid joint; greater violence may dislocate the talus out of the ankle joint. A fracture through the neck of the talus may follow extreme dorsiflexion so fierce that the neck of the talus is broken against the anterior lower margin of the tibia. Occasionally the posterior fragment of the talus may be dislocated out of the ankle joint. If the talus is dislocated it may lie subcutaneously and cause such pressure as to necrose the skin. Fractures of the talus require the expert attention of the orthopaedic surgeon, who achieves reduction partly by manipulation and partly by operative means. Serious complications are necrosis of the skin, avascular necrosis of the talus and sub-talar arthritis.

Calcaneum (Fig. 66)

Fractures of the calcaneum usually follow a fall from a height on to the heels; at the same time crush fractures of vertebrae are often sustained. The heel is tender and may show broadening if the bone has been severely

FIG. 66. Fractures of the calcaneum: (i) normal shape; (ii) fracture involving talo-calcaneal joint; (iii) fracture of greater tuberosity

compressed; bruising of the heel appears over a period of days. Movements at the sub-taloid joint are impossible or very painful. Axial and lateral radiographs are essential to reveal the extent of the fracture. The axial view is taken with the foot in full dorsiflexion, the beam of X-rays passing through the bone from its plantar surface.

Fractures of the calcaneum are very serious if there is involvement of the talo-calcaneal joints, as is usual. In the lateral radiograph the upper surface of the calcaneum may be flattened or even depressed, in which case healing is followed by sub-taloid osteoarthritis, causing pain on walking and a sense of walking on pebbles. If both legs are affected, as may well be likely, then incapacity is serious. Compression fractures are difficult to treat effectively. Operative methods of reduction and manipulation produce no better results than rest in bed and elevation of the feet until pain has subsided. Active movements are commenced as soon as possible. Bed rest is necessary for about 6 weeks, then intensive physiotherapy is encouraged to regain movements of the ankle and sub-taloid joint. Weight bearing is not permitted for six weeks. Severe disability may necessitate sub-taloid arthrodesis. Some surgeons perform this operation in severe compression fractures early after injury because of the certain development of arthritis.

Other fractures which do not involve the sub-taloid joint heal well, especially if there is no separation of the fragments. A below-knee plaster is applied for 4–5 weeks, followed by active exercises. There should be no complications from these fractures. The fracture line usually passes through the tuberosities.

Metatarsals

Metatarsal fractures are usually due to a weight falling on the foot or from some twisting injury to the forefoot. Any part of the bone may be fractured, neck, shaft or base, and several may be broken. Fracture of the base of the 5th metatarsal is common. Stress fracture of the neck of the 2nd metatarsal is described on p. 441. Fractures of metatarsals heal uneventfully with strapping. Plaster immobilisation is needed if there is great pain.

Phalanges

Fractures of the phalanges of the toes, especially the great toe, follow crushing injuries. The distal phalanx is often comminuted and the fracture may be compound. Pain is relieved by dressings or strapping. There is never any problem with union. Occasionally infection may supervene if a wound becomes contaminated.

FURTHER READING

Garden, R. S. (1961) *Low Angle Fixation in Fractures of the Femoral Neck*, J. Bone & Joint Surg., **43B**, 647.

Garden, R. S. (1964) *Stability and Union in Subcapital Fractures of the Femur*, J. Bone & Joint Surg., **46B**, 630.

Küntscher, G. B. G. (1958) *The Küntscher Method of Intramedullary Fixation*, J. Bone & Joint Surg., **46A**, 17.

Denham, R. A. (1964) *Internal Fixation for Unstable Ankle Fractures*, J. Bone & Joint Surg., **46B**, 206.

CHAPTER THIRTY-THREE

FRACTURES OF THE FACE, JAWS, SPINE AND PELVIS

INJURIES OF THE FACIAL SKELETON AND JAWS

Injuries to the face and jaws follow direct violence, a punch, a kick or often the impact of the face on the windscreen of a car. Such injuries can be serious, because swelling and bruising may cause obstruction to the airway, necessitating tracheostomy. Blood, teeth or dentures may be inhaled and cause a lung abscess. Skull fractures may be associated also with injuries to the paranasal air sinuses or the orbit. It is important in treatment that the occlusion of the teeth is accurately restored, and the function of the jaws should be as perfect as possible. Such injuries call for close liaison between the surgeon, dentist, plastic surgeon, neurosurgeon, and ear, nose and throat surgeon.

In first aid the airway must be kept clear. The patient is laid on his side and the tongue pulled forward. A sucker should be available to aspirate blood and secretions. A supporting bandage can be placed to hold the jaw in a reasonable position. First-class radiographs of the facial skeleton must be made available as soon as possible.

Mandible

Fractures of the mandible (Fig. 67) follow a blow on the jaw or accidentally during dental extraction. The commonest fracture is in a line passing

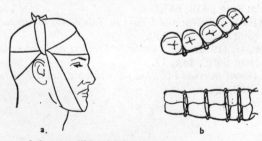

FIG. 67. Fractures of the mandible; (*a*) bandage used to support mandible; (*b*) inter-dental wiring used to immobilise fractures

between a canine tooth and a mental foramen; bilateral fractures may occur. Next in frequency is an oblique fracture just behind the angle of the mandible. The symphysis may be split, the coronoid process avulsed or the neck of one or both articular condyles may be fractured, with or without dislocation of the temporo-mandibular joint. Fractures may be unilateral or bilateral, displaced or undisplaced. Fractures of the horizontal ramus are likely to be compound into the mouth.

All fractures of the mandible must be immobilised, even if they are apparently undisplaced because the pull of powerful muscles like the pterygoids, temporalis and genial muscles tend to distract the fragments and because delayed union and infection may occur. Displacement must be corrected so that the normal occlusion of the teeth is restored.

Fixation is usually achieved by the dentist, who immobilises the fractures by interdental wiring (Fig. 67). The wires pass around and between the teeth on each jaw and lock the upper and lower teeth in perfect occlusion. Of course, the mouth cannot be opened, but patients soon find they can cope with fluids satisfactorily. Frequent syringing of the mouth after operation is important to keep the mouth clean and free of infection. Special dentures can be made for the edentulous to fix the jaws, or wires can be passed circumferentially around the fragments, which are then wired together. Another method is to insert metal pins in two planes into each fragment and to lock them in the correct position by externally fitted metal bars. Fractures of the articular condyles can be reduced by manipulation under general anaesthesia, after which the jaws are wired together. Interdental wiring is kept in position for about 4–6 weeks until union is certain.

Dislocation of the mandible may follow a blow on the jaw, manipulation of the jaw under anaesthesia (usually by the dentist) and occasionally by a deep yawn. One or both condyles may slip out of the temporo-mandibular joint. Reduction is performed under anaesthesia by firm downward pressure on the horizontal ramus, forcing the condyles around the articular prominence.

Zygomatic Arch

Fractures of the zygoma follow a blow on the side of the face. The fracture may be difficult to diagnose because of swelling and bruising, but it should always be suspected if there is tenderness over the zygomatic arch. If the arch is depressed the range of movement of the lower jaw may be limited. After the swelling has subsided there may be flattening of the side of the face and cheek that is cosmetically unsightly. Radiologically the zygomatic arches can only be seen clearly if Town's view of the base of the skull is taken so that the shape of the two arches can be compared.

If the zygoma is depressed it must be elevated under general anaesthesia. A small incision is made above the zygoma down to and through the temporalis fascia. An elevator is passed under the fascia and the fracture elevated by pressing the elevator outwards, using the side of the skull as a fulcrum.

Malar

Greater violence to the side of the face may fracture the malar bone, driving it into the maxillary antrum (Fig. 68). Unless the fracture is reduced, the cheek may be left flattened, diplopia may occur from deformity of the inferior margin of the orbit, and the infra-orbital nerve may be damaged, causing an unpleasant anaesthesia of the cheek, upper lip and upper teeth on one side. The fracture is best revealed in a view of the skull that shows the paranasal sinuses. Radiopacity of an antrum confirms haemorrhage into it.

The fracture is reduced as for fractures of the zygomatic arch. If reduc-

Fig. 68. Fracture of the zygoma with impaction into the antrum

tion is difficult the maxillary antrum must be opened by an incision made through the mouth above the upper incisor teeth (the Caldwell Luc approach). The lower margin of the orbit can then be ironed out and maintained in position by a gauze pack. Unless the infra-orbital margin is accurately reduced, anaesthesia in the distribution of the infra-orbital nerves may persist, and in addition there may be diplopia.

Anterior Facial Fractures (Fig. 69)

A blow on the nose may fracture the nasal bones, leaving an unsightly depression if the fracture is not reduced. In addition, the septum may be buckled, leading to nasal obstruction. If the bones are depressed they must be reduced under anaesthesia, using special forceps with long blades that replace the nasal bones and flatten the septum. A splint of plaster or strapping is applied externally to the nose to maintain the position.

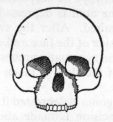

Fig. 69. Anterior facial fracture

A more severe injury may cause a fracture which passes across the nasal bones along the infra-orbital margins down through the infra-orbital foramina and through the upper jaw on both sides. The whole maxilla may be mobile and pushed back (dish-face injury). Although the displacement is gross, it may easily be missed, because it is masked by swelling of the face. In any severely bruised face anaesthesia of the cheeks should be tested for, and the upper teeth grasped and rocked to see if the maxilla is mobile. The patient should be asked if occlusion of the teeth is normal or if the teeth are numb.

The fracture is reduced under anaesthesia by special forceps with which the maxilla can be pulled forwards. Special metallic splints are made by the dentist capping the teeth of both the upper and lower jaws. The teeth are kept in perfect occlusion by the cap splints, which are screwed together so that the upper jaw is locked to the lower. The fractures are kept reduced by a metal rod that joints the cap splints to a plaster cap moulded around the head.

In the severest injuries to the face, the nose, maxilla and anterior cranial fossa are involved. Additional complications are cerebro-spinal rhinorrhoea and infection from the paranasal sinuses. Rhinorrhoea may dry up spontaneously, especially if the patient is sat up. As soon as possible, the anterior cranial fossa should be explored through an osteoplastic flap and the source of the leak discovered, either through the cribriform plate or through the frontal sinus. The defect in the dura is usually closed by a fascial graft taken from the thigh. Sulphonamides and antibiotics are prescribed during the phase of leakage, for fear of infection causing meningitis. The patient wears a 'nose bag' soaking up the cerebro-spinal fluid, and is warned against blowing his nose in case air is forced into the cranium to cause an aerocoele.

FRACTURES AND DISLOCATIONS OF THE SPINE

Fractures of the spine may follow direct violence, crushing injuries, severe flexion, extension or twisting strains. Most injuries are flexion injuries. Miners are commonly injured by roof falls on to the back. A fall from a height may cause a crush injury of vertebrae, an injury often associated with fractures of the calcaneum. Fractured vertebrae used to be common following electro-convulsion therapy, but are rare now that muscle relaxants are used. Pathological fractures are common, for example, secondary to osteoporosis or secondary carcinomas.

Vertebral fractures are classified as stable or unstable in relation to the possibility of paraplegia. In stable fractures it is usually the vertebral bodies that are fractured. In unstable fractures rupture of the interspinous and interarticular ligaments, fracture of the vertebral arch, lamina, articular facets or spines allows dislocation that may transect the cord.

The most serious complication of vertebral fracture is paraplegia, usually due to irrecoverable damage to the spinal cord caused at the time of injury. Paraplegia may, however, follow injudicious movement after injury, so in first-aid treatment, when a spinal injury is suspected, it is imperative that the patient should be moved as little as possible. Most vertebral injuries are suffered in flexion, so further flexion must be avoided by carrying the patient in the position in which he is found if that is possible, or by carrying him prone. In the general examination of the patient with a head injury it is important to examine the cervical spine clinically and radiologically, because injuries to the cervical spine are so often associated. When cervical spinal damage is suspected it is especially important to disturb the patient as little as possible in movement, for dislocation and redislocation is very common in this region.

Cervical Spine

Fractures of the atlas and axis vertebrae are rare. They may cause fatal quadriplegia because of transection of the cord above the level of innervation of the respiratory muscles. Undisplaced fractures cause pain, especially on nodding the head (from which the patient refrains and should not be encouraged to perform). The head is held immobile by muscle spasm. Radiographs taken through the open mouth show the fractures. Displacement may occur if the odontoid process is fractured or if the transverse ligament is torn. Pathological dislocation is rare, but may occur from an adjacent focus of inflammation, for example, severe tonsillitis may soften the transverse ligament, it occurs more commonly in rheumatoid arthritis.

Fractures of the lower cervical vertebrae are usually crush fractures due to severe flexion. Paraplegia is unlikely so long as there is no dislocation. A fracture dislocation may only be revealed if radiographs are taken in the lateral plane with the cervical spine in flexion; in this view slight slipping forwards of C6 vertebra on C7 may be shown. More serious fracture dislocations may occur, in which the interarticular facets become locked, causing difficulty in reduction. In paraplegia due to injury to the cervical spine radiographs often appear to be normal. In these vertebral dislocation has occurred transecting the spinal cord, followed by spontaneous replacement. The dislocation may easily recur if a flexion strain is allowed. It is therefore important in any case of injury to the cervical spine that in the first-aid treatment the patient be carried with the neck immobilised as much as possible, for example, with sand bags.

Treatment

The important decision in fractures or dislocations of the cervical spine is whether traction should be applied to the skull to prevent pressure on the spinal cord or to relieve pressure on it or to obtain reduction. Where paraplegia has occurred or where it is felt that it is a danger, then traction is applied using skull calipers. The head of the bed is raised and the calipers are attached to a weight by a cord running over a pulley at the head end of the bed. The patient is nursed on a special bed (Striker frame) which can be frequently turned to prevent pressure sores without interruption of the traction. The position is maintained for several weeks until recovery of the paraplegia or stability of the fracture is achieved. A decision must then be made as to whether the cervical spine must be fixed operatively to prevent recurrence of dislocation. Fixation is achieved by bone grafts laid along either side of the rawed spinal processes. Undisplaced stable cervical spinal fractures can be treated by immobilisation in a plaster or plastic collar. Full immobilisation of the cervical spine in plaster requires the application of a skull cap and a thoracic carapace. This is rarely necessary.

Thoracic Spine

Fractures of thoracic vertebrae are uncommon and, when they occur, should raise suspicion of a pathological fracture. Crush fractures from senile osteoporosis are probably the commonest, though secondary deposits in this region may cause collapse of vertebrae. The fractures cannot be reduced. Rest is advised until pain has subsided sufficient to allow exercises to the posterior spinal muscles. Any underlying cause is treated, for example, anabolic steroids are of value in recalcifying the vertebrae of old people. Paraplegia is a common sequel to traumatic fractures of thoracic vertebrae.

Thoraco-lumbar Region

The lower dorsal and upper lumbar vertebrae are the commonest sites of vertebral fractures. Fractures of vertebrae are likely where a mobile part of the spine adjoins an immobile part, i.e. thoraco-lumbar and cervico-thoracic regions.

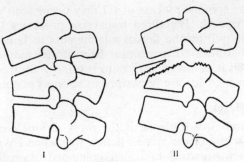

FIG. 70. Fracture of lumbar vertebrae: (i) wedge or compression fracture; (ii) fracture-dislocation

Fractures of the vertebral body are usually crush or compression fractures due to severe flexion. Typically only one vertebral body is involved, becoming wedged anteriorly (Fig. 70). Compression of the cord only occurs if there is severe comminution causing a localised angular kyphosis or if a fracture dislocation has occurred with rupture of the intervertebral ligaments or fracture of laminae or pedicles allowing slipping of one vertebra forward on the next below.

Treatment

For stable fractures, usually isolated compression injuries, rest in bed with a pillow under the lumbar spine for from 2–3 weeks is needed until the pain subsides, followed by extension exercises to the spinal muscles and a belt for spinal support. Immobilisation in a plaster jacket for 6–12 weeks may be necessary if there is severe pain. Rarely is any attempt made at reduction of the fracture by hyperextension and plaster immobilisation. The accent is upon early ambulation and building up the erector spinae muscles by extension exercises.

Unstable fractures are serious. Paraplegia may have occurred from the time of the injury or have been induced or aggravated during movement. Nowadays the tendency is to immobilise unstable fractures operatively as soon as possible, not so much in the hope of restoring function or aiding recovery of paraplegia but more of allowing intensive nursing care to be given comfortably and to prevent complications of paraplegia such as bed sores.

At operation the fracture is exposed. Dislocation of a vertebra is reduced, if necessary by removing a locked interarticular facet. The spinous processes above and below the fracture are fixed by cortical bone slabs or plates bolted on either side of the spinous processes. Fixation must be so firm that the patient can be nursed and turned frequently without great discomfort.

Spinous and Transverse Processes

Fracture of the spinous process of C7 may occur with violent strain—'clay shovellers injury'. Fractured transverse processes follow avulsion by strong muscle pull on the fascial attachments to bone. Renal injury may be associated and retroperitoneal haematoma may cause paralytic ileus. Rest in bed is enforced until pain subsides. Strapping gives some relief. Extension exercises are prescribed as soon as possible.

Traumatic Paraplegia

Paraplegia, rarely quadriplegia, is the most serious complication that may follow a fracture of the spine. Before the Second World War traumatic paraplegia was usually fatal or condemned the patient to end his days in bed in an institution, usually with suprapubic drainage of the bladder, chronic urinary infection and bed sores. Now, so long as the paraplegic is properly treated, preferably in a unit set up for this particular problem, he has an excellent chance of returning home and leading a useful life.

Most paraplegias result from unstable fractures or dislocations of the cervical or thoraco-lumbar spine. In the reception area of the hospital careful assessment of the motor power and sensation of all four limbs should be carried out. Radiographs are taken in both the lateral and antero-posterior planes. If an unstable fracture with paraplegia is diagnosed the decision must be made when to apply traction to the skull for cervical injury or to immobilise the spine in lumbar injuries.

Not all paraplegias are permanent. Some are due to concussion of the cord and are followed by complete recovery. The presence of any trace of motor power or sensation in the limb is an important prognostic sign of possible recovery. If it disappears the possibility of haemorrhage compressing the cord must be considered an indication for operative decompression. If recovery is going to occur some improvement should be obvious within 3 weeks; thereafter progress may be slow over a year or more.

Injuries of the cervical part of the spinal cord are most often recoverable. Of course if the cord is transected no recovery is possible, for regeneration cannot occur.

The level of spinal-cord injury is diagnosed from the physical signs.

Cervical Spine. Here there may be quadriplegia with a lower motor-neurone lesion of the upper limbs and upper motor-neurone lesion of the lower limbs. Above the level of C4 transection of the cord is immediately fatal because of paralysis of respiration. In injuries at the C5, C6 level the abductors of the shoulder are paralysed and the limb is held to the side; wasting of the small muscles of the hand develops. In injuries at the level of C6 and C7 the abductors and external rotators of the shoulder draw the shoulder into abduction and the upper limb into external rotation. The level of loss of sensation extends no higher than the level of T1 because the supraclavicular nerves (C3, C4 and C5) extend over the neck and clavicle.

Thoracic Spine. The upper limit of the sensory level of anaesthesia depends on the level of the damage to the spinal cord. Below the level of injury there will be anaesthesia and paralysis of the lower limbs and abdominal muscles. Paralysis is first flaccid, but after 2–3 weeks becomes spastic as the effects of concussion wear off.

Lumbar Spine. Above the level of the cauda equina the spinal cord is damaged, causing spastic paralysis of the lower limbs. If the cauda equina is affected a lower motor-neurone lesion of the legs results with loss of anal reflexes and sacral anaesthesia.

In injuries of the cervical, thoracic and upper lumbar vertebrae, the bladder becomes distended because of acute retention due to the unopposed action of the sympathetic, unopposed because of paralysis of the parasympathetic nerve supply to the bladder. When the cauda equina is damaged, because sacral nerve roots are involved, dribbling incontinence results, due to loss of the pelvic innervation of the bladder.

The urgent problems in paraplegia are treatment of the bladder and prevention of the bed sores that result from pressure on insensitive skin over the sacrum, buttocks and heels. Injuries of the spinal cord above the cauda equina are followed by acute retention of urine. This must be relieved by a fine plastic catheter of the Foley or Gibbon type passed under aseptic precautions and left *in situ.* After 2–8 weeks the lower part of the spinal cord below the site of transection recovers to allow the development of an automatic bladder. An automatic bladder can be stimulated to contract by various manoeuvres such as pressure over the bladder or by stroking the inner side of the thigh. An automatic bladder can be trained to void urine every 4 hours. Occasionally there is some difficulty in complete evacuation, in which case a partial resection of the bladder neck can be performed per urethram to reduce the volume of residual urine.

Insensitive skin must be protected by careful nursing and by turning the patient every 2 hours, night and day, on a special frame that has an anterior shell which supports the patient in the prone position. Pressure points are kept clean and gently rubbed every 4 hours with oil and spirit and kept dry with powder. By using a frame the position of the fracture can be maintained in injuries of the cervical spine, even if traction is being applied to the skull. As soon as possible, a decision must be made as to whether operative reduction of a fracture dislocation must be performed or whether spinous processes should be fixed above and below the fracture to provide stability.

As soon as the patient is fit and it is considered that he is likely to have a permanent paraplegia he should be transferred to a paraplegic unit. Initially the paraplegia is flaccid, but as the distal cord recovers spasticity becomes apparent and often very painful flexor spasms may occur. If these are very painful they can be relieved by division of appropriate anterior nerve roots—anterior rhizotomy or by intrathecal injection of phenol.

By developing the arm and trunk muscles it is possible for a man with complete paraplegia to learn to walk on special calipers, which he swings by using his unparalysed trunk muscles. Even in a chair he can engage in sports and develop hobbies and even perform a job. Psychological rehabilitation is imperative so that he can return to being a useful member of the family.

FRACTURES OF THE PELVIS

The diagnosis of a pelvic fracture is made from the nature of the injury, for example, crushing or a fall from a height. Tenderness may be felt over the site of the fracture. Bleeding may occur in the retroperitoneal tissues and in the pelvis, which may give rise to a palpable mass. Damage to the urethra may cause bleeding at the urethral meatus or retention of urine. Rectal examination may reveal a sense of bogginess in the pelvis or posterior displacement of the prostate. Fractures of the pelvis with upward displacement of the ilium or central dislocation of the femur through a fracture of the acetabulum may shorten a limb. An extensive retroperitoneal haematoma may cause paralytic ileus.

Isolated fractures of the pelvis (Fig. 71) are painful but not serious, in that complications do not occur because displacement is not a feature. The pubic rami on one side may be fractured or the blade of the ilium or the acetabulum. Such fractures require only bed rest until pain has subsided, followed by mobilisation with exercises. Weight bearing is allowed when the pelvis is no longer painful.

If the pelvic ring is disrupted, then the injury is much more serious and likely to be associated with shock and such serious complications as ruptured urethra or bladder. In compression injuries the pubic rami on both sides are fractured and pushed posteriorly; such an injury is likely to damage the intrapelvic part of the urethra or the bladder. A severe blow to the pelvis may open the pelvic ring, either by splitting the symphysis or by fracturing the pubis on one side. Separation of the fractured bones can only occur if the sacro-iliac joint is dislocated or if

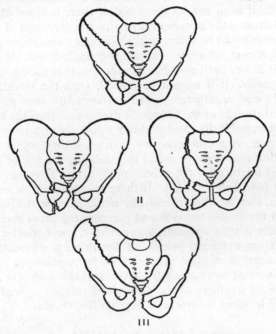

FIG. 71. Fractures of the pelvis: (i) isolated fractures; (ii) fractures of the pelvic ring (iii) fractures with displacement

there is a fracture of the ilium. The urethra may be damaged. If the sacro-iliac dislocation is not reduced prolonged backache is likely. A fall from a height is likely to cause fractures through the ilium and pubis, with upward dislocation of one side of the pelvis. The limb on that side will then show shortening.

Avulsion fractures of the pelvis due to severe muscular contraction are uncommon. The anterior superior spine, anterior inferior spine and ischial tuberosity may be avulsed. Fractures of the sacrum are rare —fissures may be seen, but rarely is there any displacement.

Falls on the bottom may cause fractures of the coccyx. These are extremely painful and cause prolonged pain. More often no fracture is found but the coccyx remains very painful for a prolonged period— coccydynia. Pain may be relieved by injections of local analgesic around the sacrococcygeal joint. Rarely is it necessary to excise the coccyx.

Treatment

In all pelvic fractures damage to the urethra should be suspected. Haemorrhage and shock may be severe and demand resuscitation. Radiographs reveal the extent of bone injury, it is particularly important to distinguish fractures of the pelvic ring from isolated fractures.

Passage of clear urine free of blood means that the urethra has not been damaged. If urine cannot be passed, if there is blood at the meatus, bogginess felt around the rectum or posterior displacement of the prostate, then the patient should be taken to the operating theatre and an attempt made to pass a catheter under full aseptic precautions. If the catheter passes it is left *in situ* until pain has subsided so that the patient may pass his urine normally. If it cannot be passed, then the bladder is opened suprapubically and a catheter passed retrogradely (see p. 394). If an extraperitoneal rupture of the bladder is diagnosed, then the bladder must be drained suprapubically, and a drain must also be inserted into the retropubic space. A urethrogram or cystogram performed immediately before operation may be very useful in localising the site of injury.

Undisplaced fractures of the pelvis and avulsion fractures require only bed rest until pain had subsided. If there is a fracture or dislocation of the pelvic ring, then an attempt must be made to close the pelvis by lying the patient on the unaffected side and pressing the ilium back into place. A strong binder is then applied. Alternatively, the patient can be slung up on slings from overhead beams. If the ilium is dislocated upwards, then traction must be applied to the leg under anaesthesia to reduce the dislocation, followed by traction for several weeks with rest in bed. For severely displaced fractures of the pelvis, bed rest is required for as long as 6 weeks and freedom from weight bearing for 3 months.

FURTHER READING

Guttmann, L. (1961) *The Management of Paraplegia*, The Medical Annual, ed. R. Bodley-Scott and R. Milnes-Walker, Wright, Bristol.

CHAPTER THIRTY-FOUR

GENERAL AFFECTIONS OF THE SKELETON

CONGENITAL OR DEVELOPMENTAL

Fragilitas Ossium (or Osteogenesis Imperfecta)

In this condition the bones are abnormally brittle or fragile for no known cause. The condition is sometimes inherited, and is often associated with a blue or grey colour of the sclera. Deafness is common. There may be varying degrees of severity. Sometimes a child is born dead with fractures of many bones sustained in utero. Less severe degrees of the affection result in multiple and repeated fractures of the long bones in childhood. The fractures are of the adult pattern showing a complete break, whereas in the very young with normal bones it is more usual to see 'greenstick' buckling. Fortunately at or after puberty the condition and strength of the bones improves and fractures occur less often. No abnormal biochemical changes can be detected.

Treatment

The fractures heal as well as fractures in normal bones, but often, because new fractures occur while old ones are healing, deformity results. Reduction of fractures and immobilisation in plaster is satisfactory, and there is a place for intramedullary nail fixation to provide some strength for the bone. As the child grows the nail may be changed for a larger one.

Achondroplasia

A failure of proliferation of bone from the epiphyseal plates during growth may occur. It is often an inherited trait, and results in an individual with limbs grossly shortened out of proportion to the trunk, which is normally developed—the traditional circus dwarf. The membrane bones are normally formed, so that the cranium is of normal size, though the base of the skull is undeveloped. The fingers are short and of equal length—trident hand. The cause is unknown, intelligence is unaffected, there are no complications.

Diaphyseal Aclasis

This is another form of abnormality at the epiphyseal plate—sometimes inherited, and of unknown aetiology. Islands of epiphyseal cells become isolated in the metaphysis of long bones and continue to proliferate to form bony outgrowths capped by cartilage that grow away from the epiphysis. These are typically grouped around the ends of the long bones. There may be only a few of these exostoses, or many hundreds, affecting all the long bones. Associated with exostoses is a failure of modelling, giving rise to misshapen ends to the bones. The protuberances may cause symptoms by pressure on adjacent structures or because of their unsightliness; they cease to grow after the epiphyses fuse. Very rarely malignancy may occur. Surgical removal is indicated if the exostoses interfere with function or if malignant change is suspected.

Multiple Chondromatosis (Dyschondroplasia: Ollier's Disease)

In this condition nests of cells become separated from the epiphyseal plate and come to lie in the medullary cavities of the bones, forming cartilaginous masses—enchondromata—that expand bone and thin the cortex, resembling a benign tumour. The metacarpals and phalanges of the hand are typical sites. Pathological fractures or deformity result from uneven growth. Curettage of the chondromata and packing of the cavities with bone chips may be necessary, or sometimes osteotomy is performed, that is operative fracture of the bones to correct deformity.

METABOLIC AND DIETARY DISEASES OF BONE

Rickets

Dietary deficiency of vitamin D and lack of sunlight may combine to cause infantile rickets. Vitamin D promotes the absorption of calcium and phosphorus from the intestine. In deficiency of vitamin D the level of serum calcium is maintained at the expense of calcification of growing parts of the bones which remain soft and uncalcified. Characteristic features of the disease are thickening of the epiphyses of long bones, with marked 'bowing' of the legs from bone softening. The costo-chondral junctions of the ribs become prominent or beaded (rickety rosary), and the attachment of the diaphragm to the softened ribs produces a horizontal depression or sulcus (Harrison's sulcus). Radiologically there is a general decrease in bone density and, at the epiphyses, there is 'cupping' and increased width and depth of the epiphyseal plate. Bowing of the legs may be obvious, causing genu valgum. Rickets becomes rare as social conditions improve, but florid rickets is again being seen in Britain in coloured immigrants who have unusual dietary habits, especially in industrial areas, where the smoky atmosphere cuts down solar ultra-violet light. The serum calcium and phosphorus levels are normal, the alkaline phosphatase is raised. Similar bone changes to those seen in infantile rickets are found in coeliac disease, renal disease in children and 'Fanconi's syndome', in which there is a renal tubular defect.

Treatment

Most cases of rickets respond well to vitamin D. Patients with severe bowing of the legs may occasionally need osteotomy for correction of deformity.

Osteomalacia

Rickets due to vitamin D deficiency may occur in adults, especially in those countries where diets are poor. The bones lack mineral salts and show an increase in osteoid tissue, which is easily deformed by pressure. Gross bowing of long bones and deformity of the pelvis often results. The narrowed pelvis is a common cause of obstetric difficulty in women. Osteomalacia is not uncommon some years after a partial gastrectomy.

Osteoporosis

A common cause of diffuse generalised bone rarefaction is senile osteoporosis. It is more common in women than men, and so may have an endocrine basis. The bones are soft and brittle; pathological fractures often result. The vertebrae are commonly wedged by 'crush' fractures and the neck of the femur softens to give rise to a varus deformity. Old ladies sometimes say they felt a crack in the hip which caused them to fall, suggesting a spontaneous fracture rather than one due to injury.

Patients suffering from osteoporosis sometimes complain of severe bone pains, particularly in the spine, relieved to some extent by anabolic steroids, which help recalcification of bones.

Scurvy

Scurvy is still sometimes seen in children in Britain, most often in immigrants who take diets grossly deficient in vitamin C or in babies who are fed for a long period with artificial feeds without vitamin C supplements. It is also seen in old people living alone on an inadequate diet. Haemorrhages occur from the gums and other mucosal surfaces. The bones are also affected by subperiosteal haemorrhages, which cause exquisite pain. Arrest of growth may occur at the epiphysis. In the acute stage the severe bony tenderness and swelling may be mistaken for acute osteomyelitis. Radiographs may show new bone formation at the site of subperiosteal haemorrhage. Epiphyseal lines are widened, and epiphyses may become separated. The condition is easily cured by giving vitamin C.

ENDOCRINE DISEASES OF BONE

Hyperparathyroidism (von Recklinghausen's Disease of Bone)

Hyperparathyroidism is characterised by diffuse osteoporosis and bone cysts, especially in the skull, mandible and phalanges. It is due to an adenoma of one of the parathyroid glands, which secretes an excess of parathormone, or to hyperplasia of all four parathyroids. There may be mental disturbance, gastro-intestinal upsets, peptic ulcer and renal symptoms due to renal-stone formation. Osteoporosis may result in bone pain, especially low backache and pathological fractures.

The diagnosis is made by recognising the clinical features, the characteristic radiographic changes in the skull and phalanges and the raised level of serum calcium. The level of phosphorus in the serum is often depressed and the serum alkaline phosphatase markedly raised. Once primary hyperparathyroidism is diagnosed, the neck should be explored and all four parathyroids displayed by a meticulous and sometimes lengthy dissection, in which the upper mediastinum may have to be exposed by splitting the sternum. The adenomatous gland is removed and immediate frozen section performed to confirm that it has arisen from a parathyroid gland; if all the parathyroids are involved by hyperplasia subtotal removal is done. After operation the serum calcium rapidly falls to normal levels; tetany may occur if the level of serum calcium becomes subnormal. The bones gradually recalcify over a period of many months, and additional calcium is given by mouth to supply the 'hungry' bones. The prognosis after removal of a parathyroid tumour depends upon the extent of renal damage that has been suffered before the diagnosis was made.

Cushing's Syndrome

Excessive secretion of adrenocortical hormones may come primarily from an adenoma or carcinoma of the adrenal or secondarily from a basophil adenoma of the pituitary. More rarely it is due to a thymic tumour or carcinoma of the bronchus. The syndrome consists of a 'moon face', obese trunk with thin limbs, hypertension, hirsutism, glycosuria, striae in the skin and osteoporosis, which may result in fractures (see p. 165).

The syndrome may also result from the prolonged administration of adrenal steroids. Occasionally severe bone damage, or even destruction of joint surfaces, results (see Chapter Thirteen).

DISEASES OF BONE OF UNKNOWN AETIOLOGY

Solitary Cyst

A solitary cyst of bone may be found in the upper humerus, tibia or femur, most often in children up to the age of puberty Pathological fracture is common, and may be the presenting feature. Healing after fracture may cure the cyst. Pain in the affected bone or a swelling are other symptoms. Radiographs show a clear area in the metaphysis, often expanding a bone but going no further than the epiphyseal plate. Treatment is to evacuate the cyst and fill the cavity with bone chips.

Fibrous Dysplasia

In monostotic fibrous dysplasia (a very rare condition) a long bone shows alteration of its architecture, with the formation of a cyst surrounded by sclerosis. There is no specific treatment, and the cause is unknown.

Several bones are affected in polyostotic fibrous dysplasia in which areas of medulla are replaced by fibrous tissue, with osteoporosis of the surrounding bone. The skull is often affected, showing a characteristically dense base and elongation of the occiput. In Albright's syndrome there is in addition sexual precocity in girls and large pale patches of cutaneous pigmentation. The level of serum calcium is normal, and there are no characteristic biochemical changes. The cause is unknown.

Paget's Disease (Osteitis Deformans)

The patient with advanced Paget's disease shows thickened 'sabre' tibiae, large clavicles, bent femora and a big domed skull. The cause is unknown, but the affected bones, though greatly thickened, are softer and more brittle than usual and have an increased blood supply, which makes them warmer than normal. The bones are liable to pathological fracture, and a small proportion develop osteosarcoma, occasionally at multiple sites. For many years only one bone may be affected. The patient may complain of pain in the affected bones, especially at night. The level of serum calcium and phosphorus is normal, but the alkaline phosphatase may be very high.

Radiographs show both sclerosis and osteoporosis. The normal bony architecture is lost, with thickening of the cortical layer due to an increase of poorly defined cancellous bone. The skull is thickened by spongy bone, the normal outline permeated and thickened by new bone formation. The increased vascularity of the bones may be so severe as to cause high-output left ventricular failure. Another complication is deafness from otosclerosis or narrowing of the bony foramen of the auditory nerve. Occasionally other nerves at the base of the skull may be affected. Thickening of the bones of the face is rare (leontiasis ossea). No effective treatment is known. Pain may be relieved by analgesics. Radiotherapy, osteotomy and guttering of bones have been used in treatment.

Rare Disorders of Bone

In *craniocleidodysostosis* the clavicles may be hypoplastic or absent, the cranium is large and the face is small. The condition is often inherited. *Osteopetrosis* (marble bones, Albers–Schönberg disease) is a condition in which bones are densely calcified and yet are prone to fracture. Stippled bones or *osteopoikilosis* is found incidentally in radiographs; the bones are stippled by small areas of dense bone. It is a condition of no pathological significance. *Melorrheostosis* is another abnormality only found accidentally on radiography. Excrescences are seen on the surface of bone that resemble the appearance of candle grease running down a candle. *Chondro-osteodystrophy* (Morquio's disease) is a hereditary or familial condition causing dwarfism. The thoracic and lumbar vertebrae are flattened and show a prominent central tongue of bone that projects anteriorly. Epiphyses are broadened, the shafts of long bones are thicker than normal. Joints may show hypermobility. *Gargoylism* is a variety of chondro-osteodystrophy in which there is dwarfism, mental defect and typically ugly features. The liver and spleen may be enlarged, corneal opacities are found. In *arachnodactyly* the fingers and toes are long and spidery. The disorder is familial. The subject is tall and thin and shows excessive mobility of the joints. Other congenital defects may be present. Dwarfism may also be due to a dysplasia of the epiphyses, which are irregular and appear mottled in radiographs. The limbs are short, but the skull and spine are unaffected, *epiphyseal dysplasia*.

FURTHER READING

Adams, J. C. (1964) *Outline of orthopaedics*, 5th ed. Livingstone, Edinburgh.

Mercer, Sir W., and Duthie, R. B. (1964) *Orthopaedic Surgery* 6th ed. Arnold, London.

CHAPTER THIRTY-FIVE

INFECTIONS OF BONES AND JOINTS

Infection of bone may follow blood-borne infection (haematogenous osteomyelitis) or occur secondary to an injury in which bone has been exposed, i.e. an open fracture or following an operation on a bone or joint. The infection may be acute or chronic.

ACUTE HAEMATOGENOUS OSTEOMYELITIS

Children are particularly liable to acute osteomyelitis, a disease that has become less common in recent years, for it is more often seen where nutrition and housing are poor. The bones are affected before epiphyseal fusion, when the nutrient vessels to the metaphyses are end arteries in which a bacterial embolus may preferentially lodge. In the rigid structure of bone the inflammatory response to acute infection causes severe tension, which ends in bone necrosis. Arteries within the Haversian canals thrombose, causing infarction. Pus may collect to form an abscess in the bone itself, but more often under the periosteum, which is lifted from the cortex. If the metaphysis lies in a joint suppurative arthritis may result.

The organism responsible for osteomyelitis is most often the *Staphylococcus aureus*. Streptococci, pneumococci and typhoid bacilli are less often found. A primary septic focus may precede the development of osteomyelitis, such as an infected wound or blister, a boil or a furuncle. From the primary focus infection spreads by the blood stream by which route organisms lodge in the metaphysis. Untreated or badly treated acute osteomyelitis may kill or become chronic, leading to crippling invalidism. Early diagnosis and treatment is curative. A delay of hours or days may result in prolonged illness or even death.

Clinical Features

A limb bone is usually affected, such as the tibia, femur or humerus, part of which becomes very painful. There is often a history of injury, but, of course, all children are liable to injury, and such a history is not necessarily reliable. The history of trauma followed by pain and tenderness in the bone may suggest a sprain or contusion, especially when the radiograph shows no abnormality. It is important to remember that in the early phase of osteomyelitis no radiographic abnormality is found, and the diagnosis should be made clinically and the condition treated before radiographic changes are seen.

Malaise, anorexia and pyrexia should arouse suspicion of bone infection. The affected bone is acutely tender in the region of the metaphysis. Later there is swelling, erythema and increased heat over the focus of infection. A nearby joint may show a sympathetic effusion. If the metaphysis lies within the joint capsule, as in the hip joint, the symptoms and signs may be suggestive of an infective arthritis with effusion. The regional lymph nodes are likely to be enlarged and tender.

Investigations

In osteomyelitis the white-cell count and erythrocyte sedimentation rate are raised—points of great value in doubtful cases. For example, the signs of a bruised bone may simulate infection, but the white-cell count and E.S.R. are unaltered. Blood culture should always be performed when the diagnosis is first made or suspected, but treatment must not wait upon its result. A radiograph of the affected bone must be performed, but is unlikely to show any change for about 10 days after the onset of infection. The earliest signs are a localised area of rarefaction or a flake of subperiosteal calcification where the periosteum has been lifted up by exudate or pus. The deep layers of the periosteum then form bone which is shown in the radiograph. In the phase of chronicity dense sclerosis with increased radiopacity of the affected part of the bone is usually seen. In the thickened area there may be evidence of cavities which contain pus or pieces of dead bone called sequestra. If the diaphysis has been infarcted by thrombosis of the nutrient artery the deeper layers of the periosteum form a thick covering of bone called the involucrum perforated by holes called cloacae made by pus.

Treatment

It is possible to cure osteomyelitis by antibiotics alone so long as treatment is started within the first 24 hours following infection. A rapid response to cloxacillin is evidenced by a fall in temperature and a decrease in the intensity of the local signs of inflammation. If this response is delayed or if treatment has been started late, then any pus under the periosteum must be released by drainage and the bone tension decompressed by drilling. The bone is exposed under anaesthesia at the maximum site of tension, the periosteum is incised and a number of drill holes made into the medulla, from which pus may discharge under some pressure. The wound is closed around a suction drain. The limb is splinted for several weeks, and if the hip joint is involved light traction is applied to the limb to prevent dislocation of the joint due to laxity of the distended capsule. Antibiotics are continued in full doses for 6 weeks to 3 months. If an organism has been cultured from the blood (in 50% of cases) its sensitivity to antibiotics can be ascertained. More and more penicillin- and tetracycline-resistant organisms are being reported, so that it is extremely important to culture the organisms rapidly and establish sensitivity.

Osteomyelitis is a grave complication of an open fracture that may end in amputation. Once infection is established, it is difficult to treat and very prone to become chronic. The diagnosis is usually made only after a purulent offensive discharge is seen exuding from the wound. Bone infection can be avoided in most open fractures by careful and thorough débridement of the wound. The skin edges are excised and all dirt and foreign bodies are removed. Any tissue of doubtful vitality is excised. The wound is irrigated with hydrogen peroxide, a good mechanical cleanser. The skin must be closed at all costs, though this often necessitates a plastic procedure. Flaps of skin can be rotated over the fracture by making relieving incisions through healthy tissue. Any skin defects are covered by split-thickness skin grafts. Tetracycline is given and the fracture immobilised. It is more important to gain skin cover and first intention healing than perfect reduction of the fracture.

CHRONIC PYOGENIC OSTEOMYELITIS

Chronicity may follow acute haematogenous osteomyelitis or infection of bone in a compound fracture. It is also a serious complication of operations on bones or joints where sepsis has followed. Where foreign bodies in the form of prostheses or nails or plates have been inserted, infection is always a hazard, and once it occurs usually indicates the need for removal of the foreign bodies in the hope of clearing up the infection. The infected bone becomes necrosed by vascular thrombosis. The dead tissue is a foreign body which slowly separates to form a sequestrum lying in a cavity filled by pus and granulations over the infected bone. An involucrum forms, perforated by openings that intermittently discharge pus on to the surface through sinuses. The infection is prone to exacerbations, with an increase of pain and pyrexia, followed by a profuse discharge of pus. Months or years may intervene between the flares of infection. A number of organisms are usually involved. Septicaemia may follow. Amyloid disease may complicate years of chronic infection. Squamous-celled carcinoma may form around the opening of a chronic sinus.

Treatment

Infection persists until the sequestrum is removed or discharged. Once a sequestrum has been demonstrated radiologically, then it should be removed and the cavity in which it lay unroofed and curetted. The cavity is packed and allowed to heal by granulation from the depths of the wound to the surface. The limb is usually immobilised in plaster. Antibiotics are given, appropriate to the sensitivity of the causative organism. This operation may need to be performed, even where a sequestrum cannot be demonstrated, if infection is severe and uncontrolled. Amputation may occasionally be necessary if severe disability follows recurrent infection and for fear of amyloid disease following years of sepsis.

Chronic osteomyelitis may complicate orthopaedic operations in which foreign bodies have been implanted—for example, plating of fractures and prostheses for joints. Such a complication is always serious, and may end in amputation. This fact is ever present in the mind of a surgeon who has to choose between the operative and non-operative methods of treatment that are available for most orthopaedic disabilities.

Brodie's Abscess

Chronic osteomyelitis may be insidious in onset, with a gradual development of pain in a bone, most often in the lower femur or upper tibia, without any acute episodes. The affected bone is tender, the white-cell count and the E.S.R. are raised. Radiography shows a radiolucent zone bounded by dense bone.

Treatment

This is the same as for chronic osteomyelitis, the cavity is unroofed and packed. Antibiotics are prescribed. The results in these cases of low-grade localised infection are rather better than in other forms of chronic osteomyelitis.

PERIOSTITIS

Inflammation or injury to the periosteum causes a tender area of thickening over the affected bone. If the periosteum is raised by haematoma or inflammatory exudate, subperiosteal bone is formed and seen radiographically as a thin layer superficial to the bone or as a densely calcified plaque. The commonest cause of periostitis is injury—for example the shin of a footballer may become irregular from periostitis of the tibia. Inflammation due to an adjacent ulcer of the leg may cause extensive new bone formation widely spread on the surface of the tibia and fibula. Very rarely nowadays is syphilis or tuberculosis a cause of periostitis or osteoperiostitis. Syphilitic periostitis may cause the typical sabre tibiae of congenital syphilis. A gumma may form in the centre of an area of periostitis and discharge on to a surface to form a gummatous ulcer. The treatment of periostitis is that of the primary disease. Fracture or neoplasm must be excluded.

In *infantile cortical hyperostosis* (Caffey's disease) infants under the age of 6 months present with swellings on a number of bones, especially the mandible, skull, scapula and long bones, which may be tender. The child may be febrile. Radiographs show subperiosteal new bone formation. Spontaneous recovery is invariable; scurvy, syphilis and osteomyelitis must be excluded.

PYOGENIC ARTHRITIS

Acute pyogenic inflammation of a joint may arise from osteomyelitis of a bone when the metaphysis lies within a joint capsule (e.g. in the hip joint) or from infection of a wound penetrating the joint. Probably the highest incidence of joint sepsis is in the fingers. The knee joint is commonly infected by a foreign body, such as a pin or needle, that enters the joint when a person is kneeling. The actual entry of the foreign body may have given rise to little or no pain. Infection is a hazard of aspiration or of operations on joints, therefore such manoeuvres must always be carried out with a full aseptic ritual in the operating theatre.

Pyogenic arthritis is a serious condition which, if it is not rapidly and effectively treated, ends either in stiffness of the joint, pathological dislocation, chronic discharging sinus and even amputation. The synovium becomes converted to granulation tissue, articular cartilage and menisci become eroded and may form sequestra. The joint space becomes obliterated by a 'pannus' of granulation tissue that creeps over the eroded surfaces and lines the damaged synovial cavity. The best result that can be expected where the joint is extensively damaged is fibrous ankylosis. Sinus formation usually follows operative drainage. Chronic discharging sinuses and pathological dislocation within the lax distended capsule are features of chronic infection. Pyogenic arthritis may also complicate tuberculous infection, especially if a sinus has formed.

Pain is felt in the joint, which becomes swollen and tense. Because the joint capsule is distended the limb lies in the 'position of function', slight flexion of the knee, flexion, abduction and external rotation of the hip, dorsiflexion of the wrist. A high swinging fever and a raised white-cell count, coupled with malaise and other signs of a severe infection, are usually present.

Severe pain on movement is the striking feature. The joint is held fixed by the spasm of surrounding muscles, and the slightest attempt at movement provokes exquisite pain. Radiography may show a foreign body and, in the early phase, widening of the joint space by the effusion. Later, rarefaction, bone destruction, diminution of the joint space due to loss of articular cartilage and finally pathological dislocation may be seen.

The diagnosis of pyogenic arthritis can be difficult. A so-called sympathetic effusion may collect due to an adjacent acute osteomyelitis. Rheumatic fever may start in one joint, an exacerbation of rheumatoid arthritis may cause great pain and swelling. A fracture with haemarthrosis may cause crippling pain, heat and tenderness. In all these conditions, unlike acute pyogenic infection, some movement can be achieved without producing increased pain. Only in pyogenic arthritis is even the slightest movement evocative of agonising pain. Finally, if there is doubt the joint must be aspirated. Aspiration is particularly indicated in children when there is a suspicion of pyogenic arthritis in the hip joint.

Treatment

As an emergency the joint is aspirated with full aseptic precautions. If pus is obtained the joint is washed out with sterile saline, following which penicillin is instilled. Antibiotics do not pass readily from the blood into synovial fluid, especially if pus is present, so a high concentration of penicillin in the joint can only be achieved by direct instillation.

Immediate microscopic examination of the aspirated fluid may give important information about the infective organism. For example, pneumococci can be demonstrated in a direct smear before culture; the presence of gram-positive cocci strongly suggests a staphylococcal lesion. The fluid is always cultured to identify the organism and its sensitivity to antibiotics. Aspiration of the joint may be repeated daily until the effusion dries up. Systemic antibiotics are given appropriate to the causative organism. The limb is splinted and the joint surfaces held apart by skin traction. No weight bearing is permitted for at least 6 weeks. Antibiotics are maintained for 3 months. If early treatment is carried out complete cure can often be obtained by aspiration and antibiotic therapy.

If treatment is ineffective or delayed and an abscess forms, then it may be necessary to open the joint, drain pus and curette out any bony foci of infection. Such a course may be necessary in interphalangeal joints, where diagnosis is often delayed (see p. 138), and the result is usually a fixed joint.

TUBERCULOSIS OF BONES AND JOINTS

The incidence of skeletal tuberculosis has strikingly decreased in recent years in Great Britain because of the widespread pasteurisation of milk and the eradication of tuberculosis in cows, measures which should result in the eventual disappearance of bovine tuberculosis. The use of streptomycin in pulmonary tuberculosis has diminished cross-infection and thus reduced the incidence of skeletal tuberculosis due to the human type of bacillus. B.C.G. vaccination of children and contacts of tuberculosis has further diminished the chances of contracting tuberculosis. Tuberculosis of bone and joint is still, however, a major problem in those parts of Asia and Africa where housing conditions and nutritional standards are poor. Most of the cases seen in Britain today occur in immigrants from Asia, Africa and Ireland.

Pathology

Tuberculosis is a chronic infection characterised by the slow formation of granulation tissue and a peculiar form of necrosis called caseation, without the signs of acute inflammation. Caseation is followed by formation of cold abscesses, which ultimately may burst to form sinuses. If sinus formation occurs, secondary pyogenic infection is inevitable. There is a tendency to healing by fibrosis, which can be hastened by rest, improvement in nutrition and by chemotherapy. Secondary pyogenic infection may be followed by healing by bone, but more often is followed by chronic sinus formation and a serious deterioration in general health threatening life or leading to amyloid disease.

The tubercle bacilli reach bones and joints via the blood stream from a primary focus in, for example, the lung, tonsil or intestine. It is hence a secondary infection resulting from a transient bacteraemia of tubercle bacilli released from the primary focus. Microscopically the disease starts with formation of tubercle follicles (see p. 62). Later tuberculous granulation tissue is produced, followed by caseation. The actual site of development of infection may be determined by injury, often of a trivial nature. The organism often lodges in the metaphyses and epiphyses of bone.

Clinical Features

There is commonly a history of tuberculosis in the family. Children and young adults are particularly prone, though flares of infection may occur at any age, with many years intervening. Before the infection becomes obvious there is often a period of malaise, with loss of weight and appetite and perhaps night sweats. When bone and joint infection becomes established there is local pain and impairment of function. Sometimes the child may complain of night starts or cries when, during sleep, muscle spasm is relaxed and slight movement causes sudden pain.

The joints most commonly affected are the hip, knee and intervertebral joints (discs). Infection may arise from infection of the synovia or in a bony focus immediately subjacent to the articular cartilage. In the spine infection may originate in the centre of the vertebral body, but more often arises from a focus near the intervertebral disc. It is a feature of tuberculosis that it eventually destroys the intervertebral discs, several of which may be involved. Tuberculous infection of joints is much more common than infection of bone alone. Rarely a focus may be found in phalanges, presenting as swelling of the phalanges, with thinning of the cortex—tuberculous dactylitis.

In a joint, local swelling and tenderness arise from thickening of the synovium. A cold abscess may form locally or track a long distance from the site of infection. For example, spinal infection may produce a cold abscess in the psoas muscle that may present in the groin or even as low down as behind the knee. Movements of the affected joint are restricted by spasm. Wasting of nearby muscles is a prominent feature of tuberculous disease. The tuberculous knee, for example, shows a very characteristic spindle-shaped enlargement of the joint, its size made apparently larger by the wasting of the thigh muscles above. When the synovial membrane is greatly thickened it can often be felt to be enlarged by polypoid masses of granulation tissue.

A sinus may form after the discharge of a cold abscess spontaneously or after aspiration. Disorganisation of joints follows spread of synovial infection and caseous granulation tissue deep to the articular cartilages, which become eroded and destroyed. Finally, the joint cavity is obliterated by fibrosis or the formation of caseous abscesses.

Investigations

Radiographs may show rarefaction in the affected bones with a haziness of the joint outlines. In purely synovial infection no bony abnormality

R

may be seen. A transient increase in the width of the joint space due to effusion becomes reduced as the articular cartilage is destroyed. As healing occurs the bones become recalcified. In the spine erosion begins on the anterior surface of the affected vertebrae adjacent to the diseased discs. Later the vertebrae collapse and become wedged. Finally, as the discs are destroyed and if healing occurs, several vertebrae may become wedged together and fused by bone, resulting in a shortening of the spine, usually with considerable angular kyphosis or gibbus. The outline of a paravertebral abscess may be seen as a soft-tissue shadow which over the years may calcify.

The E.S.R. is usually raised and the Mantoux reaction positive. However, the results of these tests must not be taken to exclude tuberculosis if they prove to be negative. It is possible for active tuberculosis to be present with a normal E.S.R. and a negative Mantoux reaction. If pus can be obtained, tubercle bacilli may sometimes be seen on direct examination. More often the diagnosis is made by culture of the organism on a Lowenstein medium or after injection of pus into a guinea-pig. If possible some histological confirmation should be obtained of tuberculosis either after excision of a regional lymph node or by biopsy of the synovial membrane. Often the diagnosis can be made from the history, signs and radiographs.

Complications

Secondary infection via a sinus is common and increases the difficulties of treatment, especially in adults. If treatment is started late the chance of preserving mobility in a joint is small. Fibrous ankylosis is the usual sequel of tuberculous joint infection, and in late cases is the aim of operative treatment. It is important that fusion of the joint should be established in the best functional position. Bony fusion usually follows pyogenic infection, though sinuses may discharge pus for a long time. In the spine the great danger is the development of paraplegia due to the direct pressure of an abscess on the spinal cord or acute kyphosis following collapse of several vertebrae. Occasionally vascular thrombosis caused by the disease process results in ischaemia of the cord with irreversible paralysis of the lower limbs. Other manifestations of tuberculosis may appear, especially in the urogenital tract (tuberculous kidney, ureter, bladder, prostate and epididymis). Pulmonary infection may also become apparent.

Treatment

The principles of treatment are threefold—rest to the part and for the whole patient, improvement of general nutrition and chemotherapy. Surgery is necessary to drain abscesses, to fix joints and sometimes to excise tuberculous foci and synovial membrane when this is predominantly affected.

Before chemotherapy was introduced rest was the only treatment available and was extremely effective, especially in children, if it could be prolonged over a period of years, for tuberculosis shows a marked tendency to spontaneous healing that is greatly aided by immobilisation. Immobilisation is achieved by splintage, in plaster of Paris or rest on special frames or plaster beds. Coupled with rest is improvement of nutrition, plenty of fresh air and sunshine. As healing progresses the patient's activity is gradually increased. Signs of satisfactory healing are an improved sense of well-being, loss of muscle spasm, absence of pyrexia, a falling E.S.R. and signs of recalcification in the radiographs. Tuberculostatic drugs are given of which streptomycin is still the most effective, especially when supplemented by *para*-aminosalicylic acid (P.A.S.) and isonicotinic acid hydrazide (I.N.A.H.). All three drugs are prescribed for six months; for a further three years P.A.S. and I.N.A.H. are given. Surgery may be required to drain abscesses and to excise isolated tuberculous foci, especially in adults, who find it difficult to spend months or years in a sanatorium. The development of paraplegia may demand acute drainage of a paraspinal abscess. After abscesses are drained they should be closed for fear of secondary infection and sinus formation.

If a joint has been so severely damaged as to lead to serious loss of mobility it is usual to speed healing by operative fusion (arthrodesis) in the position of function. Operative treatment is especially indicated in adults, in whom speedy healing is preferable to a long course of immobilisation. Early operation is increasingly being performed for tuberculosis of the spine after a period of immobilisation on a plaster bed and antibiotic therapy to avoid abscess formation and the danger of paraplegia.

SYPHILIS OF BONE

The bony manifestations of syphilis are now excessively rare. In congenital syphilis metaphysitis may occur in infants, especially of the hips. Painful joints, failure to thrive and a miserable child are features. Radiographs show sclerosis of the juxta-epiphyseal region. In older children syphilitic osteoperiostitis causes thickening of the cortex and subperiosteal new bone formation, best seen on the anterior surface of the tibiae (sabre tibiae) or over the parietal bones (Parrot's nodes). A tumour or chronic osteomyelitis may be simulated. Other bony manifestations of congenital syphilis include notching of the incisor teeth (Hutchinson's teeth) or peg-shaped molars (Moon's molars). In adults, diffuse osteoperiostitis may produce great thickening of a bone in which gummatous changes may occur and cause ulceration on to a surface. The Wassermann reaction and biopsy confirms the diagnosis. Syphilitic inflammation of bones responds rapidly to chemotherapy (see p. 67).

FURTHER READING

McSweeney, I. (1964) *Infantile Cortical Hyperostosis*, J. Bone & Joint Surg., **46B**, 153.

CHAPTER THIRTY-SIX

TUMOURS OF BONE

Tumours of bone may be benign or malignant. If malignant the tumour may be primary or secondary. A malignant tumour of bone marrow is called myeloma.

BENIGN TUMOURS

An *osteoma* is a benign tumour of cortical bone found most often on the skull or cortex of a long bone. It is hard as ivory and tends to enlarge very slowly over a number of years. No symptoms arise unless rarely when one is found growing in the external auditory meatus causing deafness, or in a paranasal air sinus, causing infection by interfering with drainage. Occasionally removal may be needed for cosmetic reasons. In the radiograph a circumscribed mass of dense cortical bone is seen, capped by cartilage. Such outgrowths of bone only need removal if they interfere with function or if they limit movement of a joint. Malignancy never occurs.

A *chondroma* is a tumour of cartilage which may arise in the medullary cavity, enchondroma or on the surface of a bone—ecchondroma. Most commonly enchondromata are found in the small bones of the hand, one of which becomes expanded, its cortex made thin by the growth.

Pathological fracture may occur. A rib is a common site for enchondroma often noticed accidentally in a radiograph or by its producing a painless swelling. Multiple enchondromata are found in a hereditary disorder called Ollier's disease. Ecchondromata arise on the surface of flat bones, and may attain a considerable size. Chondromata occasionally become malignant—chondrosarcoma.

Radiographically an enchondroma is seen as a clear circumscribed area in the centre of a bone. The outline of an ecchondroma may be made more obvious by some calcification, especially near its periphery. Chondromata should be removed with a curette, the cavity being filled by bone chips.

An *osteochondroma* is a tumour of both bone and cartilage. It is usually single, but in congenital diaphysial aclasis multiple foci are found (see p. 491). In this disorder of epiphyseal growth a stalk of bone is formed capped by a cartilaginous head pointing away from the epiphysis. Many solitary osteochondromata are made obvious by their appearance in radiographs, which show them speckled by calcification.

Osteoclastoma (giant-cell tumour of bone) is usually classified as benign, but probably stands somewhere between the rigid definitions of benign and malignant. It is always locally invasive, and occasionally becomes very rapidly growing and frankly malignant, with metastases, though this is very unusual. Young adults are usually affected, and the tumour arises in the end of a long bone, lower end of femur, upper tibia, upper humerus and lower radius.

The patient presents with pain and swelling near the end of a long bone or pathological fracture. Radiographs show a typical 'soap bubble' appearance caused by bone trabeculae crossing a large cavity in the bone. A similar appearance may be seen with a bone cyst, though this rarely extends into the epiphysis, whereas a giant-cell tumour may extend up to the articular cartilage.

The cut surface of an osteoclastoma shows it to be a circumscribed tumour, chocolate coloured and obviously very vascular. Pathological fracture may occur. Histologically the tumour is comprised of a fibrous tissue stroma containing many large multi-nucleated giant cells similar to osteoclasts. Biopsy may be necessary to confirm the diagnosis, especially when a bone cyst or some inflammatory process is suspected. Occasionally it is necessary to exclude sarcoma.

Treatment involves removal of the tumour with as wide a margin of normal tissue round it as possible without endangering function. For a tumour in the lower end of the femur a wide block is excised, often leaving only a small portion of the condyles. If the joint is greatly deformed by this procedure it may need to be fused by sliding a cortical bone graft from the tibia.

An *osteoid osteoma* is a very rare benign 'tumour' of bone only comparatively recently recognised. The patient affected by it complains of a deep boring pain in a limb bone, usually the tibia or femur, often mostly at night. The pain is characteristically relieved by aspirin. Radiologically a tiny central midus is seen surrounded by a small zone of relative translucency within the slightly expanded cortex of the shaft of a bone.

Complete relief of pain is achieved by excision of the lesion. Recurrence does not occur. The histology is that of very vascular granulation tissue.

PRIMARY MALIGNANT TUMOURS OF BONE

Of the primary bone tumours osteosarcoma, fibrosarcoma, chondrosarcoma and reticulosarcoma, *osteosarcoma* is the commonest and one of the most malignant of tumours. Its development is all the more tragic, for it so often affects children and young adults. The growth almost always arises in the metaphyseal region of long bones, causing local swelling and pain. Metastasis is early by the blood stream to the lungs. Locally there is a swelling which is hot and tender and may be so vascular as to reveal a bruit on auscultation. The joint is never invaded, but spread occurs through the periosteum, which is lifted up from the cortex, and beyond it into the soft tissues. Occasionally lymph nodes are involved, though it is much more common for spread to occur by the blood stream. Radiologically the cortex is eroded, and lifting of the periosteum is shown by subperiostial bone formation (Codman's triangle). Radiating spicules of bone appear crossing the growth (Sunray spicules).

Biopsy is necessary to confirm the diagnosis and to exclude other types of tumour and inflammation. Histologically a pleomorphic picture is seen of a very vascular tumour in which malignant cells appear to line vascular spaces. The cells themselves show a great variety of size, shape and chromatin network. The tumour tissue shows a variable attempt at bone formation.

It must be appreciated that this is a highly malignant tumour, which in many cases has metastasised before diagnosis has been made. The outlook in most cases is poor, and so it is important that amputation should not be performed unless there is some chance of long survival. High-voltage radiation therapy will cause complete cessation of growth for several months, so all children presenting with an osteogenic sarcoma without radiographic evidence of secondaries in the lung are given radiotherapy. If secondary deposits are found in the lung, then nothing should be done except to relieve pain. Occasionally amputation may be necessary for severe pain and fear of fungation.

Three months after radiotherapy, if the lungs are still radiologically clear of metastases, the limb should be amputated well proximal to the tumour, as there is now a good chance of cure. About 30% of cases can then be expected to survive 5 years free of recurrence, a salvage rate far higher than was obtained when amputation was the only treatment and in many cases was a pointless operation.

The osteosarcoma that arises in areas of Paget's disease may be multifocal, and carries a very poor prognosis. Radiotherapy is given, amputation is rarely performed. The patients are usually very old.

Fibrosarcoma of bone is a similar tumour to osteogenic sarcoma but of a lower grade of malignancy. Radiographs show osteolytic erosion of the surface of the bone. The tumour is relatively radio-resistant and amputation is the only treatment.

Chondrosarcoma of bone most often arises in flat bones such as pelvis and scapula in a pre-existing osteochondroma. Radiologically a multilocular osteolytic process is seen circumscribed by a thin shell of new bone. The tumour often remains locally invasive for some time, during which radical amputation offers a reasonable chance of cure. Amputations of the magnitude of forequarter and hindquarter amputation may be justifiable.

Ewing's tumour is a rare, highly malignant tumour which arises in the midshaft of a long bone, usually in a child or a young adult. Central erosion occurs with a marked degree of surrounding subperiosteal new bone formation resulting in a characteristic radiographic picture resembling an 'onion-skin'. Histologically the tumour is composed of sheets of small round cells with dense nuclei. Some believe this tumour to be a reticulum cell sarcoma. Others think that it is a secondary deposit from a neuroblastoma. Biopsy must be performed to exclude chronic osteomyelitis or syphilis. Treatment is by radiotherapy, followed in some cases by amputation. The prognosis is poor, spread occurs to the lungs and other bones by the blood steam.

Multiple Myeloma. In myelomatosis, a malignant disease of bone marrow, deposits of cells that look like plasma cells are found throughout the skeleton, producing 'punched-out' areas of rarefaction in radiographs. The skull, vertebrae, ribs and pelvis are most commonly affected. Bone pain is often the presenting feature. Initially there may be no radiographic change, so the diagnosis may at first be obscure. The patient is often anaemic and the E.S.R. raised. Later, Bence Jones proteose may be found in the urine. Commonly an abnormal globulin is found in the serum by electrophoresis. Biopsy of the sternal or iliac marrow is often diagnostic. The condition is uniformly fatal, usually within 2 years of its onset. Occasionally a solitary tumour is found, plasmacytoma, that may for a long time remain only locally malignant and may be excised. Treatment of myelomatosis can at best only delay the course of the disease. Radiotherapy should be tried and then cytotoxic agents such as melphalan.

Leukaemia and Hodgkin's Disease may produce deposits in bone causing osteoporotic defects in radiographs and occasionally a pathological fracture.

Lipoid Storage Diseases. There are a number of rare disorders in which certain lipoid substances accumulate in organs such as the liver, spleen and lymph nodes and in which bone deposits may be found. In such cases the bones may show radiolucent defects in radiographs. These diseases include Hand–Schüller Christian disease, Gaucher's disease and eosinophilic granuloma.

SECONDARY CARCINOMA

Secondary deposits of malignant disease are more often found in bone than primary tumours. The orthopaedic surgeon sees in a year on the average only one or two patients with a primary malignant bone tumour, whereas both he and the general surgeon will see many more cases of secondary deposits in bone. The primary growths that show a strong tendency to metastasise to bone are five—the lung, kidney, breast, thyroid, prostate and less often the adrenal. All are osteolytic except those from the prostate and, in some infants, from the adrenal. Prostatic secondary deposits are often deeply sclerosing and may closely resemble Paget's disease of bone. Pain in the bones and pathological fracture are features. Extensive secondary deposits may so replace bone marrow as to cause an anaemia characterised by the presence of nucleated red cells and primitive white cells—leucoerythroblastic anaemia.

When secondary deposits are dependent upon the hormonal environment treatment by hormones may be very effective in relieving pain. Treatment for prostatic carcinoma with stilboestrol or by orchidectomy is often extremely effective, even when metastatic deposits are widespread. It seems possible that life may even be prolonged. Hormone therapy for breast carcinoma (see p. 191) may also be effective in producing remission of those growths that are hormone dependent. Some thyroid carcinomas can be suppressed by the administration of thyroxine, and occasionally adrenal neuroblastomas respond dramatically to the administration of folic acid.

Solitary secondary deposits may be healed and rendered painless by radiotherapy. A pathological fracture may often best be reduced and immobilised by some form of internal fixation such as a Küntscher nail inserted into the medulla of the bone. Immobilisation in this way may be followed by union. Sometimes it is justifiable to remove an apparently solitary deposit, especially if the interval from the treatment of the primary tumour is long and there is evidence that the secondary is slow growing. The primary growth must be treated if it is causing symptoms, for example a hypernephroma causing bleeding or pain may justifiably be treated by nephrectomy, even though a secondary deposit may have been found.

FURTHER READING

Fairbank, Sir T. (1951) *Atlas of General Affections of the Skeleton*. E. & S. Livingstone, Edinburgh.
Collins, D. H. (1960) *Pathology of Bone*. Butterworth, London.

CHAPTER THIRTY-SEVEN

ARTHRITIS

CHRONIC ARTHRITIS

Arthritis may be acute, subacute or chronic. It may be monarticular or polyarticular. Acute synovitis with effusion may follow injury or be related to some nearby infection such as osteomyelitis. Rheumatic fever is polyarticular, but may begin in a single joint and cause difficulty in diagnosis from osteomyelitis or pyogenic arthritis. Synovitis of the hip may be difficult to diagnose from early tuberculosis or osteochondritis, often the rapid response to rest is diagnostic. Allergic reactions, for example to antitetanus serum, may cause an acute painful polyarthritis. Acute pyogenic arthritis may be simulated by gonococcal infection or Reiter's disease (urethritis, arthritis and iridocyclitis). Some cases of rheumatoid arthritis may present very acutely with a hot, painful joint. Rarely synovitis may be seen in the secondary phase of syphilis.

The commonest chronic disease of joints are rheumatoid and osteoarthritis. Tuberculosis is the commonest cause of chronic arthritis due to a specific organism. Typhoid infection is very rare. Neuropathic arthritis follows nervous disorders that lead to loss of proprioceptive sensation and pain in a joint. Gouty arthritis is a metabolic disorder of purine metabolism. In pseudo gout or chondrocalcinosis crystals of apatite are deposited in joints. Haemophiliacs may develop arthritis from recurrent haemarthroses. Osteoarthritis may occur in tunnel workers due to bubbles of nitrogen released in the bones causing bone infarcts if decompression is too rapid (caisson disease).

RHEUMATOID ARTHRITIS

Young and middle-aged adults are usually affected, more often women than men, though children and elderly people may be involved. The changes in the joints are similar to those found in the so-called collagen diseases, such as lupus erythematosus and polyarteritis nodosa.

The disease often begins fairly acutely, several joints being usually affected at once. The small joints of the hands are most often involved, especially the interphalangeal and metacarpophalangeal joints. The affected joints become painful and swollen, the swelling being mostly due to synovial thickening and effusion. Movements are restricted by joint swelling and muscle spasm. Eventually the joints become permanently damaged as granulation tissue erodes away articular cartilage and capsule.

After years of rheumatoid arthritis secondary osteoarthritic changes supervene.

The natural history of the disease is infinitely variable. Remissions and exacerbations are common. The course may be short and severe, and then may remit for years. More often there is a steady deterioration. Many patients are never seriously incommoded, and some recover completely after a minor attack. The variations in the course of the illness make for great difficulty in the assessment of any treatment which has to be empirical in the absence of knowledge of the cause of the disease.

Some patients have a temporary systemic illness at the onset. Occasionally a single joint may appear so acutely inflamed as to simulate pyogenic arthritis, but almost always other joints become affected. Rheumatic nodules composed of masses of collagen are often seen in the subcutaneous tissue, especially over the elbows and knees, often of massive size. The hands show a characteristic deformity with spindle-shaped fingers, due to the swollen interphalangeal and metacarpophalangeal joints. The fingers are fixed in flexion and the wrist in flexion and ulnar deviation. The elbows and knees become flexed, the hips adducted and flexed, the shoulders adducted. In the most severe cases almost every joint in the body, including spinal and mandibular joints, are affected. The disease may apparently burn itself out and yet leave the subject crippled by permanent deformity due to fibrous ankylosis and secondary osteoarthritic changes. Tendons, too, are affected, spontaneous rupture is common, especially in the hand, as are trigger fingers. Bursitis may arise. The E.S.R. is raised, the Rose Waaler test, in which the patient's serum agglutinates sheep red cells, is often positive. Wasting and anaemia are common.

Treatment

In the acute phase splintage of the affected joints relieves pain and prevents deformity. Aspirin, indomethacin and phenylbutazone have proved the best analgesics, although it is doubtful if they affect the course of the disease. Steroids in the form of cortisone, prednisolone or their derivatives have a powerful anti-inflammatory effect and produce great symptomatic relief. Initial enthusiasm for their use has waned in recent years, since it has been found that the high dosage needed to produce relief is associated with a marked incidence of serious side effects, including osteoporosis and even spontaneous fracture of bones, disorganisation of joints, gastro-intestinal haemorrhage and perforation of the gut. In addition, withdrawal of the drug may be followed by an exacerbation of the arthritis.

After the acute phase, physiotherapy in the form of active and passive exercises, heat and wax baths are given. Local injections of hydrocortisone into joints may give relief, but there is a danger of local osteoporosis with collapse of bone near the joint. Intramuscular injections of gold have not been so popular of recent years, but it is still believed that they have some effect.

Some grossly deformed and painful joints can be given some function with relief of pain after excision, arthrodesis or arthroplasty. For example, the elbow, hip and interphalangeal joints may require operative treatment. Ruptured tendons can be repaired or replaced. In joints such as the wrist or knee stability is more important than mobility, and in these pain can be relieved by arthrodesis. In the early phase of the disease excision of the thickened synovial membrane before cartilage erosion has occurred may be very successful in improving function, especially of the knee and joints of the fingers.

OSTEOARTHRITIS

Osteoarthritis is by far the commonest form of chronic arthritis seen in Britain and most countries with a temperate climate. It is responsible for an incalculable amount of pain and invalidism. The cause is unknown, but, whereas rheumatoid arthritis has many features akin to an inflammatory disease affecting relatively young persons, in most cases osteoarthritis is a degenerative disorder of older persons. Joints seem to wear out with advancing age; just as the arteries harden, the joints stiffen. An important but small group of arthritics have suffered some previous disease of their joints which has left the articular surfaces malaligned or irregular. Occasionally a loose body in the joint may have caused roughening of the articular cartilage. Many fractures into joints predispose to the development of osteoarthritis, perhaps only after many years have elapsed.

The disease particularly affects the large weight-bearing joints of the lower limb—such as the hip and the knee. In the fingers it is the distal interphalangeal joints that become swollen, and small bony excrescences appear at the bases of the terminal phalanges—Heberden's nodes. The articular cartilage becomes worn away, exposing bone which becomes hardened and shiny (eburnated). In this subchondral bone small cysts form, surrounded by sclerosis. At the articular margins bony spurs grow, called osteophytes. Radiographs show all these changes with evidence of loss of joint space due to the erosion of articular cartilage. The synovial membrane becomes thickened and laden with fat (lipoma arborescens). There may be a great effusion distending the capsule; sometimes herniations of the capsule filled with fluid form obvious swellings which are called Baker's cysts and are commonly visible behind the knee.

The patient notices increasing pain, especially on movement, which becomes progressively restricted. The pain is made worse by exercise, is relieved by rest and is especially worse at the end of the day. The joint is swollen to a varying degree by the effusion. Grating or crepitus can be sensed by a hand applied over a joint during movement. Nearby muscles become wasted. There may be a fixed deformity or even complete fixity (ankylosis) of the joint.

Treatment

In the older patient with mild symptoms little is needed except re-assurance, some restriction of activity, weight reduction and perhaps a walking stick. If pain is more severe physiotherapy in the form of heat, traction and exercises may be of great help supplemented by mild analgesics. More and more surgery is being offered in the early and painful stage of the disease.

The type of operation depends on the age of the patient and the state of nearby joints. Excision or arthroplasty of a joint gives a painless mobile joint at the expense of stability. Making a new joint (arthroplasty) by the insertion of a prosthesis can give mobility, but often at the expense of stability and relief of pain. Fixing the joint (arthrodesis) makes it stable, painless and immobile. A simple method of relieving pain in the hip joint is to divide the femur at the level of the lesser trochanter (sub-trochanteric osteotomy) and to displace it medially, in which position the bones unite and the joint becomes less painful. It was thought that the function of this operation was to change the lines of stress on the joint, but it is more likely that osteotomy interferes in some way with the vascularity of the femur, for a prominent pathological feature of osteoarthritis is increased vascularity.

GOUT

Gout is a disorder of purine metabolism in which there is an increase in the serum uric acid (normally below 4 mg. %). Mostly elderly people are afflicted, but although this is a fairly rare disorder, it must not be forgotten that it occurs even in the young. Joints which are particularly affected are the toes, especially the great toe and the fingers, but any joint may be involved. Gross flexion deformities of the small joints of the hands are seen, with crises of great pain and swelling. The deformity of the joints may simulate rheumatoid arthritis. Often gouty tophi, deposits of sodium biurate, are seen on the prominences of the knuckles and near the cartilages of the ears. These may ulcerate on to a surface discharging a white powdery substance. Sometimes bursae become enlarged and painful. The kidneys may show a form of chronic nephritis. Radiographs demonstrate clear, translucent, rounded areas in the affected bones due to the presence of deposits of sodium biurate, best seen near the heads of the phalanges.

Specific drugs are available for treating this condition, such as colchicine and probenecid.

NEUROPATHIC ARTHRITIS

In tabes dorsalis, syringomyelia and diabetic neuropathy joints may lose their sensory nerve supply and become disorganised. The articular cartilage becomes eroded, and the bone ends are deformed so that bizarre movements become possible. Effusion in the joints is common. The important clinical features are painlessness, gross deformity and hypermobility. The knee and hip joints are often affected in tabes dorsalis, the shoulder in syringomyelia and the joints of the foot in diabetic neuropathy. Confirmation of the diagnosis is given by the presence of Argyll Robertson's pupils (pupils that are small, do not react to light but do react to accommodation) and evidence of loss of sensation of those nerves that pass up the posterior columns of the spinal cord. There is no specific treatment. Occasionally gross mobility may require arthrodesis in someone who is otherwise relatively fit. In diabetes neuropathy is often complicated by sepsis, which may necessitate amputation of the infected insensitive tissue. Perforating ulcers are often seen in the foot beneath the metatarsal heads, painless ulcers that go deeply down to the joint beneath.

FURTHER READING

Kersley, G. D. (1962) *The Rheumatic Diseases*. Heinemann Medical Books, London.

CHAPTER THIRTY-EIGHT

THE HIP JOINT

CLINICAL EXAMINATION

Pain, limp and stiffness are the three commonest complaints produced by diseases of the hip joint. The pain is usually sited in the hip joint itself, but is also commonly referred to the knee, so examination of the hip is part of examination of the knee. Occasionally there is a history of injury but usually the onset of symptoms is insidious. Age is some guide to diagnosis, because congenital dislocation of the hip is usually diagnosed in infants, osteochondritis happens between five and ten years, slipped epiphysis around puberty, osteoarthritis and fracture occur in older people. Tuberculosis may appear at any age, but is most commonly first seen in childhood.

Examination of the hip is conducted with the patient undressed to expose the abdomen and the whole extent of both legs. The legs are placed together if possible with the pelvis level and inspected for obvious shortening or deformity. The feet, knees and hips must be inspected for deformity, shortening or lengthening. Scars of previous operations or abscesses may be seen around the hip. Wasting of muscles, especially the glutei, may be obvious. The region of the joint is palpated for areas of tenderness or swelling.

The *true length* of the legs is measured from the anterior superior iliac spine to the tip of the medial malleolus, with the anterior spines lying at the same transverse level. If there is no fixed deformity the legs can be brought together and measured, but if there is fixed deformity, then the unaffected leg must be placed in the same position as the affected leg before measurement. The *apparent length* is measured from the xiphisternum to the tip of the medial malleolus with the legs parallel.

Shortening is more often found than lengthening. *True shortening* is due to failure of development, bone disease or injury. If true shortening is found the part of the limb in which the shortening occurs should next be located. If the knees are bent to 90 degrees with the feet flat on the examination couch it becomes obvious that the shortening is below the knee if the upper level of one knee lies below its fellow. Shortening above the level of the greater trochanter of the femur is made obvious by placing the fingers on each trochanter simultaneously with the thumbs on the anterior superior iliac spines when it becomes clear if one is higher than the other. Elevation of one greater trochanter can be confirmed by drawing Nelaton's line from the anterior superior spine to the ischial tuberosity. The greater trochanter should normally lie below this line. *Apparent shortening* (Fig. 72) is due to tilting of the pelvis, which compensates for a fixed adduction deformity of the hip and so equalises the length of the legs. Measurement of the circumference of the thighs may reveal muscle wasting, and this may be a useful pointer to which hip is affected.

True lengthening is found in conditions of excessive bone growth, diffuse congenital arteriovenous anastomoses, some cases of polio-myelitis, osteomyelitis, tuberculosis and neurofibromatosis. *Apparent lengthening* is found in cases of fixed abduction deformity of the hip.

A *fixed flexion* deformity of the hip (Fig. 73) is demonstrated by flexing the unaffected leg at the hip joint until a hand under the back appreciates that the lumbar lordosis has been flattened out. If there is any degree of fixed flexion, then the affected leg will rise as the pelvis rotates.

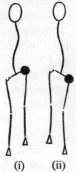

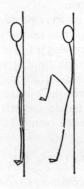

(i)   (ii)

FIG. 72 (i) Adduction of the hip leading to apparent shortening. (ii) Abduction causing apparent lengthening

FIG. 73. Thomas' fixed flexion test. Flexion of the normal hip reveals fixed flexion of the other

Movements of the hip are next examined. The range of abduction and adduction is tested with one hand on an anterior iliac spine while the other is used to move the limbs. As the limit of abduction or adduction is reached the pelvis is felt to move by the hand on the ilium. In some cases no movement may be possible at the hip joint, apparent movement being achieved by rotation of the pelvis where it joins the spine. Internal and external rotation are estimated by rolling the straightened limb or after flexing the limb at the knee and hip the leg can be used to rotate the femur. *Telescoping* is a sign of congenital dislocation of the head of the femur. It is demonstrated by flexing the hip and knee, pressing the knee down with one hand, the other being held over the greater trochanter, where it senses the movement of the head of the femur sliding up and down the side of the ilium.

The patient should next lie on his face. Inspection may disclose scars, swelling or wasting of the glutei. A spinal deformity may also be discovered. The range of extension at the hip is estimated. The patient is then asked to stand, when it may be obvious that the pelvis is elevated on the affected side if there is fixed adduction, or lowered if there is fixed abduction. The spine may show a scoliosis which compensates for the tilt in the pelvis. Trendelenburg's sign is positive if the inferior crease of the buttock falls instead of rising when the subject stands on the affected limb, indicating weakness of the glutei and lateral rotators of the hip, dislocation of the head of the femur or coxa vara (a decrease in the angle between the neck and shaft of the femur that limits abduction). The patient is asked to walk to demonstrate his limp or any other peculiarities of gait.

The central nervous system must be examined if it is suspected that pain is referred from the spine or that the arthritis is neuropathic. Claudication may be mistaken for pain due to disease of the hip joint, therefore the peripheral pulses should be checked and the feet inspected for signs of ischaemia.

The most important investigation is radiography in both the anteroposterior and lateral planes. Deformity, fracture, bone disease, widening, or narrowing of the joint space and irregularity of the joint surfaces, osteophytic lipping of the bone margins, rarefaction of bone or subchondral sclerosis may be shown. Shenton's line is traced from the upper margin of the obturator foramen down the neck of the femur. This line should have a smooth uninterrupted contour. Other investigations include a white-cell count, E.S.R. and occasionally the Mantoux test.

SYNOVITIS OF THE HIP JOINT

It is common to see infants or young adults who complain of a painful stiff hip in whom examination reveals limitation of movement. Radiography is usually negative and there is no systemic change. Most cases are due to a mild degree of effusion into the joint, but difficulty in diagnosis may arise because in the early phases of osteochondritis and tuberculosis the presentation is similar. Other possibilities are poliomyelitis, osteomyelitis, the early phase of rheumatic fever before other joints are affected and septic arthritis. Such patients are rested in bed. If there is severe pain, skin traction is applied to immobilise the joint and separate the joint surfaces. White-cell count, E.S.R. and the Mantoux test may be useful. In most patients the pain and stiffness settle rapidly, and they become symptom free with full painless movement of the hip. Others must be followed if early tuberculosis and osteochrondritis are not to be missed.

SEPTIC ARTHRITIS

Septic arthritis of the hip joint is uncommon, but it produces a serious disability unless treatment is rapidly instituted. It is usually due to osteomyelitis of the femur or acetabulum which involves the joint because the infective focus lies within the joint capsule. Suppuration rapidly destroys the articular cartilage and disorganises the joint, abscesses may discharge on to a surface. The joint capsule may become distended and allow pathological dislocation of the hip joint. Fibrous or bony ankylosis is the likely sequel unless active treatment is started early. The child is ill, febrile and irritable, screaming when any attempt is made to move the limb. The leg may be held flexed at the hip joint due to spasm of the psoas muscle. Psoas spasm may also be due to appendicitis, suppurating deep iliac lymph nodes or acute osteomyelitis of the ilium. The white-cell count shows a polymorphonuclear leucocytosis.

In the early phase of septic arthritis widening of the joint space may be seen; later the space is narrowed or absent and rarefaction of the affected bones is apparent. Pathological dislocation may occur.

If there is any suspicion of septic arthritis the hip joint must be aspirated through a needle inserted into it in a line running from just above the greater trochanter parallel to the neck of the femur. If purulent fluid is obtained it is replaced by a solution of penicillin. Skin traction is applied to the limb to immobilise it and relieve spasm. Systemic chemotherapy is given with ampicillin or cloxacillin. The organism responsible is usually the penicillinase-producing *Staphylococcus aureus*, so it is important to give a form of penicillin to which the staphylococcus is likely to be sensitive. Chemotherapy must be maintained for several weeks. Aspiration may need to be repeated if the joint becomes further distended. Weight bearing is not permitted until all signs of activity have disappeared and the radiographs are normal. If the disease has spread into the shaft of the femur, pus must be evacuated through an incision and the cortex of the bone drilled.

Very rarely nowadays syphilitic epiphysitis is seen in small infants. The child is miserable and resents movement of the hip joints. Radiographs show sclerosis of the epiphyses, fluffiness of the epiphyseal lines and periostitis of the adjoining bones. There may be other manifestations of congenital syphilis and the Wasserman reaction is positive, Yaws can present in a similar way. Treatment in either case is by penicillin.

OSTEOCHONDRITIS OF THE HEAD OF THE FEMUR (PERTHÉ'S DISEASE)

In osteochondritis the head of the femur becomes softened (Fig. 74) to such a degree that with weight bearing it becomes squashed and mushroom shaped. Over a period of 2–3 years the bone structure is reformed, but the deformed shape of the head persists and leads to osteoarthritis in adult life. The cause is unknown, but because there is often a history of injury and, because the radiological appearances are those of avascularity followed by revascularisation, it is thought most likely that trauma causes some temporary ischaemia of the femoral head. Support for this view is given by the similar radiological appearances that sometimes follow manipulative reduction of a congenitally dislocated hip.

Radiographs at first show some widening of the joint space, presumably due to effusion, followed by an increase in density of the femoral head frequently best seen in the lateral projection. Over a period of months the head becomes fragmented by newly vascularised bone until a more normal architecture is restored. If weight bearing is allowed the head becomes mushroomed and flattened, the neck of the femur becomes thicker and shorter and the angle between it and the shaft of the femur is decreased (coxa vara).

Osteochondritis of the femoral head usually occurs in boys, who complain of a painful limp between the ages of 3 and 8 years. Examination reveals limitation of abduction and internal rotation.

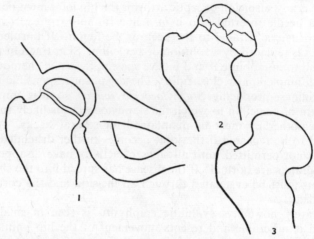

FIG. 74. Osteochondritis of the hip. (1) Widening of joint space. (2) Fragmentation and mushrooming of the head. (3) Late result a deformed flattened head, short neck and cox avara

The differential diagnosis must be made from tuberculosis. In osteochondritis the child is well and there is no evidence of any systemic upset. The E.S.R. is normal. Some movements are relatively painless unlike the tuberculous hip, in which all movements are affected. The response to bed rest is dramatic in Perthé's disease, in that pain is rapidly relieved. With the appearance of increased density of the head of the femur the diagnosis is confirmed; in tuberculosis rarefaction is seen.

The basis of treatment is to prevent deformity of the femoral head while it is soft. If there is much pain a period of rest in bed is enforced with, if necessary, skin traction to immobilise the limb and relieve pain and muscle spasm. Later a non-weight-bearing caliper is fitted in which the child can walk. This appliance must be worn until the femoral head is revascularised, a process which may take anything from 1 to 3 years. The only complication of osteochrondritis is osteoarthritis, which may require operative treatment in adult life.

TUBERCULOSIS OF THE HIP JOINT

Tuberculosis of bone and joint may occur at any age, though it is more usual in children and young adults. There may be evidence of the disease elsewhere, for example in the spine, genito-urinary tract or lung, in which foci may appear over the course of many years. Often there is a family history of tuberculous infection. The disease is blood borne from a primary focus in the tonsils, lung or gut. It may rarely be purely synovial, more often there is a focus in the head or neck of the femur or in the acetabulum (Fig. 75). The bursa deep to the gluteus medius over the greater trochanter may be the site of tuberculosis, but this focus rarely involves the hip joint.

A synovial effusion is first produced. Caseation and cold-abscess formation may lead to discharge from a sinus in the groin, buttock or over

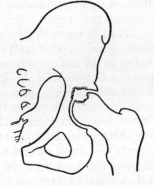

FIG. 75. Tuberculosis of the hip joint. Focus in head of femur and acetabulum

the greater trochanter. The articular cartilage and ligaments are rapidly destroyed, the joint capsule may become lax and subluxation or dislocation of the hip may occur. With early and efficient treatment a normal joint may be regained. More often fibrous ankylosis results, often incomplete and painful. Secondary septic infection via sinuses may eventually lead to bony ankylosis after healing.

Radiographs in the early phase of the disease may show some evidence of widening of the joint space and rarefaction of the affected bones. Later there is narrowing of the joint space, and evidence of destruction of bone may be revealed, sometimes with large defects in the substance of the bone suggesting caseous foci. As healing occurs recalcification is seen.

The first complaint is of pain and limping. The child may appear ill and febrile and there may be night starts and cries. The muscles around the joint waste rapidly. Movements of the joint are restricted by muscle spasm. In the early phase of effusion, which is short lived, the limb is held in slight flexion, abduction or external rotation. Later, as the muscle spasm increases, the limb is drawn into adduction and internal rotation with apparent shortening from the fixed adduction. If there is much destruction of bone true shortening is found.

Early diagnosis and treatment is essential. The E.S.R. and Mantoux test are of help. Occasionally iliac node biopsy may be diagnostic. Rest is achieved by traction on a special frame to which Thomas' splints are attached so that the limbs are rested with traction to the legs, the hips being abducted. Tuberculostatic drugs, improved nutrition and a sanatorium régime are the basis of treatment. In adults early operation is indicated after 6 months of tuberculostatic drugs, or earlier, because few adults can afford to spend perhaps 1 or 2 years in a sanatorium, a length of time which can easily be enforced in a child. Surgery is indicated to evacuate a tuberculous abscess in soft tissue or in a bony cavity or to remove a sequestrum. Later in the disease operation may be needed to stabilise an imperfect ankylosis or to correct an adduction deformity. Extra-articular methods of arthrodesis are preferred to avoid opening the diseased joint. In Brittain's operation osteotomy is combined with arthrodesis. The osteotomy, performed below the trochanters, enables the adduction deformity to be corrected, with increase in the apparent length of the limb. At the same time a bone graft is inserted between the ischial tuberosity and the femur at the site of osteotomy. Such an operation should be followed by painless ankylosis of the joint. After any operation on the hip joint immobilisation in a hip spica is needed until union is achieved, with rest in bed and full anti-tuberculous treatment with drugs. The ideal position for the fixed hip joint is neutral, except for slight flexion to allow easy sitting. After union is thought to have been achieved ambulation is allowed cautiously with a non-weight-bearing caliper. More and more weight bearing is permitted over a period of some months until the appliance is discarded. Careful observation over a period of years for evidence of activity of the disease or the development of other foci is essential.

OSTEOARTHRITIS

Osteoarthritis of the hip may be part of a generalised arthritis when both hips joints are often involved. Monarticular arthritis of the hip commonly follows previous disease usually suffered in childhood, for example congenital dislocation of the hip, osteochondritis and slipped epiphysis. The disease is much more common in Europe and North America than in the Orient. The complaint is of pain, stiffness and increasing difficulty in walking. The disease may progress at a varying speed over many years. Episodes of more severe pain and limitation of movement are common. Eventually pain may be continuous and walking severely restricted. At first abduction and rotation are particularly limited. Finally, there is severe deformity in the adducted and internally rotated position, with apparent shortening. The joint space is narrowed, the head of the femur is absorbed.

Radiographs show progressive diminution of the joint space with a narrow zone of sclerosis subjacent to the articular cartilage (sub-chondral calcification). Osteophytic lipping is seen at the margins of the acetabulum and femoral head. Small cysts may be seen in the femur and acetabulum. Eventually the head becomes deformed and the neck shortened, with some degree of coxa vara.

Many patients with osteoarthritis suffer to only a mild degree, and the disease may never progress or only slowly become worse. A walking stick may help, and some restriction of activity is essential. Analgesics are prescribed, such as aspirin to relieve pain, phenylbutazone or indomethacin may help. Reduction of weight helps to relieve symptoms. In some severe episodes of pain physiotherapy with heat and gentle exercises may be of

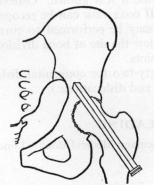

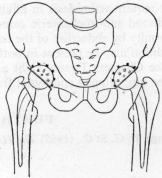

FIG. 76. Watson Jones' arthrodesis of the hip joint

FIG. 77. Total replacement of the hip joint

value. Rarely, manipulation of the joint under anaesthesia may be indicated. Osteotomy is being advised frequently in the early stages of the disease much earlier than formerly.

Operation may be needed when there is severe pain and limitation of movement. If the hip alone is affected it can be arthrodesed. In Watson Jones' operation (Fig. 76) the articular cartilage is removed from the joint surfaces and the joint immobilised by a long trifin nail driven up the neck of the femur across the joint into the ilium. For such an operation to be effective the spine and knee must be mobile and free of arthritis and the person must be fairly fit, reasonably young and active. Another method of treatment is the McMurray osteotomy dividing the femur just below the lesser trochanter which is usually performed for relief of pain in a movable joint. After division of the bone it is displaced medially towards the ischium. It may be followed by complete ankylosis of the joint. Pain is relieved probably because any operation which interferes with the blood supply of the femoral head reduces pain in the osteoarthritic hip. Arthroplasty may be performed when both hips are involved. Total replacement of the hip joint is proving to be the most satisfactory operation. The new acetabulum is cemented to the ilium by a plastic cement (Fig. 77).

COXA VARA

In coxa vara the angle between the neck of the femur and the shaft is reduced, leading to limitation of abduction. The complaint is usually of pain in the hip, especially in adult life, when osteoarthritic symptoms develop. Examination reveals some true shortening of the leg, with raising of the greater trochanter causing a limp. The cause may be a congenital deformity, the result of a slipped epiphysis, osteochondritis, an old fracture or congenital dislocation of the hip. Primary bone diseases, rickets, osteomalacia, hyperparathyroidism and Paget's disease are less common causes.

Treatment is that for the primary cause if it is known. Osteoarthritis may require arthrodesis in adult life. If coxa vara can be recognised in childhood sub-trochanteric osteotomy may be performed to correct the deformity by abduction of the femur below the site of bone division. The condition may be present in both hip joints.

(See Chapters Twenty-eight and Thirty-two for congenital dislocation of the hip; slipped epiphysis; fractures and dislocations.)

FURTHER READING

Strange, F. G. St C., (1965) *The Hip*. Heinemann Medical Books, London.

CHAPTER THIRTY-NINE

THE KNEE JOINT

CLINICAL EXAMINATION

Injuries and diseases of the knee joint cause pain, swelling and loss of movement. Locking of the knee may occur, usually in flexion, when the knee cannot be extended for perhaps hours or days and in some cases can only be extended after manipulation under general anaesthesia. The knee is prone to give way in painful conditions, especially when the thigh muscles are wasted.

Examination of the knee must be meticulous and systematic, both knees must be examined for comparisons, for so often the correct diagnosis can only be made from eliciting physical signs. The whole of both limbs must be exposed to reveal any postural deformities. The hip must always be examined, because pain referred to the knee is common in diseases of the hip joint. Inspection of the knee may disclose swelling, deformity and sometimes colour changes of the skin. Wasting of the thigh muscles may be obvious, or may only be detected by having the patient press the knees back into the examination couch, when the hands of the examiner can detect differences in the tone of the quadriceps muscles.

A large effusion in the knee joint is made clear by the shape of the swollen joint and the outline of the distended suprapatellar pouch. Patellar tap is likewise a sign of considerable effusion, the patella is tapped and felt to bounce off the articular surface of the femur. A minimal excess of fluid is detected by stroking the capsule of the joint on either side of the patella. If any fluid is present it will be seen to deform the shape of the capsule beside the patella as it is moved from side to side.

Flexion deformity of the knee of slight degree is easily missed unless a hand is slid behind the knee, when a gap is found between it and the examination couch. Attempts at full extension by pressure on the knee may be resisted by pain or muscle spasm or by a sense of springiness if a torn cartilage is interposed between the femoral and tibial condyles. Movement of the patella from side to side may reveal crepitus, a grating sensation felt when there is irregularity of the articular surfaces of the patella or femur.

Tenderness in the knee joint is best localised after flexing both knees to 90° with the feet flat on the couch. Firm pressure is applied with a thumb first over the joint line and then near it from front to back, starting on either side of the patellar ligament progressing over the collateral ligaments and behind them. Often tenderness is found to be sharply localised and may give clear evidence of injury to ligaments, menisci or bones.

Palpation of the joint may also reveal thickening of the synovial membrane, and occasionally a loose body may be felt.

The range of active and passive movement is tested. During movement, a hand placed over the joint may detect crepitus due to rough bony or cartilaginous surfaces. Excessive mobility may denote a lax capsule or ligamentous damage associated with severe wasting of the quadriceps muscle.

The integrity of the collateral ligaments is estimated by extending the knee joint and alternately abducting and adducting the leg at the joint. The knee is supported by the examiner's hand, which is placed over the side of the knee as a fulcrum and the lower leg is held with the other hand so that the leg can be firmly adducted and abducted; this reveals if the joint can be opened out on one side or the other. The cruciate ligaments are tested by flexing the knees to 90° with the feet flat on the couch. With two hands the tibia is gently pressed backwards and forwards across the femoral condyles. Abnormal mobility backwards indicates a torn or lax posterior cruciate ligament; mobility forwards, or the possibility of hyperextension at the knee joint, indicates a torn anterior cruciate ligament. In McMurray's test for a torn meniscus the knee is flexed slowly, while the foot is externally rotated. Firm pressure is exerted at the same time between one hand on the heel and the other over the top of the knee compressing the tibial and femoral condyles together across the meniscus. The test is positive if a click is felt over a point in the range of movment. In all cases of suspected knee-joint disease radiographs of both knees must be taken in both anterior and lateral planes.

EFFUSION INTO THE KNEE JOINT

Effusion into the knee joint is common and usually follows an injury. A rapid onset of swelling suggests the possibility of haemarthrosis, especially if radiographs show a fracture into the joint. Haemarthrosis may follow trivial injuries in some blood diseases, such as haemophilia, in which recurrent bloody effusions later cause arthritis.

The knee must be examined for evidence of bone disease, ligamentous or menisceal injury or a loose body. Pain and a large effusion may not allow complete examination until after a period of rest. Radiographs are essential. Arthritis of the rheumatoid or osteoarthritic type may be discovered, but this is often only an incidental finding. The possibility of gout must not be forgotten; other joints may be involved. The occurrence of synovial thickening suggests an infective element, such as tuberculosis or arthritis of the rheumatoid type. In an adult, arthritis and urethritis should suggest gonococcal arthritis or Reiter's disease. If there is severe pain and muscle spasm septic arthritis is a possible diagnosis. Occasionally osteomyelitis of a metaphysis which lies near to or within the joint capsule may simulate septic arthritis, either from pus in the joint or the development of a sympathetic effusion. Most effusions are traumatic and follow strain due to ligamentous damage, menisceal injuries or a loose body. Repeated effusions are common if there is a torn cartilage, underlying arthritis or loose bodies.

Most traumatic effusions subside in 10–14 days with rest and firm bandaging. Quadriceps exercises for 5 minutes every hour are begun as soon as pain subsides, because otherwise the muscles of the thigh waste rapidly due to inactivity and allow ligamentous laxity that slows recovery. Once the effusion has subsided, a careful examination must be made for bony disease, arthritis or injury to ligaments or menisci. Recurrent or persistent effusion, especially in children, raises the suspicion of tuberculosis. Aspiration may be indicated for a large persistent effusion, but only with full sterile precautions. Occasionally, in severe forms of arthritis, the synovial membrane may become so thickened that prominent fringes project into the joint. It is possible that in such cases acute pain in the joint with effusion may result from the nipping of one of these synovial fringes. In the infrapatellar region a large fat pad may develop, on the surface of which synovial fringes may become nipped between the patella and femoral condyles. Pain and effusion result, with tenderness sharply localised to one or both sides of the infrapatellar ligament. Another cause of repeated synovial effusion may be a recurrent dislocation of the patella, or arthritis of the patella-femoral compartment of the knee joint.

INTERNAL DERANGEMENT OF THE KNEE JOINT

Internal derangement of the knee (often abbreviated to IDK) includes injuries to ligaments both within and adjacent to the joint and also the menisci. Probably the commonest injury to the knee is a tear of a medial collateral ligament due to a severe abduction strain. Pain is felt on the inside of the knee, with tenderness most marked at the insertion of the ligament just below the joint line. Pain and effusion usually subside in a few days, and then exercises to strengthen the quadriceps muscles should be encouraged. When there is severe pain and swelling a support to the back of the knee by a slab of plaster of Paris extending from the ankle to the thigh is very comforting. A tear of the medial collateral ligament is diagnosed by springing the ligaments. Abduction of the knee is found to be very painful, and may show some laxity of the ligament. In a complete tear mobility is gross and operation to suture the ligament may be justified. Radiographs are essential in all cases of internal derangement to exclude bone disease or a loose body. Occasionally calcification may be seen in the medial ligament near the adductor tubercle, typically in horse riders who use their adductors excessively.

Lateral ligament tears are less common, but may be associated with a depressed fracture of the tibial condyle and a lateral popliteal nerve palsy.

One of the commonest and most serious injuries of the knee joint is a tear of a meniscus, a frequent accident in soccer players and miners. The mechanism of the injury is an abduction eversion strain, such as that occurring in a tackle in football when the leg is fixed, with the rest of the body pivoting at the knee. The meniscus, usually the medial, is ground between the tibial and femoral condyles so that either the anterior horn is torn or the meniscus is split longitudinally and a portion comes to lie between the condyles (bucket-handle tear), preventing full extension.

Severe pain is felt, the knee is locked in flexion and an effusion rapidly develops. Examination of the knee joint, once pain and the effusion has subsided, reveals extreme tenderness *in the joint line* over the anterior horn of the medial or, less often, the lateral semi-lunar cartilage, the maximum point of tenderness being midway between the collateral ligament and the infrapatellar ligament. Less often the area of tenderness is limited to the surface marking of the posterior horn, which is felt on the medial or lateral side of the popliteal fossa. Extension of the locked knee joint may only be achieved under general anaesthesia by manipulation. The flexed leg is alternately everted and inverted, until it can be fully extended. A pressure bandage is applied and quadriceps exercises undertaken as for a traumatic effusion. If the diagnosis is certain, if a bucket handle tear has occurred, and especially if there are recurrent attacks, the meniscus must be removed. This is not only because of the disability of pain and locking but also for fear of the late development of traumatic osteoarthritis.

Tears of the lateral meniscus are less common. Occasionally the lateral meniscus is congenitally misshapen, being thick and discoid. A loud clunk-like noise occurs on flexion, which may be associated with pain and is worrying to the patient. Cysts of the lateral cartilage form large, bony, hard swellings above the head of the fibula, so hard that an osteoma may be diagnosed by the inexperienced. The swelling characteristically disappears in flexion and is always more obvious in extension.

Operation is performed for tears, cyst formation and discoid lesions of menisci. Quadriceps exercises are practised pre-operatively. At operation a tourniquet is applied to the limb, which is then placed over the end of the table with the leg hanging down. A small anterior oblique incision is made over the joint line, between the infrapatellar and collateral ligaments, the capsule of the joint is opened and the meniscus is removed by a no-touch technique. The whole cartilage must be removed. The posterior horn is often inaccessible and occasionally has to be removed through a small separate incision made posteriorly. Following operation, a pressure bandage is applied, and as soon as pain has subsided, intensive exercises are given to the quadriceps muscles.

Injuries to the cruciate ligaments result from severe strains of the knee oint and cause serious disabilities, such as pain, giving way of the joint and eventually osteoarthritis. Injury may be associated with a fracture of the tibial spine or depression of a tibial condyle (see Chapter Thirty-two). Dislocation of the joint is inevitably associated with rupture of its ligaments and haemarthrosis, especially if there is a fracture in the joint. When the effusion has subsided, hypermobility may be elicited. Normally, with the knee flexed, it should not be possible to move the head of the tibia posteriorly or anteriorly on the femoral condyles, but if the anterior ligament is torn the tibia can be moved anteriorly, if the posterior ligament is torn the tibia can be pushed posteriorly. If the anterior cruciate ligament is completely ruptured hyperextension of the knee may be possible—genu recurvatum. In most cases intensive physiotherapy, with stress on quadriceps exercises, improves the stability of the joint. Rarely a fracture of the tibial spine may be reduced by open operation and fixation of the fragment by a pin.

CHONDROMALACIA PATELLAE

Pain and effusion in the knee may be associated with a degenerative condition of the articular cartilage of the patella, which loses its lustre, becomes softened and fibrillated. The end result is patella-femoral osteoarthritis and eventually osteoarthritis of the whole knee joint. The condition is seen in young adults, and may be bilateral. The pain is aggravated by moving the patella laterally across the femoral condyles, and eventually crepitus may be felt. Lateral radiographs may show irregularity of the posterior surface of the patella or loss of joint space between the patella and femoral condyles.

In the early phase immobilisation of the knee in a plaster shell may result in resolution. In late cases excision of the patella may be indicated if arthritis is feared or is developing. Some surgeons pare away the diseased cartilage from the articular surface of the patella.

LOOSE BODIES

Most loose bodies in the knee joint are osteocartilaginous, having a central core of bone surrounded by cartilage. These most often arise in a condition called osteochondritis dissecans which occurs in children or young adults. It is thought that trauma causes separation of a piece of bone, usually in the intercondylar notch between the femoral condyles. The damaged segment of bone is capped by articular cartilage; after some time it separates and may break loose into the joint. In the synovial fluid growth of the cartilage occurs around the bone in a characteristic way. Usually only one loose body is formed, but occasionally there are many, and the condition is then often bilateral. Osteochondritis is also seen, but much less often, in the elbow, ankle, and shoulder joints.

Loose bodies cause pain, recurrent effusion and transient locking of the joint. If the loose body is floating in the synovial fluid it may be felt in the suprapatellar pouch or occasionally elsewhere in the joint. Radiographs in the early phase of osteochondritis dissecans show an area of bone surrounded by a thin translucent zone in the intercondylar notch of the femur. Later the separated fragment may be seen in the joint, often in between the condyles, where it may have caused locking. Repeated damage to the joint surfaces may be followed by osteoarthritis.

Before separation of the fragment has occurred, immobilisation of the knee in a plaster shell for 2–3 months may be followed by healing. At a later phase the joint must be opened and the diseased segment of bone removed or if it is very large it is fixed by a pin. If the body is free it must be removed and the edges of the cavity from which it separated pared away.

Other types of loose bodies may form in the knee joint. Fibrinous bodies may follow haemarthrosis or an inflammatory synovitis. Bony fragments may derive from osteoarthritic lipping. In neuropathic arthritis bony, cartilaginous, fibrinous or fibrous loose bodies may be found. In osteoarthritis prominent fringes of synovial membrane form, which may be nipped and set free into the joint as masses of fibrous tissue. Such loose bodies are only found incidental to some operation on a joint either for diagnosis or treatment.

Recurrent dislocation of the patella must be treated operatively to prevent the development of osteoarthritis (see p. 472).

SYNOVIOMA

Tumours of the synovial membrane are rare. Synoviomata may be pedunculated tumours that project into the joint cavity, where they cause pain, swelling and locking. The tumour is usually benign. Histologically vascular fibrous tissue is found, showing a tendency to the formation of synovial clefts and the presence of tumour giant cells. Local excision is curative. Malignant synovioma is a highly malignant tumour, fortunately rare. Amputation is needed once the diagnosis has been made by biopsy.

CHRONIC ARTHRITIS OF THE KNEE JOINT

The commonest arthritic condition of the knee joint in temperate climates is *osteoarthritis*. This may be part of a primary disease with manifestations of osteoarthritis in other joints. Monarticular arthritis of the knee is likely to be due to previous injury, e.g. a fracture, menisceal or ligamentous injury, a loose body or recurrent dislocation of the patella. If a cause can be found it should, if possible, be treated. Mild degrees of osteoarthritis are controlled by analgesics, rest, a walking stick, supportive bandaging and physiotherapy. Reduction of body weight may help. The symptoms are often episodic, and relief of pain by physiotherapy may often be effective. Rarely is arthrodesis justified in a severe monarticular arthritis. Tibial osteotomy corrects deformity and maintains movement. It may arrest the progress of the disease by interfering with the blood supply of the joint.

Rheumatoid arthritis may affect the knee, but usually other joints are then involved. Severe arthritis may end in fibrous ankylosis and, as the years go by, with secondary osteoarthritic changes. In the early phase splintage to prevent deformity is coupled with physiotherapy to preserve movement. Passive exercises maintain movement, active exercises improve muscle tone. Analgesics, phenylbutazone and cortisone may help. Injection of hydrocortisone into the joint may be dramatically effective in relieving pain, but such injections are dangerous, because collapse of the joint surfaces may occur. When ankylosis has occurred in a bad position, for example, with a severe flexion deformity, arthroplasty may sometimes be justified.

Tuberculosis of the knee joint is rarely seen in Britain nowadays. It is to be suspected in a child or young adult who presents with a painless or painful chronic effusion. Synovial thickening suggests tuberculosis, though it also occurs in rheumatic joint conditions. The thigh muscles waste rapidly, leading to a characteristic spindle-shaped joint with a typically pallid skin colour. Spasm of the muscles around the joint may cause pain. Systemic evidence of tuberculosis may be present—fever, night sweats, night starts and a raised E.S.R. There may be a familial history of tuberculosis. In the early phase or where only the synovial membrane is affected there may be no radiological signs. Where the bones are affected decalcification or erosion of the bony contour may be seen. The diagnosis is made by aspiration of the joint and culture of the synovial fluid and injection of it into a guinea-pig. Biopsy of the synovial membrane may be necessary. Biopsy of a gland in the groin may give useful histological evidence of tuberculosis. The Mantoux reaction is usually performed, though it is not of great diagnostic value.

Early cases respond to immobilisation, the administration of anti-tuberculous drugs and a sanitorium régime and later synovectomy. In adults arthrodesis is performed after 6 months of tuberculostatic drug therapy. The joint is fixed with the limb straight by a compression type of arthrodesis, in which the joint is opened and the bone ends are excised. Pins are inserted transversely through the tibia and femur, which are locked together by turnbuckles so that the bones are firmly held in apposition. Bony union should be complete in about 3 months, chemotherapy is maintained for 2 years.

Haemophilic arthritis follows recurrent haemarthrosis. Fibrous ankylosis, often with flexion deformity and misshapen joints, occurs in children. Crises of bleeding can be controlled by the use of anti-haemophilic globulin.

Gonococcal arthritis may cause a swollen knee, which occasionally ankyloses. Reiter's syndrome may cause swelling of the knee joint similar to that seen in rheumatoid arthritis. Often there is considerable systemic upset, with fever, urethritis and iritis. Reiter's syndrome is treated with antibiotics and cortisone, but often recurs.

Neuropathic arthritis of the knee is usually due to tabes dorsalis. The patient shows Argyll Robertson pupils, extensor plantar responses and loss of proprioceptive sensation in the legs. The knee joint is swollen, but characteristically painless. There is gross hypermobility. Radiography shows a bizarre appearance of destruction of bone, often with hyperostosis. Treatment consists of a restraining support which is fitted, such as a caliper or knee cage.

FURTHER READING

Smillie, I. S. (1962) *Injuries of the Knee Joint.* E. & S. Livingstone, Edinburgh.
Smillie, I. S. (1960) *Osteochondritis Dissecans*, Livingstone, Edinburgh.

CHAPTER FORTY

THE SPINE

CLINICAL EXAMINATION

Spinal diseases cause pain, deformity and stiffness, the pain being commonly referred either down the arm or the leg. When it is within the distribution of the sciatic nerve it is called *sciatica*. Nerve compression and irritation may cause pain corresponding to appropriate nerve roots.

The patient is examined both from behind and in front with the subject standing to demonstrate deformity of the spine itself or other deformities, such as a short leg, squint, torticollis or evidence of spina bifida or spondylolisthesis. There may be a tuft of hair over a spina bifida. Over a spondylolisthesis (see p. 534) a prominent step may be seen between the lumbar spine and sacrum and characteristic folds of the skin lying over the iliac crest and apparent shortening of the lumbar spine. Inspection from in front may reveal torticollis, squint or prominent ribs on one side due to scoliosis.

The range of movements of the spine: flexion, extension, lateral flexion and rotation are all tested, and it is noted whether any movements are limited or cause pain. It is also observed whether deformities disappear or are made more prominent in flexion. Spasm of the erector spinae muscle may be obvious when the patient is examined from behind by the fact that the muscles stand out more than normally on one or both sides.

The patient lies prone, and any sites of tenderness are localised. Firm pressure over certain spinous processes may reveal local tenderness—other sites of lumbar tenderness are in the renal angles and over the sacro-iliac joints. The patient is then turned on to his back and the abdomen is palpated. The legs are raised singly when straight. Limitation of straight leg raising suggests pressure on the sciatic nerve roots, especially if pain is aggravated by raising the head. Pain due to hip disease may be distinguished by the fact that flexion of the hips alone, with the knee bent, is painful. If pain is produced when the knees are straightened, then tension on the sciatic nerve can be diagnosed.

The central nervous system is next examined. In the upper limb evidence of weakness and wasting of the small muscles of the hand and anaesthesia may be found. In the lower limb anaesthesia and diminished ankle and knee reflexes may be demonstrated. Pelvic examination is always essential in order to exclude a rectal neoplasm or ovarian or uterine tumour. When secondary deposits are suspected in bone the breast, lung, thyroid, prostate and kidney should be examined clinically and where indicated radiologically.

In all cases of backache and when pain is thought to be referred from the spine, radiography is essential to exclude primary bone disease, secondary deposits, congenital lesions or degenerative disease such as osteoarthritis. The serum alkaline phosphatase is often raised in osteoporosis and in Paget's disease. The acid phosphatase is raised in carcinoma of the prostate. The level of calcium and phosphorus in the serum should be estimated where hyperparathyroidism is suspected and in cases of osteoporosis.

CONGENITAL LESIONS

A congenitally wedged vertebra or hemivertebra may cause a severe degree of scoliosis or kyphoscoliosis (Fig. 78). Several vertebrae may be fused, especially in the cervical spine, an abnormality that may be associated with the Sprengel lesion of the shoulder (p. 564) or the Klippel–Feil syndrome. Spina bifida may be found in radiographs, in most cases un-

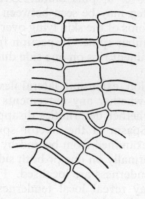

FIG. 78. Scoliosis due to congenital hemivertebra

related to any symptom. In spina bifida occulta the laminae of the lower lumbar and upper sacral vertebrae show a defect of fusion. The gap may be variable in width from a hairline crack to a wide defect. Usually the overlying skin is normal, though excessive hairiness is suggestive of spina bifida. Talipes and pes cavus may be associated, and evidence of spina bifida should always be looked for clinically and radiologically in such deformities. Less often severe constipation, urinary incontinence, paralysis and hydrocephalus may be associated.

Radiography may reveal sacralisation of the fifth lumbar vertebra or lumbarisation of the first segment of the sacrum, but such abnormalities can rarely be incriminated as a cause of backache. Spondylolisthesis is a disorder in which a defect is found in the pars interarticularis of the fifth lumbar vertebra which allows it to slip forwards on the sacrum (Fig. 79). Before movement occurs the condition is called spondylolysis. If the fifth lumbar vertebra moves forwards it takes with it the upper articular facet leaving behind the lamina, pedicle and inferior articular facet.

Another radiological sign seen in the antero-posterior view is prominence of the lower edge of the fifth lumbar vertebra which seems to lie much lower than normal. Whether the lesion is congenital or acquired is not certain.

A prolapsed intervertebral disc may be associated and the condition causes low backache or sciatica. In spondylolisis radiographs show a linear defect between the superior and inferior articular facets of the fifth lumbar vertebra. Spondylolisthesis may be clinically obvious if there is a

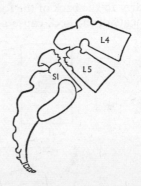

FIG. 79. Spondylolisthesis allowing slipping of L5 vertebra on S 1

step in the lumbo-sacral spine, a curious deformity that appears to shorten the lumbar spine. The lumbar vertebrae are more easily felt per abdomen than usual.

In early cases of spondylolisis or spondylolisthesis physiotherapy, rest and a spinal support are effective. In gross cases of slipping, spinal fusion may be necessary, sometimes with removal of a prolapsed intervertebral disc. Fusion by bone grafting may be achieved by an approach to the affected spines posteriorly, laterally or from the front.

PROLAPSED INTERVERTEBRAL DISC

The intervertebral disc is made up of a central nucleus of a jelly like substance—the nucleus pulposus, enclosed under tension by a fibrous ring —the annulus fibrosus. The nucleus of the disc may prolapse (Fig. 80) if the annulus is ruptured or degenerates, either into the vertebral body (Schmorl's node) or more often posteriorly to press on the spinal cord, or if more laterally placed, on nerve roots. Swelling of the nucleus may cause a prolapse that may later diminish in size with amelioration of symptoms. Osteoarthritis of intervertebral joints may follow degeneration and prolapse of the disc.

The cervical and lumbar parts of the spine are most often affected. Backache due to disc prolapse or spondylosis causes pain but no systemic manifestations—an important point when the differential diagnosis from tuberculosis and ankylosing spondylitis is being considered.

S

Cervical Spine

Cervical disc prolapse may be sudden in onset, with severe pain in the neck often radiating down the arm in the distribution of nerve roots. Torticollis and stiff neck are common. The discs above and below the sixth cervical vertebra are those most often affected, often causing pain that radiates either in the distribution of the fifth and sixth cervical nerves that is over the shoulder and down the lateral side of the upper arm, or in the area of supply of the sixth and seventh cervical nerves down the upper arm to the back of the forearm and to the back of the middle finger. Movements of the neck cause aggravation of pain, rest or traction on the

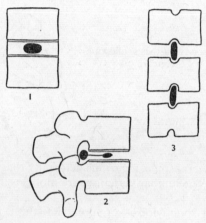

FIG. 80. (1) Intervertebral disc. (2) Posterior prolapse of nucleus pulposus. (3) Schmorl's node.

spine alleviates it. Less often signs of pressure on the cord even quadriplegia may remit. A spinal tumour may be simulated.

Massage and careful manipulation may help. A collar may be worn to limit movement of the neck made of plastic, felt or an inflatable material. More severe cases with nerve-root compression require traction by the physiotherapist for about 20 minutes every day. In very severe cases the patient is admitted to hospital, nursed on a Stryker frame with traction of the neck maintained for as long as the patient can stand it via a head harness or halter. This harness is very uncomfortable and can only be worn for limited periods. If there is evidence of cord compression with developing quadriplegia and urinary incontinence urgent decompression by laminectomy may be needed, followed by spinal fusion. It is difficult and often dangerous to attempt to remove the prolapsed disc in the cervical region.

Lumbar Spine

Prolapse of an intervertebral disc usually occurs above or below the fifth lumbar vertebra. Rarely the disc between the third and fourth lumbar vertebrae may be affected. Low backache is caused, often with evidence of compression of the fifth lumbar or first sacral nerve roots. Acute prolapse causes severe pain often following lifting. The spinal muscles go into painful spasm, and the patient describes himself as locked in agony, being unable to walk or bend. The lumbar spine is flattened and sometime scoliotic. A prolapse in the midline presses on the cord, causing backache alone. A more laterally situated prolapse may press on the adjacent nerve root. There may be numbness of the foot or diminution of the ankle reflex. Prolapse of the disc between the fifth lumbar and first sacral vertebrae causes pain, which travels down the back of the leg, after the prolapse of the disc between the fourth and fifth lumbar vertebrae the pain travels down the outside of the leg and thigh. Prolapse of the disc between the first and second lumbar vertebrae is much less common, but may cause pain in the flank, radiating to the groin, which may even simulate renal or biliary colic. Prolapse of the disc between the third and fourth

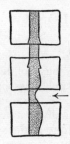

Fig. 81. Myelogram showing indentation by prolapsed intervertebral disc

lumbar vertebrae is often accompanied by a scoliosis that may change from one side to the other as the patient bends and extends—alternating scoliosis. Characteristically patients find that the pain of a prolapsed disc is aggravated by coughing and sneezing. Often in the early phase it is worse when resting in bed. Occasionally though pain and sciatica may be severe, movements of the spine are remarkably free. An important feature of disc prolapse distinguishing it from inflammatory disease, such as tuberculosis or spondylitis, is that some movements of the spine are free and painless unless symptoms are very acute, whereas in tuberculosis all movements cause pain. In addition, there are no signs of a systemic disease. Radiographs show narrowing of the disc space affected, most often between the fifth lumbar vertebra and the sacrum. Osteophytic lipping may be seen in chronic cases at the margins of the vertebrae.

The differential diagnosis includes a spinal tumour, primary bone disease or secondary carcinoma. In cases of backache the spine must therefore always be radiographed. A pelvic examination is often indicated. All sites of primary tumour that metastasise to bone must be examined, that is breast, lungs, thyroid, prostate and kidney.

In the acute phase rest is enforced for up to 6 weeks in bed on boards placed under the mattress to give a rigid support. Later a corset is fitted

in which steel stays provide a support to the spine. In some very sever
cases a plaster of Paris jacket is advised. In cases of repeated and sever
attacks of pain, or where there is evidence of nerve-root compression
operation is performed to remove the disc through a posterior approach
after removal of half of one lamina and the ligamentum flavum on one side
Rarely if compression of the cauda equina develops it must be relieved by
laminectomy as an emergency operation.

Occasionally myelography has to be performed (Fig. 81) by intratheca
injection of radio-opaque contrast medium to confirm the diagnosis of a
prolapsed disc or to eliminate the possibility of a spinal tumour, especially
f the fluid obtained by lumbar puncture indicates the possibility of a
spinal block (see p. 586).

In the thoracic spine prolapse of an intervertebral disc rarely cause
symptoms, though evidence of prolapse into the centre of vertebra i
common in Scheuermann's disease (see below).

SPONDYLOSIS

Spondylosis of the spine is a degenerative condition akin to osteo
arthritis and often part of a generalised osteoarthritis. More localised
spondylosis may follow trauma, though the actual incident may have
occurred many years previously and have been forgotten. The cervical
and lumbar vertebrae are particularly affected. The diagnostic feature
are pain, usually in a nerve-root distribution, limitation of movement and
stiffness. Many of the symptoms and signs of spondylosis are the same a
those presenting in prolapse of intervertebral discs. An element of disc
prolapse is a common feature of spondylosis, though usually the radiographic and clinical features indicate a more widespread affection of the
vertebrae than those found in disc prolapse alone.

Radiography reveals osteophytic lipping of the edges of the vertebrae
especially obvious in the lateral view. Osteophytes are particularly liable
to form around the vertebral foramina through which nerve roots pass
Narrowing of the foramina can best be seen in oblique views of the cervical
spine. Disc degeneration manifests itself in narrowing of the space between
adjacent vertebrae.

Because of the widespread radiation of pain caused by spondylosis
many conditions may be simulated. In the cervical region occipital headache, rheumatism and any cause of brachial neuritis (see p. 546) may be
mimicked. Spondylosis in the lumbar spine may give rise to symptoms
suggestive of biliary, renal or colonic pain if pain is caused in the area of
supply of the first and second lumbar nerve roots. Sciatic pain is associated with involvement of the fifth lumbar and first sacral vertebrae. The
symptoms of peripheral vascular disease are often mistaken for spondylosis
of the spine, and vice versa. The characteristic aggravation of pain on
movement caused by spondylosis and relief by rest is important in the
diagnosis. The radiological signs of vertebral osteoarthritis are so common

hat the diagnosis of pain due to spondylosis can only be made by exclusion of many other causes of backache. Gross arthritic changes may be found in the spine accidentally by radiography and in the absence of any symptoms.

The treatment for spondylosis is much the same as for prolapsed intervertebral disc. Analgesics such as aspirin are given to relieve pain, and phenylbutazone may be used. In mild cases physiotherapy gives relief by using heat in various forms and building up the strength of the spinal extensor muscles. Traction for varying periods of the day may be valuable. It is usual to recommend a spinal support, such as an abdominal corset with steel stays inserted posteriorly to limit the movement of the lumbar spine. A cervical collar made of plastic, felt or inflatable rubber can be used to immobilise the cervical spine. In some cases pain may be so severe as to require immobilisation in a plaster jacket. Operation is only used for the severest persistent symptoms or for evidence of advancing nerve pressure or where another lesion such as spinal tumour or prolapse of an intervertebral disc is suspected. Laminectomy for confirmation of the diagnosis is followed by spinal fusion with bone grafts.

ANKYLOSING SPONDYLITIS

Ankylosing spondylitis is a disease of unknown cause affecting young adults between the ages of about 15 and 40 years. Men are more often affected than women. Some features of spondylitis are similar to rheumatoid arthritis, with which it may be associated. The patients are often unwell, being thin and showing a low fever, raised E.S.R. and white-cell count and anaemia. Backache and stiffness usually sited over the sacro-iliac region is complained of first. The disease is episodic, and in mild cases may regress or never progress. In the severest cases pain and stiffness increase with each episode until the whole spine is involved. The normal spine curvatures become replaced by a single kyphosis, occasionally so acutely angled that the patient's back becomes horizontal (poker back). Acute episodes of irido-cyclitis are common. The disease tends to burn itself out over a period of years, leaving the patient severely deformed or disabled because of the generalised ankylosis. When other joints are involved by rheumatoid arthritis they, too, become ankylosed, and occasionally one sees a patient who is completely rigid in spine, hip and knee joints so that he can neither bend, sit nor walk. Rarely the cardio-vascular system is involved, with aneurysmal dilatation of the ascending aorta and aortic valve incompetence indistinguishable from that seen in syphilis, although the W.R. is negative. Death may occur from rupture of the aneurysm.

The first radiological signs are seen in the sacro-iliac joints, which become blurred, irregular and sclerosed, signs that are best shown in oblique views. Later, the spine shows calcification of the ligaments around the intervertebral discs and interarticular joints, producing in advanced cases the typical picture of a 'bamboo spine' (Fig. 82).

Treatment is difficult because the cause is unknown. In mild early cases rest, analgesics and physiotherapy to preserve movement are adequate. Steroids such as prednisolone are of use in crises. Relief of pain may be achieved with phenylbutazone. Most of the anti-inflammatory drugs used in spondylitis can, however, be dangerous if administered for long periods. Radiotherapy to the spine is probably the most effective treatment in

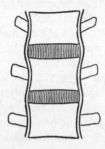

FIG. 82. 'Bamboo Spine' due to ossification of intervertebral ligaments

acute episodes, but it may sterilise women, and there are reports of its being followed by leukaemia years later. In the severe cases of poker-back deformity, osteotomy of the spine may be justified to straighten the back. Arthroplasty of the hips may allow the subject to sit.

OSTEOCHONDRITIS OF THE SPINE

The features of osteochondritis seen elsewhere in bone and joint (see p. 517) may be found in the spine, that is increased density of bone followed by fragmentation and eventually restoration of normal architecture with some deformity produced by compression while the bone is soft.

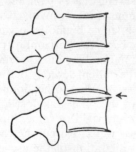

FIG. 83. Osteochondritis of the spine. Wedging of the vertebrae and fragmentation of the anterior part of the cartilaginous plates

In a child a localised angular kyphosis may be caused if one vertebral body is affected (Calvé's disease). The vertebra becomes denser and wedged anteriorly, causing pain. A proportion of these cases is due to solitary foci of eosinophilic granuloma. The differential diagnosis must be made from tuberculosis. Injury to the anterior margins of the epiphyseal plates of the lower six thoracic vertebrae occurs quite commonly in adolescence and is called Scheuermann's disease (Fig. 83). In the active phase fragmentation of the epiphyseal plates is seen radiographically, more marked anteriorly. A variable number of vertebrae become wedged anteriorly to produce a long gentle kyphosis (adolescent kyphosis). Disc degeneration with prolapse of the nucleus pulposus into the vertebral body is common (Schmorl's nodes), showing as a clear rounded defect in the vertebral body adjacent to the intervertebral discs.

Treatment is rarely needed. There may be some aching that clears spontaneously. The patient may need to be taught to improve his posture by increasing a compensatory curve in the lumbar spine. In adult life the symptoms and signs of osteoarthritis may present. Rarely rest in bed may be advised or a spinal brace be worn.

TUBERCULOSIS OF THE SPINE

Tuberculosis of the spine may occur at any age and affect any part of the spine, though usually young adults and children are most often affected.

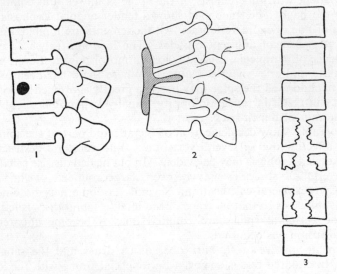

Fig. 84. Tuberculosis of the spine. (1) Vertebral focus. (2) Paravertebral abscess. (3) Involvement of several vertebrae

The thoracic and lumbar spine are the parts commonly diseased. Spinal tuberculosis may flare up at any age though apparently healed for years.

Tuberculous infection is blood-borne, giving rise to caseous foci in the vertebral bodies close to the intervertebral discs. Bony destruction leads to collapse and, as the anterior part of the vertebra is most often severely affected, it becomes wedged. Destruction of the intervertebral discs is common, and several vertebrae may be involved (Fig. 84). When the angular kyphosis is very marked the deformity is called a gibbus. The great fear is paraplegia due to pressure on the cord by caseous granulation tissue, sequestrated bone or in later years by angulation of the cord over the bony ridge that projects in a severe angular kyphosis. A cold abscess may form in the paravertebral region, where it may remain encysted and become calcified. From the cervical spine an abscess may track and present in front or behind the sternomastoid muscle, or a retro-pharyngeal abscess may be seen on inspection of the pharynx through the mouth. In the thoracic region an abscess may follow the course of an intercostal neuro-vascular bundle and point lateral to the sternum. Lumbar abscesses track within the psoas muscle, producing a fluctuant mass in the groin, often continuous with another in the iliac fossa. Cross fluctuation may be demonstrated between the two swellings. An abscess may also appear in the lumbar region just above the iliac crest. Abscesses from the sacro-iliac joint point posteriorly. Spontaneous discharge of a cold abscess leads to sinus formation, with secondary infection and sometimes amyloidosis.

The patient with tuberculosis of the spine is unwell and complains of pain in the back The spine may show a tender angular kyphosis due to collapse of one or more vertebrae. All movements are limited, and there is marked spasm of adjacent muscles. The legs must always be tested for evidence of paraplegia, especially loss of motor power. Fever, malaise, night starts and cries may be features. Where there has been extensive disease in childhood the spine may become greatly shortened by kyphosis. Healing can result in severe deformity, usually kyphoscoliosis, dwarfism and a prominent hunch-back.

Radiographs show decalcification of the affected part of the spine, with erosion affecting one or several vertebrae. With vertebral destruction an acutely angled kyphosis may be evident. In old healed disease calcification of paravertebral abscesses may be seen, large rounded swellings made evident by peripheral calcification. Several vertebrae may become fused by bony ankylosis so that no trace of the intervertebral discs is left. Only when the vertebral spines are counted does it become apparent that vertebral fusion has occurred.

Treatment involves rest, anti-tuberculous drugs and the sanatorium régime. In children rest is achieved on a special frame with the legs immobilised by skin traction to Thomas' splints attached to the frame. Kyphosis is corrected in children by angulating the bed anteriorly, slowly and cautiously. If the cervical spine is involved, then a halter or harness is worn to keep the neck still. Adults are placed on a plaster bed, no attempt is made to correct kyphosis.

Operation is performed both in adults and children after 6 weeks of anti-tuberculous drugs. The approach is to the antero-lateral aspect of the vertebrae. In the thoracic region this involves a left thoracotomy, and the rib removed can be used for preparing a suitable bone graft and bone chips after all the caseous material has been gently curetted and any sequestra removed. Alternatively, an extra-pleural route is used. The lumbar spine is approached via the ilio-lumbar region and the cervical vertebrae either via an incision along the anterior border of the sterno-mastoid or through the mouth. After operation the patient is immobilised on a plaster bed. When fusion has been successful and the disease is quiescent activity is allowed, first in a plaster jacket and then with a spinal brace. A close follow-up must be maintained throughout treatment, because flares of infection are not uncommon, and no movement should be allowed until it is certain the disease is inactive. Cold abscesses may be aspirated, if they approach the skin, with great care to prevent secondary infection.

Paraplegic symptoms and signs that arise in the early phase of infection often respond to rest and chemotherapy as the inflammatory reaction subsides. So long as the motor power is preserved, a period of rest and chemotherapy is justified. A sudden onset of paraplegia, failure of the paraplegia to respond rapidly to a period of rest for 3 or 4 weeks with chemotherapy or a recurrence of the paraplegic signs are all indications for operation. Decompression of the cord is achieved after resection of the heads of the ribs near the affected vertebrae, allowing an approach to be made to the antero-lateral aspect of the vertebral bodies to expose the theca. Caseous tissue, necrotic bone or a prominent bar of bone due to an angular kyphosis may need to be removed. Bone grafting to fuse the spine is needed at a later date. Paraplegic symptoms that develop late in the disease after healing are usually due to the severity of an angular kyphosis.

OSTEOMYELITIS OF THE SPINE

Osteomyelitis of the spine other than that due to tuberculosis is rare. The commonest organism is the staphylococcus. Typhoid osteomyelitis may also occur, causing a chronic infection.

In pyogenic osteomyelitis there is severe pain in the back, fever, malaise and a raised white-cell count. Radiographic signs may be minimal early on, though later there is calcification and a characteristic beaked appearance of the margins of the bodies of the affected vertebrae. A paravertebral abscess may form. The condition responds to a prolonged course of antibiotics, the most difficult problem is often that of diagnosis.

SCOLIOSIS AND KYPHOSIS

Scoliosis is a deformity due to deviation and rotation of the spine to one side. Kyphosis is an increase in antero-posterior curvature and is the opposite to lordosis. Kyphosis and scoliosis are often associated as a kyphoscoliosis. These deformities are either mobile or fixed. A mobile scoliosis disappears when the spine is flexed, a fixed scoliosis becomes more obvious because of vertebral rotation, which is often associated in fixed scoliosis but absent in mobile scoliosis. A mobile kyphosis can be corrected by alteration of posture or in recumbency.

A spinal deformity is usually a complex of primary and secondary or compensatory curves. The primary curve of scoliosis is usually thoracic and to the right, to which compensatory curves develop in the cervical and lumbar region. A thoracic kyphosis may be secondary to a lumbar lordosis, in turn compensating for a deformity of the hip such as coxa vara or a short leg.

Scoliosis

In the diagnosis of the cause and treatment of scoliosis the first decision to be made is whether the deformity is mobile or fixed, i.e. whether it disappears on bending or becomes more obvious (Fig. 85). The child should be carefully inspected for evidence of torticollis, squint or short leg that may cause compensatory scoliosis. If there is torticollis this must be

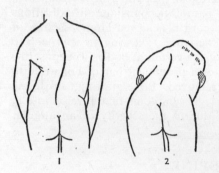

FIG. 85. (1) Scoliosis of the spine. (2) Made more obvious by flexion

treated by division of the sternomastoid at its insertion; similarly, correction of the squint or raising of the heels. Postural scoliosis is corrected by physiotherapy to improve the child's posture and develop compensatory curves.

A fixed scoliosis is made more marked by flexing the spine, which, by increasing the rotation of vertebrae, increases posterior projection of the ribs on one side. If inspection of the chest from the front shows flattening of the ribs on the side this deformity is often part of scoliosis.

Evidence of muscle weakness or wasting may indicate a previous attack of poliomyelitis. Scoliosis is a common feature of some neurological disorders such as syringomyelia, Friedreich's ataxia and neurofibromatosis. Radiographs of the spine should be carried out for evidence of congenital abnormalities of the vertebrae, such as hemi-vertebra or fusion of vertebrae. Abnormalities of the ribs may also be found. However, in most patients no obvious cause can be found for a fixed scoliosis—the so-called idiopathic group.

Scoliosis is unpredictable in its development. The majority never progress to any serious degree, but at any time in the period of growth an alarming deterioration may occur. No treatment is necessary for most patients with scoliosis except exercises to improve posture and keep the spine supple. Patients should be seen regularly at 3–6-monthly intervals and when necessary radiographed and photographed to allow the degree of deformity and any variations to be measured. Spinal braces are of little value in controlling or arresting the progress of scoliosis, but they may have to be worn when there is considerable muscle weakness, as occurs following poliomyelitis.

If it is considered that the deformity must be arrested, a period of rest in bed is advised in a plaster jacket that can be wedged on one side and then opened to correct the deformity as far as possible. When maximal reduction has been achieved an extensive spinal fusion is performed. Operative treatment is admittedly unsatisfactory at present, and new methods are being tried, such as attempts to fuse the vertebrae on one side by stapling or bone graft to allow correction to occur by controlled growth of the vertebrae. Metallic rods can be inserted enabling the vertebra to be distracted. As a rule, scoliosis usually ceases to become worse once the epiphyses of the iliac crests are seen to be completely formed in radiographs.

Kyphosis

Most kyphoses occur in the thoracic region. A mobile kyphosis may be simply due to poor posture—round shoulders. Muscle weakness from poliomyelitis or some neurological disorder, such as progressive muscular atrophy, may be the cause. Thoracic kyphosis may be compensatory to the prominent lumbar lordosis that is seen in congenital dislocation of the hip or a hip fixed in flexion. In such cases attention to posture with exercise and treatment of the primary cause, if that is possible, is all that is necessary.

A fixed kyphosis affecting the whole thoracic spine in adolescents may be due to osteochondritis of the lower thoracic vertebrae. In the young and middle-aged adult ankylosing spondylitis may be the cause. In the elderly kyphosis is very common and part of the general stooping posture of the aged, in whom the intervertebral discs degenerate and cause narrowing of the disc space and slight anterior wedging of the vertebrae. Pain may then arise due to osteoarthritic changes in the intervertebral joints. Elderly women may develop osteoporosis possibly due to a hormone change, for recalcification and some relief of pain may be derived from the administration of oestrogens or androgens or combinations of both. Crush fractures may occur spontaneously from trivial injury to osteoporotic vertebrae. The discs bulge into the decalcified vertebrae, which become biconcave in shape or wedged anteriorly. Primary bone disorders (e.g. rickets, osteomalacia and Paget's disease) may cause kyphosis and kyphosciolosis. Secondary deposits may also produce deformity.

Most of the causes of kyphosis so far enumerated cause a generalised increased curvature of the thoracic spine. A local angular kyphosis may follow tuberculosis, osteochondritis of a single vertebra or may be the result of a fracture. The possibility of a secondary deposit must not be forgotten.

The treatment of a fixed kyphosis is that of the primary disease if that is amenable to treatment. Analgesics and some form of spinal support may help. It may be necessary to treat arthritic changes in adult life with physiotherapy and a corset with extra support to the spine.

BACKACHE, SCIATICA AND BRACHIAL NEURITIS

Pain in the back, often radiating down the leg or arm, is so common that it is worth considering these complaints in detail. So many conditions are involved as to make the differential diagnosis difficult unless the

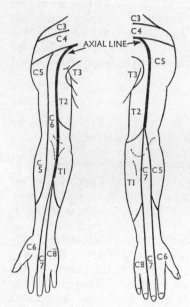

FIG. 86. Dermatomes of the upper limb

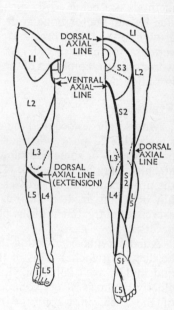

FIG. 87. Dermatomes of the lower limb

diseases that may affect the spinal cord and nerves from their origins to their terminations, are considered anatomically. This scheme does not, of course, put the conditions in order of frequency of occurrence, but indicates a logical approach by examination to establish the diagnosis. It is important in any assessment of pain in the arm and leg to discover if the distribution of pain or the abnormal neurological signs indicate a lesion of the spinal cord, the nerve roots or the peripheral nerves. If peripheral nerves are involved the level of the disease can usually be localised. Diagnosis necessitates knowledge of the distribution of the dermatomes (Figs. 86, 87) in the upper and lower limbs.

Many pains in the back or pain in the arm or leg have no detectable organic basis but full investigation and complete clinical examination must be made before resorting to such terms as fibrositis, fasciitis, lumbago, myalgia or neuritis. It must be stressed that backache and pain in the arm and leg are serious symptoms meriting full examination clinically and radiologically. Probably the commonest clinical and radiological diagnosis is of spondylosis of the spine, second comes a prolapsed intervertebral disc. Tumours of the spinal cord (see p. 585) are easily missed for long periods unless the signs of cord compression appear. In the intervertebral foramina neurofibroma of a nerve root or narrowing by osteophytes or spondylolisthesis may cause root pain.

In the upper limb nerve root pain in the C6 and C7 dermatome is often referred from cervical spondylosis. A cervical rib or costoclavicular compression may cause pain in the distribution of the lower cord (C8, T1) of the brachial plexus. Occasionally carcinoma of the apex of the lung may cause pain down the arm (Pancoast tumour) from involvement of the brachial plexus. Painful lesions around the shoulder joint include osteoarthritis of the shoulder and tears of the supraspinatus tendon. At the elbow, osteoarthritis and ulnar neuritis must be considered, at the wrist, carpal tunnel syndrome and tenosynovitis. The pain of carpal tunnel syndrome may radiate far up the arm, even to the shoulder regions and neck, and is worse at night-time.

In the lower limb sciatic pain may be due to diseases of the spine and the structures in the spinal canal. Maladies of the sacro-iliac joint or hip joints, such as osteoarthritis, spondylitis or tuberculosis may also be responsible for pain in the leg.

Abdominal diseases may cause backache, for example biliary, pancreatic or renal diseases. A gastric ulcer may penetrate the pancreas and cause pain in the back. Pelvic infection due to cervicitis and chronic salpingitis is a common cause of low lumbar backache. Pelvic tumours, primary and secondary, must be excluded by vaginal and rectal examination. True neuritis occurs with diabetes, alcoholism or infective polyneuritis.

Radiography is essential to diagnose fracture, secondary deposits and diseases of the lung, such as cancer or tuberculosis. Tuberculosis of the spine or primary bone disease, such as osteoporosis and Paget's disease, may be revealed. Unsuspected congenital lesions of the spine may be found, such as spina bifida, spondylolisis or spondylolisthesis. Osteoarthritic changes may be seen around vertebrae and their interarticular joints. Rarely a primary tumour of a vertebra, such as a haemangioma or osteoma, may be found.

FURTHER READING

Cervical Spondylosis. 1967. Ed. Lord Brain and Wilkinson, M. Heinnemann Medical Books, London.

CHAPTER FORTY-ONE

TENDONS, SKELETAL MUSCLE, BURSAE, GANGLION AND SOME NEUROLOGICAL DISORDERS

TENDONS

Injuries affecting tendons cause rupture, division and dislocation. When rupture occurs it either happens near the insertion of the tendon or at its junction with a muscle belly. The *tendo Achillis* ruptures during severe exertion when the subject feels something like a pistol shot at the ankle and experiences great pain, swelling and inability to plantarflex the ankle. Complete rupture necessitates open operation and suture of the tendon, followed by immobilisation of the leg and thigh for six weeks in a plaster shell. Physiotherapy is then needed to regain full use of the limb. Unrecognised injury may lead to severe disability and a typical shuffling gait. Partial rupture of the Achilles tendon or rupture of the plantaris muscle causes sudden severe pain in the ankle or in the calf; the subject may be running and fall to the ground, often believing the leg has been struck from behind. The ankle can still be moved, and only rest is needed until the pain has subsided, followed by exercises to regain strength. Pain usually persists for a few weeks.

The *rectus femoris* muscle may be ruptured by a strain where the muscle belly joins the quadriceps tendon. A prominent swelling forms in the thigh when the muscle contracts, but there is no disability and no need for treatment. The *patellar tendon* may be ruptured by a violent flexion strain of the knee, either at its attachment into the patella or where the patellar ligament is inserted into the tibial tubercle. The symptoms and signs suggest a patellar fracture with inability to extend the knee, and a depression may be felt at the site of rupture. The ruptured tendon must be sutured and the knee immobilised in plaster of Paris for 3 weeks, following which active rehabilitation is required to restore movements and muscle power. The tendon of the long head of *biceps humeris* may rupture at its junction with the muscle belly, usually without any obvious injury. The rupture is presumably due to degeneration of the tendon where it passes through the bicipital groove. The patient presents with a swelling in the antecubital fossa, which is made more prominent by flexion of the elbow. The condition causes no disability and requires no treatment. It is usually seen in the elderly.

Rupture of the *supraspinatus muscle* occurs at its insertion into the head of the humerus, giving rise to pain in the region of the shoulder. There may be a definite incident of trauma, sometimes with fracture of the greater tuberosity of the humerus, but more often the onset of pain is insidious and results from some degenerative condition or tendinitis in the supraspinatus muscle, where it is inserted into the greater tuberosity of the humerus. If there is a complete tear abduction cannot be initiated though, if the arm is supported through the first 15°, abduction can be completed by the deltoid muscle. Where a partial rupture has occurred or where tendinitis is the cause, the arm can be abducted fairly painlessly to about 30°, but as the greater tuberosity moves under the acromion process pain is aggravated and only relieved by external rotation of the arm, which allows it to be brought parallel to the head. As the arm is returned to the side the 'painful arc' is repeated as the tuberosity slides under the acromion process. Examination by firm pressure over the shoulder joint reveals a localised area of tenderness just below the acromion process.

The pain of supraspinatus tendinitis is very unpleasant and causes considerable limitation of movement. It is often worse at night, and may be referred to the insertion of the deltoid muscle. Radiographs may show a small area of calcification where the tendon is inserted into the greater tuberosity.

A fractured tuberosity needs no local treatment if it is not separated. If there is separation it may be pressed back under anaesthesia (see Chapter Thirty One). Rarely an open operation to fix the fragment may be justified, but only in the young. These injuries usually occur in elderly people, and the immobility that must be maintained after operation is likely in them to induce severe joint stiffness. With intensive physiotherapy the patient's movements can usually be regained and the pain subsides.

For supraspinatus tendinitis the best treatment is to inject hydrocortisone and lignocaine into the tender area of the humerus just below the acromium. Other tender spots may be found in the capsule of the shoulder, especially anteriorly, and may be due to rupture or degeneration of the tendinous insertions of any of the small rotator muscles into the joint capsule ('rotator cuff syndrome'). These may similarly be treated by injection of hydrocortisone and lignocaine which may have to be repeated at intervals of two or three weeks. Physiotherapy with heat and exercises helps to relieve pain and regains movements.

Tendons may dislocate if their fascial sheaths or the restraining bands around them are torn by injury or strain. An example of dislocation of a tendon is that of *peroneus longus*, which may be dislocated out of its groove on the calcaneum by an eversion injury. Division of tendons in wounds is most serious in the hand and at the wrist. The diagnosis and treatment of such injuries as well as diseases of tendon sheaths are described in Chapter Twelve. It may be added that non-suppurative tenosynovitis is also seen in the dorsal extensors of the foot and of the tendo Achillis. Treatment is as for tenosynovitis of the wrist extensors (see Chapter Twelve).

MUSCLES

Muscles may be injured by direct or indirect violence. Haemorrhage from the torn muscle fibres may cause a large swelling, for example the rectus abdominis muscle may be torn or even completely divided by a violent hyperextension strain or a blow on the abdomen. Tenderness in this muscle may simulate appendicitis. In old people a massive haematoma may develop in the rectus abdominis after rupture of an atherosclerotic inferior epigastric artery during an episode of severe coughing. This incident may also occur during labour.

A muscle hernia may follow incision of the fascia overlying it or where the nerves supplying muscles have been divided—for example, where fascia lata has been removed from the thigh to reinforce a hernial repair, or the weakness that may follow an operation in the loin to remove a kidney.

Inflammation of muscle is rare. Anaerobic infection (gas gangrene) causes necrosis of muscle with gas formation and a serious illness (see p. 59). Pyogenic infection may extend from a nearby septic focus. Chronic infection may be due to tuberculosis or syphilis. Gumma is rarely seen nowadays, but the sternomastoid muscle used to be a typical site. Parasitic infection by the *taenia echinococcus* may be seen in skeletal muscle. The cut surface of the muscle shows small, white, round cysts, which may be seen in radiographs because they commonly become calcified. Ossification in muscle—myositis ossificans—occurs as a complication of fractures in which osteoblasts are released into the muscle. Ectopic bone may form in abdominal scars after operation. Fibrosis of muscle may follow ischaemia, the best known being fibrosis of the forearm muscles due to damage to the brachial artery complicating a supracondylar fracture of the humerus. A similar lesion may follow damage to the popliteal artery, resulting in fibrosis of the calf muscles and clawing of the toes.

Primary tumours of skeletal muscle are rare, although they represent one of the commonest malignant conditions of childhood. Most are fibrosarcomata of varying degrees of malignancy. Histologically the tumours are spindle-celled or round-celled. Metastasis is usually by the blood stream to the lungs. Local recurrence is likely unless wide excision is performed. These tumours appear deceptively encapsuled, but shelling them out is likely to be followed by recurrence. Block dissection of the affected muscle mass with a wide excision of surrounding normal muscle without concern for any subsequent functional disability is more likely to result in a successful outcome.

A special type of slowly growing fibrosarcoma is the desmoid tumour, which occurs in the rectus abdominis muscle, especially in women who have borne children. The rectus muscle below the umbilicus is usually affected. Histology suggests a fibroma, but recurrence is likely, and when the tumour recurs it may show the histological features of fibrosarcoma.

Wide excision affords a good chance of cure, and metastasis is extremely rare. Fibromata also occur in muscle, but all should be suspected of being fibrosarcomas of a low grade of malignancy. When local resection of a fibrosarcoma of a limb is difficult or is likely to produce a useless limb amputation is essential. When recurrence occurs amputation is also usually necessary.

Rhabdomyosarcoma is a very rare, highly malignant tumour of striped muscle that should always be treated by amputation. Rhabdomyoma is a very rare benign tumour that can be treated by local excision.

BURSAE

Bursae which become enlarged may be those that are well recognised anatomically or those that may arise secondarily to pressure or irritation—adventitious bursae. For example, if a congenital or postural deformity causes prominence of a bony point, then a bursa may form in the tissues over the projection. An adventitious bursa may appear over a medial cuneiform made prominent by pes cavus, over the heel when the postero-superior angle of the calcaneum projects abnormally or over the head of the first metatarsal in hallux valgus. In such cases treatment is given to the cause of the primary condition, which is usually a postural or anatomical defect. Shoes are specially made to avoid friction on bony prominences. Soft pads of foam rubber may protect the projections from irritation. In the treatment of bunion it is usual to excise the adventitious bursa as part of the operation for hallux valgus (see p. 557).

The commonest primary bursae occur around the knee or elbow. Most arise from repeated trauma or the irritation produced by prolonged pressure. Although anatomically thirteen bursae are recognised around the knee joint, only the prepatellar bursa and the semi-membranosus bursa become enlarged in practice.

In prepatellar bursitis or housemaid's knee a subcutaneous fluctuant swelling appears over the lower part of the patella. This may be painful, and occasionally suppuration and abscess formation may occur. Inside the bursa is a clear mucinous liquid resembling synovial fluid. In chronic bursitis melon-seed bodies may be found, condensations of fibrin that cause a characteristic crepitus on palpation. In the early phase of its development the bursa may be emptied by aspiration, occasionally with cure. If the swelling recurs or is persistent, then excision via an incision lateral to the patella must be performed. It is important not to have a scar over the point of the knee, where it may cause discomfort on kneeling. If an abscess occurs it is drained by incision.

Semi-membranosus bursa is common in children. A tense fluctuant swelling is seen in the popliteal fossa on its medial side, made more obvious with the knee extended, and disappearing on flexion of the joint. Aspiration of its jelly-like content may cure. If the swelling recurs it can be excised, using a tourniquet to produce an avascular field.

Enlargement of the subcutaneous bursa over the olecranon is common, presenting as a lax fluctuant swelling. Aspiration may effect a cure, but if recurrence occurs, then excision must be performed via an incision well clear of the point of the elbow. Occasionally suppuration causes a persistent purulent discharge. If this is prolonged the whole bursa must be excised.

The subcutaneous bursae which lie over the patella and the olecranon never communicate with the underlying joint, but when they are inflamed there may be so much swelling and pain as to suggest the possibility of infection of the joint. However, a few degrees of painless movement is always possible, allowing bursitis to be distinguished from septic arthritis.

Chronic bursitis over the greater trochanter of the femur is often due to tuberculosis. The diagnosis is made after aspiration of pus or biopsy. Treatment with tuberculostatic drugs may effect a cure, occasionally excision must be performed, if only to provide a means of diagnosis. Swelling of the suprascapular bursa occurs in tuberculosis and in rheumatoid arthritis. This bursa usually communicates with the shoulder joint, which is often grossly swollen. Radiography may confirm the suspicion of tuberculosis. Aspiration of the joint may be needed to relieve tension or to provide confirmation of the diagnosis. Gouty bursitis is rare, but easily recognised if the serum uric acid level is found to be raised. There may be evidence of gout elsewhere.

FASCIITIS

Fasciitis is a loose term applied to areas of tenderness in fascia or joint capsules, usually related to a 'rheumatic condition'. Tender areas in the back may be found which appear to be related to rheumatism, whatever that may be. Tender nodules may be due to small herniations of fat through fascia which undergo necrosis. Such tender nodules may be relieved by intensive physiotherapy with deep pressure to 'break up the nodules'. Injection of local analgesic or hydrocortisone may also be effective.

In 'tennis elbow' intense pain is felt at the elbow and radiates down the forearm. Pressure over the lateral epicondyle causes pain, as does palmar flexion of the pronated wrist. Injection of the tender area with xylocaine and hydrocortisone down to the periosteum over the epicondyle is often effective in relieving pain. Radiographs of the elbow must always be performed first, to exclude any underlying bony disease or fracture.

The complaint of painful heel is common. Tenderness is found over the heel on its plantar surface over the greater tuberosity of the calcaneum. Radiography usually shows no abnormality, though occasionally a calcaneal spur may be found projecting anteriorly. Injection of 25 mg. hydrocortisone into the painful area is often effective in relieving pain. Provision of a foam rubber pad under the heel may also be effective. Rarely is it necessary to excise a calcaneal spur.

GANGLION

A ganglion is a mucinous degeneration of fibrous tissue, probably due to trauma. It occurs adjacent to tendon sheaths and the capsules of joints. A smooth swelling arises that may be fluctuant if it is lax or so tense as to give the impression of solidity. Transillumination is positive and diagnostic, but in small ganglia it may be difficult to perform. Because the cysts are closely in relation to tendons or joints, they characteristically become more fixed with movement. Histologically, all that is seen is a mucinous jelly-like fluid enclosed within a mass of fibrous tissue. There is no specific lining, and hence no specific pathology.

The commonest sites of ganglion formation are around the wrist and on the dorsum of the foot. Small tense ganglia may be very painful, especially if they are deeply sited. They are common at the root of the finger and associated with flexor tendons.

Treatment is by excision. Lax ganglia may often be ruptured by external firm pressure, but the tendency to recurrence is high. However, the condition is innocuous, and if only 50% can be cured by rupture this is a reasonably effective method of treatment, and the remainder can be excised.

Because ganglia arise from tendon sheaths and capsules, it is imperative that when they are excised the operation is performed under general anaesthesia with a tourniquet and using full aseptic precautions in an in-patient operating theatre. Excision in a bloody field as an out-patient procedure is often followed by recurrence, and more seriously may be followed by sepsis, which could involve tendon sheaths or a joint.

Although the wrist and foot are the common sites of ganglia, they may occasionally be found wherever there is connective tissue or fascia, for example, in intermuscular septa and adjacent to joints in any part of the body.

A compound palmar ganglion is a special condition found in the hand caused by tuberculosis (or rarely rheumatoid arthritis) affecting the compound palmar bursa, and this is a form of bursitis and not a true ganglion.

NEUROLOGICAL DISORDERS

Some neurological disorders come into the field of the orthopaedic surgeon because they may be confused with skeleto-muscular diseases or because in some phases of their treatment physiotherapy or operative correction may be needed.

ANTERIOR POLIOMYELITIS

The incidence of acute anterior poliomyelitis has been greatly reduced by prophylaxis by immunisation. The use of an oral vaccine of the attenuated virus (Sabin vaccine) has been found especially effective, for the virus, which is excreted in faeces, spreads to colonise entire families, and so the oral vaccine affords a wider protection than that given by injection of the killed virus (Salk vaccine).

The virus is droplet and water borne and also carried via excreta. The incidence of infection is greater in hot, dry summers, and liability to attack seems increased after any injection, excessive exercise and possibly after such operations as tonsillectomy. For these reasons, in epidemics immunisation clinics are closed and operations for tonsillectomy are often stopped.

The virus causes an acute inflammation, with destruction of groups of anterior horn cells in the spinal cord. The cells that are destroyed cannot regenerate. The recovery that is seen in anterior poliomyelitis is due to subsidence of oedema and inflammation around surviving anterior horn cells. During the phase of active infection muscles waste away, but with recovery hypertrophy may occur of those fibres that remain innervated. Other muscles can be encouraged to take over lost function by appropriate physiotherapy.

Poliomyelitis is heralded by a febrile illness that may never progress to paralysis. It is probable that most infections in epidemics are abortive, and only a small proportion go on to cause paralysis. Other symptoms may develop, such as meningism. Muscle pain is common, with severe spasm and exquisite tenderness. Abdominal pain and rigidity may simulate an acute abdominal crisis. Acute retention of urine may develop. In the phase of paralysis the limbs are usually affected with a lower motor-neurone type of lesion. Any muscles and any number of muscles may be involved. Particularly dangerous for life is involvement of the intercostal muscles leading to respiratory paralysis. If the bulbar nerves are affected there may be respiratory paralysis, with difficulty in breathing, swallowing and speaking. In doubtful cases examination of the cerebrospinal fluid may be of help in revealing an increase in cells and protein.

Treatment

In the acute stage the patient requires first-class nursing and observation, preferably in a unit allocated to the treatment of the disease. Analgesics and immobilisation of the affected limbs by sandbags help relieve pain. As soon as the pain and spasm subside, splints must be made to prevent deformity, and expert physiotherapy is given to prevent joint stiffness. Later galvanism may help prevent wasting of muscles.

When respiration is embarrassed some mechanical assistance may be essential, often with tracheostomy through a cuffed plastic tube. A mechanical respirator and tracheostomy may be needed only temporarily, but sometimes failure of recovery condemns the subject to a lifelong existence in a respirator.

Recovery of muscle power may be expected over a period of two years. During that period, and perhaps permanently, an appliance may have to be worn, for example, a spinal support for a paralysed spine, abdominal support for paralysed abdominal muscles, leg irons to assist a paralysed knee or ankle and a toe-raising spring to control a dropped foot.

Operation may help by arthrodesis of a flail joint to allow movements at other joints to be more useful. For example, the spine, the wrist, shoulder or elbow may need to be fixed in the best position for function. Tendons of unaffected muscles can be transplanted in certain instances to replace the function of paralysed muscles, for example, pectoralis major can be used to replace biceps humeris, and a wrist flexor can be inserted into the tendons of paralysed extensor muscles.

Throughout the illness and in the phase of recovery intensive skilled physiotherapy is essential, with observation by the orthopaedic surgeon who guards against the development of contractures and deformity that may hinder recovery even though muscles regain some function.

SPASTICITY (CEREBRAL PALSY)

Now that the incidence of poliomyelitis is so low, greater interest is being shown in the treatment and rehabilitation of children affected by spasticity. In years gone by many children crippled by this disease led sheltered lives and were believed ineducable. More and more it is appreciated that many of those affected are of normal or above normal intelligence and can be helped to lead a near normal life if their physical handicaps can be alleviated and if they have the right sort of education.

Spastic children have suffered brain damage perhaps in utero or during childbirth. The cerebral cortex is injured, causing a wide variety of defects of both physical and mental development. The affected muscles are weak, but show a greater tone than normal. Movements are inco-ordinate and often choreiform and athetoid. Monoplegia, hemiplegia and diplegia may be seen, and the face may be affected.

Spastic children need physiotherapy to help them control their movements. Surgical procedures can be of assistance most often by a tendon-lengthening operation. A child may be helped to walk by lengthening of the tendo Achillis if the foot is held in an equinus position by the spasticity of calf muscles. In spastic flexion of the knees the hamstrings may be detached from the tibia and reinserted into the lower end of the femur.

NEUROFIBROMATOSIS (VON RECKLINGHAUSEN'S DISEASE)

In the most severe cases of neurofibromatosis the patient is covered by thousands of small papillomata of the skin and subcutaneous neurofibromata. Patches of pigment of variable size (café-au-lait spots) are common. Overgrowths of nerves may occur (plexiform neuroma), limbs may show asymmetry of length and bulk, a spinal kyphoscoliosis is common. All degrees of this condition are seen. It is usually familial, and the tumours appear in early childhood. Often the face is spared. The condition is usually compatible with a normal life, and only causes harm if a neurofibroma develops in a bony canal. For example, in the VIIIth nerve foramen it may cause deafness, in the optic foramen blindness, in the spinal canal paraplegia. Occasionally a highly malignant neurogenic sarcoma may develop. The disease is a malformation of mesodermal tissue characterised by the development of neurinomas or schwannomas, overgrowths of Schwann cells related to tiny nerve fibres.

The orthopaedic surgeon may be called upon to deal with asymmetry of the legs. Small differences in lengths can be compensated by raising the heel of one shoe. A considerable difference is best treated by equalising the limbs by removal of a block of bone from the longer femur. Scoliosis of the spine may be due to neurofibromas in the intervertebral foramina causing unequal growth, although the exact mechanism is still unknown. Fusion of parts of the spine may be indicated before the deformity becomes too great.

FURTHER READING

London, P. S. (1967) *Care of the Injured.* Livingstone, Edinburgh.

CHAPTER FORTY-TWO

DEFORMITIES AND AMPUTATIONS

The successful repair of a congenital deformity is one of the most rewarding tasks with which a surgeon is entrusted. Great interest in the cause of these deformities has arisen since it was discovered that some of them are caused by infection and drugs reaching the foetus during the early months of pregnancy. In 1941 Gregg in Australia reported the association of rubella during the first trimester of pregnancy with the incidence of congenital cataract and malformations of the heart in the offspring. It is only when the infection occurs during the first 3 months of pregnancy that the child is likely to be affected. More recently it was discovered that certain drugs had teratogenic properties and, when taken by the mother during early pregnancy, were capable of producing abnormalities in the foetus. The most striking of these is thalidomide, and as a result of its use a number of babies are now growing up, especially in England and Germany, with absence of limbs. Complete absence of a limb is called amelia, partial absence, phocomelia. Some deformities may be due to an abnormal position of the foetus in utero, and some follow the effects of birth trauma. Another large group of deformities is inherited, some as a dominant and others as a recessive characteristic. A good example is the familial condition of diaphyseal aclasis (see p. 491), in which many individuals of the family are found to have multiple exostoses near the ends of their long bones formed as result of faulty moulding. However, for a great many congenital abnormalities no obvious cause can be discovered.

In this chapter some common deformities will be described. Many of them are sent to the paediatric or orthopaedic surgeon for correction, and therefore may also be found mentioned in other sections of this book. Deformities of the spine will be found in Chapter Forty.

DEFORMITIES OF THE FOOT

Deformities of the feet, which are usually acquired, but occasionally congenital, are so common that they will be considered first. Many of them cause pain, and this brings the patient to the surgeon.

Hallux Valgus

This common abnormality is almost only seen in people who wear shoes; it is commoner in women than in men, and is seen with increasing frequency with advancing years. It has been attributed to a short first metatarsal which is deviated medially (metatarsus primus varus), but the wearing of shoes which taper towards the front and therefore push the toe over into the valgus position is much the most important aetiological factor.

On examination the great toe is seen to be deviated to the outer side of the foot, both phalanges being affected, while the metatarsal is adducted so that the metatarso-phalangeal joint becomes prominent. Pressure of footwear on this prominence produces a chronically inflamed overlying adventitious bursa called a bunion. The metatarso-phalangeal joint usually becomes osteoarthritic with the passage of time, and there is also frequently a crowding of the toes, and often associated hammer-toe deformity, most marked of the second toe.

Treatment consists of wearing well-constructed footwear, which should be almost straight along the inner border and thus not crowd the toes. If the bunion is painful it can be excised and the underlying osteophytic metatarsal head and phalangeal base trimmed. In severe deformities, when pain seriously interferes with walking, a more radical operation is indicated, and the most favoured is Keller's. This consists of excising the overlying bunion and the base of the first phalanx, thus performing an arthroplasty between the remainder of the phalanx and the metatarsal head. The head of the metatarsal may require shaping on its medial border. After operation the patient must wear footwear that does not press on the scar and have exercises with, if necessary, faradism to improve the function of small muscles of the foot.

Hallux Rigidus

In this condition the first phalanx is flexed on the metatarsal of the great toe. There is osteoarthritis of the metatarso-phalangeal joint and pain. It may be the result of an old injury, inflammation or more rarely a congenital flexural deformity. Young people are often affected. The disability produced by minor degrees of this condition is relieved by raising the metatarsal heads with an insole which is fitted into the shoe or boot. More severe degrees require Keller's operation as described above or fusion of the joint.

Hammer Toe

This common abnormality is often painless, but painful callosities may develop due to the pressure of shoes. The cause is almost certainly ill-fitting footwear, and it commonly complicates all kinds of foot abnormalities as a secondary development. The first phalanx is hyperextended and the second and third flexed so that the proximal interphalangeal joint is directed upwards like an inverted V.

Pain is due to the callosities or corns which form over the prominent proximal interphalangeal joint. When the pain is severe the head of the first phalanx is excised and arthrodesed with the base of the second, which is trimmed to receive it.

Overlapping fifth Toe

The little toe may be so adducted that it overlaps the adjoining ones and becomes an embarrassment to its owner, it may also be painful on account of the pressure of the shoe upon it in this unnatural position. The cause in most cases is ill-fitting footwear associated with poor tone in the intrinsic muscles of the foot. Treatment in an adult is excision of the toe, which is a minor operation and cosmetically most acceptable. Occasionally in children and young adults the deformity may be corrected by division of the capsule of the joint and straightening of the toe by a plastic operation in the skin, a so-called V–Y plasty, in which the skin is incised with a V-shaped incision and sewn up like a Y.

Pes Planus

Flat foot is a normal finding in most infants and young children and also those adults who have never worn footwear, but in these adults the foot is strong, supple and symptom-free, and certainly does not call for any kind of treatment. However, it is not normal to see a foot which is painful and flat in someone accustomed to wearing shoes. It is to this condition to which the term flat foot can be applied in terms of surgical treatment.

The causes of flat foot are many. Typically it is seen in someone who has been confined to bed for an illness, and on starting to walk again finds that the feet are painful and that the normal longitudinal arch has been lost. In this case, as in so many others, the main trouble is loss of tone in the intrinsic muscles of the foot, and treatment therefore consists of improving the quality of the interossei and lumbricals. Simple exercises, such as picking up a pencil or fountain-pen cap from the floor with the toes, can be practised and faradic stimulation given to the muscles. They must not be allowed to become overtired, and some help can be provided by a resilient pad in the shoe placed just proximal to the heads of the metatarsals, the so-called insole metatarsal bar. Flat foot may also follow acute foot strain if it is not treated by proper rest and gradual return to exercise, this is especially so in young adults. It is also seen as a result of inflammation and as in the rare example of gonococcal fasciitis. Fractures of any of the bones of the foot may be complicated by pes planus, this is especially so with fractures of the os calcis. Spasm of the muscles in the peroneal compartment of the leg can pull the foot into abduction and cause severe painful flat feet, especially in children. Spastic flat foot is usually associated with arthritis of the talo-navicular joint.

The treatment of flat foot depends on the cause. If it is symptomless nothing need be done. If the onset is acute and there is much pain rest will be important, together with graduated exercises to the intrinsic muscles and occasionally some kind of metatarsal support such as an insole. With the severe untreated flat foot which is occasionally seen in adults, manipulation under an anaesthetic and fixation in a walking plaster is occasionally of help, but more radical treatment, such as arthrodesis of the small tarsal bones, especially the subastragaloid joint, is usually the only way to relieve the pain in cases with severe disability.

Pes Cavus

In this condition, which is sometimes called claw foot the longitudinal arch of the foot is exaggerated. The high arch is associated with a dropping of the forefoot, tightness of the dorsal extensor tendons and clawing of the toes. In most people the deformity is mobile and easily corrected by pressure on the ball of the great toe, thus raising the forefoot. It is almost always a congenital condition, and is often seen in association with conditions such as spina bifida. It may be acquired as a complication of poliomyelitis and Friedreich's ataxia. Most of the trouble with pes cavus stems from the difficulty of obtaining suitable good-fitting footwear, and this often has to be specially made. Usually there are no symptoms unless excessive exercises are undertaken or if boots have to be worn. Pes cavus is a common cause of disability in service recruits.

Treatment of pes cavus of a severe degree in children consists of lengthening the plantar fascia by a subcutaneous fasciotomy, followed by a vigorous stretching of it. Steindler's operation may be performed for severe cases, in this all the soft tissue, including fascia and muscle, is detached from the lower surface of the calcaneum, the deformity of the foot is corrected and maintained in plaster of Paris. In older patients very little can be done except for symptomatic treatment and the making of suitable shoes to fit the deformity. In severe cases triple arthrodesis is performed.

Metatarsalgia

Acute pain under the heads of the metatarsal bones, which the patient may describe as feeling like a stone in the shoe, is usually seen after middle age and is commoner in women. In most it is due to flattening of the transverse arch so that the metatarsal heads protrude abnormally into the sole. It can sometimes be traced to a neuroma developing on a digital nerve, possibly due to pressure from the heads of the adjoining metatarsals. Division of the nerve and excision of the neuroma may rarely be necessary to relieve the pain. Treatment must include measures to increase the tone in the small muscles of the foot and support by an insole that excludes further changes from the pressure of the metatarsal heads.

Club Foot

Talipes, by long usage, has come to mean club foot, but the origin of the word talipes from the Latin (*talus* an ankle and *pes, pedis*, a foot) indicates that it should always be qualified by a description of the deformity present. Thus, in talipes equino-varus, which is the commonest form of club foot seen, the sole faces medially and the foot is plantar flexed. Equinus means like a horse, because the patient walks on the tips of the toes, the tendo Achillis being short. The different varieties of club foot are defined as follows:

Talipes Calcaneo Valgus. The ankle is dorsi-flexed so that the patient walks on the heel. The foot is abducted at the midtarsal joint and the sole faces laterally, so that the patient walks on the inner side of the foot.

Talipes Equinus. The ankle is plantar flexed and the patient walks on the toes like a horse.

Talipes Varus. The foot is adducted at the midtarsal joint so that the sole faces medially and the patient walks on the outer side of the foot.

Combinations of the above are usually seen, the commonest being talipes equino-varus and talipes calcaneo-valgus.

Talipes Equino-varus

This is usually seen as a congenital abnormality, and is often associated with other failures of development, such as hare-lip and spina bifida. Depending on the severity of the lesion, manipulation will partly or completely correct it and, being painless, no anaesthetic is necessary. Treatment therefore begins immediately after birth, the foot being manipulated outwards and upwards and held in an over-corrected position with adhesive strapping on Denis Browne's metal splints. These are changed at 2- or 3-weekly intervals until the deformity is completely corrected, usually before 6 months of age. If there is any tendency for relapse a night splint can be worn after this age. If correction fails in the young, an operation is carried out in the soft tissues allowing remoulding of the foot (Brockman's operation).

On those rare occasions when the child is not seen until after 10 years of age and in those adults in whom the condition is acquired, usually because of poliomyelitis paralysing the extensor and peroneal muscles, treatment by manipulation under a general anaesthetic may be tried, followed by immobilisation in plaster of Paris. In most older patients, however, operative intervention is necessary, and this consists of elongation of the tendo Achillis and wedge resection of the tarsal bones, followed by triple arthrodesis of the talo-calcaneal, talo-navicular and calcaneocuboid joints.

Talipes Calcaneus

This is usually congenital, but may follow poliomyelitis affecting the calf muscles, or it may be due to trauma. If the lesion is congenital, manipulation and splinting will allow the toes to reach the ground. In those patients in whom the calf muscles are paralysed, grafting the peroneus longus tendon into the tendo Achillis may give it enough strength to hold up the heel. Shortening the tendo Achillis may be adequate if the calf muscles have been stretched as a result of trauma.

In adult club foot it is usually easy to distinguish between those which are congenital and those that are due to paralysis, since in the latter the limb is blue, cold and feels flabby, and the acquired condition is seldom bilateral.

DEFORMITIES AROUND THE KNEE JOINT

Knock knee and bow legs are common conditions for which parents bring their children to the surgeon. Fortunately, many of these abnormalities improve spontaneously with the passage of time; a few are severe. They may also develop in adult life, often as a result of faulty posture or injury.

Genu Valgum

Many children develop knock knee for no apparent cause. In Britain rickets used to be the common aetiological factor, but is rare today. On examination it will usually be seen that more than one deformity is present: the lower end of the femur bends laterally, the upper end of the tibia bends inwards and the inner condyle at the lower end of the femur may appear too large. The patella is displaced towards the outer side of the knee. If the patient is told to stand up with the knees just touching the degree of genu valgum can be measured by using a tape measure between the internal malleoli at the ankle. The condition is commoner in girls than boys, and is occasionally associated with scoliosis or some other abnormality.

Treatment is not called for if there is not much deformity, and the parents should be reassured that it will correct itself spontaneously. Wedges (0·5–1·0 cm.) can be placed under the inner side of the sole and heel of the shoe to release the strain on the inner side of the leg. Previously knock knee splints and irons were worn to attempt to correct deformity. These are not used now. If the deformity is gross, stapling of the inner side of the lower femoral and upper tibial epiphyses is performed to inhibit growth at the age of eleven or twelve years.

Genu Varum

Bow legs also used to be a complication of rickets. Usually it is difficult to find any cause in children, and the condition frequently corrects itself. A wedge-shaped addition of leather (1–2 cm.) may be put along the outer side of the sole and heel of the shoes. If an extreme deformity is present osteotomy of the tibia can be done to correct it.

Bow legs can develop as an acquired deformity in people who do much horse-back riding, and they appear to suffer no disability from this.

Genu Recurvatum

This is not a common abnormality. Laxity of the knee joint that allows a severe degree of hyperextension of the joint is usually congenital. Occasionally this abnormality follows an attack of poliomyelitis in which the flexors of the knee joint are weakened. The unopposed pull of the quadriceps subsequently results in hyperextension of the knee joint. A rupture of the anterior cruciate ligament permits genu recurvatum. Patients are rarely disabled by genu recurvatum, and operative treatment is therefore seldom needed.

Short Leg

Careful measurements often reveal small discrepancies in the length of the two legs, but occasionally one leg is found to be considerably shorter than the other as the result of a congenital abnormality. This is either due to lack of development of one of the long bones, femur or tibia or both; more rarely there is general hypoplasia of the whole limb or of one half of the body. Operations for lengthening limbs are only successful in very special circumstances, and are not generally applicable. However, raising a boot with a light cork sole will often compensate for the shortness and allow the individual to walk normally. In gross examples of disparity of length it is justifiable to consider shortening of the longer limb in young adults or epiphyseodesis in children before growth has stopped. A segment of the femur is usually removed.

ABNORMALITIES OF THE UPPER LIMB

Deformities of the fingers and hands are dealt with in the chapter on the Hand, only the wrist, elbow and shoulder are considered here.

Cubitus Valgus

If the arm is stretched out it will be seen that the forearm is a little abducted and that the angle at the elbow is about 10 degrees in men and 15 degrees in women; this is called the carrying angle. If the abduction is exaggerated the condition is called cubitus valgus. It may be congenital, but is much more frequently due to injury to the outer part of the lower epiphysis of the humerus. This often accompanies fractures of the external condyle in children, and as a result the valgus deformity increases as the years pass. Abduction at the elbow leads to stretching of the ulnar nerve where it passes behind the medial epicondyle, causing neuritis and a gradual paralysis of the intrinsic muscles of the hand. Treatment consists of transplanting the ulnar nerve to the front of the medial condyle. If the bony deformity is gross an osteotomy of the humerus can be performed in young adults to straighten it and prevent the possibility of ulnar neuritis.

Cubitus Varus

It is rare to see the forearm adducted on the arm. It is always the result of a fracture, usually a supracondylar fracture in childhood, which has united in a poor position. This deformity in no way interferes with the ulnar nerve, but if it is very insightly it can be corrected by an osteotomy of the lower end of the humerus.

Madelung's Deformity

In this condition the lower end of the ulna is very prominent, and because the ulna is longer than usual the carpus is displaced to the radial side. The condition may be inherited when it can be bilateral, but more often is the result of trauma to the lower end of the radius, which by damaging the epiphysis causes an arrest of normal growth. Despite the prominent lower end of the ulna, there is little disability, and the treatment is unnecessary. Occasionally in young persons it is justifiable to resect the lower end of the ulna and so prevent dislocation of the wrist.

Sprengel's Shoulder

Congenital elevation of the shoulder may be familial. The scapula is much smaller than on the opposite side and is situated at a higher level. The scapula is rotated towards the midline, especially at its lower pole, and there may be some restriction of shoulder movement. The abnormality is only noticeable when the patient is seen from behind, and if it is bilateral can be mistaken for a short neck. No treatment is necessary for a Sprengel's shoulder, and it is surprising how slight is the disability.

AMPUTATIONS

An amputation performed as an emergency for example after injury, can be a life-saving operation, and the decision to do it is usually not a difficult one. However, when an amputation is planned as an elective operation the decision may be indeed difficult and the surgeon well advised whenever possible to obtain a second opinion. The commonest indication for leg amputation is atherosclerotic gangrene. Skilful management postoperatively is essential if a good stump is to be obtained, and this will include firm bandaging with crêpe and elastic bandages and early physiotherapy designed to build up tone in the muscles. Amputees have special problems related to their return to work and a useful place in society, which are best catered for from an early date by the medical social worker (almoner). If a prosthesis is to be fitted, especially if it is for a lower limb, the limb fitter should be consulted as early as possible and the stump fashioned in collaboration with him. The after care of the amputee, which must of necessity be for life, is extremely important if complications are to be avoided or treated early and a prosthesis kept in good working order.

Great Britain provides a better service for amputees than any other country in the world, partly because the National Health Service ensures everyone having full access to free medical care and partly because of the provision of a national limb-fitting service with adjoining hospital facilities and workshops where limbs are made and can be serviced. Regional centres for fitting and service exist throughout the country. The immense advantages of such centralisation of effort have only one drawback a rather rigid standardisation of techniques and limb patterns, so that there is a tendency to mould the patient to the limb rather than the reverse.

Thus prostheses for Symes' and Gritti–Stokes amputations had been successfully fitted in Canada and the U.S.A. long before being accepted in Britain. On the other hand, the standard artificial leg made in Britain is unexcelled.

LOWER LIMB

Symes' Amputation

This is suitable when the part of the foot to be sacrificed permits the retention of a heel flap. The resulting stump is end-bearing, function is good, and the amputee can walk without a prosthesis in his own home. The prosthesis is a moulded plastic socket which is cosmetically acceptable as well as offering almost normal walking. Pulsatile arteries must be palpable at the ankle for the success of this amputation.

Below-knee Amputations

The optimum length of stump is 12–18 cm. measured from the line of the knee joint. As short a stump as 5 cm. can be fitted with a prosthesis with difficulty, but still is much preferable to anything that can be done with an above-knee amputation.

The prosthesis distributes the weight on the patellar tendon and each side of the tibia, but sore places often occur, and the stump shrinks for at least 6–9 months after operation. A suction socket is often preferable for this kind of prosthesis. Function is usually excellent, and bilateral below-knee amputees may even be able to walk without the help of a stick.

Above-knee Amputations

It is unusual to be able to perform disarticulation of the knee joint except after injury, but when this is possible the bulbous stump gives good end-bearing for a prosthesis. If the limb is amputated through the thigh—the longer the stump, the better the function in most cases. Occasionally a stump as short as 10 cm. can be fitted, but this is the limit of usefulness, and a short flabby stump requires a metal hip joint, pelvic band and shoulder strap.

A Gritti–Stokes' amputation is one in which the patella is attached to the end of the femur after it has been transected above the condyles. This is popular when amputation is dictated by arterial insufficiency and gives good function. The end-bearing stump so provided makes for good control because the extensor muscles remain attached to the patella and the hamstring muscles can be sutured to it. Proprioceptive function is preserved and the patient is more aware of his stump than if an above knee amputation had been performed.

Hip Disarticulation and Hindquarter Amputation

Most of these patients are happiest with crutches. If the patient is young, active and slim it is possible to fit an artificial limb using some sort of tilting table, waist band and shoulder strap.

UPPER LIMB

Wrist Disarticulation and Below-elbow Amputation

This is easily fitted with an artificial hand or hook by means of a socket into which the forearm fits. No device can ever replace the patient's own hand in usefulness, and even a single digit is worth preserving.

Elbow Disarticulation and Above-elbow Amputation

A similar prosthesis to the above is attached to an upper arm socket through a hinged elbow joint with a locking device. A sling or band goes across to the other shoulder. When a forequarter amputation has been done a light prosthesis is provided solely for cosmetic reasons.

Cineplastic prostheses are at present being actively developed in many countries, especially the U.S.S.R. and Great Britain. They consist of complicated mechanical devices, usually powered by compressed gas or electricity, which can be operated by the amputee using muscle groups which have survived the amputation. At the present time they are mostly in the experimental stage, but it seems likely that they may come into general use in the near future.

Postoperative Complications

The ideal stump is cylindrical in shape and free of tenderness and pain. Haematoma and sepsis may cause sloughing of skin flaps and even exposure of the end of the bone. Osteomyelitis of the bone may cause a sinus only cured by removal or discharge of sequestrum. Haematoma is avoided by drainage and sepsis by antibiotics. Oedema and tenderness of the stump is treated by firm bandages applied twice a day. Joint movements must be actively encouraged or contracture and stiffness may occur. A flexion contracture at the hip or knee joint is a serious handicap in walking on an artificial limb.

A painful stump or a painful phantom limb is common. Most painful stumps become pain free or tolerably so in time so drastic procedures are to be avoided. Injection of tender and painful areas with lignocaine, hydrocortisone and hyalase may be effective for a time. Rhythmic percussion of tender neuromata by a rubber covered hammer may help. Spraying the area with a volatile cooling fluid may suppress pain for some hours. Rarely paravertebral sympathetic block, sympathectomy or even cordotomy may be indicated.

FURTHER READING

Gillis, L. (1954) *Amputations*. E. S. Livingstone, Edinburgh.
Gillis, L. (1957) *Artificial Limbs*. Pitman Medical, London.

CHAPTER FORTY-THREE

THE NERVOUS SYSTEM

HEAD INJURIES

Head injuries are a common problem in surgery and likely to be commoner in the future with the increasing incidence of motor-car accidents. It has been estimated that more than one in every thousand of the population is admitted to hospital each year because of a head injury. Three-quarters of these head injuries are due to road-traffic accidents.

TYPE OF INJURY

The scalp may be lacerated and the skull severely fractured without injury to the brain. Severe brain damage may occur, however, without any obvious evidence of injury to overlying structures. Most head injuries in civil life are *dynamic*, usually due to the head striking a flat surface such as the road. The amount of damage to the brain is due to the acceleration or deceleration of the head at the moment of impact because the brain shows inertia relative to the skull, setting up shearing stresses that cause contusion, especially during rapid deceleration. A *closed* injury may be associated with little or no outward evidence of damage to the head, but severe concussion and coma is much more likely when the cranium is closed. *Static* injuries are not common. The skull may be so slowly compressed that there may be no loss of consciousness although the cranial bones are widely fractured. *Penetrating* injuries of the skull and brain are commoner in wartime; in these the damage to the brain is often so localised as not to impair consciousness.

WOUNDS OF THE SCALP

Wounds of the scalp are often serious, first because severe external bleeding may occur; such bleeding can usually be controlled by firm pressure. Secondly, a scalp wound is a portal for infection that can result in osteomyelitis of the skull, extradural abscess or even cerebral abscess or meningitis.

The skin around any scalp wound should be shaved to prevent sepsis from hair and hair follicles, to make suturing easier and the subsequent dressings more convenient. All foreign material should be removed, and devitalised tissue at the edges of the laceration excised. Tetanus immunisation must not be forgotten. If there is extensive skin loss plastic methods of repair may be necessary, especially where the scalp has been avulsed by

T

the hair being caught in a machine. The skull must be radiographed in any case of scalp wounds.

FRACTURES OF THE SKULL

Most fractures of the skull are closed, simple linear cracks or fissures which by themselves are unimportant both for treatment and in subsequent prognosis. It is the complications associated with linear fractures that are so important.

1. Haemorrhage, particularly when a fracture crosses branches of the middle meningeal artery leading to extradural haemorrhage, commonly in the temporal region.

2. Dural sinus thrombosis—a fracture crossing the sagittal sinus may cause thrombosis of the sinus leading to swelling of the brain.

3. Infection—compound fractures of the skull may open externally due to laceration of the scalp or internally, with resultant leakage of cerebrospinal fluid from the nose or ear leading to such complications as aerocoele (a pocket of air in the brain) or meningitis.

4. Damage to structures traversing the skull. The middle and inner ear, the facial and other cranial nerves may suffer damage, sometimes complete and sometimes irrecoverable.

Linear cracks in the skull are common. Gross displacement is much less often seen in which fragments of skull are depressed and tilted and may penetrate the dura and wound the underlying brain.

BRAIN INJURY

Brain damage is due to the injury and also to the effects of secondary changes such as oedema, haemorrhage and vascular thrombosis; some of which changes are preventable. It is important to assess the extent of the primary damage as soon as the patient is seen, so that secondary changes can be recognised when they occur.

The most important observation in the care of a case of head injury is the *level of consciousness* which is described under the following terms:

1. *Lucidity*
2. *Confusion*
   The patient responds to commands, but shows a variable degree of confusion; there is disorientation in time and space.
3. *Semicoma*
   The patient only responds to painful stimuli.
4. *Coma*
   The patient does not respond to any stimulus, and all reflexes are absent. On recovery of consciousness there is loss of memory for events that followed the injury for a period which varies in duration according

to the degree of trauma, this is called post-traumatic amnesia. There is also usually a loss of memory for events immediately preceding the injury, called retrograde amnesia, which may be only momentary or last for hours or even days. The duration of pre- and post-traumatic amnesia gives some indication of the severity of damage to the brain.

CONCUSSION

In this condition there is loss of consciousness for a limited period. Because, by definition, recovery is complete there is no possibility of discovering any pathological lesion. The mechanism is unknown, but the site of disturbance may well be in the brain stem. The term concussion was originally used to describe the brief stunning effect of a mild injury, but it is now thought that even this is accompanied by some degree of neuronal damage. Probably the difference between slight and severe brain injuries is quantitative rather than qualitative.

CONFUSION AND CEREBRAL IRRITATION

Confusion results from a more severe injury than that producing concussion. Microscopically changes are seen in the brain, such as haemorrhage at the site of the injury or under the pia or dura mater; there may also be small haemorrhages in the substance of the brain. The result is that unconsciousness is more prolonged and there may be local effects, such as weakness of one limb or of one side of the face and changes in speech. Since most injuries of the brain are due to shearing stresses, it is possible for most of the damage to occur in the brain on the opposite side to that of the injury, the so-called contre-coup injury.

When consciousness returns the patient often shows evidence of *cerebral irritation*, a clinical rather than a pathological conception. It is a state in which the patient shows mental irritability and resentment whenever aroused, and it is often accompanied by a severe headache. The patient, if left undisturbed, lies curled up in a position of general flexion and, because of photophobia, turns away from the light. The pulse rate is slow and of good volume. Respiration is quiet and regular.

RAISED INTRACRANIAL PRESSURE

Raised intracranial pressure after head injury may be caused by bleeding within the cavity or oedema of the brain.

Symptoms and Signs

Rising intracranial pressure is due to secondary complications of injury to the brain that may be fatal but are often remediable. Accumulating massive haemorrhage (extradural, subdural, subarachnoid or intracerebral), oedema the result of contusion of the brain and cortical laceration are the common complications causing relapse into coma.

There is a deterioration in the patient's clinical state from that recorde immediately after the accident. Thus, if the patient has been lucid afte only a momentary concussion one may expect increasingly severe heac ache, perhaps with vomiting and eventually clouding of consciousnes: If the patient has initially suffered a more severe injury and has been in state of semi-coma, then the evidence of deterioration may be moi difficult to detect. Here the signs may be increasing restlessness, a failui to respond as briskly to painful stimuli as before or the onset of unilater; or bilateral decerebrate attacks with painful stimulation. When a lat stage of cerebral displacement is reached the pupil on one side and late on both sides will become dilated and fail to react to light. At this tim respiration is usually laboured and noisy and the pulse fast. In any patier whose conscious level is deteriorating a dilating pupil is a sign for urger surgical treatment.

MANAGEMENT OF HEAD INJURIES

Although most head injuries are mild and their effects transitory, it : important that anyone who has been unconscious, no matter how briefl should be thoroughly examined neurologically, and have good radic graphs of the skull. *All those with a history of loss of consciousness, exter sive scalp lacerations or fractures of the skull should be admitted to hospit: for a period of observation*, of at least 24 hours, for fear of the develoj ment of intracranial haemorrhage. This also applies to the intoxicated (the man who is confused and smells of drink, as the course of the coi fusion may be cerebral rather than alcoholic. Witnesses or relatives shoul be closely questioned about the incident. Important questions are th duration of unconsciousness, what happened in the accident, the volun of blood lost, alcohol intake and any previous medical history.

In the observation of a patient who has suffered a head injury *the mo. important neurological assessment is the level of consciousness.* The trea ment of a patient who has been briefly unconscious and shows a fairl rapid return to normality should consist of rest in bed until the mai symptoms have subsided. Repeated neurological examinations in the earl stages are essential to exclude further complications. Fluids and a ligh diet are started as soon as the patient is able to take them. The patient i allowed out of bed as soon as there is no complaint of headache or dizz ness and after 24 hours allowed to go home. Should the headache recui then bed rest must be resumed.

In cases of coma it is often difficult to know if the patient fell due t some cause such as a stroke, fit or blackout and suffered injury, or wheth trauma was the cause of coma. The initial problem is then one of diffe ential diagnosis. Causes of unconsciousness must be considered, such a epilepsy, diabetic coma and hypoglycaemia, cerebro-vascular accident and poisoning due to alcohol or drugs.

The patient who is admitted in coma is carefully examined general nd neurologically. The head is inspected and palpated for bruising and, f there is an open wound, signs of exuding brain tissue. The ears and nose are examined for blood and cerebrospinal fluid.

Injuries are frequently multiple, and therefore examination should be made of the rest of the body. Loss of blood causes shock, chest injuries may need urgent attention, and visceral injuries in the abdomen must not be overlooked. Bowel, liver, spleen and bladder may be damaged. Brain damage may cause spasticity of both the lower extremities, whereas a spinal injury will more usually result in flaccid paralysis of the legs. Injuries to the cervical spine are easily missed unless looked for and the appropriate radiographs taken.

The level of unconsciousness must be assessed and recorded accurately. The pupils should be examined for size and reaction to light. If the pupils were equal in size and reacted to light after the injury, but one is later found larger, intracranial haemorrhage should be suspected. When both pupils are dilated and fixed soon after the injury severe damage to the brain is likely and a fatal outcome. Fixed pupils of pinpoint size suggest injury to the brain stem, but can be the effect of morphine misguidedly given. Other signs which will help in assessing the site and extent of the injury are hemiparesis, facial nerve palsy, deafness, blindness or visual-field defect and epilepsy. Papilloedema is important evidence of raised intracranial pressure. Decerebrate rigidity is a sign of severe brain-stem injury and is often coupled with pinpoint pupils and hyperpyrexia.

In the ward the level of consciousness, pulse, temperature, respiration and blood pressure are assessed and charted by the nurses. These records provide a base line for comparison if deterioration occurs later. The patient is wakened frequently to make sure that the level of consciousness is not deteriorating, the time interval between wakening depends upon the severity of the injury, often it may be as frequent as every fifteen minutes. The size of the pupils is recorded frequently. Clear instructions are left that the house surgeon must be called urgently if there is any sign of *deterioration in the level of consciousness or if the pulse, respiratory rate or blood pressure varies significantly*—possible signs of a raised intracranial pressure. Lumbar puncture is rarely of value, and should only be performed after consultation with the neurologist or neurosurgeon, as there is a danger that it may cause 'coning' in the presence of a raised intracranial pressure that forces the brain stem down to plug the foramen magnum and cause death. Its only real value is to establish a diagnosis of meningitis where there is neck stiffness or fever in association with external leakage of cerebrospinal fluid.

The first priority in a case of coma from any cause must be to maintain a clear airway. The head should be turned to one side and, if necessary, the patient is laid three-quarters prone, allowing blood and vomit to come out of the mouth freely. A sucker must be available to remove secretions and blood. If coma is deep and the cough reflex absent or impaired a tracheostomy should be performed, the tube to be inserted being made of

plastic and provided with an inflatable cuff to prevent inhalation o
secretions and blood. It is extremely important that the patient has a goo
airway, for most patients who die after a head injury die of pneumoni
from aspiration of vomit or blood. The patient's skull is radiographed o
the way to the ward, where careful regular observation is carried out.

The care of patients who are in prolonged coma requires skilled atten
tion to many points of detail if recovery is to be aided and complication
avoided, Most patients who have head injuries are incontinent of urine
catheterisation is rarely necessary, and indeed is dangerous because of it
complications. Occasionally it is necessary to catheterise a patient wh
becomes restless or even violent while comatose or semi-comatose due t
a distended bladder. Before full consciousness is regained it may b
necessary to give fluids and a fluid diet through an indwelling gastric tube
It may also be necessary to set up an intravenous infusion, especially t
replace blood loss. A careful fluid balance chart is kept. Where coma i
prolonged a diet providing 2,000 calories per day is given by gastric tube
Skilful nursing is essential, and the patient has to be turned repeatedl
and nursed on a ripple bed to prevent pressure sores. The physiotherapis
treats the patient, giving chest percussion and passive movements of th
limbs through a full range to prevent contractures. Hyperpyrexia i
treated by leaving the patient covered only by a sheet, with perhaps a
electric fan if the environmental temperature is high, but the patient shoul
not be exposed to the point of shivering. Intramuscular injection o
chlorpromazine may be useful in depressing body temperature an
metabolism. Often the brain damage is so severe that the patient remain
in deep coma until he dies—perhaps months later. Occasionally, especi
ally in children, a remarkable degree of recovery occurs.

EXTRADURAL HAEMORRHAGE

An extradural haematoma is a dreaded, though fortunately rare, com
plication of a head injury. It is usually due to a torn middle meningea
artery, but there are other possible sites of haemorrhage, for example
tearing of venous sinuses or cerebral veins where they enter venous sinuses

Symptoms and Signs

Sometimes a trivial injury may be followed by this complication. Mos
patients show a fracture in the temporal region. Haemorrhage often cause
death, because the patient may regain consciousness and be sent home
only to lapse into coma after an interval of minutes, hours or days—luci
interval. If he is intoxicated at the time of injury his stuporose conditio
may be mistaken for drunkenness, and it is not uncommon for such
person to be taken away by the police and to be found dead next day in
cell. Drunkenness must be regarded as poisoning and be an indicatio
for admission and observation.

Restlessness and headache may be complained of first, followed b dilatation of the pupil on the side of the injury. The diagnosis must be suspected and operation undertaken while the conscious level is deteriorating. By the time a fixed dilated pupil is observed, operation is usually too late. The urgency of operation varies with the rate of deterioration. If it is rapid, then operation is urgently required. If the deterioration is slow, for example, over several days, then there may be time for carotid angiography. The pulse rate usually slows and the blood pressure may rise, the respirations become deep and stertorous. If the haemorrhage continues Cheyne–Stokes type of breathing may occur, the patient becomes deeply unconscious and dies. There may, however, be no lucid interval, and deep coma may develop directly after a severe injury without the patient ever regaining consciousness.

Treatment

Urgent operation is necessary if the patient's life is to be saved. Important information lateralising the haemorrhage is given by the site of fracture, puffiness and tenderness over the fracture and a dilated pupil on the side of haemorrhage. A carotid angiogram may show vessels displaced by a space-occupying lesion. A burr hole is made through the skull in the temporal fossa on the side on which it is believed that the vessel is bleeding. Clot is evacuated and the bleeding vessels sealed with diathermy or by a metal clip or plugging the foramen spinosum with bone wax. If no haematoma is found a burr hole is made on the opposite side of the skull, since the injury may be contre-coup.

SUBDURAL HAEMATOMA

A subdural haematoma usually results from tearing of veins which connect the cerebral cortical vessels to the sagittal, transverse or sphenoparietal venous sinuses. Rarely the bleeding is acute, more usually it is chronic, and therefore the interval between injury and the resulting symptoms and signs can be spread over days or weeks.

Symptoms and Signs

An *acute subdural haemorrhage* will result in the patient never regaining consciousness after an injury. Such haemorrhages are usually rapidly fatal. In the more *chronic subdural haematoma* there may be no definite history of an injury. The patient will probably be over 50 years of age, complaining of headache and often symptoms of mental deterioration, which may be wrongly diagnosed as due to cerebrovascular disease or senile dementia. Drowsiness, apathy and even confusion follow, and there may be some dysphasia. The deterioration in the patient's condition makes it difficult for him to give any account of himself. A history of injury must be sought, however trivial, for some weeks previous to the onset of such symptoms. There may be no pupillary changes, but papilloedema may be seen.

Cerebral angiography is the best form of investigation, since it shows the site and the extent of the clot.

Treatment

Subdural haematoma is treated by making burr holes, usually over the parietal eminences, through which the blood clot may be removed by irrigation with saline after incision of the dura. The clotted blood may be difficult to remove, and sometimes the brain does not readily expand to fill the dead space unless an osteoplastic flap is turned. Subdural haematoma is commonly seen in infants as a result of birth injury, but fortunately it can be treated by 'subdural taps', that is the repeated use of aspiration through a sharp needle inserted through the outer angle of the fontanelle to evacuate the blood and clot.

SPONTANEOUS INTRACRANIAL HAEMORRHAGE

Two of the commonest conditions causing spontaneous intracranial haemorrhage which have surgical importance are congenital saccular aneurysms of the Circle of Willis and arteriovenous malformations of the brain.

Sudden and frequently fatal cerebral haemorrhage may occur from rupture of a congenital aneurysm of the cerebral vessels or from arteriovenous malformations. Aneurysms usually occur on the circle of Willis, and are most often of a saccular form; fusiform aneurysms are usually atherosclerotic and rarely bleed. Bleeding may occur at any age. Haemorrhage usually presents as a sudden and blinding headache, together with vomiting. Loss of consciousness may or may not occur. Neurological deficits may or may not be present, depending on the situation of the aneurysm and whether there is any accompanying vascular spasm or intracerebral haematoma. Blood in the subarachnoid space causes cerebral irritation with meningism, painful neck rigidity and a positive Kernig's sign. Lumbar puncture is essential for diagnosis. The C.S.F. is found mixed with blood. After a few hours the supernatant fluid of a centrifuged specimen is coloured yellow, an important diagnostic point in differentiating bleeding from a traumatic lumbar puncture from intracranial haemorrhage. Angiography is necessary to demonstrate the site of the aneurysm and in the first place is usually a study of both internal carotid arteries, as 85% of aneurysms lie on the anterior half of the Circle of Willis; 15% of aneurysms are multiple.

The treatment of an aneurysm is aimed at preventing further haemorrhage, and should be carried out as soon as the patient has recovered from bleeding. The basis of treatment is either to divert the arterial stream from the aneurysmal neck or to obliterate the sac. The operation may be ligation of the common carotid artery in the neck or an intracranial operation, the choice depending on the site of the aneurysm. Should the aneurysm be in a suitable position, it may be exposed, the neck of the sac clipped off or bleeding vessels coagulated or ligatured. Application of a graft of muscle to the wall of the aneurysm may be used.

Arteriovenous malformations are a less frequent cause of intracranial haemorrhage or epilepsy. With haemorrhage there is frequently an intra-cerebral haematoma, which may cause a contralateral hemiparesis. The ideal treatment is excision of the fistulae with ligation of the feeding arteries, if that is possible. Many malformations are at present inoperable because of their size and complexity or their strategic situation in the brain.

INFLAMMATORY CONDITIONS

Cerebral Abscess

More than 50% of cerebral abscesses result from the extension of in-flammation from the middle ear. The temporo-parietal area of the cerebrum or the cerebellum is usually affected. Infection of the brain may also complicate frontal, sphenoidal and ethmoidal sinusitis. Although the spread may be by direct continuity, more commonly it is by way of vessels, and so the abscess is sited within the brain substance separated from the original source of infection by an apparently healthy layer of brain tissue and membranes.

Another cause of brain abscess is septic thrombosis of the intracranial venous sinuses, the lateral sinus may thrombose secondary to middle-ear infection and the cavernous sinus secondary to infection on the face. A brain abscess may follow open fractures or penetrating wounds of the skull, especially around foreign bodies or from infected and inadequately treated scalp wounds. Abscesses may arise as a result of infection spread by the blood stream, particularly in pyaemia. The source of the infected emboli may be bronchiectasis, lung abscess, empyema, osteomyelitis and septic endocarditis, but in these days of antibiotics such causes are quite rare. Some types of congenital heart disease are particularly prone to present with cerebral abscess, e.g. atrial septal defect.

At first there is an acute encephalitis around the focus of infection with marked local oedema, one of the causes of raised intracranial pressure. Usually in 3-4 weeks a more chronic abscess is formed with a tough wall due to peripheral gliosis. Typically the abscess is single, but occasionally there may be several. Sometimes the abscess cavity is loculated, and this may present difficulties in its efficient drainage during treatment.

Symptoms and Signs

The early features are toxaemia and fever, often with focal signs indi-cating a cerebral lesion. With progress the abscess becomes localised and the toxaemia less. The picture is then more of a focal cerebral lesion of rapid onset, with headache, vomiting and drowsiness. The localising neurological signs will depend on the site of the abscess. It is important to note that a diagnosis of cerebral abscess does not require the presence of fever. If the abscess is in the temporal lobe there may be weakness of the opposite side of the face, if it is in the left hemisphere there may be dysphasia in a right-handed person. With cerebellar abscesses there may be giddiness, nystagmus and ataxia. A frontal lobe abscess may produce no localising signs at all. Usually in temporal or cerebellar abscess there is a previous history of middle-ear disease.

Lumbar puncture is useful in the diagnosis of cerebral abscess. The pressure of the cerebrospinal fluid may be raised, and great care must be taken in withdrawing fluid slowly to minimise the risk of a 'pressure cone'. The level of protein in the fluid is raised above the upper limit of normal (20 mg. %) to about 40–100 mg. % or more. There is pleocytosis, the number of white cells rising from the normal of 5–10 per cu. mm. to about 200 cu. mm. If there is associated meningitis the number of cells will be much higher.

Accurate localisation of the abscess is of great importance in diagnosis and treatment. Localisation is achieved on the basis of the neurological signs and the history of the previous illness, for example, ear disease. Further aid in localisation is given by electroencephalography; in the majority of cases air studies or angiography is required.

Treatment

Most abscesses develop from an acute or subacute focus of inflammation, and the symptoms in the early stages may be largely due to oedema causing raised intracranial pressure. The speed of development of raised intracranial pressure may occasionally be very rapid and necessitate urgent measures to save life, such as the administration of intravenously administered dehydrating agents or aspiration of pus.

The essentials of treatment for any cerebral abscess are to give antibiotics both into the abscess cavity and systemically, to drain the pus and deal with any primary focus of infection, such as mastoid or sinus disease. A sulphonamide or an antibiotic which penetrates into the cerebrospinal fluid should be given to control the diffuse inflammatory process. The abscess is localised accurately by the neurological signs, ventriculography, electroencephalography and arteriography. A burr hole is then made over the site of the abscess, which is aspirated by means of a blunt brain needle. The resistance felt in passing the needle gives an index of the localisation and chronicity of the abscess by indicating the quality of the pyogenic membrane. Pus is aspirated and the abscess cavity filled with 2–3 ml. of the appropriate antibiotic, usually penicillin and streptomycin, together with a fine suspension of barium to outline the cavity of the abscess radiologically. Sensitivity tests are carried out on the organisms cultured from the pus. Radiography shows the size of the abscess outlined by the barium to become smaller if treatment is effective. Aspiration is repeated as required, usually every few days. The primary focus of infection must also be treated. With repeated aspiration the majority of abscesses eventually heal and leave only a small scar. It is rare nowadays for abscesses to be excised at any stage.

Extradural and Subdural Abscess

An abscess outside or under the dura mater may result from the same kind of primary infections that lead to cerebral abscess, usually by direct spread, but instead of the inflammatory process penetrating the brain tissue, it stops at a more superficial level. The commonest causes include middle-ear disease, infection of an extradural or subdural haematoma following injury and also as a result of open fractures and osteomyelitis of the skull.

The signs of increased intracranial pressure together with fever suggest that pus is forming, but on the whole localising signs are less common with pus on the surface of the brain than with intracerebral abscess formation.

Treatment is urgent, for the patient is gravely ill. Antibiotics are given systemically and locally and the pus is drained. Any primary focus is also dealt with.

Infective Thrombosis of Intracranial Venous Sinuses

Infective sinus thrombosis is a rare complication of infection in the head and neck region because of the wide usage of antibiotics. When it occurs it is a very serious condition, for the mortality is high. It is always secondary to some focus of infection. It may come from the middle ear, or from infection of the paranasal air sinuses. Other likely sources of infection are boils and carbuncles on the face or in and around the orbit. More rarely it may arise from infection of the scalp or skull. Surgical treatment is hardly ever needed nowadays because the infective element of the condition usually responds to antibiotics, which also prevent the complication of pyaemia due to infected fragments of thrombus breaking off into the venous circulation.

Veins pass directly from the area of the face lateral to the nose and from the orbital region to the cavernous sinus. Inflammation in these areas must always be treated as potentially serious. Infection of the middle ear may result in thrombosis of the lateral sinus.

In cavernous sinus thrombosis the patient is seriously ill with a high, swinging fever. Signs of pyaemia and those of raised intracranial pressure may become apparent. Exophthalmos develops with great orbital congestion and oedema of the conjunctiva. There may be ocular paralysis, with hyperaesthesia in the area of supply of the first division of the fifth nerve. Drainage of the septic focus on the face or orbit is carried out and a suitable antibiotic given.

Meningitis

Inflammation of the arachnoid and pial membranes is usually acute due to the meningococcus, streptococcus, pneumococcus and staphylococcus. Other types of organism, such as the tubercle bacillus and certain viruses, may also cause meningitis. The surgeon is most likely to be concerned with meningitis which results from an adjacent focus of inflammation. The commonest is infection of the mastoid air cells, next in frequency is frontal sinusitis. Meningitis may also complicate open fractures or gunshot wounds of the head. Rarely it may follow lumbar puncture or spinal infections. Even a scalp wound may result in meningitis if it is not adequately treated.

The infection spreads swiftly throughout the whole of the subarachnoid space involving the cortex of the brain. Often the symptoms appear with astonishing rapidity. There is severe headache and frequently vomiting. There may be irritability, followed by delirium and signs of cerebral compression. Photophobia is common. There is spasm of muscles, particularly those of the neck, leading to head retraction. The onset of the condition may be heralded by rigors and a high temperature.

Lumbar puncture is essential both for diagnosis and for treatment. The cerebrospinal fluid is under increased pressure and may be turbid or frankly purulent when penicillin and streptomycin are given intrathecally and systemically. A soluble sulphonamide such as sulphadimidine is given orally or intravenously and its level in the cerebrospinal fluid kept at about 12–15 mg./100 ml. The organisms in the fluid should be identified and their sensitivity to antibiotics determined so that the most suitable antibiotics can be used. Skilled nursing is essential, as these patients are often mentally disturbed and may become delirious.

CEREBRAL NEOPLASMS

Varieties

Tumours can arise from brain tissue, blood vessels, meninges and skull.

1. *Glioma*

This is the commonest type of brain tumour, and arises from neuro glia, the connective tissue of the central nervous system. Gliomas account for nearly 50% of intracranial tumours. There are four main types.

(a) *Astrocytoma* is the commonest type of glioma presenting all grades of malignancy. Many can be benign, but the majority, in the cerebral hemispheres, are malignant. It is the common tumour of the cerebrum in the adult and of the cerebellum in the child. The most malignant form of astrocytoma is that formerly termed glioblastoma multiforme.

(b) *Ependymoma* occurs mainly in children, arising in the ventricles, especially the fourth ventricle.

(c) *Oligodendroglioma* is seen mainly in adults in the cerebral cortex. It is often heavily calcified, a feature of radio-diagnostic significance.

(d) *Medulloblastoma* typically occurs in childhood as a very malignant tumour of the cerebellum arising in the midline. It is prone to disseminate throughout the nervous system. The microscopic appearance is very variable.

2. Tumours Arising from the Meninges

Meningiomas account for 20% of cerebral tumours. They consist of sheets of endothelial cells. They are benign and do not give rise to metastases. Very often they can be successfully removed, but there may be difficulty due to position or vascularity. They arise from the arachnoid and occur at both the base and vertex of the cranium. Occasionally there are changes in the overlying skull which produce a characteristic radiological appearance with increased vascular markings and hyperostosis.

The interest taken in meningiomas is out of all proportion to the frequency of their occurrence, probably because adequate surgical excision often results in a cure. Few cranial tumours of other types can be as radically treated as some meningiomas.

3. Tumours Arising from the Skull

Primary skull tumours are extremely rare—they include benign osteoma and malignant sarcoma. Sarcoma occasionally complicates Paget's disease of the skull. Secondary tumours are more common, and may be carcinomata, melanomata and sarcomata. The carcinomas which may be expected to metastasise to the skull are bronchial, renal, mammary, thyroid and, in children, adrenal. It should also be remembered that the skull is commonly affected by Paget's disease, multiple myelomatosis and hyperparathyroidism, and a solitary focus of one of these diseases may mimic a primary tumour.

4. Neuromas

Tumours of nerves and nerve roots do not arise from nerve cells themselves, but from their supporting cells—the Schwann cells. Because of the differences of opinion that exist over the origin of these cells a variety of names are used for tumours arising from them: schwannoma, neurilemmoma, neurofibroma, neuroma and neurinoma. The most common example is the acoustic neuroma which arises from the sheath of the eighth nerve in the cerebello-pontine angle and causes deafness and signs of a space-occupying lesion. People with generalised neurofibromatosis may develop bilateral acoustic neuromas.

5. Metastatic Neoplasms

These constitute 15–20% of all cerebral tumours. The most frequent site of the primary tumour is in the bronchus, kidney, breast, prostate, stomach and from malignant melanomata of the skin. Almost 25% of patients dying with carcinoma of the bronchus are found to have cerebral secondaries.

Symptoms and Signs

(a) General

The tumours listed above are very diverse in nature and tend to have an individual life history and symptomatology. However, sooner or later they reveal their presence as space-occupying lesions by causing increased intracranial pressure. Two-thirds of patients with cerebral tumours present the classical triad of *headache, vomiting and papilloedema*. Mental disorder of some kind is common, such as personality change, drowsiness, dementia and coma. Headache, vomiting and papilloedema, if they occur individually, can indicate a wide variety of diseases, but together the triad is almost pathognomonic of a space-occupying lesion within the skull.

The general effects of cerebral tumours are first produced by the effect of displacement of brain tissue, for example, between the various cranial compartments. Displacement towards the base of the skull may result in third-nerve palsy and in the more chronic condition sixth-nerve palsy, the result of tentorial herniation. Herniation of the brain stem and cerebellar tonsils may plug the foramen magnum, which acutely, may cause sudden failure of respiration and death unless the herniation is relieved by operation. It must be remembered that within the rigid structure of the skull the cranial cavity is divided by dural septa into compartments, so that a rise of pressure in one compartment must be followed by herniation into another.

The second effect of a cerebral tumour is obstruction causing hydrocephalus. Obstruction is particularly likely in those tumours arising in the ventricles. A tumour in the third ventricle will obstruct both lateral ventricles. In the fourth ventricle a tumour obstructs the lateral and third ventricles and the aqueduct. Impaction at the foramen magnum may also result in obstruction to the outlets of the fourth ventricle leading to accumulation of cerebrospinal fluid. Obstruction may produce false localising signs, including basal nuclear and even hypothalamic impairment, so that the patient may present with syndromes akin to Parkinsonism, hypopituitarism and various defects of memory.

(b) *Local*

Localising signs will depend very much on the situation of the tumour, and the following are typical examples:

Frontal Lobe: lack of initiative or ambition, personal neglect, inappropriate behaviour and epileptiform attacks. As the mass extends backwards, there may be weakness of the face and arms. If it extends deeply into the internal capsule there may be spastic hemiparesis. In the posterior part of the left frontal lobe there may be dysphasic and dysarthric difficulties.

Parietal Lobe: loss of discriminatory sensation, visual field defects, interference with body scheme and various forms of apraxia.

Temporal Lobe: disorders of language, temporal lobe seizures and visual field defects.

Occipital Lobe: homonymous hemianopia.

Cerebellum: inco-ordination, vertigo and nystagmus. Interference with the function of the fifth and eleventh cranial nerves where they lie close to the cerebellum and brain stem.

Cerebello-pontine Angle: Paralysis of the seventh and eighth nerves and cerebellar signs.

Mid-brain, Pons and Medulla: involvement of cranial nerves and the various long tracts.

Hypothalamus: abnormalities of alimentary function, temperature control, metabolic control and also water balance.

If the lesion is in a so-called silent area of the brain, such as the frontal lobe, there may be no obvious localising symptoms or signs.

PITUITARY TUMOURS

Most pituitary tumours have attention drawn to them because the optic chiasma is compressed with loss of the outer part of the visual fields —bitemporal hemianopia. Sometimes one optic tract is affected first— homonymous hemianopia. The pressure of the tumour as it enlarges results in increasing impairment of function of the optic chiasma and later of one and then both optic nerves till eventually blindness is complete.

Most pituitary adenomata arise in the anterior lobe and are classified by the staining reaction of their cells into chromophobe and chromophil adenomata, the latter being either eosinophil or basophil. In addition, a congenital lesion near to the pituitary, the Rathke pouch cyst or cranio-pharyngioma, may by its proximity grow and destroy the pituitary and chiasma, though often not producing symptoms until puberty or adult life.

1. A *chromophobe tumour* consists of non-granular cells and is associated with hypopituitarism. In children this results either in Froehlich's adiposo-genital syndrome (the fat boy of Peckham) or Lorain's syndrome, the well-proportioned infantile dwarf. In adults sexual desire is lost and amenor-rhoea is common.

2. *Eosinophil tumours* are formed of granular eosinophils resembling the normal cells of the anterior lobe and giving rise to symptoms of hyperpituitarism—gigantism in young people and acromegaly with over-growth of the skull, spine and extremities in adults.

3. *Basophilic tumours* are usually associated with adrenal cortical hyperplasia and result in Cushing's syndrome (see p. 165).

Diagnosis of Intracranial Tumours

A careful history is taken of the patient and his relatives, for the patient may be an unreliable witness. The time sequence of events in the patient's history may be of great importance.

Full examination of the central nervous system is essential and repeated so that any change in signs may be noted. Radiographs of the skull may show an enlargement of the sella turcica in pituitary tumours, erosion of the skull and enlargement of the meningeal channels in meningiomata. The internal auditory meatus is enlarged by an acoustic neurinoma, calcified tumours may be demonstrated. Displacement of the calcified pineal body from the midline offers important evidence of raised intra-cranial pressure.

Certain special tests may be indicated, for example full examination of the visual fields on a screen and tests of otological function. Electro-encephalography is sometimes of help if slow delta waves can be picked up in the vicinity of a tumour. The pressure, chemistry and cytology of the cerebrospinal fluid may give valuable diagnostic data. Lumbar air encephalography, in which some of the fluid in the ventricles is replaced by air, will indicate any distortion of the ventricles in the brain and may localise the site of the tumour. Angiography, in which a radiopaque sub-stance is injected into the common carotid artery and sometimes the vertebral, visualises the various phases of the circulation within the skull. It is of the greatest value in the diagnosis of vascular malformations such as aneurysms but is also of help in outlining abnormal vascularity in tumours within the brain substance or showing displacement of vessels by a tumour. When papilloedema is present, lumbar puncture and the injection of air into the ventricles may be dangerous because release of pressure in the spinal canal and posterior fossa may result in herniation of the brain through the tentorial opening or the foramen magnum, with resultant sudden arrest of respiration.

Brain scanning with radioactive isotopes is now proving an extremely efficient and certain way of detecting the presence of single or multiple tumours within the skull, and has the added advantage that it can be per-formed without admission to hospital. In some hands the various types of tumours can be identified from the scanning picture. An isotope of mercury is now most often used which is concentrated in the tumour after its intravenous injection.

Treatment

Some intracranial tumours are relatively slow growing and encapsulated, and can be removed with a good prospect of cure. Because of rapid growth, infiltration or site many can only be treated in a palliative way. The majority of gliomata are rapidly growing and invasive, and cannot be completely removed. Sometimes incomplete excision may be worth while and may relieve symptoms temporarily At other times it is unwise to do more than perform biopsy of the tumour to confirm diagnosis. Malignant astrocytomas, the glioblastoma of adults and the cerebellar medullo-blastoma of children fall into this rapidly growing group. The majority of meningiomas and pituitary tumours are removable, as are many acoustic nerve tumours. It is always important to diagnose a cerebral tumour as early as possible and, when possible, to identify it by a biopsy.

To approach tumours in the anterior fossa or in the region of the pituitary, an osteoplastic flap is usually raised in the frontal region. To approach the middle fossa, a similar flap may be raised in the temporal region. When it is necessary to enter the posterior fossa most of the occipital bone is removed through a 'cross-bow' incision posteriorly.

CRANIAL NERVE LESIONS

The Olfactory Nerve lies wholly in the anterior fossa of the skull. Fractures through this area or pressure on the nerve for any other cause may result in disturbance or complete loss of smell. Anosmia is a very common and unpleasant sequel of fracture of the skull because taste and smell are so closely allied.

The Optic Nerve may be injured following fractures. Compression by tumours, particularly in the pituitary fossa, may interfere with its function. Tumours, haemorrhage and inflammation in the orbital region may injure the nerve, resulting in optic neuritis, optic atrophy or even blindness.

Nerves III, IV and VI may be affected by trauma, pituitary tumours, aneurysms or inflammatory conditions, particularly in the region of the cavernous sinus. When all three nerves are involved there is paralysis of all the muscles of the eye; quite often the ophthalmic branch of the trigeminal is also involved and there is anaesthesia of the cornea and forehead.

Trigeminal Nerve (V). Trigeminal neuralgia or tic douloureux incapacitates the patient with paroxysms of agonising pain. Typically the paroxysmal attacks of pain begin in the area supplied by second or third divisions of the nerve and only later spread to involve the first. They may be triggered off by quite trivial stimuli such as a cold wind, shaving or touching certain points on the face or in the mouth—trigger areas. Usually there is neither sensory nor motor paralysis. The cause of tic douloureux is unknown.

First of all an examination is carried out to exclude dental, ophthalmic and sinus disease. Diseases of the central nervous system must also be excluded. Relief of pain by analgesics is rarely successful except in the mildest cases. Recently the drug 'tegretol' has been found most effective. Injection of the trigeminal (gasserian) ganglion with 90% alcohol is used in treatment as is surgical division of the fifth nerve proximal to the ganglion. The injection is performed via a needle guided through the foramen ovale. Long periods of relief, even permanent relief, may follow injection with alcohol. More recently, injection of 5% phenol in myodil has been found effective in relieving pain without diminishing sensation, but usually not with results so long lasting as with alcohol. At the present time more patients are being treated by operation than formerly. The main disadvantage of alcohol injection is that the cornea is rendered insensitive as the method does not allow sparing of the ophthalmic division of the nerve. The patient has to wear protective spectacles and must be warned about the dangers of an anaesthetic cornea—foreign bodies and infection.

At operation the lower two divisions of the trigeminal nerve are divided proximal to the ganglion preserving the first division and the motor root. The fibres conducting facial pain can also be divided in the medulla to leave the cutaneous supply of other modalities of the trigeminal nerve intact, but this is a big procedure for patients who have trigeminal neuralgia, many of whom are old and feeble.

Facial Nerve (*VII*). 1. A lesion *within the brain* may be supranuclear or infranuclear. In supranuclear lesions only the lower half of the face is paralysed, since the upper part receives bilateral innervation. 2. Lesions within the *petrous bone* are caused by fractures of the base of the skull, middle ear inflammation or injury during an operation on the mastoid antrum or middle ear. In such a case there is complete paralysis of one side of the face. In Bell's palsy this lesion occurs quite suddenly for no known reason with, in most cases, spontaneous recovery. It is possibly due to a virus infection. Taste in the area supplied by the chorda tympani nerve may be impaired if the geniculate ganglion is involved. 3. Lesions *outside the skull* may be due to malignant growths of the parotid gland or due to the facial nerve being injured during operations on this gland. The result is partial or complete paralysis of one side of the face with asymmetry and inability to close the eye or whistle.

The treatment depends upon the lesion. If the nerve has been divided at operation or by injury it should, if possible, be exposed and sutured. An autograft of a segment of cutaneous nerve may be inserted if the ends cannot be approximated. It is also possible to restore tone to the facial muscles by anastomosing the proximal part of the hypoglossal nerve to the distal end of the facial. Facio-hypoglossal anastomosis is the standard procedure when the facial nerve has been sacrificed in the removal of an acoustic nerve tumour.

Most cases of Bell's palsy recover spontaneously in about six weeks; those that do not recover may be helped by decompression of the nerve in its bony canal. Galvanism is used to prevent atrophy of muscles, and the angle of the mouth can be splinted by a wire slipped over the ears or a flange attached to a denture. When facial paralysis is permanent fascial strips may be placed subcutaneously, extending from the zygomatic arch to the upper and lower lips in the midline and also to the angle of the mouth to prevent it from drooping.

The Auditory Nerve (*VIII*) may be injured in a fracture of the base of the skull. Sometimes it is the site of a neurinoma.

The Glossopharyngeal and Vagus Nerves (*IX* and *X*) are rarely involved in intracranial lesions. The ninth to the twelfth nerves arise in the posterior fossa, but are rarely damaged by fractures of the base of the skull. The nerves may be involved by intracranial tumour and inflammation. Lesions of the glossopharyngeal nerve cause interference with sensation of the back of the tongue; when the vagus nerve is involved there is paralysis of the vocal cord on the same side. If the pharyngeal plexus is involved difficulty in swallowing and speaking may result.

Glossopharyngeal neuralgia is a rare symptom in which pain in the throat is brought on by swallowing. This pain can be very severe and may require intracranial section of the nerve.

The Spinal Accessory and Hypoglossal Nerves (*XI* and *XII*) are rarely involved in intracranial lesions, but they may be injured during operations on the neck, particularly removal of lymph nodes or even a sebaceous cyst n the posterior triangle. The spinal accessory supplies the sternomastoid and trapezius muscles, paralysis of which leads to a drooping shoulder and inability to shrug the shoulder. Paralysis of the hypoglossal nerve produces atrophy of half of the tongue, so that when it is protruded it points towards the affected side.

SPINAL-CORD LESIONS

Most lesions of the spinal cord arise from diseases or injuries of the vertebral bodies. Perhaps the commonest lesion of all is a fracture-dislocation of the spine. Diseases of the vertebrae, such as tuberculosis and metastases, involve the cord and nerves by direct extension and cause collapse of the vertebrae with pressure on the cord. Spinal tumours may be extradural or intradural. Intradural tumours may be intramedullary (that is inside the cord) or extramedullary.

Extradural tumours present with symptoms and signs of irritation of nerve roots preceding the signs of pressure on the cord. Other conditions, such as a prolapsed intravertebral disc, in the lumbar or less commonly the cervical region, may produce identical symptoms. The commonest tumours are secondary deposits. Sarcoma, reticulosis, chordoma and neurofibroma are also found. A neurofibroma may be 'dumb-bell' in shape, the smaller portion lying within the neural canal and the larger portion projecting through an intervertebral foramen and encroaching into the thorax. Chordoma is a painful eroding tumour found in the sacral region which destroys bone and nerves. The course is slow over a number of years.

Intradural tumours may be extramedullary or less often intramedullary. The most important of the extramedullary tumours are meningiomas and neurinomas. The anterior or posterior roots tend to be involved first; the proximal level of the sensory and motor changes depends on the site of the tumour. Symptoms due to pressure on nerve roots may be followed some months later by symptoms of pressure on the cord itself. Later there may be the Brown–Séquard hemisection phenomena, with weakness and loss of vibration sense on the same side as the lesion and loss of pain on the opposite side. Paraplegia will follow if pressure is not relieved.

Intramedullary tumours are usually gliomas, angiomas or ependymomas. Paralysis may occur on both sides, or sometimes may be of the crossed type, where there is anaesthesia on one side and paralysis and hyperaesthesia on the other. Dissociated sensory loss may occur. With intramedullary tumours it is the cord signs which present first, while the root pains tend to occur later. Interference with the urinary sphincters usually appears early.

Symptoms

Symptoms due to compression of the cord by a tumour are usually chronic in onset, rarely acute. Chronic compression causes symptoms often spread over years before the correct diagnosis is made. Pain is usually the first complaint often referred to the distribution of a nerve root for example, a girdle pain in the trunk. A cough or sneeze, which raises intrathecal pressure, or movement of the spine causes acute lancinating root pain. Pain from a tumour is often worse when the person affected is lying in bed, unlike that caused by a prolapsed intervertebral disc. As time passes, weakness and wasting of muscle groups occurs, and there may be spasticity and sensory changes according to the position of the tumour. There may be trouble with the vesical or anal sphincters, but this usually occurs late.

At each end of the spinal column, that is in the foramen magnum and lumbosacral region, diagnosis may be especially difficult. In the foramen magnum cranial nerves may also be affected and, while the sensory loss may be restricted to the neck, all four limbs may show motor weakness. The roominess of the lumbo-sacral canal allows big tumours to develop with few signs, but bony involvement may make spinal movement difficult and painful.

The signs of a tumour depend on the site and segmental level of the lesion. Compression of anterior horn cells produces a lower motor neurone lesion, with wasting and weakness in the muscles of the affected segments. Compression of the long tracts in the cord produces spastic weakness, increased reflexes, extensor plantar responses and a loss of superficial sensation below the level of the lesion.

Investigations

1. Radiography of the spine, anteroposterior, lateral and oblique views should be taken. Erosion of bone or some other bony abnormality is seen in nearly 50% of patients with spinal tumours.
2. Lumbar puncture will reveal a raised protein content in the cerebrospinal fluid, which may be yellow (xanthochromia) or low in pressure. In addition, Queckenstedt's test may show that a spinal block is present due to compression of the cord by the neoplasm.
3. Myelography consists of introducing an opaque medium—myodil—into the spinal subarachnoid space. This is the only means of localising with precision the obstructed area, and enables the surgeon to perform laminectomy at the correct level.

Treatment

The diagnosis having been established, laminectomy is performed and if possible, the tumour is removed. The removal of the tumour and laminae help in decompression of the cord. Acute paraplegia demands an emergency operation.

Sacrococcygeal Tumours

These tumours are congenital in origin and arise from anomalous development or persistence of rudimentary structures. Frequently they are solid or cystic teratomas or dermoid cysts between the rectum and coccyx or over the surface of the sacrum. Occasionally they include recognisable parts, for example, a limb. Some tumours are thought to arise from the notochord, neurenteric canal or post-anal gut. This is a common site for chordoma. Radiographs provide much the best evidence of the extent of these tumours.

Treatment

Teratomas should be removed by dissection after excision of the coccyx and wide opening of both ischio rectal fossae; the prognosis is good if the tumour is benign and completely removed. Chordomas tend to recur, some are sensitive to radiotherapy.

SPINA BIFIDA

In spina bifida there is a failure of fusion in the midline of the structures which cover and protect the spinal cord. In its mildest form spina bifida is only discovered on radiography of the spine, when a gap is seen in the bony neural arches of one or more vertebrae, usually in the lumbo-sacral region—*spina bifida occulta*. There may be a tuft of hair or tell-tale haemangioma in the skin overlying it, a talipes deformity of the foot may be associated.

When a swelling overlies the bony defect it is called *spina bifida cystica*. The degree of disability depends on the extent to which the spinal cord and nerve roots are incorporated in the walls of the sac. Three-quarters of these lesions occur in the lumbo-sacral region, but any part of the spinal column may be involved. Rarely the swelling occurs to one side of the midline. *Meningocele* is a cystic swelling overlying the spine composed only of spinal membranes containing cerebrospinal fluid. Despite its name, there is often some degree of maldevelopment of the cord and nerve roots, with resulting weakness and deformity of the legs and dysfunction of the sphincters controlling the bladder and bowel. *Meningomyelocele* is a serious abnormality of development in which the spinal cord runs over the convexity of the sac and the spinal roots traverse its walls, a fact which can be demonstrated by transillumination. There is always weakness or even flaccidity of the lower limbs, and often incontinence of urine and faeces. A number of those who survive later develop hydrocephalus due to the Arnold–Chiari malformation. In this the cerebellar tonsils prolapse into the foramen magnum and obstruct the circulation of cerebrospinal fluid.

Treatment

A sinus track, a dermal sinus, may rarely be seen in the sacral or occipital region connecting the dural cavity with the skin. Cerebrospinal fluid may be discharged, meningitis is a hazard. Infection may accumulate around the spinal cord and leave the patient paraplegic, therefore such tracks should be excised. No treatment is necessary for spina bifida occulta; in many patients its existence remains undiscovered unless radiographs are taken.

The treatment of meningocele and meningomyelocele has completely changed in recent years from the old attitude of conservatism and covering the swelling with a pad. Today all these babies are operated upon as soon after birth as possible, preferably within the first 24 hours. The walls of the sac are excised using the greatest care to spare all nervous tissue, cord and roots, which are gently replaced in the spinal canal. Flaps of fascia are raised on each side from the overlying erector spinae muscles, and primary skin closure is obtained, if necessary by laterally placed relieving incisions. The baby is nursed with the head end of the cot lowered to prevent leakage of cerebrospinal fluid. Orthopaedic care will be necessary for the weak lower limbs, and any associated abnormality, such as talipes or congenital dislocation of the hips, which are fairly frequently associated. If there is incontinence of urine an ileal bladder is constructed before the child is of school age.

Closure of a meningocele may be followed by hydrocephalus, so the circumference of the skull is measured regularly to detect the onset of any enlargement early. In some patients spontaneous arrest of hydrocephalus occurs, but in others treatment is required because the head continues to enlarge. Most success has attended the insertion of a Spitzholter or Pudenz valve, by which the excess cerebrospinal fluid is led into a jugular vein via a plastic tube.

THE PERIPHERAL NERVOUS SYSTEM
PERIPHERAL NERVE INJURIES

When a nerve is injured new axons have to grow down from the site of injury, reach appropriate end organs and mature so that impulses can be conveyed along the new fibres. Regeneration of nerve implies restoration of function, both sensory and motor.

STRUCTURE OF NERVES

The axon is surrounded by a Schwann cell. Outside this there is a tube of more rigid collagenous material called the *Schwann tube*. The composition of the wall of the tube and the inter-connecting collagenous material between individual axons is called the *endoneurium*. Each nerve trunk is composed of fascicles, each surrounded by a sheath called the *perineurium*. In turn these fascicles are bound together by the *epineurium* to form a single trunk.

TYPES OF INJURY

The best way to understand nerve injuries is to classify them into the following three groups:

1. *Pressure (Neuropraxia)*. Light pressure, applied for a considerable time, can lead to loss of conduction along the nerve fibres. However, there is no peripheral Wallerian degeneration. The cause is believed to be a disturbance of the myelin around the axon at the site of the lesion. Recovery is rapid, within 2–3 weeks of injury, and is complete.

2. *Crush (Axonotmesis)*. When a nerve trunk is crushed there is Wallerian degeneration of the axons distal to the site of the lesion. However, the supporting tubes remain intact, and the regenerating axons can grow back along their original tubes to their old end organs. Recovery in such instances is complete. However, in clinical practice there is frequently additional destruction of the supporting structures within the nerve trunk, with consequently diminished return of function.

3. *Division of Nerve (Neurotmesis)*. This is complete severance of the nerve. When the axons regenerate they are frequently guided into inappropriate Schwann tubes, thus reaching endings quite different from those with which they were originally connected. Recovery under these circumstances is never complete, although occasionally remarkably good functional results may occur.

In clinical practice the three basic types of lesion described above are frequently mixed. *Compression* may result from crutches or splints or internally by tumours, aneurysms, cervical rib or osteoarthritic excrescences. In addition, the nerves may be involved in fibrous tissue in a scar or by callus in the healing of a fracture. The results resemble those of a pressure lesion initially, but at a later date fibrosis may occur within the nerve trunk with permanent interference with nerve conduction. Contusion of a nerve may be caused by an external injury, or may be associated with a fracture or dislocation. In many instances this resembles a pressure lesion, and signs of recovery appear fairly soon after injury. Recovery is excellent unless there has been destruction of the supporting tissues within the nerve trunk.

Traction Injuries occur most often in the brachial plexus as a birth injury or after trauma, such as dislocation of the shoulder or too energetic attempts at reduction. Sometimes there is incomplete division of a nerve, the results depending on which fibres have suffered injury.

Degeneration

Following a crush injury or division of a nerve there is immediate degeneration distal to the site of the lesion. This consists in the breaking up of the axon and the lipoprotein contained in the Schwann cell membrane. These droplets are removed by macrophages. The Schwann cells, however, within the rigid Schwann tube begin to multiply, and in large fibres increase by as much as thirteen-fold, 25 days after the lesion. The

Schwann tubes and the cells within them are essential for the guidance of the regenerating axons.

Regeneration after Crush or Division

Following a crush injury the axon grows back as a main growth cone along the same tube to its original ending. Once the axon matures so that it can convey appropriate impulses, the recovery of function is perfect.

In contrast, the results following severance of a nerve trunk are quite different. The essential factors here are the downgrowth of the axon from the proximal nerve stump and the outgrowth of Schwann cells from the distal stump. The growing axons are guided across the gap by contact with the Schwann cells. Quite frequently they are guided into the wrong Schwann tubes, so that eventually they connect up with inappropriate end organs. It is because of this that recovery of function is never perfect after division of a nerve.

The rate of return of function along an axon is approximately 1 mm. per day. This approximation allows the surgeon to form a rough calculation of when recovery can be hoped for after nerve suture. It should be remembered, however, that before recovery can occur there must be a downgrowth of axons, connection with appropriate endings and a maturation of the fibres so that impulses can be conveyed along them. This accounts for the fact that while the apparent rate of return of function is of the order of 1 mm. a day, the rate of growth of axon tips is about 4–5 mm. per day.

Symptoms and Signs

1. *Paralysis of Muscles* supplied by the nerve occurs, and quite soon afterwards, within weeks, there is commencing wasting and deformity due to the unopposed action of synergistic muscles.

2. *Sensory Changes.* Sensation in the area supplied by the nerve is lost but this may be smaller than expected because of the overlap from neighbouring nerves. Tendon reflexes are lost.

3. *Vasomotor Changes.* In addition to atrophy of the muscle there is loss of blood supply and atrophy of the skin. Trophic ulceration may occur, and there is loss of sweating. Rarefaction of bone sometimes occurs.

Following complete division of a nerve a bulbous projection or neuroma forms on the proximal stump. This is composed of axons turning back on themselves, Schwann cells and fibroblasts. Similarly, in the distal cut end there is a smaller neuroma composed largely of Schwann cells.

Treatment

When a nerve has been completely divided it has to be sutured. This suture may be primary or delayed. Following a clean cut of the nerve, for example during an operation, by a piece of glass or knife wound, many surgeons advocate immediate suture. Nevertheless, the majority of injuries are best treated by delayed suture 3–4 weeks after the injury. At the primary operation the wound is excised and any foreign material removed. Infection is controlled by antibiotics. Three to four weeks later there should be complete healing of the wound, and suture of the nerve at this stage can then be conducted under safer conditions. In addition to this, 3–4 weeks after the original injury it is easier to recognise the extent of damage to the nerve trunks, and accurate resection of any neuromas can be performed. In addition to this the epineurium is toughened at this stage, which makes suturing of the prepared nerve ends easier.

Lastly, the migration of Schwann cells from the distal stump has reached a peak at this stage, and results in more efficient guidance of growing axon tips across the gap into the distal tubes. Fine silk is used to suture the nerve ends, which should be orientated one to another as nearly as possible in their original position. Tension must be avoided in suturing nerves, and if necessary to achieve this the trunks may be mobilised or transposed. When incomplete division is suspected a policy of wait and see is usually adopted. If, however, after the calculated time for recovery of sensory or motor function this has not taken place, then the nerve should be explored. Nerve suture should not be delayed for longer than 6 months, since the Schwann tubes then begin to shrink in size, and permanent degenerative changes begin to occur in nerve endings. Nevertheless, acceptable results have been attained following exploration and suture as long as a year or more after injury to the nerve.

In all nerve injuries of limbs well-planned physiotherapy is of the greatest importance. The limbs should be splinted with light material in the appropriate position. Active and passive movements should be carried out to prevent stiffening of the joints and atrophy of muscles. Galvanism helps to retard atrophy of the muscles.

In general, it can be said that suture of nerves after division, give useful functional results in about half the cases. However, recovery varies considerably, and is dependent on many factors. On the whole, the larger the nerve trunk, the more proximal the lesion and the more heterogenous the constituent fibres of the nerve, the greater the chances of misdirection of growing fibres with consequent poor recovery. In addition to this the more delicate the function performed by the muscle, the more integrated is the return required, and consequently the poorer the chances of a useful recovery.

RADIAL NERVE LESIONS

The commonest site of injury is where the radial nerve winds round the mid-shaft of the humerus. Here it can be injured at the time of fracture or compressed against the bone, for example, by a crush. There is paralysis of the triceps, supinators and extensors of the wrist and digits. This results in wrist-drop. However, the terminal phalanges can still be extended by means of the interossei and lumbrical muscles, which are supplied by the ulnar and median nerves. There is practically no loss of sensation. It is important that the hand and arm be supported in all radial nerve injuries to prevent the ill effects of wrist-drop. Physiotherapy and splinting are essential. Nerve suture at the common site of injury of the radial nerve gives comparatively good results. In long-standing cases when re-innervation of the muscles is impossible, due to atrophy of the muscles or loss of the nerve, some of the flexor tendons of the wrist can be transplanted to the insertion of the extensors of the fingers to produce a more useful hand.

MEDIAN NERVE LESIONS

The usual site of injury of this nerve is at the wrist; frequently the flexor tendons are divided at the same site. There is paralysis of the opponens pollicis, abductor pollicis, part of flexor pollicis brevis and the outer two lumbricals. Although true opposition of the thumb to the little finger is impossible, it may be simulated by use of the unparalysed flexors and adductors. There is wasting of the thenar eminence and sensory loss over the lateral part of the palm of the hand, including the thumb, index and middle fingers. Posteriorly, sensation is lost on the terminal two-thirds of the middle and index finger and the terminal one-half of the thumb. Less commonly the median nerve may be injured at the elbow and, when this happens, the pronators and the majority of the flexors of the wrist and fingers are all paralysed. Nevertheless, the fingers, except for the index, can still be flexed to some extent by the flexor digitorum profundus.

Nerve suture should be carried out in the usual way, since effective re-innervation of the intrinsic muscles of the hand is essential for a good result. The precision of function of these muscles requires accurate re-innervation, and for this reason the prognosis is sometimes unfavourable. Nevertheless, extremely good results following a division at the wrist can be obtained in the young.

Carpal Tunnel Syndrome

This syndrome is due to pressure on the median nerve as it passes under the flexor retinaculum. It results in pain, numbness and weakness in the median nerve distribution. The syndrome is almost only seen in women, and is especially common at about the menopause. The pain is worst at night-time, and the patient often obtains relief by cooling the hands outside the bedclothes. Treatment initially consists of resting the wrist with application of a splint which holds the joint in the neutral position. The splint should be worn both day and night. This treatment may be augmented by injections of hydrocortisone around the carpal ligament. Should the symptoms not be relieved, operation should be carried out. This consists of division of the flexor retinaculum with decompression of the median nerve.

ULNAR NERVE LESIONS

This nerve is most commonly injured at the elbow, usually at the time of dislocation or fracture at that site. It may be injured in wounds at the wrist level. There is paralysis of the interossei, the inner two lumbrical muscles, adductor pollicis and hypothenar muscles. Wasting, particularly between the metacarpal bones and of the hypothenar eminence, follows. The fingers assume the position of hyperextension proximally and flexion distally; this position is called main-en-griffe. If the injury is above the level of the elbow the flexor carpi ulnaris and part of the flexor digitorum profundus are also affected. Sensory changes occur over the medial half of the hand, both anteriorly and posteriorly. This includes the small finger and the medial half of the ring finger anteriorly and posteriorly.

Following division of the nerve, suture in the usual way should be carried out. Occasionally pressure symptoms on the nerve occur following injuries in the region of the elbow. Sometimes they occur when there is a pronounced cubitus valgus deformity of the elbow, presumably resulting in stretching or repeated minor trauma to the nerve. In these patients the ulnar nerve may be transplanted from its posterior position to the front of the elbow joint.

THORACIC INLET SYNDROME

This condition is characterised by pressure on the nerves or vessels as they cross the first rib. Several factors may be involved in the pressure: (1) cervical rib or similar congenital remnant; (2) pressure on the plexus by the scalenus anterior muscle; (3) stretching of the plexus over the first rib, especially when there is an abnormally low contribution of nerve roots to the plexus (post-fixed plexus).

In all of these conditions there are symptoms of pressure on the eighth cervical and first thoracic nerves. The symptoms are those of pain and paraesthesia, with sometimes weakness of the small muscles of the hand. These may be accompanied by vascular changes, mostly coldness and pallor of the hand. The vascular symptoms may be due to narrowing or thrombosis of the subclavian artery. Sometimes an aneurysm of the sub-clavian artery forms distal to a cervical rib (post-stenotic dilatation). Emboli from the aneurysm may cause digital gangrene. Characteristically the symptoms are worse at night when the patient is fatigued. Very often they occur in middle-aged women. The symptoms may be closely simulated by other conditions, such as cervical prolapsed disc, osteoarthritis and spondylosis of the cervical spine, and more rarely spinal-cord disease, such as syringomyelia. Occasionally a peripheral lesion, such as the carpal tunnel syndrome, may simulate the condition.

Treatment

In the first place this should be conservative. Exercises are carried out to strengthen the muscles of the shoulder girdle and to improve posture.

The patient should avoid carrying heavy objects. Should the symptoms persist and become worse, then operation may be considered. The type of operation depends on the findings. A cervical rib or other vestigial remnant should be removed; occasionally division of the scalenus anterior muscle may benefit the patient. Rarely, if compression of the neurovascular bundle is suspected between the clavicle and first rib, the inner end of the first rib is resected—costoclavicular compression.

BRACHIAL PLEXUS LESIONS

The majority of these lesions are due to traction; birth injury or after dislocation of the shoulder or its too energetic reduction. Complete plexus injury results in paralysis of the whole arm and complete anaesthesia of the limb. The pupil may be contracted on the same side, since the sympathetic nerve roots in that region may be injured. The innervation of the serratus anterior and rhomboid muscles escapes. Should the constituents of the brachial plexus be divided in an injury, then the results following suture are extremely poor. A useless limb may have to be amputated. Following a traction injury, however, there may be considerable recovery of function, and indeed, this may eventually be complete. The two main varieties of brachial plexus injury are:

Upper-arm Type (Erb-Duchenne)

The upper trunk (C5 and C6) is injured, and this results in paralysis of the deltoid, biceps, brachialis, brachioradialis and most of the rotators of the shoulder joint. There is no loss of sensation in the arm.

Lower-arm Type (Klumpke)

The lower trunk (C8 and T1) is involved, and there is paralysis of the flexors of the wrist and fingers and of the intrinsic muscles of the hand.

There is anaesthesia of the inner side of the arm, forearm and hand. Whenever there has been an actual rupture of the nerve plexuses the results are so uniformly poor that reconstructive operations, for example, arthrodesis of the shoulder, should be considered as soon as it is clear that function is not returning.

SCIATIC NERVE LESIONS

Injuries of the sciatic nerve are fairly rare in civil life. It is often said that suture of the sciatic nerve gives hopeless results. This is not entirely true. In about 50% of patients there is a useful return of function to the muscles of the calf, and pain on deep pressure in the foot may be felt. The resultant functions in the limb may be quite useful, and saves amputation.

Sciatic pain is very commonly seen in clinical practice (see p. 546). The chief causes are prolapsed lumbar or lumbo-sacral intervertebral disc, osteoarthritis of the lumbar vertebrae and the sacro-iliac joints and more rarely infiltration of nerves by malignant disease arising in the pelvis.

LATERAL POPLITEAL NERVE LESIONS

This nerve may be injured where it winds round the neck of the fibula. Pressure from splints or some similar mechanism is common. Following injury to the nerve there is paralysis of the dorsal flexors of the ankle and peroneal muscles. This results in foot-drop and anaesthesia of the lateral area of the leg and foot. The results of suture of this nerve are only fair, and the great majority of people require a toe-raising spring to correct foot drop. When nerve suture has failed the foot may be kept raised by transplantation of flexor tendons to the extensor aspect of the foot, and sometimes arthrodesis of the subtaloid joint is required to stabilise the foot.

THE AUTONOMIC NERVOUS SYSTEM

This system is composed of two parts—the sympathetic and para-sympathetic. The endings of sympathetic nerves release adrenaline and noradrenaline; on the other hand, the parasympathetic nerves release acetylcholine. The two systems therefore frequently have mutually antagonistic actions on smooth muscle, cardiac muscle and glandular structures.

SYMPATHETIC SYSTEM

These nerves arise from the spinal cord, from the first thoracic to the second or third lumbar segments. Preganglionic fibres (myelinated) emerge with the anterior motor roots, having taken origin from the lateral columns of the spinal cord. They pass by way of the white rami com-municantes to the corresponding sympathetic ganglia, or they pass through these to synapse in a ganglion at another level. The second link is the postganglionic fibre (unmyelinated), which passes from these ganglia back to the spinal nerves by way of the grey rami communicantes; some are distributed via nerve trunks which are composed entirely of sym-pathetic fibres.

Although the highest point of emergence of preganglionic fibres is the first thoracic segment, the sympathetic nerves are continued in a cranial direction through the cervical chain. Here there are three main ganglia—the lowest of these is called the stellate ganglion and represents the fusion of the inferior cervical and first thoracic ganglia. The superior cervical ganglia give rise to postganglionic fibres which are distributed to the eye, the skin, salivary glands and other structures in the head and neck. The lowest point of emergence from the cord of the sympathetic preganglionic fibres is from the second or third lumbar segments. However, the sympathetic nerves are prolonged downwards as the hypogastric plexuses, which in turn give rise to sympathetic fibres, which are distributed to abdominal viscera.

Sympathetic nerves supply vaso-constrictor fibres to almost all blood vessels in the skin, cerebral and visceral vessels; possibly the only exceptions are the arteries supplying the myocardium. Stimulation of sympathetic fibres to the appropriate viscera increases the heart rate, dilates bronchi and inhibits peristalsis in the stomach and intestines. Pain arising from the gastro-intestinal tract is mainly carried along afferent fibres in the sympathetic pathways. However, other afferent fibres arise, for example, in the stomach and small intestine, from pressure receptors and pH receptors, and travel by way of the vagus nerve.

Interruption of sympathetic nerves results in vasodilatation and absence of sweating in the affected area of the skin. Injury to the cervical sympathetic results in Horner's syndrome—this is a contraction of the pupil on the same side (meiosis), ptosis (drooped eyelid) and enophthalmos (sunken eyeball).

The operation of sympathectomy is most frequently carried out for vascular disease of the lower limb. The second and third lumbar ganglia on the affected side are usually removed; this is a preganglionic sympathectomy, and is in most cases complete from the level of the knee downwards. It results in dilation of the skin vessels of the lower limb and a loss of sweating there. The results are usually permanent if the operation is complete.

Less frequently sympathectomy is carried out for diseases of the upper limb. Here again the aim is usually a preganglionic sympathectomy, removing the upper thoracic chain on the affected side, including the second and third thoracic ganglia. The stellate ganglion is spared to avoid causing a Horner's syndrome and also the accompanying vasocongestion of the nasal air passages. Sympathectomy in the case of the upper limb tends to be incomplete, and the effects of the operation may only last for about a year. This applies particularly to vasodilatation in the hand and arm; loss of sweating, however, is often a permanent feature.

Sympathectomy is carried out for a variety of conditions:

1. *Vascular Disorders.* The commonest of these is atherosclerosis. Before carrying out sympathectomy, tests may be performed to discover how much the vessels are capable of dilating. Other conditions include Raynaud's disease, Raynaud's phenomenon and thromboangiitis obliterans.

2. *Hyperidrosis.* Excessive sweating is successfully treated in the upper limb or lower limb by sympathectomy.

3. *Pain,* for example causalgia, is frequently alleviated by sympathectomy. Certain types of dysmenorrhoea may be helped by a presacral sympathectomy.

4. *Ulceration* due to inadequate blood supply of the skin may be helped by sympathectomy, as may the painful blue limb which follows an attack of poliomyelitis.

PARASYMPATHETIC SYSTEM

The parasympathetic fibres arise from the brain and from the central segment of the spinal cord. They are distributed with the cranial nerves III, VII, IX and particularly X. In addition, they are distributed in the second, third and fourth sacral nerves. For the most part they antagonise the effects of the sympathetic nerves, for example causing the pupil to contract. Like the sympathetic nerves, they have preganglionic fibres which synapse in ganglia with postganglionic fibres and are in turn distributed to the various viscera. Examples at the cranial end of this system are the ciliary and spheno-palatine ganglia.

The vagus nerves are distributed to the heart, lungs, oesophagus, stomach, small bowel and to the proximal part of the large intestine. They contain preganglionic fibres which synapse with the intrinsic nerve plexuses within the bowel wall. The ganglia in this situation are mainly aggregated into Auerbach's and Meissner's plexuses. From these ganglia, postganglionic fibres arise and supply the smooth muscle and various secreting glands of the viscera. These efferent fibres are motor to the smooth muscle of the alimentary tract and to the secretory glands, but they inhibit the heart. They also cause constriction of the smooth muscle of the bronchioles. One point not previously recognised is that the vagus nerves contain numerous afferent fibres; these are not pain-conducting fibres, but arise from pH and pressure receptors in the stomach and small bowel.

Section of the vagus nerves to the stomach is now frequently carried out in the treatment of duodenal ulcer (see Chapter Twenty).

THE SURGERY OF INTRACTABLE PAIN

Causalgia

A small number of patients with nerve lesions develop severe and frequently intractable burning pain followed by marked trophic changes in a limb. This condition occurs most frequently after incomplete division of a nerve, and is typically seen in lesions of the cords of the brachial plexus, the median nerve and, less commonly, the sciatic nerve. All of these nerves contain large numbers of sympathetic fibres. It is believed that the cause of this pain is the formation of artificial synapses between individual axons at the site of injury. Thus, impulses passing down sympathetic fibres can jump across at this site and pass upwards and downwards along adjacent sensory fibres. They can thus cause pain by impulses travelling centrally or cause trophic changes via impulses passing peripherally.

The tendency is for the pain of causalgia to pass off spontaneously after months or years. In the first place the treatment is conservative; the patient is sedated and appropriate analgesics, such as codeine used. However, should the pain persist, sympathectomy is performed and proves successful in relieving pain in a high proportion of patients.

Phantom limb pain

Following amputation of a limb there arises in a small proportion of patients pain which appears to be coming from a part of the vanished limb. The pain usually starts 24–48 hours after amputation; on rare occasions it may arise years after the operation. As in causalgia, there is a spontaneous tendency for the pain to disappear.

Operations for Intractable Pain

There are a variety of other conditions which give rise to intractable pain and which may necessitate interruption of sensory fibres. When analgesics are ineffective and when the patient's expectation of life is sufficient to justify another operation one or more of the following procedures may be carried out:

1. *Peripheral Nerves.* A nerve in which the motor function is unimportant may be divided or removed, *neurectomy*. For example, a small segment may be excised from an intercostal nerve if it is the site of intercostal neuralgia.

2. *Sensory Nerve Roots.* Posterior *rhizotomy* or interruption of the sensory roots may be carried out by surgery or by the injection of alcohol or phenol intrathecally. It is necessary to interrupt adjacent posterior nerve roots, since there is a considerable overlap in the peripheral distribution of the sensory fibres.

3. *Spinal Cord.* Pain-carrying fibres can be interrupted by division of the spinothalamic tract; this interrupts conduction of pain and temperature sensation from the opposite side of the body. It can be performed at an appropriate level usually at T1 or T2, but occasionally division of the tract in the cervical region may be necessary for pain arising in the upper limb or thorax. This operation is called *cordotomy*.

4. *Sympathetic Nerves.* Division of sympathetic nerves, *sympathectomy*, may be successful in allaying the pain in causalgia, ischaemic pain usually in the lower limb and certain forms of visceral pain, for example, dysmenorrhoea or angina.

5. *The Brain.* When all efforts to relieve an intolerable pain have failed it only remains to modify its quality of appreciation by the higher centres. This may be achieved by the operation of *leucotomy*.

FURTHER READING

Potter, J. M. (1961) *The Practical Management of Head Injuries.* 2nd ed., Lloyd-Luke, London.
Jennett, W. B. 1964 *An Introduction to Neurosurgery* Heinemann, London.
Walton, J. *Subarachnoid Haemorrhage* Livingstone, Edinburgh.

INDEX

Apraxia, 580
Arachnodactyly, 496
Argyll–Robertson pupils, 515, 532
Arnold–Chiari malformation, 587
Arterial disease, 84–100
  embolus, 98–100
  grafting, 88
  haemorrhage, 6–7, 94–95
  injury, 94–96, 440, 447, 457, 470
    causing gangrene, 94, 95, 96, 440;
      peripheral ischaemia, 94; throm-
      bosis, 95
  stenosis, 91–92
  ulcers, 106
Arteriography (*see also* Angiography *and*
    Aortography)
  lower limb, 86–87
Arteriovenous fistula, 94, 96, 101, 106,
    107
Artery, brachial, injury in fractures, 457
  calcification of media, 93
  carotid ligation of, 574
    stenosis of, 92
  mesenteric stenosis of superior, 92
  renal, stenosis of, 91–92, 377
  vertebral, stenosis of, 92
Arthritis, 511–515
  ankylosing spondylitis, 539
  gonococcal, 68, 511, 531
  in ulcerative colitis, 314, 315
  neuropathic, 514–515, 531–532
  of hip, 518–519, 522–524
  of knee, 530–532
  of spine, 538–543
  osteoarthritis, 432, 447, 464, 472, 473,
    477, 478, 513–514, 520, 528, 529,
    530
  rheumatoid, 511–513
    tendon rupture in, 142
  septic, 497, 500–502 (*see also* Septic
    arthritis)
  tuberculous, 502–505, 521–522
Arthrodesis, Brittain's (hip), 522
  extra-articular, 522
  in hammer toe, 558
  in osteoarthritis, 514
  in rheumatoid arthritis, 513
  of ankle, 479
  of hip, 432, 522, 523
  of knee, 530, 531
  of neck, 484, 488
  of shoulder, 594
  of spine, 486, 536, 539
  of wrist, 464
  sub-taloid, 479, 560, 561, 595
  Watson-Jones' (hip), 523

Arthrogram, hip, 432
Arthroplasty, in osteoarthritis, 514
  in rheumatoid arthritis, 513
  of hip, 432, 468, 524, 540
  of knee, 531
  of toe, 559
Artificial kidney, 367, 369, 440
Ascheim–Zondek test, 412
Ascites, 250
  in constrictive pericarditis, 225
  in liver failure, 342–346
  malignant, 250
Asphyxia, traumatic, 203–204
Astrocytoma, 578, 582
Asymmetry of legs, 556, 563
Atelectasis, 208, 210
Atherosclerosis, 84–94
  aetiology of, 84
  common sites of, 85
  diabetic, 93–94
  in lower limb, 85–89
    investigations of, 86–87
    symptoms and signs of, 85–86
    treatment of, 87–89
Atresia, ileal, 427
  oesophageal, 424–425
  rectal, 428–429
Atrial septal defect, 221–222
Auditory nerve, 584
Auricle, accessory, 184
Auscultation of abdomen, 240, 426
Austin–Moore prosthesis, 468, 523, 524
Autoclaving, 53–54
Auto-immune disease, in salivary glands,
    174
  in thyroid, 158
Automatic bladder, 388, 487
Autonomic nervous system, 595–597
Avascular necrosis, 446, 463, 464, 466,
    467, 468
Axonotmesis, 589

B.C.G. vaccine, 45, 61
Bacitracin, 49
Backache, 535, 537, 539, 542, 546–547
Back-fire injury, 462, 463
Bacteraemia, 44
Bacterial toxins, 43–44, 45
Baker's cyst, 513
Balanitis, 390, 419–420
Bamboo spine, 539–540
Bandages
  pressure, in treatment of leg ulcers,
    107–108
    heavy elastic, 108, 112
    crepe, 108